The Process *of* Gender

Jennifer A. Linde
Arizona State University

Belle A. Edson
Arizona State University

KENDALL/HUNT PUBLISHING COMPANY
4050 Westmark Drive   Dubuque, Iowa 52002

Contents

Preface

The Process of Gender is the beginning of a conversation that we hope you will continue to have for many years to come. Although all of us have lived in a "gendered body" for our entire life, many of us have never taken the time to consider the implications of that experience. We have not been asked to critically examine the ways that our gender has impacted our values, attitudes, behaviors, and experiences. This book is designed to prompt you to begin or continue that examination.

Gender is a multi-disciplinary concept. It is studied in biology, sociology, psychology, anthropology, etc. . . . We want to introduce you to the study of gender within the context of human communication. In our discipline we are interested in the ways that gender influences the process of communication behavior. For example, gender is a dominant component of the way that we understand and use language. In the field of communication we presume that language helps us to construct our world and that we are also constructed by the language that surrounds us, the language that we learn, the language that is used to describe and define us and the language that helps us to construct our very responses to the world and to others in that world.

In human communication, the study of gender is approached from a wide variety of methodological perspectives. Quantitative methods (surveys, questionnaires, interviews, experiments) allow us to understand how people think and act in regards to gendered communication in their lives. Qualitative methods (textual analysis, ethnography, participant observation) allow us to examine more in-depth human responses to the topic of gender. A short list of the ways that communication scholars study gender includes: the role of gender in relational communication, the influence of gender on perceptions of public address, the ways that language development is linked to gendered behavioral expectations, how bodies exist and communicate within a gendered context, and gender as a cultural construct.

Students of communication clearly understand the impact that gender has on the construction and interpretations of messages. Our students often remark that communicating with someone from another gender is like speaking to someone from a different world! Our ability to grasp the influence that gender has on our perception and interpretation of messages, our use of language and nonverbal displays, and our positions of power and privilege in society is vital to our ability to learn and practice effective communication.

We view gender as a process. Like any process, it is a something that is influenced by its surroundings, can easily change, and never truly comes to a definitive end. Gender can be studied as an organic concept, something fluid and flexible, and something that is both fascinating and never-ending. As we study gender and communication as a process you will begin to understand that it is best to experience the topic as a critical thinker. You will be offered frameworks for understanding the process of gender and these, in turn, should provide you with the ability to examine gendered communication from a critical perspective. So, we don't just learn about gendered pronoun use (he and she), we learn how this simple act of communication influences and is influenced by the process of gender.

We encourage you to approach the material presented in this book as an introduction to gender within a variety of contexts. We hope that it prompts you to want to learn more about this fascinating dimension of the communication process.

Jennifer A. Linde
Belle A. Edson

Introduction

To study gender and communication is to study a complex concept that has strong application to your life. Consider your motives for taking a class on gender and communication. Do you want to learn more about how gender affects your friendships and romantic relationships? Do you want to understand how you can enhance, modify, or completely change your gendered communication to benefit you in work settings? As a woman, do you worry about the statistics that suggest that you that you will more than likely be affected by gendered violence in your lifetime? As a man, do you find yourself responding to an increased pressure from the media to be both "buff" and "beautiful?" To study gender and communication inevitably means that you study yourself. So, as you engage in the experience of learning about the topic of gender, you will also be learning about many things that have direct application to your life.

You will undoubtedly be challenged by the material presented in your gender and communication course. You will probably find that your lifelong notions of what it means to be a woman or a man are not the fixed ideas that you had previously thought. You may find yourself examining your personal values in relationship to the topics of the course. You may even experience some frustration as your newly formed understanding of gender begins to affect the ways that you view your favorite television program, converse with a co-worker, or even the ways that you notice gendered nonverbal displays in public spaces. To be open to the material of this course means that you will need to engage it with an open mind. You will learn a great deal about gender and communication if you refrain from quick judgments about unfamiliar ideas and instead be willing to read, listen, talk, and possibly confront personal biases that you may bring to the topic. You have spent a lifetime constructing your personal gender identity. You now have an opportunity to learn how others define themselves in terms of gender. You now have an opportunity to engage in the process of gender.

This textbook is comprised of 19 published readings about gender and communication as well as discussion questions and exercises that provide additional ways to examine the material. The readings are divided into six sections. These include: *The Process of Defining Gender, The Process of Becoming Gendered, The Process of Communicating Gender, The Process of Examining Gendered Violence, The Process of Understanding Gender in Social Systems,* and *The Process of Critiquing Gender.* Each section is designed to build upon your understanding of the process of gender and communication.

Part One, *The Process of Defining Gender,* will introduce you to terms and definitions associated with the study of gender. You will read and learn about a variety of labels that have been given to gendered phenomena. You will be exposed to scholarly definitions, discussions, and disagreements about how we should define and use the term *gender.* Articles: Lorber raises the question of whether or not gender is a social or biological construct. Hass offers information on the legal debate regarding genital reconstruction surgery for those born with intersex conditions. Wood articulates the similarities and differences between feminist standpoint theory and muted group theory.

Part Two, *The Process of Becoming Gendered* is an exploration of the ways that people form identities in relationship to gender. You will be asked to interrogate assumptions about femininity and masculinity and learn about the possibility of gender as a fluid concept. Articles: Martin examines the ways that gender is taught to children in pre-school settings. Boyle, Smith, and Liao examine the psychological motivations and effects of genital surgery for adult women. Ashcraft and Flores evaluate modern performances of masculinity as they pertain to race and class.

Part Three, *The Process of Communicating Gender,* is concerned with understanding the influence that gender has on human communication. You will read about the implications of gender based language and nonverbal displays and study the impact that gender has on the communication within friendships and romantic relationships. Articles: Kramarae addresses important questions about muted group theory. This theory is often used to analyze the ways that subordinate groups in society are "muted," or not allowed to speak. Gilbert describes her experiences performing masculinity. Harvey makes connections between hegemonic masculinity, nonprofessional athletics, and male friendships.

Part Four, *The Process of Examining Gendered Violence* gives you an opportunity to read about the ways that gender intersects with violent human behavior. Articles: Philips writes about the masculine practice of *punking*. Wood examines the discourse surrounding intimate partner violence. Kahn writes about the ways that college women *label* their experiences of sexual assault.

Part Five, *The Process of Gender in Social Systems,* allows you to examine broad societal institutions in regards to how they are influenced by gendered communication. In this section we will discuss the impact that gender has on workplace communication, educational organizations in the United States, and the media. Articles: Niemi challenges the claim that there is gender equity in the American school system by studying middle school students' gender and academic identities. Railton and Watson discuss music videos' portrayals of women's sexuality. Squires and Brouwer analyze the frames that dominant media use in their presentation of "passing." Nadesan and Trethewey evaluate the strategies that popular success literature offer to women who participate in corporate organizational settings.

Part Six, *The Process of Critiquing Gender* provides you with a critical framework for understanding gender and communication. You will study historical social movements that are motivated to change attitudes, policies and laws pertaining to gender. Articles: Gallagher and Wood address the impact of shifting gender ideals on conservative Protestants. MacLean offers an historical accounting of the women's movement. Mohan and Schultz describe their experiences working with men in a community anti-violence program.

1

The Process of Defining Gender

The first step in the process of learning about gender and communication is to understand key terms and concepts that you will use throughout this book. In "The Process of Defining Gender," we provide you with rather simple definitions for very complicated concepts. We believe that these definitions will allow you to begin to communicate and learn about gender. These definitions will serve as building blocks to a more complex understanding of gender and communication. We also introduce you to theories of gender that help explain the ways that human beings experience gender in their lives.

We have included three articles in this section that provide in-depth discussion and analysis of some of the concepts from our list.

Concepts

Sex

Intersex

Gender

Gender Identity

Gender Presentation

Gender Role

Androgyny

Basic Concepts

Sex: Sex is a term that refers to the innate biological characteristics of an individual based on genitalia, chromosomes, and hormones. We use the terms *female* and *male* when we are discussing a person's sex.

Intersex: Intersex refers to individuals who are born with ambiguous sex traits. This may include indistinguishably male or female chromosomes and/or genitalia.

Gender: Gender is a psychologically, culturally, and often politically constructed term. It is a learned concept and its meaning changes within diverse contexts. Gender is a process. We most often use the terms *man, masculine, woman, feminine,* and the prefix *trans* when discussing a person's gender.

Gender Identity: Gender identity refers to a person's internal definition and interpretation of *self* in relationship to gender. This identity may or may not depend on the person's biological sex.

Gender Presentation: Gender presentation refers to the ways that individuals communicate their gender to others. This presentation (or performance) of gender involves elements of both verbal and nonverbal communication.

Gender Role: This term refers to the social role that accompanies gender. Members of a society are often rewarded or punished for the degree to which they accommodate the expectation of their gender role.

Androgyny: Androgyny is a term that is used to describe people or behaviors that possess qualities we typically associate with both genders. It is often considered to be a blurring or neutralizing of the gender binaries of feminine and masculine.

Terms

Naturalness

Categories
of sex

Ideology

Social
practices

BELIEVING IS SEEING
Biology as Ideology

JUDITH LORBER

This article is about the "naturalness" of gendered behaviors and social categories. What we believe is that there are two sexes that correspond to the production of two genders. This binary leads to the formation of social inequality whereby men are afforded more status than women and males are viewed as more important than females.

Western ideology takes biology as the cause, and behavior and social statuses as the effects, and then proceeds to construct biological dichotomies to justify the "naturalness" of gendered behavior and gendered social statuses. What we believe is what we see—two sexes producing two genders. The process, however, goes the other way: gender constructs social bodies to be different and unequal. The content of the two sets of constructed social categories, "females and males" and "women and men," is so varied that their use in research without further specification renders the results spurious.

Until the eighteenth century, Western philosophers and scientists thought that there was one sex and that women's internal genitalia were the inverse of men's external genitalia: the womb and vagina were the penis and scrotum turned inside out (Laqueur 1990). Current Western thinking sees women and men as so different physically as to sometimes seem two species. The bodies, which have been mapped inside and out for hundreds of years, have not changed. What has changed are the justifications for gender inequality. When the social position of all human beings was believed to be set by natural law or was considered God-given, biology was irrelevant; women and men of different classes all had their assigned places. When scientists began to question the divine basis of social order and replaced faith with empirical knowledge, what they saw was that women were very different from men in that they had wombs and menstruated. Such anatomical differences destined them for an entirely different social life from men.

In actuality, the basic bodily material *is* the same for females and males, and except for procreative hormones and organs, female and male human beings have similar bodies (Naftolin and Butz 1981). Furthermore, as has been known since the middle of the nineteenth century, male and female genitalia develop from the same fetal tissue, and so infants can be born with ambiguous genitalia (Money and Ehrhardt 1972). When they are, biology is used quite arbitrarily in sex assignment. Suzanne Kessler (1990) interviewed six medical specialists in pediatric intersexuality and found that whether an infant with XY chromosomes and anomalous genitalia was categorized as a boy or a girl depended on the size of the penis—if a penis was very small, the child was categorized as a girl, and sex-change surgery was used to make an artificial vagina. In the late nineteenth century, the presence or absence of ovaries was the determining criterion of gender assignment for hermaphrodites because a woman who could not procreate was not a complete woman (Kessler 1990, 20).

Yet in Western societies, we see two discrete sexes and two distinguishable genders because our society is built on two classes of people, "women" and "men." Once the gender category is given, the attributes of the person are also gendered: Whatever a "woman" is has to be "female"; whatever a "man" is has to be "male." Analyzing the social processes that construct the categories we call "female and male," "women and men," and "homosexual and heterosexual" uncovers the ideology and power differentials congealed in these categories (Foucault 1978). This article will use two familiar areas of social life—sports and technological competence—to show how myriad physiological differences are transformed into similar-appearing, gendered social bodies. My perspective goes beyond accepted feminist views that gender is a cultural overlay that modifies physiological sex differences. That perspective assumes either that there are two fairly similar sexes distorted by social practices into two genders with purposefully different characteristics or that there are two sexes whose essential differences are rendered unequal by social practices. I am arguing that bodies differ in many ways physiologically, but they are completely transformed by social practices to fit into the salient categories of a society, the most pervasive of which are "female" and "male" and "women" and "men."

Neither sex nor gender are pure categories. Combinations of incongruous genes, genitalia, and hormonal input are ignored in sex categorization, just as combinations of incongruous physiology, identity, sexuality, appearance, and behavior are ignored in the social construction of gender statuses. Menstruation, lactation, and gestation do not demarcate women from men. Only some women are pregnant and then only some of the time; some women do not have a uterus or ovaries. Some women have stopped menstruating temporarily, others have reached menopause, and some have had hysterectomies. Some women breastfeed some of the time, but some men lactate (Jaggar 1983, 165fn). Menstruation, lactation, and gestation are individual experiences of womanhood (Levesque-Lopman 1988), but not determinants of the social category "woman," or even "female." Similarly, "men are not always sperm-producers, and in fact, not all sperm producers are men. A male-to-female transsexual, prior to surgery, can be socially a woman, though still potentially (or actually) capable of spermatogenesis" (Kessler and McKenna [1978] 1985, 2).

When gender assignment is contested in sports, where the categories of competitors are rigidly divided into women and men, chromosomes are now used to determine in which category the athlete is to compete. However, an anomaly common enough to be found in several women at every major international sports competition are XY chromosomes that have not produced male anatomy or physiology because of a genetic defect. Because these women are women in every way significant for sports competition, the prestigious International Amateur Athletic Federation has urged that sex be determined by simple genital inspection (Kolata 1992). Transsexuals would pass this test, but it took a lawsuit for Renée Richards, a male-to-female transsexual, to be able to play tournament tennis as a woman, despite his male sex chromosomes (Richards 1983). Oddly, neither basis for gender categorization—chromosomes nor genitalia—has anything to do with sports prowess (Birrell and Cole 1990).

In the Olympics, in cases of chromosomal ambiguity, women must undergo "a battery of gynecological and physical exams to see if she is 'female enough' to compete. Men are not tested" (Carlson 1991, 26). The purpose is not to categorize women and men accurately, but to make sure men don't enter women's competitions, where, it is felt, they will have the advantage of size and strength. This practice sounds fair only because it is assumed that all men are similar in size and strength and different from all women. Yet in Olympics boxing and wrestling matches, men are matched within weight classes. Some women might similarly successfully compete with some men in many sports. Women did not run in marathons until about twenty years ago. In twenty years of marathon competition, women have reduced their finish times by more than one-and-one-half hours; they are expected to run as fast as men in that race by 1998 and might catch up with men's running times in races of other lengths within the next 50 years because they are increasing their fastest speeds more rapidly than are men (Fausto-Sterling 1985, 213–18).

The reliance on only two sex and gender categories in the biological and social sciences is as epistemologically spurious as the reliance on chromosomal or genital tests to group athletes. Most research designs do not investigate whether physical skills or physical abilities are really more or less common in women and men (Epstein 1988).They start out with two social categories ("women," "men"), assume they are biologically different ("female," "male"), look for similarities among them and differences between them, and attribute what they have found for the social categories to sex differences (Gelman, Collman, and Maccoby 1986). These designs rarely question the categorization of their subjects into two and only two groups, even though they often find more significant within-group differences than between-group differences (Hyde 1990). The social construction perspective on sex and gender suggests that instead of starting with the two presumed dichotomies in each category—female, male; woman, man—it might be more useful in gender studies to group patterns of behavior and only then look for identifying markers of the people likely to enact such behaviors.

What Sports Illustrate

Competitive sports have become, for boys and men, as players and as spectators, a way of constructing a masculine identity, a legitimated outlet for violence and aggression, and an avenue for upward mobility (Dunning 1986; Kemper 1990, 167–206; Messner 1992). For men in Western societies, physical competence is an important marker of masculinity (Fine 1987; Glassner 1992; Majors 1990). In professional and collegiate sports, physiological differences are invoked to justify women's secondary status, despite the clear evidence that gender status overrides physiological capabilities. Assumptions about women's physiology have influenced rules of competition; subsequent sports performances then validate how women and men are treated in sports competitions.

Gymnastic equipment is geared to slim, wiry, prepubescent girls and not to mature women; conversely, men's gymnastic equipment is tailored for muscular, mature men, not slim, wiry prepubescent boys. Boys could compete with girls, but are not allowed to; women gymnasts are left out entirely. Girl gymnasts are just that—little girls who will be disqualified as soon as they grow up (Vecsey 1990). Men gymnasts have men's status. In women's basketball, the size of the ball and rules for handling the ball change the style of play to "a slower, less intense, and less exciting modification of the 'regular' or men's game" (Watson 1987, 441). In the 1992 Winter Olympics, men figure skaters were required to complete three triple jumps in their required program; women figure skaters were forbidden to do more than *one*. These rules penalized artistic men skaters and athletic women skaters (Janofsky 1992). For the most part, Western sports are built on physically trained men's bodies:

> Speed, size, and strength seem to be the essence of sports. Women *are* naturally inferior at "sports" so conceived.
>
> But if women had been the historically dominant sex, our concept of sport would no doubt have evolved differently. Competitions emphasizing flexibility, balance, strength, timing, and small size might dominate Sunday afternoon television and offer salaries in six figures. (English 1982, 266, emphasis in original)

Organized sports are big businesses and, thus, who has access and at what level is a distributive or equity issue. The overall status of women and men athletes is an economic, political, and ideological issue that has less to do with individual physiological capabilities than with their cultural and social meaning and who defines and profits from them (Messner and Sabo 1990; Slatton and Birrell 1984). Twenty years after the passage of Title IX of the U.S. Civil Rights Act, which forbade gender inequality in any school receiving federal funds, the *goal* for collegiate sports in the next five years is 60 percent men, 40 percent women in sports participation, scholarships, and funding (Moran 1992).

How access and distribution of rewards (prestigious and financial) are justified is an ideological, even moral, issue (Birrell 1988, 473–76; Hargreaves 1982). One way is that men athletes are glorified and women athletes ignored in the mass media. Messner and his colleagues found that in 1989, in TV sports news in the United States, men's sports got 92 percent of the coverage and women's sports 5 percent, with the rest mixed or gender-neutral (Messner, Duncan, and Jensen 1993). In 1990, in four of the top-selling newspapers in the United States, stories on men's sports outnumbered those on women's sports 23 to 1. Messner and his colleagues also found an implicit hierarchy in naming, with women athletes most likely to be called by first names, followed by Black men athletes, and only white men athletes routinely referred to by their last names. Similarly, women's collegiate sports teams are named or marked in ways that symbolically feminize and trivialize them—the men's team is called Tigers, the women's Kittens (Eitzen and Baca Zinn 1989).

Assumptions about men's and women's bodies and their capacities are crafted in ways that make unequal access and distribution of rewards acceptable (Hudson 1978; Messner 1988). Media images of modern men athletes glorify their strength and power, even their violence (Hargreaves 1986). Media images of modern women athletes tend to focus on feminine beauty and grace (so they are not really athletes) or on their thin, small, wiry androgynous bodies (so they are not really women). In coverage of the Olympics,

> loving and detailed attention is paid to pixie-like gymnasts; special and extended coverage is given to graceful and dazzling figure skaters; the camera painstakingly records the fluid movements of swimmers and divers. And then, in a blinding flash of fragmented images, viewers

> see a few minutes of volleyball, basketball, speed skating, track and field, and alpine skiing, as television gives its nod to the mere existence of these events. (Boutilier and SanGiovanni 1983, 190)

Extraordinary feats by women athletes who were presented as mature adults might force sports organizers and audiences to rethink their stereotypes of women's capabilities, the way elves, mermaids, and ice queens do not. Sports, therefore, construct men's bodies to be powerful; women's bodies to be sexual. As Connell says,

> The meanings in the bodily sense of masculinity concern, above all else, the superiority of men to women, and the exaltation of hegemonic masculinity over other groups of men which is essential for the domination of women. (1987, 85)

In the late 1970s, as women entered more and more athletic competitions, supposedly good scientific studies showed that women who exercised intensely would cease menstruating because they would not have enough body fat to sustain ovulation (Brozan 1978). When one set of researchers did a yearlong study that compared 66 women—21 who were training for a marathon, 22 who ran more than an hour a week, and 23 who did less than an hour of aerobic exercise a week—they discovered that only 20 percent of the women in any of these groups had "normal" menstrual cycles every month (Prior et al. 1990). The dangers of intensive training for women's fertility therefore were exaggerated as women began to compete successfully in arenas formerly closed to them.

Given the association of sports with masculinity in the United States, women athletes have to manage a contradictory status. One study of women college basketball players found that although they "did athlete" on the court—"pushing, shoving, fouling, hard running, fast breaks, defense, obscenities and sweat" (Watson 1987, 441), they "did woman" off the court, using the locker room as their staging area:

> While it typically took fifteen minutes to prepare for the game, it took approximately fifteen minutes after the game to shower and remove the sweat of an athlete, *and* it took another thirty minutes to dress, apply make-up and style hair. It did not seem to matter whether the players were going out into the public or getting on a van for a long ride home. Average dressing time and rituals did not change. (Watson 1987, 443)

Another way women manage these status dilemmas is to redefine the activity or its result as feminine or womanly (Mangan and Park 1987). Thus women bodybuilders claim that "flex appeal is sex appeal" (Duff and Hong 1984, 378).

Such a redefinition of women's physicality affirms the ideological subtext of sports that physical strength is men's prerogative and justifies men's physical and sexual domination of women (Hargreaves 1986; Messner 1992, 164–72; Olson 1990; Theberge 1987; Willis 1982). When women demonstrate physical strength, they are labeled unfeminine:

> It's threatening to one's takeability, one's rapeability, one's femininity, to be strong and physically self-possessed. To be able to resist rape, not to communicate rapeability with one's body, to hold one's body for uses and meanings other than that can transform what *being a woman means*. (MacKinnon 1987, 122, emphasis in original)

Resistance to that transformation, ironically, was evident in the policies of American women physical education professionals throughout most of the twentieth century. They minimized exertion, maximized a feminine appearance and manner, and left organized sports competition to men (Birrell 1988, 461–62; Mangan and Park 1987).

Dirty Little Secrets

As sports construct gendered bodies, technology constructs gendered skills. Meta-analysis of studies of gender differences in spatial and mathematical ability have found that men have a large advantage in ability to mentally rotate an image, a moderate advantage in a visual perception of horizontality and verticality and in mathematical performance, and a small advantage in ability to pick a figure out of a field (Hyde 1990). It could be argued that these advantages explain why, within the short space of time that computers have become ubiquitous in offices, schools, and homes, work on them and with them has become gendered: Men create, program, and market computers, make war and produce science and art with them; women microwire them in computer factories and enter data in computerized offices; boys play games, socialize, and commit crimes with computers; girls are rarely seen in computer clubs, camps, and classrooms. But women were hired as computer programmers in the 1940s because

> the work seemed to resemble simple clerical tasks. In fact, however, programming demanded complex skills in abstract logic, mathematics, electrical circuitry, and machinery, all of which . . . women used to perform in their work. Once programming was recognized as "intellectually demanding," it became attractive to men. (Donato 1990, 170)

A woman mathematician and pioneer in data processing, Grace M. Hopper, was famous for her work on programming language (Perry and Greber 1990, 86). By the 1960s, programming was split into more and less skilled specialties, and the entry of women into the computer field in the 1970s and 1980s was confined to the lower-paid specialties. At each stage, employers invoked women's and men's purportedly natural capabilities for the jobs for which they were hired (Cockburn 1983, 1985; Donato 1990; Hartmann 1987; Hartmann, Kraut, and Tilly 1986; Kramer and Lehman 1990; Wright et al. 1987; Zimmerman 1983).

It is the taken-for-grantedness of such everyday gendered behavior that gives credence to the belief that the widespread differences in what women and men do must come from biology. To take one ordinarily unremarked scenario: In modern societies, if a man and woman who are a couple are in a car together, he is much more likely to take the wheel than she is, even if she is the more competent driver. Molly Haskell calls this taken-for-granted phenomenon "the dirty little secret of marriage: the husband-lousy-driver syndrome" (1989, 26). Men drive cars whether they are good drivers or not because men and machines are a "natural" combination (Scharff 1991). But the ability to drive gives one mobility; it is a form of social power.

In the early days of the automobile, feminists co-opted the symbolism of mobility as emancipation: "Donning goggles and dusters, wielding tire irons and tool kits, taking the wheel, they announced their intention to move beyond the bounds of women's place" (Scharff 1991, 68). Driving enabled them to campaign for women's suffrage in parts of the United States not served by public transportation, and they effectively used motorcades and speaking from cars as campaign tactics (Scharff 1991, 67–88). Sandra Gilbert also notes that during World War I, women's ability to drive was physically, mentally, and even sensually liberating:

> For nurses and ambulance drivers, women doctors and women messengers, the phenomenon of modern battle was very different from that experienced by entrenched combatants. Finally given a chance to take the wheel, these post-Victorian girls raced motorcars along foreign roads like adventurers exploring new lands, while their brothers dug deeper into the mud of France. . . . Retrieving the wounded and the dead from deadly positions, these once-decorous daughters had at last been allowed to prove their valor, and they swooped over the wastelands of the war with the energetic love of Wagnerian Valkyries, their mobility alone transporting countless immobilized heroes to safe havens. (1983, 438–39)

Not incidentally, women in the United States and England got the vote for their war efforts in World War I.

Social Bodies and the Bathroom Problem

People of the same racial ethnic group and social class are roughly the same size and shape—but there are many varieties of bodies. People have different genitalia, different secondary sex characteristics, different contributions to procreation, different orgasmic experiences, different patterns of illness and aging. Each of us experiences our bodies differently, and these experiences change as we grow, age, sicken, and die. The bodies of pregnant and nonpregnant women, short and tall people, those with intact and functioning limbs and those whose bodies are physically challenged are all different. But the salient categories of a society group these attributes in ways that ride roughshod over individual experiences and more meaningful clusters of people.

I am not saying that physical differences between male and female bodies don't exist, but that these differences are socially meaningless until social practices transform them into social facts. West Point Military Academy's curriculum is designed to produce leaders, and physical competence is used as a significant measure of leadership ability (Yoder 1989). When women were accepted as West Point cadets, it became clear that the tests of physical competence, such as rapidly scaling an eight-foot wall, had been constructed for male physiques—pulling oneself up and over using upper-body strength. Rather than devise tests of physical competence for women, West Point provided boosters that mostly women used—but that lost them test points—in the case of the wall, a platform. Finally, the women themselves figured out how to use their bodies successfully. Janice Yoder describes this situation:

> I was observing this obstacle one day, when a woman approached the wall in the old prescribed way, got her fingertips grip, and did an unusual thing: she walked her dangling legs up the wall until she was in a position where both her hands and feet were atop the wall. She then simply pulled up her sagging bottom and went over. She solved the problem by capitalizing on one of women's physical assets: lower-body strength. (1989, 530)

In short, if West Point is going to measure leadership capability by physical strength, women's pelvises will do just as well as men's shoulders.

The social transformation of female and male physiology into a condition of inequality is well illustrated by the bathroom problem. Most buildings that have gender-segregated bathrooms have an equal number for women and for men. Where there are crowds, there are always long lines in front of women's bathrooms but rarely in front of men's bathrooms. The cultural, physiological, and demographic combinations of clothing, frequency of urination, menstruation, and child care add up to generally greater bathroom use by women than men. Thus, although an equal number of bathrooms seems fair, equity would mean more women's bathrooms or allowing women to use men's bathrooms for a certain amount of time (Molotch 1988).

The bathroom problem is the outcome of the way gendered bodies are differentially evaluated in Western cultures: Men's social bodies are the measure of what is "human." Gray's *Anatomy*, in use for 100 years, well into the twentieth century, presented the human body as male. The female body was shown only where it differed from the male (Laqueur 1990, 166–67). Denise Riley says that if we envisage women's bodies, men's bodies, and human bodies "as a triangle of identifications, then it is rarely an equilateral triangle in which both sexes are pitched at matching distances from the apex of the human" (1988, 197). Catharine MacKinnon also contends that in Western society, universal "humanness" is male because

> virtually every quality that distinguishes men from women is already affirmatively compensated in this society. Men's physiology defines most sports, their needs define auto and health insurance coverage, their socially defined biographies define workplace expectations and successful career patterns, their perspectives and concerns define quality in scholarship, their experiences and obsessions define merit, their objectification of life defines art, their military service defines citizenship, their presence defines family, their inability to get along with each other—their wars and rulerships—define history, their image defines god, and their genitals define sex. For each of their differences from women, what amounts to an affirmative action plan is in effect, otherwise known as the structure and values of American society. (1987, 36)

The Paradox of Human Nature

Gendered people do not emerge from physiology or hormones but from the exigencies of the social order, mostly, from the need for a reliable division of the work of food production and the social (not physical) reproduction of new members. The moral imperatives of religion and cultural representations reinforce the boundary lines among genders and ensure that what is demanded, what is permitted, and what is tabooed for the people in each gender is well-known and followed by most. Political power, control of scarce resources, and, if necessary, violence uphold the gendered social order in the face of resistance and rebellion. Most people, however, voluntarily go along with their society's prescriptions for those of their gender status because the norms and expectations get built into their sense of worth and identity as a certain kind of human being and because they believe their society's way is the natural way. These beliefs emerge from the imagery that pervades the way we think, the way we see and hear and speak, the way we fantasize, and the way we feel. There is no core or bedrock human nature below these endlessly looping processes of the social production of sex and gender, self and other, identity and psyche, each of which is a "complex cultural construction" (Butler 1990, 36). The paradox of "human nature" is that it is *always* a manifestation of cultural meanings, social relationships, and power politics—"not biology, but culture, becomes destiny" (Butler 1990, 8).

Feminist inquiry has long questioned the conventional categories of social science, but much of the current work in feminist sociology has not gone beyond adding the universal category "women" to the universal category "men." Our current debates over the global assumptions of only two categories and the insistence that they must be nuanced to include race and class are steps in the direction I would like to see feminist research go, but race and class are *also* global categories (Collins 1990; Spelman 1988). Deconstructing sex, sexuality, and gender reveals many possible categories embedded in the social experiences and social practices of what Dorothy Smith calls the "everyday/everynight world" (1990, 31–57). These emergent categories group some people together for comparison with other people without prior assumptions about who is like whom. Categories can be broken up and people regrouped differently into new categories for comparison. This process of discovering categories from similarities and differences in people's behavior or responses can be more meaningful for feminist research than discovering similarities and differences between "females" and "males" or "women" and "men" because the social construction of the conventional sex and gender categories already assumes differences between them and similarities among them. When we rely only on the conventional categories of sex and gender, we end up finding what we looked for—we see what we believe, whether it is that "females" and "males" are essentially different or that "women" and "men" are essentially the same.

REFERENCES

Birrell, Susan J. 1988. Discourses on the gender/sport relationship: From women in sport to gender relations. In *Exercise and sport science reviews.* Vol. 16, edited by Kent Pandolf. New York: Macmillan.

Birrell, Susan J., and Sheryl L. Cole. 1990. Double fault: Renée Richards and the construction and naturalization of difference. *Sociology of Sport Journal* 7:1–21.

Boutilier, Mary A., and Lucinda SanGiovanni. 1983. *The sporting woman.* Champaign, IL: Human Kinetics.

Brozan, Nadine. 1978. Training linked to disruption of female reproductive cycle. *New York Times,* 17 April.

Butler, Judith. 1990. *Gender trouble: Feminism and the subversion of identity.* New York and London: Routledge & Kegan Paul.

Carlson, Alison. 1991. When is a woman not a woman? *Women's Sport and Fitness* March: 24–29.

Cockburn, Cynthia. 1983. *Brothers: Male dominance and technological change.* London: Pluto.

———. 1985. *Machinery of dominance: Women, men and technical know-how.* London: Pluto.

Collins, Patricia Hill. 1990. *Black feminist thought: Knowledge, consciousness, and the politics of empowerment.* Boston: Unwin Hyman.

Connell, R. W. 1987. *Gender and power.* Stanford, CA: Stanford University Press.

Donato, Katharine M. 1990. Programming for change? The growing demand for women systems analysts. In *Job queues, gender queues: Explaining women's inroads into male occupations,* written and edited by Barbara F. Reskin and Patricia A. Roos. Philadelphia: Temple University Press.

Duff, Robert W., and Lawrence K. Hong, 1984. Self-images of women bodybuilders. *Sociology of Sport Journal* 2:374–80.

Dunning, Eric. 1986. Sport as a male preserve: Notes on the social sources of masculine identity and its transformations. *Theory, Culture and Society* 3:79–90.

Eitzen, D. Stanley, and Maxine Baca Zinn. 1989. The deathleticization of women: The naming and gender marking of collegiate sport teams. *Sociology of Sport Journal* 6:362–70.

English, Jane. 1982. Sex equality in sports. In *Femininity, masculinity, and androgyny,* edited by Mary Vetterling-Braggin. Boston: Littlefield, Adams.

Epstein, Cynthia Fuchs. 1988. *Deceptive distinctions: Sex, gender and the social order.* New Haven, CT: Yale University Press.

Fausto-Sterling, Anne. 1985. *Myths of gender: Biological theories about women and men.* New York: Basic Books.

Fine, Gary Alan. 1987. *With the boys: Little League baseball and preadolescent culture.* Chicago: University of Chicago Press.

Foucault, Michel. 1978. *The history of sexuality: An introduction.* Translated by Robert Hurley. New York: Pantheon.

Gelman, Susan A., Pamela Collman, and Eleanor E. Maccoby. 1986. Inferring properties from categories versus inferring categories from properties: The case of gender. *Child Development* 57:396–404.

Gilbert, Sandra M. 1983. Soldier's heart: Literary men, literary women, and the Great War. *Signs: Journal of Women in Culture and Society* 8:422–50.

Glassner, Barry. 1992. Men and muscles. In *Men's lives,* edited by Michael S. Kimmel and Michael A. Messner. New York: Macmillan.

Hargreaves, Jennifer A., ed. 1982. *Sport, culture, and ideology.* London: Routledge & Kegan Paul.

———. 1986. Where's the virtue? Where's the grace? A discussion of the social production of gender relations in and through sport. *Theory, Culture, and Society* 3:109–21.

Hartmann, Heidi I., ed. 1987. *Computer chips and paper clips: Technology and women's employment.* Vol. 2. Washington, DC: National Academy Press.

Hartmann, Heidi I., Robert E. Kraut, and Louise A. Tilly, eds. 1986. *Computer chips and paper clips: Technology and women's employment.* Vol. 1. Washington, DC: National Academy Press.

Haskell, Molly. 1989. Hers: He drives me crazy. *New York Times Magazine,* 24 September, 26, 28.

Hudson, Jackie. 1978. Physical parameters used for female exclusion from law enforcement and athletics. In *Women and sport: From myth to reality,* edited by Carole A. Oglesby. Philadelphia: Lea and Febiger.

Hyde, Janet Shibley. 1990. Meta-analysis and the psychology of gender differences. *Signs: Journal of Women in Culture and Society* 16:55–73.

Jaggar, Alison M. 1983. *Feminist politics and human nature.* Totowa, NJ: Rowman & Allanheld.

Janofsky, Michael. 1992. Yamaguchi has the delicate and golden touch. *New York Times,* 22 February.

Kemper, Theodore D. 1990. *Social structure and testosterone: Explorations of the socio-bio-social chain.* Brunswick, NJ: Rutgers University Press.

Kessler, Suzanne J. 1990. The medical construction of gender: Case management of intersexed infants. *Signs: Journal of Women in Culture and Society* 16:3–26.

Kessler, Suzanne J., and Wendy McKenna. [1978] 1985. *Gender: An ethnomethodological approach.* Chicago: University of Chicago Press.

Kolata, Gina. 1992. Track federation urges end to gene test for femaleness. *New York Times,* 12 February.

Kramer, Pamela E., and Sheila Lehman. 1990. Mismeasuring women: A critique of research on computer ability and avoidance. *Signs: Journal of Women in Culture and Society* 16:158–72.

Laqueur, Thomas. 1990. *Making sex: Body and gender from the Greeks to Freud.* Cambridge, MA: Harvard University Press.

Levesque-Lopman, Louise. 1988. *Claiming reality: Phenomenology and women's experience.* Totowa, NJ: Rowman & Littlefield.

MacKinnon, Catharine. 1987. *Feminism unmodified.* Cambridge, MA: Harvard University Press.

Majors, Richard. 1990. Cool pose: Black masculinity in sports. In *Sport, men, and the gender order: Critical feminist perspectives,* edited by Michael A. Messner and Donald F. Sabo. Champaign, IL: Human Kinetics.

Mangan, J. A., and Roberta J. Park. 1987. *From fair sex to feminism: Sport and the socialization of women in the industrial and post-industrial eras.* London: Frank Cass.

Messner, Michael A. 1988. Sports and male domination: The female athlete as contested ideological terrain. *Sociology of Sport Journal* 5:197–211.

———. 1992. *Power at play: Sports and the problem of masculinity.* Boston: Beacon Press.

Messner, Michael A., Margaret Carlisle Duncan, and Kerry Jensen. 1993. Separating the men from the girls: The gendered language of televised sports. *Gender & Society* 7:121–37.

Messner, Michael A., and Donald F. Sabo, eds. 1990. *Sport, men, and the gender order: Critical feminist perspectives.* Champaign, IL: Human Kinetics.

Molotch, Harvey. 1988. The restroom and equal opportunity. *Sociological Forum* 3:128–32.

Money, John, and Anke A. Ehrhardt. 1972. *Man & woman, boy & girl.* Baltimore, MD: Johns Hopkins University Press.

Moran, Malcolm. 1992. Title IX: A 20-year search for equity. *New York Times* Sports Section, 21, 22, 23 June.

Naftolin, F., and E. Butz, eds. 1981. Sexual dimorphism. *Science* 211:1263–1324.

Olson, Wendy. 1990. Beyond Title IX: Toward an agenda for women and sports in the 1990s. *Yale Journal of Law and Feminism* 3:105–51.

Perry, Ruth, and Lisa Greber. 1990. Women and computers: An introduction. *Signs: Journal of Women in Culture and Society* 16:74–101.

Prior, Jerilynn C., Yvette M. Yigna, Martin T. Shechter, and Arthur E. Burgess. 1990. Spinal bone loss and ovulatory disturbances. *New England Journal of Medicine* 323:1221–27.

Richards, Renée, with Jack Ames. 1983. *Second serve.* New York: Stein and Day.

Riley, Denise. 1988. *Am I that name? Feminism and the category of women in history.* Minneapolis: University of Minnesota Press.

Scharff, Virginia. 1991. *Taking the wheel: Women and the coming of the motor age.* New York: Free Press.

Slatton, Bonnie, and Susan Birrell. 1984. The politics of women's sport. *Arena Review* 8.

Smith, Dorothy E. 1990. *The conceptual practices of power: A feminist sociology of knowledge.* Toronto: University of Toronto Press.

Spelman, Elizabeth. 1988. *Inessential woman: Problems of exclusion in feminist thought.* Boston: Beacon Press.

Theberge, Nancy. 1987. Sport and women's empowerment. *Women's Studies International Forum* 10:387–93.

Vecsey, George. 1990. Cathy Rigby, unlike Peter, did grow up. *New York Times* Sports Section, 19 December.

Watson, Tracey. 1987. Women athletes and athletic women: The dilemmas and contradictions of managing incongruent identities. *Sociological Inquiry* 57:431–46.

Willis, Paul. 1982. Women in sport in ideology. In *Sport, culture, and ideology,* edited by Jennifer A. Hargreaves. London: Routledge & Kegan Paul.

Wright, Barbara Drygulski et al., eds. 1987. *Women, work, and technology: Transformations.* Ann Arbor: University of Michigan Press.

Yoder, Janice D. 1989. Women at West Point: Lessons for token women in male-dominated occupations. In *Women: A feminist perspective,* edited by Jo Freeman. 4th ed. Palo Alto, CA: Mayfield.

Zimmerman, Jan, ed. 1983. *The technological woman: Interfacing with tomorrow.* New York: Praeger.

Voicing Your Opinion
Believing Is Seeing:
Biology as Ideology

Judith Lorber

1. Respond to Lorber's assertion that "neither sex nor gender are pure categories." What does the author mean in this statement? What implications might this statement have in your understanding of gender and communication?

   _____

   _____

   _____

   _____

   _____

2. What is your experience with competitive sports? Have you witnessed or experienced any of the sex/gender issues discussed in the article? How do you respond to Lorber's suggestion that assumptions about men's and women's bodies influence the way they are treated as athletes?

   _____

   _____

   _____

   _____

   _____

3. How is Lorber using common human activities such as driving and using public bathrooms as a basis for her argument? Does this argument reflect any of your own opinions or experiences?

   _____

   _____

   _____

   _____

   _____

Terms
Intersex
Genital
reconstruction
Genital
normalization

WHO WILL MAKE ROOM FOR THE INTERSEXED?

♂ ♀

KATE HAAS

This article discusses the legal and medical response to individuals born with intersex conditions. A person is considered intersexed if they are born with sexual characteristics that are not clearly male or female. Genital reconstruction is almost always done when these individuals are babies, therefore allowing parents the ability to name their child as "girl" or "boy." This piece argues that genital reconstruction is rarely medically necessary and that the U.S. Constitution may need to be changed to protect the rights of intersexed individuals.

I. Introduction

Between 1.7 and 4% of the world population is born with intersex conditions, having primary and secondary sexual characteristics that are neither clearly male nor female.[1] The current recommended treatment for an infant born with an intersex condition is genital reconstruction surgery to render the child as clearly sexed either male or female.[2] Every day in the United States, five children are subjected to genital reconstruction surgery that may leave them with permanent physical and emotional scars.[3] Despite efforts by intersexed people to educate the medical community about their rejection of infant genital reconstruction surgery, the American medical community has not yet accepted the fact that differences in genital size and shape do not necessarily require surgical correction.[4]

Genital reconstruction surgery may involve removing part or all of the penis and scrotum or clitoris and labia of a child, remodeling a penis or creating a vaginal opening.[5] While the initial surgery is typically performed in the first month of a child's life, genital reconstruction surgery is not only performed on infants.[6] Older children may be subjected to multiple operations to construct "functional" vaginas, to repair "damaged" penises, and to remove internal sex organs.[7] Personal accounts written by intersexed adults indicate that some children have been subjected to unwanted surgery throughout their childhood and teenage years without a truthful explanation of their condition.[8]

Genital reconstruction is rarely medically necessary.[9] Physicians perform the surgeries so that intersexed children will not be psychologically harmed when they realize that they are different from their peers.[10] Physicians remove external signs that children are intersexed, believing that this will prevent the child and the child's family from questioning the child's gender.[11] However, intersexed children may very well feel more confused about their gender if they are raised without any explanation about their intersex condition or input into their future treatment options.[12] The medical community's current practice focuses solely on genital appearance, discounting the fact that chromosomes also affect individuals' gender identities and personalities.[13]

Operating on children out of a belief that it is crucial for children to have genitals that conform to male/female norms ignores the fact that even the best reconstruction surgery is never perfect.[14] Genital reconstruction surgery may result in scarred genitals, an inability to achieve orgasm, or an inability to reproduce naturally or through artificial insemination.[15] The community-held belief that an individual's ability to engage in intercourse is essential, even without orgasm or reproductive capability, seems to govern the decision to perform genital surgery on many otherwise healthy, intersexed children.[16]

Despite the intersex community's rejection of genital reconstruction surgery, no U.S. court has examined the legality of performing these operations without the individual child's consent.[17] By contrast, Colombian courts have heard three such cases and have created a new standard for evaluating a parent's right to consent to genital reconstruction surgery for their minor children.[18] In response to the Colombian rulings and pressure from intersex activists, the American Bar Association recently proposed a resolution recommending that physicians adopt the heightened informed consent procedures required by the Colombian Constitutional Court decisions.[19]

This Article questions whether genital reconstruction surgery is necessary in the Twenty-first Century. Part II discusses the history and current preferred "treatment" for intersex conditions. Part III explains the groundbreaking Colombian Appellate Court decisions prohibiting parental consent for genital reconstruction on children over the age of five, and establishing a heightened informed consent doctrine for younger children. Part IV analyzes the protection that current U.S. law could provide to intersexed children. Part V explores how international law may influence decisions regarding the treatment of intersexed children.

II. A History of Collusion: Destroying Evidence of Ambiguous Genitals

The term "intersex" is used to describe a variety of conditions in which a fetus develops differently than a typical XX female or XY male.[20] Some intersexed children are born with "normal" male or female external genitals that do not correspond to their hormones.[21] Others are born with a noticeable combination of male and female external features, and still others have visually male or female external characteristics that correspond to their chromosomes but do not correspond to their internal gonads.[22] Individuals who are considered intersexed may also be born with matching male chromosomes, gonads, and genitals but suffer childhood disease or accident that results in full or partial loss of their penis.[23] The loss of a penis may lead physicians to recommend that a boy be sexually reassigned as female.[24] Although the conditions differ, the commonality of intersexed people is that their gonads, chromosomes, and external genitalia do not coincide to form a typical male or female.[25] The current American medical treatment of intersexuals is to alter the individual's internal and external gonads to sex them as either clearly male or clearly female.[26]

Medical "treatment" of intersexuals has only been practiced in the United States since the 1930s.[27] During that period, the medical community determined that intersexed people were truly male or female but had not fully developed in the womb.[28] Hormone treatments and surgical interventions were meant to complete the formation of an intersexed adult into a "normal" man or woman.[29] By the 1950s, physicians were able to identify most intersex conditions at birth and began operating immediately on intersexed children to eliminate any physical differences.[30]

Prior to the treatment of intersexuality in the United States, intersexed Americans were treated as either male or female according to their dominant physical characteristics.[31] This strict male/female delineation is not used in all countries though. Other cultures have treated intersexuals differently, either as a third sex, neither male nor female, or as natural sexual variations of the male or female sex.[32] Alternatively, some societies still accept intersexed people without clearly defining their sex at birth.[33]

For instance, within small communities in the Dominican Republic and Papua New Guinea, there is a hereditary intersex condition known as 5-alpha reductase deficiency that occurs with a relatively high frequency.[34] This condition causes male children to be born with very small or unrecognizable penises.[35] During puberty, the children's male hormones cause their penises to grow and other secondary male sexual characteristics to develop.[36] Most of these children are raised as girls and begin living as men when they reach puberty.[37] These communities have accepted these intersexuals without genital reconstruction surgery.[38] In the United States, however, a child with the same condition would likely be surgically altered at birth, raised as a girl and treated with hormones to prevent the onset of male physical development.[39]

Genital reconstruction surgery became standard practice in the United States through the efforts of John Money, a Johns Hopkins University professor.[40] Money introduced the theory that children are not born with a gender identity, but rather form an understanding of gender through their social upbringing.[41]

He based this theory on early research done with intersexed children who were surgically altered at birth and raised as either male or female.[42] Money's research found that children who were born with exactly the same genetic makeup and physical appearance fared equally well when raised as either females or males. He concluded that chromosomes did not make any difference in gender differentiation, and that children could be successfully reared as either sex irrespective of their anatomy or chromosomal make-up.[43] Money attempted to prove his theory by demonstrating that a "normal" male child could be successfully raised as a female with Bruce Reimer.[44]

In 1972, Money made public his experimental sex reassignment surgery on a twenty-two-month-old male child named Bruce Reimer who had been accidentally castrated during a routine circumcision.[45] The doctor who examined Reimer shortly after the accident believed that he would be unable to live a normal sexual life as an adolescent and would grow up feeling incomplete and physically defective.[46] Money's solution was to perform a sex change operation on baby Bruce and to have his parents raise him as a girl named Brenda. During Brenda's childhood, Money removed all of "his" internal reproductive organs. As Brenda approached puberty "she" was given female hormones to trigger breast development and other female secondary characteristics.[47] By removing Brenda's gonads, Money destroyed Brenda's reproductive capability. However, Money believed that by changing Brenda's sex, he would make it possible for her to engage in intercourse and marry.[48]

Early reports of Money's experiment claimed that the operation was successful and that Brenda was a happy, healthy girl.[49] Money's research was published throughout the world, convincing doctors that gender was a societal construct, and therefore intersexed children could be raised unconditionally as either male or female.[50] He believed that the only way to ensure that both the family and the child would accept the child's gender was if the child's genitals looked clearly male or female. Based on this theory, babies born with ambiguous genitals or small penises and baby boys who were accidentally castrated were surgically altered and raised as females.[51] Similarly, children born with mixed genitalia, gonads, and chromosomes were surgically altered to fit the definition of a "normal" male or female.[52] Following U.S. lead, other countries also began to practice routine genital reconstruction surgery on intersexed infants.[53]

Despite the widespread use of genital reconstruction surgery, there is no research showing that intersexuals benefit psychologically from the surgery performed on them as infants and toddlers.[54] No follow-up studies were ever done on adult intersexuals who underwent genital reconstruction surgery as children.[55] In the late 1980s, researchers attempting to disprove Money's gender identity theory began searching for Brenda, the subject of Money's highly publicized research.[56] The boy who was raised as a girl was now living as a man and had changed his name to David.[57] In 1997, Milton Diamond and Keith Sigmundson published an article rebutting the results of Money's famous gender research.[58] The publicity caused by Diamond and Sigmundson's article led to a biography of Reimer by John Colapinto. When Colapinto interviewed Reimer in 1997, Reimer admitted that he had always been certain that he was not a girl, despite being deceived by his doctor and his family.[59]

Reimer suffered emotional duress at all stages of his development, despite the corrective surgery that was meant to make him "normal." In his biography of Reimer, Colapinto describes the painful experiences that Reimer suffered throughout his childhood and teenage years.[60] During her childhood, Brenda did not fit in with her peers and felt isolated and confused.[61] As early as kindergarten, other children teased Brenda about her masculinity and failure to adopt "girl's play."[62] Although her kindergarten teacher was not initially told of her sex change, the teacher reported realizing that Brenda was very different from other girls.[63]

In addition to her failure to fit in socially, Brenda was constantly reminded that she was different by her parents and Dr. Money. During her visits to John Hopkins, Money would often force her to engage in sexual role-play with her twin brother in order to enforce that she was a girl and he was a boy.[64] Her genitals were scarred and painful as a child and she hated to look at them.[65] She became suspicious that something terrible had been done to her, primarily due to the frequent doctor's visits with John Money. During these visits, Dr. Money and his associates questioned Brenda about her genitals and her gender identity.[66] Rather than enforcing her gender identity, the medical intervention compounded the trauma caused by her medical condition.

One particularly traumatic procedure inflicted on intersexed children was not discussed in the biography of David Reimer. Intersexed children who have artificially created vaginas must undergo vaginal dilation procedures throughout their early childhood.[67] In order to ensure that the newly created vaginal opening does not close up, the child's parents must insert an object into the child's vagina on a daily basis.[68] This procedure has sexual implications that may be emotionally traumatic for many children.

As a teenager, Reimer rejected his assigned sex and refused to take his female hormones. He reported engaging in typically male behavior throughout his teens. He dressed as a male, chose a trade school for mechanics, and even began urinating standing up.[69] When Reimer's parents finally told him that he was born male, he immediately chose to adopt a male identity and changed his name to David.[70] He had a penis constructed and implanted, and underwent breast reduction surgery to rid himself of the breasts developed through estrogen therapy.[71] There is no procedure that can replace the gonads that were removed as part of Reimer's sex reassignment surgery. There is also no cure for the deception that he experienced upon learning that his parents and doctors had lied to him about many aspects of his life.[72] The trauma of learning about his condition caused David to attempt suicide on several occasions.[73]

David is now married and has adopted his wife's children.[74] His story reads as a happy ending to many people. However, David could have avoided the gender dysphoria, loss of reproductive capability, and many years of therapy that resulted from genital reconstruction surgery. These experiences are not atypical in the intersexed community. According to many intersexed activists, the comfort of being raised in a clear gender role does not outweigh the pain of deception or the physical side effects associated with the surgery.[75]

Despite the emotional and physical scars that people like David Reimer face from genital reconstruction surgery, the majority of American physicians continue to encourage early childhood surgery.[76] In some cases, physicians have insisted on performing genital reconstruction surgery on teenagers without their consent.[77]

In 1993, an intersexed activist named Cheryl Chase began a support and advocacy group for intersexed adults called the Intersex Society of North America ("ISNA").[78] Chase was born with a large clitoris, which was removed when she was an infant.[79] When she was eight years old, her internal gonads were removed without her knowledge or consent.[80] Because of the surgery, she is no longer capable of having her own children or obtaining orgasm.[81] Today, Chase and other advocates are vocal about their hope for a moratorium on the invasive treatment of intersexed children.[82]

ISNA members have contributed significantly to the debate over genital reconstruction surgery by providing personal insight into the effects of surgery on intersexed adults. As of the late 1990s, more than 400 intersexed individuals from around the world contacted ISNA and recounted stories similar to Ms. Chase's.[83] According to ISNA, sex change operations and genital normalizing surgeries should not be performed on children until the child has the ability to consent personally to the operation.[84]

At this point, there is insufficient proof that intersexed adults who are not operated on fair any worse than intersexed adults who have had genital reconstruction surgery as children.[85] The only research that has been done on intersexed adults who have not been surgically altered also comes from John Money. In the 1940s, prior to his well-known study on Reimer, Money interviewed many intersexed adults about their gender identity and upbringing.[86] To his surprise, he found that intersexed adults who had not undergone genital reconstruction surgery had a gender identity comparable to other adult males and females.[87] Unfortunately this research was done as part of Money's doctoral thesis and was never published.[88]

III. The Colombian Constitutional Court's Ruling

Public authorities, the medical community and the citizens in general must make room for these people who have been silenced until now.[89]

In 1995, Colombia's highest court, the Constitutional Court, addressed the legality of performing gender reconstruction surgery on children.[90] The Constitutional Court has issued three decisions on the constitutionality of genital reconstruction surgery, and, as of the publication date of this Article, it is the only court in the world to have rendered an opinion on this issue.[91] The first case that the court considered was brought by a teenage boy who had been raised as a girl under circumstances very much like David Reimer's.[92] Several years after this first case, the court decided two other cases involving children born with intersex conditions.[93] These three cases have limited parents' rights to choose genital reconstruction surgery for their children in Colombia.

The first case, *Sentencia No. T-477/95* [hereinafter *Gonzalez*], involved a male infant who was accidentally castrated during circumcision and was subsequently subjected to a sex change operation.[94] His physicians performed the sex change operation so that his genitals would conform to societal norms and he would be capable of sexual intercourse as an adult.[95] As a teenager, Gonzalez learned of the operation and sued the doctors and hospital that allowed the operation to be performed without his consent.[96] The Colombian Constitutional Court heard Gonzalez's appeal and found that this operation violated the boy's fundamental right to human dignity and gender identity.[97] The court based its decisions on the Colombian Constitution and the international covenant on human rights guaranteed by the Inter-American Court of Human Rights.[98] The court ruled that doctors could not alter the gender of a patient, regardless of the patient's age, without the patient's own informed consent.[99]

Several years after *Gonzalez,* the parents of two children born with intersex conditions brought their cases to court seeking the authority to consent to surgery on behalf of their minor children.[100] In both cases, the children's physicians had recommended genital reconstruction surgery, but refused to perform the surgery without each child's consent.[101] For the first time in the world, a court addressed the issue of whether parents should be allowed to consent to genital reconstruction surgery on their intersexed children. Although these cases were not identical to *Gonzalez,* the hospital feared that if it performed genital reconstruction surgery on any child without the child's consent, it could be held liable under *Gonzalez.*[102] The Colombian Constitutional Court heard both cases on appeal.[103]

In *Sentencia No. SU-337/99* [hereinafter *Ramos*], the Colombian Constitutional Court considered the case of an eight-year-old intersexed child raised as a girl and diagnosed with male pseudo-hermaphroditism.[104] Ramos was born with XY (male) chromosomes but due to her inability to process male hormones, her external genitalia did not fully develop.[105] Ramos had a small penis (three centimeters), folds of skin that did not contain testicles, male gonads, and a urinal opening at the base of her perineum.[106]

According to the documents received at the trial court level, Ramos' doctors were not aware that she was intersexed until she was three years old.[107] Until that point, Ramos' mother had raised her as a girl without questioning whether she might not have female chromosomes. When Ramos' pediatrician became aware that the child was intersexed, the doctor recommended that she receive genital reconstruction surgery to remove her small penis and gonads and to construct a vagina.[108] The doctor recommended the sex change operation because although Ramos had a small penis, it would never grow to the size of a typical penis, and it would never function properly.[109] Additionally, Ramos had been raised as a girl thus far, had a female name, wore feminine clothing, and identified with the social role of Colombian women.[110]

Ramos' mother brought this action to force the hospital to accept her consent on behalf of Ramos so that the doctors could proceed with the surgery.[111] Ramos' mother alleged that if the hospital waited to perform surgery until Ramos could consent for herself, the child would be psychologically harmed because she would grow up without a clear gender identity.[112]

However despite being raised female, the trial court found that Ramos' gender was ambiguous because "in some aspects she behaves like a woman and in some aspects like a man."[113] It also concluded that every person should have the right to develop his or her own gender identity as a part of the development of his or her personality.[114] The trial court stated that nobody could determine with the gender identity of this child would be except for the child herself, denying Ramos' mother the right to consent to surgery.[115] Ramos' mother appealed the case to the Constitutional Court.

By the time the case was heard on appeal, Ramos was eight years old.[116] After considering medical information and briefs from experts around the world, the Constitutional Court upheld the trial court's decision denying Ramos' mother the right to consent to genital reconstruction surgery for her child.[117] In its decision, the court referred extensively to the Colombian Constitution, as well as international laws and norms.[118]

The court considered the gravity of the procedure and the negative effects it could have on the child if she were to reject her assigned sex, and found that substitute judgment should not be allowed. The Constitutional Court quoted the trial court's opinion, noting that it would be wrong for anyone to consent to a sex change operation other than the child herself.[119] In reaching its conclusion, the court discussed the lack of evidence of any psychological harm to children that are not operated on, and the existence of actual evidence of psychological harm to children that have had such operations.[120]

The *Ramos* decision did not seem to rely on the individual facts of the case, but rather on the over-reaching harm of the surgery as compared to the unproven benefits. However in its next case, the Constitutional Court seems to have made its decision based on the individual facts of the case, primarily that the surgery had already been performed with no major problems.[121]

In the Constitutional Court's next decision, *Sentencia No. T-551/99* [hereinafter *Cruz*],[122] the court relied heavily on the information provided in *Ramos.*[123] However, the decision in *Cruz* was substantially weaker than both of the previous decisions, limiting its prior holdings to children over the age of five.[124]

Cruz was born with XX (female) chromosomes and male external genitalia.[125] Her parents were seeking to have her clitoris/penis removed or reduced in size so that she would look more female.[126] At the age of two, Cruz was already aware that her genitals were different from those of her family members.[127] However since Cruz was much younger then Ramos, the trial court did not rely on facts regarding Cruz's own gender identity. After hearing the case, the trial court held that Cruz's parents could consent to genital reconstruction surgery on her behalf if their consent was "informed."[128]

Cruz was only three years old when the case was brought to the attention of the Constitutional Court and had already undergone genital reconstruction surgery.[129] The Constitutional Court decided to hear the case in order to set a standard for the lower courts to follow in the future.[130] The court found that Cruz's parents did not really understand the implications of the operation on their child's life. Believing that their child would be "normalized" by the procedure, the parents were given the impression that surgery was their only option.[131] Since the parents were not properly informed about the procedure or provided alternative options, the court held that Cruz's rights had been violated despite her young age.[132] Although it was too late to make any changes in the decision that was already made for Cruz, the court ordered that an interdisciplinary team be put together to support the child and her family in the future.[133]

In this decision, the court could have followed its reasoning in *Ramos* to ban parental consent to genital reconstruction surgeries on all children.[134] However, instead of following its own precedent, the court decided that parents should be allowed to consent to surgery on children under age five.[135] The court explained that Cruz was too young to have formed a gender identity.[136] By prohibiting parental consent for the surgery, the court stated that it would be intruding into the realm of family privacy.[137] The court also stated that prohibiting this surgery altogether would be like a social experiment in which children were the subjects.[138] Had it decided to prohibit the surgery on young children, the intersexed children following this case would be the first children in the country to be prohibited from obtaining sex assignment/reconstruction surgery.[139]

While deciding not to make room for the intersexed, the court made clear that it did not intend to leave the decision whether to operate at the full discretion of the parents either. It reasoned that parents might be fearful of intersex conditions and discriminate against their children, consenting to operations not truly in the child's best interest.[140] Finally, the court concluded that the medical community should establish a protocol allowing parents to consent to genital reconstruction surgery only after they establish that it is truly in their child's best interest, creating a new form of "qualified and persistent, informed consent."[141]

The court in *Cruz* gave Colombian parents the right to substitute judgment for infants and young children who have already achieved consciousness of their bodies; however, parents can only give consent after fully understanding the consequences of the surgery for their child. In *Cruz,* the court clarified that its decision to withhold parental consent in *Ramos* was based on the fact that Ramos was eight years old when her case was decided.[142] *Cruz* narrowed the individual consent doctrine to apply to children over the age of five, holding that intersexed children over the age of five must give their informed consent before undergoing genital reconstruction surgery.[143]

In *Cruz,* the court determined that in order for parental consent to genital reconstruction surgery to be valid for children under the age of five, three criteria must be met: (i) detailed information must be provided, and the parent must be informed of the pros and cons that have sparked the current debate; (ii) the consent must be in writing, to formalize the decision and to ensure its seriousness; and (iii) the authorization must be given in stages.[144] This last qualification is intended to permit the parents the time to bond with their child the way that he or she is, and not to make a prejudicial decision based on shock at the baby's appearance.[145] The court stated that it would be up to the medical community and the legislature to determine the specific details for the consent procedure.[146]

Doctors generally recommend surgery for intersexed children at birth.[147] Ramos' mother was forced to wait until Ramos was eight years old only because the trial court originally denied permission for her to give consent for the operation.[148] However important the investigation and dicta was in *Ramos,* most intersexed children will not benefit from it. Most often, surgery will be performed when the child is still an infant and only the heightened informed consent will be directly applicable to them.[149] By limiting the holding of *Ramos* in *Cruz* to children over the age of five, the court diminished the significance of *Ramos.*

All three of the Colombian Court's decisions could have fundamentally altered the individual rights of intersexed children in Colombia. Instead, they have only given the parents of intersexed children the right to more information before they consent to genital reconstruction surgery. Perhaps some parents will obtain enough information to decide to decline these operations. However, in the end, it is still the parent and not the child who will be able to determine what gender the child will be, whether the child will be able to reproduce, and who the child will be allowed to marry. Given the opportunity to make a huge difference in the lives of intersexed people around the world, the Colombian Court's decision did not adequately protect this "marginalized and forgotten minority."[150]

Despite the Colombian Court's reticence about banning infant genital reconstruction surgery, Colombian law still provides far more protection for intersex children then current American law. The Colombian Court's decisions have increased the world's awareness of the problems with genital reconstruction surgery and reopened the medical debate regarding genital reconstruction surgery in the United States.

IV. Making Room for Intersexuals in the United States

The United States does not currently provide any procedural protection for intersexed children. In the United States, doctors are not required to receive the consent of intersexed children before performing genital reconstruction surgery.[151] Neither are parents routinely given sufficient information to make an informed decision on their child's behalf.[152] Currently, the United States lacks even the standard for informed consent instituted after the Colombian Court's final decision in *Cruz*.[153]

Thus far, there has been no legal challenge brought on behalf of intersexed children in the United States. Intersexed adults who have inquired about suing their doctors for performing genital reconstruction surgery that altered their gender have met resistance.[154] Intersexed adults have been told that because the doctors followed standard medical practice when they performed the surgery, the doctors are not liable for medical malpractice.[155]

Unlike the Colombian Constitution, the U.S. Constitution does not have specific provisions protecting a child's right to bodily integrity. However, the Constitution has been interpreted to protect privacy rights, including the right to marry and reproduce, and the right to bodily integrity generally.[156] Common law also provides some protection for children when there is no "informed" consent, or when a parent's consent or lack of consent to medical treatment is found to be contrary to the child's best interest.[157] In addition to case law supporting the need for informed consent and the best interest of the child, there are recent federal and state statutes protecting female children from genital mutilation.[158] Thus, while no intersexed Americans have successfully sued a physician or hospital for conducting early genital reconstructive surgery, they may have grounds to sue based on female genital mutilation laws, the constitutional right to privacy and lack of informed consent by their parents.

A. Constitutional Protection for Intersexuals: Leaving Room for an Open Future

The U.S. Constitution protects individuals from overreaching government power through the Fourteenth Amendment, which states "No state shall make or enforce any law which shall abridge the privileges or immunities of citizens of the United States, nor shall any state deprive any person of life, liberty, or property, without due process of law . . ."[159] The U.S. Supreme Court has interpreted the Fourteenth Amendment as protecting individuals from government action that infringes upon certain "fundamental rights" considered "implicit in the concept of ordered liberty."[160]

The Supreme Court has found that the right to bodily autonomy, the right to choose whether or not to reproduce, the right to marry, and the right to make decisions about how to raise children are all fundamental privacy rights.[161] The government may not violate a person's liberty by infringing any of these rights without first proving in a court of law that there is a compelling state interest that must be served, and that the method that the government is using is narrowly tailored to achieve a compelling governmental interest.[162]

Historically, children have not been accorded the same constitutional rights as adults. A child's parents and the government are allowed to restrict some rights that would be held fundamental for an adult.[163] The Supreme Court has also recognized a fundamental right to family privacy, according parents a high degree of respect regarding decisions they make about their child's upbringing.[164] This includes the choices parents make regarding their children's medical care.[165] Despite the Fourteenth Amendment right to family privacy, the parents' rights must be weighed against the children's rights to be protected against harm. The doctrine of parens patriae articulates the government's interest in protecting the rights of vulnerable individuals from harm.[166]

The doctrine of parens patriae allows the government to interfere with parents' choices about how to raise their children when the children may be harmed because of the parents' actions or inactions.[167] Generally, the government interferes with parental decisions under laws prohibiting parental abuse or neglect.[168] In the case of intersexed children, the government may have reason to override the parents' decision to perform surgery if the surgery would harm the child.

The Fourteenth Amendment does not prohibit an individual from violating another individual's fundamental rights. Thus, a child cannot generally sue a hospital or a physician for an infringement of his or her constitutional rights. For there to be a constitutional violation, there must be state action.[169] If genital reconstruction surgery is performed at a state hospital, then there is state action allowing the child to sue the hospital directly. If the surgery is conducted at a private hospital, there may not be state action. In that case, in order to implicate the Fourteenth Amendment, an intersexed child who is about to be subjected to genital reconstruction surgery must seek an injunction against the hospital prior to the surgery.[170] If a judge orders the surgery to progress, there is state action, and the child may claim a constitutional violation.[171] If the child successfully claims that the surgery violates a fundamental right, then in order for the court to order the surgery over the objection of the child or his or her court appointed representative, the proponents must prove, by clear and convincing evidence, that the surgery is in the child's best interest.[172] This standard is high, and in order to prevail, the proponent of the surgery must establish that there are no less restrictive means to accomplish the same result.[173] Since there are no studies proving that genital reconstruction surgery psychologically benefits children, and there are testimonial accounts that genital reconstruction surgery causes psychological and physical trauma, it is unlikely that the court would find that there was clear and convincing evidence of best interest.

1. Bodily Integrity: If It Works, Don't Fix It

Included in the Fourteenth Amendment right to privacy is the right to bodily autonomy, which protects individuals from intrusion by the government into their health care decisions.[174] This right includes the right to choose to forego medical treatment, even if foregoing treatment may result in death.[175] For the most part, children are not accorded the right to choose medical treatment or to choose to forego medical treatment without parental consent, despite the fact that it has been found to be a fundamental right.[176] The reason that parents are allowed to consent for children is that a child may not be able to understand fully the consequences of their own consent because of their age or inexperience.[177]

There are several exceptions to the rule requiring parental consent to treatment. The first exception accepted by several states by statute is the "mature minor" exception.[178] Minors who are considered mature enough to make their own medical decisions need not obtain parental consent to medical treatment, and may object to medical treatment that their parents choose for them.[179]

Many states have also provided exceptions to parental consent requirements for children seeking treatment for drug addiction, mental health treatment, and testing and treatment for sexually transmitted diseases.[180] The logic behind these exceptions is that these treatments are very personal, and if required to seek parental consent, many children would forego treatment. If children could not be treated for HIV, drug addiction, or mental illness, they would likely place themselves and others in danger.[181]

These exceptions take into account the fact that parents do not always act in their child's best interest, and a child may suffer abuse or psychological harm if required to seek parental consent to certain treatments. The right to choose whether or not to undergo genital reconstruction surgery should be an exception to the general rule allowing parental consent to treatment of minors. Genital reconstruction surgery is a personal choice that children should be allowed to make on their own in certain circumstances, or, at a minimum, in conjunction with their parents. It is difficult for many children to learn about their intersexuality. However, it is also hard for children to learn to cope with pregnancy, drug addiction, mental illness, or their HIV positive status. In contrast to intersex conditions, all of the above medical conditions are free of parental consent requirements under certain circumstances.

Genital reconstruction surgery is arguably the ultimate infringement of an individual's bodily autonomy. Genital reconstruction surgery can cause a child significant psychological and physical harm.[182] For these reasons, parents should not be allowed to make the decision to alter surgically their child's genitals without the child's consent absent clear and convincing evidence that it is in the child's best interest. If the state participates by allowing the procedure to be performed at a state hospital or by ordering the procedure over the child's objection, then there may be a constitutional violation of the child's right to bodily autonomy under the Fourteenth Amendment.

2. Reproduction: Gonads Cannot Be Replaced

The right to choose whether or not to reproduce is a fundamental right and, accordingly, certain restrictions are placed on the government's right to interfere with decisions bearing on reproduction.[183] For example, all minors regardless of age have the right to seek an abortion without undue burden from the state, though the state may act to ensure that a woman's decision is informed.[184] Therefore, even when state law requires minors to receive parental consent before seeking an abortion, minors are permitted a judicial bypass, allowing them the right to prove to a court that they are mature enough to make the decision to have an abortion without parental consent.[185] Children may also have the right to seek contraception, treatment for pregnancy, and childbirth without parental consent.[186]

Because reproduction is a fundamental right, parents are limited in their ability to consent to sterilization procedures for their children. Generally, sterilization is raised in the context of a parent who wants to sterilize a handicapped child to protect the child from the harm of a dangerous pregnancy. If there is an objection made by the child or an advocate for the child, then a court cannot order the procedure against the child's objections without affording the child due process.[187] The child must be appointed an independent guardian *ad litem,* and receive a fair trial at which the court must determine by clear and convincing evidence that the operation to remove the child's gonads will be in the child's best interest.[188]

As with all people, some intersexed adults do not have the ability to reproduce even without genital reconstruction surgery.[189] Others will retain their full reproductive capacity even after the surgery is performed.[190] However, some intersexuals have the ability to reproduce either naturally or artificially and are denied that right by the removal of their gonads and other reproductive organs. For those children whose gonads are removed to complete their physical transformation, their fundamental right to reproduce has been violated. For example, a child born with male chromosomes and sexed at birth as female will have her gonads removed, thus, effectively sterilizing her.

Based on the lack of evidence of the effectiveness of genital reconstruction surgery, it would be difficult for a court to determine that this procedure is clearly in the child's best interest. If there are pros and cons to performing the surgery, the court must decide in a manner that will not violate the child's fundamental right to reproduce.[191]

3. Marriage: Determining Gender Determines Sexuality

Genital reconstruction surgery may inhibit or completely interfere with a child's fundamental right to marry. In the United States, there are currently no states in which it is legal to marry someone of the same sex.[192] In 1993, several gay couples challenged the prohibition against same-sex marriages under the Hawaii Constitution.[193] The Hawaii Supreme Court ruled in favor of the plaintiffs and allowed the first gay couples to marry legally.[194] In reaction to the ruling, the Hawaii state legislature immediately amended their own constitution to prohibit same-sex marriages.[195] The federal government reacted to the first gay marriages by passing the Defense of Marriage Act, which allows states to refuse to recognize same-sex marriages that are legally valid in another state.[196] Given that 3% of the world population does not fit into a clearly defined sex and still engage in marriage and child birth, it would be wise to re-think this prohibition.

However, given the laws as they currently stand, genital reconstruction surgically defines an intersexed person as male or female, thus, prohibiting them from marriage to a person of their "same" gender. Intersexuals are in a unique position before they undergo genital reconstruction surgery because they can petition the court to change their legal gender from female to male or male to female without having to undergo a sex change operation. They must prove that they are intersexed, that they have unclear genitals, and that they identify as the opposite sex, and their birth certificate may be altered.[197]

Once an intersexed person has undergone genital reconstruction surgery making his or her genitals clearly male or female, he or she cannot then choose to change his or her birth certificate without having a second round of surgeries performed.[198] For example, if a child born with male chromosomes or mixed chromosomes is surgically assigned a female gender at birth, that individual would be prohibited from marrying a female later in life without first undergoing another sex change operation.[199] In this case, if the initial gender reconstruction surgery had not been performed, this person would be considered a male, not a homosexual female, and thus would have a fundamental right to marry.

By choosing a gender for the child and performing reconstruction surgery at birth, the doctors may be infringing on an individual's ability to marry as an adult. The imposition of additional surgery to change their assigned sex would add such high financial and emotional costs on the individual that it may prohibit some, otherwise qualified, intersexuals from marrying.

B. Taking a First Step: Informing Parents That Their Child Is Intersexed

Physicians must receive informed consent from all patients before they treat them for any medical condition.[200] If physicians fail to obtain informed consent from their patients, they may be liable for medical malpractice.[201] Under the informed consent doctrine, a patient may even choose to refuse life saving treatment after weighing their treatment options.[202] The informed consent doctrine originated in the tort doctrine of battery, which includes intentionally touching a person in a way that they find harmful or offensive.[203] The surgical removal of part or all of a child's genitals must only be done after receiving informed consent or it may be considered battery.

Absent a recognized exception allowing children to consent to their own medical treatment, parents will generally be allowed to give or withhold consent for medical treatment on behalf of their children. In the United States, genital reconstruction surgery is not currently a procedure that children are allowed to consent or object to without their parents' participation. For informed consent to be valid, the parents must be informed of the nature and consequence of their child's medical condition, as well as the various treatment options available.

The Colombian standard of informed consent ensures that doctors provide parents with all of the known information about intersex conditions over a prolonged period of time. Doctors must provide surgical and non-surgical options for treatment, and refer parents to support organizations for intersexed individuals.[204] This model ensures that parents are not deceived about their child's prognosis, and that they understand that genital reconstruction surgery is not the only solution for their child.

In the United States, parents of intersexed children are not given enough information to make a truly informed decision about their child's treatment.[205] Some parents are not told that their child is intersexed, but instead that their child is a girl or boy with "unfinished" genitals that the doctor will repair with surgery.[206] Physicians may also tell the parents that their baby will have "normal" genitals after surgery.[207] Surgery may make the child's genitals look more clearly male or female, but it will also leave scarring and possibly diminish sexual functions.[208] Generally, more than one surgery is needed to alter completely the genital appearance, and the average number of surgeries is three or more.[209] Surgery and check-ups will continue through the child's early years and may be extremely stressful for the child and his or her parents.[210]

Additionally, parents must understand that while surgery will make intersexed children look more similar to their peers, it will not change their chromosomes. Even with hormone therapy, many intersexed youth will endure gender dysphoria.[211] They may feel confused about their gender despite having genitals that look clearly male or female. Intersexed adults may decide that their assigned gender is not their gender of choice. This might prompt the desire for additional, more complicated surgeries to perform a complete sex change operation.[212] Most of these facts are not presented to the parents of intersexed children at the time that they approve genital reconstruction surgery.[213] If parents are encouraged to consent to surgery without being told of the risks and side effects, their consent is not truly informed.

There are several exceptions to the rule for informed consent. The first exception is when there is a medical emergency and a person's life or health is in immediate danger, the doctors may proceed with a procedure if they have not received instructions to the contrary.[214] Most intersexed infants are not in any immediate danger that would exempt a physician from receiving informed consent to operate.[215] Even when intersexed infants have medical conditions that require surgical intervention on an emergency basis, the emergency aid can be given without removing any part of the child's body that is not immediately harming the child.[216] Physicians have relied upon the emergency doctrine to perform full sex change operations on children.[217] The argument is that if a parent were to learn that their child was intersexed, they might raise their child without a clear gender identity thus causing the child psychological harm.[218]

Additionally, under the guise of an emergency situation, parents are placed under unnecessary time pressure to decide whether or not to consent to surgery. They are encourage to make a decision about surgery in the first few weeks of their newborn's life. During the first few weeks after giving birth, parents may be stressed and anxious about their newborn's condition. They should be given more time to become accustomed to their child's body before doctors recommend surgery that is not medically necessary. This pressure forces parents to make decisions without seeking outside information to determine if there is a true medical necessity for the surgery.[219] In some cases, children have been operated on even after their parents explicitly refused to give consent.[220]

The emergency doctrine was not meant to prevent hypothetical psychological harm to the patient or their parents, but to prevent death or serious impairment to a patient in an emergency situation.[221] Physicians should not surgically remove or alter any part of an intersexed child's genitals without informed consent absent a true medical emergency.

A doctor may also be exempt from explaining the exact nature of the illness or treatment if it would be unsafe for the patient because it would cause them extreme physical or mental duress that would deteriorate their condition.[222] This exception has also been used by physicians to lie to parents or disguise the truth so that they will raise their child without any doubts as to the child's gender.[223] Reportedly, doctors do not explain intersex conditions to parents because they do not want to shock them.[224] Parents are frequently told that their child must be operated on in order to repair a minor birth defect. Doctors do not always tell the parents the chromosomal make-up of their child, or explain the ramifications of gender reassignment.[225] Although the parents may feel distressed upon learning of the child's condition, the parents' distress is not enough to exempt doctors from fully explaining the whole condition and the treatment options.[226] The emergency exception applies to the patient's condition, not to the parents' reaction to the patient's condition.

Additionally, if parents do not understand that their child was born intersexed, they will not be in a position to understand the issues their child may later develop and his or her potential for gender dysphoria. If the exceptions to informed consent were extended to prevent harmful parental reactions to differences in their child, doctors would have free reign to repair all congenital abnormalities at the parent's cost without informing the parent of the abnormality or obtaining their consent for the surgery. The exceptions to the informed consent doctrine were clearly not meant to extend this far.

C. Genital Mutilation: Equal Protection for Intersexed Children

Intersex children may also have a claim for medical malpractice based on violation of the law prohibiting female genital mutilation.[227] In 1996, Congress passed the Criminalization of Female Genital Mutilation Act.[228] Five states have also individually criminalized female genital mutilation.[229]

The process of removing or altering the genitalia of intersexed children is a form of genital mutilation as defined by the statute.[230] The law prohibits anyone from authorizing or performing an operation on a female child to remove all or part of her genitals for other than health reasons.[231] The statute explicitly covers ritual circumcisions, even if the child herself believes in the religious or cultural significance of the procedure.[232] In section 116(c), the law specifically states that no account shall be taken of the effect of any belief that has led the person or their family to demand the operation.[233] This Act holds the physician liable even if the family believed that the operation would be in the child's best interest and it was standard practice in their ethnic or religious community.[234]

According to the Act, the only way that genital operations can be legally performed on female children in the United States is if the doctor can show that under section 116(b)(1), it is necessary for the health of the person on whom it is performed.[235] As the Colombian Constitutional Court found through its extensive international research, there is no evidence that most surgery performed on intersexed children is done for other than psychological reasons.[236]

When an intersexed child is operated on to normalize his or her genitals, it is also part of a cultural tradition. Parents want their child to look like other children in Western countries, or as close to "normal" as possible.[237] In some Native American cultures, India, the Dominican Republic, and Papua New Guinea, intersexed people are accepted in society and occupy a specific cultural and social position.[238] In those cultures it would not be considered beneficial to the child to alter the child's genitals.

In the United States, intersexed children are operated on in order to make them look like other children who are not intersexed. Although some medical conditions might endanger intersexed children and therefore make the operations beneficial, this is not usually the case.[239] Most doctors who agree with genital operations for intersexed children claim that the surgery is necessary to protect their mental health.[240] However, no studies have been done that support the question of whether or not genital reconstruction and hormones actually protect the mental health of the patient any better then counseling and education.[241]

More than 400 intersexed people internationally have contacted ISNA in support of its opposition to genital reconstruction surgery on children.[242] The Constitutional Court of Colombia noted that doctors could not find any intersexed people willing to speak in support of such surgery on children.[243]

The congressional findings on the practice of female genital mutilation in the United States are particularly relevant to the issue of genital surgery on intersexed children. In particular, Congress found that female genital mutilation harms women both physically and psychologically.[244] They found that the practice violates both federal and state constitutional and statutory laws.[245]

The damaging physical and psychological effects of genital reconstruction surgery are identical to the effects of ritual female circumcision. In both cases, the surgery may result in pain, scarring, and the inability to achieve orgasm.[246] Congressional findings that females should not be subjected to the loss of any part of their genitalia for cultural reasons is directly applicable to intersexed children.

The Act indicates that parents do not have the right to give consent to nonessential genital surgery and doctors do not have the right to perform such surgery even if it will make the children assimilate with their ethnic and religious community.[247] The statute only applies to female children.[248] If taken as such, the statute may violate equal protection.[249] However, the Act does not define "female" by genetic make-up or external characteristics. Arguably, most intersexed children fall under one definition of "female" or another. Thus, intersexed children who have their clitoris reduced or other genital parts removed seem to have a strong claim of assault under the Female Genital Mutilation Act.

V. Sexual Diversity and the International Community

The United States should consider international standards for the treatment of children when considering the legality of genital reconstruction surgery. One of the main standards by which to judge the international consensus on children's rights is the Convention on the Rights of the Child.[250] The United States was one of only two United Nations member countries that did not sign the Convention on the Rights of the Child.[251] Despite the fact that the United States has not signed the Convention, it is an internationally accepted standard that should be considered by U.S. healthcare practitioners.

The Convention recognizes the rights of children independent of their parents by allowing them to veto parents' decisions on issues of health, education, and religious upbringing.[252] The Convention specifically states that a child should have input into all decisions affecting him or her.[253] Because the decision to alter a child's genitals will forever change the course of the child's life, particular care should be taken to involve the child in this decision.

The second international agreement that is relevant to the treatment of intersexuals is the Nuremberg Code, signed by the United States after World War II.[254] The Nuremberg Code prohibits countries from conducting experimental medical treatments on patients without their express informed consent.[255] Since genital reconstruction surgery has only been in practice during the last thirty years and no studies have been done to prove the procedures effectiveness, critics argue that genital reconstruction surgery is still experimental.[256] If the procedure is an experimental procedure, then the level of consent required should be higher.

Other countries look to the U.S. medical establishment in developing standards of care.[257] It is important for intersexed children around the world that doctors within the United States make a concerted effort to provide parents and children with all available knowledge regarding intersex conditions before making the recommendation to perform genital reconstruction surgery.

VI. Conclusion

Through its research and publication of many of the facts about intersex genital surgery, the Colombian Court has opened up a worldwide medical, ethical, and legal debate. However, rather than following the Colombian Court's decision, the world should heed the court's advice. Diversity should not be "a factor of violence and exclusion," but rather it should be "an irreplaceable source of social wealth."[258] The court, paraphrasing Johns Hopkins University professor, Dr. William Reiner, challenges the world to listen to intersexuals and to learn to coexist with them.[259]

With those words in mind, future legal decisions in the United States and abroad should prohibit hospitals from performing childhood genital reconstruction surgery when it is not medically necessary. The current insistence on genital "normalizing" surgery can be explained by our society's obsession with physical appearance and our fear of people who are "different."[260] However, as the Americans with Disabilities Act and other anti-discrimination laws integrate more and more people with different physical characteristics and abilities, society will begin to accept physical differences as a natural and positive part of being human.[261] At the point that our society makes room for the intersexed through laws prohibiting gender reassignment surgery and unnecessary genital reconstruction surgery on children, then people will begin to acknowledge the existence of intersexuals. When faced with the fact that 3% of the population has chromosomes, genitals, and sexual characteristics that are different, teachers will need to modify sex education courses. Ideally, children will learn that every individual has unique sexual characteristics that help make up their gender identity and sexual preference. Through open discussions of growth and sexual development, intersexed children will learn that they are not alone, and others will learn that intersexuality is a common condition that may effect someone they know.[262]

ENDNOTES

1. ANNE FAUSTO-STERLING, SEXING THE BODY: GENDER POLITICS AND THE CONSTRUCTION OF SEXUALITY 51 (2000) (reporting that 1.7% of the population may be intersexed); Julie A. Greenberg, *Defining Male and Female: Intersexuality and the Collision Between Law end Biology,* 41 ARIZ, L. REV. 265, 267 (1999) (reporting that Johns Hopkins sex researcher John Money estimates the number of people born with ambiguous genitals at 4%). Historically, people with intersex conditions were referred to as "hermaphrodites" but this word has been rejected as embodying many of the misperceptions and mistreatment of intersexed people. Raven Kaldera, *American Boyz Intersexuality Flyer, at* http:www.amboyz.org/intersection/flyerprint.html (last visited Mar. 27, 2004).

2. Hazel Glenn Beh &. Milton Diamond, *An Emerging Ethical and Medical Dilemma: Should Physicians Perform Sex Assignment Surgery on Infants with Ambiguous Genitalia?,* 7 MICH. J. GENDER & L. 1, 3 (2000): FAUSTO-STERLING. *supra* note 1, at 45; *see infra* note 4.

3. Emi Koyama, *Suggested Guidelines for Non-Intersex Individuals Writing About Intersexuality and Intersex People, at* http://isna.org/faq/writing-guidelines.html (last visited Mar. 27, 2004). *But see* Beh & Diamond, *supra* note 2, at 17 (estimating the number of sex reassignments in the United States at 100 to 200 annually).

4. Kishka-Kamari Ford. *"First Do No Harm"—The Fiction of Legal Parental Consent to Genital-Normalizing Surgery on Intersexed Infants.* 19 YALE L. & POL'Y REV. 469, 471 (2001).

5. FAUSTO-STERLING, *supra* note 1, at 61–63.

6. *Id.* at 45; Ford *supra* note 4, at 471; Sentencia No. SU-337/99 (Colom.), *available at* http://www.isna.org/Colombia/case1-partJ.html (last visited Mar. 27, 2004) (hereinafter Ramos). There are currently no published English translations of the three Colombian cases referred to in this Article. E-mail from Cheryl Chase, founding director of Intersex Society of North America ("ISNA") (Mar. 19. 2002) (on file with the author).

7. FAUSTO-STERLING, *supra* note 1, at 62. 84–85.

8. *Id.* at 84. Fausto-Sterling recounts the story of a twelve-year-old intersexed girl named Angela Moreno who lost her ability to orgasm after having her enlarged clitoris removed without her consent. She was told that she had ovarian cancer and was going to have a hysterectomy performed. Later she discovered she never had ovaries. Instead, she had testes that were also removed during the procedure. *Id.*

9. *Id.* at 63–65; Ford, *supra* note 4, at 476–77.

10. FAUSTO-STERLING, *supra* note 1, at 63–65; Ford, *supra* note 4, at 476–77, According to Ford, "medical professionals admit that it is the psychosocial problem of intersex that makes it an emergency." *Id.*

11. FAUSTO-STERLING, *supra* note 1, at 64–65; Beh & Diamond, *supra* note 2, at 51.

12. *See* FAUSTO-STERLING, *supra* note 1, at 84; Beh & Diamond, *supra* note 2, at 2; JOHN COLAPINTO, AS NATURE MADE HIM: THE BOY WHO WAS RAISED AS A GIRL 143–50, 212–13 (2000). In his book, Colapinto vividly describes the gender dysphoria and sexual confusion of David Reinier, a boy raised

as a girl after his penis was destroyed during a botched circumcision. *Id.* at 143–50. This biographical account of Reimer's life was written with the cooperation and participation of Reimer himself who sat for more than 100 hours of interviews and allowed the author access to all of his confidential files and medical records. *Id.* at xvii. Colapinto also discusses other children who have suffered extreme gender dysphoria growing up without being informed of their condition. One fourteen-year-old girl described in the book dropped out of high school and threatened suicide if she could not have reconstructive surgery to make her a boy. Testing revealed that she was intersexed, having male chromosomes and female external genitalia. *Id.* at 212.

13. COLAPINTO, *supra* note 12. at 32; FAUSTO-STERLING, *supra* note 1, at 46. Fausto-Sterling cites Johns Hopkins researcher John Money. "From the sum total of hermaphroditic evidence, the conclusion that emerges is that sexual behavior and orientation as male or female does not have an innate, instinctive basis." *id.*

14. FAUSTO-STERLING, *supra* note 1, at 85–87.

15. *Id.* at 58, 80, 85–87.

16. *Id.* at 57–58. Doctors consider a penis adequate if, as a child is able to stand while urinating and, as an adult is able to engage in vaginal intercourse. *Id. See also* Ford, *supra* note 4, at 471 (stating the "penis will be deemed 'adequate' at birth if it is no less than 2.5 centimeters long when stretched").

17. Ford, *supra* note 4, at 474.

18. Julie A. Greenberg & Cheryl Chase, *Colombia's Highest Court Restricts Surgery on Intersex Children, at* http://www.isna.org/colombia/background.html (last visited Mar. 27, 2004) (synthesizing in English the three Colombian cases to which this Article will refer).

19. E-mail from Alyson Meiselman, Liaison Representative of NLGLA (Aug. 19, 2002) (on file with author). The American Bar Association ("ABA") resolution was proposed by the International Law and Practice Section regarding surgical alteration of intersexed infants. The memorandum was drafted for the ABA Commission on Women in the Profession. *Id.* The resolution will be voted on by the House of Delegates at the August 2003 ABA meeting in San Francisco, California. E-mail from Alyson Meiselman, Liaison Representative of NLGLA (April 29, 2003) (on file with author). A draft of the proposed resolution is available at http://www.kindredspiritlakeside.homestead.com/ P_ABA.html (last visited Mar. 27, 2004).

20. FAUSTO-STERLING, *supra* note 1, at 36–39, 48–54.

21. *Id.*

22. *Id.* at 48–54. The most common forms of intersexuality are: Congenital Adrenal Hyperplasia, which affects children with XX chromosomes and is otherwise referred to as "female pseudo-hermaphrodite"; Androgen Insensitivity Syndrome, which affects children with XY chromosomes and is also referred to as "male pseudo-hermaphrodite"; Gonadal Dysgenesis, which predominantly affects children with XX chromosomes; Hypospadias, which affects children with XX chromosomes; Turner Syndrome, which affects children with XO chromosomes and causes these children to lack some feminine characteristics such as breast growth and menstruation; and Klinefelter Syndrome, which affects children with XXY chromosomes and causes these children to lack some external male characteristics. *Id.*

23. *Id.* at 66.

24. Beh & Diamond, *supra* note 2, at 3; *see* COLAPINTO, *supra* note 12, at 32.

25. FAUSTO-STERLING, *supra* note 1, at 51.

26. *Id.* at 56–63; Beh & Diamond, *supra* note 2, at 3.

27. FAUSTO-STERLING, *supra* note 1, at 40.

28. *Id.*

29. *Id.*

30. *Id.* at 44–45.

31. *Id.* at 40.

32. *Id.* at 33.

33. *Id.* at 109. For example, the Dominican Republic and Papua New Guinea acknowledge a "third type of child," however, they still recognize only two gender roles. *Id.*

34. *Id.*

35. *Id.*

36. *Id.*

37. *Id.*

38. *Id.*

39. *Id.*

40. COLAPINTO, *supra* note 12, at 39. Colapinto quotes Dr. Benjamin Rosenberg, a leading psychologist specialized in sexual identity, as saying, "Money was 'the leader—the front-runner on everything having to do with mixed sex and hermaphrodites . . . .'" *Id.*

41. *Id.* at 32–35; Ford, *supra* note 4, at 471.

42. COLAPINTO, *supra* note 12, at 32.

43. *Id.* at 32–35.

44. *Id.* at 50, 67–68, 70.

45. *Id.* at 65. John Money presented the case at the annual meeting of the American Association for the Advancement of Science on December 28, 1972.

46. *Id.* at 16.

47. *Id.* at 131.

48. *Id.* at 50. Money envisioned Brenda marrying a man and engaging in vaginal intercourse. *Id.*

49. *Id.* at 65–71.

50. *Id.* "The twins case was quickly enshrined in myriad textbooks ranging from the social sciences to pediatric urology and endocrinology." *Id.* at 70.

51. Ford, *supra* note 4, at 471–73; Beh & Diamond, *supra* note 2, at 3.

52. Ford, *supra* note 4, at 471; Beh & Diamond, *supra* note 2, at 3.

53. COLAPINTO, *supra* note 12, at 75.

54. Summary of Sentencia No. SU-337/99 (Colom.), at 4 [hereinafter Ramos Summary] (on file with author). The Colombian Court asked for follow-up studies on intersexed children and was not able to obtain any. *Id.;* COLAPINTO, *supra* note 12, at 233–35. There have been several cases of genetic males raised as females that were not followed until recently. *Id.* at 273–75; *see also* FAUSTO-STERLING, *supra* note 1, at 80–91 (providing statistics and personal accounts of intersexuals who received surgery during childhood).

55. Ramos Summary, *supra* note 54, at 4.

56. COLAPINTO, *supra* note 12, at 208–09. Milton Diamond, an outspoken opponent of John Money put out an advertisement searching for Brenda in the 1980s. With the help of Keith Sigmundson, he tracked down the subject of Money's famous study. *Id.* at 199, 208–09.

57. *Id.* at 208.

58. *Id.* at 214. The article was published in the *Archives of Pediatrics and Adolescent Medicine* in March 1997. *Id.*

59. *Id.* at 216.

60. *Id.* at 60–63, 145–50.

61. *Id.*

62. *Id.* at 60–63.

63. *Id.* Due to Reimer's negative behavior at school, she was referred to a guidance counselor in the first grade. Brenda's parents then allowed her doctor to speak with her guidance counselor and her teacher about her condition. *Id.* at 63–64.

64. *Id.* at 87.

65. *Id.* at 92.

66. *Id.* at 80.

67. Ramos Summary, *supra,* note 54, at 9; Kaldera, *supra* note 1.

68. Kaldera, *supra* note 1.

69. COLAPINTO, *supra* note 12, at 190–95.

70. *Id.* at 180–85.

71. *Id.* at 184.

72. *Id.* at 267. The Reimer family moved after Brenda's sex change operation and her parents created stories about other parts of their family history in order to hide the truth from her. *Id.* at 100–01, 106, 267.

73. *Id.* at 188.

74. *Id.* at 195.

75. *Id.* at 218–20; Alice Dreger, *Why Do We Need ISNA?,* ISNA NEWS, May 2001, *at* http://isna.org/newsletter/may2001/may2001.html. Because of the private nature of the topic many intersexed adults are hesitant about talking of their experiences. *Id.;* FAUSTO-STERLING, *supra* note 1, at 85. The ISNA website provides links to personal accounts written by intersexed adults, press releases, medical information, and other resources.

76. FAUSTO-STERLING, *supra* note 1, at 45–50.

77. *Id.* at 84.

78. *Id.* at 80; Intersex Society of North America, ISNA NEWS, Feb. 2001, *at* http://isna.org/newsletter/feb2001.html.

79. FAUSTO-STERLING, *supra* note 1, at 80.

80. *Id.*

81. *See id.* at 81; ABCNews.com, *Intersex Babies: Controversy Over Operating to Change Ambiguous Genitalia,* Apr. 19, 2002, *at* http://abcnews.go.com/sections/2020/DailyNews/2020_intersex_020419.html; COLAPINTO, *supra* note 12, at 217–18.

82. COLAPINTO, *supra* note 12, at 220.

83. *Id.* at 218.

84. *Id.* at 220; Intersex Society of North America, ISNA's Amicus Brief on Intersex Genital Surgery, Feb. 7, 1998, *available at* http://isna.org/colombia/brief.html.

85. COLAPINTO, *supra* note 12, 233–34; FAUSTO-STERLING, *supra* note 1, at 94–95.

86. COLAPINTO, *supra* note 12, at 233–35.

87. *Id.* at 234. The study included interviews with ten intersexed adults who had not been operated on as infants. The study found that genital appearance only plays a small part in a person's formation of gender identity.

88. *Id.*

89. Ramos Summary, *supra* note 54, at 10.

90. Greenberg & Chase, *supra* note 18.

91. *Id.*

92. *Id.*

93. *Id.*

94. *Id.* The first intersex case was heard by the Constitutional Court of Colombia in 1995. This case is available at the Intersex Society of North America website, at http://www.isna.org/colombia/t-477-95.html (last visited Mar. 27, 2004). Although the case has not been officially translated, the original Spanish text of this decision and the two subsequent decisions can be found on the website. E-Mail from Cheryl Chase, founding director of ISNA (March 19, 2002) (on file with author). For purposes of this Article, I referred to my own translation as well as to summaries of the cases forwarded in an e-mail by Cheryl Chase, written by Sydney Levy, ISNA Board of Directors (March 19, 2002) (on file with author). The names in all three decisions were changed by the Colombian court to maintain the privacy of the individuals involved. Ramos Summary, *supra* note 54, at 2. The court

refers to the cases by number and initials. This Article will refer to each case with a fictitious surname to avoid confusion.

95. Translation of Sentencia No. T-477/95 (Colom.), at 11–12 [hereinafter Gonzalez Translation] (on file with author).

96. *Id.* at 7.

97. *Id.* at 14–16.

98. *Id.* at 4–5, 14–15. CONSTITUCION POLITICA DE COLOMBIA, *translated in* CONSTITUTIONS OF THE WORLD (1998).

99. Gonzalez Translation, *supra* note 95, at 15; *see* Greenberg & Chase, *supra* note 18.

100. Ramos Summary, *supra* note 54, at 1; Translation of Sentencia No. T-551/99 (Colom.), at 1 [hereinafter Cruz Translation] (on file with author).

101. Ramos Summary, *supra* note 54, at 1; Cruz Translation, *supra* note 100, at 1.

102. Ramos Summary, *supra* note 54, at 2.

103. *Id.* at 1; Cruz Translation, *supra* note 100, at 1, 6.

104. Ramos, *supra* note 6. Throughout the case, the court refers to Ramos with female pronouns and so I will also refer to her as female.

105. Ramos Summary, *supra* note 54, at 1, 3.

106. *Id.* at 1.

107. *Id.*

108. *Id.*

109. *Id.*

110. *Id.* at 4.

111. *Id.* at 1.

112. *Id.* at 1.

113. *Id.* at 2. The Constitutional Court quotes directly from the trial court opinion.

114. *Id.*

115. *Id.*

116. *Id.* at 9.

117. *Id.* The court examined the nature and frequency of cases of intersexuality, the various medical procedures considered acceptable by the medical community, the urgency and necessity of the procedures, and the optimal age at which surgery should be performed. *Id.* at 2. Finally, the court looked at whether there were any studies showing the beneficial or detrimental effects of surgery. *Id.* The court stated that in response to its request for information it had received numerous documents, most of which concurred. *Id.* at 3. In the United States, Germany, and Colombia (up until this point), surgery on the external genitalia is performed as soon as possible after the birth of the infant, usually within the first week. *Id.* at 4. The internal gonads are generally removed during adolescence. *Id.* According to medical experts, the surgery is done immediately so that the parents will not raise their child without a clear gender role. *Id.* Doctors also hope to prevent the child from becoming confused about their gender and deciding to change their assigned sex in the future. *Id.* When the ambiguity is not discovered at birth, such as in the case of Ramos, the child is usually assigned the gender that the parents have raised him or her with thus far. *Id.* Proponents of the surgery argue that if the child's genitals do not conform to their social sex, their parents may feel uncomfortable with the child's ambiguity. *Id.* at 5. In addition, the child may be teased by their peers and develop low self-esteem or other psychological problems. *Id.* In opposition to the surgery, the court received an amicus brief from ISNA to which it often references in its opinion. *Id. See* Intersex Society of North America, ISNA's Amicus Brief on Intersex Genital Surgery, Nov. 7, 1998, *available at* http://isna.org/colombia/brief.html. Critiques of the surgery include lack of informed consent by parents, lack of long-term studies, and random choice of sex assignment by doctors and parents. Ramos Summary, *supra* note 54, at 4. The court was not able to locate any follow-up studies that had been done on the effectiveness of these

medical procedures. *Id.* The court referred to the Nuremberg Code that prohibits research and experimentation on human subjects without the individual's consent. *Id.* at 6–7.

118. *See The International Covenant on Civil and Political Rights, Article 7,* G.A. res. 2200A.(XXI), 21 U.N. GAOR Supp. (No.16) at 52, U.N. Doc. A/6316 (1966), 999 U.N.T.S. 171, entered into force Mar. 23, 1976, *available at* http://www.umn.edu/humanrts/instree/b3ccpr.htm. "No one shall be subjected to torture or to cruel, inhuman or degrading treatment or punishment. In particular, no one shall be subjected without his free consent to medical or scientific experimentation." *Id.* art. 7. In *Ramos,* the Colombian Constitutional Court explores the legal dilemma created by the doctor's mandate to help the patient in whatever way possible stemming from the benevolence principle in Articles 44 and 49 of the Colombian Constitution; the patient's right to have access to science and technology from Articles 13 and 49 of the Constitution; versus the patient's right to autonomy and physical integrity, from Articles 1, 12, 16 and 44. Ramos Summary, *supra* note 54, at 6. The court also mentions the advancement of science that is encouraged by allowing doctors to develop new techniques through experimentation without strict judicial control. *Id.* The court states that these constitutional principles may often be in contradiction. *Id.* The court's decision is controlled by the principles of autonomy in Article I, and the preservation of the life and health of the people in Articles 2 and 46. *Id.* at 7. Thus, the court concludes that people must have more autonomy to consent to procedures that are risky to their life and health. *Id.; see also* Levy, *supra* note 94; CONSTITUCION POLITICA DE COLOMBIA, *supra* note 98, arts. 1, 2, 12, 13, 16, 44, 46, 49.

119. Ramos Summary, *supra* note 54, at 9.

120. *Id.*

121. Sentencia No. T-551/99 (Colom.), *available at* http://www.isna.org/colombia/case2.html (last visited Mar. 27, 2004) [hereinafter Cruz].

122. *Id.*

123. Cruz Translation, *supra* note 100.

124. *Id.* at 16, 24; *see* Levy, *supra* note 94, at 6.

125. Cruz Translation, *supra* note 100, at 1–2.

126. *Id.*

127. *Id.* at 1; *see* Levy, *supra* note 94, at 6.

128. Cruz Translation, *supra* note 100, at 3.

129. *Id.* at 1–2, 21.

130. *Id.* at 18, 22.

131. *Id.* at 21; *see* Levy, *supra* note 94, at 6.

132. Cruz Translation, *supra* note 100, at 21; *see* Levy, *supra* note 94, at 6.

133. Cruz Translation, *supra* note 100, at 22–23, 26.

134. *Id.* at 9.

135. *Id.* at 15–16.

136. *Id.* at 13, 15, 23.

137. *Id.* at 14, 17–18.

138. *Id.*

139. *See id.*

140. *Id.* at 17–18.

141. *Id.* at 18–20.

142. *Id.* at 15.

143. *Id.* at 15–16, 24.

144. *Id.* at 18.

145. *Id.* at 19–20.

146. *Id.* at 21, 25.

147. Ramos Summary, *supra* note 54, at 4.

148. *Id.* at 9.

149. *Id.* at 7–8.

150. Cruz Translation, *supra* note 100, at 23.

151. Beh & Diamond, *supra* note 2, at 38–39.

152. Ramos Summary, *supra* note 54, at 4.

153. Glenn M. Burton, *General Discussion of Legal Issues Affecting Sexual Assignment of Intersex Infants Born with Ambiguous Genitalia,* § IIG, at http://www.isna.org/library/burton2002.html (last visited Mar. 27, 2004).

154. Beh & Diamond, *supra* note 2, at 2.

155. *See* Helling v. Carey, 519 P.2d 981, 983 (Wash. 1974). A physician may be negligent even if they follow customary medical practice. *Id.; see* Burton, *supra* note 153, § IIA. Burton writes that the American Board of Pediatrics added an addendum to their 1996 recommendation for early surgical intervention acknowledging the recent debate over infant genital reconstruction surgery. *Id.*

156. Loving v. Virginia, 388 U.S. 1, 12 (1967) (holding that the right to marry is fundamental); Skinner v. Oklahoma, 316 U.S. 535, 541 (1942) (holding that the right to reproduce is fundamental); Rochin v. California, 342 U.S. 165, 172–73 (1952) (holding that the right to bodily integrity is fundamental).

157. *See* Parham v. J. R., 442 U.S. 584, 606–07 (1979) (holding that a parent can involuntarily commit a minor child for mental health treatment as long as the treatment is determined to be in the child's best interest by an independent determination). The Court stated that there should be an independent examination to determine that parents were not using that hospital as a "dumping ground." *Id.* at 598. *See also In re* Rosebush, 491 N.W.2d 633, 640 (1992) (recognizing the best interest standard applies for determining whether life saving treatment should be provided for a minor child against the parent's wishes).

158. *E.g.,* 18 U.S.C § 116 (2000).

159. U.S. Const. amend. XIV, § 1.

160. Gideon v. Wainwright, 372 U.S. 335, 342 (1963).

161. Washington v. Glucksberg, 521 U.S. 702, 720 (1997); Planned Parenthood of Southeastern Pa. v. Casey, 505 U.S. 833, 851 (1994) ("Our law affords constitutional protection to personal decisions relating to marriage, procreation, contraception, family relationships, child rearing, and education," (citing Carey v. Population Services International, 431 U.S. 678 (1977)).

162. *Washington,* 521 U.S. at 721 ("The 14th Amendment 'forbids the government to infringe . . . 'fundamental' interests at all, no matter what process is provided, unless the infringement is narrowly tailored to serve a compelling state interest.'" (quoting Reno v. Flores, 507 U.S. 292, 302 (1993)).

163. *Casey,* 505 U.S. at 899. Although the Court reaffirmed that women have a constitutional right to seek an abortion without undue burden, a state may require minors to seek a parent's consent for an abortion provided that there is an adequate judicial bypass procedure. *Id.* In an earlier case, the Supreme Court stated "our cases show that although children generally are protected by the same constitutional guarantees against governmental deprivations as are adults, the State is entitled to adjust its legal system to account for children's vulnerability and their needs for 'concern, . . . sympathy, and . . . paternal attention.'" Bellotti v. Baird, 443 U.S. 622, 635 (1979).

164. Lassiter v. Dep't of Social Services of Durham County 452 U.S. 18, 39 (1981); *see* Wisconsin v. Yoder, 406 U.S. 205, 232–34 (1972); Pierce v. Society of Sisters of the Holy Names of Jesus and Mary, 268 U.S. 510, 534–35 (1925); Meyer v. Nebraska, 262 U.S. 390, 399 (1923).

165. Parham v. J. R., 442 U.S. 584, 602–04 (1979) ("The fact that a child may balk at hospitalization or complain about a parental refusal to provide cosmetic surgery does not diminish the parents' authority to decide what is best for the child.").

166. *Id.* "The court is not without constitutional control over parental discretion in dealing with children when their physical or mental health is jeopardized." *Id.* at 603. "The parent's interests in a child must be balanced against the State's long-recognized interests as parens patriae." Troxel v. Granville, 530 U.S. 57, 88 (2000). *See also* Prince v. Massachusetts, 321 U.S. 158 (1944). In *Prince,* the

Supreme Court examines the parents' right to have their child distribute religious material on the street. *Id.* The Court allowed the state to limit parent's power in this regard stating, "Parents may be free to become martyrs themselves. But it does not follow they are free, in identical circumstances, to make martyrs of their children before they have reached the age of full and legal discretion when they can make that choice for themselves." *Id.* at 170.

167. Elizabeth J. Sher, *Choosing for Children: Adjudicating Medical Care Disputes Between Parents and the State,* 58 N.Y.U. L. REV. 157, 169–70, 170 n.57 (1983); Jennifer Trahan, *Constitutional Law: Parental Denial of a Child's Medical Treatment for Religious Reasons,* 1989 ANN. SURV. AM. L. 307, 309 (1990). Trahan has divided the medical neglect cases into three categories: those where the child's death is imminent; those where there is no imminent harm; and those where the child is endangered but death is not imminent. *Id.* at 314–15. In most cases, courts will interfere when death is imminent and where the child is endangered even where death is not imminent. However, when there is no risk of imminent death, the parent's religious rights and privacy rights are weighed against the state's parens patriae rights. *Id. See also In re* Richardson, 284 So.2d 185, 187 (1973) (denying parents' request to consent to son's kidney donation for the benefit of his sister where it was not found to be in the son's own best interest).

168. Child Abuse Prevention and Treatment Act of 1996, Pub. L. No. 93-247, 88 Stat. 4 (codified in sections of 42 U.S.C. §§ 5101-5116i (2000)); Adoption and Safe Families Act of 1997, Pub. L. No. 105-89, 111 Stat. 2117 (1997); *see Lassiter,* 452 U.S. at 34 (citing various statutes in support of decision to uphold a termination of parental rights).

169. U.S. CONST. amend. XIV, § 1 ("No state shall make or enforce any law which shall abridge the privileges or immunities of citizens of the United States; nor shall any state deprive any person of life, liberty, or property without due process of law; nor deny to any person within its jurisdiction the equal protection of the laws."); Shelley v. Kraemer, 334 U.S. 1, 13 (1948) ("[A]ction inhibited by the first section of the Fourteenth Amendment is only such action as may fairly be said to be that of the States. That Amendment erects no shield against merely private conduct, however discriminatory or wrongful." (citing the Civil Rights Cases, 109 U.S. 3 (1883))); *see also* Moose Lodge No. 107 v. Irvis, 407 US. 163, 173 (1972).

170. *See Shelley,* 334 U.S. at 14.

171. *Id.* ("That the action of state courts and of judicial officers in their official capacities is to be regarded as action of the State within the meaning of the Fourteenth Amendment, is a proposition which has long been established by decisions of this Court."); *see also* Lugar v. Edmonson Oil Co., Inc., 457 U.S. 922, 942 (1982).

172. Estate of CW, 640 A.2d 427 (Pa. Super. Ct. 1994); Matter of Guardianship of Hayes, 608 P.2d 635 (Wash. 1980); Elizabeth S. Scott, *Sterilization of Mentally Retarded Persons: Reproductive Rights and Family Privacy,* 1986 DUKE L.J. 806, 818 (1986).

173. *Estate of CW,* 640 A.2d at 428; *Matter of Guardianship of Hayes,* 608 P.2d at 641.

174. Rochin v. California, 342 U.S. 165, 172–73 (1952).

175. Cruzan v. Director, Mo. Dep't of Health, 497 U.S. 261 (1990).

176. Parham v. J. R., 442 U.S. 584, 603 (1979); Lawrence Schlam & Joseph P. Wood, *Informed Consent to the Medical Treatment of Minors: Law & Practice,* 10 HEALTH MATRIX 141, 142 (2000); *see* Andrew Popper, *Averting Malpractice by Information: Informed Consent in the Pediatric Treatment Environment,* 47 DEPAUL L. REV. 819 (1998).

177. Schlam & Wood, *supra* note 176, at 147–49.

178. *Id.* at 151.

179. *Id.* at 143.

180. *Id.* at 166–68.

181. *Id.* at 167.

182. FAUSTO-STERLING, *supra* note 1, at 81.

183. Eisenstadt v. Baird, 405 U.S. 438, 453 (1972). The Court stated that it is the right of the individual to decide "whether to bear or beget children." *Id.*

184. Planned Parenthood of Southeastern Pa. v. Casey, 505 U.S. 833, 899–901 (1994).

185. Planned Parenthood of Central Mo. v. Danforth, 428 U.S. 52 (1976); Bellotti v. Baird, 443 U.S. 622 (1979).

186. *Casey,* 505 U.S. at 833 (abortion); Carey v. Population Serv. Int'l, 431 U.S. 678 (1977) (contraception); *see also* Schlam & Wood, *supra* note 176, at 166.

187. Estate of CW, 640 A.2d 427 (Pa. Super. Ct. 1994).

188. *Id.; see In re* Guardianship of Hayes, 608 P.2d 635 (Wash. 1980). In limited circumstances, parents can consent for their incompetent children to be sterilized to protect them from harmful pregnancies. *Id.* at 638. However, there are strict procedural guidelines that the court follows before allowing parental consent. *Id.* at 639. The following guidelines must be followed: (1) the child must be represented by a disinterested guardian ad litem; (2) the child must be incapable of making her own decision about sterilization; and (3) the child must be unlikely to develop sufficiently to make an informed judgment about sterilization in the foreseeable future. *Id.* at 641. Even after the court establishes the listed criteria, the parent or guardian seeking an incompetent's sterilization must prove by clear, cogent, and convincing evidence that there is a need for contraception. *Id.* First the judge must find that the individual is physically capable of procreation, *Id.* Second the judge must find that she is likely to engage in sexual activity at the present or in the near future under circumstances likely to result in pregnancy, *Id.* Finally the judge must determine that the nature and extent of the individual's disability, as determined by empirical evidence and not solely on the basis of standardized tests, renders him or her permanently incapable of caring for a child, even with reasonable assistance, *Id.*

189. Reproductive rights will not be infringed for those intersexed children who are incapable of producing sperm or eggs or who do not have a functional uterus.

190. Reproductive rights will also not be infringed for intersexed children who have clitoral reduction surgery and do not have their gonads or uterus removed.

191. *Estate of CW,* 640 A.2d at 427.

192. However, in Vermont, same-sex couples may seek a civil union, pursuant to Vt. St T.15 § 1201. These civil unions may not be recognized by other states. *See* William C. Duncan, *Civil Unions in Vermont: Where to Go From Here?,* 11 WIDENER J PUB. L. 361, 373–76 (2002). In addition, the Massachusetts Supreme Judicial Court held in *Goodridge v. Dep't of Public Health,* that barring an individual from the protections, benefits, and obligations of civil marriage solely because that person would marry a person of the same sex violates the Massachusetts Constitution and stayed the judgment for 180 days to permit the Legislature take action. 798 N.E.2d 941 (Mass. 2003).

193. Baehr v. Lewin, 852 P.2d 44 (Haw. 1993): Baehr v. Miike, No. 91-1394, 1996 WL 694235 (Haw. Cir. Ct. Dec. 3 1996).

194. *Lewin,* 852 P.2d at 67.

195. HAW. CONST, art. 1, § 23; *see also* Baehr v. Miike. No. 91-1394, 1996 WL 694235 (Cir. Ct. Haw. Dec. 3, 1996). The Hawaii Constitution was amended by voter referendum shortly before the decision was rendered in *Baehr v. Miike.* David Orgon Coolidge, *The Hawai'i Marriage Amendment: Its Origins, Meaning and Fate,* 22 U. HAW. L. REV. 19, 82, 101 (2000).

196. Defense of Marriage Act. 28 U.S.C. § 1738C (1996).

197. Lynn E. Harris, *Born True Hermaphrodite, at* http://www.angelfire.com/ca2/BornHermaphrodite (last visited Mar. 27, 2004). The Superior Court, County of Los Angeles, granted the two-part request of Lynn Elizabeth Harris, Case No. 437625, changing the name and legal sex on her birth certificate from Lynn Elizabeth Harris to Lynn Edward Harris, and from female to male, respectively. *Id.*

198. *See In re* Estate of Gardiner, 22 P.3d 1086 (Kan. Ct. App. 2001). Most court cases discussing the legality of changing birth certificates, names or gender identification only consider chromosomes as one factor in determining a person's legal gender. *Id.* The main factor that courts consider is the genitalia of the individual requesting a legal change of status, *Id.* In this case involving a male to female transsexual, the court discusses intersex conditions extensively in explaining the difficulty in determining legal gender. *Id.*

199. Burton, *supra* note 153, § IIIC. Burton cites Littleton v. Prange, 9 S.W.3d 223 (Tex. App. 1999). In *Littleton v. Prange,* a male to female transsexual legally changed her birth certificate to female and

married. 9 S.W.3d at 224–25. However, the court found that she was not a legal spouse because she was born male and thus was unable to sue for the wrongful death of her husband. *Id.* at 225–26.

200. Cruzan v. Mo. Dep't of Health, 497 U.S. 261, 269 (1990). "This notion of bodily integrity has been embodied in the requirement that informed consent is generally required for medical treatment. Justice Corcozo, while on the Court of Appeals of New York, aptly described this doctrine: Every Human being of adult years and sound mind has a right to determine what shall be done with his own body; and a surgeon who performs an operation without his patient's consent commits an assault, for which he is liable in damages." *Id.*

201. *Id.*

202. *See id.* at 279.

203. *See* Washington v. Glucksberg, 521 U.S. 702, 725 (1997).

204. Cruz Translation, *supra* note 100, at 18–21.

205. Beh & Diamond, *supra* note 2, at 47–48.

206. Fausto-Sterling, *supra* note 1, at 64–65.

207. Beh & Diamond, *supra* note 2, at 47; Ford, *supra* note 4, at 483–84.

208. Ford, *supra* note 4, at 483.

209. Fausto-Sterling, *supra* note 1, at 86.

210. Ford, *supra* note 4, at 485.

211. *Id.* at 484.

212. *Id.*

213. *See* Beh & Diamond, *supra* note 2, at 48–52.

214. Burton, *supra* note 153, § 11F; Ford, *supra* note 4, at 475–76; *see also* Canterbury v. Spence, 464 F.2d 772, 788–89 (1972).

215. Ford, *supra* note 4, at 476.

216. Intersex Society of North America, *ISNA's Recommendations for Treatment,* 1994, *at* http://isna.org/library/recommendations.html (1994). Although not always medical emergencies, some conditions can be painful and require early surgery. *Id.* Intersex activists opposing genital reconstruction surgery generally do not oppose surgery for these cases which may include "severe second or third degree hypospadias (with extensive exposed mucosal tissue vulnerable to infection), chordec (extensive enough to cause pain), bladder exstrophy, and imperforate anus." *Id.*

217. Ramos Summary, *supra* note 54. at 3. *See* Beh & Diamond, *supra* note 2, at 44.

218. Beh & Diamond, *supra* note 2, at 45.

219. *See id.* at 11–12.

220. Fausto-Stirling, *supra* note 1, at 84.

221. American Medical Association, Code of Medical Ethics § E-8.08, *available at* http://www.ama-assn.org/ama/pub/category/2503.html (last updated Dec. 22, 2003). The American Medical Association defines informed consent as "a basic social policy for which exceptions are permitted: (1) where the patient is unconscious or otherwise incapable of consenting and harm from failure to treat is imminent; or (2) when risk disclosure poses such a serious psychological threat of detriment to the patient as to be medically contraindicated. Social policy does not accept the paternalistic view that the physician may remain silent because divulgence might prompt the patient to forego needed therapy. Rational, informed patients should not be expected to act uniformly, even under similar circumstances, in agreeing to or refusing treatment." *Id.*

222. Beh & Diamond, *supra* note 2, at 36.

223. *See id.* at 48.

224. *Id.* 47–50.

225. Ramos Summary, *supra* note 54, at 4. *See* Beh & Diamond, *supra* note 2, at 48, 53.

226. Beh & Diamond, *supra* note 2, at 37–38.

227. 18 U.S.C. § 116 (2000).

228. *Id.*

229. Bruce A. Robinson, *Female Genital Mutilation in North America & Europe, at* http://www. religioustolerance.org/fem_cira.htm (last updated Jan. 22, 2004). "FGM has . . . been criminalized at the state level in California, Minnesota, North Dakota, Rhode Island, and Tennessee." *Id.*

230. 18 U.S.C. § 116.

231. *Id.*

232. *Id.*

233. *Id.* § 116(c).

234. *Id.* § 116.

235. *Id.* § 116(b)(1).

236. *See* Beh & Diamond, *supra* note 2, at 46; FAUSTO-STERLING, *supra* note 1, at 58.

237. FAUSTO-STERLING, *supra* note 1, at 48, 51.

238. *Id.* at 109.

239. *Id.* at 52, 55, 58. Intersexed children with Congenital Adrenal Hyperplasia may develop problems with salt metabolism, which could be life threatening if not treated with cortisone. *Id.* at 52. Some intersexed babies may have an increased rate of urinary tract infections possibly leading to kidney damage. *Id.* at 58.

240. Beh & Diamond, *supra* note 2, at 46; FAUSTO-STERLING, *supra* note 1, at 58.

241. Ramos Summary, *supra* note 54, at 4; Kaldera, *supra* note 1, at 4.

242. COLAPINTO, *supra* note 12, at 218.

243. Ramos, *supra* note 6.

244. 18 U.S.C. § 116.

245. Pub. L. No. 104-208, div. C, § 645(a). 110 Stat. 3009-709 (1996) (codified as amended at 18 U.S.C. § 116 (2000)). "The Congress finds that—(1) The practice of female genital mutilation is carried out by members of certain cultural and religious groups within the United States; (2) the practice of female genital mutilation often results in the occurrence of physical and psychological health effects that harm the women involved; (3) such mutilation infringes upon the guarantees of rights secured by Federal and State law, both statutory and constitutional; (4) the unique circumstances surrounding the practice of female genital mutilation place it beyond the ability of any single State or local jurisdiction to control; (5) the practice of female genital mutilation can be prohibited without abridging the exercise of any rights guaranteed under the first amendment to the Constitution or under any other law; and (6) Congress has the affirmative power under section 8 of Article 1, the necessary and proper clause, section 5 of the fourteenth Amendment, as well as under the treaty clause, to the Constitution to enact such legislation." *Id.*

246. FAUSTO-STERLING, *supra* note 1, at 85–86.

247. *See* 18 U.S.C. § 116.

248. *Id.*

249. Craig v. Boren, 429 U.S. 190. 197–98 (1976). Equal protection claims brought on the basis of gender must meet intermediate scrutiny; thus, the government must show that there is a legitimate state interest in treating the sexes differently, and that this statute is substantially related to a legitimate government interest. *Id.*

250. *Convention on the Rights of the Child,* G.A. Res. 44/25, U.N. GAOR. 44th Sess., Supp. No. 49, at 167, U.N. Doc. A/44/49 (1989}, *available at* http://www.un.org/documents/ga/res/44/a44r025.htm

251. *Id.* The other country that did not sign the convention was Somalia. *See* Office of the United Nations High Commissioner for Human Rights, *Status of the Ratification of the Convention on the Rights of the Child* (Nov. 4, 2003), *available at* http://www.unhchr.ch/html/menu2/6/crc/treaties/status-cre.htm.

252. *Convention on the Rights of the Child, supra* note 250.

253. *Id.*

254. *Trials of War Criminals Before the Nuremberg Military Tribunals Under Control Council Law No. 10 (1946–1949)* [*Nuremberg Code*], *available at* http://www.umn.edu/humanrts/instree/nuremberg.html [hereinafter *Nuremberg Code*]; Grimes v. Kennedy Krieger Institute, Inc. 782 A.2d 807 (2001). This case discusses experimental research on children in the United States without informed consent, *Id.* at 811. The court in that case stated, "The Nuremberg Code is the most complete and authoritative statement of the law of informed consent to human experimentation. It is also part of international common law and may be applied, in both civil and criminal cases, by state, federal and municipal courts in the United States." *Id.* at 835 [internal quotations omitted]. The court refers to the text of the Nuremberg Code to support its conclusion that the consent to the research was invalid, "The voluntary consent of the human subject is absolutely essential. This means that the person involved should have legal capacity to give consent; should be so situated as to be able to exercise free power of choice, without the intervention of any element of force, fraud, deceit, duress, over-reaching, or other ulterior form of constraint or coercion; and *should have sufficient knowledge and comprehension of the elements of the subject matter involved as to enable him to make an understanding and enlightened decision.*" *Id.*

255. *Nuremberg Code, supra* note 254.

256. In *Ramos,* the court explores the experimental nature of the surgery and its possible violation of the Nuremberg Code. Ramos Summary, *supra* note 54, at 6.

257. COLAPINTO, *supra* note 12, at 75.

258. Cruz Translation, *supra* note 100, at 25.

259. *Id.; sea* Greenberg & Chase, *supra* note 18.

260. *Cf.* Ryken Grattet & Valerie Jenness, *Examining the Boundaries of Hate Crime Law: Disabilities and the 'Dilemma of Difference,'* 91 J. CRIM. L & CRIMINOLOGY 653 (2001) (exploring the susceptibility of minority groups to hale crimes).

261. Americans with Disabilities Act of 1990 [ADA], 42 U.S.C. § 12101, (2000). The ADA was enacted in the face of discrimination against individuals with disabilities in all areas of life. *Id.* The purpose of the ADA is to ensure inclusion of individuals with disabilities in employment, education, public accommodations, and government services. *Id.*

262. FAUSTO-STERLING, *supra* note 1.

Voicing Your Opinion
Who Will Make Room for the Intersexed?
Kate Haas

1. Do you believe that the United States should provide legal protection for intersex children? If so, what type of protection might that include? Should there be laws that allow parents to make sex assignment choices for their intersex children? Should the medical community be allowed to make those choices?

_____

_____

_____

_____

_____

2. Haas mentions small communities in the Dominican Republic and Papua New Guinea where male children who are born with small or unrecognizable penises are raised as girls until they develop male sexual characteristics during puberty. At this point in their lives, these children begin living as men. What might be the impact on our understanding of sex/gender formation if this was a policy that the United States had regarding children born with intersex conditions? Can you imagine this as a common practice in the United States? Why or why not?

_____

_____

_____

_____

_____

3. What ethical concerns are raised in the discussion of sex assignment for children born with intersex conditions? How might these concerns be addressed by parents, the medical community, and society in general?

_____

_____

_____

_____

_____

Terms
Feminist
standpoint
theory
Marxism
Muted group
theory
Social location

FEMINIST STANDPOINT THEORY AND MUTED GROUP THEORY Commonalities and Divergences

JULIA T. WOOD

This article is about two theories that help us frame gender experiences. The first is *feminist standpoint theory*, which suggests that patriarchal societies naturalize "male" and "female" divisions. This naturalization process makes it seem normal and right that women are subordinate to men. This theory, which is based in Marxism, suggests that the work we do and the activities we engage in shape our identities and consciousness. Feminist standpoint theory articulates a critical position regarding the "naturalization" of gender. *Muted group theory* is similar and suggests that some groups are more dominant in a culture than others. The subordinate group does not have access to power and therefore is muted—meaning easily silenced or not heard.

Origins of Feminist Standpoint Theory

Feminist standpoint theory is one theory in the group of standpoint theories. Others focus on standpoints defined by, for instance, race-ethnicity and sexual orientation. It was not until the 1980s that feminist standpoint theory was developed and named by feminist social scientists working primarily in sociology and political theory. The first stage of theorizing included work by scholars such as Patricia Hill Collins (1986), Donna Haraway (1988, 1997), Sandra Harding, (1991, 1993), Nancy Hartsock (1983), Hiliary Rose (1983), and Dorothy Smith (1987).

Like all standpoint theories, feminist standpoint theory is indebted to Marxist analysis. Just as Marxist theorizing examines how capitalism naturalizes bourgeois and proletariat class divisions, so does feminist standpoint theory analyze how patriarchy naturalizes male and female divisions, making it seem natural, right, unremarkable that women are subordinate to men. Feminist standpoint theory draws especially on the Marxist claim that the work we do—the activities in which we engage—shape our identities and consciousness and, by extension, our knowledge. Just as Marxist analysis starts from the material conditions of the proletariat, feminist standpoint starts from the material conditions of women's lives.

For feminist standpoint theory, a key claim is that women's lives are systematically and structurally different from the men's lives and, that these differences produce different (and differently complete) knowledges. To a significant extent, then, social location shapes the social, symbolic, and material conditions and insights common to a group of people.

From Social Location to Feminist Standpoint

That claim is a necessary basis for feminist standpoint theory, but it does not specifically get us to the key concept of standpoint. It highlights women's social location and claims that their social location shapes women's lives in material, as well as social and symbolic, ways. This asserts only that social locations shape lives and, specifically, that women's social location shapes their lives in ways distinct from men's lives. But social location is *not* standpoint. A standpoint is achieved—earned through critical reflection on power relations and through engaging in the struggle required to construct an oppositional stance. Being a woman does not necessarily confer a feminist standpoint. Because social location and standpoint are so frequently conflated, let me emphasize the distinction one more time: A feminist standpoint grows out of (that is, it is *shaped by,* rather than essentially given) the social location of women's lives. Feminist standpoint can, *but does not necessarily,* arise from being female.

Because standpoint resists, or opposes, the dominant worldview, it is necessarily political. This means, as Haraway (1988) has noted, that standpoints "are not innocent" (p. 584). It follows that the dominant worldview, or perspective, cannot be a standpoint. It is a position; it is a social location; it provides a perspective on social life; but it is not a standpoint because it does not grow out of critical reflection on its genesis and character and is not oppositional to itself (i.e., the dominant worldview).

From Feminist Standpoint to Feminist Standpoint Theory

We need to move one more step to get from feminist standpoint to feminist standpoint theory. A feminist standpoint can be achieved through critical reflection on power relations and their consequences. However, achieving a feminist standpoint does not necessarily make one a theorist, other than in the sense that we are all naïve theorists. Achieving a feminist standpoint, then, does not mean one is capable of describing, explaining, predicting, increasing understanding, and/or critiquing, which are the business of theory. Feminist standpoint theory offers a critique of existing power relations between women and men and the inequality they produce. It does so by developing an epistemology for constructing knowledge from women's experiences. Standpoint theory asks what we know if we start from a subordinated group's experiences. Feminist standpoint theory asks what we know if we start from women's lives.

Starting from women's lives—from the material, everyday routines that compose them—immediately raises questions about what counts as knowledge. The dominant ideology claims that the only acceptable knowledge comes from science, which relies on objectivity and separation of scientist and object of knowledge. Standpoint theorists reject restricting knowledge in this manner and, instead, consider how admitting subjectivity and placing knower and known on the same plane generate knowledge.

Key Claims of Feminist Standpoint Theory

Perhaps the most concise way to summarize feminist standpoint theory is to explicate its key arguments.

1. Society is structured by power relations, which result in unequal social locations for women and men: Men are the dominant, privileged, or centered group, and women are a subordinate, disadvantaged, or marginalized group. These common conditions shape the experiences of women and men. In turn, the experiences that are open and closed to women and men shape what they know and how they understand cultural life.

2. Subordinate social locations are more likely than privileged social locations to generate knowledge that is "more accurate" or "less false." This is because (a) members of privileged groups have a vested interest in not seeing oppression and inequity that accompany and, indeed, makes possible their privilege; (b) members of marginalized groups are more likely to understand both their location and the social location of more powerful groups than the converse; (c) political analyses of oppression are more likely to be encountered and explored by members of subordinate groups. Although many standpoint scholars assert that subordinate social locations necessarily produce better knowledge than privileged locations, this is not assumed by all standpoint scholars. I will elaborate this point later in the article.

3. The outsider-within is a privileged epistemological position because it entails double consciousness, being at once outside of the dominant group and intimately within that group in ways that allow observation and understanding of that group. For instance, a live-in Latina maid is not a member of the

employing family that belongs to the privileged group, but she has access to the minute details of their private lives.

4. Standpoint refers not simply to location or experience, but to a critical understanding of location and experience as part of—and shaped by—larger social and political contexts and, specifically, discourses. By implication, a standpoint is an intellectual achievement that reflects—and necessarily entails—political consciousness. Standpoints are not automatically given based on biology or any other essential factor. Instead, they are earned through political struggle that creates *oppositional* stances based on recognition of and resistance to dominant worldview.

5. Any individual can have multiple standpoints that are shaped by membership in groups defined by sex, race-ethnicity, sexual orientation, economic class, etc.

I will not attempt to summarize muted group theory since that is done by others contributing to this special issue. Instead, I turn now to a discussion of similarities and differences between feminist standpoint theory and muted group theory.

Feminist Standpoint Theory and Muted Group Theory: Convergences and Divergences

Readers who are familiar with muted group theory have probably already sensed similarities between it and the foregoing description of feminist standpoint theory. Less obvious perhaps, are divergences between the two theories.

Connections Between the Theories

I perceive three particularly important points of convergence between feminist standpoint theory and muted group theory. First, both theories recognize that societies are structured hierarchically, designating some groups as dominant, or centered, and other groups as subordinate, or marginal. Thus, both theories acknowledge the operation of power relations in cultural life.

Second, both theories value the lives and the knowledge of subordinated groups. Beginning with Shirley Ardener's (1978) and Edwin Ardener's (1975) groundbreaking work, muted group theory has recognized that women's voices are muted in Western society so that their experiences are not fully represented in language and has argued that women's experiences merit linguistic recognition (that is, naming). Similarly, feminist standpoint theory argues that women's activities and the kinds of knowledge making practices they cultivate are underrepresented and are valuable.

Third, both theories are political, although in different ways. Muted group theory's political inclinations arise from its attention to the power of naming. It asserts that those who get to name the world do so from their perspectives and, by implication, that the other perspectives are suppressed. Feminist standpoint theory's political inclinations grow out of the recognition that power relations authorize designating distinct social groups and, following that, privileged or subordinate status for members of those groups. Feminist standpoint theory also focuses on the processes by which the existing power relations and the inequities they sanction are made to seem natural and right.

I am not asserting that these are the only points of convergence or overlap between muted group theory and feminist standpoint theory. Rather, I am highlighting these three convergences as particularly important affinities between the two theories.

Divergences Between the Theories

Muted group theory and feminist standpoint theory differ in certain respects, three of which I will discuss. These divergences do not necessarily signal or imply incompatibility between the two theories. I am more inclined to think they point to different and largely complementary foci that the theories choose to highlight. First, muted group theory focuses on one site where power relations are manifested: language. This calls attention to the "power of naming" (Spender, 1984a,b) and, equally important, the consequences of using a language that does not name some of your experiences. Feminist standpoint theory does not focus on language. It focuses on knowledge, the kind of knowledge and the ways of knowing that start from women's everyday activities and lives, which are structured by power relations.

Second, as I understand muted group theory, it assumes that the likelihood of having one's voice muted is linked rather directly to whether one belongs to a subordinate group such as women. Feminist standpoint theory has not drawn nearly so straight a line between being a woman (or even being in the social location designated for women) and having a feminist standpoint. A feminist standpoint requires conscious, deliberate, political struggle to understand the group(s) to which one belongs and how that group and the lives of group members have been structured by a "partial and perverse" dominant worldview. Thus, not all women earn feminist standpoints, and not all men are unable to earn feminist standpoints (Collins, 2003).

Third, the goals of muted group theory seem different from those of feminist standpoint theory. My understanding is that muted group theory has two aims: (1) to call attention to the muting of women's voices and, thus, experiences; and (2) to reform language so that women's experiences from women's perspectives are fully represented. Feminist standpoint theory, in contrast, doesn't necessarily aim to create one language or one social position. It has two aims: (1) to develop an epistemology, or method, for constructing knowledge, that is based on insights arising from women's experiences; (2) to learn from knowledge that arises from women's social locations.

Feminist standpoint theorists argue that what is learned when we start from women's lives not only provides insight into the lives of women, but also that those insights allow new understandings on the practices of the dominant group. In other words, once we look at power relations from women's lives, we are likely not only to have new insights about women and their lives, but also about men and their lives.

Challenges Confronting Feminist Standpoint Theory

All theories face challenges, and feminist standpoint theory is no exception to that rule. I want now to highlight three questions that feminist standpoint theory must address if the theory is to advance.

How Can Feminist Standpoint Theory Account for Multiple Standpoints?

Every standpoint theorist whose work I know recognizes the multiplicity of standpoints. For instance, one could have a lesbian standpoint, a feminist standpoint, and a Black standpoint, and in particular circumstances one standpoint assumes greater prominence than others. On this, standpoint theorists are clear and in agreement. What is far less clear is how we account for multiple standpoints. Certainly, we can't just add them up as if they are discrete when it seems likely that they would interact and overlap, at least at times. Standpoint theorists have not developed analytical means for dealing with multiple, probably intersecting standpoints.

The recognition of multiple standpoints that an individual may occupy has been critical in defending standpoint against charges of essentialism. Recognizing multiple standpoints allows theorists to assert they do not group all women together and ignore differences among them. But, frankly, we have not developed useful means of studying, theorizing, and even describing the dynamism of these interlocking standpoints.

Should Subordinated Social Locations Be Epistemologically Privileged?

Many standpoint theorists claim that a subordinated location produces more accurate, more complete knowledge than a privileged position for reasons noted in the first section of this paper. But some feminist standpoint theorists do not accept the claim; they reject the notion that any particular social location provides the best vantage point from which to discern truth. Hill Collins, in particular, argues that every individual has a partial view of social life, and she refuses to rank partial views on any sort of a continuum from more to less partial. Hill Collins states that subordinated social groups—black women, in the case of her work—are capable of developing unique insight into the power relations that create and uphold their subordinate location. However, Hill Collins does not argue that this unique insight is necessarily or always superior to insights that arise from other locations. Instead, she sees the "outsider within" as a position that is particularly capable of generating more complete, less false knowledge. Haraway (1988) is similarly reluctant to grant privileged epistemological status to subordinate social locations. Instead, she insists on remembering the partiality of all views and recognizing that every viewpoint is from somewhere. Hill Collins and Haraway clearly think such subordinated positions facilitate producing more accurate knowledge, but they do not absolutely guarantee it just as privileged positions do not absolutely preclude it.

I want to join Haraway and Hill Collins in resisting the idea of any absolutely privileged epistemological position. And I want to sound a cautionary note: There are dangers in romanticizing women's subordinate standpoint. This could invite embrace of subordination because of the superior knowledge it produces. With that, women would (continue to) be complicit in maintaining their subordinate positions. And this kind of valuing or revaluing of women's location and activities would be entirely consistent with dominant ideology that has always been quite willing to value women as long as they "stay in their place."

Because feminist standpoint theory is first and foremost concerned with epistemology, resolving this issue should be a priority. And resolving it should entail careful, intricate theoretical analysis that clarifies whether the theory leads to the conclusion that some social locations actually do or can produce better knowledge.

Is Feminist Standpoint Theory Naïve or Misguided in Valorizing Contradictions?

Most, if not all feminist standpoint theorists argue for the value of living with contradictions. Carole McCann and Seung-Kyung Kim (2003) give as an example "living the contradiction of doing the crucial work of caregiving in a society that does not value caregiving" (p. 280). Whether called "double consciousness" or the "outsider within position," there is consensus that living with contradictions can generate liberatory knowledge and can fuel resistance, both of which might instigate social change.

But is living with contradictions equally or more likely to generate different and undesirable consequences. For instance, many people are overwhelmed by contradictions, by being in circumstances that don't cohere. Most people who find contradictions disturbing develop ways of coping. For instance, a person might compartmentalize her worlds so that, to use Hill Collins' example, a black maid sees a certain type of food and set of manners as appropriate in the home of her employer, but keeps that separate from her views of what is appropriate in her own home. Or one might cope by refusing to live with the contradictions. In the example, the maid might quit her job or change the foods and manners in her own home to more closely resemble those in her employer's home. A third way of coping with feeling overwhelmed by contradictions is to refuse more or less consciously to recognize the contradictions. If a person does not have to see and acknowledge contradictions, they are not overwhelming. More extreme forms of undesirable responses to being overwhelmed by contradictions are to become catatonic, to have a psychotic breakdown, or to experience a schizophrenic break.

There is simply no way to justify the claim that living with contradictions has the potential only for positive outcomes, such as liberatory knowledge and resistance. Of course it has that potential. And, of course, there are other potential responses to living, which we might not want to encourage.

Summary

Feminist standpoint theory is an epistemological theory that focuses on the ways that social location shapes knowledge. In so doing, feminist standpoint theory offers a critique of existing power relations and the inequality they produce in the lives of women and men. It does so by developing an epistemological theory for constructing knowledge from the insights that arise from women's experiences.

While feminist standpoint theory has clear and important affinities with muted group theory, the two are distinct and offer distinct insights into women's social locations and their consequences. In this sense, feminist standpoint theory and muted group theory make good allies.

Voicing Your Opinion
Feminist Standpoint Theory and Muted Group Theory: Commonalities and Divergences
Julia T. Wood

1. The first key argument of feminist standpoint theory claims that "men are the dominant, privileged, or centered group." Respond to this claim with you own experiences and knowledge of the world. What is true about this statement? What is untrue about this statement? How have the values and attitudes of our society contributed to this argument?

   _____

   _____

   _____

   _____

2. The first key argument of feminist standpoint theory also claims that "women are a subordinate, disadvantaged, or marginalized group." Respond to this claim with you own experiences and knowledge of the world. What is true about this statement? What is untrue about this statement? How have the values and attitudes of our society contributed to this argument?

   _____

   _____

   _____

   _____

3. Wood suggests that the goals of muted group theory and feminist standpoint theory are to call attention to the muting of women's voices, to reform language so that women's experiences are more fully represented, and to develop a "way of knowing" based on women's experiences. How might society benefit from the goals set forth by these theories? How would *you* benefit from the goals set forth by these theories?

   _____

   _____

   _____

   _____

Observation Exercise

Instructions

Take <u>three full twenty-four hour days</u> to be critically observant of gender and communication in your world (work, school, relationships, media, etc. . . .). Take careful notes during this time and then respond to the following questions about your observations:

Questions

- What are the most significant (obvious) messages of communicated gender that you notice in your world?
- Are you *comfortable* or *uncomfortable* with these messages? Why?
- How does your gender affect your *perceptions* of the messages that you have observed and recorded?
- Would somebody else have a different response to these messages? Describe your observations to another person and ask them how they perceive these gendered messages.
- Use one or more of the terms from the readings in Part One, *The Process of Defining Gender,* to explain what you have observed. How do your observations support or contradict the information that you have read?

Suggestions

Be open-minded and curious as you begin to observe your world.

Use as many senses as possible in order to enhance your observations.

Be mindful of *who, what, when, where, why* as you are observing and taking notes.

2 The Process of Becoming Gendered

The next step in the process of learning about gender and communication is to consider how individuals come to understand, define, and present themselves in relationship to their gender. In "The Process of Becoming Gendered," we provide you with some questions to consider in regards to gender formation, gender identity, and gender presentation. We want these questions to stimulate your thinking and help you to continue to think about gender and communication as a fluid process.

We have included three articles in this section that provide in-depth discussions of topics pertaining to the ways that people establish and maintain their gender identity.

Questions to Consider

What family stories have you heard and told that help you understand what it means to be a "man" or a "woman"?

What positive rewards were you given as a child when you "performed" your gender correctly?

Were you ever criticized or punished as a child for not "performing" your gender correctly?

What are the props and costumes of ideal American femininity? What are the props and costumes of ideal American masculinity?

How does cross-dressing communicate a person's gender identity?

Do people get trapped by societal expectations of masculinity? Do people get trapped by societal expectations of femininity?

What is the relationship between gender identity and sexual identity?

How easily can a person change gender identity?

Terms
Gendered
performance
Disciplining
bodies
Bodily
instructions
Resistance

BECOMING A GENDERED BODY Practices of Preschools

KARIN A. MARTIN

♂ ♀

This article is about hidden curriculums in preschools and how we are taught as children to use our bodies. The author studied everyday movements, comportment, and use of physical space by children to determine how teachers and other adults train children to use their bodies as girls or boys. She looks at five separate sets of practices that help to create the differences: dressing up; permitting the use of relaxed behaviors versus requiring formal behaviors; controlling voices; and how teachers interact with our bodies. These differences suggest that we then learn to use our bodies differently, and it becomes the "natural" and "normal" performance of gender.

Many feminist scholars argue that the seeming naturalness of gender differences, particularly bodily difference, underlies gender inequality. Yet few researchers ask how these bodily differences are constructed. Through semistructured observation in five preschool classrooms, I examine one way that everyday movements, comportment, and use of physical space become gendered. I find that the hidden school curriculum that controls children's bodily practices in order to shape them cognitively serves another purpose as well. This hidden curriculum also turns children who are similar in bodily comportment, movement, and practice into girls and boys—children whose bodily practices differ. I identify five sets of practices that create these differences: dressing up, permitting relaxed behaviors or requiring formal behaviors, controlling voices, verbal and physical instructions regarding children's bodies by teachers, and physical interactions among children. This hidden curriculum that (partially) creates bodily differences between the genders also makes these physical differences appear and feel natural.

Social science research about bodies often focuses on women's bodies, particularly the parts of women's bodies that are most explicitly different from men's—their reproductive capacities and sexuality (E. Martin 1987; K. Martin 1996; but see Connell 1987, 1995). Men and women in the United States also hold and move their bodies differently (Birdwhistell 1970; Henley 1977; Young 1990); these differences are sometimes related to sexuality (Haug 1987) and sometimes not. On the whole, men and women sit, stand, gesture, walk, and throw differently. Generally, women's bodies are confined, their movements restricted. For example, women take smaller steps than men, sit in closed positions (arms and legs crossed across the body), take up less physical space than men, do not step, twist, or throw from the shoulder when throwing a ball, and are generally tentative when using their bodies (Birdwhistell 1970; Henley 1977; Young 1990). Some of these differences, particularly differences in motor skills (e.g., jumping, running, throwing) are seen in early childhood (Thomas and French 1985).[1] Of course, within gender, we may find individual differences, differences based on race, class, and sexuality, and differences based on size and shape of body. Yet, on average, men and women move differently.

Such differences may seem trivial in the large scheme of gender inequality. However, theoretical work by social scientists and feminists suggests that these differences may be consequential. Bodies are (unfinished) resources (Shilling 1993: 103) that must be "trained, manipulated, cajoled, coaxed, organized and in general disciplined" (Turner 1992:15). We use our bodies to construct our means of living, to take care of each other, to pleasure each other. According to Turner, ". . . social life depends upon the successful presenting, monitoring and interpreting of bodies" (p. 15). Similarly, according to Foucault (1979), controlled and disciplined bodies do more than regulate the individual body. A disciplined body creates a context for social relations. Gendered (along with "raced" and "classed") bodies create particular contexts for social relations as they signal, manage, and negotiate information about power and status. Gender relations depend on the successful gender presentation, monitoring, and interpretation of bodies (West and Zimmerman 1987). Bodies that clearly delineate gender status facilitate the maintenance of the gender hierarchy.

Our bodies are also one *site* of gender. Much postmodern feminist work (Butler 1990, 1993) suggests that gender is a performance. Microsociological work (West and Zimmerman 1987) suggests that gender is something that is "done." These two concepts, "gender performance" and "doing gender," are similar—both suggest that managed, adorned, fashioned, properly comported and moving bodies establish gender and gender relations.

Other feminist theorists (Connell 1987, 1995; Young 1990) argue that gender rests not only on the surface of the body, in performance and doing, but becomes *embodied*—becomes deeply part of whom we are physically and psychologically. According to Connell, gender becomes embedded in body postures, musculature, and tensions in our bodies.

> The social definition of men as holders of power is translated not only into mental body-images and fantasies, but into muscle tensions, posture, the feel and texture of the body. This is one of the main ways in which the power of men becomes naturalized. . . . (Connell 1987:85)

Connell (1995) suggests that masculine gender is partly a feel to one's body and that bodies are often a source of power for men. Young (1990), however, argues that bodies serve the opposite purpose for women—women's bodies are often sources of anxiety and tentativeness. She suggests that women's lack of confidence and agency are embodied and stem from an inability to move confidently in space, to take up space, to use one's body to its fullest extent. Young (1990) suggests "that the general lack of confidence that we [women] frequently have about our cognitive or leadership abilities is traceable in part to an original doubt of our body's capacity" (p. 156). Thus, these theorists suggest that gender differences in minute bodily behaviors like gesture, stance, posture, step, and throwing are significant to our understanding of gendered selves and gender inequality. This feminist theory, however, focuses on adult bodies.

Theories of the body need gendering, and feminist theories of gendered bodies need "childrening" or accounts of development. How do adult gendered bodies become gendered, if they are not naturally so? Scholars run the risk of continuing to view gendered bodies as natural if they ignore the processes that produce gendered adult bodies. Gendering of the body in childhood is the foundation on which further gendering of the body occurs throughout the life course. The gendering of children's bodies makes gender differences feel and appear natural, which allows for such bodily differences to emerge throughout the life course.

I suggest that the hidden school curriculum of disciplining the body is gendered and contributes to the embodiment of gender in childhood, making gendered bodies appear and feel natural. Sociologists of education have demonstrated that schools have hidden curriculums (Giroux and Purpel 1983; Jackson 1968). Hidden curriculums are covert lessons that schools teach, and they are often a means of social control. These curriculums include teaching about work differentially by class (Anyon 1980; Bowles and Gintis 1976; Carnoy and Levin 1985), political socialization (Wasburn 1986), and training in obedience and docility (Giroux and Purpel 1983). More recently, some theorists and researchers have examined the curriculum that disciplines the body (Carere 1987; Foucault 1979; McLaren 1986). This curriculum demands the practice of bodily control in congruence with the goals of the school as an institution. It reworks the students from the outside in on the presumption that to shape the body is to shape the mind (Carere 1987). In such a curriculum teachers constantly monitor kids' bodily movements, comportment, and practices.[2] Kids begin their day running wildly about the school grounds. Then this hidden curriculum funnels the kids into line, through the hallways, quietly into a classroom, sitting upright at their desks, focused at the front of the room, "ready to learn" (Carere 1987; McLaren 1986). According to Carere (1987), this curriculum of disciplining the body serves the curriculums that seek to shape the mind and renders children physically ready for cognitive learning.

I suggest that this hidden curriculum that controls children's bodily practices serves also to turn kids who are similar in bodily comportment, movement, and practice into girls and boys, children whose bodily practices are different. Schools are not the only producers of these differences. While the process ordinarily begins in the family, the schools' hidden curriculum further facilitates and encourages the construction of bodily differences between the genders and makes these physical differences appear and feel natural. Finally, this curriculum may be more or less hidden depending on the particular preschool and particular teachers. Some schools and teachers may see teaching children to behave like "young ladies" and "young gentlemen" as an explicit part of their curriculums.

Data and Method

The data for this study come from extensive and detailed semistructured field observations of five preschool classrooms of three to five-year-olds in a midwestern city.[3] Four of the classrooms were part of a preschool (Preschool A) located close to the campus of a large university. A few of the kids were children of faculty members, more were children of staff and administrators, and many were not associated with the university. Many of the kids who attended Preschool A attended part-time. Although teachers at this school paid some attention to issues of race and gender equity, issues of diversity were not as large a part of the curriculum as they are at some preschools (Jordan and Cowan 1995; Van Ausdale and Feagin 1996). The fifth classroom was located at Preschool B, a preschool run by a Catholic church in the same city as Preschool A. The kids who attended Preschool B were children of young working professionals, many of whom lived in the vicinity of the preschool. These children attended preschool "full-time"—five days a week for most of the day.

The curriculums and routines of the two preschools were similar with two exceptions. First, there was some religious instruction in Preschool B, although many of the kids were not Catholic. Preschool B required children to pray before their snack, and the children's activities focused more on the religious aspects of Christian holidays than did the activities of children in Preschool A. For example, at Christmas, teachers talked to the kids about the birth of baby Jesus. At Preschool A there was little religious talk and more talk about decorating Christmas trees, making cards, and so on. The second difference between the two preschools is that Preschool B had some explicit rules that forbade violent actions at school. Posted on the wall of the playroom was the following sign (which few of the preschoolers could read)

1. No wrestling.
2. No violent play, killing games, kicking, karate, etc.
3. Bikes belong on the outside of the gym.
4. No crashing bikes.
5. Houses are for playing in not climbing on.
6. Older children are off bikes when toddlers arrive.
7. Balls should be used for catching, rolling, tossing—not slamming at people.
8. Adults and children will talk with each other about problems and not shout across the room.
9. Use equipment appropriately.

Such rules were usually directed at boys, although they were not enforced consistently. Preschool A also had some of these rules, but they were not as explicit or as clearly outlined for the teachers or the kids. For example, teachers would usually ask kids to talk about their problems or disputes (rule 8) at both schools. However, rule 2 was not in effect at Preschool A unless a game got "out of control"—became too loud, too disruptive, or "truly" violent instead of "pretend" violent. The data from these preschools represent some ways that schools may discipline children's bodies in gendered ways. As Suransky's (1982) study of five preschools suggests, the schools' and teachers' philosophies, and styles, and cultural context make dramatic differences in the content and experience of a day at preschool.

A total 112 children and 14 different teachers (five head teachers and nine aides) were observed in these classrooms.[4] All teachers were female. Forty-two percent of the kids were girls and 58 percent were boys, and they made up similar proportions in each classroom. There were 12 Asian or Asian American children, 3 Latino/a children, and 4 African American children. The remaining children were white. The children primarily came from middle-class families.

A research assistant and I observed in these classrooms about three times a week for eight months. Our observations were as unobtrusive as possible, and we interacted little with the kids, although on occasion a child would ask what we were doing or would sit next to us and "write" their own "notes." We varied our observation techniques between unstructured field observation, in which we observed the classroom in a holistic manner and recorded everyday behavior, and more structured techniques, in which we observed one part of the classroom (the block area, the dress-up area), one particular child (25 children were observed this way), one particular teacher (seven teachers were observed this way), or one set of children (boys who always play with blocks, the kids that play with the hamsters, the kids that played at the water table a lot—most children were observed this way). We observed girls and boys for equal amounts of time, and we heeded Thorne's (1993) caution about the "big man bias" in field research and were careful not to observe only the most active, outgoing, "popular" kids.

We focused on the children's physicality—body movement, use of space, and the physical contact among kids or between kids and teachers. Our field notes were usually not about "events" that occurred, but about everyday physical behavior and interaction and its regulation. Field notes were coded using the qualitative software program Hyper-Research. Categories that were coded emerged from the data and were not predetermined categories. Excerpts from field notes are presented throughout and are examples of representative patterns in the data. Tables presenting estimates of the numbers of times particular phenomena were observed provide a context for the field note excerpts. The data are subject to the observers' attention and accurate descriptions in the field notes. For instance, most micro and "neutral" physical contact between kids or among teachers and kids is probably underestimated (e.g., shoulders touching during circle time, knees bumping under the snack table). Future research might use video recordings to assess such micro events.

Results

Children's bodies are disciplined by schools. Children are physically active, and institutions like schools impose disciplinary controls that regulate children's bodies and prepare children for the larger social world. While this disciplinary control produces docile bodies (Foucault 1979), it also produces gendered bodies. As these disciplinary practices operate in different contexts, some bodies become more docile than others. I examine how the following practices contribute to a gendering of children's bodies in preschool: the effects of dressing-up or bodily adornment, the gendered nature of formal and relaxed behaviors, how the different restrictions on girls' and boys' voices limit their physicality, how teachers instruct girls' and boys' bodies, and the gendering of physical interactions between children and teachers and among the children themselves.

Bodily Adornment: Dressing Up

Perhaps the most explicit way that children's bodies become gendered is through their clothes and other bodily adornments. Here I discuss how parents gender their children through their clothes, how children's dress-up play experiments with making bodies feminine and masculine, and how this play, when it is gender normative, shapes girls' and boys' bodies differently, constraining girls' physicality.

DRESSING UP (1). The clothes that parents send kids to preschool in shape children's experiences of their bodies in gendered ways.[5] Clothes, particularly their color, signify a child's gender; gender in preschool is in fact color-coded. On average, about 61 percent of the girls wore pink clothing each day (Table 1). Boys were more likely to wear primary colors, black, fluorescent green, and orange. Boys never wore pink.

> The teacher is asking each kid during circle (the part of the day that includes formal instruction by the teacher while the children sit in a circle) what their favorite color is. Adam says black. Bill says "every color that's not pink." (Five-year-olds)

Fourteen percent of three-year-old girls wore dresses each day compared to 32 percent of five-year-old girls (Table 1). Wearing a dress limited girls' physicality in preschool. However, it is not only the dress

Table 1 Observations of Girls Wearing Dresses and the Color Pink: Five Preschool Classrooms

Observation	N	Percent
Girls wearing something pink	54	61
Girls wearing dresses	21	24
3-year-old girls	6	14
5-year-old girls	15	32
Number of observations	89	100
3-year-old girls	42	47
5-year-old girls	47	53

Note: In 12 observation sessions, what the children were wearing, including color of their clothing, was noted. The data in Table 1 come from coded field notes. There were no instances of boys wearing pink or dresses, and no age differences among girls in wearing the color pink.

itself, but knowledge about how to behave in a dress that is restrictive. Many girls already knew that some behaviors were not allowed in a dress. This knowledge probably comes from the families who dress their girls in dresses.

> Vicki, wearing leggings and a dress-like shirt, is leaning over the desk to look into a "tunnel" that some other kids have built. As she leans, her dress/shirt rides up exposing her back. Jennifer (another child) walks by Vicki and as she does she pulls Vicki's shirt back over her bare skin and gives it a pat to keep it in place. It looks very much like something one's mother might do. (Five-year-olds)
>
> Four girls are sitting at a table—Cathy, Kim, Danielle, and Jesse. They are cutting play money out of paper. Cathy and Danielle have on overalls and Kim and Jesse have on dresses. Cathy puts her feet up on the table and crosses her legs at the ankle; she leans back in her chair and continues cutting her money. Danielle imitates her. They look at each other and laugh. They put their shoulders back, posturing, having fun with this new way of sitting. Kim and Jesse continue to cut and laugh with them, but do not put their feet up. (Five-year-olds)

Dresses are restrictive in other ways as well. They often are worn with tights that are experienced as uncomfortable and constraining. I observed girls constantly pulling at and rearranging their tights, trying to untwist them or pull them up. Because of their discomfort, girls spent much time attuned to and arranging their clothing and/or their bodies.

Dresses also can be lifted up, an embarrassing thing for five-year-olds if done purposely by another child. We witnessed this on only one occasion—a boy pulled up the hem of a girl's skirt up. The girl protested and the teacher told him to stop and that was the end of it. Teachers, however, lifted up girls' dresses frequently—to see if a child was dressed warmly enough, while reading a book about dresses, to see if a child was wet. Usually this was done without asking the child and was more management of the child rather than an interaction with her. Teachers were much more likely to manage girls and their clothing this way—rearranging their clothes, tucking in their shirts, fixing a ponytail gone astray.[6] Such management often puts girls' bodies under the control of another and calls girls' attentions to their appearances and bodily adornments.

DRESSING UP (2). Kids like to *play* dress-up in preschool, and all the classrooms had a dress-up corner with a variety of clothes, shoes, pocketbooks, scarves, and hats for dressing up. Classrooms tended to have more women's clothes than men's, but there were some of both, as well as some gender-neutral clothes—capes, hats, and vests that were not clearly for men or women—and some items that were clearly costumes, such as masks of cats and dogs and clip-on tails. Girls tended to play dress-up more than boys—over one-half of dressing up was done by girls. Gender differences in the amount of time spent playing dress-up seemed to increase from age three to age five. We only observed the five-year-old boys dressing up or using clothes or costumes in their play three times, whereas three-year-old boys dressed up almost weekly. Five-year-old boys also did not dress up elaborately, but used one piece of clothing to animate their play. Once Phil wore large, men's winter ski gloves when he played monster. Holding up his now large, chiseled looking hands, he stomped around the classroom making monster sounds. On another occasion Brian, a child new to the classroom who attended only two days a week, walked around by himself for a long time carrying a silver pocketbook and hovering first at the edges of girls' play and then at the edges of boys' play. On the third occasion, Sam used ballet slippers to animate his play in circle.

When kids dressed up, they played at being a variety of things from kitty cats and puppies to monsters and superheroes to "fancy ladies." Some of this play was not explicitly gendered. For example, one day in November I observed three girls wearing "turkey hats" they had made. They spent a long time gobbling at each other and playing at being turkeys, but there was nothing explicitly gendered about their play. However, this kind of adornment was not the most frequent type. Children often seemed to experiment with both genders when they played dress-up. The three-year-olds tended to be more experimental in their gender dress-up than the five-year-olds, perhaps because teachers encouraged it more at this age.

> Everett and Juan are playing dress-up. Both have on "dresses" made out of material that is wrapped around them like a toga or sarong. Everett has a pocketbook and a camera over his shoulder and Juan has a pair of play binoculars on a strap over his. Everett has a scarf around his head and cape on. Juan has on big, green sunglasses. Pam (teacher) tells them, "You guys look great! Go look in the mirror." They shuffle over to the full-length mirror and look at themselves and grin, and make adjustments to their costumes. (Three-year-olds)

The five-year-old children tended to dress-up more gender normatively. Girls in particular played at being adult women.

> Frances is playing dress-up. She is walking in red shoes and carrying a pocketbook. She and two other girls, Jen and Rachel, spend between five and ten minutes looking at and talking about the guinea pigs. Then they go back to dress-up. Frances and Rachel practice walking in adult women's shoes. Their body movements are not a perfect imitation of an adult woman's walk in high heels, yet it does look like an attempt to imitate such a walk. Jen and Rachel go back to the guinea pigs, and Frances, now by herself, is turning a sheer, frilly lavender shirt around and around and around trying to figure out how to put it on. She gets it on and looks at herself in the mirror. She adds a sheer pink and lavender scarf and pink shoes. Looks in the mirror again. She walks, twisting her body—shoulders, hips, shoulders, hips—not quite a (stereotypic) feminine walk, but close. Walking in big shoes makes her take little bitty steps, like walking in heels. She shuffles in the too big shoes out into the middle of the classroom and stops by a teacher. Laura (a teacher) says, "don't you look fancy, all pink and purple." Frances smiles up at her and walks off, not twisting so much this time. She's goes back to the mirror and adds a red scarf. She looks in the mirror and is holding her arms across her chest to hold the scarf on (she can't tie it) and she is holding it with her chin too. She shuffles to block area where Jen is and then takes the clothes off and puts them back in dress-up area. (Five-year-olds)

I observed not only the children who dressed up, but the reactions of those around them to their dress. This aspect proved to be one of the most interesting parts of kids' dress-up play. Children interpreted each others' bodily adornments as gendered, even when other interpretations were plausible. For instance, one day just before Halloween, Kim dressed up and was "scary" because she was dressed as a woman:

> Kim has worn a denim skirt and tights to school today. Now she is trying to pull on a ballerina costume—pink and ruffly—over her clothes. She has a hard time getting it on. It's tight and wrinkled up and twisted when she gets it on. Her own clothes are bunched up under it. Then she puts on a mask—a woman's face. The mask material itself is a clear plastic so that skin shows through, but is sculpted to have a very Anglo nose and high cheek bones. It also has thin eyebrows, blue eye shadow, blush, and lipstick painted on it. The mask is bigger than Kim's face and head. Kim looks at herself in the mirror and spends the rest of the play time with this costume on. Intermittently she picks up a plastic pumpkin since it is Halloween season and carries that around too. Kim walks around the classroom for a long time and then runs through the block area wearing this costume. Jason yells, "Ugh! There's a woman!" He and the other boys playing blocks shriek and scatter about the block area. Kim runs back to the dress-up area as they yell. Then

throughout the afternoon she walks and skips through the center of the classroom, and every time she comes near the block boys one of them yells, "Ugh, there's the woman again!" The teacher even picks up on this and says to Kim twice, "Woman, slow down." (Five-year-olds)

The boys' shrieks indicated that Kim was scary, and this scariness is linked in their comments about her being a woman. It seems equally plausible that they could have interpreted her scary dress as a "trick-o-treater," given that it was close to Halloween and she was carrying a plastic pumpkin that kids collect candy in, or that they might have labeled her a dancer or ballerina because she was wearing a tutu. Rather, her scary dress-up was coded for her by others as "woman."

Other types of responses to girls dressing up also seemed to gender their bodies and to constrain them. For example, on two occasions I saw a teacher tie the arms of girls' dress-up shirts together so that the girls could not move their arms. They did this in fun, of course, and untied them as soon as the girls wanted them to, but I never witnessed this constraining of boys' bodies in play.

Thus, how parents gender children's bodies through dressing them and the ways children experiment with bodily adornments by dressing up make girls' and boys' bodies different and seem different to those around them. Adorning a body often genders it explicitly—signifies that it is a feminine or masculine body. Adornments also make girls movements smaller, leading girls to take up less space with their bodies and disallowing some types of movement.[7]

Formal and Relaxed Behaviors

Describing adults, Goffman (1959) defines front stage and backstage behavior:

> The backstage language consists of reciprocal first-naming, co-operative decision making, profanity, open sexual remarks, elaborate griping, smoking, rough informal dress, "sloppy" sitting and standing posture, use of dialect or substandard speech, mumbling and shouting, playful aggressivity and "kidding," inconsiderateness for the other in minor but potentially symbolic acts, minor physical self-involvements such as humming, whistling, chewing, nibbling, belching, and flatulence. The front stage behavior language can be taken as the absence (and in some sense the opposite) of this. (P. 128)

Thus, one might not expect much front stage or formal behavior in preschool, and often, especially during parents' drop-off and pick-up time, this was the case. But a given region of social life may sometimes be a backstage and sometimes a front stage. I identified several behaviors that were expected by the teachers, required by the institution, or that would be required in many institutional settings, as formal behavior. Raising one's hand, sitting "on your bottom" (not on your knees, not squatting, not lying down, not standing) during circle, covering one's nose and mouth when coughing or sneezing, or sitting upright in a chair are all formal behaviors of preschools, schools, and to some extent the larger social world. Crawling on the floor, yelling, lying down during teachers' presentations, and running through the classroom are examples of relaxed behaviors that are not allowed in preschool, schools, work settings, and many institutions of the larger social world (Henley 1977). Not all behaviors fell into one of these classifications. When kids were actively engaged in playing at the water table, for example, much of their behavior was not clearly formal or relaxed. I coded as formal and relaxed behaviors those behaviors that would be seen as such if done by adults (or children in many cases) in other social institutions for which children are being prepared.

In the classrooms in this study, boys were allowed and encouraged to pursue relaxed behaviors in a variety of ways that girls were not. Girls were more likely to be encouraged to pursue more formal behaviors. Eighty-two percent of all formal behaviors observed in these classrooms were done by girls, and only 18 percent by boys. However, 80 percent of the behaviors coded as relaxed were boys' behaviors (Table 2).

These observations do not tell us *why* boys do more relaxed behaviors and girls do more formal behaviors. Certainly many parents and others would argue that boys are more predisposed to sloppy postures, crawling on the floor, and so on. However, my observations suggest that teachers help construct this gender difference in bodily behaviors.[8] Teachers were more likely to reprimand girls for relaxed bodily movements and comportment. Sadker and Sadker (1994) found a similar result with respect to hand-raising

Table 2 Observations of Formal and Relaxed Behaviors, by Gender of Child: Five Preschool Classrooms

	Boys		Girls		Total	
Type of Behavior	N	Percent	N	Percent	N	Percent
Formal	16	18	71	82	87	100
Relaxed	86	80	21	20	107	100

Note: Structured/formal behaviors were coded from references in the field notes to formal postures, polite gestures, etc. Relaxed/informal behaviors were coded from references to informal postures, backstage demeanors, etc.

for answering teachers' questions—if hand raising is considered a formal behavior and calling out a relaxed behavior, they find that boys are more likely to call out without raising their hands and demand attention:

> Sometimes what they [boys] say has little or nothing to do with the teacher's questions. Whether male comments are insightful or irrelevant, teachers respond to them. However, when girls call out, there is a fascinating occurrence: Suddenly the teacher remembers the rule about raising your hand before you talk. (Sadker and Sadker 1994:43)

This gendered dynamic of hand-raising exists even in preschool, although our field notes do not provide enough systematic recording of hand-raising to fully assess it. However, such a dynamic applies to many bodily movements and comportment:

> The kids are sitting with their legs folded in a circle listening to Jane (the teacher) talk about dinosaurs. ("Circle" is the most formal part of their preschool education each day and is like sitting in class.) Sam has the ballet slippers on his hands and is clapping them together really loudly. He stops and does a half-somersault backward out of the circle and stays that way with his legs in the air. Jane says nothing and continues talking about dinosaurs. Sue, who is sitting next to Sam, pushes his leg out of her way. Sam sits up and is now busy trying to put the ballet shoes on over his sneakers, and he is looking at the other kids and laughing, trying to get a reaction. He is clearly not paying attention to Jane's dinosaur story and is distracting the other kids. Sam takes the shoes and claps them together again. Jane leans over and tells him to give her the shoes. Sam does, and then lies down all stretched out on the floor, arms over his head, legs apart. Adam is also lying down now, and Keith is on Sara's (the teacher's aide) lap. Rachel takes her sweater off and folds it up. The other children are focused on the teacher. After about five minutes, Jane tells Sam "I'm going to ask you to sit up." (She doesn't say anything to Adam.) But he doesn't move. Jane ignores Sam and Adam and continues with the lesson. Rachel now lies down on her back. After about ten seconds Jane says, "Sit up, Rachel." Rachel sits up and listens to what kind of painting the class will do today. (Five-year-olds)

Sam's behavior had to be more disruptive, extensive, and informal than Rachel's for the teacher to instruct him and his bodily movements to be quieter and for him to comport his body properly for circle. Note that the boys who were relaxed but not disruptive were not instructed to sit properly. It was also common for a teacher to tell a boy to stop some bodily behavior and for the boy to ignore the request and the teacher not to enforce her instructions, although she frequently repeated them.

The gendering of body movements, comportment, and acquisitions of space also happens in more subtle ways. For example, often when there was "free" time, boys spent much more time in child-structured activities than did girls. In one classroom of five-year-olds, boys' "free" time was usually spent building with blocks, climbing on blocks, or crawling on the blocks or on the floor as they worked to build with the blocks whereas girls spent much of their free time sitting at tables cutting things out of paper, drawing, sorting small pieces of blocks into categories, reading stories, and so on. Compared to boys, girls rarely crawled on the floor (except when they played kitty cats). Girls and boys did share some activities. For example, painting and reading were frequently shared, and the three-year-olds often played at fishing from a play bridge together. Following is a list from my field notes of the most common activities boys and girls did during the child-structured activity periods of the day during two randomly picked weeks of observing:

> *Boys:* played blocks (floor), played at the water table (standing and splashing), played superhero (running around and in play house), played with the car garage (floor), painted at the easel (standing).

> *Girls:* played dolls (sitting in chairs and walking around), played dress-up (standing), coloring (sitting at tables), read stories (sitting on the couch), cut out pictures (sitting at tables).

Children sorted themselves into these activities and also were sorted (or not unsorted) by teachers. For example, teachers rarely told the three boys that always played with the blocks that they had to choose a different activity that day.[9] Teachers also encouraged girls to sit at tables by suggesting table activities for them—in a sense giving them less "free" time or structuring their time more.

> It's the end of circle, and Susan (teacher) tells the kids that today they can paint their dinosaur eggs if they want to. There is a table set up with paints and brushes for those who want to do that. The kids listen and then scatter to their usual activities. Several boys are playing blocks, two boys are at the water table. Several girls are looking at the hamsters in their cage and talking about them, two girls are sitting and stringing plastic beads. Susan says across the classroom, "I need some painters, Joy, Amy, Kendall?" The girls leave the hamster cage and go to the painting table. Susan pulls out a chair so Joy can sit down. She tells them about the painting project. (Five-year-olds)

These girls spent much of the afternoon enjoying themselves painting their eggs. Simon and Jack joined them temporarily, but then went back to activities that were not teacher-structured.

Events like these that happen on a regular basis over an extended period of early childhood serve to gender children's bodies—boys come to take up more room with their bodies, to sit in more open positions, and to feel freer to do what they wish with their bodies, even in relatively formal settings. Henley (1977) finds that among adults men generally are more relaxed than women in their demeanor and women tend to have tenser postures. The looseness of body-focused functions (e.g., belching) is also more open to men than to women. In other words, men are more likely to engage in relaxed demeanors, postures, and behaviors. These data suggest that this gendering of bodies into more formal and more relaxed movements, postures, and comportment is (at least partially) constructed in early childhood by institutions like preschools.

Controlling Voice

Speaking (or yelling as is often the case with kids) is a bodily experience that involves mouth, throat, chest, diaphragm, and facial expression. Thorne (1993) writes that an elementary school teacher once told her that kids "reminded her of bumblebees, an apt image of swarms, speed, and constant motion" (p. 15). Missing from this metaphor is the buzz of the bumblebees, as a constant hum of voices comes from children's play and activities. Kids' play that is giggly, loud, or whispery makes it clear that voice is part of their bodily experiences.

Voice is an aspect of bodily experience that teachers and schools are interested in disciplining. Quiet appears to be required for learning in classrooms. Teaching appropriate levels of voice, noise, and sound disciplines children's bodies and prepares them "from the inside" to learn the school's curriculums and to participate in other social institutions.

The disciplining of children's voices is gendered. I found that girls were told to be quiet or to repeat a request in a quieter, "nicer" voice about three times more often than were boys (see Table 3). This finding is particularly interesting because boys' play was frequently much noisier. However, when boys were noisy, they were also often doing other behaviors the teacher did not allow, and perhaps the teachers focused less on voice because they were more concerned with stopping behaviors like throwing or running.

Additionally, when boys were told to "quiet down" they were told in large groups, rarely as individuals. When they were being loud and were told to be quiet, boys were often in the process of enacting what Jordan and Cowan (1995) call warrior narratives:

> A group of three boys is playing with wooden doll figures. The dolls are jumping off block towers, crashing into each other. Kevin declares loudly, "I'm the grown up." Keith replies, "I'm the police."

Table 3 Observations of Teachers Telling Children to Be Quiet, by Gender of Child: Five Preschool Classrooms

Gender	N	Percent
Girls	45	73
Boys	16	26
Total	61	100

Note: Coded from references in the field notes to instances of teachers quieting children's voices.

> They knock the figures into each other and push each other away. Phil grabs a figure from Keith. Keith picks up two more and bats one with the other toward Phil. Now all three boys are crashing the figures into each other, making them dive off towers. They're having high fun. Two more boys join the group. There are now five boys playing with the wooden dolls and the blocks. They're breaking block buildings; things are crashing; they're grabbing each other's figures and yelling loudly. Some are yelling "fire, fire" as their figures jump off the block tower. The room is very noisy. (Five-year-olds)

Girls as individuals and in groups were frequently told to lower their voices. Later that same afternoon:

> During snack time the teacher asks the kids to tell her what they like best in the snack mix. Hillary says, "Marshmallows!" loudly, vigorously, and with a swing of her arm. The teacher turns to her and says, "I'm going to ask you to say that quietly," and Hillary repeats it in a softer voice. (Five-year-olds)

These two observations represent a prominent pattern in the data. The boys playing with the wooden figures were allowed to express their fun and enthusiasm loudly whereas Hillary could not loudly express her love of marshmallows. Girls' voices are disciplined to be softer and in many ways less physical— toning down their voices tones down their physicality. Hillary emphasized "marshmallows" with a large swinging gesture of her arm the first time she answered the teacher's question, but after the teacher asked her to say it quietly she made no gestures when answering. Incidents like these that are repeated often in different contexts restrict girls' physicality.

It could be argued that context rather than gender explains the difference in how much noise is allowed in these situations. Teachers may expect more formal behavior from children sitting at the snack table than they do during semistructured activities. However, even during free play girls were frequently told to quiet down:

> Nancy, Susan, and Amy are jumping in little jumps, from the balls of their feet, almost like skipping rope without the rope. Their mouths are open and they're making a humming sound, looking at each other and giggling. Two of them keep sticking their tongues out. They seem to be having great fun. The teacher's aide sitting on the floor in front of them turns around and says "Shhh, find something else to play. Why don't you play Simon Says?" All three girls stop initially. Then Amy jumps a few more times, but without making the noise. (Five-year-olds)

By limiting the girls' voices, the teacher also limits the girls' jumping and their fun. The girls learn that their bodies are supposed to be quiet, small, and physically constrained. Although the girls did not take the teacher's suggestion to play Simon Says (a game where bodies can be moved only quietly at the order of another), they turn to play that explores quietness yet tries to maintain some of the fun they were having:

> Nancy, Susan, and Amy begin sorting a pile of little-bitty pieces of puzzles, soft blocks, Legos, and so on into categories to "help" the teacher who told them to be quiet and to clean up. The

three of them and the teacher are standing around a single small desk sorting these pieces. (Meanwhile several boys are playing blocks and their play is spread all over the middle of the room.) The teacher turns her attention to some other children. The girls continue sorting and then begin giggling to each other. As they do, they cover their mouths. This becomes a game as one imitates the other. Susan says something nonsensical that is supposed to be funny, and then she "hee-hees" while covering her mouth and looks at Nancy, to whom she has said it, who covers her mouth and "hee-hees" back. They begin putting their hands/fingers cupped over their mouths and whispering in each others' ears and then giggling quietly. They are intermittently sorting the pieces and playing the whispering game. (Five-year-olds)

Thus, the girls took the instruction to be quiet and turned it into a game. This new game made their behaviors smaller, using hands and mouths rather than legs, feet, and whole bodies. Whispering became their fun, instead of jumping and humming. Besides requiring quiet, this whispering game also was gendered in another way: The girls' behavior seemed to mimic stereotypical female gossiping. They whispered in twos and looked at the third girl as they did it and then changed roles. Perhaps the instruction to be quiet, combined with the female role of "helping," led the girls to one of their understandings of female quietness—gossip—a type of feminine quietness that is perhaps most fun.

Finally, by limiting voice teachers limit one of girls' mechanisms for resisting others' mistreatment of them. Frequently, when a girl had a dispute with another child, teachers would ask the girl to quiet down and solve the problem nicely. Teachers also asked boys to solve problems by talking, but they usually did so only with intense disputes and the instruction to talk things out never carried the instruction to talk *quietly*.

Keith is persistently threatening to knock over the building that Amy built. He is running around her with a "flying" toy horse that comes dangerously close to her building each time. She finally says, "Stop it!" in a loud voice. The teacher comes over and asks, "How do we say that, Amy?" Amy looks at Keith and says more softly, "Stop trying to knock it over." The teacher tells Keith to find some place else to play. (Five-year-olds)

Cheryl and Julie are playing at the sand table. Cheryl says to the teacher loudly, "Julie took mine away!" The teacher tells her to say it more quietly. Cheryl repeats it less loudly. The teacher tells her, "Say it a little quieter." Cheryl says it quieter, and the teacher says to Julie, "Please don't take that away from her." (Three-year-olds)

We know that women are reluctant to use their voices to protect themselves from a variety of dangers. The above observations suggest that the denial of women's voices begins at least as early as preschool, and that restricting voice, usually restricts movement as well.

Finally, there were occasions when the quietness requirement did not restrict girls' bodies. One class of three-year-olds included two Asian girls, Diane and Sue, who did not speak English. Teachers tended to talk about them and over them but rarely to them. Although these girls said little to other children and were generally quiet, they were what I term body instigators. They got attention and played with other children in more bodily ways than most girls. For example, Sue developed a game with another girl that was a sort of musical chairs. They'd race from one chair to another to see who could sit down first. Sue initiated this game by trying to squeeze into a chair with the other girl. Also, for example,

Diane starts peeking into the play cardboard house that is full of boys and one girl. She looks like she wants to go in, but the door is blocked and the house is crowded. She then goes around to the side of the house and stands with her back to it and starts bumping it with her butt. Because the house is cardboard, it buckles and moves as she does it. The teacher tells her, "Stop—no." Diane stops and then starts doing it again but more lightly. All the boys come out of the house and ask her what she's doing. Matt gets right in her face and the teacher tells him, "Tell her no." He does, but all the other boys have moved on to other activities, so she and Matt go in the house together. (Three-year-olds)

Thus, Diane and Sue's lack of voice in this English-speaking classroom led to greater physicality. There may be other ways that context (e.g., in one's neighborhood instead of school) and race, ethnicity, and class shape gender and voice that cannot be determined from these data (Goodwin 1990).

Table 4 Observations of Teachers Giving Bodily Instructions to Children, by Gender of Child: Five Preschool Classrooms

Teacher's Instruction/ Child's Response	Boys		Girls		Mixed Groups	
	N	Percent	N	Percent	N	Percent
Bodily instructions from teachers[a]	94	65	39	26	13	9
Child obeys instructions[b]	45	48	31	80	—[c]	—[c]
Undirected bodily instructions from teachers[b]	54	57	6	15	5	55

Note: Bodily instructions are coded from references in the field notes to instances of a teacher telling a child what to do with his or her body.

[a] Percentages based on a total of 146 observations.

[b] Percentages based on a total of 94 observations for boys and 39 observations for girls.

[c] In the observations of mixed groups of girls and boys, usually some obeyed and some did not. Thus an accurate count of how the groups responded is not available.

Bodily Instructions

Teachers give a lot of instructions to kids about what to do with their bodies. Of the explicit bodily instructions recorded 65 percent were directed to boys, 26 percent to girls, and the remaining 9 percent were directed to mixed groups (Table 4). These numbers suggest that boys' bodies are being disciplined more than girls. However, there is more to this story—the types of instructions that teachers give and children's responses to them are also gendered.

First, boys obeyed teachers' bodily instructions about one-half of the time (48 percent), while girls obeyed about 80 percent of the time (Table 4).[10] Boys may receive more instructions from teachers because they are less likely to follow instructions and thus are told repeatedly. Frequently I witnessed a teacher telling a boy or group of boys to stop doing something—usually running or throwing things—and the teacher repeated these instructions several times in the course of the session before (if ever) taking further action. Teachers usually did not have to repeat instructions to girls—girls either stopped on their own with the first instruction, or because the teacher forced them to stop right then. Serbin (1983) finds that boys receive a higher proportion of teachers' ". . . loud reprimands, audible to the entire group. Such patterns of response, intended as punishment, have been repeatedly demonstrated to reinforce aggression and other forms of disruptive behavior" (p. 29).

Second, teachers' instructions directed to boys' bodies were less substantive than those directed to girls. That is, teachers' instructions to boys were usually to stop doing something, to end a bodily behavior with little suggestion for other behaviors they might do. Teachers rarely told boys to change a bodily behavior. A list of teachers' instructions to boys includes: stop throwing, stop jumping, stop clapping, stop splashing, no pushing, don't cry, blocks are not for bopping, don't run, don't climb on that. Fifty-seven percent of the instructions that teachers gave boys about their physical behaviors were of this undirected type, compared with 15 percent of their instructions to girls (Table 4). In other words, teachers' instructions to girls generally were more substantive and more directive, telling girls to do a bodily behavior rather than to stop one. Teachers' instructions to girls suggested that they alter their behaviors. A list of instructions to girls includes: talk to her, don't yell, sit here, pick that up, be careful, be gentle, give it to me, put it down there. Girls may have received fewer bodily instructions than did boys, but they received more directive ones. This gender difference leaves boys a larger range of possibilities of what they might choose to do with their bodies once they have stopped a behavior, whereas girls were directed toward a defined set of options.

Table 5 Observations of Physical Interaction between Teachers and Children, by Gender of Child: Five Preschool Classrooms

Type of Contact	Boys		Girls	
	N	*Percent*	*N*	*Percent*
Positive	41	60	21	54
Negative	24	35	6	15
Neutral	3	4	12	31
Total	68	99	39	100

Note: Coded from references in field notes to bodily contact between teachers and children. Percentages may not sum to 100 due to rounding.

Physical Interaction between Teachers and Children

Teachers also physically directed kids. For example, teachers often held kids to make them stop running, tapped them to make them turn around and pay attention, or turned their faces toward them so that they would listen to verbal instructions. One-fourth of all physical contacts between teachers and children was to control children's physicality in some way, and 94 percent of such contacts were directed at boys.

Physical interaction between teachers and children was coded into three categories: positive, negative, or neutral. Physical interaction was coded as positive if it was comforting, helpful, playful, or gentle. It was coded as negative if it was disciplining, assertive (not gentle), restraining, or clearly unwanted by the child (e.g., the child pulled away). Physical interaction was coded as neutral if it seemed to have little content (e.g., shoulders touching during circle, legs touching while a teacher gave a group of kids directions for a project). About one-half of the time, when teachers touched boys or girls, it was positive. For example, the teacher and child might have bodily contact as she tied a shoe, wiped away tears, or tickled a child, or if a child took the teacher's hand or got on her lap. For girls, the remaining physical interactions included 15 percent that were disciplining or instructing the body and about one-third that were neutral (e.g., leaning over the teacher's arm while looking at a book). For boys, these figures were reversed: Only 4 percent of their physical interactions with teachers were neutral in content, and 35 percent were negative and usually included explicit disciplining and instructing of the body (see Table 5).

This disciplining of boys' bodies took a particular form. Teachers usually attempted to restrain or remove boys who had "gone too far" in their play or who had done something that could harm another child:

> Irving goes up to Jack, who is playing dress-up, and puts his arms up, makes a monster face and says, "Aaarhhh!" Jack looks startled. Irving runs and jumps in front of Jack again and says "Aaaarrhh!" again. Marie (teacher) comes from behind Irving and holds him by the shoulders and arms from behind. She bends over him and says, "Calm down." He pulls forward, and eventually she lets him go. He runs up to Jack again and growls. Marie says, "He doesn't want you to do that." (Three-year-olds)
>
> Jane (teacher) tells Jeff to pick up the blocks. He says, "I won't." She catches him and pulls him toward her by the arm. She holds him by the arm. He struggles and gets away. He jumps up and down. Other kids put the blocks away. Jane ignores Jeff. (Several minutes later.) Jeff has been throwing the blocks and now Jane pries the blocks from him and grabs him by the wrist and drags him away from the blocks by his shirt arm. He is looking up at her and pointing his finger at her and saying, "No, cut it out!" in a mocking tone. Jane is angry, but she talks to him calmly but sternly telling him he can't throw the blocks. Jeff is struggling the entire time. Jane lets go of his arm, and Jeff runs right back to the block area and walks on the blocks that are still on the floor. (Five-year-olds)

As Serbin (1983) suggests, frequent loud reprimands of boys may increase their disruptive behavior; more frequent physical disciplining interactions between teachers and boys may do so as well. Because boys more frequently than girls experienced interactions in which their bodies were physically restrained or disciplined by an adult who had more power and was angry, they may be more likely than girls to associate physical interaction with struggle and anger, and thus may be more likely to be aggressive or disruptive.

Physical Interaction among Children

Thorne (1993) demonstrates that children participate in the construction of gender differences among themselves. The preschool brings together large groups of children who engage in interactions in which they cooperate with the hidden curriculum and discipline each others bodies in gendered ways, but they also engage in interactions in which they resist this curriculum.

Girls and boys teach their same-sex peers about their bodies and physicality. Children in these observations were much more likely to imitate the physical behavior of a same-sex peer than a cross-sex peer. Children also encourage others to imitate them. Some gendered physicality develops in this way. For example, I observed one boy encouraging other boys to "take up more space" in the same way he was.

> James (one of the most active boys in the class) is walking all over the blocks that Joe, George, and Paul have built into a road. Then he starts spinning around with his arms stretched out on either side of him. He has a plastic toy cow in one hand and is yelling, "Moo." He spins through half of the classroom, other children ducking under his arms or walking around him when he comes near them. Suddenly he drops the cow and still spinning, starts shouting, "I'm a tomato! I'm a tomato!" The three boys who were playing blocks look at him and laugh. James says, "I'm a tomato!" again, and Joe says, "There's the tomato." Joe, George, and Paul continue working on their block road. James then picks up a block and lobs it in their direction and then keeps spinning throughout this half of the classroom saying he's a tomato. Joe and George look up when the block lands near them and then they get up and imitate James. Now three boys are spinning throughout much of the room, shouting that they are tomatoes. The other children in the class are trying to go about their play without getting hit by a tomato. (Five-year-olds)

The within-gender physicality of three-year-old girls and boys was more similar than it was among the five-year-olds. Among the three-year-old girls there was more rough and tumble play, more physical fighting and arguing among girls than there was among the five-year-old girls.

> During clean up, Emily and Sara argue over putting away some rope. They both pull on the ends of the rope until the teacher comes over and separates them. Emily walks around the classroom then, not cleaning anything up. She sings to herself, does a twirl, and gets in line for snack. Sara is behind her in line. Emily pushes Sara. Sara yells, "Aaahh," and hits Emily and pushes her. The teacher takes both of them out of line and talks to them about getting along and being nice to each other. (Three-year-olds)
>
> Shelly and Ann have masks on. One is a kitty and one is a doggy. They're crawling around on the floor, and they begin play wrestling—kitties and doggies fight. The teacher says to them, "Are you ok?" They stop, lift up their masks, and look worried. The teacher says, "Oh, are you wrestling? It's ok, I just wanted to make sure everyone was ok." The girls nod; they're ok. Then, they put their masks back on and crawl on the floor some more. They do not resume wrestling. (Three-year-olds)

From lessons like these, girls have learned by age five that their play with each other should not be "too rough." The physical engagement of girls with each other at age five had little rough-and-tumble play:

> Three girls leave the dress-up corner. Mary crawls on the floor as Naomi and Jennifer talk. Jennifer touches Naomi's shoulder gently as she talks to her. They are having quite a long conversation. Jennifer is explaining something to Naomi. Jennifer's gestures are adult-like except that she fiddles with Naomi's vest buttons as she talks to her. Her touching and fiddling with Naomi's clothes is very gentle, how a child might fiddle with a mom's clothing while talking to her—doing it absent-mindedly. Mary, on the floor, is pretending to be a kitty. Then Jennifer gets on the floor and is a kitty too. They are squeaking, trying to mimic a cat's meow. Naomi then puts her arm around Susan's shoulder and leads her to play kitty too. Naomi seems to be a person still, not a kitty. She is in charge of the kitties. (Five-year-olds)

Two girls are playing with the dishes and sitting at a table. Keisha touches Alice under the chin, tickles her almost, then makes her eat something pretend, then touches the corners of her mouth, telling her to smile. (Five-year-olds)

I do not mean to suggest that girls' physical engagement with each other is the opposite of boys' or that all of boys' physical contacts were rough and tumble. Boys, especially in pairs, hugged, gently guided, or helped each other climb or jump. But often, especially in groups of three or more and especially among the five-year-olds, boys' physical engagement was highly active, "rough," and frequent. Boys experienced these contacts as great fun and not as hostile or negative in any way:

Keith and Lee are jumping on the couch, diving onto it like high jumpers, colliding with each other as they do. Alan watches them and then climbs onto the back of the couch and jumps off. Keith takes a jump onto the couch, lands on Lee, and then yells, "Ouch, ouch—I hurt my private," and he runs out of the room holding onto his crotch. The teacher tells them to stop jumping on the couch. (Five-year-olds)

A group of boys is building and climbing on big, hollow, tall blocks. They're bumping into each other, crawling and stepping on each other and the blocks as they do it. They begin yelling, "Garbage can," and laughing. They put little blocks inside the big hollow ones, thus "garbage can." Mike pushes Steve away from the "garbage can" and says, "No that's not!" because he wanted to put a block that was too big into the "can." Steve quits trying and goes to get another block. (Five-year-olds)

The physical engagement of boys and girls *with each other* differed from same-sex physical engagement. Because girls' and boys' play is semi-segregated, collisions (literal and figurative) in play happen at the borders of these gender-segregated groups (Maccoby 1988; Thorne 1993). As Thorne (1993) demonstrates, not all borderwork is negative—40 percent of the physical interactions observed between girls and boys were positive or neutral (Table 6).

Ned runs over to Veronica, hipchecks her and says "can I be your friend?" and she says "yes." Ned walks away and kicks the blocks again three to four times. (Five-year-olds)

However, cross-gender interactions were more likely to be negative than same-sex interactions. In fact, physical interactions among children were twice as likely to be a negative interaction if they were between a girl and boy than if they were among same-gender peers. Approximately 30 percent of the interactions among girls and among boys were negative (hostile, angry, controlling, hurtful), whereas 60 percent of mixed-gender physical interactions were negative. Sixty percent of 113 boy-girl physical interactions were initiated by boys, 39 percent were initiated by girls, and only 1 percent of these interactions were mutually initiated.

At the borders of semi-segregated play there are physical interactions about turf and toy ownership:

Sylvia throws play money on the floor from her play pocketbook. Jon grabs it up. She wrestles him for it and pries it from his hands. In doing this she forces him onto the floor so that he's hunched forward on his knees. She gets behind him and sandwiches him on the floor as she grabs his hands and gets the money loose. Then, two minutes later, she's giving money to kids, and she gives Jon some, but apparently not enough. He gets right close to her face, inches away and loudly tells her that he wants more. He scrunches up his face, puts his arms straight down by his sides and makes fists. She steps back; he steps up close again to her face. She turns away. (Five-year-olds)

Negative interactions occur when there are "invasions" or interruptions of play among children of one gender by children of another:

Courtney is sitting on the floor with the girls who are playing "kitties." The girls have on their dress-up clothes and dress-up shoes. Phil puts on big winter gloves and then jumps in the middle of the girls on the floor. He lands on their shoes. Courtney pushes him away and then pulls her legs and clothes and stuff closer to her. She takes up less space and is sitting in a tight ball on the floor. Phil yells, "No! Aaarrhh." Julie says, "It's not nice to yell." (Five-year-olds)

Table 6 Observations of Physical Interactions among Children, by Gender of Children: Five Preschool Classrooms

| | Interactions between: | | | | | |
| | Boys | | Girls | | Boys and Girls[a] | |
Type of Interaction	N	Percent	N	Percent	N	Percent
Positive	46	70	42	66	20	18
Negative	19	29	20	31	68	60
Neutral	1	2	2	3	26	23
Total	66	101	64	100	114	101

Note: Physical interaction was coded from references in the field notes to bodily interaction between children. Bodily contact that was minor and seemingly meaningless was not recorded in field notes. For example, children brushing against each other while picking up toys was not recorded if both children ignored the contact and did not alter their actions because of it. Percentages may not sum to 100 due to rounding.

As Thorne (1993) suggests, kids create, shape, and police the borders of gender. I suggest that they do so physically. In this way, they not only sustain gender segregation, but also maintain a sense that girls and boys are physically different, that their bodies are capable of doing certain kinds of things. This sense of physical differences may make all gender differences feel and appear natural.

Conclusion

Children also sometimes resist their bodies being gendered. For example, three-year-old boys dressed up in women's clothes sometimes. Five-year-old girls played with a relaxed comportment that is normatively (hegemonically) masculine when they sat with their feet up on the desk and their chairs tipped backward. In one classroom when boys were at the height of their loud activity—running and throwing toys and blocks—girls took the opportunity to be loud too as the teachers were paying less attention to them and trying to get the boys to settle down. In individual interactions as well, girls were likely to be loud and physically assertive if a boy was being unusually so:

> José is making a plastic toy horse fly around the room, and the boys playing with the blocks are quite loud and rambunctious. José flies the toy horse right in front of Jessica's face and then zooms around her and straight toward her again. Jessica holds up her hand and waves it at him yelling, "Aaaarrrh." José flies the horse in another direction. (Five-year-olds)

These instances of resistance suggest that gendered physicalities are not natural, nor are they easily and straightforwardly acquired. This research demonstrates the many ways that practices in institutions like preschools facilitate children's acquisition of gendered physicalities.

Men and women and girls and boys fill social space with their bodies in different ways. Our everyday movements, postures, and gestures are gendered. These bodily differences enhance the seeming naturalness of sexual and reproductive differences, that then construct inequality between men and women (Butler 1990). As MacKinnon (1987) notes, "Differences are inequality's post hoc excuse . . ." (p. 8). In other words, these differences create a context for social relations in which differences confirm inequalities of power.

This research suggests one way that bodies are gendered and physical differences are constructed through social institutions and their practices. Because this gendering occurs at an early age, the seeming naturalness of such differences is further underscored. In preschool, bodies become gendered in ways that are so subtle and taken-for-granted that they come to feel and appear natural. Preschool, however, is presumably just the tip of the iceberg in the gendering of children's bodies. Families, formal schooling, and other institutions (like churches, hospitals, and workplaces) gender children's physicality as well.

Many feminist sociologists (West and Zimmerman 1987) and other feminist scholars (Butler 1990, 1993) have examined how the seeming naturalness of gender differences underlies gender inequality. They have also theorized that there are no meaningful natural differences (Butler 1990, 1993.) However, how gender differences come to feel and appear natural in the first place has been a missing piece of the puzzle.

Sociological theories of the body that describe the regulation, disciplining, and managing that social institutions do to bodies have neglected the gendered nature of these processes (Foucault 1979; Shilling 1993; Turner 1984). These data suggest that a significant part of disciplining the body consists of gendering it, even in subtle, micro, everyday ways that make gender appear natural. It is in this sense that the preschool as an institution genders children's bodies. Feminist theories about the body (Bordo 1993; Connell 1995; Young 1990), on the other hand, tend to focus on the adult gendered body and fail to consider how the body becomes gendered. This neglect may accentuate gender differences and make them seem natural. This research provides but one account of how bodies become gendered. Other accounts of how the bodies of children and adults are gendered (and raced, classed, and sexualized) are needed in various social contexts across the life course.

ENDNOTES

1. There is little research on differences in things like step size and sitting positions among children; most of the traditional developmental research on children looks at motor skills and the outcomes of those skills. "Although the outcome reflects the movement process, it does not do so perfectly and does not describe this process" (Thomas and French 1985:277). I am just as interested in differences in the process as the outcome (also see Young 1990). For a review of the developmental psychology literature on gender differences in motor skills see Thomas and French 1985; for more recent examples in this literature, see Butterfield and Loovis 1993, Plimpton and Regimbal 1992, and Smoll and Schutz 1990.

2. I use "kids" and "children" interchangeably; children themselves prefer the term "kids" (Thorne 1993:9).

3. There were three physical locations for the classrooms, but two of the classrooms had both morning and afternoon sessions with a different teacher and different student composition, resulting in five sets of teachers and students.

4. Classrooms usually contained 15 to 18 children on a given day. However, since some kids came to preschool five days a week, some three, and some two, a total of 112 different kids were observed.

5. Parents are not solely responsible for what their children wear to preschool, as they are constrained by what is available and affordable in children's clothing. More important, children, especially at ages three to five, want some say in what they wear to preschool and may insist on some outfits and object to others.

6. All of my observations of this uninteractional management were with three-year-olds. Teachers seemed to manage children's bodies more directly and with less interaction at this age than with the five-year-olds, perhaps because they could. Five-year-olds demanded explanations and interaction. This result may also be confounded with race. On at least two occasions when teachers treated girls this way, the girls were Asian students who understood little English. The teachers generally tended to interact less with non-English speaking kids and to talk about them as if they were not there more than they did with those who spoke English.

7. Although girls could take up *more* space with their dressing up—by twirling in a skirt or wearing large brimmed hats or carrying large pocketbooks—we did not observe this behavior at either preschool.

8. Throughout the paper, when I use the term "constructed," I do *not* mean that preschools create these differences or that they are the only origins of these differences. Clearly, children come to preschool with some gender differences that were created in the family or other contexts outside of preschool. My argument is that preschools reinforce these differences and build (construct) further elaborations of difference upon what children bring to preschool.

9. Once a teacher put a line of masking tape on the floor to show where the "block corner" ended because the boys playing with the blocks took up one whole end of the classroom. However, this did not work.

As the teacher was making the line on the floor, the boys told her to extend it further outward (which she did) so they could have room to play in an area in which they did not usually play, and in the end the line was ignored. The same teacher tried on another occasion to tell the boys who played with the blocks that they had to play with Legos instead. They did this, and two girls began playing with the blocks; but in short order two of the boys who were supposed to be playing Legos asked the girls if they could play with them, instead of asking the teacher. There was about 10 minutes of mixed gender play before the girls abandoned the blocks.

10. There were several cases for boys and girls in which the observer did not record the child's response.

REFERENCES

Anyon, Jean. 1980. "Social Class and the Hidden Curriculum of Work." *Journal of Education* 162:67–92.

Birdwhistell, Ray. 1970. *Kinesics and Contexts.* Philadelphia, PA: University of Pennsylvania Press.

Bordo, Susan. 1993. *Unbearable Weight.* Berkeley, CA: University of California Press.

Bowles, Samuel and Herbert Gintis. 1976. *Schooling in Capitalist America.* New York: Basic Books.

Butler, Judith. 1990. *Gender Trouble.* New York: Routledge.

———. 1993. *Bodies that Matter.* New York: Routledge.

Butterfield, Stephen and E. Michael Loovis. 1993. "Influence of Age, Sex, Balance, and Sport Participation on Development of Throwing by Children in Grades K-8." *Perceptual and Motor Skills* 76:459–64.

Carere, Sharon. 1987. "Lifeworld of Restricted Behavior." *Sociological Studies of Child Development* 2: 105–38.

Carnoy, Martin and Henry Levin. 1985. *Schooling and Work in the Democratic State.* Stanford, CA: Stanford University Press.

Connell, R. W. 1987. *Gender and Power.* Stanford, CA: Stanford University Press.

———. 1995. *Masculinities.* Berkeley, CA: University of California Press.

Foucault, Michel. 1979. *Discipline and Punish: The Birth of the Prison.* New York: Vintage Books.

Giroux, Henry and David Purpel. 1983. *The Hidden Curriculum and Moral Education.* Berkeley, CA: McCutchan.

Goffman, Erving. 1959. *The Presentation of Self in Everyday Life.* Garden City, NY: Doubleday.

Goodwin, Marjorie Harness. 1990. *He-Said-She-Said: Talk as Social Organization among Black Children.* Bloomington, IN: Indiana University Press.

Haug, Frigga. 1987. *Female Sexualization: A Collective Work of Memory.* London, England: Verso.

Henley, Nancy. 1977. *Body Politics.* New York: Simon and Schuster.

Jackson, Philip W. 1968. *Life in Classrooms.* New York: Holt, Rinehart, and Winston.

Jordan, Ellen and Angela Cowan. 1995. "Warrior Narratives in the Kindergarten Classroom: Renegotiating the Social Contract." *Gender and Society* 9:727–43.

Maccoby, Eleanor. 1988. "Gender as a Social Category." *Developmental Psychology* 24:755–65.

MacKinnon, Catharine. 1987. *Feminism Unmodified.* Cambridge, MA: Harvard University Press.

Martin, Emily. 1987. *The Woman in the Body.* Boston, MA: Beacon Press.

Martin, Karin. 1996. *Puberty, Sexuality, and the Self: Boys and Girls at Adolescence.* New York: Routledge.

McLaren, Peter. 1986. *Schooling as a Ritual Performance: Towards a Political Economy of Educational Symbols and Gestures.* London, England: Routledge and Kegan Paul.

Plimpton, Carol E. and Celia Regimbal. 1992. "Differences in Motor Proficiency According to Gender and Race." *Perceptual and Motor Skills* 74:399–402.

Sadker, Myra and David Sadker. 1994. *Failing at Fairness: How America's Schools Cheat Girls.* New York: Charles Scribner and Sons.

Serbin, Lisa. 1983. "The Hidden Curriculum: Academic Consequences of Teacher Expectations." Pp. 18–41 in *Sex Differentiation and Schooling,* edited by M. Marland. London, England: Heinemann Educational Books.

Shilling, Chris. 1993. *The Body and Social Theory.* London, England: Sage.

Smoll, Frank and Robert Schutz. 1990. "Quantifying Gender Differences in Physical Performance: A Developmental Perspective." *Developmental Psychology* 26:360–69.

Suransky, Valerie Polakow. 1982. *The Erosion of Childhood.* Chicago, IL: University of Chicago Press.

Thomas, Jerry and Karen French. 1985. "Gender Differences across Age in Motor Performance: A Meta-Analysis." *Psychological Bulletin* 98: 260–82.

Thorne, Barrie. 1993. *Gender Play: Girls and Boys in School.* New Brunswick, NJ: Rutgers University Press.

Turner, Bryan S. 1984. *The Body and Society: Explorations in Social Theory.* New York: Basil Blackwell.

———. 1992. *Regulating Bodies: Essays in Medical Sociology.* London, England: Routledge.

Van Ausdale, Debra and Joe R. Feagin. 1996. "Using Racial and Ethnic Concepts: The Critical Case of Very Young Children." *American Sociological Review* 61:779–93.

Wasburn, Philo C. 1986. "The Political Role of the American School," *Theory and Research in Social Education* 14:51–65.

West, Candace and Don Zimmerman. 1987. "Doing Gender." *Gender and Society* 1:127–51.

Young, Iris. 1990. *Throwing Like a Girl.* Bloomington, IN: Indiana University Press.

Voicing Your Opinion
Becoming a Gendered Body: Practices of Preschools
Karin A. Martin

1. Martin presents the argument that gendered is an *embodied* aspect of our identity. How is this idea informed by the tradition of sex-gendered role delineation? How do *you* experience gender at an embodied level?

   _____

   _____

   _____

   _____

   _____

2. Discuss the posted rules of behavior for Preschool B (p. 55). How do these rules reflect gender socialization? Do these rules contribute to gender socialization? If so, how?

   _____

   _____

   _____

   _____

   _____

3. Consider the idea of the hidden school curriculum. Can you recall times in your own educational experience where there was evidence of a hidden curriculum of gender?

   _____

   _____

   _____

   _____

   _____

ADULT GENITAL SURGERY FOR INTERSEX
A Solution to What Problem?

MARY E. BOYLE, SUSAN SMITH, AND LIH-MEI LIAO

This article examines the reported experiences of adult women with intersex conditions who choose to have genital surgery. This choice is examined within the contexts of gender and heterosexuality. Patients often experience passivity in dealing with surgeons prior to and during the sex assignment process. The article also examines the impact that the surgery has on the women's relational intimacy.

The desirability of routine genital surgery for infants with ambiguous genitalia is increasingly debated. But there is less discussion about intersex adults who choose genital surgery, despite evidence suggesting that the results are often unsatisfactory. This study reports on how six women with intersex conditions decided to have feminizing genital surgery and how they evaluated the outcomes. The initial analysis highlighted a chronological transition from surgery as non-dilemmatic to surgery as a serious dilemma; a version of Foucauldian discourse analysis was then used to place the women's experiences in a cultural context. The implications for psychological involvement in services for women with intersex conditions are discussed.

The term 'intersex' refers to a result of sexual differentiation and development problems in which a person's chromosomal, gonadal and/or genital characteristics cannot be unambiguously placed into our categories of male and female. Two conditions implicated in intersex outcomes are congenital adrenal hyperplasia (CAH) and androgen insensitivity syndrome (AIS). In the former, an enzyme abnormality results in a female (XX) foetus producing substantial amounts of androgens which masculinize the external genitalia to varying degrees. In AIS, an XY (male) foetus, with male gonads, produces normal amounts of androgens but lacks receptors to respond to them. The infant may have 'standard' female genitalia but without cervix, womb or ovaries (so that the condition may not be diagnosed until puberty) or may show varying degrees of masculinization of the genitals, depending on the degree of residual receptor or hormonal activity. Estimates vary, but Warne (1998) suggests that around 1/4500 live-born infants has a genital abnormality severe enough to make the immediate assignment of sex difficult.

It has been standard paediatric practice to recommend sex assignment to male or female, and then genital surgery for infants with ambiguous genitalia, with potential sexual function (erectile and penetrative potential of the phallus) a major consideration in the case of infants who might be sex-assigned as males, and fertility (presence of womb and ovaries) in the case of chromosomal females (Creighton, 2001). Because it is easier to construct a 'functional' vagina (i.e. capable of receiving a penis) than a 'functional' penis (i.e. capable of erection and penetration), surgeons have generally recommended female assignment where genital ambiguity is pronounced (Wilson & Reiner, 1998). Following sex assignment, parents have traditionally been advised to raise the child without ambiguity, which may mean that the child (and adult) receives limited information about their medical condition (Hegarty, 2000; Kessler, 2000; Wilson & Reiner, 1998). Infant surgery might be followed by further genital surgery in childhood, adolescence or adulthood, together with the administration of hormones to align the child's physical appearance to the assigned sex.

Very recently, these practices have been challenged not least through the 'coming of age' of those who had such interventions as children and, as adults, have spoken negatively of their experiences. Professionals have focused critically on reports of adults with intersex conditions choosing to change gender later in life (Meyer-Bahlburg, Gruen, & New, 1996; Reiner, 1996); on infant surgery; and on the fact that raising a child 'unambiguously' in line with the assigned sex has often meant that information has been withheld from children and adults, raising serious ethical issues, not least about consent to treatment (Fausto-Sterling, 2002; Kessler, 2000). It is also unlikely that children are not aware that they are different, given possibly evasive or incomplete answers to questions, frequent hospital visits, possible absence of menstruation, genital surgery and hormonal treatments (Wilson & Reiner, 1998).

There is, too, a lack of information on the outcomes of surgical sex assignment. Large-scale studies may remain impractical, but an increasing number of smaller-scale studies and case reports suggest that the outcomes of genital surgery, even using newer techniques, are problematic with repeat surgery usually needed after puberty if intercourse is to take place. Women also report scarring, loss of sexual sensation and pain on intercourse (Creighton, 2001; May, Boyle, & Grant, 1996; Minto, Liao, Woodhouse, Ransley, & Creighton, in press).

As a result of these concerns, a number of changes in the management of intersex have been suggested. Although there are disagreements on the desirability of sex assignment at birth, there is general agreement among those seeking changes in practice on the need to involve parents fully in decision making; to foster more open communication among parents, children and professionals; to stop viewing the birth of an infant with ambiguous genitalia as an 'emergency' (unless surgery is medically necessary) and as far as possible to delay genital and gonadal surgery until the person can give informed consent (Creighton, 2001; Kipnis & Diamond, 1998).

Rationale for the Present Study

Criticism of traditional management of intersex targets non-consensual genital surgery for infants and children. But there has been little discussion of the issues raised when intersex adults choose genital surgery (e.g. vaginal construction or clitoral reduction), almost as if 'consensual' surgery removes the need for discussion. But the study of these adult choices is important because the cultural imperatives underlying infant sex assignment, particularly the male–female dichotomy and assumptions about what male and female genitals are *for,* are also likely to impinge on expert advice about adult surgery and on decisions to accept it. In addition, studies that show surgery outcomes to be problematic raise questions about the information patients receive, the decision-making process and criteria for 'success'. The present study is concerned with the experiences of women with intersex conditions who chose genital surgery as adults (and most adult surgery is carried out on women). The study focuses on decision making for surgery, the experience of surgery itself and perceived outcomes. More specific research questions will be discussed in the analysis section.

Method

Participants

Participants were recruited from a support group for women with intersex conditions following circulation of research information on the group's website and a brief presentation by one of the authors (SS). We had hoped to recruit women who had chosen not to have surgery, although we knew this would be difficult because of high rates of genital surgery. Of the six participants only one had not had genital surgery but had instead used vaginal dilators. We will return later to issues raised by the recruitment process.

The women had a variety of medical (intersex) conditions, including complete androgen insensitivity syndrome, although none of the women had CAH. However because we were interested in what the women had in common—an intersex diagnosis and atypical genitalia—and to protect their confidentiality, only group information about non-diagnostic characteristic is given in Table 1.[1]

Table 1 Participant Characteristics

Non-diagnostic characteristics	
Total	6
Age range	27–52
Age at surgery	19–43
Type of intervention	
Clitoridectomy	1
Vaginaplasty	4
Dilators only	1
Number of operations	
One	3 participants
Two	2 participants
Relationship status	
Divorced	1
With a male partner	2 (includes divorced participant)
Not in a relationship	4
Education	
To degree level	6

Materials

INTERVIEW SCHEDULE A semi-structured interview format was chosen to balance a structure imposed by the researchers with the need to allow participants to speak about what was relevant to them. The schedule covered the women's initial decision making about surgery, their experience of surgery and the outcomes of surgery, particularly in relation to self-perception, forming intimate relationships and sexual activities.

Procedure

When ethical approvals had been obtained, women who expressed an interest in the research were given an information sheet and asked to sign a consent form; participants chose whether to be interviewed in their homes (4) or in a hospital psychology department (2). The interviews (carried out by SS) were recorded with participants' consent and took between 1.5 and two hours. The tapes were transcribed verbatim and all potentially identifying information removed from the transcript.

Analysis

Analytic Methods

The interview transcripts were analysed using two methods: interpretative phenomenological analysis (IPA; Smith, 1996) and a version of Foucauldian discourse analysis. Because these methods may be seen as representing the different epistemological traditions of realism and constructionism (although in the case of IPA, the distinction may be rather blurred; see Willig, 2001), we will discuss why this dual approach was chosen.

Our two major aims were to highlight patterns in the reported experience of intersex women who had chosen or not chosen genital surgery, and to consider the meanings of these experiences in a cultural and gendered context. IPA appeared to be the method of choice for our first aim, given its aim of conveying the quality of an individual's experience and the meanings they attach to it, while acknowledging that such experiences always involve interpretation (Smith, 1996). The strength of IPA may be its insistence on remaining with participants' accounts of their experiences and their meanings, but as Yardley (1997a) points out, we have no choice but to convey our experiences using cultural concepts and language. Willig (2001) similarly emphasizes the tensions between IPA's assumption of the representational validity of language and the possibility that language does not constitute the means of expressing our subjective experience but instead prescribes what we *can* think and feel. Willig has further argued that while IPA is able to generate rich descriptions of participants' experiences, it has not generally furthered our understanding of *why* such experiences take place or of the social, linguistic and material conditions that give rise to, and continue to shape them.

A form of discourse analysis was chosen to complement IPA because the latter's limitations are precisely in those areas focused on by discursive approaches which explicitly acknowledge the socially and linguistically mediated nature of human experience (Yardley, 1997a). Stam has also argued for more attention to discourse in health psychology, emphasizing that 'the activities [of those who provide and use biomedicine] are constituted discursively and an analysis of care-talk necessarily leads to a deconstruction of traditional categories of health care' (2000, p. 274).

A version of Foucauldian discourse analysis was therefore used here because of its particular concern with examining the relationships among the cultural availability of discursive resources, the social conditions which contribute to and are shaped by discursive resources and the ideological and power relations which are reflected in and strengthened by the use of particular discourses. Foucauldian discourse analysis is also concerned with the potential relationships between discursive practice and the construction of individual desires, as well as with 'subject positions', i.e. possibilities for feeling and acting, made available or closed down by particular discourses.

The analytic approach adopted here has much in common with material discursive psychology (e.g. Ussher, 1997; Yardley, 1997b) and, like Yardley (1997a), we would argue for the usefulness of complementing a phenomenological perspective with some form of discourse analysis. The ways in which the two approaches were combined will be discussed later.

Analysis—Process

Although different types of qualitative analysis ask different questions of and make different assumptions about the data, there is much procedural overlap because all analyses seek regularities or themes in people's accounts of events or experiences. We adopted here Taylor and Bogdan's description of themes as units obtained from patterns in, for example, 'conversation topics, vocabulary, recurring activities, meanings [and] feelings' (1984, p. 131). This type of analysis is central to IPA (Willig, 2001) and we therefore initially followed procedures outlined by Smith, Jarman and Osborn (1999) but noted that these overlap with those for discourse analysis (Parker, 1992). However, as we were concerned with the chronology of the women's experience in choosing, having and living with the outcomes of surgery, this sequence formed an overall framework for the analysis. In order to facilitate the integration of IPA and the Foucauldian discourse analysis, further specific questions were then posed of the thematically organized accounts of the women's experiences. The two parts of the analysis will be presented separately.

Results and Discussion: IPA[2]

The superordinate theme identified was that of the transition from the relative absence to the marked presence of a dilemma. Thus, the three chronological periods—before surgery, the experience of surgery and post-surgery—were characterized by a transition from experiencing surgery as largely non-dilemmatic to experiencing it as a serious dilemma. We are using 'dilemma' here in the sense discussed by Billig et al., who have argued that '[t]o experience a dilemma is to live out an opposition, so that one is divided upon it in the failure to achieve a resolution' (1988, p. 91). The transition process in the women's accounts, from relatively non-dilemmatic to dilemmatic thinking, is described below.

Before Surgery: The Absence of Dilemma

The relative absence of dilemmatic thinking, or self-argumentation, in the women's experience of choosing genital surgery can be understood in terms of three constituent themes which characterized their accounts of this process: 'conferring normality'; 'conferring sexual and relationship entitlement'; and 'doctor knows best'.

CONFERRING NORMALITY The women spoke of their feelings of being 'outsiders', even of potentially being seen as 'monsters' or 'freaks', who had become skilled at concealing the physical and emotional effects of their medical condition. Surgery was then seen as a means of conferring 'insider' status or normality:

> I felt as though I was on the outside if you like. Maybe they would talk about the things they did and often I'd give it the big, old, 'Oh yea, you know, me too.' (P6)
> I had also expected that the surgery would eliminate the [ ] I always hoped that the strong [ ] the desire for . . . a perfect female body which [ ] I'm *sure* a lot of women (laughs) *have,* I-I mean all our advertising is certainly geared towards it. And I expected that that would go away. (P3)
> I expected that I would have an ordinary heterosexual relationship. That was, that was my expectation. (P2)

But as well as feeling normal and having 'ordinary' heterosexual relationships, the women also hoped that surgery would remove the need for questions and explanations:

> . . . to find yourself in that intimate situation with [ ] a male partner [ ] and for them [ ] to [ ] make some comment about the fact that you didn't have . . . you know, a vagina. . . it would open up this whole can of worms and you'd have to kind of explain things . . . I just couldn't handle it. (P5)
> Well, if, if a guy went to [ ] to have full sex with me and he found out I was too short, there *would* be questions, I would have to explain *something.* I didn't even know [ ] myself [ ] what was wrong, you know. (P7)

These comments emphasize that it is not simply that the women feared having to explain their condition, but that they might not know what to say particularly as many had been given incomplete or misleading or no explanations when they were growing up.

CONFERRING SEXUAL AND RELATIONSHIP ENTITLEMENT This second constituent theme was closely related to the previous theme of conferring normality. The women talked not only of feeling like outsiders, but of feeling *unentitled* to 'normal' relationships:

> And if you've lived your whole life *knowing that* [ ] you know, that you—that the vagina's, like, one centimetre or whatever, um [ ] you know, you just, you just get this sort of fixation in your mind that you're not [ ] entitled, really, to have that sort of relationship. (P5)

This entitlement involved the assumption that a vagina is essential to heterosexual relationships: 'I would think it's really nice to be able to have a vagina before, or even, or *just, just to have a vagina* and then you would have a chance to have an intimate, committed relationship' (P7). The taken-for-granted connection between vaginas and relationships was also evident in doctors' reported consultations with the women: 'when the time comes you have surgery' and similar phrases implied that surgery would be necessary when the woman wanted to have an (assumed heterosexual) relationship. The idea of a vagina as a pre-condition of this was also strongly reinforced by the women's assumptions that men would 'scream'; 'freak out'; 'run off' or 'totally flip' when they discovered that the woman did not have a normal vagina.

Surgery thus had the strong appeal of a procedure which would confer normal femininity, rendering the women acceptable both to themselves and future male sexual partners; it was seen as a means of escape from a situation where concerns about the inevitability of 'discovery' led all of the women either to end relationships with men at a very early stage or not to form them at all. Notably, the woman who chose not to have surgery (but later used dilators) did so partly because at that time she could not imagine 'finding anyone'.

DOCTOR KNOWS BEST The third theme that contributed to the relatively non-dilemmatic nature of choosing surgery was 'doctor knows best'. A striking aspect of the women's accounts was the extent to which they recalled genital surgery being presented matter of factly, as generally unproblematic and desirable:

> Well, he did explain that it, you know, it might make [ ] things look a little bit different . . . I did actually ask, I said, are there not any other options that could be tried? And he said that, you know, he thought this was the best one. (P5)

> He said, these are the other alternatives, he said you *can* dilate, but you do it for months and months and—you start off tiny, it's a long drawn-out process, um, *the way* [ ] the way he described it at the time, left the impression to me that [ ] that wasn't the way to do it, that wasn't, that wasn't the way he'd recommend. (P7)

The combination of medical authority, the straightforward presentation of surgery and the consultation setting made it difficult to engage in detailed discussion of what surgery might or might not achieve:

> I think part of it could have been, well, this doctor knows what to do best, as my doctor [ ]. I was like, oh, you know best, you're the professional here, I'll, and I'll bow to your better judgement. (P6)
> Whenever I used to see the doctor, there would always be at least eight white coats sitting behind me, you know, scribbling down notes, and that's not really a time that you can then sit there and say, 'is it going to affect my orgasms?' because I could just imagine, you know, all the eyes glancing at one another and you, you just don't do it. (P5)

But the subjugation of potentially dilemmatic aspects of surgery in the medical encounter was strongly reinforced by the women's own hopes for surgery, as we discussed earlier:

> It's, it's, I'm sure they explained those things to me, it's just that I was [ ] *s-o* desperate at the time that explanations just went right on by. (P3)
> You *want* some instant resolution [ ] so you're kind of prepared to put up with [ ] the sort of [ ] side-effects, because you think, you think the overwhelming benefits are going to be [ ] overwhelming [laughs]. (P5)

For both women and doctors, then, surgery appears as the taken-for-granted means of correcting what is held to be *the* obstacle (i.e. non-typical genitalia) to an active (hetero) sexual life or, as one woman put it, 'something you've got to do' (P7).

The Experience of Surgery: An Emerging Dilemma

Two themes were identified in women's accounts of the process of surgery, and of its immediate after-effects: 'just another fanny' and 'the imperfect results'.

JUST ANOTHER FANNY This theme represents a pivotal point in tracing the emergence of dilemmatic thinking in the women's accounts because the experience of surgery marked a sharp divergence between the women's experience of surgery as a momentous event, and the routines of medical management:

> I was seeing a doctor that was going to do, you know, examine me in a way that perhaps I'd been examined half a dozen times before, and, to me, it was a big deal, whereas to him, it was just another [ ] fanny [laughs], you know . . . and I really did feel as though, you know, we were all lined up like a cattle market. You know, they just come and have a quick look and a prod and a poke, and then go off again. (P6)
> He didn't even examine me, he didn't, he just said, yea, I'll see you on the operating table . . . so, I just [ ] don't worry about it, I don't need to examine you now. (P7)
> You just went and got it done, and you got on with it, and that was it [ ] go away. (P2)

It was perhaps at this point that the women began to see themselves more as passive recipients of medical management than as people who had made an active choice:

> I just signed the consent form. I didn't have any information on, really, what he was going to do. How he was going to do it. I just sort of signed my name and that was it. [ ] I let him do what he wanted. (P2)
> So I was like, yea, OK, if that's what needs to be done, that's what needs to be done. Um [ ] and then obviously I signed the consent form . . . (P6)

THE IMPERFECT RESULTS OF SURGERY This theme bridges the immediate post-operative and the long-term outcomes of surgery and will be elaborated further in the next section. It was clear, however, that the short-term outcomes were often very different from those hoped for. One woman suffered severe post-operative infection; three experienced stenosis (closure) of the newly constructed vagina: '. . . after the first operation, because that closed up [ ] really quickly . . . it just closed up so [ ] quickly. So that was a complete waste of time, really' (P5).

Another woman (P6) described the discrepancy between her doctor's description of the procedure as 'a bit painful . . . it's only the discomfort while we're stretching you' and the 'excruciating pain' she experienced post-operatively. She described the procedures as 'acts of violation'; other women described them as 'disfiguring' and 'stigmatizing', particularly ironic comments given the power previously invested in surgery to de-stigmatize.

Post-Surgery: Surgery as Dilemma

Far from surgery being 'the end of it' as one woman had hoped, its dilemmatic aspects became increasingly salient. Two themes particularly reflect surgery's apparent failure to resolve that problems for which it was sought: surgery is net experienced as conferring 'normality' or satisfactory intimate relationships.

The women realized that post-operative procedures would be a continual reminder of difference:

> Having to have [ ] *having to go* to a doctor *every* year for a physical, rather than [ ] the assumption that, OK, when the surgery's over that's all you get for a lifetime, you know? [ ] And I didn't know that I'd . . . have to dilate. (P3)

'Having to dilate'—often necessary to keep the constructed vagina open—was a process which some women found unpleasant (one described it as 'a nightmare'), as well as a reminder of difference. It was not clear whether the women had been told beforehand that regular dilation might be necessary; some claimed not to have known, others that they might not have 'heard' the information, so great was their desire for surgery. In either case, dilation was problematic:

> I haven't been dilating, it's just painful . . . The first year I was very good at it [ ] but then, *after that* [ ] um, I think maybe, I got more sick about doing it . . . *I just worry that I'll* progressively go worse and worse and eventually have to have an [other] operation. (P7)

Nor did surgery make it easy to form intimate relationships; on the contrary, it made visible what had previously been masked;

> I felt . . . like [ ] I hadn't learned all the social sort of skills that were needed to [ ] you know to-to establish a relationship and that maybe that was the main problem, and having a vagina wouldn't really help . . . there's more going on than just vaginal length. (P5)
> *But then* I still, even though that [ ] part of the problem had been taken away, that, you know, penetrative sex could be possible, I still had all the other hang-ups, the shit that I was still carrying around. (P6)

All of the women shrill had difficulty in starting or continuing any (potentially) sexual relationship. These difficulties centered round two major pre-occupations; does it work? and, will I pass?

The women's concern over whether their altered genitals 'worked' meant that sexual encounters were seen as a test rather than an opportunity for pleasure:

> *Initially,* you know, it probably took four years, three to four years, post-operatively, before I was really able to put it to the test. (P6)
> It's like, everything is all a *test* you know, it's [ ] like with this second guy, I regarded the whole thing as, like, a test, you know, I was testing it all out sort of thing, to see if part A fitted into part B and stuff like that. (P5)
> [Intercourse] was this [ ] big [ ] kind of thing that I had to cross [ ] that I was working to understand [ ] but it didn't feel earth-shattering to be able to do that to myself [use dilators]. I still thought that the big [ ] test will be intercourse. (P4)

And, because of the need to dilate to avoid closure of the vagina, for some women, this 'test' could become a regular part of their sexual relations:

As regards functioning [ ] um [ ] I-I've only tried it out on someone four or five times, but even then, when I did try it [ ] I think I was just too conscious about [ ] um, is it long enough, and have I dilated enough in the last two days to make it, make it the right size? (P7)

But as well as needing to 'test out' the size of their vaginas against the size of their partner's penis, the women faced the continuing threat of being 'found out', in spite of the fact that one of the reasons for having surgery had been to escape this threat:

The whole scenario [sexual intimacy] is *so* filled, filled with anxiety [ ] that, you know, I just can't relax [ ] because the whole, the whole thing has become associated with [pause] you know, being wrong or being found to be wrong, uh, you know, and not being adequately equipped . . . (P5)
    I think a lot of the time I've been [ ] afraid to open up too much, or let them, let them see, or even feel, too much of my body in case they ask me about my scarring. (P7)

Even the woman who had had clitoral reduction and no vaginal surgery was not able to anticipate satisfactory sexual relationships because she had, so to speak, been found out by herself: *'Like I said,* people say they would—people wouldn't know, but I mean, I know [ ] and to me that's, that's enough. [ ] That is a stumbling block' (P2).

What these women know, of course, is not simply that they have had genital surgery, but the reason for it—that they have an intersex condition whose implications in terms of self-perception and anticipated perception by others cannot, it seems, be negated by attempting to correct the most visible outward sign. However, the dilemma faced by the women after genital alteration was not simply that it had fulfilled few of the hopes invested in it, but that there seemed to be no alternative way of solving the problems for which it had been sought. Some of the women wondered if the outcomes would have been different if they had used only dilators rather than having surgery, with their dilemma being particularly strikingly conveyed by P5, who had had two vaginoplasties, choosing the second procedure because of its assumed technical superiority, but then asking herself whether it would not have been better just to have used dilators, while also saying that 'there's more going on than just vaginal length. It's like I haven't learned, sort of, how to relate to people properly or, uh, how to sustain a relationship.' But since the women had attributed most of their relationship difficulties to their non-typical genitalia, then the only possible solution appeared to be to standardize them, a solution which did not seem to work. For some of the women, meeting 'the right man' was seen as a way out of this seemingly insoluble problem; this idea was also present in May et al.'s (1996) study of women with CAH. But the fear of being 'found out' made it difficult to see how this meeting could take place.

We have used Billig et al.'s (1988) approach to everyday thinking as dilemmatic, as an 'analytic thread' (Taylor & Bogdan, 1984) linking the themes which characterized the women's accounts of choosing and living with genital alteration. We have suggested that for these women, the process involved a transition from relatively non-dilemmatic to explicitly dilemmatic thinking. It seemed to be at the point of surgery itself that dilemmas began to be explicitly formulated, while further, post-operative dilemmas were organized around the knowledge that a complete resolution of the previously defined difficulties did not occur. Post-operatively, some of the problems of bearing the condition became apparent, no longer obscured by the authoritative appeal of a mechanical solution.

A Discursive Approach

We argued earlier that phenomenological approaches were less able to account for why people's experiences took the form they did or why particular meanings were assigned to them. We also argued, with Stam (2000) and Yardley (1997a), for the relevance of a discursive approach that acknowledges both the material and the socially constructed nature of the body and experiences associated with it. In the next sections, we therefore present a brief analysis of the women's accounts from this perspective. The analysis focuses on key questions posed by Foucault (1972): what makes particular desires, or ways of talking about things, seem reasonable? How do they come to be taken for granted? The questions emphasize the point that any particular way of talking or desiring depends for its intelligibility on often unarticulated assumptions which reflect dominant (cultural) forms of making sense of the world in any given period (Sawicki, 1991). This relates to Billig's (1991) suggestion that our private thoughts have the structure of public arguments. Thus, if our personal thinking about an issue is relatively non-argumentative, we might expect an equal lack of public argument on the issue, or taken-for-granted assumptions about 'the way things are'. We will analyze here three aspects of the women's experience in order to highlight these points: (1) choosing potentially harmful genital surgery or dilation when it was unnecessary for either reproduction (none of the women could become pregnant) or sexual pleasure; (2) the relative lack of dilemmatic thinking in choosing surgery or dilation; and (3) the complete absence of talk of enhanced sexual pleasure or enjoyment as an explicit goal or outcome. The first two of these will be discussed together.

Choosing Surgery and Choice as Non-Dilemmatic

The women's choice of surgery (or dilation) and its relatively non-dilemmatic nature, can be at least partly understood with reference to two powerful, and powerfully related, discursive constructions: two fixed sexes and the linguistic and conceptual conflation of sex with intercourse.

TWO FIXED SEXES The idea that there exist two sexes, one to each body, is so taken for granted by us, so much not a subject of day-to-day argumentation, that it is extremely difficult to see the idea as constructed and contestable, rather than natural and immutable. Dreger (1998) and Foucault (1979) have focused on the late 19th and early 20th centuries—a time when the social order was especially threatened by war and by women's demands for the vote and a greater role in public life—as the beginning of the modern preoccupation with demarcating two sexes, biologically, socially and psychologically; at this time, the 'perverse' adult—the homosexual and the hermaphrodite—was a particular object of scrutiny given their obvious capacity to threaten a dichotomous division of the sexes. Dreger (1998) and Kessler and McKenna (1978) have argued that the historical importance attributed to outward and easily checked appearance, and the later development of surgical techniques for altering genitals, contributed to a shift during the 20th century from gonads to genitals as *the* signifier of gender and to the modern centrality of genital surgery in the demarcation of two sexes. Thus when the women in this study talk about being a freak or state bluntly 'you are a freak', they are expressing the fact that culturally they are not supposed to exist. The emphasis they place on the psychologically transformative power of genital surgery to make them feel 'more feminine' and a 'normal female' is therefore not surprising.

THE CONFLATION OF SEX WITH INTERCOURSE The women, however, did not choose surgery or dilation only to *feel* more womanly but also to enable them to *act* like women, to 'have sexual relationships' with men. That this should seem to require surgical or manual alteration of the genitals in women already very capable of sexual arousal and orgasm is made at least partly comprehensible by the strong discursive conflation of (hetero) sex and intercourse (Holland, Ramazanoğlu, Scott, Sharp, & Thompson, 1990; Sanders & Reinisch, 1999), a conflation evident in the women's accounts and reinforced by medical encounters in which it seemed to be taken for granted that the women would have surgery in order to 'have sexual relationships'.

The desire for surgery or dilation as *the* means to 'have sex' was, however, also dependent on the meanings of intercourse, with penetration allowing you to 'be a woman' or being 'a yardstick of a womanly status'. Such meanings are cultural rather than purely personal. A further part of the linguistic, psychological and social importance placed on penis–vagina intercourse, however, depends on its power to signify heterosexuality; as some of the women in this study were well aware, surgical or manual alteration of the genitals in preparation for 'sex' implied a rejection of homosexuality.

The Absence of Pleasure Talk

We noted earlier that the women did not talk of enhanced sexual enjoyment as a goal or outcome of genital surgery or dilation. On the contrary, there was explicit acknowledgement of *not* enjoying intercourse after surgery: 'To be honest, it was just like a dead weight [ ] inside, which sounds strange, but it was [ ] I, I don't know, I didn't know how [ ] I could get enjoyment from it' (P7). This lack of talk about enhanced sexual pleasure as a goal is also evident in surgical outcome studies (e.g. Azziz, Jones, & Rock, 1990; Azziz, Mulaikal, Migeon, Jones, & Rock, 1986) whose criteria for 'success' or 'normal sexual function' or 'fully satisfactory intercourse' do not include sexual enjoyment, but simply the woman's ability to accommodate a penis without pain or discomfort. Similarly, intercourse (like dilators) was presented to some of the women in this study as part of post-operative maintenance, as a way of keeping the vagina open, as one woman put it, 'for the biggest size [of penis]' (P7).

The de-emphasis of women's sexual pleasure might be explained by the potentially more important psychological meanings of possessing a vagina and having intercourse, which were discussed earlier. But the striking lack of pleasure talk in both the literature and from the women themselves, also needs to be understood in a cultural context which has generally privileged male sexual pleasure over female (Hollway, 1989; Maxwell & Boyle, 1995; Ramazanoğlu & Holland, 1993). And in Azziz et al.'s study, surgery was considered a 'partial success' even if the woman experienced discomfort during intercourse, provided this 'did not fully impair penetration' (1990, p. 24). Not surprisingly, then, the women in this study often conveyed the impression that although they expected to gain psychologically from surgery or dilation, these procedures were also undertaken for imaginary future male partners who, it was assumed, would not accept a relationship which could not include vaginal intercourse.

Discussion

Methodological Issues

All of the participants were recruited from a support group for women with intersex conditions; this may have produced a sample with more similar (and possibly negative) experiences than would have been the case had more varied recruitment methods been used. The sample was also small and none of the women had CAH. There are, however, several reasons for assuming that these factors may not significantly compromise the study's validity. First, we made no attempt to suggest an interest in negative experiences of surgery. Second, the women all spoke unprompted of differences of views and experiences within the group. Third, aspects of the women's experiences are corroborated by the most recent data on sexual function collected by medical practitioners (Minto, Liao, Conway, & Creighton, in press; Minto et al., in press). Lastly, the women's experiences not only made sense in terms of well-researched constructions of sexuality and gender, but their accounts of sexual and relationship problems following surgery were very similar to those reported by May et al. (1996) for women with CAH, all of whom had been recruited from medical records for a broader study of quality of life.

It is nevertheless important to extend research to larger samples. Barthold and Aaronson (2002), noting the sparse outcome data on genital surgery, have also called for research using 'objective criteria' to evaluate outcome. But it is important to be very cautious about 'objectivity', given the implicit assumptions that may inform criteria used for 'success'. We would also argue for the routine inclusion of methods that allow women to give their own accounts of outcomes.

The participants had also had surgery some years ago (from the mid-1970s to the mid-1990s) and while this allows the evaluation of longer-term outcomes, it might be argued that procedures have improved since then. Wilson and Reiner (1998) caution strongly against this argument, given the lack of systematic evaluation of newer techniques and the lack of evidence that their results are superior (see also Creighton, 2001; Kessler, 2002). We were also unable to detect any clear differences in the accounts in terms of when the women had had surgery.

Clinical Implications

The study has highlighted some of the 'dominant ways of making sense of the world' (Sawicki, 1991, p. 104), which appear to shape both the desire for genital surgery and its medical provision. These include the dichotomous construction of sex; the conflation of genitals and gender; and the conflation of heterosexual relationships with intercourse. When the psychological and behavioural ideals implied by these constructions cannot be achieved by material alterations to the genitals, then a serious dilemma ensues, whose only solution appears to be more of the same (further surgery or dilation) or a fantasy partner. Yet neither of these solutions arguably provides a basis for constructive psychological input either to women with intersex conditions or to the medical professionals involved in their care.

We would like to suggest several changes to practice, focusing first on the issue of informed consent. Clinical teams would need to (re-)consider what information to give women and how best to explore their understanding of its implications, as well as avoiding the usual presupposition that a vagina or clitoris of certain dimensions are pre-conditions of 'sex'. The possibility that surgery might damage the very thing that it tries to fix—appearance and 'normal' sexual function—must be entertained, as should the fact that surgery may not remove the possibility of having to give explanations to partners or bring about an ideal relationship.

Second, in direct work with women, a major aim would be to encourage more 'self-argumentation' at an early point rather than seeing surgery as the inevitable and only 'solution'. It is possible to increase personal control of social interaction in general, including disclosure situations, and to explore alternative avenues of satisfaction—sexual and non-sexual (Liao, in press). For women who do choose surgery or dilation, the priorities may be the management of their limitations and the development of sexual relationships which focus on mutual pleasure rather than the 'testing' of surgically or mechanically altered genitals.

It is, finally, worth noting that the social, familial and medical secrecy which has surrounded intersex, together with the pursuit of surgical and mechanical solutions, has resulted in doctors, patients and their families having little vocabulary with which to discuss the condition and the experience of living with it beyond that of its most visible sign—the non-typical genitalia. It is no surprise, then, that the 'solution' of genital alteration should be so readily offered and accepted. Recent calls for more open discussion of alternatives to infant and child surgery, as well as a greater emphasis on psychological aspects of intersex, may help provide a future context in which it is possible to talk—and think—about intersex and its management with richer vocabularies and conceptual frameworks than has traditionally been the case.

ENDNOTES

1. Participants are numbered 2–7. No quotations are provided from P1. who volunteered for the research because she wished to talk about her experiences of intersex but surgery was not an issue for her or her doctors.
2. Key to transcript notation: [ ] = noticeable pause in speech; . . . = text omitted; [abc] = text inserted by authors for clarification; *abc* = said with emphasis.

REFERENCES

Azziz, R., Jones, H. W., & Rock, J. A. (1990). Androgen-insensitivity syndrome: Long-term results of surgical vaginal creation. *Journal of Gynecological Surgery, 6,* 23–26.

Azziz, R., Mulaikal, R. M., Migeon, C. J., Jones, H. W., & Rock, J. A. (1986). Congenital adrenal hyperplasia: Long-term results following vaginal reconstruction. *Fertility and Sterility, 46,* 1011–1014.

Barthold, J. S., & Aaronson, I. A. (2002). Editorial. *Dialogues in Pediatric Urology, 25,* 1–2.

Billig, M. (1991). *Ideology and opinions.* London: Sage Publications.

Billig, M., Condor, S., Edwards, D., Gane, M., Middleton, D., & Radley, A. (1988). *Ideological dilemmas: A social psychology of everyday thinking.* London: Sage Publications.

Creighton, S. (2001). Surgery for intersex. *Journal of the Royal Society of Medicine, 94,* 218–220.

Dreger, A. (1998). *Hermaphrodites and the medical invention of sex.* Boston, MA: Harvard University Press.

Fausto-Sterling, A. (2002). Gender identification and assignment in intersex children. *Dialogues in Pediatric Urology, 25,* 4–5.

Foucault, M. (1972). *The archaeology of knowledge.* London: Tavistock.

Foucault, M. (1979). *The history of sexuality, vol. 1: An introduction.* London: Allen Lane.

Hegarty, P. (2000). Intersex activism, feminism and psychology: Opening a dialogue on theory, research and clinical practice. *Feminism and Psychology, 10,* 117–132.

Holland, J., Ramazanoğlu, C., Scott, S., Sharp, S., & Thompson, T. (1990). *Don't die of ignorance . . . I nearly died of embarrassment.* WRAP Paper 2. London: Tufnell Press.

Hollway, W. (1989). *Subjectivity and method in psychology: Gender, meaning and science.* London: Sage Publications.

Kessler, S. J. (2000). *Lessons from the intersexed.* New York: Rutgers University Press.

Kessler, S. J. (2002). Questioning assumptions about gender assignment in cases of intersexuality. *Dialogues in Pediatric Urology, 25,* 3–4.

Kessler, S., & McKenna, W. (1978). *Gender: An ethnomethodological approach.* Chicago, IL: University of Chicago Press.

Kipnis, K., & Diamond, M. (1998). Pediatric ethics and the surgical assignment of sex. *Journal of Clinical Ethics, 9,* 398–410.

Liao, L. M. (in press). Learning to assist women born with atypical genitalia: Journey through ignorance, taboo and dilemmas. *Journal of Reproductive and Infant Psychology.*

Maxwell, C., &. Boyle, M. (1995). Risky heterosexual practices amongst women over 30: Gender, power and long-term relationships. *AIDS Care, 7,* 277–293.

May, B., Boyle, M., & Grant, D. (1996). A comparative study of sexual experiences: Women with diabetes and women with congenital adrenal hyperplasia due to 21-hydroxilase deficiency. *Journal of Health Psychology, 1,* 479–492.

Meyer-Bahlburg, H. F. L., Gruen, R. S., & New, M. I. (1996). Gender change from female to male in classical congenital adrenal hyperplasia. *Hormones and Behavior, 30,* 319–332.

Minto, C. L., Liao, L. M., Conway, G. S., & Creighton, S. M. (in press). Sexual function and complete androgen insensitivity syndrome. *Fertility and Sterility.*

Minto, C. L., Liao, L. M., Woodhouse, C. R., Ransley, P., & Creighton, S. M. (in press). Adult outcomes of childhood clitoral surgery for ambiguous genitalia. *Lancet.*

Parker, I. (1992). *Discourse dynamics: Critical analysis for social and individual psychology.* London: Routledge.

Ramazanoğlu, C., & Holland, J. (1993). Women's sexuality and men's appropriation of desire. In C. Ramazanoğlu (Ed.), *Up against Foucault: Explorations of some tensions between Foucault and feminism* (pp. 239–264). London: Routledge.

Reiner, W. G. (1996). Case study: Sex reassignment in a teenage girl. *Journal of the American Academy of Child and Adolescent Psychiatry, 35,* 799–803.

Sanders, S. A., & Reinisch, J. M. (1999). Would you say you 'had sex' if . . . ? *Journal of the American Medical Association, 281,* 275–277.

Sawicki, J. (1991). *Disciplining Foucault: Feminism, power and the body.* New York: Routledge.

Smith, J. (1996). Beyond the divide between cognition and discourse: Using interpretative phenomenological analysis in health psychology. *Psychology and Health, 11,* 261–271.

Smith, J. A., Jarman, M., & Osborn, M. (1999). Doing interpretative phenomenological analysis. In M. Murray & K. Chamberlain (Eds.), *Qualitative health psychology: Theories and methods* (pp. 218–40). London: Sage Publications.

Stam, H. (2000). Theorizing health and illness: Functionalism, subjectivity and reflexivity. *Journal of Health Psychology, 5,* 273–283.

Taylor, S., & Bogdan, R. (1984). *Introduction to qualitative research methods,* 2nd edn. New York: Wiley.

Ussher, J. (Ed.). (1997). *Body talk: The material and discursive regulation of sexuality, madness and reproduction.* London: Routledge.

Warne, G. (1998). Advances and challenges with intersex disorders. *Reproduction, Fertility and Development, 10,* 79–85.

Willig, C. (2001). *Introducing qualitative research in psychology: Adventures in theory and method.* Buckingham: Open University Press.

Wilson, B. E., & Reiner, W. G. (1998) Management of intersex: A shifting paradigm. *Journal of Clinical Ethics, 9,* 360–369.

Yardley, L. (1997a). Introducing material-discursive approaches to health and illness. In L. Yardley (Ed.), *Material discourses of health and illness* (pp. 1–24). London: Routledge.

Yardley, L. (Ed.). (1997b). *Material discourses of health and illness.* London: Routledge.

Voicing Your Opinion
Adult Genital Surgery for Intersex: A Solution to What Problem?
Mary E. Boyle, Susan Smith, and Lih-Mei Liao

1. Boyle, Smith, and Liao's research identifies three reasons why the subjects of the study made the choice to have genital surgery. The first two reasons relate to the idea of wanting to be able to engage in "normal" heterosexual relationships. How does your understanding of the concept of heteronormativity affect your understanding of these reasons?

2. The women in this study chose to change their physical bodies to accommodate an identity that was emotional, intellectual, and psychological. Are there other instances where people alter or change their bodies in order to accommodate a desire to be something/someone different?

3. The authors mention the presence of secrecy in relationship to intersex identity, as well as the secrecy that revolves around the decision to have genital surgery. What might happen if there was no need for secrecy in regards to this topic? How would the discourses that surround the topic of intersexuality change if this was not a taboo or secret topic? How does the presence of secrecy affect the ways that society perceives intersexed individuals?

Terms

Professional
masculinity

Civilized/
primitive
masculinity

Masculinity as
discourse and
performance

Negotiation of
masculinity in
private/public
spheres

Hegemonic
masculinity

Neurasthenia

SLAVES WITH WHITE COLLARS Persistent Performances of Masculinity in Crisis

KAREN LEE ASHCRAFT AND LISA A. FLORES

This article is about masculinity in white-collar professions. It looks at how masculinity is defined as civilized/ primitive and at how masculinity is performed. The article deals with the issue of private versus public spheres, hegemonic masculinity, and an historically popular disease called neurasthenia. The article charts these issues through exploration of two films, *In the Company of Men* and *Fight Club*.

Recent trends in popular culture suggest an emerging discourse of professional masculinity in crisis. This essay examines two illustrative films. Fight Club *and* In the Company of Men, *whose characters bemoan the impending demise of the masculine businessman. To revive him, they (re)turn to what we call a "civilized/primitive" masculinity, embodied by the hardened white man who finds healing in wounds. This subjectivity shrouds the race and class hierarchy on which it rests by overtly appealing to gender division. The current discourse of dominant men in crisis bears remarkable resemblance to historical narratives of masculinity in decline. Ultimately, we argue that this pattern reveals chronic conflicts embedded in particular performance of masculinity and thus, potential vulnerabilities in patriarchal capitalism.*

The whole generation is womanized; the masculine tone is passing out of the world; it's a feminine, a nervous, hysterical, chattering, canting age, an age of hollow phrases and false delicacy and exaggerated solicitudes and coddled sensibilities, which, if we don't soon look out, will usher in the reign of mediocrity, of the feeblest and flattest and the most pretentious that has ever been.

Basil Ransom, *The Bostonians,* 1886 (qtd. in Rotundo 252)

I swear it's not a world of men [. . .] It is a world of clockwatchers, bureaucrats, office holders. It's a fucked-up world. No adventure in it [. . .] We're the members of a dying breed.

Ricky, *Glengarry, Glen Ross,* 1992

From sitcoms to social movements, commercial campaigns to scholarship, we are witnessing the growth of interest in men as men. Increasingly, US representations of manhood converge on the claim that masculinity is in the midst of crisis. The rise of men's movements like the Promise Keepers and mythopoetic men, not to mention popular television programs like *The Man Show,* suggest the broad resonance of this crisis narrative and the perceived need for curative forms of manliness. Though scholars have begun to examine the alleged crisis (e.g., Horrocks: Robinson), few have attended to the particular role of work, and those who have tend to stress working-class frailties (e.g., Faludi; Fine, Weis, Addelston, and Marusza).

In this essay, we spotlight the performance of a subjectivity that has drawn little direct discussion. Specifically, we trace an emerging discourse that offers identity politics to white/collar[1] men. To focus our analysis of this freshly politicized subjectivity, we explore two illustrative yet distinct film performances: *Fight Club* and *In the Company of Men*. The discourse that weaves across these texts mourns the imminent collapse of the corporate man, over-civilized and emasculated by allied obligations to work and women. To rebuild this haggard creature, the films (re)turn to what we call a "civilized/primitive" masculinity, embodied by the hardened white man who finds healing in wounds. This resilient figure obscures the race and class hierarchy on which it rests by explicitly appealing to gender division, if not outright misogyny. The current discourse of dominant men in crisis bears conspicuous resemblance to other historical discourses, such as a similar narrative of threatened masculinity in play one century ago. Ultimately, we argue that this pattern reveals chronic conflicts embedded in the ongoing performance of white/collar masculinity and so, potential vulnerabilities in patriarchal capitalism.

Organizing Masculinity

Research on masculinity has become a truly interdisciplinary venture, including feminist analyses that span rhetorical, historical, psychoanalytic, and sociological perspectives. Below, we clarify our interest in the meeting of dominant masculinities and labor identities. We begin by establishing our conception of masculinity and, more specifically, the role of discourse and performance in the social construction of gender. We then narrow our focus to professional masculinity, drawing upon relevant historical and contemporary discourses of gender, labor, and identity to theorize enduring dilemmas that appear to haunt white/collar performances. Our theoretical frame integrates insights gleaned from three principal literatures: masculinity and film studies, feminist and critical organization research, and historical accounts of masculinity rhetoric.

Studying and Defining Men and Masculinity

Scholarly interest in masculinity continues its dramatic rise. A recent proliferation of monographs, anthologies, and journals confirms the development of a diverse body of work that interrogates gender identities and explores how masculine forms relate to patriarchal systems.[2] This research has generated pivotal insights that inform our work. For example, masculinity may be conceptually detached from actual male bodies (Cheng "Men") and broadly defined as "the set of images, values, interests, and activities held important to a successful achievement of male adulthood" (Jeffords *Remasculinization* xii). Masculinity is not a stable or unified phenomenon; its meanings shift over time and in relation to culture, context, and person (Spitzack "Production"). Multiple narratives of manhood abound at once, and the subjectivities and practices they enable engender differential, consequential performances of power and resistance (Corey; Mechling and Mechling; Nakayama "Significance"). More specifically, theories of intersectionality push us to recognize that gender identity is inevitably raced and classed (C. Crenshaw; K. Crenshaw; Dace; Orbe). Thus, talk of "men" and "the masculine"—however generalized—always refers to a type of masculinity (Dines; Eng; Wiegman).

Most masculinity studies coalesce around a concern shared with feminist scholarship: the need to mark masculinity and men as gendered subjects. In particular, scholars challenge the invisibility of dominant masculinities, since all forms of manhood do not enjoy similar privilege. Hence, the term "hegemonic masculinity" has come to capture the socially constructed, institutionalized yet shifting form of masculinist identity that systematically dominates femininities and alternative masculinities (Connell "Big Picture" and *Gender;* Donaldson). Ironically, studies of hegemonic masculinity run the risk of re-centering the subject they seek to dismantle: white, heterosexual, middle-class men (Robinson).[3] Not oblivious to such danger, many masculinity scholars assume the risk to shatter illusions of homogenous, indelibly privileged male selves (e.g., Eng; Mumby; Spitzack "Theorizing"). In a similar vein, we stress how popular performances of masculinity offer identity politics to middle-class, heterosexual, white men. Accordingly, we do not directly study men *per se* but rather discourses of dominant masculinity.

Masculinity as Discourse and Performance: Filmic Fragments

By "discourse," we refer to temporarily fixed (i.e., predictable but not determined), coherent (though also conflicted), abstract, and dispersed social narratives about people, objects, and events. Multiple discourses (e.g., of masculinity and race) circulate and intersect at once, although some enjoy greater institutional support, and so, "look" and "feel" more persuasive than others (Hall "Signification" and "The Work"). Discourses generate possible conditions in that they enable ways of seeing, being, and doing (Laclau and Mouffe). In dramaturgical terms, they supply social actors with roles and scripts, with rough guides to public and mundane performances of identity and social relations. Discourses—of gender, for example—come to life and assume concrete form as we perform and thus, affirm or revise the possibilities they offer. In this sense, accomplishing gender necessarily entails performance, whether improvised in the mundane moments of everyday life or memorialized on screen for countless witnesses (Butler; West and Zimmerman).

Appearing in various mediated forms, discourses are dynamic and partial. While we may select various texts (e.g., popular films or literature, interview data) for analysis, we do not presume that any one contains nor completely represents a discourse; rather, apparently discrete texts can be understood as fragments of larger narratives (McGee). Attention to complementary *and* contradictory strands enables a contextual analysis, for texts do not exist in cultural vacuums but become promiscuous players in larger social structures. Although various public texts comprise cultural discourses, we stress popular culture, and specifically, film. Our discursive approach to film highlights vocabularies and ideologies of masculinity, necessarily excluding empirical claims about male behaviors or psyches. This is not to say that we see no connection between filmic and other performances of gender, such as those found in mundane interaction. Rather, we take interest in film performance as it shapes the social imagination, extending invitations to "new" performances of subjectivity in everyday life. In short, we treat film as a meta-performance wherein actors recognized as such articulate gendered possibilities for social actors. We are especially concerned with how film performances both highlight and obscure intersections of masculinity with other facets of identity. This focus reflects our aim to understand how "representational intersectionality" operates in popular performances (K. Crenshaw). In other words, we explore how "symbolic images applied to different race, class, and gender groups interact in maintaining systems of domination and subordination" (Collins 33). When not qualified in political terms, masculinity discourse tends to summon a homogenous, static image that is white, middle-class, and heterosexual (Mandziuk).

Guiding our venture is a considerable body of work on gender and film.[4] In particular, some feminist film scholars criticize a tendency to take masculinity as given, thereby perpetuating the notion that it is a fixed entity occupying the space of privilege (e.g., Cohan and Hark; Wiegman). In an effort to rupture its silence and normativity, these authors investigate performances of masculinity in film, targeting race, class, and sexuality as central poles around which masculinities converge and diverge (e.g., Beavers; Dyer *White;* Jeffords *Hard;* Tusker "Fists"). Not surprisingly, this work extends the larger interest in hegemonic masculinity, demonstrating the flexibility with which it co-opts discourses of race, class, and sexuality without deposing its white, heterosexual, and middle-class footing.[5]

To complicate masculinity, some film scholars have turned to the male body, observing contrasting bodily depictions and their relationship to dominant and subordinated identities.[6] This work has uncovered the centrality of hard bodies to hegemonic masculinity (e.g., Jeffords *Hard;* Tasker *Spectacular;* and S. Willis). Additionally, it indicates visual pleasures available through voyeuristic attention to the male body and heterosexual anxieties aroused by male-on-male gazing.[7]

Masculinities That Work

The masculinity and film literature yields crucial insights, but a key question remains understudied: How do forms of labor facilitate distinctive masculine performances? Certainly, film scholars acknowledge the importance of work to masculinity. Yet they tend to stress a limited range of working (class) subjects, as evident in their extensive attention to action films featuring soldiers and police officers. While Jeffords provides a convincing chronicle of the reign of hard-body masculinity in the 1980s, she does not address connections with professional identity *(Hard).* Similarly, Robinson's provocative account of white male crisis rhetoric concentrates elsewhere, though the book's cover figures a white businessman, briefcase and cell phone in tow. Such cursory attention to labor, much less the professions, is striking, particularly given professed scholarly interest in the meeting of masculinities and class. Moreover, work has anchored US white, middle-class manhood since the early 19th century (Rotundo; Trujillo).

Organizational scholars are poised to provide the most nuanced treatment of masculinity and work. Though they have begun to do so, the majority of gendered organization research addresses the professional dilemmas of white, middle-class women.[8] This work guides us to the import of two historical formations: the discourse of separate spheres (i.e., public and private) and the discourse of gender difference (i.e., masculine and feminine as complementary opposites).[9] Still today, these notions intersect in a manner so familiar as to barely necessitate review. The public realm is commonly seen as the legitimate site of production and politics, the more "natural" turf of men/masculinity. Divorced from "real" labor, the private sphere is linked to intimacy, sexuality, reproduction, emotion, and domestic concerns, deemed the expertise of women/femininity (Martin; Mills and Chiaramonte). Feminist scholars compellingly contend that the discourses of public-private and gender difference come together to naturalize workplace control and exclusion of femininities (Acker).

While these accounts enhance our understanding of some women's subordination, they also neglect a different consequence of the same discursive union. Namely, some men are expected to travel competently across spheres, although the masculine is aligned with only one. As the spheres are thought to entail opposing demands and habits, white masculine subjectivity bears a sort of schizophrenia or double bind. Consequently, many men may struggle to negotiate selves that work in public and private. Recent scholarship indicates another layer of the paradox: expectations for civilized *and* primitive male selves in public *and* private arenas (Bordo; Robinson; Rotundo). At least in the US, the civilized-primitive dualism evokes slippery evolutionary images of man-savage-animal, tinged with racial hierarchy (Bederman). Though diluted, such racist meanings hang on the tips of our tongues, and the dualism still serves as a powerful way to (racially) mark approaches to violence and sexuality (e.g., primitive release, civilized restraint) (Orbe; Sloop). Moreover, the dualism remains one of the primary ways we distinguish types of work (e.g., manual or mental labor), suggesting that constructions of class are also deeply raced.

Forms of public labor have long been coded in terms of how they blend masculinity with the primitive-civilized. For example, organizational scholars have begun to explore how blue-collar labor produces a primitive masculinity replete with images of raw physicality—hard, hands-on work performed by dirty, sweaty bodies (e.g., Collinson; Gibson and Papa; P. Willis). Accordingly, working-class subjects enjoy (suffer?) closer ties to primal, near-bestial savagery and sexuality (Gherardi). Such coding will likely shape the way in which masculinity dilemmas manifest themselves. For example, primitive blue-collar masculinity can dominate the "soft" private and even "soften" (i.e., feminize, make impotent) its white-collar superiors. Simultaneously, it is prone to charges of being uncivilized, which depict working-class men as dumb, juvenile, or overgrown brutes.

Since white-collar labor leans toward the civilized pole, we might expect scholars to find mirror-image vulnerabilities. To the contrary, the burgeoning literature on managerial masculinity implies that corporate life furnishes a persistent, resilient home for white male dominance, despite dramatic changes in capitalism and the organization of work.[10] Like film theorists, then, organization scholars tend to presume intact the uniform, enduring, and seamless reign of businessmen. In addition, they have scarcely begun to address race (Ashcraft and Allen; Nkomo). We seek to redress these oversights by problematizing the performance of white/collar masculinity.

Professional Masculinity: Voices of Crisis from the Turn of the Centuries

As we hinted above, white/collar masculinity is susceptible to feminization, given its reputed lack of physicality and bureaucratic sterility, suppression of the body, self-imposed discipline, and obligatory ingratiation. Perhaps tellingly, professional discourses summon the primitive and civilized at once. Consider this dizzying array of business imagery: the corporate jungle, the rational actor, unbridled competition and aggression, self-discipline and impulse-control, intellectual (i.e., "clean") labor, dog-cat-dog world. We argue that white/collar masculinity straddles both primitive and civilized poles; to overstress one is to risk failure at the other and, therefore, to render masculinity, professionalism, or whiteness suspect. In this sense, a chronic anxiety plagues professional identity, as it is no simple feat to perform hard and soft, primitive and civilized at once, especially given their varying depiction as unequal opposites. For help in this thorny endeavor, white/collar masculinity depends on affiliation with other gender, race, and class discourses. For instance, it can appeal to images of dark savagery or working-class men as powerfully primal *and* subordinate (i.e., professional minds dominate primitive bodies). At times, it can affiliate with white women, who become a taming force that nurtures the advancement of civilization. Upon inspection, each alliance sparks its own vulnerabilities. For example, if civilization is emphasized and associated with whiteness, white women can stake a claim to equality; if an essential male primitive is stressed, men of color and diverse class can do so. How can professional masculinity draw on these discourses without undermining itself? How can white/collar masculinity retain its race, class, and gender dominance all at once? How are these tensions discursively and performatively managed? Or perhaps first, how *were* they managed?

FROM CIVILIZED RESTRAINT TO PRIMITIVE PASSIONS: TURNING THE LAST CENTURY. This is not the first time that public representations of dominant masculinity in crisis have circulated in the US. For example, a similar surge of crisis discourse surfaced around the turn of the last century. That wave is worth reviewing not only due to arresting parallels, but because "our lives a century later are still bound by this reshaping of manhood" (Rotundo 222). Attention to historical context can expose the political economies that give rise to particular gendered discourses—or, put with different emphasis, the political and material circumstances that such discourses struggle to manage.

Rotundo identifies a change in hegemonic masculinity between the 18th and 19th centuries: from a communal manhood based on moral community obligations to a self-made manhood proven by individual work achievement. In the late 19th century, the notion of masculinity in crisis swept the country. The principal fear was that men, especially white professionals, were overcivilized to the point of impending extinction. Two key changes in capitalist labor arrangements lay at the core of the crisis narrative: (a) the increasingly bureaucratic nature of work minimized opportunities for entrepreneurial achievement, trading independence for subordination to other men; and (b) women began to infringe on the public sphere (Bederman; Rotundo). Among other ways, the crisis narrative materialized in a medical discourse of "neurasthenia," a nervous disorder thought to result from overcivilization and, specifically, too much mentally stimulating work. The US saw an outbreak of male neurasthenia diagnoses between 1880 and 1910, and those deemed at greatest risk "were middle- and upper-class businessmen and professionals whose highly evolved bodies had been physically weakened by advances in civilization" (Bederman 87). Widespread worry about the alleged disease flagged a puzzling paradox: "Only white male bodies had the capacity to be truly civilized. Yet, at the same time, civilization destroyed white male bodies. How could powerful, civilized manhood be saved?" (Bederman 88).

In response to the crisis narrative, public discourse of the time embraced "natural" male passions long disciplined out of white men. As Bordo summarizes, "fantasies of recovering an unspoiled, primitive masculinity began to emerge, and with them, a 'flood of animal metaphors' poured forth to animate a new conception of masculinity. White men drew on the images and ideology of the savage Other to help them articulate this emerging construction of 'passionate manhood'" (249). In the new subjectivity, "savages and animals fade together," as "middle-class men [. . .] were drawn to both groups for the same qualities" (Rotundo 229). What became of white civilized professionalism amid this turn to the primitive? Bederman argues that, rather than discursive division or death, it allied with the primitive, joining contradictory notions of manhood with " 'civilization's larger narrative of millennial advancement toward a higher race and perfect manhood" (218). But white/collar man's anxiety would persist, for his was a conflicted and contestable right to the primitive.

MODERN MAN'S NEURASTHENIA? CONTEMPORARY CRIES OF CRISIS. Recently, abundant public and scholarly discourse has converged on another so-called masculinity crisis (Faludi; Horrocks; Robinson). Those who trace it to work stress the fragility of working-class identities, weakened by economic and social conditions (e.g., Fine et al.). We tease out a strand of discourse that has garnered less attention. Specifically, we argue that public performances of white/collar masculinity in crisis are gaining momentum and bear startling resemblance to themes from the last turn of the century. Consider the rash of recent films that portray mounting tension between professional men and work: *Falling Down* (1989); *Glengarry, Glen Ross* (1992); *Disclosure* (1994); *Wolf* (1994); *In the Company of Men* (1997); *Office Space* (1999); *American Beauty* (1999); *Fight Club* (1999); *The Big Kahuna* (2000); and *Boiler Room* (2000)—to name a few. In contrast to the usual films featuring men at work, this trend suggests that corporations amount to an increasingly inadequate stage that stifles and emasculates the performance of white/collar masculinity. Evidence suggests some similarities to the early 20th century, even a familiar yearning for the primitive. Bordo details how "today, with many men feeling that women—particularly feminists—have been pushing them around for a couple of decades, the idea of a return to manhood 'in the raw' has a fresh, contemporary appeal" (251).

Across most current scholarship, then, the hegemony of white/collar masculinity appears relatively smooth, even when marked. Despite growing testament to the ambiguities of masculinity, we continue to neglect how even the most dominant forms require relentless maintenance. This gap becomes pressing in an age of patriarchal and managerial capitalism, for which the professional subject is a central character (Deetz and Mumby). The dearth of attention to white/collar dilemmas also contributes to the continued invisibility of multiple intersections in masculinity. Accordingly, we highlight how professional masculinity depends upon discourses of race, class, sexuality, and labor.

Healing Wounds: Violence and the Civilized/Primitive

To interrogate white/collar masculinity, we selected two films that shoulder its tensions and manage them in seemingly contradictory ways: *In the Company of Men,* a critically acclaimed independent film, and *Fight Club,* a Hollywood blockbuster based on the best-selling novel of the same name. Two questions organize our analysis: How do the films stage the masculinity crisis, and what performances bring comfort and resolution?

The Wounds of the White/Collar Man

As soon as we meet them, the men of both films inform us that something has gone wrong. Women and work are at varying degrees of fault, and the situation is dire. Below, we trace how the films convey the professional man's breaking point, and we identify common themes of crisis.

IN THE COMPANY OF MEN. This film follows the lives of two corporate men on a six-week assignment at a non-specific company in Anytown, USA. In the opening scenes, we meet the two central characters, clad in standard business attire and waiting in an airport courtesy lounge, Howard—a glaringly insecure, sulky man recently promoted to manage the project—marvels that he has just been slapped by a woman from whom he simply asked the time. Chad Piercewell, an attractive and swaggering figure, is Howard's old college friend and new underling. For Chad, the slap epitomizes the sorry state of businessmen's lives. In the airport, on the plane, and in a restaurant at their destination, the two men proceed to mourn the "doom" they face "as a race—men like us, guys who care a smidgen about the workplace, their women." They trade tales of abandonment and rejection by the women in their lives, interspersed with cautionary words about vile colleagues and maddening corporate politics. Howard observes that, "everything—work, these women—feel like they're getting out of balance, don't they?" Chad concurs, "Yeah, they really do, Howard [. . .] We ought to do something about it." Soon after, Chad professes the urgency of the situation: "Circle the date on this one, big guy. If we keep playing along with this pick-up-the-check, can't-a-girl-change-her mind crap—we can't even tell a joke in the workplace—there's gonna be hell to pay down the line, no doubt about it. We need to put our foot down pronto." Despite Howard's formal rank, Chad immediately surfaces as the alpha male. He almost single-handedly articulates the crisis and aggressively solicits Howard's help in addressing it. Howard meekly assents, interjecting the occasional "I hear ya."

It is thus in the first few minutes of the film that work and women are linked together as the cause of professional men's impending downfall. In brief, women expect men's sensitivity in romantic and work relationships, as well as their financial support. Yet women offer nothing but ingratitude and abuse in return. Men give and give, while women bite the hand that feeds them. What's more, corporations have become a sterilized den of thieves, thanks in part to women's invasion and a merciless corporate elite. Women control us; corporations consume us; and if this continues, the common businessman will soon be extinct. The situation demands immediate action. And—make no mistake—that action is a noble struggle to reclaim something lost, to restore a rightful order.

FIGHT CLUB. This film begins at its end. The two main characters, a nameless narrator and Tyler Durden, are engaged in a conversation laden with tense expectancy. Immediately, the intimacy between the two is apparent, as are the profound differences that divide them. The narrator sits small and tentative, curiously un/dressed in his boxer shorts. Tyler stands in a pose that exudes militaristic power; and in his sleeveless tight shirt and low-slung camouflage pants, he vibrates with a sexual intensity enhanced by his hardened body and muscled arms.

In flashback style, the narrator takes us back to a time when he was a numbed shell of a man. Corporate servitude engulfs him. He is locked in a sterile, white/collar world where mere imitations of life abound: "Everything's a copy of a copy of a copy." Bureaucratic objectification and meaningless existence emerge in techno-jargon, as he dully asks his boss: "You want me to deprioritize my current reports until you advise of a status upgrade?" Corporate control threatens complete takeover; even scientific dreams of space exploration can only produce "the IBM stellarsphere, the Microsoft Galaxy, Planet Starbucks." Service to the company enables a second crippling factor: an obsession with material perfection as defined by corporate gods. This all-encompassing materialism sucks men into illusions of identity. Wondering what "kind of dining set defines me as a person," the narrator seeks to create the perfect home, an absolute replica of a catalog image. Consumed by consumption, young businessmen are, in Tyler's words, "by-products of a lifestyle obsession" who occupy ornamental bodies and spaces (Bordo; Faludi).

Part of a "generation raised by women," Tyler and the narrator suffer from the absence of men in their lives. They are children of divorce—of fathers who abandoned them to "franchise" new lives and families. They are victims of fathers' false promises about careers, marriage, and social responsibility. Even God, the ultimate father, is absent and uncaring. A sense of utter disposability and despondency floods their experience. Nobody's heroes, they enjoy no great moment in history, for the noble wars of the past belong to other men. As Tyler later proclaims, "Our great war is a spiritual war [. . .] Our great depression is our lives." These young men are not simply denied access to the masculine; they are invaded by femininity on all sides. Early in the film, the narrator frames his tale around women: "I realized that all of this [. . .] had something to do with a girl named Marla Singer." Beyond the physical presence of women, the feminine threatens to overtake. We witness the narrator battle his insomniac stupor with feminized tools, including "Martha Stewart" materialism, sleeping pills, meditation, and therapeutic retreats to his "inner cave." Weak and impotent, he finds temporary relief in a new addiction, support groups. During his first attendance—to a testicular cancer group called "Remaining men together"—he meets Bob, a one-time body-building champion now literally castrated. Nestled between Bob's "bitch tits," the narrator finds release through sobbing, temporarily curing his insomnia. The threat of the feminine emerges further in the form of Marla, another "tourist" on the therapy circuit. Her presence at the support groups disrupts the narrator's relief, plunging him back into insomnia and desperation.

In short, *Fight Club* codes the corporate world and all its trappings—bureaucratic sedation, materialism, isolation, deception, and the crushing presence of things feminine—as a force that kills men. Tyler captures this subordination when he asks, "Now, why do guys like you and I know what a duvet is? Is this essential to our survival in the hunter-gatherer sense of the word?" As Tyler explains, young men have become "slaves with white collars," stuck in "jobs we hate, so we can buy shit we don't need." They must mobilize and fight to regain control, if not life.

PRODUCING THE WOUNDED CORPORATE FIGURE. Despite different takes on whether corporations are conducive to masculinity, the white/collar men of both films are united by their search for more dignified, satisfying identities, if not outright revenge. They share a keen sense that work and women are not as they once were. Jobs are more competitive; corporate environments are increasingly cruel and hygienic; and the possibility of a secure future looms ever distant and unsatisfying. Women bear the blame for many of these changes, and their intrusions and orders have become unbearable. Specifically, women have feminized and disabled men with conflicting demands for emotional, financial, and political support and sensitive, over-civilized behavior. To make matters worse, "woman" is the ultimate source of men's corporate bondage; it is largely because of her that men subject themselves to the whims and abuses of an elusive, all-powerful, corporate elite. It is no longer tolerable that her insidious presence grows with her confusing list of demands. In theoretical terms, she is unraveling an ambivalent web of dominance, duty, and resentment that has long sutured relations between white, middle-class masculinity and femininity (Lyman; Rotundo). Or, as film critic Hershenson puts it, "the old roles continue to crumble" and "you're pretty much on your own, buddy" (par. 3).

Given this discourse of wounded businessmen, it is not surprising that the central characters of each film define their quest as resistance to an oppression that, as one film critic noted, is "worth rising up against" (Smith par. 2). They do not experience the crisis in their lives as a disruption of male privilege that might facilitate more inclusive social relations. On the contrary, they perceive it as injustice and violence—a thing expected but denied, a promise wrongly snatched away (Hearn "Organization"; Linstead). In this way, men's collective corporate dominance becomes eclipsed by the individual man's personal experience of powerlessness (Hamada; Horrocks).

As to what must be done, the characters concur on a few points. First, any "new manhood" premised on men's exploration and development of the traditionally feminine is grossly insufficient. They fear their status as drained, cloned, impotent "yes men" who perform meaningless work at others' bidding. They mourn the passing of an age when work was a world of adventurous, virile men. As one critic of *Fight Club* remarked, "Nice is over and hard is where it's at" (Watson par. 2). Second, they believe their load is too heavy, and something must give. Chad takes a first step to freedom when he lets go of caring: "You know why I'm still chipper? Big grin on my face, Howie? . . . Because I realized something [. . .] I do not give a shit, not about anybody." Meanwhile, Tyler liberates the narrator from the promise of corporate success, the throes of materialism, and all debilitating fears, goading him to hit bottom: "It's only after we've lost everything that we're free to do anything." Both films imply that if one rejects the rules of the current game, he becomes free to write, play, and win his own game. However, this requires a radical switch from a passive to an active approach to life. Chad announces, "Life is for the taking, is it not?"

At the end of the day, a man who continues to obey the rules will be an impotent, feminized bureaucrat who has sold his soul to borrow the power of others. It is in imaginative, daring manipulation of the rules or bold, outright rebellion that a real man can be made. Next, we trace two disparate paths toward healing the wounded white/collar man. While *In the Company of Men* depicts a professional jungle ruled by the sadistic warrior, *Fight Club* nurtures a corps of masochistic soldiers who burn that jungle to the ground.

Business as Sadistic Sport—*In the Company of Men*

As Chad and Howard sip scotch and commiserate over their crisis, Chad devises a "refreshing" and "very therapeutic" scheme to "fuck somebody up for good" and "restore a little dignity to our lives":

> Say we were to find some gal [. . .] just vulnerable as hell [. . .] disfigured in some way [. . .]
> just some woman who is pretty sure that life—and I mean a full, healthy sexual life, romance, stuff
> like that—is just lost to her forever. Anyhow, we take a girl of that type [. . .] and we both hit her.
> You know, small talk, a dinner date, flowers [. . .] see an ice show, something like that. And we
> just do it, you know, you and me, upping the ante all the time. And suddenly she's got two men;
> she's calling her mom; she's wearing makeup again. And on we play and on and on. Then one
> day, out goes the rug and us pulling it hard. And Jill? She just comes rumbling after [. . .] Trust
> me, she'll be reaching for the sleeping pills within a week, and we will laugh about this 'til we are
> very old men.

Though initially hesitant, Howard consents by the end of the evening like a kid caving to peer pressure. Soon after, Chad meets Christine, a young deaf woman employed in the company's typing pool. Given her evident vulnerabilities, Chad concludes that she's a perfect target and takes her out. Goaded by Chad, Howard agrees to court her as well. The rest of the film follows Chad and Howard's pursuit of two shared and parallel projects: they work, date Christine, and swap stories about both. Before long, it becomes clear that the twin projects are proceeding differently. Howard develops what he sees as genuine feelings for Christine, while Christine falls for Chad. Even worse, Howard's first management assignment unravels; he and Chad discuss faulty reports and other mishaps that perturb the guys at the home office. Ultimately, Christine rejects Howard, proclaiming her love for Chad, and Howard is demoted from his management position. Chad callously discards a devastated Christine, returning home to a promotion and his live-in girlfriend. Despite his cruel cons in business and romance, Chad's world only improves. Despite Howard's tireless efforts to be "the good guy" (at least in his eyes), his world collapses. The film concludes with a smug and smirking Chad, enjoying his lover's services, juxtaposed against a pathetically collapsing Howard, whose strident screams—"Listen to me . . . Listen, listen, listen!"—fall on Christine's deaf ears.

What can we learn about healing white/collar masculinity from such a disturbing tale? We begin by elucidating the film's depiction of dominant and subordinate, potent and impotent, masculinities. Chad's character reveals that performing victory over and at the expense of opponents is the core passion and proof of manliness. Any man is entitled to compete, but only those with "big, brass ones" can win. Climbing the corporate hierarchy is the only game that counts, and all other contests are mere training for the ultimate competition among men. So how does a man win the all-important sport of business, thereby earning and haunting his superior balls?

From the striking contrast between Chad and Howard, we learn that a potent man carefully and constantly hones specific aptitudes. Chief among these is a fundamental suspicion of everyone. Throughout, Chad cautions Howard to expect betrayal—to "watch your back," "cover your ass," to "be careful" of this "bunch of vultures" hovering to "feed on my insides"—citing various company men to build his case for an ever-vigilant, always-defensive ethos. Chad's paranoia does not discriminate; he warns that one should be especially wary of the company of women, who are all made of "meat and gristle and hatred just simmering." Women lie in wait to ambush men, and they'll "kick you straight in the teeth" just "when you start to feel sorry" for them.

A basic distrust and disgust for humanity calls for a second key aptitude: ruthless, unflinching, impenitent violence toward others. To sustain his startling ability to "not give a shit," Chad objectifies the targets of his violence. When presented with personalizing details about someone, Chad routinely dismisses or ignores the information. For example, when a co-worker cagily observes that Christine is a "nice girl [. . .] types like 95 a minute [. . .] she's kind of pretty," Chad rises to leave and retorts, "Anyway, see you later," in the shrill, dolphin-like tone with which he imitates Christine's voice. Chad paints all people as useless caricatures, pure enemies to be decimated, disposable things. Frequently, he whets and validates his paranoia, rehearsing the dehumanization of possible targets. In one scene, for instance, with co-workers, he reviews colleagues depicted in a company newsletter: "I hate this guy. Oh, I hate that guy too. He's a little bastard [. . .] Oh, I hate that dude right there [. . .] one of those from Pittsburgh. Oh, he sucks dick [. . .] Oh man, I despise that dude. Sales rep from Indiana [. . .] Now, he's a new breed of fuck, like a special strain of fucker. Oh, I hate that little prissy cocksucker." Importantly, a wary and violent stance is more than a necessary survival strategy for the corporate winner; it is his primary source of pleasure. Chad's newsletter review is far more than an angry, vicious outburst. It is playful, cunning, and hilarious; and he joyously savors the moment. Likewise, with a twisted smile, Chad eagerly asks his various victims "So how does it feel?" and relishes their palpable shock and pain. In this sense, the vigilant violence practiced by the corporate victor is profoundly sadistic.

Thus far, the corporation is characterized as a specific sort of jungle; it's a kill-or-be-killed, every-man-for-himself world in which only the strongest survive. Accordingly, a successful businessman sees himself as perpetually wounded and all others as the possible cause. For white masculinity, "the threat of castration is everywhere present and everywhere hidden" (Holmlund 153). For this reason, the corporate jungle entails guerilla warfare, which real men enjoy. Success under these conditions requires a third aptitude: relentless self-interest, often cloaked as partnership. That is, a man must be politically savvy enough to know when his interests can be served by temporary alliance with others. Such coalitions require a form of hypocrisy: the effective performance of feelings one does not allow himself to actually experience. Chad brilliantly executes this feat with Christine and Howard, who respectively mistake him for a sincere lover and friend. Chad further displays his charlatan skills in the newsletter scene described above. When his amused and admiring co-workers ask if he likes a colleague who just left the room (and with whom he had just exchanged pleasant conversation), he casually responds, "Him? You kiddin' me? I hate that prick." Throughout the film, Chad's capacity for persuasive kindness followed by swift malice goes unrivaled. As he observes to his girlfriend at the end of the film, "When I get working, I can sound like practically anyone." Conversely, one of Howard's key frailties becomes his inability to discern performance from authenticity. With both Chad and Christine, he confuses instrumental alliance with meaningful relationship and, worse yet, falls prey to his own feeble performances.

Victory amid corporate guerilla warfare requires an additional aptitude for constant and stringent control of self and others. In Chad's words, "Never lose control [. . .] that is the total key to the universe." As indicated above, a man of suspicion and sadism keeps a tight reign on the emotions he feels, much less publicly displays. He also disciplines his body such that, ironically, it appears to require no control. For example, Chad limits himself to more refined forms of violence: clever verbal attacks, never physical brawls. He wears the corporate uniform with comfort and confidence, head and shoulders erect, body rarely prone. In striking contrast, Howard's body appears in endless disarray. We watch him eat, defecate, and vomit; and these bodily functions seem exceptionally awkward and time-consuming, akin to a "leaking" feminized body (Trethewey). Moreover, we see and hear that Howard stoops to physical scraps with women, which create a visual effect more akin to a "catfight" than domestic violence. And while assertive Chad grabs every opportunity to seize an upper hand, bumbling Howard tends to babble on toward embarrassment.

Finally, a man who would win the corporate game never retreats to the petty comforts found in the company of boys. In the film, corporate losers are synonymous with boys. Two characters vividly occupy this position and expose the perils of a boy's world. The most prominent is Howard, tellingly referred to as

"Howie" by Chad. We listen to Howie vie for freedom from his mother and ex-fiancé; we then watch him brace for similar bondage when he recycles an old engagement ring and shops for china with Christine in mind. The second character is a Black intern, who appears in a brief and poignant scene discussed later. For now, it is sufficient to note that Chad assails the intern group as a "bunch of juvenile fuckers" who mistake work for "summer camp" and "still want their mommies wiping their bottoms every time they go potty." Hence, a boy's world is suspect because it is subject to domineering women and because its members are too infantile and negligent to comprehend the rules that distinguish life in the company of men.

In sum, a man who is susceptible to human trust and care, whose conscience impedes violent pleasures, who cannot uphold the masquerade, and who lacks control of himself and others is a despicable figure—a corporate loser, a soft boy. Howie embodies this pitifully impotent creature. By the film's conclusion, he loses more than his managerial voice and metaphorical balls to a virile corporate warrior; he is literally rendered silent by a gullible, feminine "handicap" who dared to claim the right to choose among suitors. Whereas *In the Company of Men* marks the corporate world as the space in which real masculinity can emerge, the players of *Fight Club* treat corporations as the very site that tames, emasculates, and so, must be destroyed.

Masochism: To Wage War Against the Corporation—*Fight Club*

Over beers at a local dive, Tyler reframes the recent explosion of the narrator's condo and possessions. The loss is opportunity, not tragedy: "I say never be complete [. . .] I say let's evolve." Devoid of the material goods he so desperately sought, the narrator should see the demolition as freedom. Intrigued but skeptical, he wavers, unable to let go of his perfectly dissatisfying life.

Emerging from the bar, Tyler invites the narrator to hit him. With that first hesitant punch, they launch "Fight Club," an underground club "for men only" in which pairs of men brawl to the cheers of on-lookers, gladiator-style. Its exponential national growth attests to its resonance, and men everywhere are drawn to it as a site that exposes and celebrates men's wounds. Eventually, Fight Club evolves into war, and Project Mayhem—a militaristic venture in which Tyler and his all-male corps fight the corporate enemy—is born. Meanwhile, we witness the narrator's increasing attraction to Tyler and his jealousy over Tyler's relationships with others, including Marla. We also see the narrator's growth, from slumping to swaggering, as well as his moral struggle with Tyler's boyish and reckless approach to life. The film climaxes when we learn, with the narrator, that he and Tyler are literally the same person. In his desperate attempt to escape his sedated life, the narrator created a persona embodying all he is not. With this split personality, the narrator and Tyler manifest the classic double bind of masculinity (Bordo; Robinson; Rotundo). As the film ends, the narrator attempts to heal himself, ironically by killing Tyler and turning to Marla.

The narrator and Tyler's youthful approach to healing includes various escapades into mischief and malice. Defining manhood as boyish rebellion, the film promotes a visceral manliness in which men strip their corporate attire and (re)turn to a primitive age filled with physical contests. Adventure replaces work, and pranks expose social niceties. The antithesis of masculinity is the man afraid to fight, controlled by social demands rather than raw instinct. Such men are mindless robots.

An initial step toward men's "evolution" entails rejection of materialism and conspicuous consumption. If, as Tyler believes, "the things you own end up owning you," then a simplistic life devoid of "things" enables growth. Violent and complete separation is necessary, and Tyler models a life free from senseless spending. Suddenly homeless, the narrator moves in with Tyler. Living in a dilapidated house, filled with bare, stained mattresses and rust-red water, Tyler and the narrator cut themselves off from the material world. This lifestyle frees them from the hold of image-based masculinity promoted by the likes of Gucci and Calvin Klein. Tyler helps the narrator as well as the men of Fight Club and Project Mayhem see that "You are not your job, you're not how much money you have in the bank, you're not the car you drive, you're not the contents of your wallet, you're not your—*fucking-khakis.*"

Evolution requires this brutal honesty to expose and reject the lies of fathers. Ultimately, men must uncover social myths and fabrications about masculinity. Tyler forces men to hear the truth: "We've all been raised on television to believe that one day we'd all be millionaires and movie gods and rock stars, but we won't. And we're slowly learning that fact, and we're very, very pissed off." Reveling in their anger at this betrayal, the men of Fight Club and Project Mayhem join Tyler in sharing these difficult lessons. Tyler's chant—"You are not special; you are not a unique or beautiful snowflake"—becomes a lesson shared among the soldiers of Project Mayhem. Only upon learning these truths can men sever the ties that enslave them and unleash their stifled selves. A primary arena for such enlightenment is Fight Club.

Prior to joining Fight Club, members are living lies, performing a fraudulent masculinity akin to femininity. This emasculating masquerade emerges in the narrator's early addiction to therapy groups, where he finds life by mimicking disability and impending death. A phony pretending to be wounded, the narrator craves the pain he witnesses in others. Tyler provides the cure in Fight Club. In brutal, bloody fights, the narrator learns to feel and wear pain with pride. Unlike the "bitch tits" that prove Bob's pain, the bruises, scars, and blood the narrator sports stand as virile wounds. A far cry from the zombie-like plod that plagued his early life, he is soon strutting down the street, parading ugly bruises and utter disregard for social decorum, openly scoffing at colleagues obsessed with corporate efficiency and whether they can "get the icon in cornflower blue." In stark contrast to stuffed-shirt corporate conformity, the narrator becomes deliberately disheveled, shirt untucked and tie askew. Rather than acquiescing, the narrator flaunts disrespect, finally bullying his boss. He reflects on his own behavior, "I used to be such a nice guy."

Fight Club adds more than fleeting bruises and scars; it engenders a ritualistic and masochistic fascination with pain (Robinson). Violence is a stimulating addiction. The narrator and Tyler bask in its glow, pushing the body to its ultimate limits. We witness Tyler pour lye onto the narrator's hand and hold him still until he can relish the exquisite pain. We watch Tyler viciously beaten, begging for more with orgasmic overtures: "That's right Lou, get it out [. . .] ooh yeeaah [. . .] oooh Loouu." Why this masochism? Burned and beaten, the narrator learns the limits of his body and uncovers new strength. Even as he hits bottom, he is not defeated, evincing a warrior-like mentality in which he refuses to die. Parallels to Schwarzenegger's and Stallone's hard-body, action-adventure masculinity, in which wounds are redemptive, are compelling (Jeffords *Hard*). As Savran maintains, white masculinity has developed a pain fixation, "torturing himself to prove his masculinity" (par. 4).

Importantly, Fight Club and Project Mayhem enable the creation of male bonds and intimacies, advancing evolution by recentering men in men's lives. Joy emerges among the men as they roll around, punching, beating, touching each other. As victims, they forge bonds in their shared identity. Victor and defeated embrace, anticipating their next encounter. These ties that bind prepare men to engage battle and defeat the corporate enemy. And Project Mayhem provides the site. A sort of boot-camp, Project Mayhem spawns an army of soldiers—young men with shaved heads and black uniforms who destroy corporate art and coffee franchises, who start fires in corporate buildings, who infiltrate local businesses. That war must be declared and corporations defeated is more than metaphor. Project Mayhem becomes a tightly organized, minutely planned operation (ironically, bureaucratic in structure). It allows neither weakness nor vulnerability); it accepts neither tears nor regret over casualties; it admits no diversions to its ultimate goal—destruction of the corporate enemy and liberation of its subjects. Men and masculinity will not be under siege.

Haunting the narrator throughout much of this war is the (feminine) fear of uncontrolled excessive masculinity. While the lure of the hard body is desirable and the moral quest to regain it important, the rebellious mentality of Tyler is often frightening and intense. Ultimately, the narrator knows that the wild boy must be contained, and thus the film concludes with the narrator's recognition of and gratitude for the lessons learned. With this realization, he destroys Tyler.

For Chad, Tyler, and his narrator apprentice, sadistic or masochistic violence awakens a businessman's taste for virility and pleasure. Next, we consider how these complementary tales of hegemonic masculinity—one that dominates, one that resists the corporation—respond to the contemporary discourse of crisis.

Across the Films: Traces and Implications of the "New" Professional

Modern Neurasthenia: Managing Masculine Double Binds

The films do not simply cure modern neurasthenia tensions; rather, they relish a perpetual sense of anxiety and unrest. First, neither film articulates the reconciliation of men's public and private selves. *In the Company of Men* marks the private as indulgent excess—a source of softening or weakening that disables a man's paranoid violence. For instance, Howard is ultimately ruined by myriad vulnerabilities to private virtues (e.g., morality, love), regulating figures, (e.g., mothers, fiancés), and bodily leaks. Trilling with the private stunts his capacity for sadism and renders him an incompetent manager—of his work, his ties to women, and even his own body. He caves and confesses the plot against Christine when he smells defeat and, ostensibly, when he begins to care for her. It is no coincidence that these sensations develop simultaneously. In a Chad-like logic, Howard is foolish enough to seek solace and healing in private relationships, or at least in their public markers. Thus, in the face of corporate loss and an increasingly shaky friendship with Chad, he is frantic to possess romance and prove some semblance of virility. Child designed the game with this in mind, for he enticed Howard with assurances that "no matter what happens after [. . .] jumped over for promotions, wife runs off with some biochemist [. . .] we would always have this thing to fall back on. Could always say, 'Yeah fine. But they never got me like we got her.'" In this light, even if Howard could win Christine, it would prove a hollow victory. For in the company of real men, the private realm we know is dead, resurrected in the image and service of the corporate jungle.

Fight Club offers another way to maneuver. Neurasthenic from corporate over-civilization and engulfed by the private to the point of symbolic castration, the narrator literally develops a split personality to reconcile the competing demands of masculinity. His discovery of the primal pleasures of fight helps him to overcome his fears and to see, accept, even cherish his wounds. By forging male intimacy through violent contact and a shared goal or moral quest, Fight Club and Project Mayhem offer men—especially young ones who live in the shadow of great heroes and memories—the opportunity to play at war and learn its manly lessons. Emerging from this military space, which has historically lent men a public/private means to foster hard bodies, the narrator can engage the private and reach out to Marla with fewer fears of future emasculation.

In brief, whereas Chad scorns the world of women, saving a mask to perform within it. *Fight Club's* narrator destroys Chad's corporate jungle and returns to the private a stronger man. Yet both films remain leery of the private as a safe space for masculinity. Both reify the need for hard bodies and public balls as a kind of armor against the private. And, though in opposite ways, both mark the resilient male body as a public figure and corporate product.

Second, neither film consistently embraces nor rejects the primitive and civilized. Indeed, the characters approach this masculine dialectic as a constant juggling act. On the one hand, both films ironically imply that men must rediscover the primitive to rescue civilization. Concurrently, these primitive habits must be curbed by civilized norms. Rationality, restraint, and strategic duplicity package the primitive in civilized form *In the Company of Men;* in *Fight Club,* vague notions of morality, honor, and human connection serve as civilizing tools. We contend that, despite manifold differences, both films construct a civilized/primitive subjectivity that allows professional men to hold conflicting selves together in temporary, partial, adaptable, and strategic performances, however loose their grip might be. For example, Chad alternately performs calculated control with apparent sensitivity (e.g., courting Christine, befriending Howard) and raw aggression-derived genitalia: "Listen, you got a pair the kind that men are carrying around, you practically wear 'em on your sleeve. That's what business is all about—who's sporting the nastiest sac of venom and who is willing to use it." For Chad, "the idea that real manliness (and sexuality vitality and zest for life) is to be found outside man-made culture is merged with the idea of the workplace as the man-made jungle where a man might realize himself, if he's the right sort of animal" (Bordo 253). In a different civilized/primitive performance, Tyler embodies a primal physicality, rationalized by his social consciousness; later, his primitive club assumes militaristic, near-bureaucratic form. Determined to erase external controls of men, Tyler ironically assumes the role of corporate father, ruling over a rule-governed and hierarchical entity. Eventually, the narrator internalizes Tyler's lessons in primal pain but slays his primitive excess in the name of ethics. In sharp contrast to the other characters, Howard remains the archetypal neurasthenic, a transparent impostor who confuses strategic performance with an "authentic" self. As he succumbs to, or becomes, the performance, he cannot adjust to changing primitive/civilized demands and, consequently, gets consumed by both.

In sum, the films cast the primitive/civilized as a masculine dialectical tension with many possible and creative performances. Central to managing this dialectic is the elusive quest for an ideal blend of control and excess. At various times, Chad, Tyler, and the narrator portray a keen sense of the shifting faces the two may take, the fine line between them, and the dangers wrought by too much of either. As a result, the characters develop adoration *and* loathing for control and excess—a flexible stance that allows them to invoke one to tame the other and, thereby, to manage shifting accountabilities to the primitive/civilized.

Ultimately, we argue that neither film moves to heal the battered white/collar man. While *Fight Club* incessantly pushes him to reopen his wounds and celebrate them as spectacle, *In the Company of Men* harbors the ubiquitous threat of bruises to fuel the fire of violence directed outward. Put simply, the wounds don't need to be healed; they *are* a healing force, creating an already broken and thus unbreakable professional body. Hence, the display of wounds becomes indefinitely central to the performance of professional masculinity, which finds stimulation in the notion that it too is injured (Jeffords *Hard;* Savran). In this sense, civilized/primitive subjectivity stakes a claim to identity politics for white/collar men (Robinson). Below, we consider how this professional character plays with other politicized subjects.

Gender, Race, Sexuality, Class, and the Civilized/Primitive

FOR MEN ONLY, BUT WHICH ONES? While some (e.g., white) masculinities and femininities lay claim to diverse dimensions of the civilized (e.g., scientific rationality, private virtues), the films insist that only men can access the primitive. The primitive emerges as a suppressed male essence, which is presumably available to all men. Significantly, across the films, only white men get to teach the primitive, and their primary pupils are other white men. However, two strikingly parallel scenes depict pupils of color. In the first, Chad chastises a young Black intern—one of the "juvenile fuckers" at "summer camp" alluded to earlier. The pretense of their meeting is that Chad is graciously showing the intern the ropes, "rolling out the opportunity" for him to "hang with the money people." When the intern shrugs off Chad's initial advice, Chad demands gratefulness from his student: "You know, I could've held back on this [. . .] let you figure out life all on your little lonesome. But I think I would've been doing you a disservice [. . .] cherish this." Chad stresses his confusion over whether the intern's name is "Keith" or "Keif" and sniggers at Keif's pronunciation of "axe": "Let me give you a professional tip. The word is *ask.*" With his arm around Keif, Chad informs him that he needs "the big brass ones" to climb the corporate ladder: "Let's see 'em then, these clankers of yours." When Keif hesitates and mumbles a disbelieving protest, Chad removes all doubt of his command: "Show–Me–Your–Balls!" After Keif complies, Chad asks him to fetch a cup of coffee on his way out: "Black's fine."

Like Chad, Tyler excels in his role as teacher, even with the most difficult lessons. Viewers watch as Tyler, embarking on a "human sacrifice," drags an Asian/American clerk out of the convenience store where he works, pushes him to his knees, and holds a gun to his head. Perusing the clerk's wallet, Tyler announces, "Raymond, you are going to die [. . .] There's going to be nothing left of your face." Tyler discovers Raymond's school ID and asks, "what'd you study, Raymond?" Violently shaking, Raymond stutters, "st-st-st-stuff," at which Tyler hits Raymond with the gun, demanding "I asked you, what'd you study?" Unsatisfied with the answer, Tyler continues, "Why? [. . .] What'd you want to be, Raymond K. Hessel?" As the clerk continues to sob, Tyler cocks the gun and repeats, "The question—Raymond, was— What–Did–You–Want–To Be?" Finally, Tyler releases Raymond, warning that he will return to see that Raymond is pursuing his goals. Mockingly, as Raymond runs off, Tyler taunts, "Run, Forrest, Run." Questioned by the narrator as to the point, Tyler proclaims assuredly that Raymond's life will now have meaning.

In both powerful scenes, the tone of white men's teaching takes a dramatic turn that reveals the ways in which civilized/primitive masculinity entails racialized performance. With their primary and most serious (white) pupils, the teachers devote extensive time and adopts a tone of relative equality and intimacy. Tyler acts as a buddy mentor who guides his chief trainee through the primitive; Chad too engages Howard as a chummy peer and a possible player, despite his agenda to the contrary. With men of color, the tone is contrastingly brief, distant, condescending, and violent; and the relation shifts from mentor-apprentice to (abusive) father-boy or tyrant-minion. These peons apparently necessitate a harsher hand and deserve to be put in their place. As such, both films invite audiences to gaze upon these racially marked and crumbling bodies. We watch Keif nervously undo his pants; we witness Raymond shaking and sobbing. While both films provide space to morally question these violent moments, they simultaneously fix or mark racial difference as visibly and immediately other (S. Willis).[11] Moreover, both scenes underscore the inability of these pupils to rightfully claim civilized/primitive subjectivity. Keif could have it all if only he would stop "screwing around," start using his head, and speak professionally (i.e., get civilized, where civilized equals white), Raymond could find a new life if he would stop blubbering like a sissy and grab his future by the horns (i.e., get primitive in pursuit of career achievements—a whitened primitive, not to mention an ironic message, for a work-suspicious film). The films' reliance on familiar racial imagery here (e.g., Black man as dumb primal brute, Asian man as over-cultured and effeminate) needs little elaboration (e.g., Dines; Eng).

The notion of white men as teachers of the primitive is telling, for it rejects the conventional discourse of the primitive as the domain of dark savage rapists (Bederman). We suggest that white masculinity can now appropriate the teaching role precisely because the emerging ideal embraces a *civilized*/primitive masculinity. This flexibility in itself marks whiteness, for dark masculinities are granted access only to savage primal modes or feminized civil ones (Dines; Eng). It is also notable that the mentors of both films grant white pupils more serious and sustained attention. These insights come together in Chad's depiction of the masculinity crisis: "OK, well we're doomed then, seriously, as a race." Chad characterizes white/collar men as an advanced civilization, entitled to "put our foot down" and damned unless they do. In this light, going primitive becomes a means of (white) race preservation. Handily, the primitive no longer threatens to taint the white man with dark savage excess, because the sophisticated white primitive retains a firm foothold in—and, actually, aims to serve and protect—civilization (Bederman).

In the Company of Men self-consciously exposes raced and classed restrictions as to which men can pull off the performance of civilized/primitive subjectivity. In addition to the Chad-Keif scene, we hear Howard denounce his working-class heritage as a quaintly impotent "Norman Rockwell" life. *Fight Club* appears less self-conscious about its class and racial limitations. With its more visually diverse membership, *Fight Club* extends a civilized/primitive brotherhood to men of all ages, races, and classes. Indeed, a Black man enjoys pummeling the narrator in one scene (though the narrator is in the midst of explaining that Fight Club is not about winning or losing). And oddly, while Fight Club develops in response to professional neurasthenia, its members are increasingly working class. By mid-film, for example, Tyler pronounces the significance of his army of men as he threatens to castrate a police commissioner: "Look, the people you are after are the people you depend on. We cook your meals; we haul your trash; we connect your calls; we drive your ambulances. We guard you while you sleep." The centrality of anti-materialism to Fight Club also reaches out to men of diverse class. At the same time, it erases racial wounds, subordinating all other injuries to those inflicted by a faceless corporate capitalism. Strategically here, through the creation of all-male clubs with trans-racial memberships, the discourse co-opts contemporary ideological debates, particularly racial ones, to its own ends (Hanke; S. Willis). Men of color are invited to act, but only in those secondary roles approved by white directors. A similar effect is produced by the film's age appeals. Although men of various ages initially flock to Fight Club, most of the key players that emerge are young, lean, white boy-men. And besides the MTV-feel of the film, the main source of identification between the narrator and Marla is a kind of "Gen X" despondency: drifting young adults discarded by divorced parents, disillusioned by American dreams, skeptical of traditional work ethics, and so forth. This youthful emphasis further serves to conceal the white, middle-class character of this generational narrative.

THE FEMININE, EFFEMINATE, AND MANLY DESIRE. The masculine identities and bonds that surface in the films are opposed to and explicitly deny the feminine. Women and things feminized appear soft, weak, hypersensitive, overcivilized, frazzled, psychobabbling, indecisive, disabled, unduly restrained yet too excessive—dripping with private (non-)sensibilities. Paradoxically, women and the feminine are also decidedly threatening, for they pose seductive entrapment. Worse yet, they rule the private realm but then refuse to be contained there. Their strides in the company of men exacerbate men's neurasthenic anxieties. It is this final and most recent violation that seems to spawn the intensified loathing and vigorous misogyny at work in these films. Simply put, femininities are menacing because they are intruding, exposing, captivating, captive-making, and necessary all at once (Horrocks). Donning the primitive helps a man stand strong amid the feminine, in part because it restores his control of it. The evolution of the relationship between Marla and the narrator nicely illustrates the point. Initially, Marla calls the shots, assertively defending her therapy group turf. Yet as Fight Club grows, she becomes increasingly neurotic and dependent. By the film's end, the relation of control has flipped: Marla feels ruined by the newly alive and virile narrator, who then rescues her and, by implication, earns her affection.

The enhanced misogyny that suffuses both films is also colored with race hierarchy. While all men may join the war, invitations are neither equal nor sufficient to disrupt racial superiority (Wiegman). As hinted earlier, Tyler's first "human sacrifice" victim becomes the symbolic equivalent of a wimpering woman, whereas Chad dismisses Keif as an ignorant boy. As such, the Asian/American clerk is a far cry from the male primitive, while the Black intern is little but primal. These scenes surface more than the import of historically racialized access to the civilized and primitive. Namely, masculinities of color are also evaluated according to their degree of closeness to things feminine. And femininities are all the more odious when expressed in a male body. After all, the obese, castrated Bob is the only Project Mayhem soldier to die in battle.

As the latter point implies, the racist and misogynist civilized/primitive is also homophobic, as revealed by Chad's choice of profanities (e.g. "prissy cocksucker") in the newsletter review scene. And while *Fight Club* flirts with the homosocial, it concludes with compulsory heterosexuality (Wittig). Yet, in seeming contradiction, the civilized/primitive can engender homoeroticism. For example, the male bonds built in *Fight Club* are joined by homosocial desire (Roper; Sedgwick). Tyler's beautifully virile physicality brings this hunger to *Fight Club*. His flamboyant apparel, ranging from vibrant vintage to hipster to camouflage to a pastel coffee-cup bathrobe, marks him as spectacle. In scene after scene, the camera hovers lovingly over his sculpted, tanned, near-naked form, as it struts around the house or writhes around on a filthy floor, interlocked with various men. That men patently adore Tyler's body is made permissible in interesting ways. First, the narrator's relationship with Tyler is fraught with the symbolism of heterosexual courtship and marriage. On their first evening together, Tyler directs the narrator to "cut the foreplay" and ask if he can spend the night. The conclusion of their first physical brawl is laden with sexual imagery: With glazed, satisfied expressions, the two share a cigarette and a beer, musing, "We should do this again sometime." After the men move in together, the narrator's cynical references to "playing Ozzie and Harriet" depict the two as a less-than-ideal married couple. We watch the narrator gaze at Tyler in the bathtub; we observe his possessive and admiring smirks when he watches Tyler fight. Later, the narrator interprets Tyler's budding interest in a young, lithe, beautiful, blonde Fight Club member—referred to as "Angel Face"—as a sort of extramarital affair. Like a spurned lover, the narrator nips the affair in the bud by destroying Angel's face in a fight, proclaiming an "inflamed sense of rejection." Meanwhile, the potential for romantic relations between Tyler and the narrator is denied by Tyler's "sportfucking" of Marla, coupled with the narrator's own muted attraction to Marla. Here, we are assured that the homoerotic is not the homosexual, while the heterosexuality of both men gets affirmed. The narrator is hardly the only man in the film who gazes on Tyler with yearning awe; but Fight Club soon adopts the frame of war, which construes such desire as hero worship and the intense physical intimacy of bonds forged in battle. But only the white male body appears worthy of worship. Although all members arrive with an "ass made of cookie dough" and come away "carved out of wood," Tyler's stylishly primal and brutally militaristic body remains special throughout, supporting Jeffords claim that hard body masculinity was never meant to include anyone but white men *(Hard)*.

In the Company of Men also toys with the homoerotic in a less frequent and visible but more explicitly racialized way. Arguably, Chad's interest in Keif's balls reflects his curiosity about the mythic genitalia of Black men (hooks *Outlaw*). Chad bluntly deflects any such reading by avowing, "I'm not a homo, Keith," and recasting the scenario as an evaluation of whether Keif is "man enough" for management. This frame negates Chad's possible desire and diffuses the threat of primitive Black bodies and sexuality, affirming the superiority of Chad's civilized/primitive masculinity in the name of corporate prowess. Taken together, the human sacrifice and Keif scenes emasculate the bodies of men of color and enforce the entitled strength and beauty of the white male body. This is not surprising, for discourses of the dangers of Black male bodies (Dines; Orbe), of the lewd nature of Latino bodies (Berg), and of the feminized Asian/American male bodies (Nakayama "Show/down") encumber the formation of a civilized/primitive body of color.

In sum, the characters of both films use intensified—and, usually, misogynist and homophobic—gender division to seduce a civilized/primitive brotherhood composed of all races and classes. However, it seems that the "unfortunate" inability of all but white men to adapt to both sides of this malleable self will preclude them from potent performance. Through such powerful discursive tactics, professional masculinity can once again manage to morph yet retain its gender, race, and class dominance all at once.

Conclusion

Thus far, we have traced two parallel yet divergent threads of a contemporary discourse of white/collar men in crisis. Like the crisis narrative a century ago, these fragments are all about manhood threatened by feminizing forces. But this time around, corporations are figured as *the* emasculating force, sterilized by women's civilization. This novel motif suggests the need to attend to the ways in which work enables and constrains the performance of hegemonic masculinity.

White men have long been construed as public characters. In the 19th century, the stage shifted from community to work, where it has largely remained until now. The crisis narrative that ensued eventually rescued business by crafting it as a jungle of men, fertile ground for potent masculinity (Bederman; Rotundo). Today, amid serious public clamor for quality of work life and fashionably derisive caricatures like Dilbert, corporate ground seems ever more barren. In short, contemporary discourse casts suspicion on the white collar, as well as the notion that a man is defined by his professional achievements and material possessions. In the discourse chronicled here, white/collar masculinity alternately appears as socially destructive, as hinted by *In the Company of Men's* satirical tone, or as personally dissatisfying, as in *Fight Club.* As noted earlier, these films are part of a recent surge of works that explore the failings of white/ collar masculinity. Arguably, many of these films—such as *American Beauty* (1999), *Office Space* (1999), and *Wolf* (1994)—also take up with the neurasthenic tensions analyzed here and depict disabling contradictions between corporate life and a potent masculine self. Ours may well be a time when hegemonic masculinity flirts with a new public home.

In this sense, the critique embedded in the rise of such films is penetrating, pushing men to seek other options. For example, both films analyzed here open space for criticizing hegemonic masculinity, especially *In the Company of Men,* whose tongue-in-cheek caricature is captured by Chad "Piercewell." While *Fight Club* does not extend the same invitation, the narrator and occasionally Tyler perform discomfort with moral excess: And in the final moments of both films, we are left with empty images: Howard screaming at the deaf Christine, Chad gloating in the sexual adulation of his lover, radical Tyler destroyed by the narrator, and a dazed and confused narrator. We submit that these spaces constitute a window of opportunity through which to re-vision dominant masculinity. Whereas corporations have long supplied an institutional anchor for white, middle-class masculinity, they now ironically become the force that strips this weary subject of his manhood. In this way, the characters' perceptions of personal powerlessness—however whiny, victimizing, or otherwise perilous—facilitates the sort of resistance that could undermine patriarchal, managerial capitalism, which depends on white/collar men to devote themselves to a game they will likely lose (Donaldson). If the present discourse continues to gain steam, we suspect that the nature of corporate commitment will have to change or white, middle-class masculinity may drift toward another public base.

Lest we sound too optimistic, we acknowledge at least two discursive hitches to sustainable resistance. First, the essay reveals the tremendous historical weight and contemporary pressure of the neurasthenic paradox, which demands that white/collar men (among others) simultaneously perform accountability to conflicting expectations for civilized and primitive selves in public and private arenas. Alternation between soft, sensitive and hard, violent masculinities constitutes one cultural means of managing this dilemma. Indeed, violence has become a familiar balm for embattled professional men (Hearn "Organization"; Linstead). We maintain that feminist and other calls for masculinity transformation must take seriously the difficulty of navigating this tension.

A second catch follows our analysis of the political relations at work in the film. Specifically, even if white, middle-class masculinity begins to dislodge from corporations, there is no reason to believe it will lose hold of its race, class, sexuality, and gender dominance. Consider, for example, what we learn about possibilities from the film tales. In general, we are offered four potential subject positions: (a) the debilitated neurasthenic (i.e., Howie, early narrator); (b) the eternally suspicious and sadistic corporate fighter (i.e., Chad); (c) the wild, masochistic boy rebel, playfully and maliciously violent (i.e., Tyler); and (d) the morally conflicted young man who killed him, only to (re)join with a woman (i.e., "evolved" narrator). Option one is immediately undermined, and the others are never embraced. To different degrees, these faulty performances of masculinity concede the inevitability of the hegemonic masculinities they seek to disrupt. Certainly, *In the Company of Men* is less at fault in this regard, yet even it depends on the audience to supply a critique frame and to connect its more and less subtle dots between gender, race, homophobia, and classism. That not everyone can or will do so becomes evident in some public reactions to the film. One viewer, frustrated by a recent romantic break-up, noted, "I actually walked out of the movie with a smile" (Kohn par. 5). Another critic observed that Chad is "so charming that he's irresistible, but what a poisonous man—just the type who often makes it in business" (Hershenson par. 9).

Alone, these twin caveats leave us with a final caution: Hegemonic masculinity remains an elastic, "historically mobile relation" (Connell *Masculinities* 77). Temporarily itinerant, perhaps. In search of a more supportive stage. But definitely not daunted.

ENDNOTES

1. Throughout the essay, our use of "white/collar" is meant to mark the masculinity's race and class profile, without subordinating one to another.

2. In addition to journals such as *Men and Masculinities* and *Journal of Men's Studies,* see for instance. Brittan: Brod and Kaufman: Hearn and Morgan: Kimmel and Messner: Segal: Seidler *Rediscovering* and *Unreasonable:* and Stecopoulos and Uebel.

3. This concern is shared among scholars of whiteness, for whom the parallel fear of reinscribing white dominance exists in tension with the desire to render it visible (e.g., Flores and Moon: Projansky and Ono).

4. See, for instance, Byars: de Lauretis *Alice* and *Technologies;* Mulvey "Afterthoughts" and "Visual": Penley: Powrie; and van Zoonen.

5. See, for instance, Bird: hooks *Reel;* Jeffords *Hard;* Tasker "Dumb" and *Spectacular;* and S. Willis.

6. See Bordo: Dyer *White;* Kirkham and Thumin *You Tarzan;* Ray; and Tasker "Fists."

7. Such arguments are explored in Cohan; Dyer "Rock"; Fuchs; Neale; and Stukator.

8. For discussions of masculinity and work, see Alvesson; Cheng *Masculinities:* Collinson and Hearn "Naming", *Men,* and "Men"; and Mumby. Studies of women and work include Ashcraft "Empowering" and "Managing"; Buzzanell: Konck and Kitch; Marshall; Pringle; Rosener; and Trethewey.

9. For an extended account of the rise of these formations and their implications for masculinity, see Rotundo.

10. See, for instance, Burris; Hearn *Men* and "Deconstructing": Kerfoot and Knights; Kilduff and Mehra.

11. As we later clarify, *In the Company of Men* marks race more self-consciously and purposefully than *Fight Club,* where it appears incidental.

REFERENCES

Acker, Joan. "Hierarchies, Jobs, Bodies: A Theory of Gendered Organizations." *Gender and Society* 4 1990: 139–58.

Alvesson, Mats. "Gender Relations and Identity at Work: A Case Study of Masculinities and Femininities in an Advertising Agency." *Human Relations* 51 (1998): 969–1005.

American Beauty. Dir. Sam Mendes. Universal Studios, 1999.

Ashcraft, Karen Lee. "Empowering 'Professional' Relationship: Organizational Communication Meets Feminist Practice." *Management Communication Quarterly* 13 (2000): 347–92.

———. "Managing Maternity Leave: A Qualitative Analysis of Temporary Executive Succession." *Administrative Science Quarterly* 44 (1999): 40–80.

Ashcraft, Karen Lee, and Brenda J. Allen. "The Racial Foundation of Organizational Communication." *Communication Theory,* 13 (2003): 5–38.

Beavers, Herman. " 'The Cool Pose': Intersectionality, Masculinity, and Quiescence in the Comedy and Films of Richard Pryor and Eddie Murphy." Stecopoulos and Uebel 253–85.

Bederman, Gail. (1995). *Manliness and Civilization: A Cultural History of Gender and Race in the United States, 1880–1917.* Chicago: U of Chicago P, 1995.

Berg, Charles Ramirez. "Stereotyping of Films in General and of the Hispanic in Particular." *Latin Looks: Images of Latinas and Latinos in the U.S. Media.* Ed. Clara E. Rodriguez. Boulder: Westview, 1997, 104–20.

The Big Kahuna. Dir. John Swanbeck. Universal Studies, 2000.

Bird, Sharon R. "Welcome to the Men's Club: Homosociality and the Maintenance of Hegemonic Masculinity." *Gender and Society* 10 (1996): 120–32.

Boiler Room. Dir. Ben Younger. New Line Studios, 2000.

Bordo, Susan. *The Male Body: A New Look at Men in Public and in Private.* New York: Farrar, Straus, and Giroux, 1999.

Brittan, Arthur. *Masculinity and Power.* New York: Basil Blackwell, 1989.

Brod, Harry, and Michael Kaufman, eds. *Theorizing Masculinities.* Thousand Oaks: Sage, 1994.

Burris, Beverly H. "Technocracy, Patriarchy, and Management." Collinson and Hearn 61–77.

Butler, Judith. *Gender Trouble: Feminism and the Subversion of Identity.* New York: Routledge, 1990.

Buzzanell, Patrice M. "Reframing the Glass Ceiling as a Socially Constructed Process. Implications for Understanding and Change." *Communication Monographs* 62 (1995): 327–54.

Byars, Jackie. "Gazes/Voices/Power: Expanding Psychoanalysis for Feminist Film and Television." *Female Spectators: Looking at Film and Television.* Ed. E. Deidre Pribam. New York: Verso, 1998. 110–31.

Cheng, Cliff, ed. *Masculinities in Organizations.* Thousand Oaks, CA: Sage, 1996.

———. "Men and Masculinities are not Necessarily Synonymous: Thoughts on Organizational Behavior and Occupational Sociology." Cheng xi–xx.

Cohan, Steven. "Masquerading as the American Male in the Fifties: *Picnic.* William Holden and the Spectacle of Masculinity in Hollywood Film." *Camera Obscura* 25/26 (1991): 43–72.

Cohan, Steven and Ina Rae Hark, eds. *Screening the Male: Exploring Masculinities in Hollywood Cinema.* New York: Routledge, 1993.

Collins, Patricia Hill. "Toward a New Vision: Race, Class, and Gender as Categories of Analysis and Connection." *Race, Sex and Class* 1 (1993): 25–45.

Collinson, David L. " 'Engineering Humour': Masculinity, Joking, and Conflict in Shop-floor Relations." *Organization Studies* 9 (1988): 181–99.

Collinson, David L. and Jeff Hearn, eds. *Men as Managers, Managers as Men.* Thousand Oaks, CA: Sage, 1996.

———. " 'Men' at 'Work': Multiple Masculinities/Multiple Workplaces." *Understanding Masculinities: Social Relations and Cultural Arenas.* Ed. In Mairtin Mac an Ghaill. Buckingham, UK: Open UP, 61–76.

———. "Naming Men as Men: Implications for Work. Organization and Management." *Gender Work, and Organization* 1 (1994): 2–22.

Connell, R. W. "The Big Picture: Masculinities in Recent World History." *Theory and Society* 22 (1993): 597–623.

———. *Gender and Power.* Palo Alto, CA: Stanford UP, 1987.

———. *Masculinities.* Berkeley: U of California P, 1995.

Corey, Frederick C. "Masculine Drag." *Critical Studies in Media Communication* 17 (2000): 108–10.

Crenshaw, Carrie. "Women in the Gulf War: Toward an Intersectional Feminist Rhetorical Criticism." *Howard Journal of Communications* 8 (1997): 219–35.

Crenshaw, Kimberlie. "Mapping the Margins: Intersectionality, Identity Politics, and Violence Against Women of Color." *Stanford Law Review* 43 (1991): 1241–99.

Dace, Karen L. " 'Had Judas Been a Black Man . . .': Politics, Race, and Gender in African America." *Judgment Calls: Rhetoric, Politics, and Indeterminacy.* Ed. John M. Sloop and James P. McDaniel. Boulder: Westview, 1998, 163–81.

De Lauretis, Teresa. *Alice Doesn't: Feminism, Semiotics, Cinema.* Bloomington: Indiana UP, 1984.

De Lauretis, Teresa. *Technologies of Gender: Essays on Theory, Film, and Fiction.* Bloomington: Indiana UP, 1987.

Deetz, Stan, and Dennis Mumby. "Power, Discourse, and the Workplace: Reclaiming the Critical Tradition." *Communication Yearbook* 13 (1990): 18–47.

Dines, Gail. "*King Kong* and the White Woman: Hustler Magazine and the Demonization of Black Masculinity." *Violence Against Women* 4.3 (1998). 24 Aug. 2000 <http://ehostvgw3.epnet.com/ehost1.asp>.

Disclosure. Dir. Barry Levinson. Warner Brothers, 1994.

Donaldson, Mike. "What is Hegemonic Masculinity?" *Theory and Society* 22 (1993): 643–58.

Dyer, Richard. "Rock—The Last Guy You'd Have Figured?" *You Tarzan: Masculinity, Movies and Men.* Ed. Pat Kirkham and Janet Thumin. New York: St. Martin's Press, 1993. 27–34.

———. *White.* New York: Routledge, 1997.

Eng, David L. *Racial Castration: Managing Masculinity in Asian America.* Durham: Duke UP, 2001.

Falling Down. Dir. Joel Schumaker. Warner Brothers, 1993.

Faludi, Susan. *Stiffed: The Betrayal of the American Man.* New York: William Morrow, 1999.

Fight Club. Dir. David Fincher. Twentieth Century Fox, 1999.

Fine, Michelle, Lois Weis, Judi Addelston, and Julia Marusza. "(In)secure Times: Constructing White Working-class Masculinities in the Late 20th Century." *Gender and Society* 11 (1997): 568.

Flores, Lisa A., and Dreama G. Moon. "Rethinking race, revealing dilemmas: Imagining a new racial subject in *Race Traitor.*" *Western Journal of Communication* 66 (2002): 181–207.

Fuchs, Cynthia J. "The Buddy Politic." Cohan and Hark 194–210.

Gherardi, Silvia. *Gender, Symbolism, and Organizational Cultures.* Newbury Park, CA: Sage, 1995.

Glengarry, Glen Ross. Dir. James Foley. Artisan Entertainment, 1992.

Gibson, Melissa K., and Michael J. Papa. "The Mud, the Blood, and the Beer Guys: Organizational Osmosis in Blue-collar Work Groups." *Journal of Applied Communication Research* 28 (2000): 66–86.

Hall, Stuart. "Signification, Representation, Ideology: Althusser and the Poststructuralist Debates." *Critical Studies in Mass Communication* 2 (1985): 91–114.

———. "The Work of Representation. *Representation: Cultural Representations and Signifying Practices.* Ed. Stuart Hall, London: Sage/Open UP, 1997, 13–64.

Hamada, Tomako. "Unwrapping Euro-American Masculinity in a Japanese Multinational Corporation." Cheng 160–76.

Hanke, Robert. "Hegemonic Masculinity in *thirtysomething.*" *Critical Studies in Mass Communication* 7 (1990): 231–48.

Hearn, Jeff. "Deconstructing the Dominant: Making the One(s) the Other(s). *Organization* 3 (1996): 611–26.

———. *Men in the Public Eye: The Construction and Deconstruction of Public Men and Public Patriarchies.* New York: Routledge, 1992.

———. "The Organization of Violence: Men, Gender Relations, Organizations, and Violences." *Human Relations* 47 (1994): 731–54.

Hearn, Jeff and David Morgan, eds. *Men, Masculinities and Social Theory.* London: Unwin Hyman, 1990.

Hershenson, Karen. "In the Company of Men." *The News-Times.* 15 Sep. 1997, 6 Sep. 2000 <http://www.newstimes.com/archive97/sep1597/mvd.htm>.

Holmlund, Chris. "Visible Difference and Flex Appeal: The Body, Sex, Sexuality, and Race in the 'Pumping Iron' Films." *Out of Bounds: Sports, Media, and the Politics of Identity.* Ed. Aaron Baker and Todd Boyd. Bloomington: Indiana UP, 1997, 145–60.

hooks, bell. *Outlaw Culture: Resisting Representations.* New York: Routledge, 1994.

———. *Reel to Real: Race, Sex and Class at the Movies.* New York: Routledge, 1996.

Horrocks, Roger. *Masculinity in Crisis.* New York: St. Martin's Press, 1994.

In the Company of Men. Dir. Neil LaBute. Tristar, 1997.

Jeffords, Susan. *Hard Bodies: Hollywood Masculinity in the Reagan Era.* New Brunswick: Rutgers UP, 1994.

———. *The Remasculinization of America: Gender and the Vietnam War.* Bloomington: Indiana UP, 1989.

Kerfoot, Deborah, and David Knights. "Management, Masculinity and Manipulation: From Paternalism to Corporate Strategy in Financial Services in Britain." *Journal of Management Studies* 30 (1993): 659–77.

Kilduff, Martin, and Ajay Mehra. "Hegemonic Masculinity Among the Elite: Power, Identity, and Homophily in Social Networks." Cheng 115–29.

Kimmel, Michael, and Michael Messner, eds. *Men's Lives,* 2nd ed. Boston: Allyn & Bacon, 1995.

Kirkham, Pat, and Janet Thumim. eds. *Me Jane: Masculinity, Movies and Women.* New York: St. Martin's Press, 1995.

———. *You Tarzan: Masculinity, Movies and Men.* New York: St. Martin's Press, 1993.

Kohn, Dan. "In the Company of Men." 12 Sep. 1997. 6 Sep. 2000 <http://xent.ics.uci.edu/FoRKo-archive/sept97/0080.html>.

Konek, Carol Wolfe, and Sally L. Kitch, eds. *Women and Careers: Issues and Challenges.* Thousand Oaks: Sage, 1994.

Laclau, Ernesto, and Chantale Mouffe. *Hegemony and Socialist Strategy: Towards a Radical Democratic Politics.* London: Verso, 1985.

Linstead, Stephen. "Abjection and Organization: Men, Violence, and Management." *Human Relations* 50 (1997): 1115–45.

Lyman, Peter. "The Fraternal Bond as a Joking Relationship: A Case Study of the Role of Sexist Jokes in Male Group Bonding." Kimmel and Messner 86–96.

Mandziuk, Roseann M. "Necessary Vigilance: Feminist Critiques of Masculinity." *Critical Studies in Media Communication* 17 (2000): 105–8.

Marshall, Judi. "Viewing Organizational Communication From a Feminist Perspective: A Critique and Some Offerings." *Communication Yearbook* 16 (1993): 122–43.

Martin, Joanne. "Deconstructing Organizational Taboos: The Suppression of Gender Conflict in Organizations." *Organization Science* 1 (1990): 339–59.

McGee, Michael Calvin. "Text, Context, and the Fragmentation of Contemporary Culture." *Western Journal of Communication* 54 (1990): 274–89.

Mechling, Elizabeth W., and Jay Mechling. "The Jung and the Restless: The Mythopoetic Men's Movement." *Southern Communication Journal* 59 (1994): 97–111.

Mills, Albert, and Peter Chiaramonte. "Organization as Gendered Communication Act." *Canadian Journal of Communication* 16 (1991): 381–98.

Mulvey, Laura. "Afterthoughts on 'Visual Pleasure and Narrative Cinema.'" *Feminism and Film Theory*. Ed. Constance Penley. New York: Routledge, 1988, 69–79.

———. "Visual Pleasure and Narrative Cinema." *Screen* 16 (1975): 6–18.

Mumby, Dennis K. "Organizing Men: Power, Discourse, and the Social Construction of Masculinity in the Workplace." *Communication Theory* 8 (1998): 164–83.

Nakayama, Thomas K. "Show/down Time: 'Race,' Gender, Sexuality, and Popular Culture." *Critical Studies in Mass Communication* 11 (1994): 162–79.

———. "The Significance of 'Race' and Masculinities." *Critical Studies in Media Communication* 17 (2000): 111–13.

Neale, Steve. "Masculinity as Spectacle: Reflections on Men and Masculinity in Mainstream Cinema." Prologue. Cohan and Hark 9–20.

Nkomo, Stella M. "The Emperor Has No Clothes: Rewriting 'Race in Organizations.'" *Academy of Management Review* 17 (1992): 487–513.

Office Space. Dir. Mike Judge. Twentieth Century Fox, 1999.

Orbe, Mark P. "Constructions of Reality on MTV's 'The Real World': An Analysis of the Restrictive Coding of Black Masculinity." *Southern Communication Journal* 64 (1998): 32–47.

Penley, Constance, ed. *Feminism and Film Theory*. New York: Routledge, 1988.

Powrie, Phil. *French Cinema in the 1980s: Nostalgia and the Crisis of Masculinity*. Oxford: Clarendon, 1997.

Pringle, Rosemary. "Bureaucracy, Rationality, and Sexuality: The Case of Secretaries." *The Sexuality of Organization*. Ed. Jeff Hearn, Deborah Sheppard, Peta, Tancred-Sheriff, and Gibson Burell. Newbury Park, CA: Sage, 1989, 158–77.

Projansky, Sarah, and Kent A. Ono. "Strategic Whiteness as Cinematic Racial Politics." *Whiteness: The Communication of Social Identity*. Ed. Thomas K. Nakayama and Judith N. Martin. Thousand Oaks, CA: Sage, 1999, 149–74.

Ray, Sid. "Hunks, History, and Homophobia: Masculinity Politics in *Braveheart* and *Edward II*." *Film and History* 29 (1999): 22–31.

Robinson, Sally. *Marked Men: White Masculinity in Crisis*. New York: Columbia UP, 2000.

Roper, Michael. " 'Seduction and Succession': Circuits of Homosocial Desire in Management." Collinson and Hearn 210–26.

Rosener, Judy B. "Ways Women Lead." *Harvard Business Review* 6 (1990): 119–25.

Rotundo, E. Anthony. *American Manhood: Transformations in Masculinity From the Revolution in the Modern Era*. New York: Basic Books, 1993.

Savran, David. "The Sadomasochist in the Closet: White Masculinity and the Culture of Victimization." *Differences: A Journal of Feminist Cultural Studies* 8 (1996). 13 Jun. 2001 <www.softlineweb.com/softlineweb/bin/KaStasGw.exe>.

Sedgwick, Eve K. *Between Men: English Literature and Male Homosocial Desire*. New York: Columbia UP, 1985.

Segal, Lynne. *Slow Motion: Changing Masculinities, Changing Men*. New Brunswick: Rutgers UP, 1990.

Seidler, Victor J. *Rediscovering Masculinity: Reason, Language and Sexuality*. New York: Routledge, 1989.

———. *Unreasonable Men: Masculinity and Social Theory*. New York: Routledge, 1994.

Sloop, John M. "Mike Tyson and the Perils of Discursive Constraints: Boxing, Race, and the Assumption of Guilt." *Out of Bounds: Sports, Media, and the Politics of Identity*. Ed. Aaron Baker and Todd Boyd. Bloomington: Indiana UP, 1997, 102–22.

Smith, Christopher. " 'Fight Club' Worth Catching in Video Version." *Bangor Daily News*. 27 April 2000. 6 Sep. 2000 <http://proquest.umi.com/pqdweb>.

Spitzack, Carole. "The Production of Masculinity in Interpersonal Communication." *Communication Theory* 8 (1998): 143–64.

———. "Theorizing Masculinity Across the Field: An Intradisciplinary Conversation." *Communication Theory* 8 (1998): 141–43.

Stecopoulos, Harry, and Michael Uebel, eds. *Race and the Subject of Masculinities.* Durham: Duke UP, 1997.

Stukator, Angela. " 'Soft Males,' 'Flying Boys,' and 'White Knights': New Masculinity in *The Fisher King.*" *Literature Film Quarterly* 25 (1997): 214–21.

Tasker, Yvonne. "Dumb Movies for Dumb People: Masculinity, the Body, and the Voice in Contemporary Action Cinema." Cohan and Hark 230–44.

———. "Fists of Fury: Discourses of Race and Masculinity in the Martial Arts Cinema." Stecoupoulos and Uebel 315–36.

———. *Spectacular Bodies: Gender, Genre and the Action Cinema.* New York: Routledge, 1993.

Trethewey, Angela. "Disciplined Bodies: Women's Embodied Identities at Work." *Organization Studies* 20 (1999): 423–50.

Trujillo, Nick. "Hegemonic Masculinity on the Mound: Media Representations of Nolan Ryan and American Sports Culture." *Critical Studies in Mass Communication* 8 (1991): 290–308.

Van Zoonen, Liesbet. *Feminist Media Studies.* Thousand Oaks, CA: Sage, 1994.

Watson, Shane. "Give Us Manly Men with Stubby Fingers!: Shane Watson on the Macho Revival." *The Guardian.* 26 May 2000. 6 Sep. 2000 <http:/www.proquest.umi/pqdweb>.

West, Candace, and Don H. Zimmerman. "Doing Gender." *Gender and Society.* 1 (1987): 125–51.

Wiegman, Robyn. "Feminism, 'The Boyz,' and Other Matters Regarding the Male." Cohan and Hark 173–93.

Willis, Paul. *Learning to Labor: How Working Class Kids Get Working Class Jobs.* New York: Columbia UP, 1977.

Willis, Sharon. *High Contrast: Race and Gender in Contemporary Hollywood Film.* Durham: Duke UP, 1997.

Wittig, Monique. *The Straight Mind and Other Essays.* Boston: Beacon, 1992.

Wolf. Dir. Mike Nichols, Columbia, 1994.

Voicing Your Opinion
Slaves with White Collars: Persistent Performances of Masculinity in Crisis
Karen Lee Ashcraft and Lisa A. Flores

1. Do you see evidence of hegemonic masculinity in other forms of media? How is this type of masculinity presented? What is the intention of this portrayal of men/masculinity? What is the effect that this presentation has on boys and men?

_____

_____

_____

_____

_____

2. How have patriarchal systems impacted your life? Do you work to resist or challenge patriarchal thinking? Why or why not?

_____

_____

_____

_____

_____

3. What current films and movies portray rigid gender identities? Are there any films or movies that portray alternative perspectives? What impact do these films and movies have on the ways that people present their gender identities?

_____

_____

_____

_____

_____

Taking a Position

Instructions

Write a paper that asserts a position regarding one of the topics listed on this page. These topics relate to the information discussed in Part Two, *The Process of Becoming Gendered.*

- **Explain your understanding of the term.** Use two academic sources to support this understanding. You should utilize research that will help you promote the position that you intend to take in your paper. For example, if you have chosen to argue that masculinity is a biological construct that is strongly influenced by the sex hormone testosterone, your sources should offer information regarding biological approaches to gender development or specific information about the influence of testosterone on masculine communication.

- **State a position that you are taking in regards to the term.** This should be articulated in a clear and concise way. (No more than three sentences.)

- **Write a thorough explanation of your position.** You should have at least three supporting statements for your position and offer multiple examples of why you believe these statements to be valid in relationship to the communication of gender identity.

- **Address any obvious and/or subtle disputes to your position.** Why would someone disagree with you or take a different position? What might that be? How does your position respond or challenge these disputes?

Suggestions

Think carefully about your position before you write about it. Your position should reflect a strongly supported opinion that you hold.

Make sure that you are asserting *your* position rather than attacking another's position.

Choose useful and credible academic sources to back up your position.

Topics

transgender	intersexuality	femininity
masculinity	heterosexuality	heteronormativity
transexuality	queer	androgyny

3 The Process of Communicating Gender

The Impact of Communication

The next step in the process of learning about gender and communication is to specifically focus on elements of gendered communication behavior in relationship to the ways that people use and interpret verbal and nonverbal cues. We consider verbal cues to be those pertaining to written or spoken language. Nonverbal cues are all forms of communication that are not considered verbal. These include facial expressions, body movement, the use of touch, and so on.

In *"The Process of Communicating Gender,"* we examine the ways that language formation and usage are influenced by familial and societal expectations of gender. We also look at the effects that gendered language has on women and men. Are there instances when language fails us because of the expectations we face as gendered individuals? What are the links between gendered use of language and our perceptions of women and men? How does societal power influence gendered communication displays?

This section also examines the ways that language and nonverbal communication operate within our personal relationships. What is the role of masculinity or femininity in the development of close personal relationships? How are these relationships positioned within a society that has specific norms for gendered verbal and nonverbal communication?

We have included three articles in this section that cover a variety of topics that pertain to gendered communication. The articles explore theories of gendered language usage, nonverbal performances of gender, and masculine communication within friendships.

Terms
Language
practices
Muted groups
Theory
building

MUTED GROUP THEORY[1] AND COMMUNICATION
Asking Dangerous Questions

CHERIS KRAMARAE

This article is about muted group theory and whether women are more constrained than men in what they can say, when, and with what results. Language has always been constructed primarily by men, so language reflects men's experiences, leaving women muted. The article looks at whether the theory is outdated, and whether we have ignored language as an important component of knowledge building. The article also examines whether or not muted group theory addresses multicultural and global issues.

B y using "Dangerous Questions" in my title, I mean to encourage questions that push us into considering some thoughts that may feel shaky—about language and communication and the relation to our linguistic, social, legal, economic and environmental existence. In short I begin with uncertainties.

My own interest in the muted group theory came from uncertainty and lots of questions about women and language. In the late 1970s, I had a contract to write a book (*Women and Men Speaking: Frameworks for Analysis*) on what was then called "language and sex" research. I was searching for a theoretical framework through which to discuss the various studies that had been done under that topic, and finally realized I was more interested in the very differing and useful questions that arise from each of the theories I was considering than in finding one that worked "best." Among the final four theories I chose was muted group theory (Ardener 1975).

It was liberating to consider and assess the theories individually, seeing whether they seem to align with experiences, my own and others, and the existing feminist research findings; and whether the theories seemed useful in guiding further study. The assumptions, scope, and uses of each varied. Each provided a kind of a story, or an outline, introducing fresh ways of seeing the world, and helping the exploration of some of the concerns we have.

When the focus is on women, men and communication, the muted group theory suggests the following:

- In many situations, women are more constrained than are men in what they can say, when, and with what results.

- Accepted language practices have been constructed primarily by men in order to express their experiences. This means that women are constrained (muted).

A similar problem exists for other groups in our culture that are in asymmetrical relationships. Interest and concern are about not just gender differences, but a range of other marginalizing differences as well (including race, sexuality, age, and class).

Muted group theory suggests that people attached or assigned to subordinate groups may have a lot to say, but they tend to have relatively little power to say it without getting into a lot of trouble. Their speech is disrespected by those in the dominant positions; their knowledge is not considered sufficient for public decision-making or policy making processes of that culture; their experiences are interpreted for them by others; and they are encouraged to see themselves as represented in the dominant discourse. The theory further suggests that an important way that a group maintains its dominance is by stifling and belittling the speech and ideas of those they label as outside the privileged circle.

In the past decades the muted group theory has encouraged attention to the knowledge and mutedness of many women. Many in our field have found that muted group theory has helped inform us about how power functions in our talk and writing, and language. It, along with other frameworks, has encouraged many of us in the U.S. and the U.K. to investigate the restrictions of a white, middle-class, hetero-male oriented language upon those whose perspectives of the world may be quite different.

Now-Three Plus Decades Later, What's a Woman and Her Communication Theories to Do?

Theory is not a word I use a lot. I can more easily talk about ideas, concepts, analyses, interpretations, and frameworks. Certainly, in the past, most academic social theories have not been any close friends of mine. Most of the theories have seemed to encode the interests, experiences, and beliefs of cultural others. Male-centered social science theories have so often been so damaging to so many women. And, as bell hooks points out, even feminist theory is often of little assistance to women trying to bring about changes in their everyday situations (1990, 9). (See Foss, Foss and Griffin [1999] for critiques of communication theories and reconceptualizations of scholarship and theory; also see Orb, this issue) on uses of theorizing.

In recent years there has been a lot of theorizing that deals explicitly with efforts to include the knowledges and creativities of many women as well as those of men; those theories are usually labeled feminist theories and are often marginalized, their exploratory potential still often limited to discussions in campus gender and women's studies classes.

Academic theorizing often has political consequences for pedagogy, as well as for issues and actions way beyond the classroom. So it's valuable to take a look at what we want from communication theory and theories. We can always change our minds, and should, as the social dimensions of the world, and our understanding, of those dimensions change. Right now, I am interested in theories that

- Help me make sense of relationships, and provide a connection of issues in my own life and the world more generally.

- Encourage me to consider and learn from the experiences of others, as I learn how environments and experiences shape the way each of us thinks and acts.

- Help me challenge the adequacy of male-centered science and social science based on theories that so often have mislabeled or ignored the varied and persistent material conditions of women's lives. I want analytical tools to make gender politics more visible to myself and others.

- Help me work, with others, on constructive social change in meaningful, healthy, and useful political practices.

Theories in academe usually come from faculty mentors, intellectual interests and training—and personal experiences. Charlene Spretnak writes about the process through which our understandings of the world can grow through an "embodied epistemology" (Spretnak 1991, 149). There is, of course, no universal woman, women's experience, or women's movement. Any feminist theory needs to deal with diversity and divisions, including such hierarchies as class, race, age, sexual orientation. Years ago, Sandra Harding warned against trying to ground feminism in a single political-philosophical theory (1986, 664). Decades ago, The Combahee River Collective (1983) pointed out that white women in the U.S. have made little effort to understand and lessen racism in our own thinking.

Muted group theory resonates with many, including many women and men of color; I know this from the messages I receive from students and others. For many, the theory is real and compelling. It helps explain what's going on in a way that is easily understood, believable, and useful. (In fact, I often think the muted group theory is too easily "understood." Often students do not explore beyond the brief description of the theory offered in textbooks.) So the interest in the theory continues. Yet, among those feminists who would label themselves as theorists and researchers, there does not seem to be a lot of explicit interest in muted group theory outside communication research. However, I do not think that this is because it is closely considered and then rejected as not being of value. Very similar concepts are often talked about under other names and descriptions.

Just a couple examples: Marilyn Frye has written, "[W]omen's existence is both absolutely necessary to and irresolvably problematic for the dominant reality" as the unseen "background" whose labors ensure the seamless performances of those whose identity is "foreground" (1983, 166–67). She uses the metaphor of the stage, with the stagehands, women, as those who work in the background while the men (primarily Anglo, economically affluent, Christian, heterosexual) repeatedly enact a fictionalized reality naturalized through its repetition. Jennifer Hornsby writes, "The use of language as it is passed down to her can seem to falsify a woman's experience, and present an obstacle to discussing it authentically. Women have been described as 'silenced' (Hornsby 2000, 88). She cites Tillie Olsen's discussions of silence (1978), and Catherine MacKinnon's (1987) claim that "pornography silences women." So, is there still a need for the muted group theory?

Is the Muted Theory Now Outdated?

Has it lost its oomph? Where is the radical, and sheer joy of discovery and defiance? In the 1970s and 1980s the muted group theory challenged the status quo, of academe at least. While many women reading and discussing the theory thought it made sense of their own lives, many other academics thought it wasn't proper—theoretically and politically. It certainly wasn't like any of the theories in introductory communication texts then. It was pretty radical.

If the muted group theory now isn't as exciting as it once seemed, this is due in part to its success and the success of theories and actions related to it. Shirley and Edwin Ardener suggested that there are "dominant modes of expression in any society which have been generated by the dominant structure within it" (E. Ardener 1975, 20). They wrote that women, due to their structural places in society, have different models of reality. Their perspectives are "muted" because they do not form part of the dominant communication system of the society. These days many people say about this, "Yeah. And?"

So the theory isn't as daring and exciting as it once was. In addition, feminist defiance now seems more muted. There is not as much against the grain transgressive behavior on campuses and U.S. communities. So, is the muted group theory really outdated or . . . ?

Is Our Focus on the Latest in Academic Theorizing Limiting Our Imagination and Understanding?

It is informative to read the "old" feminist work from the 1970s and 1980s in the U.S. (Leathwood 2004, 456) and many other countries, and to see just how radical many of the writings and actions of feminists remain to our eyes and ears. We certainly should not ignore or throw out this theorizing without a lot of deep consideration. Often in academe, many of us have a tendency to make past writings seem simplistic and ineffective, in order to promote the newness and excitement of our new ideas. Often the presentation of the older ideas are false or incomplete. (E.g., there was a lot of critical discussion of difference and identity in the 1970s, but one wouldn't also get a sense of this from contemporary feminist theorizing.) Diana Leonard (2000) cautions that, since the 1980s, feminists have grown up with "just a caricature" of what was achieved by earlier feminism. I join the others who encourage us all to go back and look at the work of earlier theorists and activists. (See discussion of this in, for example, McLaughlin 2003; Rowland and Klein 1996; Stanley and Wise 2000). Many feminists have offered us a rich variety of adventuresome, creative, and profound ideas. In inspecting and respecting their work, we can interrogate their ideas, consider the insights of women of many experiences, and build on their contributions.

Can We Take the Very UnAmerican (or Unmodern) Stance of Thinking That We Do Not Necessarily Have Better Questions, Ideas, Answers, Solutions Than All Those Who Have Come Before?

Can we think of ourselves as related to, and students of, many other generations? Can we learn from their experiences and words? Can we learn anything useful today from looking at the force of the various prohibitions against women speaking in various locations, to various people—and the creativity with which they have responded to such proscriptions? (See, for example, analysis of the rhetoric of women through the 19th and 20th centuries, Campbell 1989).

It might be a real surprise for many people to learn that the "strong-minded women" publishing in the 1860s have a lot to say to us about a lot of "contemporary issues" such as false generics; the constant labeling of women's speech as different and inferior to men's; the belittling use of terms of endearment such as "doll" and "angel"; the restrictions on women's voices in "public" places; the exclusive language of the churches; the double standard of sexual activity; the "disgrace" of Harvard and Yale in their treatment of women; street harassment; rape; wife beatings; the danger to women of the military; the bondage of fashion; equal pay for equal work; and the arrest of prostitutes but not of the men visiting them. In words they described as "hard as cannonballs," they criticized the "Noodledom" and the "Mandom" that laughs at independent women, and the "mischievous words" such as *white* and *male* used in legal documents. Their word coinages and their critique of the form and content of men's talk often seems very fresh (and, alas, still very radical) today. For example, they advised women to "honor their own names and then keep them" whether married or unmarried. (See Rakow and Kramarae 1991; Russo and Kramarae 1991.)

Those of us interested in the muted group theory can see that more than 100 years ago, women were talking about the different perspectives of women and men because of their different experiences. They were talking about the assumed primacy of men's vision and the danger it poses to everyone. And they were often doing it with great insight, visionary passion, invention, and humor.

Because the work of these earlier strong-minded women was not carried forward in traditional analyses and bibliographies, Betty Friedan didn't know about them and so had to write of the "problem with no name." Edwin Ardener wrote of "The Problem." The strong-minded women of the 19th century had many descriptive names for the many related problems they experienced. Thanks to the work of many feminist historians, we now at least know the names of some of these women, yet we seldom extend our reading and thinking about our history and culture beyond the time and publications of our own adulthood. It's an exclusion that limits our imagination and understanding.

When we are looking for the theory and practice to guide our social revolution, we need to search for and mine our feminist past. Today, in thinking about how we speak, many academics are more likely to make reference to Aristotle and Plato of Greek antiquity than to the many women who during the past 150 years have focused on who speaks about what, when, where and why and with what consequences. *They* dared to speak and write, but their voices have since been muted.

Has Language and Communication Study Lost Its Importance in Feminist Theorizing?

In 1994 bell hooks wrote: "Recent discussions of diversity and multiculturalism tend to downplay or ignore the questions of language" (173). During the 1960s, 1970s and 1980s, language critiquing was very important to feminist ideology. Linguistic reform was important for our thinking about ourselves, our culture, and possibilities for change. The representations and images of women and men were scrutinized and critiqued, and alternatives offered. However, in the 1980s and 1990s, criticisms of the sexist and racist language used by dominant individuals, groups, and institutions gave way to projects of locating and understanding differences within the category of "women," a word which has been broken open with discussions of representations, self-identity, and lived experience.

Many recent books of feminist theory have pages of discussions of body, desire, difference, sexuality, globalization, queerness, postcolonialism, pleasure, identity, and gender—but relatively few explicit discussions of the ways language and communication practices impose restrictions, and offer some solutions, to social problems.

Interest in destabilizing many key terms (e.g., of sexual differences) continues, but seemingly mostly as efforts to sort out meanings. Stated much too simply, while there was once heavy critique of the language of the "oppressors," now there is much reflection among feminists about being bodies in the world. (Of course, academic feminists have always been involved in many projects. But I mention here some of the most publicized theoretical debates.[2])

Knowledge remains language-based. But lately there isn't as much interest in what social injustices are reflected by language, what is missing in language, and how it can be reworked.[3] This has implications for how much interest in muted group theory that we can expect from feminist theorists.

The study of language is both more serious and less central than it was 30 years ago. While there are many current books that focus on the terminology of feminist theory, with intense explorations of such terms as gender, sex, gay, queer, heterosexuality, identity, body, and difference, at least in U.S. academic feminism there is not as much mucking about with the language. Some words are contested, but few words are created. Current academic writing about contested terms is more likely to stay within institutional methods of deconstruction and politics. Many of our concerns are now less revolutionary and much more institutionalized. There is less talk these days about the magic of, and discomfort with, the words we use, and less talk about alternative ways of communicating. While people in communication studies continue to closely inspect language usage and forms of communication, this study no longer is considered a core concern of feminists in all disciplines. There do not seem to be many groups of Gloriously Growling Guerilla Girls inside academe these days.

We might want to revisit and refresh our conversations about our language and communication. In talking about a vital activity of the women's movement, Dorothy Smith (2004) writes about the importance of women's getting together as women, speaking together as women, and discovering dimensions of "our" experience that had no previous expressions or explanations (265). In this context, "women" is, she writes, particularly nonexclusive and open-ended, always subject to the disruption of women who enter speaking from difference experiences (265). Although power relationships will always operate, they operate within common situated and political structures. Many women share many common problems, if not a common outlook (McLaughlin 2003, 68). A critical reconsideration of the muted group theory suggests that gender conceptions are still worthy of being taken seriously but it does not require an assumption that all the differences are between women's and men's experiences.

Does Muted Group Theory Differ from Standpoint Theory?

The interest, in standpoint theory, of the ways that politics, culture, and language function as "prison-houses" of "conventional" knowledge, is closely related to the interest in muted group theory. The linkages between the theories can be seen when looking at some central standpoint arguments:

- Societal hierarchies include divisions of race, ethnicity, sexuality, gender, and class.
- The resulting sexual division of labor means that women and men are likely to have different understandings of the world.
- People in privileged positions do not acknowledge the processes that place them in their position and have a vested interest in not seeing those processes.
- The viewpoints of marginalized people reveal the bias of the privileged positions.
- Recognizing and understanding the problems of the marginalized can help resolve major social problems and create a better society for everyone.
- There is no view from nowhere, no neutral observers. (See the discussion in McLaughlin 2003, 56, 60–61; and Wood, this issue.)

One way muted group theory and standpoint theory differ is in the point of view involved. The muted group theorist is likely to look out on the social landscape and see/hear the groups she then describes. The standpoint theorist is more apt to listen to the labels individuals use to describe their places in society. Both theories are concerned about labels and language use and exclusion, although the uses of muted group theory are often more directly focused on the ways women's and men's world views are reflected or not in the language and at the amount and types of speech practices of women and men.

Neither muted group theory nor standpoint theory suggest that any individual or group has the only truth, but both argue for the importance of challenging and providing alternatives to dominant explanations of the way the world works. As one writer, drawing on the work on Black feminist standpoint perspectives by Patricia Hill Collins and others, warns, "Challenges to oppressive ideas about the inferiority of Black people are unlikely to come from the dominant modes of thought which produced the ideas in the first place" (McLaughlin 2003, 64).

What about the Questions of Essentialism?

How can we use the muted group theory yet avoid the mistaken generalizations about people and language, wherever the errors have come from—intent, sloppy thinking and talking, ignorance, ethnocentrism . . . ?

While the muted group theory grows out of and respects cultural differences of many sorts, some users of the theory may rather too easily neglect the complexities of gender, class, and race domination. Some people using the theory have boxed oppression within discrete, binary categories, e.g., women/men; AfricanAmericans/EuroAmericans. A focus only on the categories of women and men, or white and non-white, for example, is simplistic and ignores other forms of struggle, as women of color, in particular, have made very clear during the past decades. Universalistic, ahistorical categories are not useful in promoting alternative ways of seeing the world and our places in it. Differences need to be considered in many, changing ways—including as experience, as social relations, as subjectivity and as identity (Brah 1992).

However, María Lugones (1991) and Marilyn Frye (2000) caution that claiming theoretical concern about essentialism may be a cover for worries about difficult, direct, and responsible engagement with women of color. As they argue, calling "anti-essentialism" a cure for racism, sexism and ethnocentrism in feminist theorizing may foreclose the needed investigation and analysis of the kinds of generalizations, errors and mistakes involved.

Further, our accusations of feminist theories as essentialist often portray our most groundbreaking, intellectual "mothers" as merely unsophisticated, simplistic, and way, way passé. As Marilyn Frye (2000) points out, when we make those easy accusations we add to the historical process of burying some of the most creative women thinkers, who have helped us, as feminists, get to our current questions and critiques (55). We need to go back to original sources to see that most feminist theorists, including those using the muted group theory, have recognized that women are not a homogeneous mass.

Does Muted Group Theory Deal Adequately with the Complexities of Gender, Class, and Race Domination—i.e., with All the Networks within the Networks?

No, but what theory does? Who knows and can adequately explain the complexities? No one, which is why we call them complexities. However, most feminist theorists are trying. The popular presentation of gender and language research is something else. Gender relations and tensions are easier (seemingly less sensitive) for most media personnel to deal with than are race or class relations and tensions.

For example, the two-culture approach to "gender troubles" continues to receive a lot of attention in the "popular media." We've all heard the simple generalizations from talk show hosts. Many people don't want to deal with power issues or actual situations. The "two, separate but equal, cultures" explanation is an easy, comfortable one for them. So, they argue, of course there are "misunderstandings" when speakers of these two cultures come together.

Not so, suggests the muted group theory. When power differentials are present "misunderstandings between cultures" won't do as an explanation. Yet there's been a problem even with much of our more nuanced discussions when race and gender become moribund categories. I'm not sure that the muted group theory helps us a lot in thinking about the shifts in groups and identities that each of us makes all the time. These days, most of us know, and know to say, that identity is never unitary and is seldom consistent. And that it is often imposed, not chosen.

We can say this, but how do we express this knowledge in our theorizing and other actions? For example, Evelynn Hammonds asks the following Difficult and Critical Questions:

> . . . if the sexualities of black women have been shaped by silence, erasure, and invisibility in dominant discourses, then are black lesbian sexualities doubly silenced? What methodologies are available to read and understand this perceived void and gauge its direct and indirect effects on that which is visible? (2002, 261)

Women of color and lesbian feminists have suggested that the "multiple jeopardy" of their lives raises serious questions about the validity of any generalizations based on gender. If gender is always meshed with race, class, ethnicity and sexual orientation, when what framework that isolates gender is of any value (Hawkesworth 2000, 142–143)?[4]

These musings and thinking about the future of muted group theory lead to even further questions, which need to be explored as we move ahead since our time and space for query here are inevitably limited. Among those questions are the following:

How Can (If It Can) Muted Group Theory Help Us Attend More to Matters of Class? In What Ways Can Muted Group Theory Encourage and Assist Us in Understanding the Relationship of Mutedness and Large Economic Structures?

When We Use Muted Group Theory, Do We Name the "Oppressed" but Not the "Oppressors"?

Inferring but not stating the agent may be an act of self-protection. However, fixing names to the ones we call "oppressors" may be necessary in order to have clear discussions about the perceived source of problems and remedies. (See discussion in Salem 1980.)

Have We Been Specific Enough about the Types of "Obstacles," "Power," "Dominance," and "Repression"?

What Language Do We Use in Talking and Writing about the Theory? Do Many of Us Use "Safe," "High," "Man-Made" Academic Language?

When We Talk about "Languages" Do We Try to Understand the Spaces between and Among Lexicon; Syntax; Language; Dialects? Between What Is Written and What Is Spoken?

What about Nonverbals? Can We Use the Muted Group Theory to Help Us Discuss the Many Ways We Communicate or "Talk Behind Backs"?

How Is the Muted Group Theory Related to the Communities of Practice Analytical Framework and Ideas about Change?

As the framework is elaborated by Penny Eckert and Sally McConnell-Ginet (1992), studying the informal and institutionalized practices in a community acknowledges that people speak out of aspects of identity that include age, ethnicity and social status—as well as the gender expectations that wash around us locally and beyond. This framework encourages us to see the practices of a community as not static but subject to contestation and change (Walsh 2001, 206). In this way it usefully expands the basic principles of the muted group theory.

Does the Muted Group Theory Encourage Talk of Victimization?

I would suggest that used simplistically, it could. However, it has often been used to encourage us to search for many kinds of resistance, defiance. For me, the theory and related theories, along with some fortunate access to publishers, led me to work with many others on a feminist dictionary and a feminist encyclopedia. Part of that work was illustrating how the construction and maintenance of gendered inequality has led many "victims" to many acts of resistance.

Are We Too Ready to Hear Similarities in the Silence and Mutedness Across Groups and Situations? Or Too Ready to Equate Silence and Mutedness?

This issue of silence is one of those fraught with complexity. For some it is "to be broken, shattered, shredded; . . . through which one must pass in order to join one's voice . . ." to others (Yamamoto, 1993, 131). For others silence may involve culturally appropriate interaction. Silence isn't always a problem to be "solved," although it *is* something to be understood. Silence is not only a result of oppression, nor is it synonymous with passivity. It can be alive with possibilities and welcomed (Stone 2002, 16–41). There is the silence that provides meditative clarity; a gift from all the noises of urban life; a time of respect for ourselves; a feeling of connectedness when experienced with others; a rest from the imperative and compulsion to speak. And it can also be a protection that should not be pried away by well-wishing others.

Silence is as complex as speech.

bell hooks has written about how being pushed to the margins and recognizing that *can* lead to a self-determined voice, at least over a period of time. She initially learned to "talk a talk that was itself a silence" and experienced intense confusion in her efforts to speak and write (1989, 6–7). As she points out, silence can be a protective, necessary, and proper response. More recently she has written about the "broken voice" of many African Americans, pointing out that when you "hear the broken voice you also hear the pain contained within that brokenness—a speech of suffering; often it's that sound nobody wants to hear" (2004, 153). However, she continues by writing that marginality is more than deprivation, it is also the site of radical possibility, of resistance (156).

How Global Is the Muted Group Theory? And Is Muted Group Theory Useful When Studying Globalization?

(See Hellinger and Bussmann 2001 for a wide-ranging discussion of labeling-meaning systems, problems and transformations in many languages and cultures.)

To say that race and gender are relational and dynamic categories, involved in local, national, and global power is easy. But beyond that . . . is difficult

Most of us English speakers don't read the work of feminists and other activists writing in other languages, even if translations are available. Those feminists who speak several languages, and those who feel the global dominance of English, often speak particularly meaningfully of the colonizing forces of a dominant language group. English has come to be the language of worldwide commerce, with the muting of voices/perspectives in other languages in many situations. Current questions and discussions of identity in U.S. feminism usually do not seem to have an immediate link to global economic and environment issues.

Today we need once again to collectively figure out how to empower more participants around the world. Who is speaking and writing about women's rights, citizenship and political representation? Further, whose interpretive voices are heard, whose voices are muted or silenced?

What Would a Revised Muted Group Theory Look Like?

One of my questions here would be: How organic, how whole, can we make our theories? Muted group theory certainly is made to deal with many kinds of human hierarchies and domination. But it doesn't seem immediately valuable in helping us with our increasing, if dragging, sensibility that our environments are not "natural" adversaries of humans, and that humans are only a member, a very enmeshed member (along with trees, salmon, creeks, newts), of this universe.

On one level we know that all life is connected. But separation is a widely practiced illusion, one that many of us are good at and one that aids in the creation of sexism and racism. Letting go of the "us and them" mentality and all the ways we hold ourselves separate is quite a task. Theories can help us challenge established practices, in part by listening to those who see assumptions where most of us see only what is a given.

Poet and theorist Adrienne Rich gives us earthy advice:

> Theory—the seeing of patterns, showing the forest as well as the trees—theory can be a dew that rises from the earth and collects in the rain clouds and returns to the earth over and over. But if it doesn't smell of the earth, it isn't good for the earth. (1986, 213–214)

In sum, the muted group theory is one resource that has provided assistance for many people, in guiding some of our thoughts and actions about communication. It has been used to make gender and race politics more visible and to highlight some reasons and potential solutions for the disarray and violence many of us see all around. Theories can be enabling, but they can also be harmful, so they need to be chosen and used carefully. We need to ask healthy dangerous questions of our theories.

ENDNOTES

1. Because some students are confused by the "Muted" in Muted Group Theory, I have tried some other labels. With a playful nod to Shirley Ardener, I mention several of them here.

   Muffling Action Theory: Muffling as in deadening sounds, or making obscure. But it sounds too car-repair-ish. Maybe Muffled Group Theory.

   The Hushing Theory: Hushing as in quieting. But it sounds too library-based.

   Voiced-Over Theory: Voiced-over as in covered up. But it sounds as if the theory is voiced-over.

   Smothered Voices Theory: As in concealed, suppressed, extinguished. And smothered includes an "other". But it sounds a bit like mushroom sauce over potatoes.

   Stifled Group Theory: As in interrupted, cut off, limited by the exercise of power or control. Calls up some Archie Bunker images, but it seems to work.

2. Of course, interest in the power and possibility of language continues in many places, particularly by those in communication and philosophy. Influential theorists such as Luce Irigaray continue to revise and thicken their analysis of language in terms of cultural change. (See, for example, Deutscher [2002].) Judith Butler (2001) takes the current academic debates about the terms "sex" and "gender" into a discussion of their current uses and effects in international politics. Sharon Marcus writes of rape "as a scripted interaction that takes place in language" (2002, 172); she argues that the grammar of violence identifies women as objects of violence and of property (175).

3. This is not to ignore the important reclaiming of such previously derogatory labels such as bitch, ho', black, nigger, and queer (see Chen 2001, 241–243). bell hooks (2004) writes about her continued use of "old codes, words like 'struggle, marginality, resistance'," knowing that they are no longer popular or "cool" but knowing that they evoke and affirm important political legacies, and that they can be renewed and given new meanings (159).

4. See, for example, Elena Stone's 2002 account of voice and silence, as she sought out and listened to "ordinary people" saying "extraordinary things" about their experience and knowledge. See also Joanna Kadi (2000) who writes, "Puh-lease. Everybody in my neighborhood . . . grasped the idea [of multiple realities] with no problem. We lived it. We had our reality, the bosses had theirs, and we understood them both. Theorists like W. E. B. Du Bois wrote about double consciousness, whereby African Americans are aware of their own reality as well as that of white people, at the turn of the [last] century" (334). She goes on to say that academic theorists don't attribute these ideas to people of color or the working-class people who have lived and understood them for centuries. Instead, academics steal these ideas and clothe them in language so inaccessible that only a few can discuss them (334).

Voicing Your Opinion
Muted Group Theory and Communication: Asking Dangerous Questions
Cheris Kramarae

1. What labels do you use to talk about gender? How/what do these labels include, exclude, erase, and imply?

   _____

   _____

   _____

   _____

   _____

2. The author writes about the ways that muted group theory helps us think about how people experience shifts in identities. We understand that it is important to look at intersections of identity as they pertain to the topic of gender. What communication have you witnessed and experienced at the intersections of class, race, sexuality, and gender? What language do we use to navigate these intersections? What changes in language do you anticipate as we continue to recognize gender as a multifaceted concept?

   _____

   _____

   _____

   _____

   _____

3. What might your world (family, work, school, etc.) be like if the history of muted groups could be changed? What impact might the past have on the present if we had historical discursive inclusion from *all* groups of people? What groups are currently muted? How will the muting of these groups affect your world in the future?

   _____

   _____

   _____

   _____

   _____

Terms
Male behavior
Female behavior
Identity
Transformation

MY LIFE AS A MAN

ELIZABETH GILBERT

This article chronicles a woman transforming herself into a man and what she learns about nonverbal communication—how to sit, how to act, what to say, what to wear, how to behave so that the general public interacts with her as a man.

My penis is made of birdseed. Allow me to be more precise. My penis is a common unlubricated, unribbed, latex Trojan condom, stuffed with birdseed. I could have stuffed it with cotton balls, or I could have been lazy and just shoved a sock down my pants, but I was advised by a famous drag king that a condom stuffed with birdseed really makes your best penis. And the drag king, it turns out, was absolutely correct in her advice.

My birdseed penis is indeed dense, pliant and reassuringly solid. And it's always semierect, which is probably more than you can say for yours.

Admittedly, my penis is not the biggest in the world. Believe me, I've seen some penises in my day, and I know what's out there. My penis is modest, just under six inches long. Sure, I could have made it bigger—birdseed is cheap, after all—but I don't need to define my masculinity in this manner. I don't need to attach my entire self-identity to my penis. Because I know who I am, goddamn it.

I am Luke Gilbert. I am a *man*. Hear me roar.

The first time I was ever mistaken for a boy, I was 6 years old. I was at the county fair with my beautiful older sister, who had the long blond tresses one typically associates with storybook princesses. I had short messy hair, and I had scabs all over my body from falling out of trees. My beautiful sister ordered a snow cone. The lady at the booth asked, "Doesn't your little brother want one, too?"

I was mortified. I cried all day.

The last time I was mistaken for a boy was only a few weeks ago. I was eating in a Denny's with my husband, and the waitress said, "You fellas want some more coffee?"

This time I didn't cry. It didn't even bother me, because I've grown accustomed to people making the mistake. Frankly, I can understand why they do. I'm afraid I'm not the most feminine creature on the planet. I don't exactly wish to hint that Janet Reno and I were separated at birth, but I do wear my hair short, I am tall, I have broad shoulders and a strong jaw, and I have never really understood the principles of cosmetics. In many cultures, this would make me a man already. In some very primitive cultures, this would actually make me a king.

But sometime after the Denny's incident, I decided, *Ah, to hell with it. If you can't beat 'em, join 'em.* What would it take, I began to wonder, for me to actually transform into a man? To live that way for an entire week? To try to fool everyone?

It could be amusing. I've always been a little titillated by the fantasy of transformation. (I hope to God I'm not the only person who daydreams about how I would change my identity to escape the FBI should there ever be a nationwide manhunt for me due to, say, a bum murder rap.)

Spending a week trying to pass as a man could also be the most intimate way yet for me to explore my lifelong fascination with men. I've always been fixated by men. I spend a lot of time in their company, very comfortable and happy there. And one of my favorite feelings is the fleeting sense I get when I'm with a group of guys who have become so relaxed around me that they've forgotten I am not one of them: They have permitted me to slip invisibly inside their most secret world. And what better way to explore that feeling (and push it) than by actually becoming a man; if only for a moment?

Fortunately, I have plenty of male friends who rally to my assistance, all eager to see me become the best man I can possibly be. And they all have wise counsel to offer about exactly How to Be a Guy:

"Interrupt people with impunity from now on," says Reggie. "Curse recklessly. And never apologize."

"Never talk about your feelings," says Scott. "Only talk about your accomplishments."

"The minute the conversation turns from something that directly involves you," says Bill, "let your mind wander and start looking around the room to see if there's anything nearby you can have sex with."

"If you need to win an argument," says David, "just repeat the last thing the guy you're fighting with said to you, but say it much louder."

So I'm thinking about all this, and I'm realizing that I already do all this stuff. I always win arguments, I'm shamefully slow to apologize, I can't imagine how I could possibly curse any more than I already goddamn do, I've spent the better part of my life looking around to see what's available to have sex with, I can't shut up about my accomplishments, and I'm probably interrupting you right this moment.

Another one of my friends warns, "You do this story, people are gonna talk. People might think you're gay." Aside from honestly not caring what people think, I'm not worried about this possibility at all. I'm worried about something else entirely: that this transformation thing might be *too easy* for me to pull off.

What I'm afraid I'll learn is that I'm *already* a man.

My real coach in this endeavor, though, is a woman. Her name is Diane Torr. Diane is a performance artist who has made her life's work the exploration of gender transformation. As a famous drag king, she has been turning herself into a man for twenty years. She is also known for running workshops wherein groups of women gather and become men for a day.

I call Diane and explain my goal, which is not merely to dress up in some silly costume but to genuinely pass as male and to stay in character for a week.

"That's a tough goal," Diane says, sounding dubious. "It's one thing to play with gender for the afternoon, but really putting yourself out there in the world as a man takes a lot of balls, so to speak. . . ."

Diane agrees to give me a private workshop on Monday. She tells me to spend the weekend preparing for my male life and buying new clothes. Before hanging up, I ask Diane a question I never thought I would ever have to ask anybody:

"What should I bring in terms of genitalia?"

This is when she informs me of the ingredients for my penis.

"Of course," I said calmly.

I write *birdseed* on my hand, underline it twice and make a mental note to stay away from the aviary next week.

I spend the weekend investing my character.

One thing is immediately clear: I will have to be younger. I'm 31 years old, and I look it, but with my smooth skin, I will look boyish as a man. So I decide I will be 21 years old for the first time in a decade.

As for my character, I decide to keep it simple and become Luke Gilbert—a midwestern kid new to the city, whose entire background is cribbed from my husband, whose life I know as well as my own.

Luke is bright but a slacker. He really doesn't give a damn about his clothes, for instance. Believe me, I know—I'm the one who shopped for Luke all weekend. By Sunday night, Luke owns several pairs of boring Dockers in various shades of khaki, which he wears baggy. He has Adidas sneakers. He has some boxy short-sleeve button-down shirts in brown plaids. He has a corduroy jacket, a bike messengers's bag, a few baseball caps and clean underwear. He also has, I'm sorry to report, a really skinny neck.

I haven't even met Luke yet, but I'm beginning to get the feeling he's a real friggin' geek.

The transformation begins painlessly enough.

It starts with my hair. Rayya, my regular hairdresser, spends the morning undoing all her work of the past months—darkening out my brightest blond highlights; making me drab, brownish, inconsequential; chopping off my sassy Dixie Chick pixie locks and leaving me with a blunt cut.

"Don't wash it all week," Rayya advises. "Get good and greasy; you'll look more like a guy."

Once the hair is done, Diane Torr gets to work on me. She moves like a pro, quick and competent. Together we stuff my condom ("This is the arts-and-crafts portion of the workshop!"), and Diane helps me insert it into my Calvins. She asks if I want my penis to favor the left or right side. Being a traditionalist, I select the right. Diane adjusts me and backs away; I look down and there it is—my semierect penis, bulging slightly against my briefs. I cannot stop staring at it and don't mind saying that it freaks me out to no end. Then she tries to hide my breasts. To be perfectly honest, my breasts are embarrassingly easy to make disappear. Diane expertly binds them down with wide Ace bandages. Breathing isn't easy, but my chest looks pretty flat now—in fact, with a men's undershirt on, I almost look as if I have well-developed pectoral muscles.

But my ass? Ah, here we encounter a more troublesome situation. I don't want to boast, but I have a big, fat, round ass. You could lop off huge chunks of my ass, make a nice osso buco out of it, serve it up to a family of four and still eat the leftovers for a week. This is a women's ass, unmistakably. But once I'm fully in costume, I turn around before the mirror and see that I'm going to be OK. The baggy, low-slung pants are good ass camouflage, and the boxy plaid shirt completely eliminates any sign of my waist, so I don't have the girlie hourglass thing happening. I'm a little pear-shaped, perhaps, but let us not kid ourselves, people. There are pear-shaped men out there, walking among us every day.

Then Diane starts on my facial transformation. She has brought crepe hair—thin ropes of artificial hair in various colors, which she trims down to a pile of golden brown stubble. I elect, in homage to Tom Waits, to go with just a small soul patch, a minigoatee, right under my bottom lip. Diane dabs my face with spirit gum—a kind of skin-friendly rubber cement—and presses the hair onto me. It makes for a shockingly good effect. I suggest sideburns, too, and we apply these, making me look like every 21-year-old male art student I've ever seen. Then we muss up and darken by eyebrows. A light shadow of brown under my nose gives me a hint of a mustache. When I look in the mirror, I can't stop laughing. *I am a goddamn man, man!*

Well, more or less.

Diane looks me over critically. "Your jaw is good. Your height is good. But you should stop laughing. It makes you look too friendly, too accessible, too feminine." I stop laughing. She stares at me. "Let's see your walk."

I head across the floor, hands in my pockets.

"Not bad," Diane says, impressed.

Well, I've been practicing. I'm borrowing my walk from Tim Goodwin, a guy I went to high school with. Tim was short and slight but an amazing basketball player (we all called him "Tim Godwin"), and he had an athletic, knee-knocking strut that was very cool. There's also a slouch involved in this walk. But it's—and this is hard to explain—a *stiff* slouch. Years of yoga have made me really limber, but as Luke, I need to drop that ease of motion with my body, because men are not nearly as physically free as women. Watch the way a man turns his head: His whole upper torso turns with it. Unless he's a dancer or a baseball pitcher, he's probably operating his entire body on a ramrod, unyielding axis. On the other hand, watch the way a woman drinks from a bottle. She'll probably tilt her whole head back to accommodate the object, whereas a man would probably hold his neck stiff, tilting the bottle at a sharp angle, making the bottle accommodate *him*. Being a man, it seems, is sometimes just about not budging.

Diane goes on to coach my voice, telling me to lower the timbre and narrow the range. She warns me against making statements that come out as questions, which women do constantly (such as when you ask a woman where she grew up and she replies, "Just outside Cleveland?"). But I don't do that begging-for-approval voice anyway, so this is no problem. As I'd suspected, in fact, all this turning-male stuff is coming too easily to me.

But then Diane says, "Your eyes are going to be the real problem. They're too animated, too bright. When you look at people, you're still too engaged and interested. You need to lose that sparkle, because it's giving you away."

The rest of the afternoon, she's on me about my eyes. She says I'm too flirtatious with my eyes, too encouraging, too appreciative, too attentive, too *available*. I need to intercept all those behaviors, Diane says, and erase them. Because all that stuff is "shorthand for girl." Girls typically flirt and engage and appreciate and attend; men typically don't. It's too generous for men to give themselves away in such a manner. Too dangerous, even. Granted, there are men in this world who are engaging, attentive and sparkly eyed, but Luke Gilbert cannot be one of them. Luke Gilbert's looks are so on the border of being feminine already that I can't afford to express any behavior that is "shorthand for girl," or my cover is blown. I can only emit the most stereotypical masculine code, not wanting to offer people even the faintest hint that I'm anything but a man.

Which means that gradually throughout Monday afternoon, I find myself shutting down my entire personality, one degree at a time. It's very similar to the way I had to shut down my range of physical expression, pulling in my gestures and stiffening up my body. Similarly, I must not budge emotionally. I feel as if I'm closing down a factory, silencing all the humming machines of my character, pulling shut the gates, sending home the workers. All my most animated and familiar facial expressions have to go, and with them go all my most animated and familiar emotions. Ultimately, I am left with only two options for expression—boredom and aggression. Only with boredom and aggression do I truly feel male. It's not a feeling I like at all, by the way. In fact, I am amazed by how much I don't like it. We've been laughing and joking and relating all morning, but slowly now, as I turn into Luke, I feel the whole room chill.

Toward the end of the afternoon, Diane gives me her best and most disturbing piece of advice.

"Don't look at the world from the surface of your eyeballs," she says. "All your feminine availability emanates from there. Set your gaze back in your head. Try to get the feeling that your gaze originates from two inches behind the surface of your eyeballs, from where your optic nerves begin in your brain. Keep it right there."

Immediately, I get what she's saying. I pull my gaze back. I don't know how I appear from the outside, but the internal effect is appalling. I feel—for the first time in my life—a dense barrier rise before my vision, keeping me at a palpable distance from the world, roping me off from the people in the room. I feel dead eyed. I feel like a reptile. I feel my whole face change, settling into a hard mask.

Everyone in the room steps back. Rayya, my hairdresser, whistles under her breath and says, "Whoaaa . . . you got the guy vibe happenin' now, Luke."

Slouching and bored, I mutter a stony thanks.

Diane finally takes me outside, and we stroll down the street together. She has dressed in drag, too. She's now Danny King—a pompous little man who works in a Pittsburgh department store. She seems perfectly at ease on the street, but I feel cagey and nervous out here in the broad daylight, certain that everyone in the world can see that my face is covered with fake hair and rubber cement and discomfort. The only thing that helps me feel even remotely relaxed is the basketball I'm loosely carrying under my arm—a prop so familiar to me in real life that it helps put me at ease in disguise. We head to a nearby basketball court. We have a small crowd following us—my hairdresser, the makeup artist, a photographer. Diane and I pose for photos under the hoop. I set my basketball down, and almost immediately, a young and muscular black guy comes over and scoops it off the pavement.

"Hey," he says to the crowd. "Whose basketball is this?"

Now, if you want to learn how to define your personal space as a man, you could do worse than take lessons from this guy. His every motion is offense and aggression. He leads with his chest and chin, and he's got a hard and cold set of eyes.

"I said, whose basketball is this?" he repeats, warning with his tone that he doesn't want to have to ask again.

"It's hers," says my hairdresser, pointing at me.

"Hers?" The young man looks at me and snorts in disgust. "What are you talkin' about, *hers?* That ain't no *her.* That's a guy."

My first gender victory!

But there's no time to celebrate this moment, because this aggressive and intimidating person needs to be dealt with. Now, here's the thing. Everyone on the court is intimidated by this guy, but I am not. In this tense moment, mind you, I have stopped thinking like Luke Gilbert; I'm back to thinking like Liz Gilbert. And Liz Gilbert always thinks she can manage men. I don't know if it's from years of tending bar, or if it's from living in lunatic-filled New York City, or if it's just a ridiculous (and dangerously naive) sense of personal safety, but I have always believed in my heart that I can disarm any man's aggression. I do it by paying close attention to the aggressive man's face and finding the right blend of flirtation, friendliness and confidence to put on my face to set him at ease, to remind him: *You don't wanna hurt me; you wanna like me.* I've done this a million times before. Which is why I'm looking at this scary guy and I'm thinking, *Give me thirty seconds with him and he'll be on my side.*

I step forward. I open up my whole face in a big smile and say teasingly, "Yeah, that's my basketball, man. Why, you wanna play? You think you can take me?"

"You don't know nothin' about this game," he says.

In my flirtiest possible voice, I say, "Oh, I know a *little* somethin' about this game. . . ."

The guy takes a menacing step forward, narrows his eyes and growls, "You don't know *shit* about this game."

This is when I snap to attention. This is when I realize I'm on the verge of getting my face punched. What the hell am I doing? This guy honestly thinks I'm a man! Therefore, my whole cute, tomboyish, I'm-just-one-of-the-guys act is not working. One-of-the-guys doesn't work when you actually *are* one of the guys. I have forgotten that I am Luke Gilbert—a little white loser on a basketball court who has just challenged and pissed off and *flirted* with an already volatile large black man. I have made a very bad choice here. I've only been on the job as a male for a few minutes, but it appears as though I'm about to earn myself a good old-fashioned New York City ass-kicking.

He takes another step forward and repeats, "You don't know shit about nothin'."

"You're right, man," I say. I drop my eyes from his. I lower my voice, collapse my posture, show my submission. I am a stray dog, backing away from a fight, head down, tail tucked. "Sorry, man. I was just kidding. I don't know anything about basketball."

"Yeah, that's right," says the guy, satisfied now that he has dominated me. "You don't know shit."

He drops the ball and walks away. My heart is slamming. I'm angry at my own carelessness and frightened by my newfound helplessness. Luke didn't know how to handle that guy on the court, and Luke almost got thrown a beating as a result (and would have deserved it, too—the moron). Realizing this makes me feel suddenly vulnerable, suddenly aware of how small I've become.

My hands, for instance, which have always seemed big and capable to me, suddenly appear rather dainty when I think of them as a man's hands. My arms, so sturdy only hours before, are now the thin arms of a weenie-boy. I've lost this comfortable feeling I've always carried through the world of being strong and brave. A five-foot-nine-inch, 140-pound woman can be a pretty tough character, after all. But a five-foot-nine-inch, 140-pound man? Kinda small, kinda wussy. . . .

I take myself out to dinner that night and eat my first steak of the week. The waitress gives me little notice until I ask where the men's room is. Then she hesitates. She looks at me hard for a fast moment. I might be paranoid, but it certainly seems that she's wondering what the hell I am. And then she makes a quick decision, the way we all make decisions about weird people we meet from time to time. She decides: *OK, if you say so.* If I claim to be a man, then she'll let me be one. She points me to the men's room.

I use the bathroom in the stall without incident. But I'm not happy about her reaction. I decide that tomorrow morning I'll add more facial hair, give myself a thicker goatee. Maybe even get glasses.

On the walk home, I'm so distracted by thoughts of how to improve my chances of passing that I don't even notice when my penis comes loose. Before I know it, the thing has slipped out of my briefs, tumbled down my pant leg and fallen onto the sidewalk at my feet. I pick up my penis and stuff it into my pocket, trying hard not to make eye contact with anyone.

My world-famously tolerant husband seems to have no trouble with my transformation at first. He unwinds my breast bandages every night before bed and listens with patience to my complaints about my itching beard. In the mornings before work, he binds up my breasts again and lends me his spice-scented deodorant so I can smell more masculine. We vie for mirror space in the bathroom as he shaves off his daily stubble and I apply mine. We eat our cereal together, I take my birth control pills, I pack my penis back into my slacks. . . .

It's all very domestic.

Still, by Wednesday morning, my husband confesses that he doesn't want to hang around with me in public anymore. Not as long as I'm Luke. It's not that he's grossed out by my physical transformation, or threatened by the sexual politics at play, or embarrassed by the possibility of exposure. It's simply this: He is deeply, emotionally unsettled by my new personality.

"I miss you," he says. "It's seriously depressing for me to be around you this way."

What's upsetting to Michael is that as a man, I can't give him what he has become accustomed to getting from me as a woman. And I'm not talking about sex. Sex can always be arranged, even this week. (Although I do make a point now of falling asleep immediately after it's over, just to stay in character.) What Michael hates is that I don't engage him anymore. As Luke, I don't laugh at my husband's jokes or ask him about his day. Hell, as Luke, I don't even have a husband—just another drinking buddy whose jokes and workday concerns I don't really care about. Michael, still seeing his wife under her goatee, keeps thinking I'm mad at him, or—worse—bored by him. But I can't attend to him on this, can't reassure him, or I risk coming across like a girl.

The thing is, I don't like Luke's personality any more than Michael does. As Luke, I feel completely and totally bound—and not just because of the tight bandage wrapped around my chest. I keep thinking back to my drag-king workshop, when Diane Torr talked about "intercepting learned feminine habits." She spoke of those learned feminine habits in slightly disparaging terms. Women, she said, are too attentive, too concerned about the feelings of others, too *available*. This idea of women as lost in empathy is certainly a standard tenet of feminism (Oprah calls it the Disease to Please), and, yes, there are many women who drown in their own overavailability. But I've never personally felt that attentiveness and engagement are liabilities. As a writer—indeed, as a *human being*—I think the most exciting way you can interact with this fantastic and capricious world is by being completely available to it. Peel me wide open; availability is my power. I would so much rather be vulnerable and experience existence than be strong and defend myself from it. And if that makes me a girlie-girl, then so be it—I'll be a goddamn girlie-girl.

Only, this week I'm not a girl at all. I'm Luke Gilbert. And poor Luke, I must say, is completely cut off from the human experience. The guy is looking at the world from a place two inches behind his eyeballs. No wonder my husband hates being around him. I'm not crazy about him myself.

On Wednesday afternoon, my friend Cree agrees to pose as my fiancée so we can shop for an engagement ring. The jeweler, recognizing that I'm the guy and therefore the one with the cash, is completely attentive to me, completely ignoring the lady. This is fine with me. The lady keeps asking about sizing and number of carats and quality, anyhow, when all I care about is price. The lady and I actually have a little tiff about this subject, right there in the store ("All you ever care about is money!" she accuses me), and we decide to not to buy a ring that day. The jeweler shoots me a sympathetic look on our way out.

I get the same sympathetic look from the waiter that night at the vegetarian restaurant where I have taken my "girlfriend" Jana for a date. Jana does all the ordering while I banter with the guy, saying, "I don't know anything about this kind of rabbit food. Before I started dating her, it was nothing but burritos and beer for me."

The waiter replies, "Well, sir, that's who keeps us in business—women. I mean, look around. Practically everyone in this restaurant is female."

Yes, I notice, practically everyone in this restaurant is female.

"That's good for me and you, though, right?" I say to the waiter, and he gives me a sly wink when my girlfriend isn't looking.

Later that night, I'm walking home alone. Just ahead of me, a blond woman steps out of a bar, alone. She's screamingly sexy. She's got all the props—the long hair, the tiny skirt, the skimpy top, the wobbly stiletto heels, the eternal legs. I walk right behind this woman for several blocks and observe the tsunami she causes on 23rd Street in every man she passes—everyone has to react to her somehow. What amazes me, though, is how many of the men end up interacting with *me* after passing *her*. What happens is this: She saunters by, the guy stares at her in astonishment and then makes a comment about her to me because I'm the next man on the scene. So we have a little moment together, the guy and me, in which we share an experience. We get to bond. It's an icebreaker for us.

The best is the older construction worker who checks out the babe, then raises his eyebrows at me and declares: "Fandango!"

"You said it!" I say, but when I walk on by, he seems a little disappointed that I haven't stuck around to talk more about it with him.

This kind of interaction happens more than a dozen times within three blocks. Until I start wondering whether this is actually the game. Until I start suspecting that these guys maybe don't want to talk to the girl at all, that maybe they just desperately want to talk to *one another*.

Suddenly, I see this sexy woman in front of me as being just like sports; she's an excuse for men to try to talk to one another. She's like the Knicks, only prettier—a connection for people who otherwise cannot connect at all. It's a very big job, but I don't know if she even realizes she's doing it.

The next day, feeling confident in my manhood now, I wander into the most famous Armed Forces Recruiting center in the country—the one located right in the heart of Times Square, where decades of young men and runaways have enlisted in moments of desperation after having spent all their money on whores and booze. I'm wearing my baseball cap backward, and I am carrying my brilliant new prop of young manhood: a sixteen-ounce bottle of Mountain Dew. I am greeted by a trim, serious staff sergeant, who does not give so much as a blink of indication that he thinks I'm anything but what I say I am—namely, Luke Gilbert, a slackabout guy who is absolutely clueless as to what to do with the rest of his life.

"I dunno, dude," I say. My posture is appalling. My disrespect in calling this NCO "dude" is appalling. I am the very picture of a kid who needs his wussy ass whipped into manhood by the United States Armed Services. "My dad thinks maybe I should enlist. You guys pay for college, right?"

"What branch of the military are you interested in, son?" asks the sergeant.

"I dunno. . . ." I gaze around at the posters on the walls as though this is the first I've heard there were different branches in the military. My eyes alight on the image of a soaring fighter plane, and I point to that. "That looks cool, dude. Airplanes . . ."

"It is cool," says the sergeant, who is smiling now, too. Turns out he's an air-force officer himself. He tells me I made the right choice. "You into driving fast, man?"

"Yeah," I shrug. "I guess. . . ."

"You'll love flying fast, then, man. You wanna punch holes in the sky?"

"Yeah." I shrug again. "I guess. . . ."

"You into that Rambo stuff, man?"

Am I into that *Rambo* stuff? Did he just say that? Is this line actually part of the official United States Armed Services recruiting pitch? Do they say this to girls, too? *Am I into that Rambo stuff?*

"Yeah," I say. I take a long swig of my Mountain Dew without tilting my head back to accommodate the bottle. "Rambo stuff is pretty excellent."

"We can get you there, Luke," says the staff sergeant. "You can do anything you want in the air force."

We talk for a while about basic training and military housing and college-tuition programs. He gives me a bunch of brochures. This is going so well and so smoothly now that I can't help messing with the man.

"You know what I'm really into, though?" I say.

"What's that, Luke?"

"Musical theater." I offer this for no reason I will ever be able to understand.

His facial expression does not change, but his eyes go a little dead on me. "Oh, yeah?"

"Yeah," I continue. "I was in a bunch of plays in high school. Singing, dancing. We did *Gypsy.* I like that stuff a lot. Can I do stuff like that in the air force?"

I have to give this man his full credit. He doesn't choke. He takes out a pen and writes something down on a business card for me.

"Tops in Blue," he says. "That's the name of the air-force performing troupe. They travel all over the world, singing and dancing. All that stuff you like. They're very good. Better than anything you'll see on Broadway. Maybe you could join up with them."

"Tops in Blue," I repeat, really enthusiastic now. "That's awesome! You mean, I could sing and dance but still be in the air force? Still do that Rambo stuff?"

"You can do anything you want in the air force, Luke."

"This is wicked awesome," I say.

Finished with our business now, we shake hands. But as I'm walking out the door and back into the bustle of Times Square, the staff sergeant has one last thing to say.

"Hey, Luke! Promise me you won't chill out on enlisting! Make it happen, man! Don't lose the fire!"

"I won't lose the fire!" I yell back at him. "I promise!"

My buddy Peter Richmond takes me out to a ball game that evening. Peter knows a lot about sports (happening, in fact, to have spent the past decade writing about that subject for this very magazine), and he determines that we must go see the Mets play, because Shea Stadium is ten times more macho than Yankee Stadium. Indeed, the game is a great celebration of masculinity. Everywhere around me, I see and smell masculinity, pure and obvious.

A few rows away from us, a fight breaks out between two enormous guys who relentlessly pound the living hell out of each other until even more enormous security guards drag them apart. When I ask Peter if he has any idea what this violent tussle was all about, he replies, "My guess is they were disagreeing with each other about something."

Behind me are three boys all under the age of 11, brothers who are studying classic guy behavior under the masterful care of their dad. The boys keep screaming down to the field that Atlanta Braves slugger Chipper Jones is a fuckin' faggot, a fuckin' homo, a fuckin' pussy, etc. All the while, their sage father nods and beams at his boys with approval.

Yes, my grasshoppers, you have learned well. Chipper Jones is a fuckin' pussy, and soon you will be men. . . .

After watching Glendon Rusch pitch seven innings of shutout ball, I realize I have reached a great milestone in my life. It is time to go to the bathroom. Let me clarify—it is time to go to the bathroom in the men's room at Shea Stadium.

"Pete," I say, "I'm going in there."

He reads my face and knows immediately what I'm talking about. Gravely, he asks, "Do you need me to come with you, Luke?"

"No. This is something I need to do on my own."

Peter understands. "Sometimes a girl's gotta do what a guy's gotta do," he says.

It is a long walk to the men's room at Shea Stadium when you're just a nervous girl with a dream and a crotch full of birdseed. My knees are rickety with real fear, but I decide to approach this task as if it were a bank holdup: I'll hit it quick, do the job in a flash, then bolt for the exit before anyone gets a good look at me. I figure I'll be back at my seat in forty-eight seconds.

What I do not count on, though, is the line. There is, it turns out, a massive line in which I must wait for ten minutes with dozens of other men. I have never seen a line for a men's room in my life (isn't that the whole goddamn point of being a guy?), and then I realize—of course, of course, I'm at a baseball game; it's nothing but men here. I look longingly over to the women's bathroom across the hall, which for the first time in human history stands vacant and welcoming. Finally, my line pushes forward and I enter the inner sanctum. I am verily overwhelmed by what I see. This is not some hygienic genderless rest room of some kindly New York bistro; this is the piss trench of Satan himself. The place reeks, the floor is soaked, and the air is filthy. There are men everywhere, and they are urinating on everything.

At last a stall opens up and I make my move. There's no lock. The door remains slightly ajar. I remain calm. I perform swiftly. I am buckling up my pants and readjusting my penis when I notice him. There is an 8-year-old boy watching me through the wide crack in the stall door. *How long has he been standing there? What has he seen?* Or—a more troubling thought—*what* hasn't *he seen?* Our eyes meet. I'm scared, but he's more scared. He's pale and panicked, like that Amish boy in *Witness* right after he sees the murder in the train-station toilet. I hold the kid's gaze as I finish adjusting my trousers. He can't look away from me. Nor I from him. I narrow my eyes at him and summon all my mighty powers of feminine communication to convey this simple message in my stare: *So help me God, kid, if you breathe a word of my secret to anyone, I will hunt you down, I will find out where you live, I will come to your house in the middle of the night, and I will dress your goddamn mother up like this.*

The boy backs away slowly. I exit the men's room fast. I don't even bother to wash my hands. Then again, neither does anyone else in here.

Final score: Mets 1, Braves 0.

Friday afternoon I head uptown to check out the auto show at the convention center. I mill around there for a couple of hours, talking to other men about the features of the new Lincoln SUVs. For some reason, I decide it is here at the auto show that I will commence my attempt to pick up girls—the ultimate test of my manhood. I spot two cute young ones standing in the lobby and make my first approach. My move is based completely on advice from a guidebook I have recently purchased called *How to Pick Up Girls!* This book has been most informative, filled with some of the most appallingly bad advice I've ever encountered. According to the book, asking for information is a good way to break the ice with women. So when I finally make my move, I begin by asking, "Excuse me, do you young ladies know where the ticket booth is?"

"No," says the tall one.

We are standing thirteen feet away from the ticket booth.

"Do you maybe wanna go find the ticket booth with me?" I ask.

The short one speaks, arching her brows and saying icily: "Our *husbands* are buying us tickets, OK?"

I'm tempted to reply, "Hey, I have a husband, too, bitch, but that wouldn't keep me from showing a little *common human politeness* to a nervous girlie-man with patchy facial hair who approaches me at a friggin' auto show!"

But instead I shrug and say merely, "Well, enjoy the cars, girls. . . ."

After a few more hours of similar encounters, it gradually dawns on me that an auto show is perhaps not the best place in the world to cruise for chicks. Any chick at an auto show is probably there with some guy. Or else she's the kind of chick who goes to auto shows alone, and that kind of chick probably doesn't go for wussy guys like me. Disappointed, I head for the men's room. I stare in the mirror above the sink.

Women hate you, the mirror tells me.

But I'm not such an unattractive guy, I protest inwardly, trying to get my confidence back up. *A little nerdy but not unattractive. I just need to find the kind of girl who likes that sort of thing. But where?*

That night, taking a friend's advice, I go out drinking in the East Village, where seven out of ten young men look just like Luke Gilbert. I end up at a bar that is crawling with really cute pierced-nosed girls. I'm wondering whom I should try to pick up when an opportunity falls into my lap. A pretty red-haired girl in a black camisole walks into the bar alone. She has cool tattoos all over her arms. The bouncer says to her, "Hey, Darcy, where's your crowd tonight?"

"Everyone copped out," Darcy says. "I'm flying solo."

"So lemme buy you a drink," I call over from the bar.

"Rum and Coke," she says, and comes over to sit next to me.

Fandango!

We get to talking. Darcy's funny, friendly, from Tennessee. She tells me all about her roommate problems. She asks me about myself, but I don't share—Luke Gilbert is not available for sharing. Instead, I compliment Darcy on her pretty starfish necklace, which Darcy tells me was a gift from a childhood neighbor who was like a grandmother to her. I ask Darcy about her job, and she tells me she works for a publishing house that prints obscure journals with titles like *Catfish Enthusiast Monthly*.

"Damn, and here I just let my subscription to *Catfish Enthusiast Monthly* run out," I say, and she laughs. Darcy actually does that flirty thing girls do sometimes where they laugh and touch your arm and move closer toward you all at the same time. I know this move. I've been doing this move my whole life. And it is with this move and this touch and this laugh that I lose my desire to play this game anymore, because Darcy, I can tell, actually likes Luke Gilbert. Which is incredible, considering that Luke is a sullen, detached, stiff guy who can't make eye contact with the world. But she still likes him. This should feel like a victory, but all I feel like is a complete shitheel. Darcy is nice. And here I'm lying to her already.

Now I really *am* a guy.

"You know what, Darcy?" I say. "I have to go. I'm supposed to hook up with some friends for dinner."

She looks a little hurt. But not as hurt as she would look if, say, we dated for a month and then she found out the truth about me.

I give her a little kiss good-bye on the cheek.

"You're great," I tell her.

And then I'm done.

Undoing It All Takes a Few Days

Rubbing alcohol gets the last of the spirit gum and fake hair off my face. I pluck my eyebrows and put on my softest bra (my skin has become chafed from days of binding and taping). I scatter my penis across the sidewalk for the pigeons. I make an appointment to get my hair lightened again. I go to yoga class and reawaken the idea of movement in my body. I cannot wait to get rid of this gender, which I have not enjoyed. But it's a tricky process, because I'm still walking like Luke, still standing like Luke, still thinking like Luke.

In fact, I don't really get my inner Liz back until the next weekend. It's not until the next Saturday night, when I am sitting at a bar on my own big fat ass, wearing my own girlie jeans, talking to an off-duty New York City fireman, that I really come back into myself. The fireman and I are both out with big groups, but somehow we peel off into our own private conversation. Which quickly gets serious. I ask him to tell me about the crucifix around his neck, and he says he's been leaning on God pretty hard this year. I want to know why. The fireman starts telling me about how his beloved father died this winter, and then his fiancée left him, and now the pressures of his work are starting to kill him, and there are times when he just wishes he could cry but he doesn't want people to see him like that. My guy friends are all playing darts in the corner, but I'm the one sitting here listening to this fireman tell me about how he never cries because his dad was such a hard-ass Irish cop, don'tcha know, because he was raised to hang so tough.

I'm looking right into this guy. I'm not touching him at all, but I'm giving him my entire self. He needs me right now, to tell all this to. He can have me. I've got my eyes locked on him, and I can feel how bad he wants to cry, and with my entire face I am telling this man: *Tell me everything.*

He says, "Maybe I was hard on her, maybe that's why she left me, but I was so worried about my father. . . ."

The fireman digs at his eye with a fist. I hand him a bar napkin. He blows his nose. He keeps talking. I keep listening. He can talk to me all night because I am unbound and I am wide-open. I'm open around the clock, open twenty-four hours a day; I never close. I'm really concerned for this guy, but I'm smiling while he spills his story because it feels so good to catch it. It feels so good to be myself again, to be open for business again—open once more for the rewarding and honest human business of complete *availability*.

Voicing Your Opinion
My Life as a Man
Elizabeth Gilbert

1. How are the author's experiences informed by the notion of gender as a performance? Was it more important for the author to *look* like a man or *act* like a man? Why?

   _____

   _____

   _____

   _____

   _____

   _____

2. Discuss Gilbert's experiences in relationship to the topic of nonverbal communication and agency. In what ways did her new gender allow for a greater sense of mental, physical and emotional control?

   _____

   _____

   _____

   _____

   _____

3. How does the author go about the "undoing" of Luke's gender? Why does this involve a large amount of time and effort? What does this suggest about the construction of gender via nonverbal communication?

   _____

   _____

   _____

   _____

   _____

   _____

139

Terms

Positional
identity

Relational
identity

Influence
of sports

Use of space

Symbolic
women

Covert intimacy

HEGEMONIC MASCULINITY, FRIENDSHIP, AND GROUP FORMATION IN AN ATHLETIC SUBCULTURE ♂ ♀

STEVEN J. HARVEY

This article is about how men create friendships within an athletic team. It examines the influence of sports teams on men's relationships and describes how men express intimacy within a team atmosphere. This atmosphere is influenced by men's team member status, the exclusion of women from the team, and the framing of the team as a band of brothers.

This qualitative study examines the construction of masculinity in a group of adult male athletes. A baseball team was selected consisting of twelve, white, middle-class athletes ranging between the ages of 18 and 30 years. This article examines the way hegemonic masculinity affects the formation of friendships and groups within the team subculture.

Male friendships were once believed to be strong, deep, and lasting, while female relationships were characterized as steeped in gossip, pettiness, and shallowness (Gilder, 1973; Tiger, 1969). However, such views of friendships became the target of criticism by feminist researchers (Messner, 1992a). Researchers found that many male friendships were, at times, built upon a foundation of destructive competition, homophobia, and emotional impoverishment (Balswick, 1976; Farrell, 1975; Fasteau, 1974; Messner, 1992a; Morin & Garfinkel, 1978).

By the mid-1980s, emotional boundaries, especially when contrasted to female relationships, characterized male friendships. According to Gilligan (1982) and Rubin (1983), men developed more "positional" identities, fearing intimacy, whereas women developed "relational" identities, fearing separation. Stated another way, the difference between male and female relationships was that women enjoy "deep, meaningful, and lasting friendships, while men have a number of shallow, superficial, and unsatisfactory acquaintances" (quoted in Messner, 1992a). In Rubin's (1985) words, male friendships are characterized by "bonding without intimacy," while female friendships emphasize more talk and sharing of intimate feelings. Male friendships are predicated more on external activities through which men can share the same emotional experience without having to reveal any details about their personal lives.

Sport provides a cultural avenue for men to share mutual experiences with other males that are often based on hegemonic masculinity. Male relationships in sport are complicated by what Reisman (1953) termed "antagonistic cooperation," which refers to a contradiction between what is portrayed to the public and what actually happens within the structure of the team. For example, while teams try to promote a "family" image and an unflinching esprit de corps, the day-to-day web of relationships among teammates is riddled with competition, often pitting one teammate against another. As Lasch (1979) observed, the "cult of teamwork conceals the struggle for survival" (p. 209). There is an intricate flux between friendly cooperation and antagonistic competition among teammates for playing time, awards,

141

accolades, and playing positions on the team. Consequently, male friendships in sport often unfold within a set of external experiences that allow men to experience mutual emotional responses from triumph to defeat, without encouraging an open exchange of intimate feelings and emotions via verbal communication.

A few researchers believe that it is misleading to compare male and female relationships based on a model of women's relationships (Swain, 1989) because it "belies the depth of affection that so many of these men express[ed] for each other" (Messner, 1992a; p. 223). Yet, when the examination of male friendships reveals such a detrimental effect on the quality and intimacy of the male relationship, it is difficult not to contrast and compare. The effect of the examination of male friendships in sport is one that has provided and continues to provide an understanding of the role that hegemonic masculine values play in the perpetuation of female subordination and gender inequality.

This article will discuss how a group of adult male baseball players negotiated the end of their athletic careers. Through a variety of qualitative research methods, this ethnographic work explored the impact of the social arena of sport on the construction of hegemonic masculinity among adult, nonprofessional athletes. The article begins with an analysis of how these male athletes organized themselves into distinct groups along hegemonic lines. The article then ties group development to the sex segregation of male athletes and provides an analysis of the male bonding effect sport has on the men who participate. Next, the article details how these male athletes shared their athletic lives with each other. Finally, there will be some concluding remarks on the effect of athletic participation for these men.

Methods

During the summer of 1997, I conducted an ethnographic study on a rural/suburban baseball team (I'll call it Bordertown) that consisted of twelve adult males who ranged in age from 18 to 30 and who came from white, middle-income backgrounds. The league that these men participated in was considered highly competitive and lasted approximately eight months. Utilizing three qualitative research methods, specifically non-participant observation, participant observation, and in-depth interviews, the study explored the social institution of sport and its impact on the way adult male athletes constructed their hegemonic masculinity.

In February of 1997, I initiated what would be an eight-month qualitative study that would take me through Bordertown's competitive summer sport season. The team was a highly competitive one that participated in local and regional competitions. Many of the team members played collegiate baseball, and some had professional tryouts with major league teams. I began my data collection with non-participant observation and observed the team preparing for its upcoming season. The practices were held at the local high school and were often in rainy, cold-weather conditions. This phase of the data collection allowed me to familiarize myself with the players, as well as individual and group dynamics, and facilitated the identification of a team hierarchy.

The Bordertown men were from white, middle-income families, attended some level of higher education, and held white-collar jobs, with the exception of Tony and Joe, who worked with a landscaping company and the Bordertown highway department, respectively. The other players' jobs were: physical education teacher, science teacher, sales manager, stockbroker, head of security, and other professional positions. The players who did not work full-time were either in college, or, in Bobby's case, high school. Most of the team played on multiple sport teams and participated in athletics several days a week. To them, sport was more than a hobby; it was their passion.

For the entire pre-season, I concentrated on non-participant observation. After several weeks, I began to interact with the team and became acquainted with each on a more personal level. It was at this juncture that I initiated the second phase of my data collection and began to interview. The interviews were conducted in a semistructured manner with prepared questions. They were tape-recorded and transcribed for accuracy and were pivotal in the transition from non-participant to participant observation.

The last phase of data collection was participant observation. During the remainder of the season, I interacted with the players on a personal level, talking to players on the bench, seeing players at local functions, going to local bars with them, and engaging in personal conversations that covered a range of topics from marriage to family life, to relationships, to school, and so on. This phase of data collection provided the "richest" data and allowed me, in a removed sense, to become a part of the team culture.

The data were transcribed and separated into non-participant and participant observation data and interviews. These two groups of data were then coded and categorized along different themes. This analysis was completed by hand, with several themes emerging from the data. This article is a portion from a larger study and examines the role sport played in the male grouping process. All of the players' names and the location of the team have been changed.

The Formation of Men's Groups in the Bordertown Team

The sporting environment brings men together and provides them with group norms, well-defined goals, and social acceptance. The formation of friendships within the team subculture revolves around the formation and maintenance of groups (Farr, 1992; Fasteau, 1974; Klein, 1991). Indeed, the processes surrounding group formation played an intricate role in the way the Bordertown baseball players developed their personal relationships. Within the team, there were three groups: a core group, a central group, and a peripheral group (see Figure 1). The core group consisted of Tony and Tom and, alongside it, the central group was composed of seven players. Three members of this central group (Joe, Bud, and Adam) would sometimes enter and exit the core group depending on changing situations and individual behavior. The other members of the central group (Buck, Pat, Kev, and Chuck) did not venture into the core leadership group. The remaining players (Bobby and Tim) and the player/coach (Al) made up the peripheral group. Women and males that were perceived not to fit into the team subculture populated the margins of this three-group team structure. These "marginalized" male outsiders were described basically as non-hegemonic males, that is, those who did not measure up to the manly character traits that were prioritized among the team members.

The three-group structure was readily recognized by the majority of the team and described by several players. Tom explained that there was a "nucleus of guys like myself, Tony, Joe, Bud, who like to do things. And the other guys just kind of get attached on the outside, and they work their way in." Similarly, Al, the coach, discussed how he adjusted his coaching around the implicitly defined groups:

> I think there's a nucleus that, if you keep them happy, everyone else feeds off of them. The nucleus here would be Tony, Tom. . . . Maybe just Tony and Tom. Because everybody else . . . I don't need to keep Buck happy because he'll be there all the time. I don't need to keep Joe happy because he'll always be there. . . . I can go all the way down the line, but the two guys I want to keep happy are Tony and Tom because everybody seems to feed off of them.

As Al explained, the existence of a "nucleus" within the team structure helped establish an overall emotional stability and exerted an impact on the way the players felt about themselves and others. Identifying Tony and Tom as the core group of the team, Al explained that the team's overall well-being depended a good deal on whether he could keep those two men happy. This was the first example of the team's internal divisions.

It was evident that the team accepted the internal division of players into groups as a natural and legitimate component of team life. While the players demonstrated a clear understanding of the internal divisions,

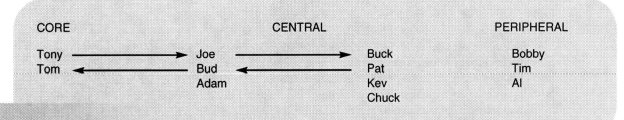

Figure 1
Male Grouping Model

they were less aware of how the divisions developed. From my perspective, it was clear that the groups were defined along hegemonic lines. Clearly, the most "macho" males occupied the positions in the core group. These men tended to be more aggressive, athletically talented, domineering, and vocal. While the core group usually contained only two men, a few more players fluctuated between the core group and the central group. I observed that movement in and out of the core group depended on the extent that a "bordering" player demonstrated hegemonic behavior. When the bordering players behaved in an aggressive and domineering manner, they temporarily became core group members. For example, when Adam began to discuss his sexual exploits with Tony or Tom, he became a central or core player and impacted the focus of the team at that moment. When Adam was quiet or talking to parents or other people in the stands, he removed himself from the core group and de-emphasized his role in determining team behavior. The temporary core group status was maintained until the players reverted back to less-hegemonic behavior. The central group consisted of players who were most often influenced by the behavior of the core group players and who ostensibly valued hegemonic qualities. The players who occupied the peripheral group tended to be less aggressive, domineering, and vocal, lacking the hegemonic masculine qualities that the core group members possessed.

Similar to the divisions of the baseball team, Thorne (1993) examined how "borders" were developed between young children on a playground. An important part of her analysis was the role that the control of space played in the maintenance of divisions between the boys and girls. Like the core group of the Bordertown baseball team, the boys dominated and controlled up to ten times more space than the girls. This "control of space (was viewed) as a pattern of claimed entitlement," prohibiting less aggressive teammates from contributing to team activities and behavior (Thorne, 1993, p. 83). For instance, during home field competitions, Tim and Bobby were often found off to the side or ten to fifteen feet away from the rest of the players. The central players were located at the score table behind the backstop, while the core players placed themselves in the dugout, closest to the action of the game and directly between the fans and home plate. The players rarely varied from these positions.

The development of the three groups within the baseball team played an intricate role in constructing and maintaining hegemonic masculinity. These groups developed a strong sense of commitment among the members that was largely "impenetrable" by outside individuals. Unlike Thorne's (1993) research, where the borders between the boys and girls fluctuated, it was very unlikely that an individual in the peripheral group would occupy a position in the core group for any significant length of time, if at all. Hence, the maintenance of masculine hegemony in the team subculture was, in part, secured by the internal, unyielding divisions of the team.

During the interviews, the Bordertown players pointed toward the athletic experience as a kind of "segregation effect." In other words, they described how they felt different from other people and, even though it was due to their privileged status, they perceived themselves as outsiders looking in. Segregation was not viewed negatively, rather it was seen as a "privileged separation" that the players were lucky to be a part of. Many of these players reflected that, as high school students, they remembered being viewed differently. The following narration describes the segregation that these players experienced as a result of their athletic participation.

Joe: I look at it this way. In high school you had different types of people. You had the athletes or jocks and then you had the "dirtbags." You know, different types of people. You know I thought that in high school I was looked upon and respected. You know? And it kind of made you feel good. You know? You know you had the pep rallies or home coming. I kind of felt like I was special to be out there and in front of the crowd. I always thought that it was kind of special. Because for me, I felt that I was fortunate and gifted enough to be able to play sports. So you know, some people aren't.

Joe and the other players were very aware of the segregation that they developed for themselves. Buck explained that "people on the outside, they see but they don't understand. You know? I want to say that it's almost like an inside joke type thing, but it goes deeper than being just that trivial."

In summary, the role that group formations play within the all-male environment of sport was crucial to the way each male navigated through the sporting experience. Within the Bordertown team, the players identified two major effects of male grouping: segregation and privileged status. Divided along hegemonic lines, these groups played a large role in the activities of the baseball team. Moreover, the groups served to control access to the team by limiting participation to those individuals who were athletically inclined. Those who were located in the core group very often dictated what activities were done and who participated. The further you were from the core group, the less significant your participation became and the less likely you were to fall under the hegemonic identity that was so clearly defined by core group membership.

Sex Segregation and Brotherhood

The formation of men's groups is intricately tied to sex segregation. Sport has played a crucial role in the spatial segregation of men and women in the United States. From the time boys are first introduced to organized sport (through elementary, middle, and high school, to organized adult athletic leagues) sport serves as a site where men can isolate themselves from the women in their lives. This isolation provides a spatial barrier between the sexes that allows male athletes to freely practice and maintain the "rituals" that perpetuate hegemonic masculinity (Sabo & Runfola, 1980).

Spain (1992) examined the spatial foundations of men's friendships and power by exploring the significance of the segregated "ceremonial hut" in non-industrial societies. This examination yielded many important findings with respect to the maintenance of the privileged male society, regardless of industrial status. Spain (1992) found that grouping along gender lines becomes a mechanism for controlling power by limiting access to the rituals and practices of the dominant group. Like the racially defined caste system in India, gender is often at the root of group identities (Spain, 1992).

The men of Bordertown reported that they were very aware of the gender segregation that sport had afforded them. Tom, a physical education teacher and coach at a local high school, explained that sport provides males with the opportunity to "group" together. In addition, he explained that this social phenomenon resulted from a boy's tendency to form friendships through association in comparison to a girl's tendency to develop friendships through more personal contact.

SH: Which do you think, the son or the daughter, would sport play a bigger role for? If either. In other words, would sport benefit one or the other more?

Tom: You see I'm looking at it from a skewed opinion anyway because I'm a male. I would say the male, without a doubt. Because of the different groups that a male can get into. Girls it seems, from the teaching standpoint, the groups aren't as distinguished. Where the guys it seems like the jocks just stay together and the "brainiacs" and the "dirties." So I think that it would affect the guy more than the girl. Without a doubt.

SH: What about benefit?

Tom: I think the same thing. I think that it would affect a son in a more positive way than it would affect a female. Not to say that it wouldn't affect a female in a positive way.

SH: Why?

Tom: Just because, from a teaching standpoint, seeing the girls. Girls can have one friend and be happy. You don't see that with guys in high school. They don't have one good friend that they are in classes with, that they go to their lockers with. That they do everything together. Guys, you don't see that. Girls, you do. So a guy seems to need more of a group setting to be successful. And where else could you get that group type setting but in an athletic team. That's the best place.

Simmel (1950) once explained that, although the purpose of all-male clubs is to "emphasize differences between men and women, not all males are admitted" (p. 364). The exclusion of such males relegates them to an outside position as "symbolic women" and emphasizes the hegemonic attributes that are a part of the sporting environment but not a part of every man's repertoire (Spain, 1992, p. 61).

During the interviews many of the players, after describing certain aspects about the sporting experience, asked me if I was an athlete. Upon confirming that I was an athlete, players would often respond "You know then," or "You know what I'm talking about." This "question and confirmation" ritual indicates that these men believe that one must be an athlete to understand the athletic experience. If an individual lacks athletic experience, whether male or female, then he or she will remain on the outside looking in. In addition, like Tom's "brainiacs and dirties" and Joe's "dirtbags," these outsiders are often relegated to a lower status to further support their exclusion.

The Bordertown players looked back on their sporting experiences with extreme fondness and nostalgia. Most of them referred to each other or their past teammates as "brothers." This cultural practice of ascribing familial qualities to teams and teammates only served to further the segregation dynamics of the team. By augmenting one's friendships to status of "brotherhood," these athletes cemented the "bonds" that tied the team together and reinforced the cohesion that, in turn, was a key factor in maintaining team loyalty and segregation.

The Bordertown team subculture served as an environment safe from the inclusion of females, but also those males that did not meet the hegemonic standards established within its socially defined boundaries. The commitment to athletic participation secured men's privileged status and, at the same time, legitimated their higher social status. In terms of informal power, sport provides a venue in which "men's authority can be expressed without challenge from women." (Spain, 1992, p. 71). In addition, it was the perception of the players that the "bonds" that were formed from athletic participation lasted long after sport participation ends. These "bonds" were evidenced by the fact that these players had grown from young boys into men and are still playing sports together like they did when they were children. As Chuck indicated, not only do athletes remain close with their fellow teammates, they maintain these friendships far beyond their sporting experience. Chuck explained:

> The friendships that you make are the friendships that you will have the rest of your life. And you always talk about those times because you have something in common. That's partly the reason why you keep them. Because they're probably the only people who remember how good you really were or what you did. You know? Most other people really don't care.

It was evident that a primary function of sport was to provide an environment that promoted hegemonic male attributes while simultaneously segregating athletes from those who might criticize or challenge their values and beliefs. What was clear from the discussions with the Bordertown players was that sport was a safe environment to develop and maintain their male friendships in ways that were consonant with hegemonic masculinity.

Sharing the Sports Experience

A fundamental difference between male and female relationships is the dependence on verbal communication by women and the dependence on mutual, goal-oriented activities by men. Swain (1989) argued that the importance of this difference is only a matter of perspective and that men can have friendships deeply rooted in emotional connections just as women can. He criticized a strict adherence to a feminist perspective and articulates that it is unfair to judge men's friendships according to a female point of view. In addition, Swain (1989) states that "men's friendships are in fact characterized by a 'covert style of intimacy'" (p. 71).

Regardless of the differences between theorists, the overriding explanation for the closeness of these men was attributed to the competitive nature of sport. While it should not downplay that sport offers a possible venue for sharing one's intimate feelings, for the average player, sport continues to support friendships built around shared competitive experiences. Adam ascribed the ability to build strong friendships with mutual participation in competitive athletics this way.

> The competition, I think . . . I think that because of the fact that every one of you are competitors. If you weren't, you wouldn't be playing. I think that that's pretty standard. I think that by winning, and pulling through tough situations together, you all feel the same way. I think that it's that feeling that you all share that brings you closer. Like I know for a fact that when we (his college team) beat the number one team in the country, a big upset and everything. After that game, everybody was going around and hugging each other, running around and doing everything. And after that, everybody is just a little bit closer.

After describing this event to me, I asked Adam, "Were there guys on the team that you maybe didn't like too much who, after you won that game, you found yourself hugging?"

Adam: Yeah, there were.

SH: So how do you explain that?

Adam: Well it's the emotion of the time and no one thought we could do it. I mean I think that it was the situation. You know? It was in front of 5,600 fans and we upset them. But even after that, the team was closer. Not just that night. We were a tighter group. And maybe I can't explain that. But I'm just saying that maybe it's because we went through it. And you work so hard for the same goal. It's the competitiveness. And I also think that is vice versa. When you start losing, you just don't seem to mix that well.

Adam suggested that there was great value placed on the "mutual sharing" of emotional "highs." When a team wins and all of the players feel the same way, the team becomes closer as a result. Like Adam, Al described the effect winning had on him and his teammates.

I think that it's just a natural thing that you want to be the best. And if and when you do, you climb another notch on your personal ladder. It's an uplifting experience. And when everybody experiences it together, there's just some kind of energy that happens that just makes it even better. And it doesn't wear off.

These explanations have extended the discourse on why these men, through their mutual experiences, built such deep emotional friendships. Adam and Al explained that it was not just the competitive nature of sport but the results of the competition that influence their relationships. Whether or not a team was winning or losing played an integral role in how the Bordertown men developed and, more importantly, maintained their friendships. I observed that the positive results of a competition also strengthened team solidarity as well as the division of team groups.

There has been extensive research in the area of friendship building among men (Farr, 1992; Gilligan, 1982; Rubin, 1985, 1983; Spain, 1992). What has been revealed is that men fear developing intimate bonds with other males because of how others might perceive it. Frequently, men are hesitant to develop male friendships based on intimacy because of the anxiety about being labeled homosexual. Rubin (1985) explains that for heterosexual males there is a tremendous amount of concern regarding intimate interaction with other males because they believe such behavior might be construed as homosexual activity.

As a result of placing excessive emphasis on sharing an experience rather than interpersonal communication, these Bordertown athletes placed a great value in the experiential "bonds" that developed between teammates. The players' views of the importance behind bonding and developing the "family" image are illustrated in Kev's comments.

Kev: You know? There is a bond there. Like when we went out on Friday night. You know it does bring you together. It has to. You become like a family because everybody has to communicate . . . and the infield and the outfield are different spots, but you have to know what's going on.

Kev: Ah, well . . . first we went up to the bar that sponsors us. You should come with us. What does going out do? You just talk about the game and you talk about things that have nothing to do with the game. You just kind of get to know everybody better. You know? You just learn to relax. Like Tom and me. He has been on my case all year for sliding into first (base). You know? Just good humor. Because I shaved my "beard" and now he calls me "beardless." You know? It kind of just loosens you up. Because sometimes you let the game take over and you should just have fun. And that's what I'm there to have. And I think they're doing it too. And I think that it's just to relax everybody . . . I think that it brings everyone together and gets us to know each other better. For some maybe it's a psychological thing. I know that (the professional team that I work with) does it just for that reason.

Kev clearly emphasized these shared experiences as a way to bring players together "like a family." The "bonding" experience he described as banter between players brought the players closer. Kev suggested during an interview that I should "go out with them" as a way of getting to know the team better. This shows, perhaps, that he placed a greater value on the experience rather than the verbal exchange of personal details of one's life.

The prescription of "hanging out with the boys" was given high priority by many of the players. These excursions were not limited to just the Bordertown team, however. On one occasion, after a game was canceled, the Bordertown players went to a bar and discovered that the team they were supposed to play was already there. Tom described the events that occurred that day:

When we went to North Tonsville and we ended up not playing, we were all just standing there. And we knew everyone because we have played with all of them before. And we all wound up at the same bar, by chance. And we all drank, played pool, shot darts, and played horse shoes. It was great. I mean talk about male bonding there. It wasn't that we all knew each other. It was because we all had a common bond and a common goal: To play and have fun in baseball. But it was neat. It was the first time I had experienced that. It was the first time I saw two teams at the same bar and having fun together. And we were all mixed up. So what goes on in the field, I don't know. Like I said, you sweat with these guys, and you're in the trenches with them. You try to pull through for them. You try to get that hit or make that play that will maybe end that inning and save you a couple of runs. And you grow from that. It gives you something to talk about when we go out. And we bust on each other. It's never that you can't harass anyone. We all know what happens.

Just as Kev explained it, Tom narrated the type of "intense" bonding that could occur in a group situation. Interestingly, Tom described his teammates' activities with the other team as "competitive" or "heterosexual masculine" behavior (Herek, 1987). Tom portrayed his connection with his teammates as one that was forged in the "trenches," built on their mutual "sweat." Using the very common "war" analogy, Tom reinforced the strength of the "bond" between him and his fellow teammates.

In addition to the bonding mentioned by Tom, he also described "busting" on each other as a way to build their friendships. This practice often took the form of nicknames and escaped only a few of the team players. What was interesting about the practice of nicknaming teammates was that it crossed over from field to social activity and back to field again. This practice served a triple purpose: first, it served to re-solidity the importance of the bonding experience; it served an assimilation function into the team culture, reaffirming established groups within the team and occasionally setting new parameters to adjust group structure; and finally, it alienated those who did not participate in traditional male bonding activities. This alienation served as additional support for the way a male was expected to behave in the sporting environment. In the following narration, Buck explains the "nicknaming process."

SH: Does nicknaming bring you guys closer?

Buck: Oh yeah! There's that male bonding thing all over again. Anything you do we'll find out and someone will come up with a nickname. Like I said, you missed some of the great ones that went around in the field. Pre-season is the best because everyone is loose, not as serious and we go out. Like on Saturday night and ah, you know? We'll have four or five different things happen. And next Monday we come into practice . . . I was like "Remember that? Did you see what happened?" Or someone will come up and say something.

There was a definite connection between nicknaming and participation in group activities. Observations revealed that the nicknames were most often created by the players in the core group or, less often, worked out between the core group and the central group members. In addition, the ones who had the most nicknames were the players who most often participated in the bonding process during external activities. Again, these players were those men who were in the core and central groups. In the following narration, Bobby and Tim describe the importance of the nicknaming process.

Bobby: Nicknames. That's probably more common in baseball than anything. I think that it has to do with why baseball players are so superstitious. I mean they call me Big Bob, because of my height. And ah, we have a lot of nicknames. And I think that that's just a part of baseball. You know? Guys joking back with guys. Having fun.

SH: What if you didn't have a nickname, what would you think?

Bobby: I think that having a nickname kind of brings me together with the guys. It kind of makes me feel more welcomed. You know? "Here's Big Bob." Instead of "Here's Bobby." It makes you feel a part of the team.

Tim: I think that (nicknaming is) kind of important. It brings the team together and gives people an identity on the field that it doesn't off the field. Or maybe not so much on and off the field but to the team players. And you're almost a different person. Whatever problems you had before at work or you're gonna have after the game is over, are kind of deferred by the moniker. I think that it's a really important part, a very healthy part of the game.

Only two players on the Bordertown team did not receive a nickname—Bobby and Tim. Bobby's nickname, "Big Bob," came from his high school team, and Tim never received a nickname. Both of these players were members of the peripheral group and rarely, if at all, participated in external activities. In addition, neither player mixed to any great degree with the other players, and both left the team before the season ended.

The creation and assignment of a nickname meant that a player was accepted by the members of the core and central groups. Hence, the nicknaming process was linked to the team's bonding activities and helped to determine who would be accommodated by changes in the group structure and who remained on the outside. This marginalization resulted from an "interplay" between players where exchanges were often characterized by aggressive verbal "jousts" and the "flexing" of one's hegemonic muscles. When a player was unable or unwilling to keep up with the more dominant players, they were subjgated to a lower status within the team hierarchy. This lower status and devaluation, as the nicknaming process demonstrated, was difficult, if not impossible, to overcome.

During my participant observation, the team generated a nickname for me. Tony nicknamed me "Dr. Green," after an actor in a popular television series. The awarding of a nickname occurred after I had bonded with the Bordertown men throughout the season. Unlike Bobby and Tim, I participated in many outside activities with the players such as going to bars, dancing, and drinking. In the following field notes, I describe one such occasion where I had the opportunity to go out with several of the players. Field Notes: After a close win, the players decided that they would go out to a city bar. Many of the players, Tom, Tony, Joe, Adam, and Pat, personally invited me to go out with them. The players who met at the bar included Tom, Tony, Joe, Bud, Adam, Pat, and Buck as well as Tom and Tony's girlfriends, Lynn and Jen, respectively, and another male friend, Jeff. During the night, the players separated into their respective groups. Tony, Tom, Joe, and Adam danced together on the dance floor and stayed in a tight circle. Both Tony and Tom paid close attention to their girlfriends and showed many public displays of affection. At one point during the night, Tony, Tom, and Joe climbed on a three-tiered box in the middle of the dance floor and essentially drew the attention of the people in the bar that were located around the dance floor. Their "outlandish" dancing and laughing often drew the attention of surrounding individuals. Away from those four on the dance floor, Bud, Pat, and Jeff watched and joked about how "crazy" their friends were. Usually walking around the bar, Buck was occupied with meeting a particular woman that he had been talking to for the past few weeks. During the night, I spent time with each of the groups and Buck at their respective places in the bar.

Like many of the bonding experiences that the players described, I was quickly assimilated into their group dynamics; e.g., I met Tony and Tom's girlfriends and spoke with them briefly, had beer bought for me by two of the players, walked with Buck while he tried to locate and talk with the woman he was interested in, danced with Adam, Tony, Tom, and Joe, and sat with Pat, Bud, and Jeff as they critiqued their friends on the dance floor.

These experiences revealed to me that the barriers between the groups were well established and that the behavior of the group members was extremely consistent across a variety of settings, both on and off the field. The core members were often the center of attention, they appeared to be more "successful" with meeting and talking with women, and they controlled the way the team positioned itself within the bar. For example, when the core members were at the bar ordering drinks, the rest of the players were also in the vicinity. When the core members decided to go to the dance floor, the central group members located in chairs so that they could watch their teammates dance. On several occasions, Pat and Bud commented on how crazy their friends were and that they would not do that. Bud explained that if he had more to drink and was "wasted," he would probably be out there, yet enjoyed watching his friends make "fools of themselves."

Clearly the above "night out" typified the male grouping model that defines the structure of the Bordertown team. In addition, the trip to the bar is one example that demonstrated the connections between group positioning and willingness to model hegemonic masculinity. As defined by one's acceptance into the core group, those members must be willing to be sexually aggressive, highly vocal, outlandish, and domineering. With respect to those players that were positioned between the core and central group, their acceptance into the core group was contingent upon their willingness to participate in core group behavior. Finally, for those members located in the central group, their behavior was most often defined by the way the core group decided to behave. The central group members were often incidental in the decision-making process. As for the peripheral group, their participation is all but irrelevant in the grand scheme of things. They were always invited to participate, but never expected to choose that option.

Conclusion

This article focused on the importance of the male grouping process within the hegemonic environment of sport. The analysis of the Bordertown team revealed that groups within the team structure were divided along hegemonic lines. In addition, these divisions played a significant role in the development of the team culture and definitions of acceptable behavior. Indeed, the formation and interaction of male groups in the team subculture reflected and perpetuated the hegemonic environment of sport. From participant and non-participant observation as well as personal interviews, a four-tier male grouping model was discerned. The Bordertown team was divided into three groups, the core, the central, and the peripheral, as well as an exterior group that contained women and non-hegemonic males. This model played a pivotal role in defining the team culture, team dynamics, and the perpetuation of male hegemony.

Observations and interviews with players showed that the male grouping process was closely linked to sex segregation and the privileging of men's status in relation to one another and women in general.

Initially, sport served as an arena where the exclusion of females was legitimated and "naturalized" in the minds of the young male athletes. The pattern of gender segregation was not limited to just women but also to men who did not display traditional hegemonic characteristics like aggression, domination, and loud banter. The absence of women and non-hegemonic males facilitated the practice of rituals and traditions that perpetuate the hegemonic environment of sport.

The perceptions of the athletes, that relationships were built upon mutually shared experiences, coupled with the development of internal team groupings, provide evidence for the connection between "bonding" and the establishment of a team hierarchy. Like the boys and girls in Thorne's analysis of "borderwork," the Bordertown players used the mutual exchange that occurred during activities to establish boundaries between hegemonic and non-hegemonic players. Their perceptions, formed through their participation in external activities and the long-standing hegemonic traditions of male sport, laid the foundation from which groups evolved. This seemingly natural evolution resulted from the interplay between athletes and the establishment of physical and emotional dominance. The culmination was a hierarchy that, at its foundation, prioritized hegemonic masculinity and marginalized non-hegemonic players.

The male grouping process deals with the perceived privileged status of the athletes and the sports they played. Many of the players stated that they felt different from other, non-athletic kids growing up and very often privileged to be able to participate in sport. This feeling of being placed at a higher status was often demonstrated by the identification of non-athletes as "dirtbags," "brainiacs," or "dirties." Concurrently, the practice of celebrating athletic participation in the form of pep rallies and homecoming further served to place the athlete higher than those who did not participate in sport.

The players often commented that their athletic participation served to alienate them from other people. They were aware of the fact that people identified them as a "baseball player" or a "basketball player" rather than a person with a name. While these players did not like being separated from other people, they often prioritized their sporting activity and accepted the few negative effects that they perceived were a part of the "game."

Men's group dynamics in the team subculture also influenced their relationships with women. The men of Bordertown explained that it was a "natural" tendency for men to group together and, in contrast, for women to have only a few close friends. They also felt that sport was a more appropriate activity for males than for females. This emphasis on sport as an all-male activity as well as the high priority given to athletic participation was also expressed through beliefs that "familial" qualities permeated relationships among teammates. By comparing the team to a family and teammates to brothers, the Bordertown baseball players not only solidified their group identity but also their separation from all those who were not a part of the team. In short, the family discourse helped to integrate team members while segregating them from others.

The final section detailed how these men described how they bonded with their teammates. As a result of the fear of being perceived as homosexual, many of these men placed greater emphasis on less intimate forms of "bonding." This limitation on the extent an athlete was willing to communicate intimately with another male prevented the Bordertown players from developing truly intimate relationships.

Finally, the process of nicknaming teammates revealed that this practice was an assimilation technique that emphasized player participation in "bonding" activities. This was best demonstrated by the value that Tim and Bobby placed on receiving a nickname even though they never actually were given one. As a result of the nicknaming process, the groups became more defined and those who did not participate in off-field activities received no nickname and became further isolated from the core and central groups.

Examining male friendships from the perspective of this research, it is difficult to say that men's friendships do indeed represent meaningful, intimate relationships. Rather, through their mutual experiences in sport, the male relationship develops a deep connection that is based not on shared interpersonal communication, but on shared emotional experiences. This lack of intimacy relates directly to the emphasis these players placed on their athletic competition and the heightened emotional response that resulted from victory. Consequently, and consistent with the research of the mid-1980s, male friendships remain largely dependent on the external experience rather than the sharing of intimate emotions.

The argument of this article has been that the groups that developed within the Bordertown baseball team served three purposes: first, they segregated the players along hegemonic lines; second, they provided hegemonic standards on which privileged status was awarded; and third, they isolated the non-hegemonic players from the rest of the team. Therefore, this internal male grouping mirrors the social institution of sport in the broader social structure. In other words, where sport serves to limit the access of women and non-hegemonic men to the practices and rituals of the dominant group; the core and central groups within the Bordertown team limit the access of the less hegemonic athletes to positions of power and influence within the team structure. Consequently, the role the male grouping process played was one that legitimized hegemonic masculinity and perpetuated the privileged male status in our society.

REFERENCES

Balswick, J. (1976). The inexpressive male: A tragedy of American society. In D. David & R. Brannon (Eds.), The forty-nine percent majority (pp. 55–67). Reading, MA: Addison-Wesley.

Farr, K. A. (1992). Dominance bonding through the good old boys sociability group. In M. Kimmel & M. Messner (Eds.), Men's lives (2nd ed., pp. 403–417). New York: Macmillan.

Farrell, W. (1975). The liberated man. New York: Bantam.

Fasteau, M. F. (1974). The male machine. New York: McGraw Hill.

Gilder, G. (1973). Sexual suicide. New York: Baton.

Gilligan, C. (1982). In a different voice: Psychological theory and women's development. Cambridge: Harvard University Press.

Herek, G. (1987). On heterosexual masculinity: Some psychical consequences of the social construction of gender and sexuality. In M. Kimmel (Ed.), Changing men: New directions in research on men and masculinity (pp. 68–82). Newbury Park, CA: Sage.

Klein, A. (1991). Sugarball: The American game, the Dominican dream. New Haven: Yale University Press.

Lasch, C. (1979). The culture of narcissism. New York: Warner.

Messner, M. (1992a). Like family: Power, intimacy, and sexuality in male athlete's friendships. In P. Nardi (Ed.), Men's friendships (pp. 215–237). London: Sage.

Messner, M. (1992b). Power at play: Sports and the problem of masculinity. Boston: Beacon Press.

Morin, S. F., & Garfinkel, E. M. (1978). Male homophobia. Journal of Social Issues, 34(1), 29–47.

Reisman, D. (1953). The lonely crowd: A study of the changing American character. New Haven: Yale University Press.

Rubin, L. B. (1983). Intimate strangers: Men and women together. New York: Harper & Row.

Rubin, L. B. (1985). Just friends: The role of relationships in our lives. New York: Harper & Row.

Sabo, D., & Runfola, R. (1980). Jock: Sports and male identity. Englewood Cliffs, NJ: Prentice Hall.

Simmel, G. (1950). The sociology of George Simmel (K. Wolf, Ed.). New York: Free Press.

Spain, D. (1992). The spatial foundation of men's friendships. In P. Nardi (Ed.), Men's friendships (pp. 59–73). London: Sage.

Swain, S. (1989). Covert intimacy: Closeness in men's friendships. In B. J. Risman & P. Schwartz (Eds.), Gender in intimate relationships: A microstructural approach (pp. 71–86). Belmont, CA: Wadsworth.

Thorne, B. (1993). Gender play: Girls and boys in school. New Brunswick, NJ: Rutgers University Press.

Tiger, L. (1969). Men in groups. London: Nelson.

Voicing Your Opinion
Hegemonic Masculinity, Friendship, and Group Formation in an Athletic Subculture
Steven J. Harvey

1. Harvey describes a series of behaviors by the Bordertown players that function to create in-group and out-group status for the team. Have you witnessed or experienced this in other all-male groups? Is this behavior typically isolated to sports activities? If so, why?

   _____

   _____

   _____

   _____

   _____

2. Are some sports more likely to create the type of hegemonic masculinity that Harvey describes in his research? Do you think that this is more likely to happen to baseball teams rather than other sports teams? Is this less likely to happen in sports that are more regularly played by women (such as basketball or soccer)?

   _____

   _____

   _____

   _____

   _____

3. What is the relationship between competition and bonding in all-male groups? Is competition an important component of American masculinity? How are boys taught to appreciate and engage in competition in sports?

   _____

   _____

   _____

   _____

   _____

Further Investigation . . .

Instructions

Investigate a specific topic regarding gendered language, nonverbal communication, and gendered communication in personal relationships. These topics relate to the readings and course discussion raised in Part Three, *The Process of Communicating Gender.*

1. You must read and summarize *three* academic sources that pertain to your chosen topic. These sources should come from scholarly journals and academic research from published books. You may not use popular press articles or internet websites. Each summary must include the following information:

   • The title, author and/or editor, publication date, and journal title (if applicable).

   • A two paragraph summary of the significant information in the source. If you are using a book you should summarize only the chapter(s) that you have read.

2. Describe what you have learned. This is not a request for a re-summary of the information from the first section! Instead, you should think about how the information affects you and how it engages your curiosity. What surprised you? What connections can you make to other information you have learned about gender and communication? What is your intellectual and/or emotional response to this information? What might you *do* with this information?

Suggestions

Pick a topic that truly interests you and/or has an impact on your education or your life.

Take the time to find sources that help you investigate your topic in a thorough manner. Do not just "settle" for the first article that you find on the topic.

Read a variety of types of research about your topic. You might also consider looking for information from multiple disciplinary perspectives.

Topics

masculine generic language	gender and intimacy
sexist language	second shift
patrilineality and name changes	masculine friendships
muted group theory	feminine friendships
essentialism	the heterosexual script
performativity	hegemonic masculinity
agency and nonverbal communication	covert intimacy in masculine friendships

4 The Process of Examining Gendered Violence

In this section we examine the ways that human violence is linked to gender. The presence of gendered violence in personal relationships and public spheres can be an overwhelming topic to investigate. It is important to understand that gendered violence is something that happens every day. It is both a problem that affects people at a personal level as well as a phenomenon that can be identified as a public health issue. You will read about sexual harassment, sexual assault, intimate partner violence, and the ways that gendered communication can produce and magnify these types of violence.

Definitions to Consider

Sexual Assault: Federal laws in the United States use the terms *forcible* and *nonforcible* to describe sexual acts. A forcible sexual offense is one that happens against a person's will; including a sex act that occurs when the victim cannot give consent. A nonforcible sexual offense refers to sexual acts that occur when the victim is under the age of statutory consent.

Intimate Partner Violence: Acts of violence between people who are involved in close intimate relationships. These may include acts of intimidation, violent assault, coercion, emotional control, and verbal abuse.

Cycle of Violence: This cycle occurs in intimate relationships and is identified by three phases: tension, explosion, and remorse. Tension escalates in the first phase when the abusive partner communicates threats and exerts control. The second phase involves an explosion of violent behavior. The third phase is marked by remorse and partner forgiveness. This cycle will continue until it is broken by one or both of the people involved in it.

Stalking: Intentional stalking occurs when a person makes a direct or indirect threat to another person and creates a fear of violence in that person.

Sexual Harassment: The Equal Employment Opportunity Commission of the United States defines sexual harassment as unwelcome sexual advances, requests for sexual favors, and other verbal or physical conduct of a sexual nature constitutes sexual harassment when submission to or rejection of this conduct explicitly or implicitly affects an individual's employment, unreasonably interferes with an individual's work performance or creates an intimidating, hostile or offensive work environment.

PUNKING AND BULLYING Strategies in Middle School, High School, and Beyond ♂ ♀

DEBBY A. PHILLIPS

This article is about a fairly common practice among young men—*punking,* which means to harass, either verbally or physically. The author outlines a definition of *punking* and explains how this practice can lead to bullying behaviors. This article offers interesting suggestions about the role that media play in teaching boys to shame others and about how punking becomes an acceptable rite of passage into the masculine world.

Punking is a practice of verbal and physical violence, humiliation, and shaming usually done in public by males to other males. This definition is based on interviews and discussion groups with 32 adolescent boys and on media sources within which adolescent males are embedded. Discourse analysis findings reveal that punking terminology and behaviors are usually interchangeable with bullying terminology and behaviors. Both practices are purposeful strategies taken up and used by many boys to affirm masculinity norms of toughness, strength, dominance, and control. Implications from this research promote a shift in understandings of how masculinity norms are achieved. Further, the research suggests that by bringing critical attention to social accountability for production of unhealthy norms and the violent practices that affirm these norms, we might well extend the scope and focus of intervention into harmful practices of violence, such as punking and bullying.

Punking is a practice of verbal and physical violence, humiliation, and shaming usually done in public by males to other males (Phillips, 2000). In the research presented here, punking was commonly used by adolescent boys and usually described interchangeably with bullying. Bullying is defined as

a specific type of aggression in which 1) the behavior is intended to harm or disturb, 2) the behavior occurs repeatedly over time, and 3) there is an imbalance of power, with a more powerful person or group attacking a less powerful one. (Nansel, Overpeck, Pilla, et al., 2001)

Using this definition to measure the prevalence of bullying behaviors among 15,686 United States youth in Grades 6 through 10, Nansel, Overpeck, Pilla, et al. (2001) indicate the extent of bullying in this country. They found that 26% of the boys reported bullying others sometimes ("moderate") to weekly ("frequent"), whereas 21% of boys reported being bullied sometimes or weekly (pp. 2096–2097). These statistics translate into millions of boys, nationally, participating in bullying either as a bully, a victim, or both. In addition to this direct participation, millions of youths and adults participate through witnessing these behaviors.

Bullying has received increased attention during the past 20 years. In 1993, the American Association of University Women (AAUW, 1993) published *Hostile Hallways,* a survey of the normalcy of bullying and sexual harassment in United States schools. Two thirds of the boys surveyed were identified as sexual harassers and bullies. Boys reported acting alone, in boy groups, and sometimes in boy/girl groups. In addition, boys were identified as the most common victims of bullying and harassment, including homophobic ridiculing and taunts. Unlike girls, however, who could recall details of harassment, boys experienced these practices so often that many had difficulty remembering their first experience.

In addition to high prevalence, research shows that there are immediate and long-term negative consequences associated with bullying. Victims, perpetrators, and young men who have experience as both victims and perpetrators are at risk for alcohol abuse, cigarette smoking, use of other forms of violence, and antisocial behaviors (Nansel, Overpeck, Haynie, et al. 2003; Nansel, Overpeck, Pilla, et al., 2001; Olweus, 1994). Other sequelae of bullying include poor psychosocial adjustment and academic achievement, loneliness, rejection, depression, anxiety, and poor self-esteem (Hawker & Boulton, 2000; Nansel, Overpeck, Pilla, et al., 2001).

In the wake of the 1999 Columbine High School killings and other publicized examples of youth school violence, bullying gained increased public attention. Many of the perpetrators of these violent practices had been male victims of earlier bullying by other boys. During this "Columbine period," men of all ages who had been bullied in childhood and adolescence spoke up publicly and urged a redefinition of bullying from "natural" and "normal" to serious, harmful, and traumatizing. Males victimized by bullying practices took the opportunity to publicly tell their stories. For example, Savage (1999), a middle-aged Euro-American male, wrote,

> Like most students [in high school], I lived in fear of the small slights and public humiliations used to enforce the rigid high school caste system. . . . Students lived in fear of physical violence. There was a boy named Marty at my school . . . who was beaten up daily for years. Jocks would rip his clothes, knowing that his parents could not afford to buy him a new uniform, and he would piss his pants rather than risk being caught alone in the bathroom. He couldn't walk the halls without being called a fag, and freshmen would beat him up to impress older kids. . . . While I didn't suffer the extreme abuse some of my friends did, I was fucked with enough to spend four years fantasizing about blowing up my high school and everyone in it. (p. 8)

As bullying began to be named as not normal or acceptable, federal and state governments moved to prohibit it, using Title IX of the 1972 Federal Education Amendments, which prohibits harassing behavior in schools and school-sponsored contexts. Under Title IX, harassment includes a pattern of behavior or a single incident perpetrated by anyone that creates an intimidating or hostile environment in which the targeted person cannot work or learn. Additionally, the Equal Protection Clause of the 14th Amendment of the United States Constitution has been used to protect against bullying, stating that schools are responsible for equally protecting all students and that all citizens are due equal protection under the law. Lastly, states such as Washington have instituted antibullying acts that are enforced statewide in schools (Washington State PTA/Safe Schools Coalition, 2003).

Traditionally, practices of male violence have been assumed to be caused by pathology. In this view, bullying results from a malfunctioning brain incapable of making "correct" moral judgments and/or from a failure of social mores to keep innate biological male "tendencies" from emerging (Gilligan, 1997). From these perspectives, research and intervention focus on individual pathology and individual change. This approach to male violence diverts attention away from social norms for boys and men and from the violent practices that affirm the norms. Moreover, it directs attention away from social responsibility and accountability for supporting and reproducing these norms.

However, an alternative view of male violence derives from the belief that practices of male violence are too widespread and frequent to be solely considered problems of deviant individuals or groups detached from the cultural milieu that continually (re)births them and shapes them as male. In this view, male violence is understood as a tragic problem of how Western societies construct, reproduce, and enforce "norms" of masculinity constituting the "ideal" as superior, in control, strong, tough, respected, and infallible (Gilligan, 1997; Kimmel, 1996; Petersen, 1998; Phillips, 2000). From this perspective, practices of violence are strategies that work to affirm the norm when other strategies to achieve or maintain the "norm" fail or are unattainable. From this alternative perspective, boys and men are not born violent or with innate violent tendencies. But they *are* born into a culture that produces a narrow and pervasive view of normal or ideal masculinity and practices of violence as ways to achieve or maintain some sense of being a "normal" man.

Recently, Daro, Edleson, and Pinderhughes (2004) noted that youth violence, child maltreatment, and domestic violence share characteristics and common causal pathways. They called for diverse kinds of research to better understand the complexities of violence and a "more holistic approach to research among these three types of violence . . . rooted in an understanding of the relationships among variables in a system of violence production" (p. 293). The work presented here moves in this direction.

This research and current prevalence statistics show that despite local, state, and federal efforts, punking and bullying continue to be pervasive. This article draws on qualitative data on punking and bullying from a larger study, *Exploring New Directions for Ending Practices of Male Violence: Masculinity, Adolescent Boys, and Culture* (Phillips, 2000). Through interviews and discussion groups, all the adolescent boys in this study talked about a common violent practice called punking, discussed the purposes and effects of punking, and illustrated its prevalence as a strategy used to affirm masculine gender identity when other means of achieving current masculinity norms are unavailable (Phillips, 2000, 2005). These findings may shed light on the larger arena of male violence, especially in contributing new understandings of structural and environmental factors as root causes in society that contribute to the shared variance among all forms of male violence.

Methods

This research was conducted in a large, urban public middle school and high school. Participants were recruited from flyers distributed in classes, and parental and participant consents were obtained. Thirty-two 12- to 18-year-old ethnically and economically diverse adolescent boys took part in the study. Among this group of boys, 7 identified as African-American, 16 as White, 3 as Native American, 3 as Hispanic, and 3 as Southeast Asian. Beyond the 1- to 2-hour interviews, 22 of these boys also participated in one of three discussion groups—two middle school groups and one high school group—with each group meeting weekly for 5 weeks. Both the interviews and the discussion groups were audiotaped, and the tapes were later transcribed.

The interviews and discussion groups began with open questions and then progressed with follow-up questions based on information participants brought forward. In both cases, participants were regularly reminded that they could pass on any question or topic. Beginning questions included "What is it like to be a teenage boy in society today?" "What makes a boy popular?" "What TV shows do you like?" "Who are your favorite characters and why?" "What's it like in your family?" and "Who do you hang out with and why?"

In addition to interview and discussion-group discourses, data were collected from numerous media sources such as TV shows popular with the study participants. In taking media seriously, Giroux (1995) argues that "under the rubric of fun, entertainment, and escape, massive public spheres are being produced through representations and social practices that appear too 'innocent' to be worthy of political analysis" (p. 45). Examined for norms of masculinity were 23 episodes of TV, 51 front pages of a large-city newspaper, video and computer games, and radio and TV news (Phillips, 2001). Themes, topics, and beliefs from groups and interviews were assessed in the media data and were brought back to the groups and interviews for discussion.

Discourse analysis was used to explore the boys' conversations and the media conversations (Hollway, 1989, 1995; Hollway & Jefferson, 2000; Phillips, 2001). Discourse analysis assumes that boys are not born with innate discourses about themselves, violence, or the world around them. Instead, it suggests that they take up or position themselves in the cultural explanations that are available and/or dominant in their world. According to this analytical approach, when adolescent boys take up and enact cultural understandings or discourses, those discourses are reproduced. From this perspective, descriptions and explanations of masculinity vary depending on context, on a boy's history in cultural discourses, and on how he may want to represent himself. Furthermore, study participants' experiential accounts and media representations offer crucial sites of cultural reproduction for research on practices of violence, such as punking and bullying, and especially on the purposes served by punking and bullying and their connections to developing identity.

Media data sources and transcripts from the interviews and discussion groups were analyzed for dominant themes and how those themes materialized in boys' lives. Eight dominant cultural discourses emerged. Besides punking and bullying, the seven other dominant discourses were labeled *Popularity and the Necessity of an Outcast, Discourses of Daring and Risk, Heterosexuality and Homophobia, Slick Masculinity: In Your Face, Masculinity as Domestic Incompetence, Enforcing Masculinity: Discourses of*

Violence, and *Fathers and Sons: Bonding and the Reproduction of Hegemonic Masculinity* (Phillips, 2000, 2001, 2005).

Findings

The larger study findings reveal that "ideal" masculinity is represented and produced through numerous cultural discourses such as dominance, superiority, control or authority, strength, toughness, willingness and ability to fight, White race, financial wealth, heterosexuality, and athleticism (Phillips, 2000, 2005). Boys in the study identified this ideal as the way to be "popular." Pathways to "popularity" included name-brand clothes, large or tall size, slim and muscular body, economic resources (family trips, cars, home, material goods), and Whiteness, in addition to athleticism (school teams, right sports), heterosexuality (liked by popular, ideal girls), strength, toughness, ability to fight and win fights (publicly), popularity with boys (lots of guy friends), and respect and/or getting respect (Phillips, 2000, 2001, 2005).

The adolescent male and media discourses examined in the study identified nonnormative males as "outcasts." Pathways to this representation and identity included wearing off-brand clothes (less expensive) and tight pants, being scrubby, geeky, wimpy, weak, and small, in addition to being smart or shy, wearing glasses, and being classified as nerdy, poor, homosexual, nonathletic and not into sports, and unwilling to fight. The findings on adolescent male popularity and the outcast are reported in detail elsewhere (Phillips, 2000, 2001, 2005).

Overall, the qualitative data reveal that practices of punking and bullying are strategies to achieve or maintain identity as a popular and normal male and to create and reproduce inferior or outcast male identities. The following exemplars represent consensus opinions across the 32 participants, with small amounts of variation dependent on the boy's experience with participating as a perpetrator, victim, both, or observer. That is, all of the participants described how punking worked, who did it to whom, and why. Likewise, the media exemplars for this study were drawn from numerous possible examples and rendered similar findings. What follows offers the most salient aspects of cultural discourses constructing punking and bullying as masculinity practices revealed by the study.

Describing Punking and Bullying Victimization

Sam was one of the first boys that I interviewed and the first who articulated a daily lived experience of being punked. A Euro-American high school student who is "above average" in academics, Sam claims that he is "not popular" because he is not in one of the popular cliques made up of "preps and the jocks" who are "basically just rich." He would like to be "bigger, stronger, better looking, and more popular" because he would then "have more friends," and when a boy is popular, "there's just like so many other open doors." From Sam's identity on the margins of popular or normative masculinity, he clearly describes punking as part of his life since at least middle school. Sam offers

> It's basically putting someone down completely, you know. Punking can be, like, taking their lunch box and not giving it back, um, you know. Slapping someone, and he doesn't do anything about it . . . And it can be verbal abuse just from, you know, ranking on 'em, like "you're ugly, you're funny-looking."
> *Debby:* It's verbal and physical?
> *Sam:* Verbal abuse. Totally, totally like, uh, making someone do something or, you know, like, someone who punks someone is usually someone who has, like, total authority over that person. Like, that person won't do anything about it. Punking is more physical, actually . . . Punking is just overall overpowering the person, telling him off.

Like Sam, the majority of boys in the study reported that punking is usually done in public ("that's how it works") and that the punker usually has an advantage of size, age, or reputation that signifies or represents him as a punker. Sam offers that punking involves "picking on someone that's smaller, throwing them around, or mouthing off at someone." He argues that, "They [punkers] can do anything. Throw stuff at 'em; make fun of 'em in front of the whole class. So many people get thrown around and stuff." Sam attributes his being punked regularly to not being popular and "basically" because "I'm skinny and I'm short (5'8")."

Initially, in middle school, Sam responded violently to punking, tapping into other normative practices of violence, such as fighting. Over time, however, he came to understand himself and his identity differently as a result of punking. Currently, occupying a position or identity on the margins of masculinity as a "wimp," or a boy who does not fight back, Sam continues to take up common understandings about punking, commenting that being punked "makes you stronger." The following excerpt provides a sense of this repositioning and the denial/minimalization that allows Sam to "accept" the inevitability of punking.

> *Sam:* Well, in seventh grade, you know, I'd get this stuff [punking] and I got hella pissed off. And then in eighth grade it was so regular to, like, be thrown against the lockers, picked on, swung around and stuff, you just get used to it after a while.
> *Debby:* So when it first happened in seventh grade, did you get pretty angry?
> *Sam:* Oh, yeah. I mean, I was devastated. I hated it. I got all pissed off, you know. I did little, little drawings of me killing the person and stuff. I mean, I was just pissed off. One time I flipped out and just kicked a guy. Threw him down and got all pissed off.
> *Debby:* And you think it makes you tougher? Stronger or something?
> *Sam:* Yeah, it makes you, if it happens again, you know, you get used to it. But if it happened to someone that's never been punked before, they're gonna be devastated.

Intervention by an adult is clearly not an option to Sam because "snitching," or telling an adult, reinforces the boy's marginalized status and enables "legitimate" escalation of punking. When asked if he thought that I should do something about this repetitive practice, he responded adamantly, "NO! Because if you actually do something, you're gonna make it worse. That's the thing. Cuz if I told on someone, then it's, like, fffffffff." Not only would the punking get worse, but, Sam continued, "Then you're screwed. You might as well just leave the school. Cuz all his friends are just gonna be . . . That's what sucks about it, if you're not popular." [He laughs.]

Sam claims he has "gotten used to it," and now "doesn't really care." When I questioned this, he responded, "Well, I mean, I CARE. Of course I do. But, I mean, not nearly as much as I used to." When I asked Sam if he expected the punking to continue, he sighed and replied in a whisper, "Yeah. . . . Oh, well. It's the life of a boy teenager when you're young."

Sam's account of the normalized practices of punking resonates with accounts provided by boys in the study who occupied positions on the margins of masculinity. His seemingly stable "identity" as a not popular or ideal male adolescent is, at least partly, created and reproduced through the repetitive practices of punking.

Lewis, a Euro-American middle schooler, is also frequently punked, but the effects of this practice materialize in ways that are both similar to and different from Sam's experiences. Similar to Sam, Lewis's positioning on the margins is exploited and reproduced by boys occupying less-marginalized positions in relation to the widely circulated norms. His experience illustrates that punking moves the punker closer to masculinity norms, and it further marginalizes Lewis. When I asked Lewis to tell me about punking, he responded,

> *Lewis:* OK, it's like, if somebody just comes up and slaps you in the back of your head, that's a big punk, that's when you get punked. Like, you feel stupid because somebody does something to you. . . .
> *Debby:* Yeah?
> *Lewis:* It's just, like, something that goes on. Like, somebody'll call me a name and they're like, "Oh, you got punked." It's just like, basically like teasing somebody. Only sometimes it gets, like, uh . . . violent or something. And it turns into a fight.

"Popular people [boys]," Lewis argues, punk because "it makes 'em more popular and it shows that they can, [and that] they're cool." Lewis laughs, "[It] makes me even more unpopular." According to Lewis, it is primarily strong boys that punk other boys. "That's how come they punk people. Cuz they're stronger and they can beat 'em up. If you're weak, you can try. But it usually doesn't happen cuz they end up punking you." Lewis says that this does not make him angry because "I don't care what people think about me."

Later in his interview, Lewis provides further evidence that practices such as punking are normalized and accepted.

> *Debby:* Hmm. Does it happen, like, in classes, in the hall, outside?
>
> *Lewis:* Oh, in classes, in the halls, just about everywhere. Like, somebody who's gonna punk me will say something to me in class, and act like they're talking to me regular, so teachers don't even pay attention to 'em. Like Clyde, he'll just act like he's talking about the work that we're supposed to be doing, then he'll punk me. If the teacher turns and looks at him, he'll just be like, "Oh, did you do this last night on your project?"

When I asked Lewis how he responded to being punked, he said, "I don't care," and then he reiterated Sam's fear about telling a teacher. "I can't tell cuz I can't be a snitch. I [would] get beat up." Lewis explains that most boys who are punked feel trapped. "[If] they snitch off somebody, they're gonna get beat up eventually. Like, I told on Clyde, and he beat me up during gym class last semester. Not very badly, but . . ." I asked Lewis if he thought that punking would go away when he got older. He responded, "only if you get stronger and become more popular. I doubt it's ever gonna go away, to weaker people, no." I then asked Lewis if "some boys spot weaker boys?" and his reply indicated the powerful reiterative, visceral effects of the practices of punking: "Yeah. Phew! Attack it like rabid dogs."

Eric, a very small, Southeast Asian, older high school student who was previously a violent gang member, provides a last explication of punking. He states, "I never get punked, I wouldn't be havin' it." He describes why certain boys get punked: "The weaker of a person you are, the more you get punked. As, more of a victim. It's hard to explain. Do you know Phil? That kid gets punked so much." According to Eric, Phil and other boys are regularly punked

> because . . . he doesn't get bitter after he gets punked, I guess. You know, like, kids [boys] throw him down on the ground and almost break his arm and stuff. And he's like, he cries and stuff and everybody laughs at him. And then he gets up and he's, like, "Why are you guys like this? And why don't you just be my friend?" Stuff like that, you know. But, you gotta be smarter than that, just to say that. You gotta come up with something that's gonna make them respect you. It's all lack of respect. Basically, he's punking himself for future. Yeah.

According to the cultural understandings Eric has taken up, boys such as Phil, to avoid being punked, need to represent themselves differently and move closer to the norm. That is, they "basically just gotta get some balls and go do whatever you gotta do, instead of trying to make friends with 'em."

Perpetrating Punking and Bullying

Many of the boys in the interviews described punking other boys, and in the discussion groups, it was a frequent topic of conversation. Several accounts stood out in that they revealed the complexity and contradictions embedded in discourses producing masculine identities and practices of punking. Several boys in the study describe regularly punking other boys in elementary, middle, and/or high school and as a current, strategic practice "when necessary." Many of these boys also disclosed that they had been repeatedly punked by other boys at some point when they were younger.

Mike, a Euro-American high school student, for example, was regularly punked by other boys when he was 9 to 11 years old. He has worked hard to renegotiate his masculine identity through establishing a claim to respect through violence to self and others. Mike has learned to box, enabling him to punk and beat up most other boys, and he pushes his body to destructive limits in skateboarding. At the time of the interview, Mike was in high school and feeling pretty good about himself. Mike describes punking:

> It's an act of being really stupid! Like, all right, man, if you're gonna punk somebody, basically, man, you just go up to 'em and you're, like, "Pocket check." And you be, like, you gotta empty out all your pockets, man . . . If, this guy was, like, really scared of the bully, he'd be like, "Oh, OK," and he's [bully's] like, "Pocket check," and he'd take all your stuff and he'd be pushing you around, and he'd be calling you a little bitch and all that, and he'd be, like, "Oh, you're nothing." You know, that's being a punk, man.

Mike admits he is a "bully," but he also takes up contradictory discourses that question these practices. "I mean, I'm kinda like that sometimes. But I try, I try not to be like that. I try to just be, like, 'Yeah, whatever, man.'"

When asked if boys of the same age punk each other, Mike responded by describing some of the negotiation that occurs:

> Yeah. It could be the same age. It's just a matter of being . . . tough, man, look, there could be a kid who's like, really good at fighting and he's all buff, you know. But there could be a kid, same size, same age, just doesn't know how to fight and he's not that strong. The kid who knows how to fight and is strong is gonna come up to that kid and be, like, "What, bitch?" You know, he's gonna start punking on him.

In both of Mike's excerpts, the feminizing ("bitch") language is produced by misogynist discourses available for boys to objectify and humiliate other boys as they also objectify and degrade women. This language can be understood as a resource for normative masculinity and for the production of marginalized masculinity. Calling a boy a "bitch," for example, is an act of marginalization. Research has yet to question the use of this language to marginalize other men, but it has examined the negative effects of these discourses for men and their interactions with women (Boxley, Lawrance, & Gruchow, 1995; Lisak, Hopper, & Song, 1996).

Mike went on to disclose that he "used to be a punker" himself. He found it hard to move out of this position, and his identity and reputation stuck with him even after he moved to a new school.

> Like, in seventh grade, I was not trying to get suspended. The SECOND day of school, and this guy, he just, like, wouldn't leave me alone. He kept on punching me all day, man. And at the end of the day I fought him, man. And then I got suspended and that just started a chain.

Mike's experiences seem to give him some empathy for boys that are punked as well as some understanding of possible consequences of punking. He distinguishes his current practices from punking by arguing that the current practices are "messing around."

> *Mike:* Yeah, I've been punked, man. It's not fun, man. And, I mean, I don't really punk people. I just kinda mess with them. You know, I'll walk up and I'm like, "Wassup, man? Oh, what do you have in your lunch bag?" I never really take anything from 'em. I'm just kinda messin' with 'em, you know?
> *Debby:* Yeah.
> *Mike:* It's fun. But I still might try not to do that cuz, you know, it makes 'em like, "Oh, man." People don't normally like that when you fuck with 'em.
> *Debby:* Yeah.
> *Mike:* And, you know, people fuck with me and I don't really like it. And so, I mean, why would those other people? So basically, it's just someone doin' it to me, and then I'm doin' it to them, and they might be doin' it to someone else . . .

Nick, an African-American middle school student, offered similar understandings of the practice and its social functions. The discourses he takes up reproduce a particular cultural understanding of masculinity, violence, and social control. Phrases such as "know your role" and "know your place" were common aspects of the particular discourses within which Nick and some of the other boys were embedded. When asked about punking, the following conversation ensued:

> *Debby:* What is punking?
> *Nick:* Like, if someone was talking and I said, "SHUT UP!!" And he just shut up. They just got punked. I mean, like, they know better. It's just funny, a lot of boys do it.
> *Debby:* And is it verbal?
> *Nick:* Sometimes. You can hem somebody up.
> *Debby:* You can what?
> *Nick:* Hem somebody up. Just grab 'em, and boom, right against the wall. Hem 'em up. That's, like, a punk, too. But, it's called "hem 'em up."
> *Debby:* And who does it to who? Would you do it to a bigger kid or an older kid?
> *Nick:* I have. There's, like, this one kid who rode our bus once. And he was, like, talking to this other guy, and I was like, "Will you shut the f—up!" Right? Cuz he's like, you know, a nerd. And he's like, "God, what's your problem?" I said, "Know your role and sit in the seat, right? And don't talk." He didn't say anything 'til I got off the bus. [He laughs.]

> *Debby:* And was that a punk?
> *Nick:* Um-hmm! He was getting annoying. He talks too much.

Nick and other boys in the study implicitly and explicitly blame punking on the boy being punked. That is, being punked is the victim's "fault." Nick describes another incident in which he punked a boy because the boy is "always talking about people." I asked Nick to explain "talking too much."

> *Nick:* He wants to get his ass beat. He talks about people. Too much. He'll talk about people, like, to his friends and stuff. And then his friends will go back and tell us, "That person was talking about you." I'll wait for him to say somethin' else. And then, I won't even confront him, I'll just push him on the back.
> *Debby:* You push him?
> *Nick:* No, push him from the back. And then I'll start something like, "Why are you throwin' me shit?" And if he has nothin' to say, then we're fightin'. That time he had nothin' to say. I say, "Why are you talking shit?" He was just, like, sitting there, and he didn't say anything. So I hit him! Cuz he didn't have a response. And I hit him again. And again. Then he finally swung back.

Similar to many of the boys in the study, Nick emphasized that punking only affirmed normative masculinity if it was done in front of an "audience." When I asked Nick if someone broke up a punking incident he had described, he exclaimed,

> *Nick:* Break it up? No! Everyone was encouraging us. Everyone goes, "Hit him back! Hit him! Hit him!" Like, all around. It's in front of other people.
> *Debby:* And is that important?
> *Nick:* Um-hmm. It's important. To make sure everybody knows . . .

Nick assumes that all boys should know the "rules" and that some boys want to be punked because it makes them "popular." Several boys in the study mentioned this popularity-enhancing and seemingly contradictory aspect of being punked. One participant said that it makes a boy "part of the group." Nick clarified why he would not explain the rules to a boy he repeatedly punks.

> *Nick:* Cuz! He should know! I'm not gonna go over there and 'splain to him, "OK, you say one more thing, you're gonna get hurt." He should know.
> *Debby:* Why?
> *Nick:* Because. It's his fault. We shouldn't have to 'splain to him, "OK, are you ready to get beat up cuz you said this? You should know not to say this, or that."
> *Debby:* Why does he keep doing it then?
> *Nick:* Cuz he's tryin' to get popular. He is popular cuz everybody knows him, and everybody wants to hurt him. That's about it. Everybody knows his name.

Similar to Nick, Tom, a Euro-American, "popular" middle school student, claims that, perhaps, the boys do not mind being punked. "There's some kids who just get punked so much that they don't mind, cuz nobody likes 'em anyway. So it doesn't bother 'em." He continues, "Maybe it bothers them, but I don't think they . . . they don't show it." Tom starts to blame these boys, the "stupid people," for being punked and then says, "Well not stupid people, but just unpopular people. Like, the people who play Pokémon and stuff, they get punked a lot." Tom claims that they get punked because they "aren't tough enough to get back what was taken from them."

He contrasts this response to how he would feel if he got punked: "I'd be really embarrassed. Cuz, like, nobody does that to me. So either I'd probably go do something to that person who did it, or I'd, like . . . I don't know." Tom agrees that a benefit of being popular is that he does not usually get punked.

Chris, a Euro-American ninth-grade student, describes some other complexities of punking when he provides details of verbal punking or "smack talk." Metaphorically, smack talk, as Chris describes it, invokes being smacked in the face with words. One effect of smack talk is social control. For example, it makes other boys stop talking. More powerfully, as Chris reports, for most boys, being smacked produces humiliation and shame.

> *Chris:* Punking is anything you do to mess with somebody else. Beating them up, calling them names. Smack talk.

Debby: Smack talk?

Chris: Smack talk. [He laughs.] Oh, well, there's the more immature stuff that the younger people do where you talk about their mother. You know, then there's just really nasty stuff where you're, like, "You fuck your mother up the ass." Stuff like that. It's gross, but it pisses them off good.

Debby: Oh.

Chris: And there's telling 'em how weak they are. Like, telling them they're, like, a fat fuck or something.

Debby: Seem to get to boys?

Chris: Yeah. Oh, and about being gay. Yes, that's the big one. Not just calling him gay. Like, a teacher here is gay. So you say, like, "So how would you like to be in the teacher's back room?" You know, because "The Back Room" is, like, some place, it's rumored, you know . . . It's, like, "You jump in the back room, don't you?" I mean, it's not good, it's not nice, but . . .

Debby: And the purpose of smack talk?

Chris: Humiliate 'em. Yeah, cuz if they get humiliated enough, they'll stop talking, most of the time. You know, without conflict.

Debby: And the purpose?

Chris: Powerful. Powerful is a big, big part.

When asked to explain the different positions in the practices of punking, such as "who does it to who?" Chris explicates a hierarchy of punking, including punking as a form of initiation that, like fraternity hazing, functions to make boys "one . . . of the family."

Chris: Well, a lot of boys punk smaller boys, you know, to gain personal power at their expense. And then there are irritating boys. Uh, like this one kid . . . He's all, [in a crying voice] "I'm gonna beat you up!" And we're like, "Oh, right."

Debby: OK. So it's usually bigger kids to littler kids, and boys to boys?

Chris: Well, yeah, the majority of punking is with boys your same age, like, eighth graders mess with the seventh graders a lot, and also there's the kind of punking that you do just to initiate 'em. You know. To make them one of the family. . . .

Debby: OK. How does that work?

Chris: Well, like, Keith, he'll, uh, playfully beat up, like, seventh graders. And, he'll pick 'em up and hold 'em upside down and jump up and down. Stuff like that.

Debby: Just out of the blue?

Chris: Just out of the blue. Oh, yeah. And, um, he'll, whenever they say something, he just stands up and goes, "YOU'RE EXPELLED!! SHUT UP!!!" And stuff like that.

Debby: And then that works to do what?

Chris: Nothing. It's just something fun. That's kinda like, what sevvies [seventh graders] get. And then when they're eighth graders, they get to dish it out. That's just the way it is.

Debby: OK. And then do 10th graders do it to ninth graders?

Chris: No, ninth graders will get froshed, which is the same thing except more seriously tossed in bodies of water. Or they'll be cellophaned or they'll be duct-taped to a wall.

Chris's account of punking as a means of "initiating" boys resonates with a 2000 Northwest newspaper story describing a "possibly not uncommon fraternity practice" of binding a male college student's wrists and ankles with duct tape and leaving him somewhere alone. In this case, after going to bed, a student was tied up and barricaded in a room. He was discovered when a fire broke out at the fraternity and other residents told the firefighters about the tied up member still in the house. Fraternity members said that this practice was not unusual and it was done "for fun." Taking up similar discourses to distinguish a "criminal" practice from a "normal" practice of fun masculinities, school officials and police debated whether this incident was a "case of hazing" or merely "a prank." As a misdemeanor, "hazing" is considered more serious than "a prank" (Eskenazi, 2000; PI staff and News Service, 2000).

Humiliating others for fun is a common practice in punking that also shows up in the media. For example, it is a constant theme produced by the Bart Simpson character on the TV show *The Simpsons,* the most frequently watched TV show by the majority of the boys in the study. Whole episodes of *The Simpsons* are commonly built on Bart's elaborate practices of punking, and most episodes have at least some examples. For instance, in an episode in which Bart and his family go to a flight show on a military base, Bart verbally humiliates the military parking attendant by saying, "Way to guard the parking lot, top gun." In another episode, Bart tries to prove that "nerds [marginalized boys and girls] conduct electricity."

To prove his point, he repeatedly shocks his very intelligent younger sister, Lisa, whose character signifies a nerd. Another punking example is in an episode in which Lisa and her "genius" [marginalized] friends are verbally and physically punked by large, mean guys who will not move away from the park gazebo that the genius group has reserved. The dominant, in-control male characters who take the reserved gazebo are signified by large size, muscular bodies, verbal and physical practices of punking, toughness, and dominance.

Highlighting punking as a strategy intentionally done in public, Chris describes it as "showing off" and stresses that it's "not personal."

> *Chris:* Well, no, [you don't do it when you're alone] because it's also kind of an attention thing. [It happens] all the time. Hallways, classrooms, everywhere, all the time, anywhere. And, um, there's no point to do it just to the person, cuz then that means you have a personal thing going, if you do it when they're alone. But if you're doing it in front of other people, just to be cool or just to do it, um, it's kinda hard to explain. But, it's mean to do it if you're just alone because then you're doing it actually to be mean to them. But if you're doing it with other people around, you're doing it to show off, basically.
> *Debby:* So it's not as much about that one kid you're doing it to?
> *Chris:* No, no, it's, it's . . . it's weird.
> *Debby:* It sounds like it helps the person who's punking . . .
> *Chris:* Oh, yeah. And, of course, you know, you want all your friends to sit, to stand around and go, "Yeahhhh, do this, do that, drop him there. Let's go put him in the garbage can." Stuff like that. But if no one's there [to watch], then why bother? [He laughs.]

The idea that punking is not a personal attack on another boy but is a strategy necessary to affirm normative masculine identity in front of others underscores the objectification of the boy who is punked. Through the practices of punking and the discourses producing normative masculinity, nonnormative masculinity is a necessary object or resource to draw on and use to affirm normative identity. Similarly, Messerschmidt (2000a, 2000b) found that adolescent boys in his study strategically used sexual violence against girls and boys to overcome their marginalization from the masculinity norms, thereby representing themselves, temporarily, as "normal" males.

Discussion

Although this study is limited by a relatively small sample size of individuals drawn from one middle school and high school, the media sources are pervasive across the United States and beyond. Together, these data sources provide evidence of how United States culture represents and practices its norms of masculinity. This study shows that punking is a significant, identity-producing, everyday practice in boys' lives. Historically, this practice has come under the innocent and naturalized guise of "roughhousing," "aggressiveness," "bullying," and "boys will be boys." However, the conclusions drawn here represent an alternative way of viewing punking and bullying and of understandings men and male violence (Gilligan, 1997).

The accounts of masculinity provided by study participants and the media sources do not represent fixed male identities or innate masculinity. They represent harmful and dangerous cultural representations or discourses that function to victimize particular men and to maintain the "ideal." There are many other ways of participating in these discourses. Not included here, for example, are the ways teachers, other professionals, parents, and female students participate in and reproduce these discourses and practices as normative.

Punking and bullying position the recipient of these practices on the margins of masculinity. Occupying a position on the margins of masculinity often produces shame that can be devastating both immediately and in the long term (Connell, 1995; Garbarino, 1999; Gilligan, 1997; Kimmel, 1996; Real, 1997). Garbarino notes that some boys react immediately to ridicule and shaming, whereas other boys horde the shame they feel but remember every incident of ridicule and humiliation.

Shame can be measured in many ways. One way is to examine violent practices such as punking and bullying as a reflection of the high stakes invested in achieving or maintaining positioning or identity as "normal" and avoiding the shame of marginalization. In other words, what is at stake to avoid shame can be existence itself, existence as a "normal man" in the dominant belief system of patriarchal Western society.

Although relatively small in scope, this study represents common experiences also cited by others. Garbarino (1999), for example, uncovered the "pride or death" theme resounding through his interviews with adolescent boys in jail for violent crimes. Rejection, humiliation, shame, and anger repeatedly surfaced as effects of marginalization from the norm. One teenage boy demonstrated for Garbarino how to walk, look, and talk "tough," commenting that this performance was crucial to his identity and to his survival. He told Garbarino,

> You take any crap from anyone and you get marked as a pussy. . . . And if you get marked as a pussy, your life is hell. Man, you could get to a point where you would rather die than live that way. (p. 144)

Shame comes from being produced as an abnormal man, signified by "pussy" or wimp in the context of the male ideal.

Gilligan (1997) also documents the negative impact of marginalization that punking can have on men. Through his work with violent male criminals in a state prison system, he uncovered severe consequences of marginalization by verbal, physical, and sexual violence. Accounts provided by the male inmates are similar to those provided by the boys in Garbarino's study as well as those provided by boys and media sources in this study. Defying marginalization, for example, one inmate told Gilligan that he would sacrifice everything for his "pride, dignity, and self esteem" (p. 106). He continued,

> and I'll kill every motherfucker in that cellblock if I have to in order to get it. My life ain't worth nothin' if I take somebody disrespectin' me and callin' me punk asshole faggot and going "Ha! Ha!" at me. Life ain't worth livin' if there ain't nothin' worth dyin' for. If you ain't got pride, you don't got nothin'. (p. 106)

Although the language of Gilligan's quotation may be different from some of the language in the boys' accounts, it reflects a shared, public, dominant discourse about normative constructions of masculinity that produces significant consequences for those included and *excluded* from the norm. To be a "not normal" male in a cultural context in which the male norm is ever present, respected, and rewarded is often shameful and humiliating on a conscious and unconscious level.

Infallibility, dominance, toughness, and the ability and willingness to fight construct normative masculinity in this culture (Gilligan, 1997; Messerschmidt, 2000a, 2000b; Phillips, 2000, 2005). The most visible alternatives to this norm are ridiculed, humiliated, shamed, portrayed as inadequate, and violently perpetrated against. To be positioned or portrayed as an heir to repeated acts of humiliation and violence is not a "free" choice made by boys and men. Only through the binary ideology of gender and masculinity (normal/not normal) does it appear as a choice. For the norm to exist, non-normative masculinity must also exist. This is the nature of binary ideology.

As available resources for demonstrating that a person is a normal boy or man, punking and bullying to shore up the two poles of the masculine gender-identity binary. Further, constructing identity categories such as "a punker" (boy who punks) and a "punk" (boy who is punked) supports pervasive discourses that divide men into normative and non-normative groups.

How masculinity and male violence are conceptualized greatly influences professional approaches to mental-health and criminal-justice treatment, to identity and psychosocial development, and to social-context acceptance and resistance. Profound differences result from locating unhealthy male behaviors or "norms" such as aggression and violence within the *natural* male body instead of locating them in the cultural context as social strategies necessary to be a "normal" man. Neither of these views is adequate to completely explain and address male violence. However, because the prevailing, innate view has done little, historically, to prevent or decrease male violence, the view that discourse analysis reveals in this study warrants significantly more consideration.

Seeing masculinity and male violence as primarily socially constructed implies we should hold society more accountable both for the production of unhealthy norms and for the violent practices that affirm them. This shift would extend the scope and focus of prevention and intervention into harmful practices such as punking and other forms of male violence. This research provides evidence of cultural discourses of masculinity taken up and reproduced through their enactment by adolescent boys and in popular media. These discourses circulate locally, nationally, and globally. When consciously and unconsciously taken up by boys, girls, men, and women as frameworks of understanding, available discourses of masculinity are reproduced, and through this participation, implicate each one of us in the reproduction of unhealthy and destructive masculinity norms.

Implications of this kind of research and perspective are enormous for all professionals but especially for those invested in healthy growth and development, mental health, criminal justice, antiviolence, and trauma. Underlying the implications is the notion of change and the question of what needs changing—that is, the possibility of changing "innate" characteristics or tendencies in individual boys and men *or* the possibility of changing social constructions at every level of society (individual, family, community, nation . . .), even if they are "life giving" in the sense that males are given "life" as normal/not normal from the cultural norms that precede them.

Repetitive performances of masculinity discourses and practices produce that of which they "speak," the "ideal" and the "outcast" (Butler, 1990/1999, 1997; Phillips, 2005, 2006). Similarly repetitiveness of punking and bullying practices produces the norm, however variability in the "performance" of these practices reveals the fragility of the constructed norms that punking and bullying reinforce. The facts that these norms are tenuous and that the patriarchal order they protect is constitutively unstable are signals of the possibility of change. Repetitive interruption of these common cultural discourses and practices is key to removing practices such as punking as a normative aspect of male gender development and identity.

Change will not be easy. The depth of cultural and individual investment in the hegemonic norm of masculinity is extensive. Reproduced in numerous cultural arenas, the norm and its esteemed position in dominant, ideological belief systems of Western societies are historically sustained and continuously reproduced. Unable to exist outside the cultural language that constitutes a society's reality, boys and men lay claim to normative identities within this belief system (Silverman, 1992). It is possible, however, through close, critical examination of the practices of masculinities, to grasp the depth of investment in current unhealthy norms and to consciously resist them and the violence practices that affirm them.

REFERENCES

American Association of University Women. (1993). *Hostile hallways: The AAUW survey on sexual harassment in America's schools.* Washington, DC.

Boxley, J., Lawrance, L., & Gruchow, H. (1995). A preliminary study of eight grade students' attitudes toward rape myths and women's roles. *Journal of School Health, 65*(3), 96–100.

Butler, J. (1990/1999). *Gender trouble: Feminism and the subversion of identity.* New York: Routledge.

Butler, J. (1997). *The psychic life of power.* Stanford, CA: Stanford University Press.

Connell, R. W. (1995). *Masculinities.* Berkeley: University of California Press.

Daro, D., Edleson, J. L., & Pinderhughes, H. (2004). Finding common ground in the study of child maltreatment, youth violence, and adult domestic violence. *Journal of Interpersonal Violence, 19*(3), 282–298.

Eskenazi, S. (2000, February 20). Bound man found as fire damages WSU frat house. *Seattle Times,* B6.

Garbarino, J. (1999). *Lost boys: Why our sons turn violent and how we can save them.* New York: Free Press.

Gilligan, J. (1997). *Violence: Reflections on a national epidemic.* New York: Vintage.

Giroux, H. A. (1995). Memory and pedagogy in the "wonderful world of Disney": Beyond the politics of innocence. In E. Bell, L. Haas, & L. Sells (Eds.), *From mouse to mermaid: The politics of film, gender, and culture* (pp. 43–61). Bloomington: Indiana University Press.

Hawker, D. S. J., & Boulton, M. J. (2000). Twenty years' research on peer victimization and psychosocial maladjustment: A meta-analytic review of cross-sectional studies. *Journal of Child Psychology and Psychiatry, 41,* 441–455.

Hollway, W. (1989). *Subjectivity and method in psychology: Gender, meaning and science.* London: Sage.

Hollway, W. (1995). Feminist discourses and women's heterosexual desire. In S. Wilkinson & C. Kitzinger (Eds.), *Feminism and discourse: Psychological perspectives* (pp. 86–105). London: Sage.

Hollway, W., & Jefferson, T. (2000). *Doing qualitative research differently.* London: Sage.

Kimmel, M. (1996). *Manhood in America.* New York: Free Press.

Lisak, D., Hopper, J., & Song, P. (1996). Factors in the cycle of violence: Gender rigidity and emotional constriction. *Journal of Traumatic Stress, 9*(4), 721–741.

Messerschmidt, J. W. (2000a). Becoming "real men": Adolescent masculinity: challenges and sexual violence. *Men and Masculinities, 2*(3), 286–307.

Messerschmidt, J. W. (2000b). *Nine lives: Adolescent masculinities, the body, and violence.* Boulder, CO: Westview.

Nansel, T. R., Overpeck, M. D., Haynie, D. L., Ruan, W. J., & Scheidt, P. C. (2003). Relationships between bullying and violence among US youth. *Archives of Pediatrics and Adolescent Medicine, 157*(4), 348–353.

Nansel, T. R., Overpeck, M., Pilla, R. S., Ruan, W. J., Simons-Morton, B., & Scheidt, P. (2001). Bullying behaviors among US youth. *Journal of the American Medical Association, 285*(16), 2094–2100.

Olweus, D. (1994). Annotation: Bullying at school: Basic facts and effects of a school based intervention program. *Journal of Child Psychology and Psychiatry, 35,* 1171–1190.

Petersen, A. (1998). *Unmasking the masculine: "Men" and "identity" in a skeptical age.* London: Sage.

Phillips, D. A. (2000). Exploring new directions for ending practices of male violence: Masculinity, adolescent boys, and culture. *Dissertation Abstracts International, 61*(11B), 5800.

Phillips, D. A. (2001). Methodology for social accountability: Multiple methods and feminist, poststructural, psychoanalytic discourse analysis. *Advances in Nursing Science, 23*(4), 49–66.

Phillips, D. A. (2005) Reproducing normative and marginalized masculinities: Adolescent male popularity and the outcast. *Nursing Inquiry, 12*(3), 219–230.

Phillips, D. A. (2006) Masculinity, male development, gender, and identity: Modern and post-modern. *Issues in Mental Health Nursing, 27,* 103 123.

PI staff and News Service. (2000, February 20). Police look into "prank" on WSU's Greek row. *Seattle Post Intelligencer,* pp. B1, B3.

Real, T. (1997). *I don't want to talk about it: Overcoming the secret legacy of male depression.* New York: Fireside.

Savage, D. (1999, May 5). Fear the geek: Littleton's silver lining. *The Stranger,* p. 8.

Silverman, K. (1992). *Male subjectivity at the margins.* New York: Routledge.

Washington State PTA/ Safe Schools Coalition. (2003). Bullying report in brief. Retrieved July 10, 2004, from www.safeschoolscoalition.org.

Voicing Your Opinion
Punking and Bullying: Strategies in Middle School, High School, and Beyond

Debby A. Phillips

1. Respond to the study's findings regarding the representation of "ideal" masculinity. How do categories such as "superiority," "toughness," and "athleticism" intersect with your understanding of adolescent male "popularity?"

_____

_____

_____

_____

_____

2. Which stories from the interviews were the most informative for you? Did the participants offer examples of punking and bullying that surprised you or shocked you? If so; which ones? If not; why not?

_____

_____

_____

_____

_____

3. Respond to Phillips' suggestion that teachers, parents and female students participate in destructive discourses about adolescent masculinity. How is this done? How do teachers, parents, and female students contribute to the problem?

_____

_____

_____

_____

_____

MONSTERS AND VICTIMS
Male Felons' Accounts of
Intimate Partner Violence ♂ ♀

JULIA T. WOOD

This article is about male prisoners and how they speak about being violent to women in their lives. How do these men account for the violence with their intimate partner, and how do they understand what it means to be a man in our culture? The author looks at justifications for the violence, how the men dissociate themselves from the violence, and how they view the concept of manhood.

Previous research on men who commit intimate partner violence has addressed two questions: (1) how can researchers and clinicians classify men's accounts of intimate partner violence?, and (2) do men who engage in intimate partner violence subscribe to particular codes of manhood? The present study linked these two questions by asking how men account for their own intimate partner violence and how their accounts draw upon understandings of manhood. Grounded theory analysis of interviews with 22 incarcerated men identified three categories of themes in participants' accounts of intimate partner violence: justifications ('she disrespected me as a man;' 'a man has a right to control his woman;' 'she provoked me;' 'she took it'); dissociations ('I am not the abusive type;' 'my violence was limited, and abusers don't limit their abuse'); and remorse ('I regret I abused her'). Divergence among these representations of violent men's reasons for violence and previous typologies reflects this study's focus on insiders' views of behavior. Also, the themes that emerged from participants were informed by conflicting, although not wholly independent, codes of manhood that circulate in U.S. cultural life. Attention to violent men's sense-making strategies and contradictory narratives of manhood suggests opportunities for intervention and rehabilitation.

I got ready to shoot 'em, and the reason I didn't do it—you're not going to believe it—my baby's lying right there. (Tank, 47 years old)

A woman's kind of like a dog. You got to break 'em. A dog don't do right, you beat it 'til it do what you say. It either leave or be broke. Same with women. (Demetrius, 23 years old)

My mother was an alcoholic . . . I was taken from my mother and placed in foster care, which I believe caused the great trauma of my life. (Winston, 37 years old)

I feel disgusted with myself. At the same time I feel like I be relieving a whole lot of anger that's on my mind. I mean, I feel good at one point, and then at another point, I feel bad. But I be feeling good 'cause I done got the stress off my chest and all that, but at the same time, I be hurting her. (Magic, 40 years old)

These words came from four inmates in a medium-security prison in the south-eastern U.S. The first speaker locked his wife in an oversized safe and her lover in a car trunk for four days, but he did not kill them, because he did not want to alarm his infant daughter. By telling me this dramatic story, the speaker, Tank, was testing me as inmates routinely do when new people enter their territory. He was also telling the truth: official records documented his story. The second man displays his assumption that he is entitled to train women to comply with his wishes. Winston, the third man, blames traumas he experienced for his violence toward women. And Magic, the final speaker, voices contradictory feelings—disgust and relief—about assaulting his wife. Are these men monsters, or victims, or both? Or are such categories themselves inadequate for understanding the complex motives and meanings given by men who engage in intimate partner violence?

Most academic and lay work on intimate partner violence, including my own (Wood, 2000, 2001), has focused on female victims of male violence. Similarly, most activist efforts and social services affiliated with domestic violence seek to provide legal, emotional, and practical support to female victims. This article, in contrast, examines a group of men's perspectives on intimate partner violence and its relationship to cultural codes of manhood. Although attention to women who suffer violence from male partners is essential, it does not address the primary source of the problem: men who harm their wives and girlfriends. Trying to understand men who harm their intimate partners is not at odds with denouncing violence against women, which must be condemned without qualification. Indeed, more effective strategies of intervention may not be possible until and unless some effort is made to understand the perspectives of men who commit intimate partner violence.

Review of the Literature

Initially, intimate partner violence was construed as a unitary phenomenon (i.e., that there was just one type of partner violence). Beginning in the 1990s, however, researchers began to differentiate between types of intimate partner violence. In 1995, for example, Johnson identified two major sub-types: (i) patriarchal terrorism, later renamed *intimate terrorism,* which is motivated by desires (usually men's) for general relationship control, is less common, and is more likely to involve frequent or severe violence; and (ii) common couple violence, later renamed *situational couple violence,* which is more common, is practiced by both sexes, and is less likely to involve frequent or severe violence. Jacobson and Gottman (1998) also identified two types of violent men, what the termed 'pit bulls' and 'cobras,' both of which fit within Johnson's category of intimate terrorists.

Johnson and his colleagues (Johnson, 1995, 2001; Johnson, Conklin, & Menon, 2002; Johnson & Ferraro, 2000; Proceedings of the National Institute of Justice Gender Symmetry Workshop, 2000) later expanded the typology to include four sub-types, which take context into account: (i) *situational couple violence,* which occurs in the context of a noncontrolling relationship; (ii) *violent resistance,* which is self-defense or fighting back against a violent, controlling partner; (iii) *intimate terrorism,* which is violence perpetrated by one partner who desires control over the other partner; and (iv) *mutual violent control* in which both partners are violent and controlling. Johnson (2001) draws a particularly clear line between situational couple violence, which is not characterized by attempts to exert control and less often involves severe violence, and intimate terrorism in which one partner—usually the man—is more likely to inflict severe and multiple types of violence in order to control the other partner—usually a woman.

Intimate terrorism is the most extreme and dangerous kind of intimate partner violence. Each year in the U.S., 4 million incidents of violence against women by intimate partners are reported (National Coalition Against Domestic Violence, 1999); of these reports, 1000 include murders by boyfriends or husbands (http://www.fbi.gov/ucr/cius_00/contents.pdf; for other discussions of its prevalence, see Tjaden & Thoennes, 1998). Intimate partner violence is not restricted to particular race-ethnicities or socio-economic statuses (Bachman & Saltzman, 1995; Goldner, Penn, Sheinberg, & Walker, 1990; Goode, 2001; Jacobson & Gurman, 1986), nor is it restricted to adults. In a comprehensive study of dating violence, 20% of girls between the ages of 14 and 18 reported they had been hit, slapped, shoved, or forced to have sex by a male date (Goode, 2001). These are conservative figures that summarize only *reported* cases of intimate partner violence; many incidents go unreported.

Some researchers (e.g., Archer, 2000a, 2000b; O'Leary, 2000; Straus, 1999) claim that intimate partner violence is practiced fairly equally by men and women. A majority of clinicians and researchers (see Goldner et al., 1990; Jacobson & Gottman, 1998; Johnson & Ferraro, 2000), however, do not accept that claim. Both sexes may engage in some types of intimate partner violence, but men are more likely than women to engage in intimate terrorism (Johnson, 2001). Further, many researchers argue that men and women have distinct motivations for engaging in intimate partner violence: although both men and women may be motivated by anger and hurt, women are more likely to become violent in self-defense than in offense (Campbell, 1993); men are more likely to become violent as a means to gain or retain control.

Research on men who inflict violence on intimate partners has highlighted the troubling connection between men's efforts to control others, particularly women, and codes of masculinity that are prevalent in many societies (Kimmel, 1996, 2002; Lloyd 1999; Lloyd & Emery, 2000; Messner, 1997). Some researchers assert that men who engage in intimate partner violence identify with and embody *in extremis* widely accepted cultural ideologies that promote masculine authority and aggression. Building on this insight, researchers (e.g., Bogaert. 2001; Boyd, 2002; Caron & Carter, 1997; Daley & Onwuegbuzie, 2000; Dutton, 1986, 1998; Dutton & Galant, 1997; Kinney, Smith, & Donzella, 2001; Petrick, Olson, & Subotnik, 1994) report that men who identify strongly with traditional Western codes of manhood often feel, or fear, that they do not measure up to those codes. Attempting to shore up their masculine self-concept, they may try to control others, particularly those who are physically weaker than they are. Concurring, Faludi (1999) reports that some men who enact violence against wives and girlfriends do so as a means of claiming the power and status they see as a birthright of manhood.

There has been some effort to understand and classify men's views of intimate partner violence. Extending Scott and Lyman's (1968) classic work on accounts to the study of intimate partner violence, researchers (e.g., Bograd, 1988; Eisikovits & Buchbinder, 2000; Eisikovits & Edleson, 1986; Hearn, 1998; Hyden & McCarthy, 1994) grouped male batterers' accounts into two categories: *justifications* and *excuses*. Justifications acknowledge responsibility for an act, but deny the act's wrongfulness or inappropriateness (e.g., 'I did it, and I had a right to do it.') or downplay the severity of the act (e.g., 'What I did wasn't all that bad.'). Excuses admit an act was bad, but do not accept full responsibility for committing it (e.g., 'It was a bad thing to do, but it was not my fault.').

These classifications are, however, based on *outsiders'* views. That is, *researchers and clinicians* have labeled meanings and motives in men's accounts of intimate partner violence. Researchers and clinicians may not agree with violent men's perceptions, but understanding violent men's views of themselves and their actions is a necessary starting point for efforts at intervention and rehabilitation. It seems important, therefore, to attempt to understand men's accounts of intimate partner violence and of themselves as men from the men's point of view—the insiders' view.

This study explored the perceptions of men who have engaged in intimate partner violence. Based on previous research, the study asked whether there are connections between how men who engage in intimate partner violence (i) represent their actions, and (ii) view manhood. To pursue that broad question, two specific research questions were posed.

RQ1: Are themes in insiders' accounts of their intimate partner violence consistent with the categories of justifications and excuses that have been advanced in previous research, derived from *outsiders'* accounts?

RQ2: Which views of manhood, if any, are evident in participants' accounts of intimate partner violence?

Methods

Participants

Participants were 22 men who were serving time in a medium-security prison in the south-eastern U.S. The men represented a range of races and ethnicities: thirteen were African American, seven were white (including two who identified as Italian Americans); one was Mexican American; and one was of mixed ethnicity. The ages of participants ranged from 23 to 54 years. All of the men had volunteered to participate in STOP, a 13-week program to change men who abuse partners. STOP is an acronym: S—Survey the situation; T—Think about consequences; O—consider Options to violence; P—Prevent violence. In volunteering for the STOP program, these men self-identified as having committed intimate partner violence, although at the time of the study some participants were serving sentences for other crimes. Before conducting interviews, I spent six months visiting the prison. During this period, I developed relationships with the prison staff and talked with prisoners in casual conversations not related to violence or my study. By the time of the interviews, I knew each participant by name, and we had a short history of interacting. I conducted all interviews before the STOP class began.

Protecting At-Risk Participants

Because inmates are subject to risks not faced by most research subjects, they are designated an 'at-risk group' whose rights require special protections. Inmates often fear retribution if they do not participate in a project approved by correctional staff. As a group, inmates also have limited education, so they might be unable to read consent forms and give informed consent. Also, inmates might harass peers for participating. An additional danger is that an inmate might divulge an unrecorded crime, which a researcher must report to authorities. Perhaps the greatest risk to prisoners, however, is that interviews might be overheard by correctional staff, who are present customarily when any nonstaff person is with an inmate.

Steps were taken to minimize risks to participants. First, the director of the STOP program, the prison superintendent, and I informed the inmates that participating or not participating in the study would not affect their privileges, treatment, or length of sentences. Second, I read the consent form and discussed it in ordinary language. Third, I conducted all interviews in an area of the prison that inmates enter routinely for a variety of reasons, so other inmates did not know whether men coming into this area were participating in the study. Fourth, at the outset of each interview I warned the participant that if he mentioned a crime for which he had not been arrested, I had to inform the authorities. No participants disclosed crimes that obligated me to inform administrators. Finally, to eliminate the possibility that correctional staff could overhear interviews, I asked permission to interview each participant in a private office behind a closed door with no guard present. Given participants' histories of violence, my request entailed legal risks for the Department of Corrections and personal danger for me. My request was granted when I waived my right to hold the Department of Corrections responsible for any harm I might experience during the study.

Interviews

Interviews were conducted over a two-week period and ranged from 25 to 75 minutes. After audiotaping interviews, I transcribed the tapes, producing a total of 227 single-spaced pages. I opened each interview with this statement:

> I'm trying to understand *your* perspective on violence in your relationships with women. I'd like for you to think of a relationship in which you were violent toward a woman and tell me what happened as long as that does not involve telling me about a crime for which you have not been arrested. In telling me what happened, please describe why you did what you did, how you felt at the time, and how you saw yourself in those situations.

Each participant then told the story of his relationship or relationships in his own way. Stories offer not only information about experiences, but more importantly insight into attitudes, feelings, thoughts, meanings, and reasoning (Bochner, Ellis, & Tillmann-Healy, 1997; Vangelisti, Crumley, & Baker, 1999). Interviews were minimally structured to allow participants to tell their stories in their own words and in sequences that made sense to them. During the interviews, my comments were limited to prompts to encourage clarification or elaboration. I did not redirect participants if they ventured into topics that seemed tangential to me. For instance, many participants talked at length about nuclear families and work problems. I assumed that these topics were not unrelated to accounts of violence, but were relevant within participants' perspectives.

Analysis

This study relied on inductive analysis as informed by grounded theory (Bulmer, 1979; Glaser, 1978, 1992; Glaser & Strauss, 1967; Strauss, 1987), which accords priority to participants' perspectives and meanings. Eschewing a priori theoretic constructs or coding schemes, grounded theory analysts comb data for emergent themes that reflect key thoughts, feelings, and meanings in participants' worlds. The process of constant comparative analysis, which involves concurrent interviewing and analysis (Strauss & Corbin, 1990), leads researchers to reshape and refine themes continuously. Thus, themes gleaned from interviews conducted late in the research process are tested against, and used to reanalyze, interviews conducted early in the research process. This mode of analysis compels researchers to revisit interpretations of early interviews through the lens of what emerges later in the research process (Charmaz, 1983; Lempert, 1996).

The accepted standard for assessing interpretive research based on grounded theory is *verification* (Creswell, 1998; Dougherty, 2001a), which requires asking whether interpretations provide *a* (not necessarily *the*) reasonable explanation of the phenomena under study. Five verification procedures were used. First, factual details of participants' stories were compared with information available in their files and from correctional staff. Second, attention was paid to extra-interview information that indicated participants' candor in interviews. For example, one participant asked for a copy of the tape. He said he had told me what it was like to be him and why he was violent. He thought if his girlfriend heard the tape, she would understand him. Other participants agreed that the tapes would be a good way to explain themselves to the women in their lives. I gave a copy of the interview tape to any participant who wanted it. Another indicator of participants' candor came from Joseph Marinello, who taught the STOP class that followed interviews. He told me that in class discussions, several participants had said the interview was the first time they had spoken openly about violence toward the women in their lives. Third, after preliminary analysis, I discussed themes with participants and asked if the themes 'seem right to you.'

The fourth verification procedure was included to minimize the likelihood of idiosyncratic interpretation by establishing standards for what constituted a theme. Following previously published thematic analyses (Owen, 1984, 1985; Shank-Krusciewitz & Wood, 2001; Wood, 2001), two standards were applied to data: (i) to count as a theme in a given participant's interview, an idea must recur a minimum of three times; and (ii) to count as a theme across participants, the theme had to surface in at least half of the interviews. Finally, in presenting results, I provide extensive quotations from participants. This comprises a form of face validity by allowing readers to assess the fit between data and themes I identify (Dougherty, 2001a, 2001b). All names used are pseudonyms, and participants' language is unedited.

Results

In the discussion that follows, I present excerpts from interviews to foreground the men's voices and allow readers to appraise my interpretations of the men's words and meanings. I then show how these themes draw upon two views of manhood that were woven into participants' accounts.

Research Question One: Themes in Men's Accounts of Intimate Partner Violence

Seven themes characterized insiders' accounts of intimate partner violence, and these were grouped into three categories: *justifications, dissociations,* and *remorse.* The category of justifications parallels that identified by previous researchers: it includes themes that represent violence as reasonable or appropriate; it also includes what previous researchers have called excuses, although I resist the use of the label, as it can be seen as representing an outsider's judgment, not that of participants in this study. In addition, there was a category of accounts best labeled as 'dissociations,' because from the insiders' perspective these functioned to differentiate or disassociate participants from 'real abusers.' I also identified a category of remorse, which is a subset of the category 'apologies' found in previous research. Table 1 arrays the three categories and the themes within each, identifies the number of participants who referenced each theme, and shows the number of times each theme appeared across interviews.

Justifications

Consistent with findings from previous research, *all* participants offered what can be labeled 'justifications' for their violence. Justifications are accounts that accept responsibility, but explain why an action was appropriate, reasonable, necessary, within the actor's right, or that the action was not as bad as perceived. Four interrelated themes comprise this category and reflect primarily a sense of the men's 'rights.'

Table 1 Categories of Themes in Men's ($N = 22$) Accounts of Violence

Theme	Number of Participants Citing Theme	Total Number of References to Theme
Justifications		
She disrespected me as a man.	22	146
A man has a right to control his woman.	18	57
She provoked me.	22	68
She took it.	13	42
Dissociations		
I am not the abusive type.	17	62
My violence was limited.	16	51
Remorse		
I regret that I abused her.	12	39

SHE DISRESPECTED ME AS A MAN. By far the most prominent theme was that violence against a wife or girlfriend was a *legitimate response* to being disrespected as a man. Reflecting a fierce sense that being a man means being in charge and being deferred to by women, this theme inflected every participant's account. Some men felt wives or girlfriends challenged their manhood by not being appropriately deferential. Kordell made the point forcefully when he said, 'most men gotta feel like they gotta be in charge. You ain't gonna smart ass Kordell, not if you're my woman. I ain't gonna put up with you. I'm not gonna let you talk to me any kinda way.' Melvin felt disrespected when he asked his girlfriend where she had been, and he said, 'I really didn't like her tone of voice . . . I felt that I had been disrespected.' Another man explained that he 'had to' discipline his girlfriend because she was 'getting more sassy. Okay, it's time to really break her down, like, Whoa! You getting way out of line now. You done crossed the line.'

Demetrius offered a similar view when he slated, 'by them [women] saying the wrong things, it's just like "right now I just really don't wanna hear what you have to say. Stay in your place and clear your position."' One participant became violent when his girlfriend insulted 'the ego, the pride, the male pride.' G. W. put it this way: 'She spose to be home when I get there. I get there, she's not there. That makes me feel disrespected.' Weeks felt disrespected when his wife didn't want to have sex one morning: 'I was wanting to make love to her and she turn her back to me, and it made me mad. So I hit her in the mouth and I swole up her lip real bad. I mean, It was real bad; I mean deep.'

Some men felt disrespected when they perceived women as challenging men's right to independence. Wyatt felt his wife intruded on his autonomy when she asked about his activities: 'And I'd come home, and she'd want to know every move I'd made, and I felt like she was invading in my privacy.' Kendrick felt disrespected when his partner asked where he was going. He said, 'a man, he's supposed to run the household. So if you're a man, you ain't really gotta—ah, how do you put it—I ain't gotta answer to my old lady. If I wanna go somewhere, I'm gonna go. I shouldn't have to tell her.'

Other men became violent when they perceived their partners as doubting their ability as breadwinners, particularly if the men themselves doubted it. During a time of financial stress, Demetrius's wife asked him, 'How's we gonna get by this month? What we gonna do?' Describing how he felt when his wife raised the question, Demetrius said, 'it's like you ain't believing in me . . . you don't too much believe in me. It felt like stepping on my pride, like you didn't believe in me. As far as a male, the worst thing you can do is hurt his pride, because you just done took everything away from him.' Concurring, Ricardo said, 'I couldn't really get a decent job to provide for my family. I didn't feel like a man . . . I'd go back home and I'd have to hear her mouth, so that led to abuse and problems.' Echoing this, another participant said that he beat his girlfriend because she was 'downin' me all the time . . . saying I wasn't ever gonna be nothing, couldn't hold a job.'

A MAN HAS A RIGHT TO CONTROL/DISCIPLINE HIS WOMAN. Present in 18 of the 22 interviews was the theme that a man is entitled to use violence to discipline his female partner(s). This theme seems to undergird the first theme of justification in that if a man assumes he is entitled to discipline and control his wife or girlfriend, then it is appropriate to respond with violence to perceived disrespect of his manhood. From participants' perspectives, *it is a man's right to use violence to discipline and control women.* Like many men who abuse, Wyatt recalled learning in his family of origin that a man has a right to assault his wife: 'I'd seen my dad drink, and my dad would abuse my mom real bad. And, it was sort of like those things are supposed to happen, you know what I mean?' Echoing this, George recalled, 'you seen your mother was abused, then you abused, so as I growed up, I seen that it was okay to do that. Didn't nobody tell me that it was wrong, so after I got on my own, I was abusive.' Similarly, as he grew up, Winston 'witnessed my father beating my mother, beating her black and blue.' Moses traced his violent behavior to 'me watching my mother get beaten from my stepfather. He would jump on her.'

Nonfamilial relationships also informed some participants' belief that men are entitled to abuse wives and girlfriends. Melvin explained that his father had left when he was an infant, so he had to look elsewhere to 'learn how to be a man. And I learned from hanging around the older people and drawing that knowledge out of their heads, and that has helped me conduct myself in a macho manner.' Miguel credited gangs with teaching him that men are justified in abusing women physically and sexually: 'Through the gangs, when they [new members] get initiated, coming in they beat or sex them [females] down or whatever.' Demetrius also looked to other men for guidance about manhood. Explaining what he learned from other men, Demetrius said, 'I see a lot of guys tame their woman, intimidate her. I get a rush out of it—control 'em intimidate 'em, tell 'em who can be their friends.'

In invoking this theme, participants emphasized that they used violence to 'keep women in their place.' Kendrick explained that his wife was 'the type of person where if she feel like she can get away with something, she gonna push it to the extreme, so you nip it in the bud. If you don't nip it in the bud, she gonna keep pushing.' When the women in his life wouldn't accept his terms, Moses blamed them for his violence: 'I wanted them to think this way, but they wouldn't. And it caused me to go into a rage of violence.' Jackson assaulted his wife 'when I wanted something that she would have stored away and she wouldn't give it to me.' Caleb used violence to teach his wife that, 'she's a mother first of all. That's how it is. She's not only a mother, but she's a wife. That's her primary objective.' According to Weeks, 'you wanna control. I mean, that's where the hitting comes from. To put fear in 'em.'

SHE PROVOKED ME. The following two categories could have been labeled as 'excuses,' because they place the choice/blame for the action outside of the abuser. Just as in the earlier cases, however, the 'excuses' were based in larger systems of justification that make the men's responses 'reasonable.' For example, several participants justified their violence explicitly as a response to women's general provocations. Moses maintained, 'I was really provoked into doing mostly what I was doing.' Echoing this, Walter said, 'she was provoking me and stuff.' Other men offered these examples: 'she do something to provoke me,' 'they provoke me so bad to act out my behavior,' and 'I been provoked so bad, I don't even wanna be bothered with you [a woman] no more.'

Many men specifically pinpointed *verbal aggravation* as provocation. Gabe recalled, 'I'm coming home every day and she's constantly bickering about something, constantly bickering, and that's where her mouth was.' Similarly, Magic perceived his wife as provoking him by 'nagging and nagging and nagging . . . I be like, "All right, all right, just keep on doing it. You're irritating me."' With sadness, Kordell remembered that his girlfriend provoked him with 'verbal things. Some of the stuff was unforgiving. Some of it was unbearable. She pushed me all the way to the limit. Enough is enough and then you feel like you have to do whatever you have to do to take care of that moment. It just get violent.' George similarly stated, 'she do something, at the time it tick me off—pushed that button.' Moses recounted hitting his girlfriend after he thought an argument about money had ended, but 'she started at it again, so I hit her.'

SHE TOOK IT. Completing the category of justifications was a theme that could, but should not from the men's perspectives, be labeled an 'excuse.' The examples in this theme asserted that women who tolerated violence licensed more of the same; in other words, participants perceived the women's acceptance of violence as justifying continued abuse and/or demonstrating that the abuse was not problematic. Reflecting on several women he had beaten, Demetrius said, 'If I can just hit you, you know what I mean, anytime I feel like it, I can just keep on going.' Agreeing, another man said the abuse began early in his marriage: 'I started dishing it out, she started taking it, like we were meant to do it.'

Twenty-nine-year-old Gabe recalled that, after he beat his wife the first time, she left but quickly returned. Gabe paused, then added, 'it was kind of like once she came back, it was kind of like in my mind she accepted it. So now I can view this as acceptable behavior. It's okay for me to do it.' Explaining how his girlfriends' toleration of 'minor' abuses led him to see more serious violence as acceptable, Miguel said, 'it'll start with just a slap or a push. Then once you get that push or slap in, that's when it get to the black eye, then all the real bad—trying to break arms and legs and all that.' To support his belief that women who do not leave violent men give permission for continued violence, one man asked, 'If he mean to you, what the hell you stay with him for?' As if to answer, Kordell said, 'I believe they *wanted* that. If you don't like how I treat you, you gonna eventually leave. If a person continues to put up with something, then that's a choice that they make.'

DISSOCIATIONS. The category of justifications focused on men's 'rights' or the 'rightfulness' of their actions. A second category of themes involved participants' dissociating, or disconnecting, themselves from their violence or from identities as 'real abusers.' Whereas justifications acknowledge the violence and maintain that it is warranted, dissociations distinguish particular kinds of violence from 'real abuse' and differentiate men who inflict limited violence from 'real abusers.' Two themes comprise this category.

I'M NOT REALLY THE ABUSIVE TYPE. Seventeen participants maintained that they were not 'really abusive,' and they used three strategies to maintain this stance. One was to dissociate specific violent acts from being abusers. Explicating this, Ricardo stated, 'I was abusive, you know, but I wasn't really the abusive type.' After describing how he stabbed his girlfriend, Jackson shook his head and said, 'I still ask myself today, "Was that really me? Did I actually do what I did?"' Insisting that the 'real him' didn't want to hurt his wife, Gabe stated that 'I really didn't mean to do it, I didn't wanna do it. It just happened.' Other men stated, 'I hit her in the eye—she had to get stitches, but I didn't mean to;' 'I knowed, *knowed* this ain't me;' and 'I didn't mean to do it. And really, deep down in my heart, that ain't me. That ain't me, yeah.' Perhaps the most remarkable dissociation of violence came from G. W., a 44-year-old man who opened his interview with two sentences: 'I'm not really what you say a violent person. My crime is for killing a girlfriend.'

Some participants deployed a second, related strategy to distinguish themselves from 'real' abusers. They emphasized that, unlike 'real abusers,' they did not enjoy hurting women. After describing his assaults on two wives, Wyatt noted that, 'I never did want to hit my wives.' Ricardo insisted, 'I never really enjoyed putting my hands on a woman. I'm not that type of person.' Tank noted that, although he had beaten and confined two women, he was not like really abusive men because 'I could have killed 'em just like that, but that wasn't in my heart.' Likewise, Jackson concluded his account of an attack on his wife by saying he had not enjoyed it because 'I don't think I got the killer blood in me.'

A third strategy of maintaining they were not abusers was to attribute violence to external causes that made them not their 'real selves.' External factors that participants saw as making them not their real selves included alcohol and other drugs and medical problems. In Scott and Lyman's (1968) typology citing an external cause for action is classified as an excuse. Yet from participants' perspectives, external causes do not so much excuse their actions *as separate their 'real selves' from those actions.* Miguel contrasted his 'real self' to the self he became when he drank: 'I never had a bad relationship when I won't drinking. It's like two people 'cause when I won't drinking or using drugs, I could handle a relationship.' Gabe, on the other hand, attributed his violent rages to medical problems that distorted who he really was: 'There's a reason, an actual physical reason for it. I'm not crazy.' Likewise, Alan claimed his assaults on women were 'on account of the medication I was taking [that] made me do what I did.' Forty-seven-year-old Weeks said, 'I haven't been a bad person. I was a sick person. When I wasn't using drugs or drinking, I'm one of the better persons that you wanna be around.'

Some participants made more global attributions to external forces that destroyed their 'real selves.' Summarizing a history of troubles that had 'warped' his real self, one man said, 'Hell, I've been hurt since I was five years old.' Others offered similarly broad accounts of circumstances that had twisted them. 'It seemed like nobody wouldn't give me no chance out there;' 'I had lost my son. I'd lost my wife, and I thought I'd lost my family and everything else. I just had so much anger I guess.' As with other forms of dissociation, external attributions would be viewed as an excuse from an outsider's perspective. From participants' perspectives, however, external attributions were construed as more legitimate, reasonable explanations of why they—their real selves—were not abusers.

MY VIOLENCE WAS LIMITED. Data in this study echoed the finding of previous research (Bograd, 1988; Hearn, 1998) that men who engage in intimate partner violence often minimize their violence. However, the label *minimization* does not capture how this theme functioned for participants. From their perspectives, the limits they observed set them apart from real abusers. Sixteen participants dissociated themselves from 'batterers' by drawing a clear line between what they did and the kinds of violence that they associated with 'real batterers.' Ricardo said, 'I was abusive to her, but I wasn't abusive *every* night, *every* weekend, stuff like that. A lot of women out there going through that—*every* day, *every* week, and that's bad.' Comparing himself with what he considered real abusers, Walter reflected that they 'acted out on impulses. I have acted out on impulses, but mine is not as bad as theirs.'

Some men dissociated themselves from really abusive men by pointing out that they had not inflicted the injury they could have and would have if they had been 'real abusers.' Jackson, for example, noted that he stabbed his wife only once: 'I stabbed her. I couldn't go in but so far, then I came back out, but I couldn't do it no more.' Explaining why it was not so bad for him to lock two women up for four days, Tank said, 'I knocked them out, but I didn't hurt them. I had guns on me, but I didn't kill nobody.' When Antonio beat his wife's face so badly that even he couldn't bear to look at her, he reasoned that he hadn't 'hit her as hard as I could. I mean, to me, it was only a taste of what she could have got.'

A third way men defined their violence as more limited than that of really abusive men was to point out boundaries they observed. For Weeks, the boundary was pregnancy. 'I did smack her a couple of times when she wasn't pregnant, but when she was pregnant I never put my hands on her.' Other men drew the limit at what they perceived as 'serious assault.' Sidney used mental games to control women and prided himself on the fact that 'I don't hit women,' Caleb, too, noted that after hitting his girlfriend once, 'I never hit her again ever. I was more mental.' Dennis remarked that 'I've never been beating my mates, but there mighta been some occasions where I might have crossed the line with verbal and emotional abuse.' Likewise, Magic said, 'I'd just push her or shake her or push her head or something like that. It wouldn't be really violent as far as cutting and shooting and brutally beating.' In similar fashion, G. W. said, 'I was getting like joy—I see she upset from things I'm saying, I just keep right on bringing it. That was good enough for me. Ain't no need for me to walk up and hit her.'

Remorse

In addition to other justifications and dissociations, more than half of the participants expressed remorse over intimate partner violence, a process that can be seen as a specific form within a category of accounts called *apologies* (Scully & Marolla, 1984). In suggesting remorse, these participants acknowledged both their violence *and* its wrongness. A single theme defines this category.

I REGRET THAT I ABUSED HER. Twelve participants acknowledged they had hurt women and stated that they regret their actions. The following comments illustrate this theme:

> In a couple of days [after beating his wife], I feel guilty for what I done.
> I was so ashamed of myself. It was shame betook me. And I be sitting in the back seat and she sitting in the front seat . . . and it was shame.
> After a minute, you feel guilty about it. You look back on it like that's wrong.
> I think it's wrong in a way, 'cause no woman should be beaten like that.
> I was ashamed. I felt less than a man when I did those things.
> I actually, really hurt somebody I love. That's something I don't wanna feel no more.

The category of remorse entails admitting being violent toward women and experiencing regret for having done so, whereas the category of dissociation resists identifying as an abusive man, and justifications resist seeing the action as harmful or outside the bounds of normative expectations. In different ways, justification, dissociation, and remorse suggest avenues for rehabilitation.

At the same time, statements of remorse should not necessarily be accepted at face value. Researchers and clinicians would be wise to recognize not only their potential for rehabilitative efforts but also the possibility that statements of remorse are strategic acts designed to win favor or redemption. Apologies are well documented as part of the 'honeymoon phase' in the cycle of violence. As Scully and Marolla (1984) noted in their analysis of convicted rapists' accounts, 'an apology allows a person to admit guilt while at the same time seeking a pardon by signaling that the event should not be considered a fair representation of what the person is really like' (p. 541). Often, however, apologies—as well as violence—continue throughout the course of a violent relationship.

Research Question Two: Views of Manhood

Participants' accounts invoked understandings of manhood that are consistent with previously summarized research that has suggested, but not actually explored, intersections between men's intimate partner violence and their views of what it means to be a man. Woven through the interviews were two contradictory, although not entirely independent, views of manhood. Both understandings of manhood are firmly ensconced in U.S. cultural narratives of masculinity and heterosexual relationships. All participants invoked the narrative that men are dominant and superior to women, and this theme surfaced 96 times in interviews. In addition, 13 participants expressed the view that men protect and do not hurt women; this theme surfaced 53 times in interviews.

Men as Dominant and Superior

Every participant alluded to what may be termed a 'patriarchal' view of manhood that holds that men are superior to women and are entitled to sex and other attention from their wives and girlfriends, that women are supposed to please and defer to men, that men have the right to control and discipline women, and that women should center their lives around men, although men are entitled to independence. Numerous researchers have noted that cultural practices may legitimate this view of manhood by approving of men who are dominant, powerful, and controlling and approving of females who 'stand by their man,' no matter how men treat them (Adams, Towns, & Gavey, 1995; Coan, Gottman, Babcock, & Jacobson, 1997; Kimmel, 1996, 2002; Meyers, 1997).

Participants articulated a patriarchal view of manhood that holds that men should be in charge of relationships. The 'naturalness' of male domination is clear in Gabe's reflection that, 'I fell into the pants and she fell into the dress, just natural as can be. I started dishing it out, she just started taking it. It was natural.' Said another man, 'I was the man in the relationship. I was always brought up like, a man's s'posed to be more in control of a relationship.' Echoing this, Demetrius stated, 'Things got to go my way or no way. I mean I respect, respect your woman's opinion, but I just feel they had to go my way or no way at all.' Concurring, Kendrick said, 'A man, he's supposed to run the household. So if you're a man, you ain't really gotta, I ain't gotta answer to my old lady. But with *her,* she wanna go somewhere, she's supposed to come to me and say "I wanna go to such and such. I wanna do such and such." That's the way I was brought up. It's still in me.' Almost repeating Kendrick, another man said, 'As far as like the man being the head of the household, it's kind of old fashioned, but I believe it.'

In addition to emphasizing that men should be in control, the patriarchal view of manhood assumes that women should serve, please, and cater to men. Explaining this facet of the patriarchal view, G. W. said that a woman should 'find out what kind of respect or what kind of leeway he [her man] want, that's what you give him. Talk to him in a respectful way.' More starkly expressing the idea that women should cater to men, Gabe said, 'I didn't want her to have a life away from home. I wanted to be the center of her world.' For Gabe, being the center of his wife's world meant, 'I had her basically trained to fix my supper and wash my clothes. She wouldn't dare let me get up outta my chair, fix my own drink. I didn't *wanna* get up, fix my own drink. And then she kinda got tired of it. [I'd say] "Bitch, fix me something to drink." And if she didn't, then it would just start all over again.' Agreeing, Melvin said, 'I'm the man. You do what I say. I say "jump," you just say "how high?"'

Male aggression and violence also fit within the patriarchal view of manhood. As G. W. explained, 'The only way she can respect her man, her man gotta be aggressive, gotta be violent.'

Expressing a similar sentiment, Kordell stated, 'Me, as a man, I felt that I had to break a woman down.' Explicitly linking manhood to controlling women, two other men remarked, 'I remember the phrase, "you're the man of the house now." So I had to be the one to discipline;' and 'Men gotta be in charge, so I got you [a woman]. And I can handle her.' What happens if a woman fails to show proper deference? According to Demetrius, that is an insult to her man's pride that justifies violence from the man: 'As far as a male, the worst thing you can do is hurt his pride. You just be prepared for war right there.'

For other participants, the patriarchal view of manhood was how they saw 'real men,' *but they were unsure that they personally embodied that ideal.* Demanding a woman's respect and subservience seemed to be means to bolster their sense of their manhood. Clearly articulating the relationship between his violence toward a woman and his insecurity in his manhood, Weeks concluded his description of pummeling his wife's face by saying, 'My self-esteem was real low and that's why I put her on my level.' In explaining why he was violent toward his wife and girlfriend, Moses compared himself with 'successful men' he knew: 'I felt helpless. I mean, I see all my other partners out there—they got these fine cars, and I ain't got my car . . . I couldn't really do nothing.' Explaining why he beat his partner, Demetrius said, 'I hadn't finished school or nothing. I mean, I knew we couldn't live off no fast food restaurant paycheck. I mean, it sorta hurt me, my pride . . . I hadn't did nothing with my life.' In the most explicit statement of feeling he failed to measure up to his ideals of manhood, Ricardo said, 'I couldn't get a decent job . . . I didn't feel like I could take, uh, like I was the provider, you know what I'm saying. I didn't feel like a man.'

As these excerpts show, the patriarchal view of manhood is evident in accounts of men who feel they are 'real men' as well as in accounts of men who fear they do not measure up to the code of manhood they endorse and admire. Men who believe they personally embody this ideal of manhood feel that they are entitled to control relationships and women, be deferred to and catered to by women, and use disciplined violence to enforce their male entitlements. Men who are not confident that they measure up to the patriarchal view of manhood use control and violence to enforce women's deference, which gives them some assurance that in the realm of private relationships they are and are perceived as 'real men.'

Men as Protectors of Women

Thirteen participants invoked a second understanding of manhood that was in some tension with the patriarchal view. The second understanding of manhood invokes a code of chivalry that requires that men respect and take care of women and never abuse them. This view of manhood is also well established in many cultures. Although not all participants who professed this view consistently embodied it, they voiced high regard for it as an ideal.

In explaining the view of men as protectors of women, participants emphasized the wrongness of men's violence against women. Said Sidney, 'I don't hit women, I don't believe a real man ever hits a woman. No man needs to do that. If he does, he's got trouble upstairs. He is mentally ill if he's hitting a woman.' Further separating hitting women from being a man, Kendrick stated, 'That don't make me a man for jumping on a woman.' Tony agreed, citing his mother as the source of this view: 'My mama always taught me you're not supposed to put your hands on a woman.' Concurring, Dennis asserted that, 'As far as a man fighting a woman, that's a no-no. . . . It takes a sorry man to jump on a woman,' and Weeks insisted that, 'Men don't hit on—no matter what—a real man don't hit his female, his queen.'

Also entailed in the view that men are protectors of women was the clear sense that men should safeguard wives and girlfriends. According to Wyatt, 'I believe a man should take care of the woman, a man should take care of his wife.' Said another participant, 'I'm here to protect you and take care of you [a female]. I have to respect them all, no matter what, and don't put no hands on them.' Summing up, Dennis said, 'I put all women on pedestals.'

Acknowledging Tension in the Two Views

These two views of manhood share the assumption of male superiority, although one view is clearly more pro-social than the other. Further, these two views of manhood were not wholly independent in participants' accounts. Thirteen participants expressed belief in both views. For example, there was a clear contrast between Sidney's adamant avowal that, 'I don't hit women. I don't believe a real man ever hits a woman. A real man don't hit a woman', and his insistence that men do not tolerate disrespect from women: 'You control her without that [hitting].' Sidney resolved the contradiction by controlling women in ways he perceived as compatible with being 'a real man' who does not resort to physical violence against women. Other participants did not resolve so easily the tension between their views of real men as controlling their women and as respecting and protecting their women. At an abstract level, they reported feeling it was wrong for men to hurt women, but at a concrete level they asserted that they were entitled or compelled to hurt the particular women with whom they had intimate relationships.

In a recent book, Felson (2002) argues that both the culture and individual men subscribe to a chivalrous code, which holds that men should protect women. Felson claims that 'violence against women [is] not an expression of sexism' (p. ix) because 'chivalry leads men to protect women, not harm them' (p. 5). The data in this study do not support Felson's claims. Instead, my data demonstrate that some men who engage in intimate partner violence recognize the cultural code of chivalry but *violate it in their own relationships with wives and girlfriends.* My data further suggest that some men subscribe to chivalry as an abstract code, but they do not necessarily draw upon it in their relationships with wives and girlfriends. In other words, some men may believe that men should protect women in general and mothers and daughters in particular. However, my data show that chivalry does not automatically find its way into some men's relationships with wives and girlfriends, and it does not deter some men from intimate partner violence.

Discussion

Previous research has classified men's accounts of violence against women into two categories: excuses, which are attributions to forces outside of actors' control; and justifications that advance reasons why violence was appropriate or less problematic than others may perceive. The themes and categories identified in the present study, although not inconsistent with those reported in prior work, offer an actor-focused interpretation of men's intimate partner violence. Consistent with previous classification systems, this study found that certain types of *justifications* predominated in men's accounts of their intimate partner violence. It also identified *dissociations* as a category in men's accounts of intimate partner violence. A third, but much less common, category of men's accounts was expressed *remorse* for having harmed women.

Although from an outsider's perspective, some justifications and dissociations may be perceived as excuses, that label does not represent well how participants viewed their actions. 'Excuses' does not capture—and, in fact, misrepresents—how these accounts work for men who commit intimate partner violence. For example, the label 'excuses' obscures many participants' active repudiation of identification with 'abuser' or 'really violent' men. These men did not admire abusers and did not identify with that category of men. Also, participants asserted that, in limiting the degree or frequency of intimate partner violence they inflicted, they evaded the category of abusers *because real abusers do not limit their violence.* Labeling these accounts as *dissociations* suggests important approaches to rehabilitation, as it provides a new perspective on ways in which the offenders view their actions.

Finally, this study noted remorse as category in men's accounts of intimate partner violence. More than half of the participants in this study expressed remorse for having hurt wives and girlfriends. If genuine, remorse might be a foundation for rehabilitation and change. Yet, as I suggested previously, it may be unwise to accept remorse at face value. It is not difficult to express regret after having done something wrong. Whether that regret prevents future wrongs is another matter. As George commented when I asked him what he would tell his daughters about avoiding violent relationships, 'I tell 'em, if he ever abuse you, get out of the relationship . . . Sometimes an apology really don't solve a problem. You might say "I'm sorry" today, and a month later, you be doin' the same thing.'

This article also reveals dueling narratives of manhood in participants' accounts of their intimate partner violence. The first narrative, which *all* participants referenced, regards men as entitled to dominate and control their women either because they are 'real men' or—ironically—because they feel that they personally do not measure up to ideals of manhood that they admire. Men who identify with a patriarchal narrative of manhood may use violence to exercise their assumed entitlements and bolster their esteem. More than half of the participants also resonated with, but reported that they could not live up to, a second narrative of manhood that defines men as protectors of women. Men who identified with this narrative espoused the belief that men should not be violent toward women. Yet they felt unable to stop being violent or believed that they were even entitled to be violent to their own intimate partners.

Most participants who invoked this view of manhood linked protecting women less to their intimate partners than to either *women in the abstract* or to *specific females,* most notably mothers and daughters. Dennis, for example, said. 'I got a mother, I got daughters and all . . . I put all women, or most women, on pedestals.' Similarly, Ricardo said that, 'I feel for the women that's in an abusive relationship.' Felson's (2002) claim that men embrace a code of chivalry should be tempered to note that men may act and feel more chivalrous toward mothers, daughters, and women in the abstract than toward intimate partners. Although revering women in the abstract, participants saw their violence against other specific women in their lives as legitimate. Exemplifying the distinction between male violence against women in general and a particular man's violence against his intimate partner, Miguel said, 'I can't stand it if I'm with you and you hittin' your wife, I can't stand it. I can't stand it if nobody else do it, but I do it.'

Directions for Future Study

This study suggests three avenues for future research on male intimate partner violence. First, scholars and clinicians should attempt to replicate the present study with men who have not been incarcerated. Because scholarship to date has made little effort to understand 'normal' men's views of manhood and male violence against intimates, we do not know how similar or dissimilar their views would be to those of participants in this study. Most of the participants in this study fit into Johnson and Ferraro's (2000) category of *intimate terrorists.* Men without criminal histories might enact other types of intimate partner violence and different themes and views of manhood might surface in their accounts.

Second, researchers should work with staff at correctional institutions and elsewhere to develop and assess programs that aim to reduce men's intimate partner violence. This study and previous research (Dobash & Dobash, 2000; Dobash, Dobash, Cavanagh, & Lewis, 1999) suggest that one key to diminishing men's intimate partner violence is teaching them to change how they think about manhood and about male–female relationships. Effective efforts to do so—to change men's intimate partner violence—must take into account the perspectives of men who commit this crime. This study begins the process of illuminating insiders' understandings of men who engage in intimate partner violence. Reading accounts from insiders' perspectives clarifies perpetrators' ways of making sense of themselves and their actions. Without accepting or endorsing their logic, understanding it is a key to developing programs that have potential to alter their perspectives and their account-making strategies.

A third direction for future study is intimate partner violence committed by some women. Many participants in this study recounted cruel verbal attacks that wives and girlfriends inflicted on them. Obviously, participants might have crafted their accounts to preserve face. Yet we should not dismiss the possibility that they reported actual abuse directed at them by women in their lives. Some research supports participants' claims that women inflict violence, including physical, on intimate partners (Lamb, 1999) and that situational couple violence is not unusual (Johnson, 1995). Without lessening efforts to denounce and diminish males' intimate partner violence, we should recognize and denounce intimate partner violence committed by some women, and we should also interrogate the underlying assumption that verbal and emotional assaults are not really abusive.

Rearticulating Cultural Codes of Manhood

In addition to identifying themes in participants' accounts of violence against women, this study calls attention to two narratives of manhood: perhaps two of many that co-exist in U.S. (and other) cultures. Each narrative may offer a kind of truth about participants in this study and, more broadly, about multiple and not entirely consistent codes of manhood that circulate in Western culture. The goal of severing manhood from intimate partner violence informs the STOP course. In an interview, STOP instructor, Joseph Marinello, defined the program's mission as helping men redefine what it means to be a man. Noting that culture is diverse and fragmented, Comaroff and Comaroff (1991) insist that any cultural field is an 'often contested and only partially integrated mosaic of narratives' (p. 29). Participants in this study reflect the larger culture's multiple and competing narratives of manhood. Participants also demonstrate the possibility of reworking existing narratives and, by extension, re-forming themselves as men. Recognizing fluid and multiple ways of defining and embodying manhood cultivates at least a fragile hope that some men can cast themselves into a narrative that unshackles manhood from intimate partner violence.

That hope is fortified by comments from three participants with whom I spoke after they had completed the STOP class. Explaining what they had learned in the class, they offered a vision of masculine identity and power that resoundingly rejects intimate partner violence. I close with their words.

> Weeks: A real man don't hit his female. That's not being a man at all. That's being a chump. You don't let nobody pull your strings and be a puppet.
>> Ricardo: It takes really strong man to walk away after a woman cuts (verbally) you.
>> Kendrick: That don't make me a man for jumping on a woman.

REFERENCES

Adams, P., Towns, A., & Gavey, N. (1995). Dominance and entitlement: The rhetoric men use to discuss their violence toward women. *Discourse & Society, 6,* 387–06.

Archer, J. (2000a). Sex differences in aggression between heterosexual partners; A meta-analytic review. *Psychological Bulletin, 126,* 651–680.

Archer, J. (2000b). Sex differences in physical aggression to partners: A reply to Frieze (2000), O'Leary (2000), and White, Smith, Koss, and Figueredo (2000). *Psychological Bulletin, 126,* 697–702.

Bachman. R., & Saltzman, L. (1995). *Violence against women: Estimates from the redesigned survey. NCJ-154348.* Washington, DC: Bureau of Justice Statistics, US Department of Justice.

Bochner, A., Ellis, C., & Tillmann-Healy, L. (1997). Relationships as stories. In S. W. Duck (Ed.), *Handbook of personal relationships: Theory, research and interventions* (2nd ed., pp. 307–324). Chichester: Wiley.

Bogaert, A. (2001.). Personality, individual differences, and preferences for the sexual media. *Archives of Sexual Behavior, 30,* 29–53.

Bograd, M. (1988). How battered women and abusive men account for domestic violence: Excuses, justifications, or explanations. In G. Finkelhor, J. Kirkpatrick, & M. Straus (Eds.), *Coping with family violence: Research and policy perspectives* (pp. 60–77). Newbury Park, CA: Sage.

Boyd, N. (2002). *Beast within: Why men are violent.* Vancouver, BC: Groundwood/Greystone Books.

Bulmer, M. (1979). Concepts in the analysis of qualitative data. *Sociological Review, 27,* 651–677.

Campbell, A. (1993). *Men, women, and aggression.* New York: Basic Books.

Caron, S., & Carter, D. (1997). The relationships among sex role orientation, egalitarianism, attitudes toward sexuality, and attitudes toward violence against women. *Journal of Social Psychology, 137,* 568–577.

Charmaz, K. (1983). The grounded theory method: An explication and interpretation. In R. Emerson (Ed.), *Contemporary field research* (pp. 109–126). Boston: Little, Brown.

Coan, J., Gottman, J., Babcock, J., & Jacobson, N. (1997). Battering and the male rejection of influence from women. *Aggressive Behavior, 23,* 375–388.

Comaroff, J., & Comaroff, J., (1991). *Of revelation and revolution: Christianity, colonialism, and consciousness in South Africa* (Vol. 1). Chicago:University of Chicago Press.

Creswell, J. W. (1998). *Qualitative inquiry and research design: Choosing among five traditions.* Thousand Oaks, CA: Sage.

Daley, C., & Onwuegbuzie, A. (2000). Relationship between sex-role attitudes and attitudes toward violence among incarcerated male juvenile offenders. *Psychological Reports, 87,* 552–554.

Dobash, R., & Dobash, R. P. (2000). Evaluating criminal justice interventions for domestic violence. *Crime and Delinquency, 46,* 252–270.

Dobash, R., Dobash, R. P., Cavanagh, K., &. Lewis, R. (1999). *Changing violent men.* Thousand Oaks, CA: Sage.

Dougherty, D. (2001a). Sexual harassment as (dys)functional process: A feminist standpoint analysis. *Journal of Applied Communication Research, 29,* 372–402.

Dougherty, D. (2001b, November). *Towards a theoretical understanding of feminist standpoint processes in organizations.* Paper presented at the National Communication Association Conference. Atlanta, GA.

Dutton, D. (1986). Wife assaulters' explanation for assault: The neutralization of self-punishment. *Canadian Journal of Behavioral Science, 18,* 381–390.

Dutton. D. (1998). *The abusive personality.* New York: Guilford Press.

Dutton, D., & Galant, S. (1997). *The batterer: A psychological profile.* New York: Harper-Collins.

Eisikovits, Z., & Buchbinder, E. (2000). Talking violent: A phenomenological study of metaphors battering men use. *Violence Against Women, 3,*482–498.

Eisikovits, Z., & Edleson, J. (1986). *Violence in the family: A study of men who batter.* New York: Harry Frank Guggenheim Foundation.

Faludi, S. (1999). *Stiffed: The betrayal of the American man.* New York: Morrow.

Felson, R. (2002). *Violence and gender reexamined.* Washington, DC: American Psychological Association.

Glaser, B. (1978), *Theoretical sensitivity.* Mill Valley, CA: Sociology Press.

Glaser, B. (1992). *Basics of grounded theory analysis.* Mill Valley, CA: Sociology Press.

Glaser, B., & Strauss, A. (1967). *The discovery of grounded theory.* Chicago: Aldine de Gruyter.

Goldner, V., Penn, P., Sheinberg, M., & Walker, G. (1990). Love and violence: Gender paradoxes in volatile attachments. *Family Process, 19,* 343–364.

Goode, E. (2001, August 1). 20% of girls report abuse by a date. *Raleigh News and Observer,* 10A.

Hearn, J. (1998). *The violences of men: How men talk about and how agencies respond so men's violence to women.* Thousand Oaks, CA: Sage.

Hyden, M., & McCarthy, I. (1994). Woman battering and father–daughter incest disclosure: Discourses of denial and acknowledgement. *Discourse & Society, 5,* 543–65.

Jacobson, N., & Gottman, J. (1998). *When men batter women.* New York: Simon and Schuster.

Jacobson, N., & Gurman, A. (Eds.). (1986). *Clinical handbook of marital therapy.* New York: Guilford Press.

Johnson, M. P, (1995). Patriarchal terrorism and common couple violence: Two forms of violence against women. *Journal of Marriage and the Family, 57,* 283–294.

Johnson, M. P. (2001). Conflict and control: Symmetry and asymmetry in domestic violence. In A. Booth, A. Crouter, & M. Clements (Eds.), *Couples in conflict* (pp. 95–104). Mahwah, NJ: Erlbaum.

Johnson, M. P., Conklin, V., & Menon, N. (2002, November). *The effects of different types of domestic violence on women: Intimate terrorism vs. situational couple violence.* Paper presented at the National Council on Family Relations annual meeting, Houston, Texas.

Johnson, M. P., & Ferraro, K. J. (2000). Research on domestic violence in the 1990s: Making distinctions. *Journal of Marriage and the Family, 62,* 948–963.

Kimmel, M. (1996). *Manhood.* New York: Free Press.

Kimmel, M. (2002, February 8). Gender, class and terrorism *Chronicle of Higher Education,* B11–B12.

Kinney, T., Smith, B, & Donzella, B. (2001). The influence of sex, gender, self-discrepancies, and self-awareness of anger and verbal aggressiveness among U.S. college students. *Journal of Social Psychology, 141,* 245–275.

Lamb, S. (Ed.). (1999). *New versions of victims.* New York: University Press.

Lempert, L. (1996). Women's strategies for survival: Developing agency in abusive relationships. *Journal of Family Violence, 11,* 269–289

Lloyd, S. A. (1999). The interpersonal and communication dynamics of wife battering. In X. B. Arriga & S. Oskamp (Eds.), *Violence in intimate relationships* (pp. 91–111). Thousand Oaks, CA: Sage.

Lloyd, S. A., & Emery, B. (2000). *The dark side of courtship: Physical and sexual aggression.* Thousand Oaks, CA: Sage.

Messner, M. (1997). *Politics of masculinities: Men in movements.* Thousand Oaks. CA: Sage.

Meyers, M. (1997). *News coverage violence against women: Engendering blame.* Thousand Oaks: Sage.

National Coalition Against Domestic Violence. (1999). Available (accessed 10 July 1999): http://www.ncadv.org

O'Leary, K. (2000). Are women really more aggressive than men in intimate relationships? Comment on Archer (2000). *Psychological Bulletin, 126,* 685–689.

Owen, W. (1984). Interpretive themes in relational communication. *Quarterly Journal of Speech, 70,* 274–286.

Owen, W. (1985). Thematic metaphors in relational communication: A conceptual framework. *Western Journal of Speech Communication, 49,* 1–13.

Petrick, N., Olson, R., & Subotnik, L. (1994). Powerlessness and the need to control: The male abuser's dilemma. *Journal of Interpersonal Violence, 9,* 278–285.

Proceedings of the National Institute of Justice Gender Symmetry Workshop. (2000, November 20). Available: http://www.ojp.usdoj.gov/nij/vawaprog/

Scott, M., & Lyman, S. (1968). Accounts. *American Sociological Review, 33,* 46–62.

Scully, D., & Marolla, J. (1984). Convicted rapists' vocabulary of motives: Excuses and justifications. *Social Problems, 31,* 530–544.

Shank-Krusciewitz, E., & Wood, J. T. (2001). 'He was our child from the moment we walked in that room:' Entrance stories of adoptive parents. *Journal of Social and Personal Relationships, 18,* 785–803.

Straus, M. (1999). The controversy over domestic violence by women: A methodological, theoretical and sociology of science analysis. In X. B. Arriaga & S. Oscamp (Eds.), *Violence in intimate relationships* (pp. 17–44): Thousand Oaks, CA: Sage.

Strauss, A. (1987). *Qualitative analysis for social scientists.* Cambridge: Cambridge University Press.

Strauss, A., & Corbin, J. (1990). *Basics of qualitative analysis.* Newbury Park, CA: Sage.

Tjaden, P., & Thoennes, N. (1998). *Prevalence, incidence, and consequences of violence against women: Findings from the National Violence Against Women Survey,* Atlanta, GA: Center for Disease Control and Prevention, Center for Injury Prevention and Control.

Vangelisti, A., Crumley, L., & Baker. J. (1999). Family portraits: Stories as standards for family relationships. *Journal of Social and Personal Relationships, 16,* 335–368.

Wood, J. T. (2000). 'That wasn't the real him:' Women's dissociation of violence from the men who enact it. *Qualitative Research in Review, 1,* 1–7.

Wood, J. T. (2001). The normalization of violence in heterosexual romantic relationships: Women's narratives of love and violence. *Journal of Social and Personal Relationships, 18,* 239–261.

Voicing Your Opinion
Monsters and Victims: Male Felons'
Accounts of Intimate Partner Violence
Julia T. Wood

1. Respond to Faludi's assertion (as quoted in Wood's article) that some men enact violence against wives and girlfriends as a means of claiming the power and status they see as a birthright of manhood. How does this assertion help us to understand intimate violence enacted by men? How might violence-prevention groups and violence educators use this information in their work?

   _____

   _____

   _____

   _____

2. Wood identifies a theme of men's accounts of violence that she names, "She took it." Read through this section in the article and then consider the question that many people ask: "Why do women remain in abusive relationships?" How does the information from the article complicate this question? How does this information contribute to your understanding of communication between men and women?

   _____

   _____

   _____

   _____

3. Participants in the study identify their thematic understanding of manhood as "men as dominant and superior," and "men as protectors of women." What is the relationship between these themes? How do these themes create and sustain patriarchal thinking and contribute to cultural narratives about masculinity?

   _____

   _____

   _____

   _____

Terms

Sexual
experience
survey

Situations
around rape

Knowing or
understanding
the legal
definition
of rape

WHAT COLLEGE WOMEN DO AND DO NOT EXPERIENCE AS RAPE

ARNOLD S. KAHN

This article is about labeling situations as rape or not. Women are more likely to label a situation as rape if the male is not a romantic partner, and if the sexual act occurred in childhood. Women are more likely to label an experience as something other than rape if a boyfriend is involved, if the woman had been drinking, or if the act was something other than penile/vaginal intercourse.

College women who did (n = 33) and did not (n = 56) label their sexual assault experience as rape provided written descriptions of their sexual assaults. From these descriptions we identified eight different sexual assault situations. Women who labeled their experience as rape were most likely to have been assaulted forcefully by an acquaintance, awakened to an acquaintance performing sexual acts on them, or experienced the assault as a child. Women were least likely to call their experience rape if they submitted to whining, begging boyfriend, gave in to a man because of being emotionally needy, were assaulted by a boyfriend, were severely impaired by alcohol or drugs and unable to resist, or were forced to engage in oral or digital sex. Observers who read these descriptions generally agreed with the victims regarding whether or not the experience constituted rape, although they could not agree on whether or not forced oral or digital intercourse or forced intercourse by a boyfriend constituted rape.

Since 1989, together with my colleagues and students, I have conducted research on rape and sexual assault. One particular stream of this research has focused on what determines whether or not a woman labels her sexual assault experience as rape. In this paper I briefly summarize what we know about labeling one's experience as rape and then focus on a very recent study that provides some new data regarding this process.

Researchers who study rape typically use a form of the Sexual Experience Survey (SES) (Koss & Gidycz, 1985) in which women respond *yes* or *no* to a series of questions concerning sexual behaviors. If a woman answers yes to one or more critical questions about her sexual experiences she has likely experienced rape. Research shows that a large percentage of women who answer yes to one or more of the critical SES questions, suggesting they had been raped, respond no when asked the direct question, "Have you ever been raped by a man?" That is, these women had an experience that appears to have been one of rape, but they did not label their experience as one of rape. Koss (1985) referred to these women as "hidden rape victims," women who experienced acts that seemed to fit the legal definition of rape, but who did not conceive of themselves as victims or survivors of rape. In our past research we have referred to these women as "unacknowledged rape victims" (Kahn, Mathie, & Torgler, 1994; Kahn & Mathie, 2000). This terminology, however, has problems. It assumes that these women did in fact experience rape, something we do not know for sure, and it favors the scientist's definition of rape over the definition of the research participant herself. Thus, I will refer to these women as "women who do not call their experience rape," rather than "hidden victims" or "unacknowledged victims."

Past research has shown that a large percentage of women, ranging from 48% (Kahn et al., 1994) to 73% (Koss, Dinero, Seibel, & Cox, 1988), who respond yes to one or more of the SES items, suggesting they had an experience that might legally be rape, respond no to the question, "Have you ever been raped by a man?" In most studies the percentage is over 50% of the sample of possible rape victims.

Why Women Do Not Label Their Sexual Assault as Rape

What leads a woman to call or not call her experience rape? A number of researchers have searched for differences in women's personalities or attitudes, or in women's experiences, that would differentiate those who called their experience rape from those who did not. This research has uncovered a number of predictors that appear to distinguish between these two groups. Compared with women who called their experience rape, women who did not label their experience as rape were more likely to have been assaulted by someone they knew well, often a romantic partner (Kahn, Jackson, Kully, Badger, & Halvorsen, 2003; Koss, 1985). These women were also more likely to have a rape script of a very violent stranger rape rather than one of an acquaintance rape (Bondurant, 2001; Kahn et al., 1994). They also experienced less assailant force than women who called their experience rape (Bondurant, 2001; Emmers-Sommer & Allen, 1999; Kahn et al., 1994; Kahn et al., 2003; Layman, Gidycz, & Lynn, 1996; Schwartz & Leggett, 1999). Finally, although women who did not label their experience as rape had negative emotional reactions during and after the incident, these negative emotional reactions were not as strong as those of women who called their experience rape (Kahn et al., 1994; Kahn & Mathie, 2000; Kahn et al., 2003). Inconsistent results have been found for alcohol use and victim self-blame (Bondurant, 2001; Frazier & Seales, 1997; Kahn & Mathie, 2000; Kahn et al., 2003; Layman et al., 1996; Pitts & Schwartz, 1993; Schwartz & Leggett, 1999). Interestingly, no personality, attitude, or demographic difference has differentiated women who do and do not label their assault experience as rape (Bondurant, 2001; Kahn et al., 1994; Koss, 1985; Levine-MacCombie & Koss, 1986). In short, women who do not call their experience rape tend to see rape as a violent act committed by a stranger, but were themselves assaulted by someone they knew well, often a romantic partner, who did not use a great deal of force. These women experienced strong, negative emotional reactions to their assault, but their reactions were not as strong as women who called their experience rape.

What Actually Happened?

Past research trying to differentiate women who did and did not label their sexual assault experiences as rape has not directly examined what actually happened when the assault occurred. That is, did women who called their assault rape encounter a different set of events than those who did not call their assault rape? In a recent study (Kahn et al., 2003) my students and I did just that: we asked women to tell us what happened to them before, during, and after their assault experience. The details of the method and quantitative findings have been published elsewhere (Kahn et al., 2003). Here I will first summarize the quantitative findings from this study and then focus on some of the qualitative findings (Study One). Then I will include some new data that have not yet been published (Study Two). Because in this research we were interested in what women would and would not label as rape, we created a version of the SES that included a variety of assault behaviors (see Kahn et al., 2003, for a complete description), some of which would not meet a strict legal definition of rape in some locations.

Study One

Method

We distributed questionnaires to 504 female college students, 90% of whom were Caucasian and 51% of whom were first-year students. We told participants, in groups of 4–25, that we were studying how people perceive stressful events. The women first completed a questionnaire in which they indicated yes, uncertain or maybe, or no to 16 questions regarding criminal or aggressive acts or attitudes, including the crucial question, "Have you ever been raped by a man?" Next they completed a version of the SES. If a participant answered yes to at least one of seven critical questions, they were considered a possible rape victim. We then asked these women to turn to the next page where they found the following instructions:

Please take a few moments to describe in detail the circumstances of this experience. If there was more than one experience, respond about the one you remember best. How did this experience come about? What occurred during the experience? What did he do? What did you do? Remember that this survey is anonymous, and there is no way to match your survey or this description with you. Therefore, be as candid as you feel comfortable. Please write your response on the two sheets of blank paper provided and then continue on the next printed page.[1]

We considered a woman to have labeled her experience as rape if she answered yes to the question about having been raped and yes to one or more of the critical SES questions. We considered a woman not to have labeled her experience as rape if she answered no to the question about having been raped and yes to one or more of the critical SES questions. We considered a woman uncertain as to whether she had been raped if she answered yes to one of the critical SES questions and maybe/uncertain to the question about having been raped.

Of the 504 participants, 13 chose not to complete the survey. Of the 491 remaining women, 33 (6.5%) called an experience they had rape, 56 (11.4%) did not label an experience they had as rape, 8 (1.6%) were uncertain whether an experience they had was rape or not, and 394 (80.2%) indicated they had not been the victim of a sexual assault. Since only eight women chose the maybe/uncertain alternative, I will not report results from these participants.

Four individuals previously unassociated with this research each read all the assault descriptions and independently classified them into types of sexual assault situations. The four then met together, agreed upon the assault situations, and provided criteria for differentiating each situation from the others. We then gave the assault descriptions, the assault situations, and criteria for assigning assaults to situations to three other people not previously involved in this research. Each of these people independently categorized each description into one of the assault situations. Based on disagreements by these categorizers, we again reviewed and modified the situations and their criteria, producing a final set of eight sexual assault situations, with an additional ninth "other" category. We gave the women's descriptions and the revised situations and their criteria to three different people who had not previously been involved in this research, and asked them to place each assault description into one of the nine situations. The average interrater reliability was 83.5%.

Results

The quantitative results, reported in Kahn et al. (2003) revealed that women who labeled their situation as rape were (a) more likely to have been assaulted by a nonromantic partner, (b) more likely to have experienced extremely high negative affect after the experience, (c) less likely to be assaulted by an assailant who was intoxicated, and (d) more likely to have experienced forceful male aggression in other sexual encounters with men. Here I wish to further explore the qualitative findings from the participants' descriptions of their assault experiences. The following constitute the eight different assault situations.

Submit to boyfriend involved, after repeated no's, giving in to a boyfriend's continued begging, whining, or arguing for sex. The woman did not want to have sex, but wanted to please him, keep peace, or feared he might become violent.

> My boyfriend of a year and I were home alone together. In prior weeks he had been very agitated at my lack of interest in intimacy and my lack of patience with his temper. His recent outbursts had caused me to distrust him. His manner towards me was angry, but he didn't actually threaten me at this time. In an attempt to appease his anger and prevent another outburst of anger, I consented to his repeated advances and requests for sex. It was so degrading.

Childhood included sexual acts performed by older cousins, a babysitter, or a close family member when the woman was in middle school or younger.

Forced sex acts occurred when a man, regardless of her relationship with him, used force to obtain or perform oral or digital sex.

> I was drunk. He forced me into the bathroom with him. He was drunk, too. He pushed me down so that I was on my knees and undid his pants, basically forcing his penis in my mouth and moving my head. I said stop a lot of times.

Emotionally needy involved situations in which the woman was emotionally unstable and needy, often following the breakup of a relationship. She did not want to have intercourse and told the man so, but eventually gave in to the man because he seemed to care for her.

> I genuinely didn't want to have sex, told him so. However, I was going through a rough time, just broken up with a serious boyfriend and felt insecure, hurt, lonely, etc., etc. This guy made me feel better about myself, told me I had no reason to be lonely, he wanted me, he wanted to help with the pain, etc. I ended up having sex with him because I believed he cared about me even though I didn't think it was right because I wanted the pain of the former breakup to quit.

Dominating boyfriend involved an older, larger boyfriend who used threats or force to obtain sexual intercourse. The woman tried to resist but could not.

> At my senior beach week I had been dating my boyfriend for about a month . . . We got into bed, unclothed, and started "messing around." After a few minutes I wanted to stop, but obviously he didn't. He held my arms down and I was on my stomach and he tried to perform anal intercourse, but I squirmed and screamed at him until he stopped . . . P.S. It hurt like hell and I left him the next day.

Forceful acquaintance involved an acquaintance who would not yield to a woman's pleas to stop and used force, threats, or coercion to obtain sexual intercourse. The following occurred during her senior year in high school when the woman turned down a schoolmate's request for a date:

> He got angry and told me that I was a tease and he slapped me across the face. So I pulled open the door to my car and tried to get away, but he grabbed my arm and forced me into the back seat. All I remember after that was crying and trying to push him off me. When he had finished he left me in the back seat of my car bleeding and barely conscious.

Asleep or tricked involved either a woman awaking to find a man performing sexual acts on her, or the man had promised no penile penetration yet did so anyway, but the woman was not immediately aware of it, unfamiliar with the "feel" of penetration.

> He promised me that he would sleep on the couch and I could have his bed. I woke up later that night with him on top of me. I told him to stop but he wouldn't. He continued and managed to take my clothes off. After raping me he rolled over and went to sleep.

Severe impairment occurred when the woman was severely impaired by alcohol or drugs and had neither the presence of mind nor the ability to resist the man, who had intercourse with her.

> We were drunk. I didn't have control over myself and I didn't have the cognitive ability to say NO. I can't remember everything, but I know we had sex and if I were sober it would not have happened. I just could not control myself at all.

Table 1 displays the number of women who called their experience rape and those who did not for each assault situation. Three situations, asleep or tricked, forceful acquaintance, and childhood accounted for over three-fourths (76.67%) of the descriptions provided by women who called their situation rape. Only four women who did not call their experience rape wrote descriptions that fell into one of these categories. Five situations, severe impairment, submit, forced sex acts, dominating boyfriend, and emotionally needy accounted for 85.1% of the descriptions provided by women who did not call their experience rape. Only seven women who called their experience rape wrote descriptions that fit into one of these five categories.

Discussion

The main finding from these qualitative results suggest that those women who labeled their experience as rape, for the most part, encountered very different assault situations from those who did not call their experience rape. Women were more likely to label their situation as rape when the assailant was someone other

Table 1 Frequencies of Each Assault Situation as a Function of Whether the Woman Labeled Her Experience as Rape or Not Rape

Situation	Labeled Rape	Not Labeled Rape
Submit	3	13
Childhood	3	0
Forced Sex Acts	0	7
Emotionally Needy	1	2
Dominating Boyfriend	0	4
Forceful Acquaintance	8	0
Asleep or Tricked	12	4
Severe Impairment	3	14
Other	0	5
Total	30	49

than their boyfriend, who either used force to obtain intercourse or started to perform sexual acts while they were asleep, waking them up. Women also labeled as rape sexual acts which had occurred in childhood. Women were more likely to label their experience as something other than rape when the experience occurred with a boyfriend, whether submitting to his repeated pleas or giving in to his threats and force, when the woman was too impaired by alcohol or drugs to effectively resist the man, when the sexual act was something other than penile/vaginal intercourse, and when the woman gave in to intercourse because she was emotionally needy.

I should note that 15 of the 45 descriptions written by women who did not label their situation as rape fell into two categories, submit and emotionally needy. Both of these situations would probably not meet the criteria in most states to be admitted as rape and appear to more closely resemble what has been called unwanted sex (O'Sullivan & Allgeier, 1998; Sprecher, Hatfield, Cortese, Potapova, & Levitskaya, 1994; Walker, 1997), that is, having intercourse to please a partner when a person did not desire it.

Study Two

In her interviews with women who had experienced rape, Phillips (2000) discussed situations in which a woman did not view her experience as rape, but when asked how she would describe the identical experience if it had happened to a friend, she gave a very different interpretation.

> If my roommate came home and told me the exact same story had happened to her, I'd tell her, "You call the hotline, you call the police! You're a victim! That guy raped you and you should report it!" Wow! But I don't know. For her it would be rape. For me it was just so complicated (p. 154).

We were interested in whether naïve observers, like some of Phillips' participants, would be more likely than the women who wrote about their experience to label the situation as one of rape. Phillips found that her participants denied their victimization, in part, to preserve their view of themselves as mature adults who can handle situations, and in part because their experiences were complicated and did not match the "true victim" discourse that rape occurs when a stranger brutally attacks a woman who does everything possible to escape.

Method

I gave the written descriptions of the sexual assaults to four additional female undergraduate students previously unfamiliar with this research. I instructed each rater, working individually, to "Please label each situation as either 'rape,' 'not rape,' or 'not enough information provided.' Avoid using the 'not enough information provided' category; if you lean however slightly to either 'rape' or 'not rape' use one of them instead." I provided no definition of rape to the categorizers.

I then looked at the categorizations of these four naïve raters. If three or four of them categorized the description as rape, I labeled the situation one of rape. Likewise, if three or four of the raters categorized the situation as not rape, I labeled the situation as not rape. Those descriptions for which there was no agreement or for which the raters agreed that there was not sufficient information, I categorized as unclear.

Results

The raters classified 28 descriptions as rape, 32 descriptions as not rape, and were unclear or could not agree about 19 descriptions. When I compared whether or not a woman called her own experience rape with how observers labeled the same situation, I found a very strong relationship, $\chi^2(2) = 36.87$, $p < .001$, which is shown in Table 2. Those situations that participants labeled as rape were also highly likely to be labeled as rape by naïve raters. Likewise, situations that participants labeled as something other than rape were also highly likely to be called not rape by naïve raters. If we remove the 24% of the situations where the observers who classified the descriptions were uncertain or could not agree and look at percentages, the situation becomes even clearer. Nearly all, 95.6%, of the descriptions for which the victim labeled her situation as rape, the observers also called it rape. Likewise in 83.4% of the description which the victim did not call her experience rape, the observers agreed that the situation was not rape.

These results support the hypothesis that observers would be more likely to label a situation as rape than would participants. Only once did a victim label her experience as rape (3.4%) when the raters agreed rape did not occur; however, six of the descriptions that the victims themselves labeled as not rape were clearly labeled rape by the observers (12%). That is, the raters were more likely to label a description as rape than were the victims themselves.

For our final analysis I examined the eight different assault situations in terms of whether or not the observers labeled the written description as rape or not.[2] As can be seen in Table 3, the findings mirror, for the most part, the victims' own categorization as to whether the situation was one of rape. From the observers' point of view, three situations clearly constitute rape: forced intercourse during childhood, forceful intercourse by an acquaintance, and waking up to someone performing sexual acts on them, the same three situations that the women in our original study overwhelmingly called rape when it happened to them. Observers clearly viewed three other situations are not rape: submitting to pressure from a boyfriend after making it clear the woman did not want sex, an emotionally needy woman giving in to the man, and intercourse because of severe impairment and the inability to resist. These situations involved experiences that the women in our original study also tended to not label as rape. Finally, there were two situations in which it was unclear, from the observers' perspective, whether rape had occurred: forced oral or digital sex and a boyfriend using threats or actual force to obtain intercourse. Women who wrote the descriptions always labeled them as not being rape.

Discussion

For years we have been trying to understand what determines whether a woman will label her assault situation as rape or as something other than rape. From our latest research I think it is safe to say that a major contributor to a woman's decision to label a situation as rape is the nature of the situation itself. Both the victims and those who read the victims' descriptions of their experience agreed that some situations constituted rape and other situations did not.

Women, both victims and those who read victim descriptions, were most likely to label a situation as rape if sexual intercourse occurred in childhood, was forced by an acquaintance, or occurred while the woman was asleep. Three factors seem to be involved here. First, the woman had sexual intercourse when she either had no control—she was a child, asleep, or forced. Second, the assailant was someone other than her boyfriend. Third, from our quantitative data (Kahn et al., 2003) the woman experienced a very high level of trauma as a result.

Table 2 Relationship Between Participants' Label of Their Assault Situation and Observers' Label of the Same Situation

Victims' Label of Situation	Raters' Label of Situation		
	Rape	Not Rape	Not Clear
Rape	22	1	6
Not Rape	6	31	13
Total	28	32	19

Table 3 Frequency of Observers Judgments as to Whether or Not Different Assault Situations Constitute Rape

Rape Situation	Observer Label of Situation		
	Rape	Not Rape	Not Clear
Submit	1	14	3
Childhood	3	0	0
Forced Sex Acts	2	1	4
Emotionally Needy	0	3	1
Dominating Boyfriend	0	0	4
Forceful Acquaintance	10	0	0
Asleep or Tricked	11	1	4
Severe Impairment	3	12	3
Other	0	5	0

Note: Data for women who were uncertain whether or not they had experienced rape are included in these data.

Three situations, submitting to the begging, whining, or arguing by a boyfriend; having intercourse because she was emotionally needy; and being too impaired to resist intercourse with an acquaintance, all lead the majority of both victims and those who read victim accounts to believe rape had not occurred.

Although submitting to a whiny boyfriend or being emotionally needy in most cases probably does not constitute rape under most state laws, the inability to stop a man because of impairment by alcohol or drugs is considered rape in most jurisdictions. The written descriptions provided by these women can help us understand why they, and those who read their descriptions, did not label their experience as rape. The intoxicated women did not seem to believe they were personally at risk and they attributed their undesired intercourse not to the man's pressure or force but to their own lack of ability to think clearly or resist—the alcohol rather than the assailant took away their options to act otherwise. These women seem to have presumed that a man wilt have sex with a woman unless the woman forcefully resists, and her inability to resist seemed to mean, to her and to observers as well, that what happened was not rape. Below are some additional extracts of descriptions provided by women who said they were too intoxicated to resist but did not call their experiences rape:

> I was having a bad day and I wanted to get trashed . . . So I went to my friend's apartment . . . So
> I got really drunk and he basically totally took advantage of my weakness. Before I could get the

strength to protest, he had quickly um, penetrated me. I know that if I hadn't been so drunk I would have had the strength and I definitely would NOT have wanted to do that with him, and I would have strongly told him no and he knew that too, which is why he waited till I was hammered to do it. So I guess it doesn't really count as rape, since I was the one who wanted to get drunk.

A man who I trusted very much made me and some friends a few drinks. We played drinking games and we were all pretty drunk. After everyone was asleep, this man and I were up talking and practically begged me to let him give me oral sex. I was drunk, told him I didn't want to, but he kept at it and finally I was just like, fine. The oral sex turned into intercourse. I hadn't wanted to do anything with him at all. I was too drunk to really consider the consequences though.

In reading these descriptions, as well as the descriptions by women who submitted to their boyfriends and those who were emotionally needy, it appears these women felt they could not call what happened to them rape because they didn't resist, even if they couldn't resist because of impairment. It also appears that these women did not experience the trauma found in the descriptions by women who labeled their experience as rape (see Kahn et al., 2003). As Gavey (1999) has suggested, although rape is frequently traumatic, "not all women are traumatized by rape" (p. 70). It may be that the women who were too intoxicated to resist labeled their experience as something other than rape because they were not as traumatized as women who tried to resist and they were adapting the best they could to an unpleasant experience, attempting to "get over it," gain control for similar situations in the future, and escape the label of "victim" (see Phillips, 2000).

Finally, in two situations the victims did not label their experience as rape, but observers could not agree whether or not rape had taken place: forced sexual acts that did not involve penile/vaginal intercourse—digital or oral intercourse—and forced sexual intercourse committed by a boyfriend. Both of these situations would likely be considered rape under most state laws. With regard to digital and oral sex, research by Sanders and Reinisch (1999) suggested that only about one-third of college women consider oral sex as "having sex" and only about 10% consider manual stimulation of genitals as "having sex." To the extent women believe that the act of rape must involve penile/vaginal intercourse, one can understand how the victims of forced oral or digital sex might call their experience something other than rape. Yet it is curious that those who read the descriptions were less clear on the matter. In two descriptions the raters agreed that rape had occurred, for one description they were sure rape had not occurred, and on four descriptions they did not agree among themselves or not enough information was provided to decide whether or not rape had occurred. Clearly this is an area in need of further research and education.

Being forced to have sexual intercourse by one's boyfriend also seems to be an ambiguous situation for those who read the descriptions but not for those who wrote them. In all four cases the victims themselves did not call their experience rape, but those who read the descriptions were unable to agree with one another on any of the four scenarios. The rape by a boyfriend appears an unanticipated situation, one for which women have no script. In our earlier research on rape scripts (Kahn et al., 1994), none of our 174 participants, when asked to write their script for a typical rape, wrote a script involving a boyfriend. Women love and trust their boyfriends and rape by a boyfriend appears incomprehensible and difficult to categorize as rape.

Conclusion

My major goal in conducting this research was to determine what types of assaultive sexual experiences college women consider to be rape and what types of assaultive sexual experiences they consider to be something other than rape. To do this we included several SES items that were likely sexual assault but not rape. We found three situations that were almost always labeled as rape and five situations that were nearly always not labeled as rape. I think this research should be viewed as a first step in this regard. We were able to obtain only a limited number of retrospective descriptions of sexual assaults from predominantly White, middle-class college students. Older, less privileged women from different ethnic backgrounds may label their experiences differently. Furthermore, we developed a crude and imperfect classification system on the basis of written descriptions of sexual assaults, some of which were quite brief. In addition, an occasional written description could have fit into more than one assault situation (e.g., a woman forced by her boyfriend to perform oral sex on him while she was severely impaired by alcohol). Conducting in-depth interviews with samples of women about their assault experiences and the conditions under which they occurred appears to be necessary to further our understanding of what leads a woman to call their sexual assault rape.

I will end this article with the same words I used previously (Kahn et al., 2003). Is it important for a woman to label her experience as rape if it occurs? At the individual level it would appear that each woman is attempting, as best she can, to cope with what had happened to her. Under some conditions, such as awaking to a man performing sexual acts on her or being forced into intercourse by an acquaintance, most women appear to cope best by calling their situation one of rape. Under other conditions, such as being unable to resist because of severe intoxication or because a boyfriend forced them to have sex, most women appear to cope best by labeling what happened to them as something other than rape. Furthermore, their peers, for the most part, agree with this classification system. Should efforts be made to teach women to label their experience as rape if they have had an experience that would legally qualify as rape? Women as a group, and likely women in the future, would certainly be better off if all women who experienced legal rape labeled it as such. Such widespread acknowledgment of rape would highlight the tremendous problem of rape in our society, hold perpetrators responsible for their behavior, and likely lead to greater enforcement of rape statutes, greater prosecution of rapists, and ultimately reducing the frequency of rape. But at what cost to individual women who can better cope with what happened to them by not calling their experience rape? Are these women better off by having someone else define their experience for them? This is not a dilemma easily resolved. Perhaps the best perspective has been provided by Gavey (1999), who said of women who do not label their experience as rape:

> Feminist accounts of rape need to be able to take account of such women's experiences without, in effect, dismissing them as the result of false consciousness. Carefully listening to and theorizing such ambivalent and confusing experiences may illuminate the complex relationship between heterosexuality and rape. Moreover, it may produce feminist analyses of rape that are sympathetic to all women who are raped, no matter how they experience it (pp. 69–70).

ENDNOTES

1. It was possible that participants may have had a rape experience, but chose to describe a less distressing, nonrape situation. We had no way of determining if this occurred.

2. I have included the descriptions written by women who were uncertain as to whether or not they had experienced rape in these data.

REFERENCES

Bondurant, B. (2001). University women's acknowledgment of rape: Individual, situational, and social factors. *Violence Against Women, 7,* 294–314.

Emmers-Sommer, T. M., & Allen, M. (1999). Variables related to sexual coercion: A path model, *Journal of Social and Personal Relationships, 16,* 659–678.

Frazier, P. A., & Seales, L. M. (1997). Acquaintance rape is real rape. In M. D. Schwartz (Ed.), *Researching sexual violence against women: Methodological and personal perspectives* (pp. 54–64). Thousand Oaks, CA: Sage.

Gavey, N. (1999). "I wasn't raped, but . . .": Revisiting definitional problems in sexual victimization. In S. Lamb (Ed.), *New versions of victims: Feminists struggle with the concept* (pp. 57–61). New York: New York University Press.

Kahn, A. S., Jackson, J., Kully, C., Badger, K., & Halvorsen, J. (2003). Calling it rape: Differences in experiences of women who do or do not label their sexual assault as rape. *Psychology of Women Quarterly, 27,* 233–242.

Kahn, A. S., & Mathie, V. A. (2000). Understanding the unacknowledged rape victim. In C. B. Travis and J. W. White (Eds.) *Sexuality, society, and feminism; Psychological perspectives on women* (pp. 377–403). Washington, DC.: American Psychological Association.

Kahn, A. S., Mathie, V. A., & Torgler, C. (1994). Rape scripts and rape acknowledgment. *Psychology of Women Quarterly, 18,* 53–66.

Koss, M. P. (1985). The hidden rape victim: Personality, attitudinal, and situational characteristics. *Psychology of Women Quarterly, 9,* 193–212.

Koss, M. P., Dinero, T. E., Seibel, C., & Cox, S. (1988). Stranger, acquaintance, and date rape: Is there a difference in the victim's experience? *Psychology of Women Quarterly, 12,* 1–24.

Koss, M. P., & Gidycz, C. A. (1985). Sexual Experiences Survey: Reliability and validity. *Journal of Consulting and Clinical Psychology, 53,* 422–423.

Layman, M. J., Gidycz, C. A., & Lynn, S. J. (1996). Unacknowledged versus acknowledged rape victims: Situational factors and posttraumatic stress. *Journal of Abnormal Psychology, 105,* 124–131.

Levine-MacCombie, J., & Koss, M. P. (1986). Acquaintance rape: Effective avoidance strategies. *Psychology of Women Quarterly, 10,* 311–320.

O'Sullivan, L. F., & Allgeier, E. R. (1998). Feigning sexual desire: Consenting to unwanted sexual activity in heterosexual dating relationships. *Journal of Sex Research, 35,* 234–243.

Phillips, L. M. (2000). *Flirting with danger: Young women's reflections on sexuality and domination.* New York: New York University Press.

Pitts, V. L., & Schwartz, M. D. (1993). Promoting self-blame in hidden rape cases. *Humanity & Society, 17,* 383–398.

Sanders, S. A., & Reinisch, J. M. (1999). Would you say you "had sex" if . . . *Journal of the American Medical Association, 281,* 275–277.

Schwartz, M. D., & Leggett, M. S. (1999). Bad dates or emotional trauma? The aftermath of campus sexual assault. *Violence Against Women 5,* 251–271.

Sprecher, S., Hatfield, E., Cortese, A., Potapova, E., & Levitskaya, A. (1994). Token resistance to sexual intercourse and consent to unwanted intercourse: College students' dating experiences in three countries. *Journal of Sex Research, 31,* 125–132.

Walker, S. J. (1997). When "no" becomes "yes": Why girls and women consent to unwanted sex. *Applied and Preventive Psychology, 6,* 157–166.

Voicing Your Opinion
What College Women Do and Do Not Experience as Rape

Arnold S. Kahn

1. Would women benefit from understanding the legal definition of rape? How might this understanding influence studies like the one presented in this article?

   _____

   _____

   _____

   _____

   _____

   _____

2. How might college men categorize the incidents of assault situations described in Kahn's research? Is it important to include college men in a discussion about the labels we use to describe rape? Why or why not?

   _____

   _____

   _____

   _____

   _____

   _____

3. What is your personal response to the eight assault descriptions identified in the article? Do you think that these labels accurately depict the experiences of college women? Why or why not?

   _____

   _____

   _____

   _____

   _____

   _____

Who Is Trying to Help?

Instructions

Learn more about organizations that are working to address gendered violence by visiting one of the websites on this list. Spend some time navigating the site and learning about the participants, their goals, and their accomplishments. Summarize your response to the website by completing the following steps:

1. Describe the content of the website. What general information was featured on the home page? Describe specific information that you discovered by following links on the site.

2. Explain how the website addresses the problem of violence in relationship to gender. Are you able to identify information that pertains to the communication of masculinity and/or femininity?

3. Link the information on the website to one or more of the topics addressed in the articles from *The Process of Examining Violence.*

Suggestions

Spend an adequate amount of time visiting the site. You may want to look at it several times before you summarize your response.

Pay attention to both the language and the images on the website.

Share what you have learned with someone else!

Websites

http://www.jacksonkatz.com
http://www.who.int/topics/gender_based_violence/en/
http://www.ovw.usdoj.gov
http://www.cdc.gov/ncipc/dvp/SV/default.htm

5 The Process of Understanding Gendered Social Systems

Beyond the Individual

The process of understanding gender continues as we examine how gendered individuals exist in social systems. Very few people live their lives as isolated individuals. Most of us have been a part of some type of educational system, we are members of social and work organizations, and we are constantly exposed to a sophisticated media that provide us with information and entertainment twenty-four hours a day! The development of our gender, and the ways that we have learned to communicate our gender, are strongly influenced by the social systems that surround us.

Schools are powerful institutions that provide individuals with the necessary tools to be competent and productive members of society. Schools are also places where girls and boys are exposed to the expectations of their gender. We are certain that you can recall school experiences that were strongly influenced by your gender. Perhaps you spoke up and joked in class as a first-grade boy and were labeled a trouble maker. Perhaps you were encouraged to take a "Life Skills" class in high school because you would need it when you "became a mother." Both the subtle and overt gendered messages in educational institutions have a way of directing us toward a particular type of gender development.

Of equal impact to our gender development is the influence of our social and work organizations. We often gather in groups to affirm our values, pursue our interests, and participate as productive and contributing members of society. You are probably quite conscious of the ways that your gender is perceived and treated in places where you have worked. Were you *not* assigned a particular project because your boss thought you weren't physically strong enough to handle it? Were you excluded from workplace conversations because it was "girl talk" and you aren't a girl? Organizations are places where our gender can have a large impact on our acceptance, our success, and the rewards that we receive.

The final topic of this section relates to the ways that media and gendered communication interact. Media are powerful in as much as they expose large populations of people to repetitive messages. This allows mediums like television and the Internet a forum to comment on gender. Media have the potential to provide those who use them with very clear expectations of gendered behavior. Media reflect our gender back to us in a variety of ways, and also exist as a vehicle for perpetuating gender stereotypes.

We have included four articles that examine the role that educational institutions, workplace settings, and media sources play in our understanding of gender.

Terms

Gender neutrality

Social formation

Social institution

Social action

Naturalization

Role of teachers

THE EMPEROR HAS NO CLOTHES
Examining the Impossible Relationship Between Gendered and Academic Identities in Middle School Students

NANCY S. NIEMI

This article is about the fiction of gender neutrality in schools. Indeed, the author finds that "girls" cannot be "good students," as those two identities do not relate to one another in the school setting. How boys are taught to be boys and girls are taught to be girls is constructed as a form of "naturalization." The school system and schools then underscore this naturalizing process.

Despite the social equity work that still needs to be done in schools and society, many researchers, politicians, and social commentators claim that gender equity work in schools has been accomplished. These people assume that actions in school lead to gender equity outside it. But, there may be two problems with this assumption: 1) achieving equity in academic work may mask still-inequitable gender work in schools and 2) girls' and boys' equal academic achievement does not promise social equality, inside or outside schools. The following study offers evidence from a recent middle school study that reveals how children's gender identities are naturalized as neutral "student" identities, making the effects of children's gender identity work invisible. This author argues that schooling at best maintains the inequity of the American gender status quo, and perhaps may work to actually lessen chances for women and men's equitable life opportunities.

Introduction

A student is a complex thing to be; many of society's expectations are heaped onto this construction of child, social class, ethnicity and gender. US society seems forever hopeful that the American dream will be realized by neutralizing students as blank slates that can be fixed and filled so that they can go on to their poetic destinies. Several decades of US and European research have exposed the fallacies behind this stubborn mythology (Willis, 1977; MacLeod, 1987; Walkerdine, 1990; Crichlow, 1991; Wexler, 1992), exposing schools as sites of simultaneous and contradictory advancement and reproduction of inequalities.

The persistent social contradictions of American schools, though less for White middle class children than for their White and non-White working class counterparts (AAUW, 1999), remain particularly confusing for those of us who are concerned about the role schooling plays in the advancement of gender equity. Much gender equity work in schools has been already accomplished (Ravitch, 1996; Pollack, 1998; Sommers, 2000), with prominent social commentators suggesting that the gender disparities in schools, if there ever were any, are gone. But, the following research suggests that student identities and gendered identities may be less compatible than anyone thought: it may be impossible to be a successful student and at the same time a successful girl or boy. The 13-year-old girls' behaviour in this study suggests that they cannot be girls and students simultaneously; their student identities cannot escape the gendered lenses through which adults and children in schools see.

The parity between girls' and boys' academic achievement in K–12[1] schooling is undeniably a significant departure from girls' and boys' unequal academic achievement in the past century (Frazier & Sadker, 1973). Within the last two decades, reports of academic disparities based in gender differences (AAUW, 1992; Mac an Ghaill, 1994; Sadker & Sadker, 1994) have not gone unheard: the differences between boys and girls' access to and success in school have changed largely for the better (AAUW, 1999). Boys' and girls' equal academic success can be attributed to a combination of good work ethics, exposure to new possibilities, participation in extra-curricular activities, and above all, good grades (AAUW, 1999, 1992). Now that girls achieve academically at the same rates or better than boys, Sommers (2000) claims that 'we should repudiate the partisanship that currently clouds the issues surrounding sex differences in schools [and] objectively educate all children fairly' (p. 74). By Sommers' interpretation of equal achievement, boys' and girls' equal success as students works in complement with children's gender identities.

Yet I maintain that children's student identities, rather than fitting over other existing social identities as Sommers (2000) suggests, are entangled within them: success in grammar, math and science, for example, is suffused with issues of poverty, language dominance and debates about girls' and boys' genetic predispositions to math (AAUW, 1999, 1992). But schools have existed and thrived historically without significant attention to the identities with which children come to school, and sometimes, when schools have tried to simultaneously fix students' social inequities as well as educate students, unfortunate consequences have resulted. Divisions by race created few schools that were separate and equal; de facto separation of students by economic class and race continues unchallenged in what is supposed to be a equal opportunity public school system, with poorer students receiving significantly fewer resources than their richer counterparts (New York State Department of Education, 2004). Girls and boys, separated less by law but by access to curricula and opportunity, have also been historically denied different futures.

Teachers and schools have done much to bring equitable treatment to all their children, treating them as 'students' despite differences in social class, ethnicity and gender. It is my contention that this treatment of children as students, while well-meaning, so sublimates the gender work that children are necessarily producing, that students and teachers cannot enact meaningful change through any identity. In particular, I will show through examples of school discourse that becoming a successful student reinforces gendered cultural expectations, while recasting gender identities as student identities that mask the gender work beneath them. I will argue that it is impossible for girls, in particular, to position themselves within discourses of academic success and femininity: they cannot be students and girls at the same time.

Background

In their 1983 Grandin School study of students' gender constructions, researchers Eisenhart and Holland noted that: 'In contrast and sometimes in overt opposition to the teachers' emphasis on children as students, the children's peer groups ignored student identities and instead stressed gender and age groups' (p. 322). Eisenhart and Holland (1983) observed that gender identities were the primary focus of the students in their study, who made a concerted effort to conceal their peer–peer interactions from school adults (p. 328). The children in my 1999 study also downplayed their student identities and constructed their school identities primarily through gender, social class and race/ethnicity, just as the children in the Grandin School study had done.

Student identities, like gender, ethnic and social class identities, have evolved as positions which children take up in order to accomplish some of the social work of society. Children, as students, find a place in school that theoretically allows them to develop the requisite skills and maturation necessary to take their place in a complex adult social structure. Student identities, at least in the Western world, are built largely on an assumed frame of middle class Whiteness (Eisenhart & Holland, 1983; Walkerdine, 1990; Mac an Ghaill, 1994), allowing them to reify the Western status quo without overt challenge. Student identities masquerade with neutered gender themes as well, as if the acquisition of knowledge, which the student is supposed to be accomplishing, happens outside the realm of gender identity development.

Yet Mac an Ghaill (1994) notes that 'sex/gender regimes are a fundamental organizing principle within the schools which underpins the individual and collective construction of student . . . subject positions' (p. 168). His 1994 study of the social construction of masculinities in secondary schools revealed that a range of feminine and masculine identities is available for students to inhabit in schools. Connell's (1995) work, too, asserted that 'masculinities come into existence as people act' (p. 208) and that both boys and girls had a range of gender identities available to them in schools. Both researchers corroborated the complex dynamics of student and gender identity work in schools.

Finders, in her 1996 study of the nature and purpose of literacy for adolescent girls, uncovered mechanisms by which schooling acts to construct gender identities even as it works to foreground student identities. She found that while girls' literacy practices in class echoed that of student identities, the girls' literate underlife (Goffman, 1974) 'displayed a tremendous sense of play' (p. 111) which they used to moderate their entry into adolescent status. Finders notes, 'The girls' literate underlife was clearly gendered . . . student-centered pedagogical practices deflected attention away from the rich complexities of students' lived experiences, creating a lens too narrow to view the power of the social dynamic' (p. 121). The data I present from White Oaks Middle School corroborates Finders' conclusions and offers evidence of the conflict created as gender identities and student identities compete in children's interactions; particularly in adolescent children's interactions.

Walkerdine (1990), perhaps more than any gender researcher within the last decade and a half, challenged schools construction of students' gender identities. She asked, 'What constructs the fiction of gender neutrality?' (p. 32). Starting from the premise that there are no 'unitary categories "boys" and "girls" ' but only people with multiple positions that are ascribed to masculine and feminine categories (p. 75) she used discourse between students and between students and teachers to illustrate how students and teachers can be positioned in a number of gendered identities and that these positions have 'real and material effects in the life chances of . . . girls' (p. 74). While her work neglected to point out that boys, even in positions of power, are equally affected by gendered positions, she nonetheless illustrated 'how [student] categories are produced as signs and how they "catch up" the subjects, position them, and in positioning, create a truth' (p. 142). By denying the complex and often masked ways in which gender becomes naturalized, power assigned to gender becomes hidden.

When gender identities are sublimated by student identities, they become even more powerful: gender feels natural as it resides in a student identity, thereby masking the ways in which gender and schooling interact. It is the unfortunate consequence of schooling in a society that still believes in the mythological power of meritocracy (Young, 1959) where the simultaneous existence of powerful gender identities and student identities become impossible. The data of White Oaks Middle School offer a glimpse of how gender identities are actively in conflict with and naturalized by student identities.

It is difficult to catch the formation of this naturalization in action. While these discursive data are contextual and fleeting (Geertz 1973, 1995), catching pieces of them in moments, in their context, is to reveal them in new light. These data are by no means comprehensive, but I believe that they provide us with a rationale for starting a newly radical conversation about girls' and boys' abilities to challenge their gender identities in school.

Poststructural Theory and Contradictory Identities in Context

These data were collected as part of a study of student gender identities in a suburban New York State school district. The Sage Creek School District is home to approximately 3300 students, grades Kindergarten through to Grade 12. It is situated in a community of 25,000 predominantly White, middle to upper middle class professionals and their families.[2] The community has a longstanding reputation for educational excellence that its members feel enhances all its residents: they carry the belief that they are academically untouchable. Real estate agents use the school district's reputation for academic superiority as a calling card for house sales in the area.

Children in the White Oaks Middle School were expected to carry student identities, with pride—to choose success. The Sage Creek Central Schools mission states, 'We expect all students to achieve their full potential for personal development and educational success' (Sage Creek Profile, 1). The middle school principal, Mr. Meyer, elaborated on this: 'We need to look at kids as learners, as individuals,' he said. 'Every kid needs a couple of pats on the back a day. We need to expect them to perform well academically—to have high standards for them and present them with opportunities' (Principal Interview 1). The principal's assertion that these 12- to 14-year-olds are 'individual learners' places them in the student identity. I suggest that positioning children as 'individual learners' makes the act of teaching less complex and the act of being a student less painful for children, as it mutes the impact of children's social identities on their understanding of how to be successful students.

But the students' discourse suggests otherwise. Despite teachers' and administrators' words that suggest children's student identities could be unchallenged by their social identities, analysis of students' discourse displays just how intertwined gender and academic achievement are. Fairclough (1995) observed that social subjects can occupy institutional subject positions that are ideologically incompatible; this is visible in the discourse of White Oaks Middle School students and teachers.

Poststructural Theory and Its Relationship to Students' Identities

Poststructuralist theory has its roots in cultural production theory, for it emphasizes the parts of the structure that make up the whole; it challenges the structural view of the whole as representative of its smaller components and allows for relationships to be the substance of analysis. Poststructuralism sees people as the building blocks of social structures, not products of them. Like cultural production theory, poststructuralism allows for the analysis of subject positions (identities) and for those subject positions to take on multiple forms. Poststructuralism, however, uses language as the analytic centerpiece. 'The idea that meanings flow back and forth from what is said to what is done, from ourselves to the world, is integral', writes Cherryholmes (1988, p. 9). Poststructuralism allows for a framework that uses a systematic analysis of language within an understanding of the fluidity of the walls between school and society.

Poststructuralist theory is one that accounts for 'the relation between language, subjectivity, social organization and power' (Weedon, 1987, p. 12). A feminist approach to poststructuralism extends the theory to understand existing gender power relations and to identify mechanisms of inequality. Feminist poststructuralist theory sees feminism as a politics directed at changing existing power relations between men and women in society. Doing so requires feminist critical research which allows us to 'understand social and cultural practices which throw light on how gender and power relations are constituted, reproduced and contested' (Weedon, 1987, p. vii).[3]

Placing acts of naturalization in a framework that facilitates the connections between the talk and actions and the larger social structure of the school allows us to understand the connections between context-specific micro actions (here, the students' and teachers' actions) and society. Fairclough (1995) offers a framework, for making these connections, stating 'It makes little sense to study verbal interactions *as if* they were unconnected with social structures' (p. 35, emphasis in original). He maintains that social structure and discourse can only be integrated through the use of micro and macro research, and that the institution must be the 'pivot' between society and local action (p. 37).

The focus on the institution as the 'pivot' between levels of society can be illustrated this way:

• Social formation (society).

• Social institution (school).

• Social action (local).

The school then, functions like a *comedia del arte* mask: half its face has ties downward to social action, to the micro-discourse of the students' and teachers' interactions, and the other half has ties upwards to the societal context in which the school sits. Fairclough argues that the relationship between these levels is not unidirectional, but rather dialectic; changes at any of the levels can influence levels up or down. Because a social institution is 'amongst other things, an apparatus of verbal interaction, or an order of discourse' (p. 38), understanding the discourse associated with a particular organization can lead to understanding the dominant and competing ideologies within that institution.

Fairclough (1995) discusses the dominant ideologies present in social institutions and the discourses used to maintain them as *ideological discourse formations,* or IDFs, created from the combination of

Pêcheux's (1982) term 'discursive formation' and Althusser's (1971) 'ideological formation'. As Fairclough further explains:

> I have referred . . . to the social institution itself as sort of a speech community and . . . ideological community; and I have claimed thai institutions construct subjects ideologically and discoursally. Institutions do indeed give the appearance of having these properties. . . . I suggest that these properties are properly attributed to the IDF, not the social institution: it is the IDF that positions subjects in relation to its own sets of speech events, participants, settings, topics, goals and simultaneously, ideological representations. (Pêcheux, 1982, p. 41)

The definition of an IDF, then, is a pattern of discursive interactions that systematically keep particular ideologies in place within an institution.

More than one IDF usually exists within an institution and it is the struggle for dominance of a particular IDF where power struggles might be visible. When an IDF is largely unchallenged, it is 'then that the norms of the IDF become the most naturalized . . . and may come to be seen as the norms of the institution itself' (p. 41). This is the case I am making with student identities in White Oaks Middle School. The power of an IDF must be continuously fought for, but that fight might not be obvious; given the possibility of an IDF being so dominant as to be thought of as the institutional norms, the group which has ideological and discoursal power may not even be status-marked.

In order for IDFs to maintain dominance, they must be supported by what Fairclough refers to as 'background knowledge.' Background knowledge is 'taken for granted knowledge . . . that subsumes 'naturalized' ideological representations which come to be seen as non-ideological "common sense" ' (p. 28). The 'student identities' and the discourse that maintains them, create in this context the IDF. In White Oaks Middle School, children's gender identities become naturalized as student identities. Since student identities are supported as the 'appropriate' and common sense identities of schooling, the children's gender identities are sublimated, although not without problem, as I present below.

How Gender Identities Are Naturalized as Student Identities

Students

There are several interactions that I Believe reveal how gender identities in this context become naturalized as student identities, forming the IDF. Below, White Oaks Middle School students are in study hall discussing the definition of the 'perfect student'. The students create a distinction between boy and girl students, unmasking the student identity as a gendered identity. I have separated the comments that describe the 'perfect female student' from the comments that challenge this construction: the girls in this conversation display their understanding that the student identity is not unproblematic. It is mostly girls who challenge the construction, but both boys and girls contribute to the construction of the 'perfect student':

Emily: [Repeating my question] What's a perfect student?
Rick: Uh, like female student?
NN: Is there a difference?
Rick: Yeah, there is a difference. The perfect female student, nice clothes, sorta shy—
Jenn: *Nice? Not nice clothes—*
Dan: Pretty and tall and like—
Jenn: *Ah, he thinks we're perfect!*
Dan: Like skinny and—
Emily: *Tall, blonde, they want them to be blonde.*
Dan: No, blondes are—
Jenn: *You're describing a Barbie doll.* [All laugh.]
Dan: I won't go there.

Jenn:	*And big boobs?*
Dan:	No, they have small boobs.
Rick:	No, but she's like Tall and she's thin and she's like I don't really know how big her boobs are but . . . I don't think it really matters, but, um—
Jenn:	*Yeah right.*
Emily:	*Hey wait, this has like nothing to do with the student.*
Jenn:	*I know.*
Emily:	*I think Barbie dolls are ugly.*
NN:	What does a perfect girl student act like in class?
Rick:	She's quiet in class—
Emily:	She does all her homework.
Dan:	Doesn't do it all at home, but gets it done.
Emily:	Passes. Always has her binder checked.
Dan:	Passes with flying colours. Never fails. Does everything, hands in her report.
Suzy:	She's always gets things on time or early and she does all the extra credit she can.
Rick:	Alright she's like, she's sorta, she's quiet she's definitely quiet.
Jenn:	*OK what girl—*
Rick:	And—
Jenn:	*—is quiet?*

Emily and Jenn counter the boys' descriptions of the perfect female student, but also contribute to the construction of the identity until Emily exposes the contradiction with 'Hey wait, this has nothing to do with the student'. Jenn concurs and Emily then directly counters their construction of the perfect female student by saying, 'I think Barbie dolls are ugly'. This comment stops the conversation for a long three seconds. But if Barbie dolls are ugly, it means by these students' definitions that 'perfect female students' must also be ugly. Since no one wants to say this, it makes sense, then, that no one responds to Emily. The students' lack of response to Emily also suggests that the girls in this conversation are negotiating contradictory discourses as Finders (1996) and Walkerdine (1990) suggest.

When I ask what this 'perfect female student' acts like in class, the students' comments again jointly construct her as long as they discuss class work. As soon as Rick says that the perfect girl is 'sorta quiet', Jenn counters by loudly asking, 'OK, what girl is quiet?'. They debate this contradictory position.

The physical description of the 'perfect female student' is that she is tall, blonde and model-like in her beauty. No matter that, as Emily notes, beauty has nothing to do with doing schoolwork: for these students, the construction of a female with these characteristics is naturalized as 'good student'. Further, Dan says that the perfect girl 'doesn't do it [her homework] all at home, but gets it done', suggesting that girls willingly participate in hiding their student identities. The perfect female student must: wear nice clothes, be beautiful like a Barbie doll, and do all her schoolwork on time and well, but hide her academic accomplishment. The girls' gender identities are naturalized as student identities, but their student identities are expected to be hidden under gender identities. These constructions create a social Catch 22: a girl is naturalized into a student, but as a student, she is supposed to be a girl in order to be a good student.

The naturalization of these girls' gender identities into student identities is clearly articulated by Emily, though her observation goes unchallenged and barely corroborated. She states that the discussion about girls' breasts 'has nothing to do with the student' but only Jenn responds with an 'I know'. The second half of the conversation reveals contradictions in the students' constructions of male students and elaborates on the construction of female students. I have denoted in bold the comments that challenge the construction of either:

NN:	So what does a perfect male student look like then?
Rick:	Can dress good.
Emily:	Pretty much everything that a female is, but—
Rick:	Glasses.

Jenn:	*Glasses? Why can't the girl have glasses?*
Rick:	'Cause the girl doesn't *wanna* wear glasses.
Jenn:	*Girls wear glasses though.*
Rick:	OK. I'm not mockin I'm just saying the girl doesn't want to wear glasses and doesn't wear glasses.
Emily:	Girls usually wear contacts.
NN:	If there's a difference between a perfect male and a perfect female student, what is it?
Rick:	He's got glasses, short hair, he's got um—
Suzy:	He's gotta be a little bit loud but not that—he can't be shy.
Rick:	No, a little bit loud.
Emily:	Not shy, a little bit. Funny.
Rick:	Sorta procrastinates but doesn't get points off for it because like he'll get it done in study hall.
Jenn:	Joke around. But gets good grades, maybe not passes every test but gets average grades, like 70s and 80s.
Emily:	[Unclear comment]
NN:	What did you just say, Emily?
Emily:	*Well, they like described the female as like perfect—*
Jenn:	I know.
Emily:	*And the male as being like a little loud, not passing every test.*
Jenn:	*It's like their dream girl.*
Emily:	*The girl has to be perfect.*
Jenn:	*A perfect girl student is like a geek, kinda, and kinda not.*
Emily:	*Too perfect. Beautiful.*
Emily:	*To be perfect, you can't be a geek.*

The students begin describing the perfect male student using physical criteria as they did with the construction of the perfect female, but they then dispense with the physical description, turning to males' behaviours and their academic and social performances. It is Emily who again interrupts, imperceptibly at first, eventually giving voice to the disparity between what perfect male and female students are supposed to be: the female has to have perfect grades and be quiet and beautiful according to the spoken description, and the male needs not to pay attention to his looks, should have less than perfect grades and should be loud.

Jenn and Emily refine their understanding of the contradiction inherent in their constructions of the perfect female and male students. Jenn notes that 'the perfect girl has to be "kinda geek and kinda not"' and Emily adds the final coda: 'to be perfect you can't be a geek'. So, the 'perfect girl student' has to possess all of the characteristics that make up the socially weak 'geek', which in this context is equivalent to a student identity.[4] The girl student has to do all her work and 'pass with flying colours', be quiet and get 'all the extra-credit she can' and at the same time she has to have the beauty and social standing of the stereotypically beautiful Barbie doll. The perfect girl student, by the students' own definition, does not and *cannot* exist. The gender standards of the culture hide in the naturalized identity that is the 'perfect female student'. Girls are expected to possess identities that in this context are completely incompatible.

The student identity for a boy also naturalizes his gender identity, though the students in this conversation do not discuss this. The perfect male student is expected to be the rowdy, outspoken boy who does not pay attention to his looks. This male student identity naturalizes the male gender identity construction in this context, and while it may seem less harmful than the female identity, it leaves no room to be any other kind of male other than the one described. Specifically, any boy who does pay attention to his looks or who 'passes everything with flying colours' as the perfect female student must do, is at risk for being a labeled a 'girl'. And, in a double cultural punch, being labeled a girl is an insult in this context, an assertion that one is gay (see Niemi, 2001, for elaboration on this point).

Girls and boys have gender identities that are naturalized as student identities. The student identity reveals, in this context however, the differing expectations for boys and girls; in White Oaks Middle School, it seems as though it is impossible to be both girl and student.

Teachers and Administrators

The adults of Sage Creek demonstrate through their discourse that they, too, try to actively prevent the influences of society and social action from entering the institution. If the institutional actors do not acknowledge what they hear or see about gender—or if they actually do not see it—then they can maintain the IDF of the student in the institution. If the efforts of the institutional actors deny the influences of society (both micro and macro), then these efforts stay accepted as a way—perhaps the only way—to make schooling successful for every student, regardless of their other identities.

Earlier I suggested how the principal's discourse naturalized students' gender identities by making them 'individuals'. The teachers naturalize gender as well. By assuming that students' academic identities override their social identities—in this case, gender—the teachers can naturalize gender and make it look as though it does not impact the student identity. In the following interaction, Ms French, an English teacher from my study, wanted to help her students identify with the characters from Shakespeare's play *The tempest*. After finishing an aural reading of the play, she asked them which character they would most like to be:

Ms French: OK. Now think for a minute. I want you to think about the characters in the play—all the different ones: Prospero, Antonio, Caliban, Miranda, Ariel, and tell me who you would choose to be in real life? [Silence while they write their answers.] Now. Raise your hand. Who would like to be Ariel? Okay, three. Who would be Miranda? Okay, Darcy, Why? [Every girl in the class raises her hand.]

Darcy: She's beautiful.

Phoebe: She gets married.

Ms French: There's no right or wrong here. What about Prospero? [All but five boys raise their hands. Then she asks the students to keep reading the play silently, and turns to talk to me.] You know, this is exactly the same thing that happened in the other class. It's distressing. Every girl in that class picked Miranda too because she was pretty and got the guy. The boys in that class said it was Prospero because of his power. Don't you think—but these are average kids. I can't imagine my high achievers doing that. Amanda, Jill, Sarah D? They would have broken the stereotype.

But, in fact, even in the high-achieving class later that day, every girl picks Miranda. Ms French, as she displays in her aside to me, wants to use high achievement—the student identity—to negate the gender work occurring in her classroom, but the students' discourse will not let her do so, at least with girls. The boys in her classes overwhelmingly picked the powerful character, Prospero, and indicated that they picked him because of his power, but the teacher does not muse about their choices. In fact, she recasts their gendered choice of power as harmless or natural by not calling attention to it. Even if it is questionable that girls pick the stereotypical choice, boys' choices are not even up for discussion, at least not with me.

The institution and its actors, as the discourse of students, teachers and administrators of Sage Creek has already demonstrated, attempt to keep out influences of macro and micro order so that school learning can occur without being challenged by those forces. Both girls and boys act and achieve as 'students', despite the clear existence of their gender identities, in a framework that supports the naturalizing of all gendered identities into student identities.

Teachers' enforcement of 'appropriate behaviour' is one more way in which gender is naturalized in this context. In an interview with my participating teachers, Mr O'Malley and Ms French, we can observe how two teachers cast children's gendered behaviour as inappropriate behaviour for school; their discourse illustrates some of the elements that contribute to making a student identity:

Mr O'Malley: Yeah. I don't think the students know that this is kind of their job that they should act a certain way in class. And I don't think that they really separate the kid. . . . It's a level of decorum. They do talk so much that sometimes you just try to keep it very structured, you know, moving forward and . . . not giving them a whole lot of

	freedom to express themselves, and it's that way because when they do it [express themselves] they don't do it in an appropriate manner.
NN:	What is that?
Mr O'Malley:	Ah, well you know it's kind of a—it's kind of like the appropriateness thing, you know like, with the Eighth Graders, just that one of maturity. It's just a huge deal and you know you can talk to them more about that, about sex and stuff, and they'll respect it. It's just the maturity level; they'll accept what you're saying and think about it rather than making fun of it or laughing.
Ms French:	There are things students should know about behaving appropriately. They have to learn that I cannot instantly gratify their needs. They cannot get out of their seats and socialize, cannot talk; they have to sit and wait. When they get older, like Twelfth Grade, they can talk about that stuff without being silly.

The expectations of these teachers seem like classroom management tools and on one level they are. Yet the discursive strategies employed by these teachers naturalize gender, as they try to keep out the social formation and the social action from the social institution. By displaying their professional understanding of what they deem as good classroom behaviour and of students' maturational development, the teachers act as gatekeepers (Erickson & Shultz 1982), forming a barrier between the whole of society—with all its influences—and the institution. Mr O'Malley says that the students should 'separate the kid', suggesting that he understands there are different identities available to students. Moreover, he admits that he tries to stop the students from expressing themselves because they do not do so 'appropriately'.

When I question him about this, Mr O'Malley refers to students' level of maturity, specifically their ability to deal with 'sex and stuff'. Herein lies a revelation of gender and students' gender identities as they are naturalized in student behaviour. Through Mr O'Malley's and Ms French's explanation that 'appropriate behaviour' in part means that they cannot talk about sex, they reveal how classroom management is also about gender. But the ideological discourse formation of 'student', in order to remain dominant, must be continuously constructed through struggle. These struggles are visible in the contradictions found in the discourse events where the students' gender identities and academic identities are juxtaposed. It is in this struggle where gender identity formation loses as the struggles to create different forms of gender identities are challenged. Gender identities are omnipresent and expected but simultaneously downplayed.

White Oaks Middle School adults seem to use discourse that supports the student identity in their attempts to block both social formation (macro) and social action (micro) from the academic work of the social institution. In effect, the teachers display that they think they can deny social identities from influencing their academic work with students.

Conclusion

Gender identities are naturalized as student identities in White Oaks Middle School. Both boys and girls are affected by this; girls, in particular, cannot exist as gendered (feminine) and academic simultaneously. Teachers and students pursue academic achievement and deny gender in this pursuit. Were gender identities able to exist side-by-side to student identities, I might be able to argue that they could coexist without harm, allowing gender to be brought in and left out as another topic of discussion and development, much as the teachers indicated they felt they could do.

Yet these four discourse examples give reason to suggest that the student identity is so opaque that it is perceived as an institutional norm, successfully obscuring the effects of any competing identities, in this case gender identities, much less those of ethnicity or social class. The adults of White Oaks Middle School did not deny that their students had gender identities, but they did believe, as their discourse showed, that they could control their students' enactment of gender in school. In the discourse events where students' gender identities were part of the interaction, the school adults either ignored the gender implications or, more often, recast the interactions as students' enactment of behaviour that was developmentally appropriate for early adolescents. The students, on the other hand, displayed a more sophisticated understanding of gender identities and their relationships to student identities, even if this understanding was not frequently—or ever—encouraged.

These four discourse examples attest to the power of dominant language practices to affect students' gender identities in spite of the academic equity that is offered in theory to all White Oaks Middle School students. Using Fairclough's (1995) framework of relationships between the levels of society allowed me to expose the naturalization of gender identities and the imposition of student identities in academic discourse. Educational researchers such as Erickson (1986), Mehan (1978) and Weedon (1987) claim that this kind of dual exposure, produced through theories of cultural production and poststructuralism, is possible. Levinson and Holland (1996) claim that by:

> . . . portray[ing] and interpret[ing] the way people actively confront the ideological and material conditions presented by schooling . . . [theories of cultural production] provide a direction for understanding . . . the production of cultural forms and [how] subjectivities form and agency develops. (Levinson & Holland, 1996, p. 14)

By portraying and interpreting the ways in which students and school adults confront and naturalize students' gender identities, I have exposed and illuminated some of the processes by which they codependently exist. Yet this is not enough.

I suggest that educators and educational researchers continue to expose the contradictions in what it means for children to be students. Without this examination, it will be easy to proclaim, as too many have already done, that the 'gender problem' in schools is over; lack of examination will also deny further exploration of the ways in which not only gender, but ethnicity and social class are heterogeneous categories in schools. White girls, for example, will continue to be told that they must be good 'students' but will understand this to mean that they must be 'Barbie dolls'. Do Black girls also hold this understanding? Do girls living in poverty feel this way? Boys, too, may continue to understand that their student performances allow them to 'joke around' while at the same time being considered a 'perfect student.' Is this understanding uncomplicated for boys, regardless of their social class? Does it change depending on the ethnicity of the girls with whom they interact? These are but a few of the questions which need be examined. If we mask the ways in which gender works in school, we lose daily chances to examine it, confront it and envision what could be.

ENDNOTES

1. K–12 schooling means Kindergarten through to Grade 12 in the United States' system of schooling; it encompasses children from roughly ages 5 through to 18.

2. Sage Creek School District and all names in this study are pseudonyms in order to protect the participants' privacy.

3. I disagree that poststructural theory must be deemed 'feminist' in order to be used to understand power relations between men and women in society; the definition of poststructuralism already takes power into account. While I absolutely agree that feminism is a politics that should and does have a place within poststructural analysis, I do not believe the theory itself is inherently feminist or masculinist. Each time poststructuralism is used within a study, its political representations should be redefined. By combining poststructural theory with an inquiry of gender and schooling, this study sets the stage for understanding the construction of students' gender identities in school and consequently how they might be related to the performance of gender equity outside of school.

4. See Niemi (2001) for extensive description and analysis of the competing student identities in this study.

REFERENCES

Althusser, L. (1971) Ideology and ideological state apparatuses, in: L. Althusser, *Lenin and philosophy and other essays* B. Brewster, (Trans) (New York, New Left Books).

American Association of University Women and American Institutes for Research (1999) *Gender gaps: where our schools still fail children* (New York, Marlowe & Co).

American Association of University Women and Wellesley College Center for Research on Women (1993) *Hostile hallways: the AAUW survey on sexual harassment in America's schools* (Washington, DC, AAUW).

American Association of University Women and American Institutes for Research on Women (1992). *How Schools shortchange girls.* (New York: Marlowe & Co.).

American Federation of Labor (1997) Trends in educational equity for girls and women, *Fact sheet: working women: equal pay,* Washington DC, 84–87.

Bowles, S. & Gintis, H. (1976) *Schooling capitalist America* (New York, Basic Books).

Cherryholmes, C. (1988) *Power and criticism: poststructural investigations in education* (New York, Teachers' College Press).

Conley, F. K. (1998) *Walking out on the boys* (New York, Farrar, Straus & Giroux).

Connell, R. W. (1987) *Gender and power* (Oxford, Basil Blackwell).

Connell, R. W. (1995) *Masculinities* (Berkeley, University of California Press).

Crichlow, W. (1991) *A social analysis of black youth commitment and disaffection in an urban high school.* Unpublished doctoral dissertation, University of Rochester, New York.

Eisenhart, M. A. & Holland, D. C. (1983) Learning gender from peers: the role of peer groups in the cultural transmission of gender, *Human Organization,* 42(4), 321–332.

Erickson, F. (1986) Qualitative methods in research on teaching, in: C. Wittrock (Ed.) *Handbook of research on teaching* (New York, MacMillan).

Erickson, F. & Shultz, J. (1982) *The counselor as gatekeeper* (New York, Academic Press).

Fairclough, N. (1992) *Discourse and social change* (Cambridge, Polity Press).

Fairclough, N. (1995) *Critical discourse analysis: the critical study of language* (New York, Longman Press).

Finders, M. J. (1996) 'Just girls': literacy and allegiance in junior high school, *Written Communication,* 13(1), 93–129.

Frazier, N. & Sadker, M. (1973) *Sexism in school and society* (New York, Harper & Row).

Geertz, C. (1973) *The interpretation of cultures* (New York, Basic Books).

Geertz, C. (1995) *After the fact, two countries, four decades, one anthropologist* (Cambridge, MA, Harvard University Press).

Goffman, E. (1974) *Frame analysis* (Boston, Northeastern University Press).

Levinson, B. A., Foley, D. E. & Holland, D. C. (Eds.) (1996) *The cultural production of the educated person. Critical ethnographies of schooling and local practice* (Albany, SUNY Press).

Mac an Ghaill, M. (1994) *The making of men, masculinities, sexualities and schooling* (Buckingham, Open University Press).

MacLeod, J. (1987) *Ain't no makin' it, leveled aspirations in a low-income neighborhood* (Boulder, CO, Westview Press).

Mehan, H. (1978) Structuring school structure, *Harvard Educational Review,* 48(1), 32–64.

National Council for Research on Women (1991) *Sexual harassment: research and resources: a report on progress.* Available online at: www.nysed.gov. [Accessed 21 March 2004].

New York State Department of Education (2003 December 11). *Board of Regents proposes major reform in state funding for the schools.* Retrieved November 2004, from *http://www.nysed.gov*

Niemi, N. (2001) *Silencing the noise of students' gender identity construction in middle school discourse.* Unpublished doctoral dissertation, University of Rochester, New York.

Pêcheux, M. (1982) *Language, semantics and ideology: stating the obvious* (London Macmillan).

Pollack, W. (1998) *Real boys: rescuing our sons from the myths of boyhood* (New York, Random House).

Ravitch, D. (1996) The gender bias myth, *Forbes,* 157(10), 168.

Sadker, D. (2002) An educator's primer on the gender war, *Phi Delta Kappan,* 84(3) 235–244.

Sadker, M. & Sadker, D. (1994) *Failing at fairness. How our schools cheat girls* (New York, Touchstone).

Sommers, C. H. (2000) *The war against boys: how misguided feminism is harming our young men* (New York, Simon & Schuster).

Walkerdine, V. (1990) *Schoolgirl fictions* (London, Verso).

Weaver-Hightower, M. (2003) The 'boy-turn' in research on gender and education, *Review of Educational Research,* 73(4), 471–498.

Weedon, C. (1987) *Feminist practice and poststructuralist theory* (New York, Basil Blackwell).

Wexler, P. (1992) *Becoming somebody: toward a social psychology of school* (London, Falmer Press).

Willis, P. E. (1977) *Learning to Labor* (Aldershot, Gower).

Young, M. (1959) *The rise of meritocracy* (New York, Random House).

Voicing Your Opinion
The Emperor Has No Clothes: Examining the Impossible Relationship Between Gendered and Academic Identities in Middle School Students

Nancy S. Niemi

1. Niemi asks middle school students to identify the "perfect" female and male student. How would *you* describe the "perfect" female and male college student? Be mindful of your use of language and evaluate how you have constructed gender identity by the way that you use words.

_____

_____

_____

_____

_____

_____

2. Do you believe that there is a possibility of creating gender neutrality in American schools? Why or why not? Is gender neutrality important in American schools? Why or why not?

_____

_____

_____

_____

_____

_____

3. Niemi points out that girls focus on how they look and boys focus on how they behave. Why does this occur? How might this affect girls as students? How might this affect boys as students?

_____

_____

_____

_____

_____

_____

Terms

Organizational
performance
Gender identity
Success
literature

PERFORMING THE ENTERPRISING SUBJECT
Gendered Strategies for Success (?)

MAJIA HOLMER NADESAN AND ANGELA TRETHEWEY

This article is about professional women and the tension they experience between their internal identity and the expectation of an external performance of gender. It introduces a discussion of the gender guidelines offered by popular literature and explores the ways that this information further complicates women's communication in work settings.

For women in contemporary corporate life, negotiating and performing a "professional" identity is a process requiring much time, energy, and self-surveillance. Yet, many women feel compelled to undertake this project despite the challenges it poses. These women often turn to popular success literature for strategies to help them craft and enact successful identities. In this essay, we analyze the popular success literature and compare its prescriptions for success with the voices of actual, successful career women. We explore the paradoxes and contradictions within and across these discourses in our efforts to deconstruct masculine constructions/performances of professionalism.

For many women in contemporary corporate life, negotiating and performing a "professional" identity is a process requiring much time, energy, and self-surveillance. Despite the emotional and physical labor that must be expended to successfully perform an exemplary identity, many women may feel that they have little choice in this matter as organizational performance measures increasingly focus on the employee's ability to embody and enact a highly prescribed image (Deetz, Martin, Nadesan). For women, performing an "appropriately" gendered professional identity is a process particularly fraught with tensions, possible missteps, and potentially irreparable consequences (Trethewey, Disciplined Bodies). Accordingly, although we recognize that many working women are too concerned with issues of survival to fixate on their "image" (Glazer, Higginbotham, Romero)—that a professional identity is indeed a luxury—we also believe there are those primarily (white) middle-class women for whom identity is a struggle on many levels.[1] Those women often turn to the popular success literature for strategies to help them craft successful identities. The popular success literature offers women performance protocols or scripts for successful organizational performance in every sense of the term.

We are interested in those organizational protocols and scripts promoted in the women's success literature and we are interested in the degree to which women appropriate or resist the literature's counsel. Informed by both Lacan and feminist thinkers, our analysis of the popular success literature suggests that its performance protocols are sites at which the discourses of enterprise and therapy intersect to discipline women's bodies and selves. Therefore, we will address the implications and potential effects that emerge when women strategize their own identities using the psychological, performative, and ultimately impossible ideal promoted within the literature on women's professional success.

We begin by turning to the popular success literature where we hear the authoritative voice of Diane, a successful woman, inform readers that women "aren't always sure what they want" because, among other reasons, they have a tendency to flip back and forth among roles including "mother, sister, wife, lover" (Brooks & Brooks 151). Diane contrasts these women who encounter "powerful" barriers, with those "successful" women who "identify as managers first, women second" (Brooks & Brooks 151). "Universally" successful women, according to Diane, manage their bodies (and sexuality) appropriately, refrain from "flipping" among alternate identities, and communicate professionally rather than emotionally. Thus, according to Diane, the professional woman is master of her internal psyche and her bodily performances.

Our analysis suggests that Diane's polarization of "women" and "manager" is merely the surface of a series of contradictory prescriptions directed toward women's workplace success. The discourse articulates "manager" as a gender-neutral, entrepreneurial ideal; however, that ideal ultimately emerges as masculine by its explicit distancing from, and rejection of, characteristics typically regarded as feminine. Women readers are encouraged to strive for success by embracing the entrepreneurial ideal while, simultaneously, they confront subtle remarks that imply that they, as women, can never hope to achieve it. In effect, the women's discourse offers readers a paradox: *Success is contingent upon realizing an entrepreneurial ideal that is ultimately held to be unattainable because of unsightly (feminine) leakages that always/already reveal their performances as charades.*

And yet, many women do in fact achieve outward measures of success including substantial salaries and high-status positions. Do they regard their everyday workplace performances as charades that are always/already threatened by the fear of being unmasked? Do they fear unsightly feminine leakages? Although it is impossible to answer these questions decisively, we find it instructive to juxtapose the discourse of success found in popular books and periodicals with individual women's voices drawn from our interviews with 20 enterprising, professional women who are all members of a chamber-of-commerce women's association.

As critical scholars, we are interested in the intersections between the women's voices and the discourse of success. However, we do not claim that there exists a one-to-one correspondence across these texts. Every text—be it an individual voice, a book, or periodical—bears the traces of multiple discourses, multiple statements about the nature and relationships among social constructs. Because of this discursive heterogeneity, every text/voice offers possibilities for multiple interpretations, for resistant readings, resistant performances. Accordingly, since our orientation as scholars is critical, we feel that it is important to identify themes that thread across texts that have the effect of reproducing social (gender/class/age/race) privilege, while still acknowledging and celebrating expressions of and possibilities for resistance. This tension between discursive closure and control on the one hand, and textual openness and resistance on the other, is a difficult one to navigate. Thus, we recognize that our reading is not exhaustive; however, we do feel that it prompts further consideration of common prescriptions for, and actual performances of, gendered organizational identities.

We begin with a brief overview of our theoretical framework before moving to our second major section, which explores the relationship between the discourse of success and professional women's voices. We conclude our essay with some critical thoughts on the relationship between discursive closure and resistance.

Theorizing Identity

The (symbolic/discursive) identities that we are interested in are representations of "successful" women found in self-help books and popular women's magazines. However, although we believe that these discursively produced identities are persuasive in their interpellations, we also recognize that the individual women we interviewed cannot be reduced to these identities. Below is our effort to map the relationships among symbolic/discursive identities, individual subjectivity, and textual interpretation.

The Symbolic, the Imaginary, and Resistance

Drawing upon Lacan, we define the symbolic as the system of signifiers that constitutes the source of all social meanings and identities. The primary, albeit suppressed signifier, or the *"point de capiton,"* is the Law of the Father, which fixes language into a stable system of differences (Lacan 154). However, although we recognize with Lacan the signifying power of patriarchy, we also acknowledge the role of other primary signifiers—particularly those pertaining to class and race—in organizing the symbolic field(s). Therefore, we argue that when the subject assumes an identity(ies) in language, s/he is always/already articulated in relation to primary signifiers that include, but are not restricted to, the Law of the Father. And yet, the positivity or fullness that these primary signifiers represent can never be *had;* they are unattainable. Indeed, individuals' identifications with *all* symbolic identities are always/already "imaginary."

In order to illustrate the imaginary nature of individuals' symbolic identifications, let us briefly turn to Lacan's discussion of the "mirror stage," wherein the infant's sense of "I" is precipitated by its (mis)recognition *(meconnaissances)* of itself us a unified, coherent bodily agent (6). As Lacan explains, this ascendancy of the jubilant I is followed by alienation as the infant realizes that his/her bodily comportment can never begin to (and never will) achieve the unified constancy of its reflection. Put simply, no one can ever *really* achieve the positivity, or fullness, of their symbolic aspirations: no one can *have* the phallus. Thus, the *process* of identification is always/already *imaginary.* For the purposes of our project, we need not delve further into Lacan's account of psychic formation. Instead, we wish to draw attention to this "gap," as it were, between the imaginary (i.e., the *process* of the individual's identification) and the symbolic sources of identification (Butler, Psychic Life 97). Rather than expressing itself as a presence, this gap engenders a *lack,* a kind of tear in the symbolic universe.

Butler draws attention to this gap because it emerges within the imaginary as "disorder," as "a site where identity is contested" (97). Butler's goal is to reclaim this gap from Lacan's more pessimistic formulation. Butler argues that Lacan fails to adequately theorize resistance because he argues that the imaginary's capacity to thwart the symbolic is limited since the former cannot turn back upon the latter to affect or reformulate it. That is, the imaginary cannot consciously transform the symbolic. Butler locates the solution to this impasse in performative practices.

Lacan, it seems, focused too exclusively on the psyche and therefore failed to give the body its due. Butler rightly points out that individuals acquire symbolically articulated identities through their (imaginary) *bodily* performances. Bodies are not passive mediums upon which symbolic discourses are inscribed. Rather, individuals are interpellated by symbolic identities which they actively (but not always consciously) perform and re-perform in time/space. As Butler (99) puts it, "This [performative] repetition or, better, iterability thus becomes the non-place of subversion, the possibility of a re-embodying of the subjectivating norm that can redirect its normativity." Repetition always/already breeds difference.

Butler therefore introduces the possibility of resistance in several ways. First, following Lacan, she provides the ontological possibility for resistance by pointing to the gaps or fissures (engendered by the imaginary), which prohibit symbolic closure.[2] Second, although these gaps cannot be mobilized directly for resistance, they may be experienced by individuals as a lack, an inconsistency, an im/possibility. Possibility thus emerges from contingency. And this is where Butler introduces her third and most important formulation of resistance. Because symbolic identities must be performed—and every performance is a repetition—the profound sense of lack may engender that "possibility of re-embodying of the subjectivating norm," redirecting and/or deflecting the normative force of the symbolic interpellation (99). This re-embodiment may be triggered by the sense of lack and/or it may be triggered by the individual's exposure to, and interpellation by, some alternative symbolic discourse. Antagonistically articulated symbolic identities would, in themselves, seem to promote that sense of lack that engenders possibility (Laclau & Mouffe; Holmer-Nadesan).

Now that we have addressed the relationships among symbolic power, individual identification, and performance/resistance, we provide a brief account of how we understand the relationship between symbolism and discourse analysis.

By moving away from Lacan's singular, pivotal signifier—the Law of the Father—we complicate our task as critics because we acknowledge the structuring effects and dislocations affected by other primary signifiers, such as those that organize race and class. Discursive complexity, heterogeneity, and the always/already possibilities for resistance complicate analysis. Although the critic may argue convincingly that a particular text instantiates a particular discourse, s/he cannot predict other readers' practices of textual interpretation. Textual interpretation is therefore a slippery process. With this in mind, when developing our analysis we remain sensitive to the inevitable slippage between what we perceive to be the textual ideal promoted in the women's success literature (i.e., our account of the preferred reading) and the interpretations and performances reported by our interviewees.

Situating Women's Discourses of Success

The women's professional success literature is a diffuse body of texts found in popular books such as *Seven Secrets of Successful Women* (Brooks & Brooks) and in advice columns found in professional trade journals (e.g., *Personnel Journal*) and women's magazines (e.g.. *Cosmopolitan*). Although diffuse in its dissemination, our reading [of articles and books published in the 1990s) indicates that the literature typically assumes the format of an advice column and therefore presumes that readers are interested in, and responsive to, the texts' "expert" interpellations. In this sense, the women's popular success literature is parallel in form to the more generic "therapeutic" self-help literature, which interpellates readers as in need of the "expert gaze," and which articulates intervention as a means of discovering deep-seated barriers to success, happiness, and self-fulfillment (see Cloud; Coyle & Grodin; DeFrancisco & O'Connor; Grodin). However, although parallel in form to the self-help genre, the women's literature on professional success focuses almost exclusively on providing strategies for achieving *workplace* success. Accordingly, the content of the literature promotes explicitly and implicitly an idealized representation of the "successful career woman." The preferred reader of the success literature is an aspiring career woman who seeks out advice on or protocols for how to perfect her workplace persona.

Reading the women's success literature, we as critics feel that the idealized representations of the successful career woman invoke the "entrepreneurial subject" described by Miller and Rose and Du Gay. The "entrepreneurial subject" is a new expression of subjectivity that has arisen at the intersection of cultural discourses of consumption and the new organizational discourses of Total Quality Management (TQM) and Business Process Reengineering (BPR). Through the process of his/her continual self-improvement, the entrepreneurial subject adds value to organizational products and services. The entrepreneurial subject consumes "innumerable training courses and seminars" in order to enhance his/her technical skill base while, simultaneously, this subject endlessly seeks to perfect his/her personal image, self-discipline, and communication skills (Miller and Rose 26). In essence, the entrepreneurial subject is an identity characterized by technical competence, style, and social adroitness (see Garsten & Grey; Nadesan). *The entrepreneurial subject, we argue, is the pivotal signifier that serves within the success literature as the symbolic source for readers' imaginary identifications.*

The success literature advises that readers' achievement of an entrepreneurial subjectivity requires (a fragmented) reflexive analysis and performance of both mind and body. Each reader is fragmented into a psychic or *"internal self,"* characterized by fears, anxieties, and weaknesses, and a *"performative self,"* which encompasses bodily image, comportment, and social skills. This fragmentation, purportedly allows the reader to act upon herself to engineer her successful adoption of the entrepreneurial ideal. Having observed this kind of fragmentation across the psychological literature. Rose claims that contemporary relations between government (in the Foucauldian sense) and subjectification have affected the development of specific techniques "intellectual techniques" and "body techniques"—that *"articulate"* and *"constitute"* the (symbolic/discursive) source of individuals' imaginary identifications (31).

Entrepreneurial prescriptions (both intellectual and bodily) for workplace success are ubiquitous. *Fortune* magazine, for example, advocates the entrepreneurial ideal stating, "Forget old notions of advancement and loyalty. In a more flexible, more chaotic world of work you're responsible for your career. For the adaptable, it's a good deal" (Sherman 50). *Fortune* magazine calls this employee the "New Organization Man" (Munk 63). Nadesan's analysis suggests that the entrepreneurial ideal is typically masculine in tone, as implied by *Fortune*'s label. Given this coding, we as critics are interested in the extent to which the women's literature for workplace success navigates the tension between a gendered ideal and the aspirations and ambitions of its female readership. We turn now to analyze the entrepreneurial ideal as it is articulated in the women's success literature and through the voices of women readers.

Analyzing Discourses/Voices of Professional Success

The popular success literature contends that there are two paths to success and both must be pursued for its realization. First, women must rid themselves of specific psychological barriers acquired during childhood gender socialization. Second, women must learn to comport their bodies in a manner that minimizes their sexuality while, simultaneously, avoids the dangers of hyper-masculinization. Accordingly, the success literature takes a fragmented approach to self-transformation by offering distinct "intellectual" and "body" performance techniques whose applications are held to guarantee success for female readers (Rose).

In developing our analysis we, as critics, elected to follow this fragmented structure. First, we explore how the literature articulates success as an end state that may be achieved only by reconstituting the psyche. We then examine the extent to which the women whom we interviewed share this understanding of success. Second, we explore those bodily techniques promoted by the literature as useful for de-sexualizing the female body. We then examine the extent to which "real" women view their bodies as posing barriers to their workplace success.

Reading Discourses of Success: Protocols for Remedying Internal Barriers

Limiting beliefs, the success literature argues, acquired in childhood gender socialization, bar women from achieving the success they deserve. As critics, we will argue that the success literature's pre-occupation with women's purported "limiting" internal states actually presupposes a homogenized construction of women's psyches that is represented as problematically *other* than the preferred entrepreneurial subject, who implicitly emerges as normatively masculine in character (see Cheng; Nadesan).

PROFESSIONAL WOMEN'S "ROLE CONFLICT." The first internal barrier women must overcome in achieving an entrepreneurial psyche is simply that, "women don't know what they want" (Brooks & Brooks). This lack of psychic certitude is often attributed by the literature to a "lack [of] self-confidence" (Glaser & Smalley 299) and/or the "fear" of success (Hyatt 20). For example, Hyatt in *The Woman's New Selling Game* explains that "there is still the fear that with success, others will resent us, threaten us; we'll lose control of our reason with the smallest amount of power and others will offer us feasts of poisoned apples!" (17). Women fear success, the literature argues, because they believe that the acquisition of power will undermine their femininity.

For example, Dowd in *Working Woman* claims that "for women, power has always had a negative aroma. It has been considered an acid that corroded femininity and sexual allure, an isolating force" (98). Consequently, the literature reasons, most women are unwilling and/or unable to relinquish their femininity and therefore end up sending "mixed-messages that are not clear and consistent" in professional contexts (Brooks & Brooks 151).

In *The Winning Image,* Gray frames this same dualistic articulation between professionalism and femininity as "role conflict" Accordingly, he states:

> The professional woman is suffering role conflict. The problem is compounded as she begins to succeed. Moving up from a subordinate—"feminine"—position to a male dominated world, she encounters the bias of 'how women should be.' Some women overreact to the conflict. At one extreme, some project an image of severity and control, especially on the job. Perhaps this is an attempt to compete with male counterparts by being recognized as equally 'masculine.' At the other extreme, perhaps, in an attempt both to attract male peers and to prove themselves, some project a very strong feminine image, an image that says 'I'm a woman, but I can stick with the best of them.' Women want jobs, particularly in management, but confusion about self-presentation is a major drawback. (16)

In Gray's terms, women experience role conflict because power and success are masculine; women's attempts to perform male identities merely heighten the visibility of their lack of fit. Conversely, some women's obstinate retention of a feminized image creates the impossible paradox of a sexualized authority figure (Tannen).

"Role conflict" is also highlighted by the literature when women's interdependent, relational (read: private) orientation is held to pollute their professional (read: public) relationships at work. For example, in helping women reframe their relational orientation, Barbieri advises, "Share no secrets, make no best friends. The office is not a pajama party" (35). Likewise, Shulte advises, "Smart office politicians know better than to confuse friendliness with friendship" (177). The advice suggests that women should abandon their normal relational strategies in favor of more masculine, utilitarian ones while again recognizing that most women find it difficult or feel conflicted about doing so.

ROLE CONFLICT'S ORIGINS: NATURE AND NURTURE. The success literature explains women's role conflict in terms of both biological and cultural factors. For example, Barbieri draws upon the seemingly inherent "nature" of males and females when claiming that "in the area of office politics, both societal conditioning and perhaps testosterone have prepped [men] to deal better than most women" (34). Dumas suggests that women's (purported) aversion to "risk-taking"—a vital dimension of the entrepreneurial personality—is biochemical in origin. Similarly, Glasser and Smalley argue that women typically "lack the backbone and know how" to make "their own rules" (Glaser & Smalley 298). Although the origin of women's role conflict is often attributed to bio-genetic factors, the women's popular success literature explicitly argues that women can learn to identify and transform inappropriate behaviors that stem from their "female" inclinations.

Women's role-conflict is also explained in terms of female gender socialization, which fosters "limiting internal belief systems" and inappropriate value orientations. In *Executive Female,* a Vice President of Coords Ceramicon Designs in Golden, Colorado, writes that "some women have not yet unlearned the limiting belief systems we were raised with" (cited in Glaser & Smalley 297). Likewise, Brooks and Brooks cite Betty Harragen in their rejection of female socialization:

> Betty Harragen writes that girls' games are outgrown early in childhood and are not resumed in adulthood because they basically have virtually no intrinsic value—they teach nothing. [. . .] Wow, did some of us women miss out on some serious development of competitive skills needed to make it in the workplace! (184–85)

In effect, femininity is articulated as both an innate and acquired limiting state. A professional woman's success depends upon its transformation.

The literature holds that women's universal, innate and socialized attributes engender a vast array of problematic behaviors including a universally implied tendency toward being "touchy-feely" as opposed to "clear-thinking" (Mindell 23). This role conflict purportedly leads to inappropriate emotional displays (Post), indecisiveness (Mindell), tendency to be "seen" as opposed to "speaking-up with confidence and convictions" (Glaser & Smalley 297), and the tendency for women to be " 'consensus-seekers'—{this can be a positive trait, but can also translate into indecisiveness on the job}" (Glaser & Smalley 298).

Women's learned and innate ways of communicating are cited as particularly detrimental to professional success. Purportedly problematic patterns of communication—inappropriate emotional displays, qualifiers, tag questions, hedges—are represented as transparent indicators of "limiting" internal states. Mindell describes women's (seemingly) emotion-laden communication as the "language of weakness" (3). For example, she warns that "Describing events or issues in terms of 'feelings' substitutes 'psychobabble' for clear thought" (4). Mindell advises readers that if they "shed the style of weakness and then weave the language of power," they will simultaneously enhance their "confidence" and will correspondingly "gain the courage to try ever more advanced skills" (15). In effect, "women's communication" is represented as more vague, less skilled, and mom rooted in affective (as opposed to cognitive) thought (see also Ancona). Worst of all, women have a tendency to ramble, to be "motormouths" (Francis 112). In a behaviorist cycle, the literature holds that the assumption of more "powerful" (i.e., concise, cognitive-rational) communication patterns will, purportedly, act back upon the mind to hone its functioning, allowing for development of "more advanced skills" (Mindell 15). Thus, Hyatt advises, "Stop whining and start winning" (27).

It is important to note that, although the discourse positions women as generally non-competitive, as a result of their problematic socialization, it does address female "sabotage," which is attributed to ruthless, jealous competition among women (Watts). Contrasting with masculine "gamesmanship" (Harragan), characteristically female sabotage is characterized as petty, irrational, immature, and ultimately driven by female insecurity and envy (Briles; Kruger; Tener). Books such as *Hardball for Women* offer women strategies for acquiring male competitive tactics.

OVERCOMING WOMEN'S SOCIALIZATION THROUGH ENTREPRENEURIAL DISCOURSE. Despite the limitations of gender socialization, the women's popular success literature is adamant that women can unlearn and/or transform dysfunctional "feminine" patterns by adopting and ultimately performing the simple therapeutic prescriptions advocated by the literature. For example, Mindell promises that "this book shows you how to use the language of power to succeed at work" (ix). Likewise, Heim states in *Hardball for Women,* that "This book is going to teach you the rules" for success (20). Looking forward, Brooks and Brooks conclude that girls are increasingly being socialized like boys, "So there's hope for the next generation!" (185).

It is important to note that we, as critics, are not endorsing rigid gender socialization. Rather, our point is to illustrate how the women's popular success literature *universalizes* and then *devalues* traits and practices coded as female or feminine because of their purported effect in "limiting" women's career success. Career success is therefore contingent upon individual women's ability to perform an entrepreneurial subjectivity that draws upon extant articulations of hegemonic masculinity, tempered by social adroitness and image awareness.

Unlike their female colleagues, male workers are represented by the literature as completely career-identified and flexible. They are rational decision-makers and strategic risk-takers. They play "hardball" with competitors, are "team players" with colleagues, manage subordinates authoritatively, and "always do what the coach says" (Heim 17). In effect, traits and practices articulated as female construct the difference against which the entrepreneurial subject takes shape. With this in mind, Brooks and Brooks claim that women's past failures at overcoming the glass ceiling can be explained by the fact that they *"hadn't evolved enough to enter a 'man's world' "* (4 italics ours). Thus, successful women "overcome" their female "tendencies" or "never had them to begin with" (Barbieri. 35).

Although the women's popular success literature centers the individual as the ultimate source of her success, its application is problematized by caveats it provides regarding its own application. Specifically, the literature provides repeated admonitions that, although women should eliminate "female" attitudes and traits, they should also avoid appearing too masculine and/or too militant. For example, Dr. Terzaghi, Ph.D., a clinical psychologist who specializes in counseling career women, is cited as cautioning women that they need to be assertive without being personally aggressive and "overbearing" (Schulte). Heim also invokes the authority of science when claiming that "Recent research has shown that behaving like a man will backfire" (20). Brooks and Brooks concur: "Men and women are generally viewed more favorably (by both men and women) when they conform to stereotypical roles" (225). In the past, women's approach to copying men "was too rigid, even hostile, rather than sportsmanlike" (Heim 5).

Arlene Ferrante-Ford summarizes the literature's ambiguous solution to the dilemma articulated above: "When women act like men, they do themselves a disservice because they get lost in trying to fit in rather than forge their own unique career paths" (cited in Watts 42). She goes on to say that women who fail to forge their unique career path, who "can't let go of the man's world approach to situations put us all at risk of losing our identity" (42). The exact nature of a career path that navigates between the masculine ideals of professionalism and the feminine pitfalls of glass-ceilings and ridicule remains to be articulated, however.

Women's Voices on Success: Internal Barriers

Although it is probably impossible to determine precisely how the popular discourse of success affects individual women who are, by most accounts successful, entrepreneurial, and confident, we are interested in exploring the question. More specifically, in the pages that follow, we read the discourse of success with and against the voices of twenty professional, (primarily) white, middle-class enterprising women. Over the course of twenty, (relatively) open-ended conversations with these self-described professional women, it became clear that many had learned from and, in fact, valued the popular discourse of success. While the women certainly do not simply echo or mimic the success discourse, their voices do force us to critically examine the ways in which women's identities are shaped in contemporary organizational life. The names of the women presented here are pseudonyms chosen by the participants.

WOMEN ARTICULATE THEIR OWN AND OTHERS' ROLE CONFLICT. One central theme found in the women's voices revolves around their efforts to navigate an identity that is at once professional and feminine. As Kim, a pharmaceutical sales representative, says, "Being a professional and being a woman, you wear numerous hats." Accordingly, nearly all of the women in our study express "role conflict" in the sense that they implicitly organize gender around a public-private dichotomy where "feminine" is relegated to the private, domestic realm. However, our respondents vary considerably both across and within their responses to this dichotomy. Most responses affirm it by valorizing the (traditional) "masculine" dictates of the public realm, while others implicitly subvert the dichotomy affirming "feminine" relational patterns in the work-context. Interestingly, those individuals who see gender as a "socialized" construct are more likely to reject traditionally feminine commitments while those who see gender as "natural" are more likely to affirm them. And yet, none sees gender as (ultimately) escapable. We return this idea in our section on performance in which feminine bodies are revealed as threatening and in need of strict controls.

Ann, a successful marketing practitioner, illustrates the tendency to organize gender around a public-private dichotomy:

> The feminine side, unfortunately, really has to go. Uh, I've been doing this for fifteen years in my own industry, and am currently at the top of my field, I would not have gotten here if I had not looked more of a male type role. Definitely. There's very few of us women who make it this far,

and they unfortunately either had to go over board in being the tough scenario, bitchy, rude, type of person. [Or] I do it a slightly different way. Um, I do it in a very quiet tone, I do it in a very controlled tone, but I'm very persistent. So either you go overboard, and become the raving maniac that they think women turn into, or you do the shifty evil way which is me. There really isn't [another way].

Ann believes that women who are successful are able to identify first and foremost as professionals, in a masculinized sense of the term, not as women. Of course, unaccustomed to power, a masculine-identified woman faces becoming a "raving maniac" or "shifty" and "evil." However, for Ann the benefits outweigh such risks. She says that she can now:

be one of the guys and still not have [to tell] the dirty jokes and still not have talk in some of the language you hear, or go to that level, but they think of you not as a woman, they think of you as a counterpart. And that is the biggest compliment. I love it when I'm thought of as one of the peers, the professionals. They can call me, they can tell me jokes if they want to, they can call for my technical ability. That is the biggest compliment I get is I'm never thought of as a woman. I'm thought of as a professional. That's very hard to acquire.

Although Ann sees herself as relatively adept at assuming a masculinized identity, another respondent, Susan, cautions that "men are real threatened by women" whose demeanor conveys the confident, assertiveness of a successful male professional.

Even while recognizing the dangers of "over-masculinization," many of our respondents regard women's traditionally "private" commitments as unwanted workplace intrusions. One of our participants, Beth Ann, a management consultant, is very critical of women who send "mixed messages" regarding their priorities, particularly when compared to men's clear and rational choices. She says, "We women must get over our hang-ups." Instead of waffling about whether we want to value family or work as a priority, we need to simply choose our priorities, as men have done. Beth Ann argues, "The man's priority has been maximum income his whole life. [He says,] 'Yes I really wanna be a father, but most of all I want maximum income,' and that's true for about 80 percent of the working men. And the women have to make their choices, too. We don't wanna make choices." Beth Ann implicitly articulates career success in opposition to "private," gendered commitments. Women's "inability" to choose simply reflects their inability to emulate the masculine model of clear, consistent decision-making. Once women make priorities clear, says Beth Ann, then the rest of their career or family choices logically follow from those priorities and their roles become explicitly articulated. Affirming the traditional public/private dichotomy, Beth Ann holds that barriers such as the "The Maternal Wall" (Painton 44) are a natural and inevitable consequence of women's role-conflict.

Similarly, Allison, a saleswoman, claims that women fail in professional relationships because they never learned that "business and friendship are two different things." Moreover, Allison reveals that she became cognizant of this problem after reading Heim's *Hardball for Women*. Allison explains, "What she says in this book is that women are taught that the relationship is more important than any other part of business. And so you will do whatever it takes to make sure the relationship is functioning. Men don't do that. That's why women work harder." According to Allison, this manifestation of role conflict, namely women's seemingly relentless focus on their relationships, even in business contexts, has the potential to hamper their performance and undermine their professionalism.

WOMEN'S REASONS FOR ROLE CONFLICT. In keeping with the discourse of success, the women in our study cite both nature and nurture as influencing women's career paths. However, as noted above, our respondents who cite feminine orientations as "natural" are more likely to affirm its workplace applications. Those that affirm strictly masculine workplace identities are more likely to see gender as a relatively malleable product of socialization.

Sunshine, a management consultant, argues that a successful professional is "supposed to be a good competitor [. . .] Now that's something that men find real important to do; however, women are taught that it's more important for everybody else to feel good and for it to be supportive." Sunshine implies that early socialization for a nurturing relational orientation later undermines women's professionalism. Similarly, Allison asserts that little girls "never learn to deal with conflict," whereas little boys' socialization processes "put them nose to nose, they shake hands and figure it out. So, that's why two men can be at each other's throats all day at the office, and at the end of the day say, 'Hey, wanna go out for a beer'?" These overt, aggressive, and ultimately more useful conflict management skills are, then, not readily available to women, suggests Allison, until, of course, they read *Hardball for Women* or some similar text.

In contrast to comments made by Sunshine and Allison, Kim, argues that women possess *intrinsic* professional acumen:

> I think that it's important to, though, to have some femininity. I really do and that's where you recognize yes, you're a woman, you're a professional, and you can somewhat separate those roles, but at the same time, we're woman, we're very sensitive, we're compassionate, we're very understanding, we can relate to people, we're empathetic, much more than a man. Those are the things that differentiate being a professional and being a woman.

While Kim's comments tend to polarize professionalism and femininity, she seems to value "feminine" workplace applications.

WOMEN'S STRUGGLES DUE TO ROLE CONFLICT. Although ambivalent in their responses to femininity, nearly all of our respondents report that they are ultimately unable to escape it. Priscilla's struggle is illustrative. Priscilla, a young financial planner, describes the difficulty that comes from trying to find an identity position that is at once not too feminine (as the popular success discourse advises) and not too masculine. Priscilla believes that, while her ability to both play and discuss competitive sports has served her well in a male-dominated field, she always chooses to display that knowledge carefully. If she is too competitive, if, for example, she plays a better round of golf than her male peers, "it hurts" her professionally. Likewise, she does not reveal to her male (or female) counterparts that she plays in and enjoys a female basketball league. She fears that her peers will see her as either "too masculine" or as a lesbian; either label, she believes, is devastating.

Given the seeming impossibility of a purely feminine professional identity *and* the dangers of over-masculinization, Sunshine suggests that "the women that I think about who have been very successful, have been women who've had their own style." And yet, like Ferrante-Ford (see above), Sunshine is unable to articulate how to carve out a path between the masculine ideals of professionalism and the feminine pitfalls of role-conflict.

Given the fear of being seen as ultra-feminine *or* hyper-masculine, many of the women in our study report that they pay particular attention to the details of dress and bodily comportment. In our next section, we address how women's struggles to contain their unruly feminine nature without appearing *too* masculine lead to a variety of bodily performance techniques.

Reading Discourse of Success: Bodily Protocols for Success

The popular success literature appropriates enterprise as a prescriptive framework for contemporary organizational life where the body is a surface to be marked by, and a site for performing, the codes of consumption and those of formal organizational sign systems. Accordingly, readers are admonished to conduct their bodies accordingly, to become entrepreneurs of their very selves, shaping their bodies and lives through performative displays. The popular success literature suggests that the body can be successfully managed by cultivating bodily regimes such as image management, style, comportment, dress, diet, and exercise.

The popular success literature encourages its readers to literally embody "masculine" values such as individualism, competitiveness, and discipline (Garsten & Grey; Nadesan). Indeed, the most winning body is described in the popular success literature as the "mesomorph (the muscular ideal)" (Gray 37). The mesomorphic body is perceived to be "stronger, more masculine, better looking, more adventurous, younger, taller, more mature, and more self-reliant" than its endomorphic and ectomorphic counterparts (Gray 37). The mesomorph is "the person we look up to, the image we expect of leaders—the image of power, strength, and guidance" (Gray 37). Clearly, not every body measures up to this ideal. Those who find themselves lacking a tall, muscular, and male body can learn to enhance their own features by wearing the appropriate clothing, improving their appearance, and cultivating the right image. This is precisely the issue that many of the popular success authors address and the issue with which many of our participants struggle.

The popular success literature presupposes that a woman's image has the potential to make or break her career. While appropriate dress or style may not guarantee success, inappropriate dress "almost ensures failure" (Molloy xi). Women are warned repeatedly by image gurus that a mistake in dress can be fatal. A recent article in *Ebony* suggests that "Those of us who are serious about our careers have invested a lot of time, effort and money in them [. . . and] it doesn't make a lot of sense to sacrifice all that by falling down in the image category" (Kinnon 31). According to *Working Woman* magazine, "There's a big difference between caring about your appearance and being able to control it. [. . .] But a well-honed image is an important professional asset, and most working women have no choice but to try" (Wadyka 102). These prescriptions make it clear that for women, a misstep in appearance and dress can be devastating for their careers.

So what, then, is an aspiring professional woman to do? The literature provides several general prescriptions that can be appropriated by every professional woman, or so it would have us believe. To deal with the image problem, women are exhorted to dress conservatively, avoid disrupting the organizational environment by appearing sexual, and to deploy the correct nonverbal signals.

SUCCESS THROUGH APPROPRIATE DRESS AND IMAGE. Dressing conservatively means that the body is displayed in very particular ways. "The business woman doesn't want to draw attention to her body. [. . .] She wants to be observed for her mind" (Townsel 66), and conservative, appropriate dress ensures that women will not draw the wrong type of attention to their bodies. Yet, negotiating an appropriate image via dress and appearance is a difficult practice. Even the prescriptive books and articles leave the reader with little in the way of specific advice on what to wear. For example, Gray suggests that the woman who has trouble being taken seriously learn to wear darker, more authoritative clothing and to tone down her make-up and jewelry. More frequently, however, the popular success literature tells women that they should *not* wear. More specifically, women are advised against appearing too feminine (Matthews), too masculine, too flashy (Molloy), or too obtrusive (Townsell). Professional image, at least for women, is primarily defined negatively, always in relation to an assumed male standard of professionalism. After all, "if a man is really good at what he does, he is often referred to as a 'diamond in the rough' and can move up in spite of a poor image" (Molloy xi). The same, unfortunately, does not hold true for women, according to the literature.

SUCCESS THROUGH APPROPRIATE SEXUALITY. Closely related to dress and image is the notion of sexuality. The popular success discourse makes clear that women should not make their bodies available to others at work, at least not in ways that may be interpreted as overtly sexual. This becomes a challenge for women who are socialized into a culture that continually objectifies women's bodies (Probyn; Russo). Matthews argues, for instance, that women should "aim to look 'business-like but feminine' rather than overtly sexy" (24). Molloy emphatically states that "no woman should ever wear sexy clothing to work" (13). Molloy goes on to argue that, although "most men enjoy an attractive woman dressed in a sexy style," they "seldom promote them or trust them with important assignments" (13). Moreover, Molloy believes that "the reaction of men is friendly compared with that of women. Our survey of 137 women who work with women who dressed in a revealing manner showed that about one-third were openly hostile" to those sexy women (13).

Women's sexuality is presupposed in the discourse of success to be so potentially disruptive to the masculinized workplace that it must be carefully monitored. By this logic, sexual harassment is a nearly inevitable consequence of women's bodies entering the workplace. Assuming its inevitability, the popular success literature implies that women should expect and develop strategies for managing what Mackoff terms "sexual tension." Specifically, Mackoff suggests that women simply lighten up and approach "sexual tension" with a sense of humor. Women's always-already sexualized bodies seem to invite comments, jokes, and advances. Women must simply learn to work around their own (assumed hetero) sexuality. The problem here is that the obvious power dimension of sexuality in general and sexual harassment in particular are excluded from consideration. Men's sexuality is viewed as unproblematic, nearly invisible. It is women who are sexed (Cockburn).

At least one popular success author suggests that women's sexual power be introduced into the workplace, however. Salmansohn, author of the (appropriately humorous and light hearted?) *How to Succeed in Business without a Penis,* argues that women should not repress their sexuality at work; rather, women should harness it for their own purposes. She argues that the woman who is totally secure in her sexuality, who is at home in her own body, will be more secure at work. Salmansohn's vision of "cleavage power" is not one shared by most authors. Salmansohn celebrates, or at least revels in, women's objectified status. What she fails to recognize is that modern consumer culture already requires the manufacturing, instrumentalizing, and partriarchal articulation of female sexuality and female desire.

Ultimately, while the literature advocates that women control their sexuality, it simultaneously implies that women's bodies and sexuality are essentially problematic because they cannot be controlled. The literature thus warns that women must be on guard against performing messages they do not intend, whether they be about sexuality or any other aspect of their intrinsically "female" identity.

SUCCESS THROUGH APPROPRIATE NONVERBAL DISPLAYS. The popular success literature acknowledges that there are bodily differences between men and women, but rather than dwell on the differences "we can't change," the literature "comments on the gestures that you can do something about" (Mindell 115). From head to toe, women are advised to control their nonverbal displays in specific, scientific-management-like style. For example, the head should be held with the chin tilted slightly upward and women should shun any "extraneous head movements," such as tossing the hair away from one's face. Mindell warns that "tightly folded knees or ankle knots show anxiety" (120). Instead, women should keep their feet flat on the ground, shoulder-width apart. Finally, the disciplined body is evidenced by the woman's smile. "As with the grammar of power, the solution [of whether to smile or not to smile] lies in control: you decide when it's appropriate to smile" (Mindell 117). These prescribed gestures, reminiscent of the 19th-century elocutionary movement (Curry), if learned and practiced, are the "powerful nonverbal moves that bring success" (Mindell 111). Again, the assumption here is that the "natural" body of the woman is other than its professional masculine counterpart. Women, says Mindell, shrink into their spaces, while ("naturally" powerful and strong) men expand into the available space. Thus, the implication is that women must learn to appropriate male behaviors. Despite this emphasis on control and masculine behaviors, women are simultaneously told that "you don't want to communicate like a man" (Mindell 117).

Finally, the literature reinforces the notion that the entrepreneurial body is disciplined, purposeful, and fit. Bordo argues that, in contemporary culture, the "firm, developed body has become a symbol of the correct *attitude;* it means that one 'cares' about oneself and how one appears to others, suggesting willpower, energy, control over infantile [or feminine] impulse, and the ability to 'shape your life' " (195). *Ebony*[3] magazine spotlights two successful, women—Antionette Malveaux, executive director of the National Black MBA Association, and Texas Congresswoman Eddie Bernice Johnson—who embody entrepreneurialism and the correct "attitude" to which Bordo refers. Both of these busy women, whose careers continually place them in the public eye, "must have a polished look at all times" (Kinnon 33). "How do they manage?" asks *Ebony* (33). Both women exercise regularly. Ms. Malveaux works out regularly with a personal trainer, and Congresswoman Johnson wakes up at 5:00 A.M. every morning to exercise at the gym. For Ms. Johnson, "Discipline is a key word" (Kinnon 33). In short, the literature indicates that the woman with the entrepreneurial spirit is able to manage her life and career successfully through shaping and disciplining her very body, in terms of its image, sexuality, and nonverbal displays.

Women's Voices on Success: Performative Barriers

The professional women we spoke to are very much interested in finding and mastering strategies that enable them to perform well at work. The strategies that seem to be most pressing for these women are not ones that require technical skills or particular abilities and knowledge; rather, professional women appear to be most concerned about "image." They appear to feel confident in their technical abilities, but it is in the performance of their professional gendered identities that they question their own choices.

WOMEN'S IMAGE PROBLEMS. As the literature suggests, the "appropriate" professional image for women is always defined in relation to a male standard, making women's ability to perform the entrepreneurial ideal more difficult. Leann, owner of a large health-care organization, argues that "men's clothes are designed so that their bodies all pretty much look alike." Thus, men can wear a standard "uniform," a navy suit, and always look professional, says Beth Ann. Women have no such professional " 'uniform' so they try to look like the males. Well, it doesn't work for the female figure because we have hips. We have chests," complains Leann.

Because women's bodies quite literally protrude into the masculine work environment, women must constantly work to make their bodies disappear. As Katie, a social-service agency director argues, "the way you look should almost be invisible, as long as the first encounter is pleasing." Vicki, vice-president of an international technology firm, makes a concerted effort to fit in and not be noticed for her gender in her male-dominated industry. She says, "I tend to dress very conservatively. For me, it's a navy blue suit with a simple colored blouse, minimalist jewelry, no doo-dads, nothing. I even go to meetings with no purse, just my glasses and my pen . . . I tend to be very conscious of not displaying anything too effusive, anything that's too bubbly, which is my normal personality." Finally, Lana, a sales manager in the hospitality industry says that women are forced to be "chameleons," continually blending in to the environment in order to succeed in business.

WOMEN NEGOTIATE SEXUALITY. Yet, even when women do attempt to blend into the professional environment, in chameleon-like fashion, their camouflage may not always work to hide their sexualized otherness. The women we spoke with warn of the dangers of revealing one's sexuality. "Plunging necklines," "short skirts," and "anything that's tight, if it gives the appearance of a figure" are all described as inappropriate. If women do not control their sexuality by wearing appropriate clothing or emitting the appropriate nonverbal signs, they may very well be mistaken for or treated as "working girls" rather than professional women.[4]

Women's own cautionary tales about avoiding sexualized displays or performances in the workplace pose something of a paradox because, within the private sphere of patriarchal culture, women experience their sexual desirability as a form of cultural capital, a fact the popular success literature largely overlooks. Cassie, for example, states, "I want to show off my figure. I'm small and I think I took nice, and I want to show that off." And yet, Cassie recognizes the illegitimacy of her desire within the public sphere as illustrated by her comment. "I mean, I won't wear something that is low-cut, you know, or things like that." Cassie's willingness to rein in her desire to make her sexual self more prominent is probably a prudent decision as one participant in our study reaffirms the disdain with which women view other women who do wear sexy clothing at work. Lana tells a story of another female saleswoman whom "always wears very short skirts" and "long red nails" and who is not afraid "to show a little leg to make a sale." When Lana learned that her fellow female professional would use her body/sexuality in this way, she said, "It just stopped me cold in my tracks and I thought, 'That's so disgusting, demeaning.'" Clearly women's bodies and sexuality are problematized in contemporary workplaces.

It is not surprising, therefore, that, women must continually find strategies to deal with their sexualized bodies in an always-already sexualized workplace (Hearn et al.). In this vein, several of the participants use humor as a way of responding to questions about sexuality at work. Other women, however, describe how they were made painfully aware of their bodies at work when male employees hugged them, stared at their breasts, or made inappropriate remarks about their bodies. Yet these women, more often than not, explain how they attempt to thwart sexual advances with grace and aplomb. Nan, a consulting-firm owner, once felt so uncomfortable when a potential client started at her breasts during a long elevator ride that she never returned to work with the offender. She relates:

> We were in the elevator, and he just like stared at my boobs the entire time. I remember feeling so uncomfortable and I just freaked out later about it. I mean, I could have no more said anything to this guy than fly. There was no way. I mean he was so blatant about it. You know? I was just totally freaked out by it, and of course you know, there's this whole "what did I do?" Then I didn't show up to do the training, instead of calling the guy. It was a totally unprofessional response. I didn't call the guy, I didn't show up to teach the class I agreed to teach.

Sadly, Nan berates herself for not tolerating sexual harassment or "sexual tension" as it is euphemistically termed in the literature. One is left to assume that a more professional response would have been to simply lighten up and laugh off the experience.

Nan's story suggests that women should always be in control of their own sexuality, and even others' responses to their sexualized bodies. Yet, Nan also reveals that she felt a decided lack of control in the context of that elevator. In our patriarchal order, menstrual blood is probably the ultimate sign of women's uncontrollable sexuality. Accordingly, one respondent recounts a particularly horrific story of "leakage." Wooing a multimillion-dollar account at lunch, our respondent recalls how "that particular time of the month" came early, causing her to bleed on her cream-colored skirt. This story was so memorable that she shared it with other women during a local women's conference and trade show. Her female conference audience was at once sympathetic and uncomfortable.

This story reveals the way patriarchal culture responds to female desire in general and vaginas in particular. Patriarchal culture attempts to discipline female desire by harnessing it for male consumption. Within this troubling logic, argues Irigaray, a woman's "sexual organ represents the *horror of nothing to see*" (353, italics original). Menstrual blood, however, points directly to the vagina, making it available to see. In so doing, it reminds us of the plurality and multiplicity of women's sex organs and desire (Irigaray).

Yet, patriarchal culture represses this view of female desire and female bodies. As a result, women "experiences herself only fragmentarily [. . .] as waste, or excess" (Irigaray 354). The narrator of the "bloody" story appears to experience herself and her body as excessively female, as do those around her. Some women later responded to her story by saying it was not one that should be told in public. Making women's excessive bodies and sexuality available to the public, whether it is through inappropriate clothing, blood, or even narratives, is troublesome. Indeed, many of our participants seem to live in fear that they may lose hard-won credibility as a result of their undisciplined bodies.

GENDERED NONVERBAL DISPLAYS. In an effort to manage their own professional performances and identities our respondents use comportment and specific nonverbal behaviors as strategies for presenting their (potentially uncontrollable) professional bodies. In fact, Success, a college administrator, suggests that women who do not know how to manage their bodies should correct that problem, through whatever means necessary. She exclaims, "I don't care whether it's taking a modeling class, learning to walk, learning to sit, [but women should] try to build self-confidence and self-esteem" via appropriate comportment. Success believes that control over her "body language" makes others "read [her] as being confident." Similarly, Suzanne a professional image consultant, argues that women need to develop a "confident posture" and refrain from "fidgeting," or engaging in any other extraneous movement because it makes men, in particular, "nervous." Many women suggest that nonverbal strategies including good eye contact, a firm handshake, an upright (not uptight) posture, and paralinguistic markers are all external indicators of internalized control and an aestheticized, masculinized professionalism.

Emotional displays are particularly damaging nonverbal messages for professional women. Our respondents are adamant that demonstrations of seemingly excessive emotions are dangerous and damaging to women's credibility. Noticeably absent are comments about men's excessive emotional displays. Men, it seems, do not emote in public, at least not in the "inappropriate" ways that women do. Ann firmly believes that women cannot show particular types of emotions, namely sadness or frustration. She says, "Oh yeah, you had to become unemotional. There was no crying. And unfortunately, guys, women cry. [. . .] You can't show emotion [. . .] if you show any of that, you're a goner." Other participants make similar statements. A weak or overly feminine woman is as problematic as her opposite, as a hyper-masculinized one. The performative space between the two seems nearly impossible for professional women to inhabit.

While managing emotional displays and other nonverbal markers clearly moves one toward the entrepreneurial ideal, for the participants in our study, nothing displays professionalism better than a "fit" body. Almost unanimously, our participants cite "fitness" as the most important measure of professionalism. When asked to define professionalism, Beth Ann says, "I think the new standard is fit [. . .] I've seen more and more pressure to be fit in the workplace than I've ever seen before." Similarly, Sunshine contends, "We've always had standards, but I don't think we've ever put them on body types. And I think we're doing that more now. We're looking for people that exemplify those healthier lifestyles." Finally, Kim argues, "In order for you to be successful, you have to be fit, physically and emotionally, and that gives you the ability to be more productive and more efficient and more in control, more machine-like." For many of the interviewees, the connection between professionalism and fitness is almost taken for granted. Nan, for example, states that a woman with a fit body is "someone who has her life under control. And somehow, if you're like really overweight, you don't have your life under control." Finally, Success believes, "If you can control yourself [and your weight], I know that you are going to take care of me. If you can't do that for yourself, how am I to trust in whatever you're gonna do for me." For these women and many women like them, a fit, not fat, body is a marker of professionalism.

While the women in this study do not use the term "discipline" to describe their own approaches to managing their bodies, the term is certainly fitting. Women go to great lengths to avoid appearing out of control or undisciplined. Women make very careful and considered choices regarding dress. Some women delay or avoid having children. Others guard their feelings carefully and strategically. In short, women discipline their corporeal selves in the name of masculinized professionalism (Bartky; Foucault). If one can control her own body and self without appearing either too masculine or hysterical, then one may well be on the path to professional success. The strategies articulated above might suggest that women's bodies can be controlled, disciplined, and "de-gendered" to move toward the promise of the idealized entrepreneurial subjectivity. Yet, the voices of the popular success texts and our participants also threaten women's aspirations when they hint at the "truth" of women's bodies; that is, women's bodies have a tendency to leak, thereby revealing their "essential," uncontrollable, and undisciplined bodily "nature." The "truth" about women's bodies is a "nature" that is ultimately ill-equipped for life in the public, professional sphere.

Critiquing Discourses of Success

To conclude our essay we will critique the women's popular success literature by exploring its principles of operation and its potential effects. We then juxtapose our exploration of discursive control and closure with some thoughts about performance and resistance.

Discursive Control, Discursive Effects

Our reading of the women's popular success literature suggests that the discourse interpellates readers at two different levels. On the first level, the literature functions therapeutically by positioning the reader as the analyzed and the discourse as the analyst. Operating at this level, the literature urges the reader to reflect critically upon her internal and external self-dimensions so that she may engineer "successful" self-transformations. At the second level, the literature interpellates readers in relation to a specific, entrepreneurial ideal, which serves as the basis for the reader's critical self-comparison. Combining the two levels, the literature implies that fragmentation can be sutured and workplace success achieved; the reader need only invoke the entrepreneurial ideal as a standard for self-transformation.

However, our critical reading of the women's success literature suggests that its facile formula for success masks deeply-rooted contradictions that rupture the discourse's certitude and coherence. We briefly identify these contradictions before moving to unpack them. The first contradiction is that the literature promotes two, incommensurable views of women's subjectivity. Accordingly, the literature's prescriptions for success presuppose a conceptualization of the self as a disembodied, *cybernetic cogito* that is capable of self-objectification and transformation. Affecting a Cartesian dualism, the self is fragmented and objectified into mind (i.e., psyche) and body (i.e., essentialized femininity) by fixing and scrutinizing distinct internal and external barriers to success. This dualism between mind and body serves as the ground for the emergence of the *cybernetic cogito*, an autonomous, rational agent capable of acting upon its beliefs, attitudes, and body. Yet, in contradiction to the presupposition of a rational cogito, the literature also articulates for readers a second identity, one that universalizes and essentializes women's bodies and minds as inherently nurturing, passive, and undisciplined. According to the literature, these feminine traits ultimately cannot be escaped, masked, or suppressed. In effect, the literature leases the reader with two oppositionally (i.e., schizophrenically) situated identities that remain unresolved—that of cybernetic cogito, which views the body as a tool for the (rational) mind's will, and that of essentialized femininity, which transcends dualism by offering up a damning, inescapable, biological/cultural transcendental self.

The second contradiction found in the women's success literature follows from the first. The contradiction is that the literature simultaneously promises success while guaranteeing failure. Implicitly invoking the cybernetic cogito, the literature argues that women can achieve the egalitarian entrepreneurial ideal through the active process of self-transformation. That the demands of the ideal are coded as "masculine" merely reflects the "universal" truth that these behaviors/attitudes are better suited to instrumentalizing the cogito's will. However, the discourse then contradicts itself by problematizing the ease with which women readers can achieve the entrepreneurial ideal. The literature implicity warns that women's efforts to embody the masculine ideal will meet with resistance and/or will be subverted by uncontrollable (feminine) bodily leakages. The egalitarian entrepreneurial ideal therefore emerges as an impossibility.

In order to unpack these contradictions, let us, for a moment, consider this entrepreneurial ideal. In a Lacanian sense, the entrepreneurial subject serves as a substitute for the (metaphoric) phallus. The entrepreneurial subject is a common point of articulation for contemporary discourses of patriarchy, consumer culture, and business. Re-reading Lacan, we might say that it is the *point de capiton* for these discourses in that it serves as a site of condensation and stabilization for their signifiers (both within and across them). However, we wish to stress that no individual can fully *assume* this identity, although it can and does serve as a basis for the subject's mis-recognition.

The impossibility of becoming the entrepreneurial subject is revealed in ruptures that problematize the extant symbolic universe by hinting toward its contingency, its arbitrariness, and its partialness. The entrepreneurial subject is represented as an egalitarian ideal that centers the individual as the source of his or her success, which is achieved through the meritorious acquisition of skill and through the adoption of an aestheticized professional persona (see Nadesan). However, despite the self-certainty of its claims, the literature is not without ruptures that point to the elusiveness of the entrepreneurial identity. Contrary to the literature's claims, individualized success is a myth that erases the efforts of backstaged others and minimizes the effects of cultural privileges such as class, race, and national origin (Hacker; Valdivieso & Davis). Further, the discourse represents the workplace in terms that systemically exclude or minimize new organizational arrangements that hamper mobility and that exacerbate the economic and political gap between corporate elites and the majority of employees (including blue-, pink- and white-collar employees) (Allen; Deetz). Finally, the fit, ever-youthful entrepreneurial ideal lacks family commitments, never tires, and never ceases to acquire precisely those new skills that will foster innovation in his/her workplace.

In effect, the symbolic/material ruptures that signify the ultimate impossibility of realizing imaginary identifications with the entrepreneurial ideal will be experienced by both men and women. However, we argue that these ruptures are likely to be more pronounced for women because the impossibility of their imaginary identification with the entrepreneurial ideal is confounded by their simultaneous articulation by (and identification with) a patriarchal symbolic order that constructs their "minds" and "bodies" in terms of intrinsically debased otherness.

Hailed as entrepreneurial subjects by the discourse, women readers are simultaneously warned of the impossibility of their successful assumption of the identity. The discourse warns that their efforts to perform "masculine" virtues will cause them to be negatively evaluated by organizational others. Further, the discourse implies, women who assume and perform masculine cognitive and performative strategies risk denying their seemingly essential femininity, thereby *transforming themselves* into the spectacle of a (over-masculinized) female transvestite or a militant hysteric (see Brewis, Hampton, & Linstead). Hysterical symptoms (e.g., the "too serious" woman who experiences "role conflict") and inadvertent and unsightly leakages (e.g., sexualized bodies, language slips, etc.) are held to accompany the repression of women's essential femininity. Consequently, the literature intimates the impossibility of women's (successful) imaginary identification with precisely that symbolic role—the masculine entrepreneurial ideal—which it is promoting.

In effect, these articulations of the subject—*cybernetic cogito* and essentialized femininity—are fundamentally contradictory, yet they remain unresolved. The key to why the literature can bear such a contradiction can be found in the way the latter articulation attempts to explain away the former: women cannot become the entrepreneurial ideal because their inherent nature resists its mental and physical discipline. In effect, the latter articulation displaces attention from the contradictions that inhere across the two constructions of subjecthood—cybernetic cogito and essentialized femininity—by retrospectively rationalizing experiential and textually given ruptures that signify the *real* impossibility of *being* the entrepreneurial subject.

Let us illustrate this point using the women's success literature's implicit account of the militant or hyper-masculinized woman as a symptom of repressed femininity. In Zizek's reading of Lacan, the meaning of the symptom—for example, the meaning of the symptom of the over-masculinized and therefore hysterical woman—is always constructed retroactively:

> The Lacanian answer to the question: From where does the repressed return? Is therefore, paradoxically: From the future. Symptoms are meaningless traces, their meaning is not discovered, excavated from the hidden depth of the past, but constructed retroactively—the analysis produces the truth; that is, the signifying frame which gives the symptoms their symbolic place and meaning. (Zizek 55–6)

The success literature implies that the over-masculinized woman and/or unseemly bodily leakages are symptoms of repression. In contrast, Zizek instructs us to see these symptoms not as necessary givens whose meanings are "excavated," but as contingent articulations retroactively applied to explain away the ruptures engendered by the impossibility of the assumption of the entrepreneurial ideal.

In hinting toward the impossibility of assuming the entrepreneurial ideal, the women's popular success literature renders women painfully aware of their debased and shameful *otherness,* of their "limiting" internal psyches and undisciplined, hyper-sexualized bodies. In an attempt at empowering women in the face of their shame, some of the literature promotes "female" styles of leadership and/or "cleavage power" (Salmansohn 207). And yet, both of these expressions of womanly power (see Young) remain articulated within a patriarchal symbolic universe. Each exalted category—mother and lover—is constructed within a patriarchal symbolic order *for* the masculine other and each carriers with it a debased alter: the wicked stepmother and the whore. The (ontological) impossibility of realizing the exalted identity will manifest as a perceived lapse toward the debased identity.

Toward Performative Resistance

Discursive control and closure will always/already be met with resistance. Following Butler, we are interested in the opportunities for resistance that are engendered by discursive failure, by the gap that emerges between the symbolic ideal and individuals' (imaginary) performances. At one level, we can describe resistance as the unintended effects of bodily performances that necessarily introduce difference into their day-to-day enactments of (idealized) symbolic identities. Although operating at a pre-reflective level, the difference engendered by (iterable) bodily performances creates the space for more conscious and strategic acts of resistance. We turn now to explore how the gap between the idealized and performed identities engenders openness, possibility, and resistance.

One gap or fissure between the ideal entrepreneurial subject and our respondents' performances of identity on an everyday basis stems from the latter's implicit valuation of "femininity." While these successful women often describe "femininity" in rather essentializing and ambivalent terms, it is also a feature of their identities that many are largely unwilling to give up. Many of our respondents believe that women are simply better at building relationships. Even while they express misgivings about "feminine" relational orientations, many of these women also value themselves and others for building and maintaining relationships despite the fact that it takes time, effort, energy, and is often not explicitly rewarded.

While it is apparent that many of our respondents are "driven" by the entrepreneurial ideal, they also occasionally and knowingly choose to resist it. At least a few of our participants claim to know the "rules," but elect on occasion not to follow them. Katie, a social service worker, for example says that she often feels that she should dress more conservatively or more professionally, but because she values her "artistic" sensibilities, she often chooses to present a unique, creative persona to the world, knowing that it does not match the entrepreneurial ideal. She says that it is difficult, but necessary, to resist conformance to professional norms. Nan, too, explicitly critiques the discourse of success she finds in the media. She ruefully claims that, "women are seduced by the professional image." Indeed, she exclaims, "It's amazing that women are getting as far as they're getting when you think of the time and energy that they spend on this stuff [. . .] I mean, isn't it a substitute for what women could really be achieving?" Yet, Nan's resistance is ambivalent because she also identifies herself as among those who are seduced by the "professional image." She can critique it reflexively, yet she remains contained by it. However, on the one hand, her awareness of the impossibility of achieving the ideal image creates a space for potential resistance.

On the other hand, Nan's reflexive awareness may illustrate how resistance is appropriated and/or "tamed." In his analysis of hi-tech workers, Deetz observed a pattern that he describes as a "implicit Faustian bargain with the company to accept conditions of subordination for the sake of payoffs in terms of identity, financial standing, and job security" (Strategized Subordination 22). Deetz's point is that the perceived rewards for aspiring to a professional ideal may be seen as compensation for the "work" of self-strategization, although, for the women in our study, the promised identity failed to pay off as anticipated. Even given ''objective" indicators of their professional and economic success, they report that they frequently question their status, their professionalism, and their image. For example, one woman in our study, who often serves as an image consultant for other professional woman, claims that being a professional woman, for her, is confusing and overwhelming at times and so she continues to read trade publications and women's magazines (e.g., *Cosmopolitan*) to "learn what's acceptable." In short, she actively consumes the discourses of success, feeling that she still has much to learn and plenty of room to continually improve herself, just as the discourse would have her believe.

As feminist critics, and professional workers, we must acknowledge our own complicity with the discourse of success. Although we do not purchase or read the literature, we invoke its metaphors when we discuss or reflect upon our professional identities. We have discussed the horrors of menstrual leakages and the challenges of ''appropriate" dress (particularly in one-hundred-degrees-plus temperatures!). We have shared the "awkwardness" of pregnancy in the classroom and among our colleagues (Pollock), and considered how lactation subverts traditional conceptions of academic professionalism (Nadesan & Sotirin). We are professional, yet we aren't. . . .

Our own experiences indicate that the perils of the entrepreneurial subject do not belong solely to the women in our study. Although not all women may see themselves in our analysis, we hope that we have expanded the ways of reflexively considering and potentially resisting the increasing colonization of self by corporate/economic discourses of success. As Rose explains, the discourse of enterprise and the discourse of therapy intersect in ways that center the individual as the source of their success and articulate self-actualization as occurring through the assumption of the idealized entrepreneurial identity: "For the new experts of the psyche promise that modes of life that appear philosophically opposed—business success and personal growth, image management and authenticity—can be brought into alignment and achieve translatability through the ethics of the autonomous, choosing, psychological self" (Rose 157). We have pointed out that those promises, by necessity, remain empty because of the unsurpassable gap between hegemonic symbolic identities and everyday social performances. Although interesting at a theoretical level, this unsurpassable gap is more significant at a practical level for the many women who consume the women's popular success literature in their efforts to engineer an entrepreneurial personality. For them, the endless pursuit of such an identity requires constant vigilance, and the expenditure of both time and resources in the pursuit of disciplining what is articulated as an unruly psyche and an overflowing body. This work on the self ultimately inhibits women's collective political action (Cloud) and adds yet another (schizophrenic) "shift" to their already difficult lives.

ENDNOTES

1. For women of color, the challenges of negotiating a "professional" gendered identity are further amplified. In this respect, we find it interesting that the popular periodical *Ebony* seemed to surpass all other women's magazines in its emphasis on image enhancement.

2. The purported univocality and fixedness of those symbolic identities are ultimately illusory anyway: social symbolic articulations are always partial and contingent as the symbolic order is a system of differences that lacks stability, despite the anchoring effects of primary signifiers (i.e., *the points de capiton* of language) such as Lacan's Law of the Father.

3. We find it troubling that an article in *Ebony* magazine advises its readers to dress in an "unobtrusive" (read: not too black, not too ethnic?) fashion. Being seen as "unobstrusive" becomes especially challenging for women who are already underrepresented in organizational context, and therefore made "obstrusive" simply by their difference (see Spellers, 1997).

4. For an interesting discussion of the ways professional women may be mistaken for professional sex workers, see Trethewey (Disciplined Bodies).

REFERENCES

Acker, J. "Hierarchies, Jobs and Bodies: A Theory of Gendered Organizations." *Gender and Society* 4 (1990): 139–58.

Allen, B. J. "Diversity and Organizational Communication." *Journal of Applied Communication Research* 23 (1995): 143–59.

Ancona, P. " 'Genderflex' Can Help You Communicate." *The Arizona Republic* 8 Aug. 1994: E4.

Apfel, R. J. " 'With a Little Help From My Friends I Get By': Self-help Books and Psychotherapy." *Psychiatry* 59 (1996): 309–22.

Ashcraft, K. L. " 'I Wouldn't Say I'm a Feminist, But . . .': Organizational Micropractice Gender and Identity," *Management Communication Quarterly* 11 (1998): 587–604.

Ashcraft, K. L., and M. E. Pacanowsky " 'A Woman's Worse Enemy': Reflections on a Narrative of Organizational Life and Female Identity." *Journal of Applied Communication Research* 24 (1996): 217–39.

Bamer, R. " 'Seven Changes That Will Challenge Managers—and Workers.' " *The Futurist* 30 (1996): 14–8.

Barbieri, S. M. "How to Win Allies and Influence Snakes: Office Politics In the Nicer 90s." *Working Woman* 18 Aug. 1993: 34–7.

Bartky, S. "Foucault, Femininity, and the Modernization of Patriarchal Power." *Feminism and Foucault: Reflections On Resistance.* Eds. I. Diamond and L. Quinby. Boston: Northeastern UP, 1988. 61–86.

Bixler, S. *Professional Presence.* New York: G. P. Putnam's Sons, 1991.

Bordo, S. *Unbearable Weight: Feminism, Western Culture, and the Body.* Berkeley: U of California P, 1993.

Bowe, C. "The Politics of Pregnancy." *New Woman* 19 Oct. 1989: 128–32.

Brenders, D., and J. Robinson. "An Analysis of Self-help Articles: 1972–1980." *Mass Communication Research* 11 (1985): 29–35.

Briles, J. *Gender Traps: Conquering Confrontophobia, Toxic Bosses, & Other Landmines at Work.* New York: McGraw-Hill, 1996.

Brooks, D. and L. Brooks. *Seven Secrets of Successful Women: Success Strategies of the Women Who Have Made It and How You Can Follow Their Lead.* New York: McGraw-Hill, 1997.

Butler, J. *Gender Trouble: Feminism and the Subversion of Identity.* New York: Routledge, 1990.

Butler, J. *The Physic Life of Power.* Stanford: Stanford UP, 1997.

Buzzanell, P. "Gaining a Voice: Feminist Organizational Communication Theorizing." *Management Communication Quarterly* 7 (1994): 339–83.

Carnegie, D. *How To Win Friends and Influence People.* New York: Simon & Schuster, 1936.

Caudron, S. "Sexual Politics." *Personnel Journal* 74 (1995): 50–9.

Cheng, C., ed., *Masculinities in Organizations.* Thousand Oaks: Sage, 1996.

Cloud, D. L. *Control and Consolation in American Culture and Politics.* Thousand Oaks: Sage, 1998.

Cockburn, C. *In the Way of Women: Men's Resistance To Sex Equality in Organizations.* Ithaca, NY: ILR Press, 1991.

Coyle, K., and D. Grodin. "Self-help Books and the Construction of Reading: Readers and Reading in Textual Representation." *Text and Performance Quarterly* 13 (1993): 61–78.

Curry, S. S. *The Province of Expression: A Search for Principles Underlying Adequate Methods of Developing Dramatic Oratoric Delivery.* Boston: School of Expression, 1891.

Deetz, S. *Democracy in an Age of Corporate Colonization.* Albany: SUNY P, 1992.

Deetz, S. *Discursive Formations, Strategized Subordination, and Self-Surveillance: An empirical Case.* Paper presented at the annual meeting of the Speech Communication Association, San Antonio, TX. November 1995.

Deetz, S. *Transforming Communication, Transforming Business: Building Responsive and Responsible Workplaces.* Cresskill, NJ: Hampton Press, 1995.

DeFrancisco, V. L., and P. O'Connor. "A Feminist Critique of Self-help Books on Heterosexual Romance: Read 'em and Weep." *Women's Studies in Communication* 18 (1995): 217–27.

DiMare, L. "Rhetoric and Women: The Private and the Public Spheres." *Constructing and Reconstructing Gender,* Eds. L. Perry and H. Sterk Ithaca: SUNY P, 1992. 45–50.

Dowd, M. "Power: Are Women Afraid of It—or Beyond It?" *Working Woman* 16 November 1991: 98–9.

Du Gay, P. *Consumption and Identity at Work.* London: Sage, 1996.

Dumas, L. "Taking Risks in Business: Are Women Getting the Hang of It?" *Cosmopolitan* June 1991: 230–31.

Ehrenreich, B., and A. Fuentes. "Life on the Global Assembly Line." *Crisis in American Institutions.* Eds. J. H. Skolnick and E. Currie. New York: Harper Collins, 1991. 379–93.

Foucault, M. *The History of Sexuality.* Trans. R. Hurley. New York: Vintage Books, 1978.

Foucault, M. *Discipline and Punish.* Trans. A. Sheridan. New York: Vintage Books, 1979.

Francis, S. "The Biggest Crime of All: Time-Sucking." *Cosmopolitan* June 1997: 110–12.

Futrelle, D. "Help Yourself." *In These Times* 17 (1993): 33–6.

Gambrill, E. "Self-help Books: Pseudoscience in the Guise of Science?" *Skeptical Inquirer* 16 (1992): 389–99.

Garsten, C., and C. Grey. "How To Become Oneself: Discourses of Subjectivity in Post-Bureaucratic Organizations." *Organization* 4 (1997): 211–28.

Gatens, M. *Imaginary Bodies: Ethics, Power and Corporeality.* London: Routledge, 1996.

Gibbs, N. "Getting Nowhere." *Time* 3 July 1995: 17–20.

Glaser. C., and B. S. Smalley. *Swim With the Dolphins: How Women Can Succeed in Corporate America on Their Own Terms.* New York: Time Warner, 1995

Glazer, N. Y. " 'Between a Rock and a Hard Place': Racial, Ethnic, and Class Inequalities in Women's Professional Nursing Organizations." *Workplace/Women's Place,* Ed. D. Dunn. Los Angeles, CA. Roxbury, 1997: 300–04.

Gray, J. *The Winning Image,* 2nd ed. New York: AMACOM, 1993

Grodin, D. "The Interpreting Audience: The Therapeutics of Women's Self-help Book Reading." *Critical Studies in Mass Communication* 8 (1991): 404–20.

Hacker, A. *Two Nations: Black and White, Separate, Hostile, Unequal,* New York: Charles Scribner's Sons, 1992.

Harragan, B. *Games Mother Never Taught You.* New York: Warner Books, 1977.

Harragan, B. " 'Dear Betty Harragan.' " *Working Woman* Sept. 1988: 48–9.

Hearn, J., et al., eds. *The Sexuality of Organization.* Newbury Park: Sage, 1989.

Heim, P. *Hardball for Women: Winning at the Game of Business.* Los Angeles: Lowell House, 1992.

Higginbotham, E. "Black Professional Women: Job Ceilings and Employment Sectors." *Workplace/Women's Place.* Ed. D. Dunn. Los Angeles, CA: Roxbury. 1997. 234–46.

Hoban, P. "Women Who Run With the Trends." *Bazaar* January 1984: 42–44.

Holmer-Nadesan, M. "Organizational Identity and Space of Action." *Organization Studies* 17 (1996): 49–81.

Hyatt, C. *The Woman's New Selling Game.* New York: McGraw-Hill, 1998.

Irigaray, L. "The Sex Which Is Not One." *Feminisms: An Anthology of Literary Theory and Criticism.* Ed. R. R. Warhol and D. P. Herndl. New Brunswick, NJ: Rutgers University Press, 1991. 350–56.

Jagger, A. M., and P. R. Struhl. eds. *Feminists Frameworks.* New York: McGraw-Hill, 1978.

Kaufman, M. "Image." *Working Woman* 16 Oct. 1991: 101–2.

Kennedy, P. *Preparing for the Twenty-First Century.* New York: Vintage, 1993.

Kinnon, J. B. "Grooming for Career Women." *Ebony* April 1997: 30–4.

Kruger. P. "What Women Think of Women Bosses." *Working Woman* 18 June 1993: 40–3.

Lacan, J. *Ecritis: A Selection* Trans. A. Sheridan. New York: W. W. Norton, 1977.

Lincoln, Y. S., and E. G. Guba. *Naturalistic inquiry.* Newbury Park: Sage, 1985.

Mackoff, B. *What Mona Lisa Knew: A Woman's Guide to Getting Ahead in Business by Lightening Up.* Los Angeles: Lowell House, 1990.

Maisel, E. "Staying Functional in the Future: 13 Self-help Trends." *Writer's Digest* 77 January 1997: 28–9.

Martin, E. "Flexible Bodies: Health and Work in an Age of Systems." *The Ecologist* 25 (1995): 221–26.

Matthews, V. "Clothes to Suit the Occasion." *Marketing Week 21* April 1995: 24.

Miller, P., and N. Rose. "Governing Economic Life." *Economy and Society* 19 (1990): 1–31.

Miller, P., and N. Rose. "Production, Identity and Democracy." *Theory and Society.* 24 (1995): 427–67.

Mindell, P. *A Woman's Guide to the Language of Success: Communicating With Confidence and Power.* Englewood Cliffs, NJ: Prentice Hall, 1995.

Molloy, S. *New Women's Dress for Success.* New York: Time Warner, 1996.

Mumby, D. K. "Organizing Men: Power, Discourse, and the Social Construction of Masculinity(s) in the Workplace." *Communication Theory* 8 (1998): 164–83.

Mumby, D. K., and L. L. Putnam. "The Politics of Emotion: A Feminist Reading of Bounded Emotionality." *Academy of Management Review* 17 (1992): 465–86.

Munk, N. "New Organization Man." *Fortune* 16 Mar. 1998: 63–74.

Nadesan, M. "The Popular Success Literature and 'A Brave New Darwinian Workplace.' " *Consumption Markets & Culture* 3 (1999): 27–60.

Nadesan, M. and Sotirin, P. "The Romance and Science of 'Breast is Best': Discursive Contradictions and Contexts of Breast-feeding Choices." *Text and Performance Quarterly* 3 (1998): 217–33.

Painton, P. "The Maternal Wall." *Time* 10 May 1993: 44–5.

"Pay Gap Widens Between Execs, Workers." *Minneapolis Tribune* 16 June 1996. A3.

Pollock, D. *Telling Bodies Performing Birth.* New York: Columbia UP, 1999.

Post, P. "Etiquette for Today." *Good Housekeeping* May 1997: 41–4.

Probyn, E. "Theorizing Through the Body." *Women Making Meaning: New Feminist Directions in Communication.* Ed. L. Rakow, New York: Routledge, 1992. 83–99.

Romero, M. "Chicanas Modernize Domestic Service." *Workplace/Women's Place.* Ed. D. Dunn. Los Angeles, CA: Roxbury, 1997. 358–68.

Rose, N. *Inventing Ourselves: Psychology, Power and Personhood.* Cambridge: U of Cambridge P, 1996.

Russo, A. "Pornography's Active Subordination of Women: Radical Feminist Re-claim Speech Rights" *Women Making Meaning: New Feminist Directions in Communication* L. Rakow, ed. New York: Routledge, 1992: 144–66.

Salmansohn, K. *How to Succeed in Business Without a Penis: Secrets and Strategies for the Working Woman.* New York: Random House, 1996.

Sheppard, D. I. "Organizations, Power, and Sexuality: The Image and Self-image of Women Managers." *The Sexuality of Organization.* Ed. J. Hearn et al. Newbury Park: Sage, 1989. 139–57.

Sheridan, A., trans. Translator's note. *Ecritis: A Selection.* New York: W. W. Norton, 1977.

Sherman, S. "A Brave New Darwinian Workplace." *Fortune* 25 Jan. 1993: 50–6.

Simonds, W. *Women and Self-help Culture: Reading Between the Lines.* New Brunswick: Rutgers UP, 1992.

Spellers, R. E. *Happy To Be Nappy!: Embracing an Afrocentric Aesthetic for Beauty.* Manuscript submitted for publication (1997).

Stock, P. "Help I Need Somebody." *Mademoiselle* July 1994: 70.

Swiss, D. J. *Women Breaking Through: Overcoming the Final 10 Obstacles at Work.* Princeton, NJ: Peterson's/ Pacesetter Books, 1996.

Tannen, D. *Talking From 9 to 5: Women and Men in the Workplace: Language, Sex and Power.* New York: Avon, 1994.

Tener, E. "Office Politics: Getting Along with Your New Coworkers." *Cosmopolitan* December 1991: 126–28.

Townley, B. *Reframing Human Resource Management.* London: Sage, 1994.

Townsel, L. J. "Working Women: Dressing for Success." *Ebony* September 1996: 60–6.

Trethewey, A. "Disciplined Bodies: Women's Embodied Identities at Work." *Organization Studies* (1999): 423–50.

Trethewey, A. *Professional bodies: The construction of professional women's identities in and through organizational discourses.* Paper presented at the meeting of the National Communication Association. Chicago, IL. November 1997.

Trethewey, A. "Resistance, Identity, and Empowerment: A Postmodern Feminist Analysis of Clients in a Human Service Organization." *Communication Monographs* (1997): 281–301.

Turner. B. S. *The Body and Society.* Oxford: Basil Blackwell, 1984.

Valdivieso, R. and C. Davis. "US Hispanics: Challenging Issues for the 1990s." *Crisis in American Institutions.* Eds, J. H. Skolnick and F. Currie. New York Harper Collins, 1991: 192–99.

Wadyka, S. "In the Eye of the Beholder." *Working Woman* 21 October 1991: 10–1.

Watts, P., ed. "Free Advice." *Executive Female* 13 January/February (1990): 41–4.

Young, I. *Throwing Like a Girl and Other Essays in Feminist Philosophy and Social Theory.* Bloomington, IN: Indiana UP, 1990.

Zachary, G. P. "Census Bureau Confirms Eroding Wages: Low Pay, Fewer Benefits Shadow Employment Gains." *The Wall Street Journal* 25 Jan. 1995: A2.

Zizek, S. *The sublime object ideology.* London: Verso, 1989.

Voicing Your Opinion
Performing the Enterprising Subject: Gendered Strategies for Success (?)
Majia Holmer Nadesan and Angela Trethewey

1. Respond to the authors' use of the *term feminine leakage.* How do *you* define this term? What does the term imply in relationship to the construction of gender? Is there a comparable masculine term? Why or why not?

   _____

   _____

   _____

   _____

   _____

2. Reflect on your own perceptions of the "successful career woman." Is she able to achieve power and success without adopting a masculine presentation? Would you consider "power and success" to be *masculine* goals? If so, what effect might this have on women attempting to achieve them?

   _____

   _____

   _____

   _____

   _____

3. The authors introduce Judith Butler's assertions regarding performative practices of gender. Think through the information in the article and then consider the following: How might alternative symbolic discourses impact the ways that you interpret and perform gender in the workplace? In what manner would these discourses be presented? What would they include? How might these discourses be introduced into organizational communication?

   _____

   _____

   _____

   _____

   _____

Terms

Visual culture
Black bodies
Ferine
Whiteness
Music videos

NAUGHTY GIRLS AND RED-BLOODED WOMEN Representations of Female ♂ ♀ Heterosexuality in Music Video

DIANE RAILTON AND PAUL WATSON

This article is about black and white women and the portrayal of sexuality in music videos. The authors argue that black women are seen as earthy, dangerous, uncontrolled, and ferine. White women are seen as hyperstylized, controlled, and reserved in their display of sexuality. The authors suggest that these heterosexual portrayals are to be read as racial prototypes that are maintained in music videos, both in words and in images.

Introduction

There is a moment during the video for Christina Aguilera's "Can't Hold Us Down" in which she appears alongside rapper Lil' Kim. The scene is notable for a number of reasons which foreground a range of issues concerning the representation of gender and race, and their relationship to sexual behaviour. Situated within a clearly codified black urban space, the women are depicted taunting a group of predominantly black men alongside, and on behalf of, a group of predominantly black women. Their behaviour is both assertive and overtly sexual, and the video links both of these to a narrative of collective female action. The lyrics of the song they perform deal explicitly with the gender politics of heterosexual behaviour. For instance, Aguilera comments on the "common double standard of society" whereby "the guy gets all the glory the more he can score/while the girl can do the same and yet you call her a whore," a sentiment immediately reinforced by Kim who questions the hypocrisy which sees men able to "give her some head or sex her raw/but if the girl do the same then she's a whore" (Christina Aguilera featuring Lil' Kim 2002). However, it is not simply that Aguilera and Kim articulate lyrics which can be read as overtly feminist that makes the scene interesting, nor even the obvious display of "sisterly" solidarity. Rather, the interest lies in the complex and contradictory ways in which raced identity is represented both lyrically and visually. For on the one hand the lyrics refer to a universal female experience (the consistent appeal to "all my girls around the world"), while on the other hand blackness and whiteness are clearly inscribed on and through the bodies of Aguilera and Kim. Indeed, it is the precise nature of that inscription, a process in which Aguilera simultaneously performs blackness and whiteness while Kim is seen to embody "essential blackness," that not only problematises any straightforward "message" of the video, but more generally serves to highlight the very limited range of ways in which female heterosexuality continues to be represented in popular culture and the way these representations are inevitably raced.[1]

One of the reasons that these articulations of race and sex appear complex and contradictory is because they are already double articulations, for Aguilera's appropriation of tropes of blackness set in juxtaposition to Kim's *embodiment* of those tropes draws attention to and reinforces her own whiteness. Moreover, the video itself invokes and gets its meaning from familiar patterns of representation of race characteristic of popular culture generally and the pop music video more specifically. And it is these patterns of raced representation that we want to address here. Indeed, it is our contention that the generic codes of pop music videos render them particularly fertile sites for the exploration of the interdependent construction of race, sex, and gender. For race is deployed within pop music videos to not only delimit or sanction sexual behaviour, but also sex and gender signify race in ways which tend to reproduce and shore up existing hierarchical power relations.

Selling (Hetero)sexuality

All music videos, but especially pop music videos, have an avowedly commercial agenda. Indeed, while it may be possible to discuss them as, say, an art form in their own right or precisely in terms of the politics of representation, they are first and foremost a *commercial* for an associated but distinct consumer product—usually a CD. While on the one hand this is an obvious claim, on the other hand it is nevertheless an important one. Firstly, the *prima facie* commercial imperatives of the form readily enable comparisons to be made between individual instances of that form for both viewers and scholars. In other words, pop music videos are not only produced in quantity and screened in quantity, but also new examples of the form are produced and released with remarkable frequency. Moreover, the proliferation of music television channels, especially those that promote the concept of consumer choice and interactivity through such devices as SMS and phone-in "voting," institute music videos as products between which comparisons can and should be made. This, taken together with the increasing branding of music TV around specific genres of popular music, establishes a context of viewing which, at least in part, is predicated on comparison and where patterns of representation are rendered visible and thus analysable.

Secondly, and relatedly, precisely the fact of their commercial function means pop music videos overwhelmingly tend to deal in the familiar, that is, in images that their audience are likely to find comfortable and unchallenging. Indeed, producing a pleasurable experience is integral to a video's success and the familiar is one of the key pleasures of pop. As Frith argues, "Pop songs are designed both to sound familiar and, often enough, to make one regret that times and people change" (Simon Frith 2002, p. 96). One implication of this is that the pop music video offers up a distillation of the ways in which contemporary culture perceives itself through cultural production. Moreover, perhaps more than anything else, pop music video is a particularly fruitful resource for examining representations of sexual behaviour. Indeed, the third main consequence of pop music video's commercial agenda is that the performance of sexual attractiveness and availability are imbricated in the generic codes of the form itself. Frith argues "Pop videos, in short, foreground performance-as-seduction and forestall performance-as-embarrassment. If nothing else . . . video is now a key component in our understanding of music as erotic" (Frith 1996, p. 225). Which is to say, the display of the sexualised body and the potential for that body to be figured as an object of desire or fantasy are crucial to the economies of both pleasure and profit of the pop music video.

While the centrality of the display of sexual attractiveness is generic, and, as such, not in itself raced or gendered, the specific ways in which sexual attractiveness is articulated in the pop music video is, however, mediated through and determined by common-sense notions of appropriate gendered and raced behaviour. Indeed, race often becomes activated as the (over)determining factor in the possible range of gendered sexual behaviour within video performances. Finally, despite the potentially problematic nature of some of the imagery, pop music video provides one of the, still very few, mainstream cultural spaces where there are a significant number of representations of black women. One of the effects of the proliferation of music channels has been to move away from the situation described by Kaplan where black women made up only 1% of the material broadcast by MTV (E. Ann Kaplan 1997, p. 414). Indeed, on some channels, such as MTV Base and Kiss for instance, black women feature, either in a leading or subsidiary role, in the majority of videos screened. This is not to say either that such videos are what hooks has described as "places of political sanctuary where we can escape, if only for a time, white domination" (bell hooks 1992, p. 15) or for that matter an "oppositional space where our sexuality can be named and represented, where we are sexual subjects—no longer bound and trapped." (hooks 1992, p. 77). However, while pop music videos are neither a sanctuary nor oppositional space, they are, nevertheless, a place where it is possible to *see* images of black women. This in itself is both important and interesting.

Seeing Blackness, Looking for Whiteness

Given both the sheer amount of work on raced identity, as well as the diversity of methodological approaches and epistemological standpoints characteristic of it, it is difficult, not to mention problematic, to posit any meaningful generalisations about such work. However, risking violence by reduction, it is possible and useful to map some key contours within this body of work in order to more precisely situate our own intervention. Generalisations notwithstanding, there are distinctions to be made between work which discusses the social and historical raced experiences of real people in real situations and analysis which seeks to explore the construction of raced identity through images and forms of language. While the former sees race as a key category through which societies organise populations and politics in ways which tend to privilege one "race" over another, the latter focuses on the ways in which such processes and patterns of oppression and exploitation are instituted, inscribed and normalised through representation. Although the latter approach, the study of representation, is, as Dyer points out, "more limited than the study of reality" it is, nevertheless "one of the prime means by which we have any knowledge of reality." For "how anything is represented is the means by which we think and feel about that thing, by which we apprehend it" (Richard Dyer 1997, p. xiii). Moreover, in the same way that oppressive political practices have very negative consequences for certain social groups, cultural representations "have real consequences for real people, not just in the way they are treated . . . but in terms of the way representations delimit and enable what people can be in any given society" (Dyer 1993, p. 3). For us, then, to study the ways in which people are represented within and by a culture is important both in understanding how discriminatory practices are legitimated and as a way of exposing those practices precisely as discriminatory.

The overwhelming majority of studies of representations of raced identity have tended to focus, understandably, on oppressed groups. More recently, however, a body of work has begun to emerge which addresses the representation of "white" as a specific raced identity in its own right, that is to say, every bit as constructed, provisional, and historically contingent as "black," and highlighting the role that our understanding of whiteness has in oppressive and racist practices. As Giroux suggests:

> Analyzing "whiteness" as a central element of racial politics becomes useful in exploring how "whiteness" as a cultural practice promotes race-based hierarchies, how white racial identity structures the struggle over cultural and political resources, and how rights and responsibilities are defined, confirmed, or contested across diverse racial claims, (Henry A. Giroux 1997, p. 295)

These "race-based hierarchies" of power and experience are maintained, at least in part, by the invisibility, that is the non-coloured status, of white as a raced category. In other words, whereas blackness has always been constructed as a raced identity, with specific and identifiable components, whiteness has until recently been perceived as a non-raced category. This has implications, not only in relation to the real world experiences of both black and white people, but also for the ways in which we attempt to study raced representations. Indeed, as Dyer points out, it is often difficult to "see" whiteness, and thus to analyse whiteness *qua* whiteness (see Dyer 1993, 1997). For it is only when whiteness is juxtaposed to blackness that it becomes visible and apprehendable. This is unsurprising insofar as there is a long history of "black" and "white" being constructed as different races and set in contradistinction to each other through forms of representation (see Sander L. Gilman 1992; Anne McClintock 1995; Vron Ware 1992). And it is precisely this structured, hierarchical difference, the way in which black people and white people are figured as different to each other through and in representation, which secures white privilege. Moreover, one of the key sites across which difference and distinction have been inscribed and played out is on the bodies of women, and more particularly in the ways in which those bodies have been *produced* as sexed and sexualised.

It is perhaps now obvious to say that gendered identities are often constructed through tropes of heterosexuality and (hetero)sexual attractiveness, tropes which are themselves culturally and historically contingent. Less obvious, however, is the ways these tropes are mobilised differently in relation to black and white women, for black heterosexual womanhood has been historically constructed very differently to its white counterpart. For example, McClintock suggests that there is a long tradition in European culture of equating Africa, and Africans, with the sexual that dates back at least to the second century A.D. Moreover, "by the nineteenth century, popular lore had firmly established Africa as the quintessential zone of sexual aberration and anomaly." More importantly, she argues that "women figured as the epitome of sexual aberration and excess. Folklore saw them, even more than the men, as given to a lascivious venery so promiscuous as to border on the bestial" (McClintock 1995, p. 22). Similarly, in his study of the iconography of female sexuality in nineteenth-century art, literature, and medicine, Gilman argues that black female bodies were figured as "more primitive, and therefore more sexually intensive" than those of white women and, more specifically, black women's primary and secondary sexual characteristics, the genitalia and buttocks, were seen as primitive, as "animal-like," a physical sign of an uncontrolled and, indeed uncontrollable, animalistic sexuality (Gilman 1992, pp. 176–180). As such, observable physical traits, or more precisely physical differences, were mobilised to construct black women not only as different but rather as antithetical to "European sexual mores and beauty" (Gilman 1985, p. 83).

It was the buttocks of black women that often provided a focal point in the display of black physical difference insofar as they came to "function as the semantic signs of "primitive" sexual appetite and activity," their "exaggerated" size signalling other exaggerations of behaviour and temperament (Gilman 1985, p. 90). In short, Victorian discourses of evolution, of medicine, of colonisation and exploration, and of the nature of sexual desire combined and focused on the materiality of the buttocks of black women in a way that rendered those women sexual, dangerous, and Other. Black women's bodies were made available to be looked at, exhibited in their nakedness at a time when white women's bodies were corseted, covered, and hidden, in mapping *availability* on to black women's bodies and *unavailability* on to the bodies of white women, it was black women that were presented as fascinating curiosities for the entertainment of a white audience.

While nineteenth-century discourses were constructing black women as animalistically hypersexed bodies, accessible for scrutiny and pleasure, those same discourses were simultaneously constructing white women[2] as, on the one hand, civilised and restrained, and on the other hand as fragile bodies in need of protection from the sexual. Indeed, Weitz argues that the notion of white women's bodies as fragile went hand-in-hand with an emphasis on the importance of romantic love for women, thus regulating and delimiting (white) female sexual desire and behaviour (Rose Weitz 2003, p. 6). Crucial here, of course, is the production of white women as asexual, as precisely above and beyond the base needs and desires of the "primitive" body. Indeed, as Dyer suggests, "the model for white women is the Virgin Mary, a pure vessel for reproduction who is unsullied by the dark drives that reproduction entails," a notion that, when stretched to its extreme, implies that even thinking about white women and sexual activity becomes "scandalous and virtually sacrilegious" (Dyer 1997, p. 29). White women were, therefore, positioned as responsible for the restriction of sexual behaviour, the control of male sexual drives and impulses. White women's bodies not only function symbolically as the unattainable but also, in practice, were only ever attainable through the protocols of courtship, romantic love, and marriage. In other words, access to the purity of the white, female body was something that could be achieved if, and only if, the institutionalised barriers that protect it were successfully overcome. The achievement of the pure, white, female body not only renders it the property of the deserving (white) man but also locates that purity at the centre of racialised power hierarchies. Indeed, the white female was placed at the centre of a number of key nineteenth-century discourses of power. Just as the purity of white women undergirded the institution of marriage, it was also integral to narratives of empire and imperialism insofar as the white woman was located as "the locus of true whiteness" while the white man struggled in dark continents, "yearning for home and whiteness, facing the dangers and allures of darkness." As such "male imperialism is presented as done for white women as . . . the literal and socialising reproducers of the race" (Dyer 1997, p. 36).

However, it was not only white men who faced the "dangers of darkness." White women, throughout the nineteenth century, were a significant presence in colonised lands. Their role as the guardians of sexual morals and cultural refinement, sustained by the presumed asexuality of their bodies and their embodiment of virtue, positioned them not only as the civilised but also the civilisers, that is to say, the principal agents through which the process of "civilising primitive peoples" was enacted. At least in part, this "civilising of primitive peoples" took part through the introduction of Victorian domesticity into colonised lands. As McClintock argues, "In the colonies . . . the mission station became a threshold institution for transforming domesticity rooted in European gender and class roles into domesticity as controlling a colonised people" (McClintock 1995, p. 35). Indeed, the rituals of domesticity were defined around the presence of the bodies of white women as the wives, daughters, sisters and so on of white men. And it is precisely such rituals of European domesticity through which the colonies were to be cleansed of "savagery," "ignorance," and "primitive" ways. Such cleansing was not only a metaphor for the process of colonisation generally, but the colonies, by reverse implication, were symbolically located, themselves, as sites of dirt, filth, and contamination that were in need of cleaning. Cleanliness and imperialism thus became mutually reinforcing discourses, an idea illustrated in much advertising of soap and other cleaning products of the time. For instance, one advertisement for Sunlight Soap depicts two white Victorian ladies, immaculately dressed in elegant gowns, standing on either side of a pitcher and bowl, washing dishes in a spotlessly clean kitchen. The skin of their neck and shoulders is surpassed in its whiteness only by the brilliance of their dresses. Indeed, the leg-of-mutton sleeves and full skirts of those dresses irradiate the scene with a whiteness which is reflected in the sheen of the polished floor, the lustre of the porcelain crockery, and the mirror of the water. This one incongruous image of Victorian domesticity, to a large extent, exemplifies what McClintock calls the "four beloved fetishes" of civilization—soap, the mirror, light, and white clothing (McClintock 1995, p. 32). The main point here, however, is that the "cleanliness" of whiteness was set in opposition to the putative "dirtiness" of blackness and that this binarism was predicated upon, and sustained by, the juxtaposition of black and white female bodies.

Of course, this process of physically and symbolically deploying the white woman as the domesticator and civiliser was not without risk; placing the pure, white, female body in such unknown and hazardous contexts redoubles its fragility. For empire was not only acquired by white men for white women, but the putative frangibility of the white female body underpinned imperial practices and policies. The sanctity of the body was always vulnerable and in need of protection, for any violation of it was also an attack on civilisation itself. As Vron Ware suggests:

> One of the recurring themes in the history of colonial repression is the way in which the threat of real or imagined violence towards white women became a symbol of the most dangerous form of insubordination . . . Protecting the virtue of white women was the pretext for instituting draconian measures against indigenous populations in several parts of the Empire . . . White women provided a symbol of the most valuable property known to white man and it was to be protected from the ever-encroaching and disrespectful black man at all costs. (Ware 1992, p. 38)

As such, the defence of white women's bodies was intimately bound up not only with the establishment and protection of civilisation itself, but also the control and repression of black people.

These imperial discourses are only one branch of a long tradition of cultural representation which produces white and black womanhood as very different. Much of this difference turns upon a series of binary oppositions, oppositions which both disguise the complexities of lived experience and structure thinking in ways which tend to mask and shore up hierarchies of power. Simply stated, within this tradition of representation, white women are defined by asexuality in direct contrast to the presumed hypersexuality of black women. On the one hand, black women's "hypersexuality" is seen to derive from a series of apparently natural traits that link them to the animal, the primitive and the "dirty." In defining the black woman first and foremost through a series of physical characteristics, her body is not only made available to both white and black men but the buttocks of that body are figured as emblematic of black womanhood generally and the icon of black female sexuality more precisely. White women's asexuality, on the other hand, is seen precisely as a product of civilisation, a process by which the natural is regulated, ordered and thus mastered. This process produces white womanhood itself around a policed and policing body, a body which is typified by qualities of restraint, virtue, and cleanliness. If black female sexuality is literally embodied in voluptuous black buttocks, then, by contrast, white female sexuality is, strictly speaking, not embodied in frangible corporeality but is rather displaced, and ideally replaced, by a fascination with the purity of "clean white bodies and clean white clothing" (McClintock 1995, p. 211).

None of this is to suggest that these patterns of raced representation began in the nineteenth century, nor that they have simply re-emerged with the inception of the music video. On the contrary, it is possible to trace the genealogy of these definitions of blackness and whiteness from the Victorian era to the present day through various forms of popular culture. For example, both lyrically and in terms of performance, the collocation of black female sexuality, the animal, and the feral has been a continuing, albeit not always dominant, feature of black music during the twentieth century (not only the music produced by black men but also the music produced by black women artists as well). Such a continuation can be mapped through analysis of artists such as Josephine Baker, Eartha Kitt, Tina Turner, Grace Jones, Mel B (Scary Spice), who make explicit use of animals/animal skins in the presentation of themselves as sexual women, and finds its contemporary expression in performers such as Ashanti, Mary J. Blige, Monica, Destiny's Child, and perhaps most strikingly, as we discuss below, the recent solo work of Beyoncé Knowles. By the same token, the representation of white female sexuality as controlled, "civilised," and/or fragile, although often more difficult to see, is there in the appearance of vulnerability found in artists from the 1960s such as Twinkle and Marianne Faithful and the "untouchability" of the glamorous and sophisticated women singers of the 1940s and 1950s such as Peggy Lee or Jo Stafford,[3] and finds its own contemporary manifestation in artists such as Rachel Stevens, Sophie Ellis-Bexter, Victoria Beckham, and, most notably, Kylie Minogue.

The main point here, however, is that many of the iconographical markings of whiteness and blackness which characterised nineteenth-century scientific, artistic, and commercial modes of representation, and which have been replayed in every generation of the twentieth century, continue, albeit in modified form, to structure much contemporary cultural production. Indeed, given the number of social and political changes that have impacted on women's lived experiences since the Victorian era, there is a surprising, and potentially worrying, continuity in the way in which women's raced identity is represented. We now want to discuss some of the ways in which these patterns of raced representation are reproduced in contemporary pop music videos. More specifically we will discuss videos by two key contemporary pop stars, Beyoncé Knowles and Kylie Minogue. The positions they occupy at opposite ends of the spectrum of raced representation means that their work can be used to construct "ideal types" which then permit a series of further analytical comparisons to be mapped. For not only do they illustrate the similarities which serve to codify representations of black and white as internally cohesive categories, but also to compare them makes visible the different ways in which blackness and whiteness are constructed.

The Ferine and the Figurine

bell hooks suggests that popular music is one of the primary cultural locations for representations of black female sexuality. She argues that, "although contemporary thinking about black female bodies does not attempt to read the body as a sign of 'natural' racial inferiority, the fascination with black 'butts' continues . . . the protruding butt is seen as an indication of a heightened sexuality" (hooks 1992, p. 63). However, while the "protruding black butt" undoubtedly remains an important lyrical and visual feature of music videos a number of other tropes also link these contemporary representations of blackness back to Victorian modes of raced representation. Indeed, through regular and explicit references to the natural and the animal, the black female body and black sexuality continue to be figured as primal, wild, and uncontrollable. To some extent these images appeal to a culture which is, as hooks suggests, one which "is eager to reinscribe the image of black woman as sexual primitive" (hooks 1992, p. 73).

The video for Knowles' "Baby Boy" can be seen as an exemplar of this mode of representing black female sexuality (Beyoncé Knowles & Sean Paul 2004). There are a number of interrelated aspects to this. Most obviously, the locations used in the video either imply "nature" or they are set directly in nature. For the most part, the video is shot out of doors *in* nature; the jungle, the beach, and the ocean. Where the action takes place indoors there is always the threat that the outside will encroach; boundaries between indoor and outdoor are blurred by the use of "natural" materials in the architecture (wood, leather, fur), and precisely the use of louvered walls to demarcate inside from outside. In fact, so flimsy is this physical demarcation that the elements regularly find their way inside, not only the wind, which blows the hair of the dancers, but also, in one remarkable shot, the ocean floods the dancefloor and washes over the feet of the women who are dancing. Moreover, the action in the video takes place either at twilight or, predominantly, at night. The action is lit in such a way that the body of Knowles, and the other performers, is often partially obfuscated by the darkness rendering any distinction between the body and its environment uncertain. Indeed, darkness often floods the frame entirely acting as a moment of transition between different (parts of) bodies and locations.

However, although the "naturalness" of the locations is important in itself, it is the way that locations act to define the body, interact with the body, and situate the performing body that is interesting here. Indeed, Knowles' feet sink into the sand, her skin sweats from the heat, her hair is blown by the wind and soaked by the water, and, at one point, her whole body is seen half-submerged in the ocean. This interaction between the body and the environment not only functions to equate the black woman with/as nature but also works to establish the possibilities of and limits to performance. The untamed landscape is matched by the "untamed" and "uncontrolled" body of Knowles. Most notably, this uncontrollability is focused around her buttocks and her hair. Whether turned towards the camera, repeatedly and rapidly shaken during dance routines, or simply protruding from beneath her clothes, the former are constantly moving and on display. Her hair, too, is in constant motion. Whether straightened or curly, loose or tied, wet or dry, whether her body is moving or not, her hair moves or is moved: it swings as she walks, it is shaken as she dances, it is blown by the wind and fans, and it is brushed across, or away from, her face and mouth. Indeed, as hooks argues, the cascading hair of black female singers is designated as a key marker of their sexualised personae and, in fact, along with the buttocks, signifies "animalistic sexuality" (hooks 1992, p. 70).

Moreover, the many outfits that Knowles wears in the video reveal her flesh, or more precisely the very *fleshiness* of her flesh. For example, she wears a number of different skirts that are short, sit low on the hips, and are split from top to bottom on both sides. As she moves the skirts move to reveal the buttocks and emphasise the voluptuousness of her thighs. By the same token, the array of tops that she wears always allows access to both the movement of her breasts and to the flesh of the stomach and her navel. As such, it is not just Knowles' body that writhes, ripples, shakes, and bounces, but her flesh too. The costumes are designed so that we always have access to the fleshiness of the naked black body; an unruly body, that like the hair, is in constant, involuntary motion.

The final scene of the video, in which Knowles performs a dance routine on the beach at night, is a heady distillation of the ways in which the conventions of the music video continue to represent black female sexuality as feral and animalistic. This scene is especially interesting inasmuch as the performance is not motivated by the demand to add an image track to the published music track (the standard conception of the music video). In other words, the music which accompanies this sequence is, in fact, a coda, operating in excess of the audio track as it is released on CD, its presence merely licensing the availability of Knowles to the desires of the spectator. As such, in uncoupling the performance in the video from the performance on the audio track, the video, but this self-contained scene in particular, can be seen as a site where the conventions of representing black female sexuality *visually,* through the display of Knowles' body, is privileged.

Wearing only a bikini, and lit by flaming torches, fire being the only element that hitherto has not explicitly been visually depicted in the video, she is shown crawling, catlike, through the sand, and, later, rolling and writhing, orgasmically, in it. She is sweating and dirty with the sand that sticks to her, further breaching the boundary between her body and nature itself. Moreover, her dance movements become increasingly frenetic and frenzied as the sequence progresses, her out-of-controlledness climaxing when she grabs a handful of sand and flings it towards the spectator. What this sequence, along with the rest of the video, does is to reinscribe black female sexuality as first and foremost hypersexuality, primitive, feral, uncontrolled and uncontrollable. Moreover, its very uncontrollability reinscribes the black female body as available, literally to the look of the spectator and symbolically to the desires and fantasies of both black and white men.

While crude, the contrast between the video for Knowles' "Baby Boy" and the video for Minogue's "Can't Get You Out of My Head" is nevertheless instructive.[4] For if the former produces black female (hyper)sexuality as wild, savage, and animalistic, then the latter is no less proficient in producing white female (a)sexuality as pure, restrained, and controlled. Indeed, if on the one hand both women perform seduction and sexual attractiveness, on the other hand the nature of that performance is very different *vis à vis* their putative sexual availability: Knowles represents a universal availability, while Minogue's availability is always provisional, restricted, and contingent. In the end, the conception of white female sexuality inscribed in and through Minogue's body differs little from the one which emerged out of Victorian and colonial discourses.

The video opens with Kylie Minogue (2001), sitting at the wheel of a car, driving into a futuristic metropolis typified by both the clinical environment of the city and the clean lines of its skyline. Indeed, both the evident architectonic space and the sheer brilliance of the image itself characteristic of this opening sequence typify the form and content of the video generally. Not only is the video episodic, that is structured around self-contained, discrete segments, but the architectonic itself frames, informs, and limits the potentialities of Minogue's performance of white female sexuality. Most obviously, all of the locations featured in the video are architectural in the sense that they are artificial, manufactured, built environments. In other words, even when the location is rendered abstract or uncertain, it is nevertheless always and unambiguously not a *natural* environment. In fact, with the exception of human bodies—which, as we argue below, is not really an exception at all—no organic matter features in the video and, indeed, has no place in the world it constructs.

Moreover, the way that the action, the performers, and the environment are lit emphasises the clinical artificiality of both the body and the space that frames the body. Put simply, the luminescence of the image never allows shadow, tone, and certainly not darkness, to intrude into the frame. Even in the final scene, apparently set at night on a rooftop, the action is bathed in light with Minogue, herself, seeming to both emit and reflect that light. Indeed, during this scene, and throughout the video, light itself is turned into a prominent aesthetic presence as the lights in the skyscrapers "dance" in time to Minogue and stylised flares, either from the sun or some other undefined light source, regularly hit the camera, blinding the spectator. One effect of this type of lighting, of course, is that the boundaries between the white body, other bodies, and the space that they inhabit are always dearly defined, and more often than not, clearly visible.

The body in the video, and especially Minogue's body, is not only sculpted and flattened by light, but its movement is mechanised and controlled, and it is hyperstylised by its clothing and costume. For example, while on the one hand dance routines are strictly and complexly choreographed, performance itself, on the other hand, is often reduced to minimalistic, simple body movements. In one instance the dancers remain static, individually posed within an overall tableau, but for the repeated flexing of the fingers. Here, dance is reduced to the mechanised movements of the robotic body. Indeed, the controlled body, and the control of the body, defines both the choreography and the performance. Even when bodies are complexly intertwined they do not touch, connecting only through the relation of one body to the next within the totality of the overall design. Moreover, the choreography individuates the bodies of the dancers insofar as each performs a different range of movements at different times yet, at the same time, it also subordinates those bodies to the demands of the overall routine in the first instance, and, more importantly, to Minogue's performance in the final instance. For Minogue's body is the one which is privileged, always distinct and distinguished, aestheticised and exhibited for the appreciation of the spectator. She is differentiated within the totality of the choreography, positioned figuratively, and often literally, apart from the other dancers. By the same token, her movements, while limited and restricted, are not only foregrounded by the choreography but also by the salient techniques of the production process itself. Most obviously, she is the principal preoccupation of the camera: she features in almost every shot, often in close-up, and the video is structured around the demands of displaying her body. More interestingly, however, the frequent and regular use of slow motion and super-slow motion both reinforces her distinction by exempting her from the constraints of "normal" time and serves to further regulate and control the movements of her body and hair precisely by slowing down her image. Indeed, while her hair is controlled by a number of physical devices and materials—it is variously tied, sprayed, fixed or entirely covered—at moments where unruly movement is threatened, especially during dance routines, the use of slow-motion photography arrests, contains, and restrains this threat. In short, the fixity of her hair mirrors the stasis of her body, an idea most evident in the significant number of shots which feature Minogue's body, fixed, posed, and presented, not moving at all.

Moreover, in moments when Minogue's body does move it is notable that her flesh does not. This is both made apparent and made possible, in part, by the design of her costumes. On the one hand, her outfits variously constrain the flesh, cover the flesh, or reveal evidence of the armature beneath the flesh. For instance, the final outfit she is seen wearing reveals the shoulders and the knees but covers and obscures the breasts, the stomach and the hips. In other words, it directs attention towards precisely those areas of the body that are not fleshy and away from those that are. In an earlier scene the body is almost entirely covered and hidden by a white, loose-fitting tracksuit. In fact, the only bits that are revealed are the sternum, the neck, and occasionally the armpits. Indeed, these outfits display, strictly speaking, not the exterior body, the flesh of the body, but rather its interior, the architecture of the body. On the other hand, however, where the flesh is revealed, what is revealed is precisely its lack of movement, the clean lines and firm edges of its sculpture. In perhaps the most striking scene of the video, Minogue is seen wearing a brilliantly white, hooded full-length dress split from ankle to waist on both sides and with a deep cowl neck line which plunges to below the navel. The design of the dress both conceals and reveals Minogue's body and as she moves the fabric falls open to expose that the flesh of her breasts, stomach, and thighs remains firm, taut and static: the sight of her flesh set against the fluidity of the dress merely confirms the flesh's rigidity.

Indeed, more generally, this sequence presents a potent image of white female sexuality as controlled, restrained, and unavailable. The most striking aspect of this scene is precisely its thoroughgoing whiteness. Not only is Minogue dressed in white, exposing porcelain-white flesh, and performing in a totally white environment, but she is further whitened by the cleansing glare of the light. The only colour in the scene, the red of the dancers' outfits and, most notably, Minogue's lips, serves only to throw into stark relief the non-colour of everything else. The purity of the frame and the sanctity of Minogue's body are never allowed to be sullied, disturbed, or threatened by the disruption and disorder of the natural. The dancers, for instance, are dehumanised; the few movements they make are roboticised and functional, and their faces are obscured by dark, perspex visors, altering the contour of their heads and restricting their gaze. They cannot look at or touch Minogue's body, and, moreover, are rarely even in the same frame, further setting the uniqueness of Minogue apart from the uniformity of the dancers. And, of course, uniqueness is a key marker of provenance and providence: things which are unique are both valuable and vulnerable, difficult to come by in the first place and, once acquired, in need of protection and preservation.

The uniqueness of Minogue is established not only by her differentiation from the mechanised choreography of the dancers but also through the denaturalisation of her own body. More specifically, if the humanity of the dancers is reduced to the machine, then the representation of Minogue's body implies that it has transcended the human, the organic. In other words, the flawlessness of her white skin, the stillness of her hair, and the way the flesh of her body seems to resist the pull of gravity situates Minogue somewhere beyond the human and outside of the natural. Here, then, the slippage from whiteness signalling purity, cleanliness, and frangibility to whiteness as defining an "ideal" and idealised female sexuality coalesces around the figurine image of Minogue's pale skin. Ironically, the very (hyper)visibility of the body which renders it available to the look simultaneously protects if from the contaminating touch, thus securing its physical unattainability.

Conclusion

What the video for "Can't Get You Out Of My Head" presents us with, then, is an image of female sexuality which stands in stark contrast to the one produced by Knowles' "Baby Boy," While both produce images of the sexually attractive, seductive, heterosexual woman, these representations of sexuality and seduction are very different, and, in the end, are constituted through and overdetermined by the limits of the raced imaginary. While on the one hand black female sexuality continues to be constructed as hypersexuality, as animalistic, primitive, and instinctive, on the other hand white female sexuality is defined principally in terms of its asexuality, that is to say, in terms of the rejection/colonisation of instinctive behaviour through/by culture and civilisation. The ferine sexuality of the black woman renders her always and already sexually available while, by contrast, the providence of the white female body secures both the white woman's unattainability and, by extension, her desirability. If the former is depicted as an essentially natural sexuality, rooted precisely in the filth, dirt, and mess of the natural world then the latter emerges as a denaturalised sexuality, abstracted from the world, purified, cleansed of its messiness. By the same token, one implication of the "naturalness" of black sexuality is that it is inevitably embodied, anchored to, and enacted through the flesh of the body itself. The denaturalisation of white sexuality, by distinction, means that it is relatively disconnected from the corporeality of the body, residing instead in the image/vision of the body, indeed the presentation and representation of it. One of the more interesting consequences of uncoupling white female sexuality from corporeality and relocating it in the *presentation* of the body is that, unlike black sexuality, it becomes, in the final instance, mutable. Which is to say, while black female sexuality is always embodied and fixed in the flesh—precisely in the fleshiest parts of the body—white sexuality, in displacing the organics of the body, is open to redefinition. Indeed, the representation of black female sexuality implies and invokes an essential sexuality that is already in and of the world while the presentation of white female sexuality always offers the potential for reinvention. Besides, even where reinvention does not take place in any one instance, such a transformative possibility, a possibility denied to black woman, nevertheless remains. And, of course, this capacity to define and redefine privileges white in the imaginary and, moreover, this symbolic privilege is one of the key ways in which power is negotiated, performed, and ultimately secured.

To end, we want to return to the issue we began with: the *fact* of the blackness of Lil' Kim set against Christina Aguilera's *performance* of blackness. For one way to explain the complexity of that scene—a scene in which racial difference is apparently erased yet which is simultaneously predicated upon a sophisticated knowledge of the codes of racial differentiation—is to address the differing positions within, and possibilities in relation to (re)presentation that Aguilera and Kim occupy. For while Kim literally embodies black hypersexuality, her sexuality produced and defined by the site/sight of her black body, Aguilera is able to produce her sexuality through the selective and playful presentation of tropes of raced identity. Put simply, while Kim can only ever be seen as a black woman, Aguilera is allowed a far more fluid and creative engagement with both raced and sexual identity. Indeed, in presenting an image of female sexuality predicated on representations of raced identity, Aguilera's whiteness and privilege is reinscribed precisely by the possibility of such a performance in the first place, even if, in the end, that performance is only a pale imitation of Kim.

ENDNOTES

1. It is worth stressing at this point that this article is about the ways in which women are variously figured in and through forms of visual culture. As such, while on the one hand we do not wish to ignore the complexities of cultural identity and identification (Aguilera, for example, is of Irish and Ecuadorian descent and now publicly identifies herself as Latina), on the other hand what we discuss here are the *cultural tropes* of raced identity (the ways in which distinct categories of white and black structure ways of being human and ways of being a woman) that are constructed and contrasted through forms of representation.

2. The white women we discuss here, of course, are middle-class women. Indeed, representations of white working-class women differ significantly from those of middle-class women. For discussion of representations of working-class white women, see McClintock (1995) and Weitz (2003).

3. Think, for example, of the "untouchability" of singer Julie London in the 1956 film *The Girl Can't Help It* where she appears only as a vision haunting the male lead.

4. The comparison between the visual representation of the singers is particularly revealing given that the sentiments of the songs are practically identical. The lyrics of both deal with sexual obsession and fantasy, Minogue's "I Can't Get You Out of My Head/Boy Your Loving is All I Think About" matched by Knowles' "I Think About You All the Time/See You in My Dreams."

REFERENCES

Aguilera, Christina featuring Lil' Kim (videorecording) (2002) 'Can't Hold Us Down', RCA.

Dyer, Richard (1993) *The Matter of Images: Essays on Representations,* Routledge, London.

Dyer, Richard (1997) *White,* Routledge, London.

Frith, Simon (1996) *Performing Rites: Evaluating Popular Music,* Oxford University Press, Oxford.

Frith, Simon (2002) 'Pop Music', in *The Cambridge Companion to Pop and Rock,* eds Simon Frith, Will Straw & John Street, Cambridge University Press, Cambridge, pp. 93–108.

Gilman, Sander L. (1935) *Difference and Pathology: Stereotypes of Sexuality, Race And Madness,* Cornell University Press, Ithaca.

Gilman, Sander L. (1992) 'Black Bodies, White Bodies: toward an iconography of female sexuality in late 19th century art, medicine and literature', in *Race, Culture & Difference,* eds James Donald & Ali Rattansi, Sage/The Open University, London, pp. 171–197.

Giroux, Henry A. (1997) 'Racial politics and the pedagogy of whiteness', in *Whiteness: A Critical Reader,* ed. Mike Hill, New York University Press, New York, pp. 294–315.

hooks, bell (1992) *Black Looks: Race and Representation,* South End Press, Boston.

Kaplan, E. Ann (1997) 'Whose imaginary: the televisual apparatus, the female body, and textual strategies in select rock videos on MTV', in *Feminisms,* eds Sandra Kemp & Judith Squires, Oxford University Press, Oxford, pp. 410–422.

Knowles, Beyoncé & Paul, Sean (videorecording) (2003) 'Baby Boy', Columbia Records.

McClintock, Anne (1995) *Imperial Leather: Race, Gender and Sexuality in the Colonial Contest,* Routledge, New York.

Minogue, Kylie (videorecording) (2001) 'Can't Get You Out Of My Head', Capitol.

Ware, Vron (1992) *Beyond the Pale: White Women, Racism And History,* Verso, London.

Weitz, Rose (2003) 'A history of women's bodies', in *The Politics of Women's Bodies: Sexuality, Appearance and Behaviour,* ed. Rose Weitz, 2nd edn, Oxford University Press, Oxford, pp. 3–11.

Voicing Your Opinion
Naughty Girls and Red-Blooded Women: Representations of Female Heterosexuality in Music Video
Diane Railton and Paul Watson

1. Respond to the article's description of the ways that music videos present the black female body as (hyper)sexual and wild and the white female body as (a)sexual and pure. Are there videos that you have seen that support this critique?

   _____

   _____

   _____

   _____

   _____

2. In what ways do music videos influence our understanding of gender, race, class, and sexuality?

   _____

   _____

   _____

   _____

   _____

3. What influence does the genre of music have on the representation of gender in music videos? Are there similar or different patterns of representation that you can identify in pop, rock, rap, country, etc.?

   _____

   _____

   _____

   _____

   _____

Terms

Passing

Marginal
media and
dominant
media

Racial passing

Sex/gender
passing

IN/DISCERNIBLE BODIES
The Politics of Passing in Dominant and Marginal Media

CATHERINE R. SQUIRES AND DANIEL C. BROUWER

This article is about the issue of *passing* with regard to race and sex/gender. It looks at the differences between dominant media and marginal media discussions of these cases. The first case of Phipps is about racial passing and the second two cases are about sex/gender passing. The authors examine the ways that media framing of information influences public perceptions of these cases.

This essay explores news media coverage of two types of alleged "passing": passing across racial lines from Black to White and across sex lines from female to male. Textual analysis of dominant print media and print media discourses produced by and/or addressed to Blacks and queers reveals prominent frames through which news consumers are invited to perceive these events. In particular, the analysis demonstrates that both dominant and marginal social groups express the desire to fix the identities of passers in a single, discrete category, although these groups wish to do so for disparate reasons. In addition, marginal groups frame passing events within broad cultural and historical contexts in contrast to the narrow contexts framed by dominant media. Comparison of race and sex passing exposes the similarities—including community consternation about the passer—and differences—including disparate focus on civil rights rather than identity issues—between Black and queer coverage of these events. Comparison of race and sex passing also exposes the way in which dominant media correlate race passing with class passing, while sex passing is correlated to sexuality passing (that is, queer passing for heterosexual).

Passing, according to Amy Robinson (1994), can be described as the interplay between three actors or groups: the passer, who (usually) performs a privileged identity; the in-group clairvoyant, a member of the passer's non-privileged group who can see through the pass; and the "dupe," a member of the privileged group who believes the pass. In this essay, we examine two distinct types of "passing," across racial lines from Black to White and across sex lines from female to male. In the three cases that we examine, Susie Guillory Phipps, Sean O'Neill (née Sharon Clark), and Brandon Teena (née Teena Brandon) are accused of passing. That is, they are charged with performing a privileged identity (White or male) in order to mask non-privileged identities (Black or queer).[1] The subjects insist, however, that the identity they have performed is genuine. In these cases, Susie Phipps, Brandon Teena, and Sean O'Neill function as "passers." That is, in the social imaginary Susie Phipps *really is* a Black woman trying to be perceived as a White woman, and Brandon Teena and Sean O'Neill *really are* women trying to be perceived as men.[2] We construe the category of "dupes" rather broadly to refer not only to the physical and emotional intimates of Susie, Brandon, and Sean, but also to their friends and acquaintances. A second type of dupe emerges in press accounts of these cases, however—the general population consisting of readers who may imagine themselves as actual or potential victims of a pass. The category of in-group clairvoyant would include members of non-privileged groups who hold the ability to see through the pass to the "true" identity of the passer.

Upon discovery of a pass, we find that all actors have much at stake. On the one hand, these "scandals" threaten a backlash by the state and dominant populations against identity groups with whom they have complicated legal, political, and social histories. On the other hand, Blacks and queers are confronted with the seeming necessity of identity maintenance that is critical to both a politics of difference and a politics of justice. The conflict between personal identity, state entities (such as law enforcement and courts of law), and social expectations is dramatized in news coverage of these events.

The focal point of our analysis is a comparison between dominant print media discourses and the print media discourses produced by and/or addressed to Blacks and queers. We use the terms "dominant media" or "dominant discourse" to indicate the relative position of power that those media and discourses occupy. We recognize that some scholars prefer the term "mainstream media," and some prefer the term "White media"; however, we think that "dominant media" more precisely exposes the power of mainstream media to shape mainstream tastes and values. Further, we prefer "dominant" to "White" because not all consumers of this media are White. Concerning our choice of representative texts for marginal media, we recognize that in-group discourse may seem to be best represented by the writings of interracial and transgendered people rather than by the writings from the Black and queer presses. However, we examine texts from the Black and queer presses because the liminal groups to which these passers might belong did not have the same kind of media resources and exposure at the time of the cases. Indeed, the interracial movement gained speed and media vehicles only after Phipps's case had wound its way through the court system, and Brandon Teena's case was a catalyst for transgender organizing and publicity (Hale, 1998, pp. 313–314). In the cases of Brandon Teena and Sean O'Neill, cases involving the purported passing of women for men, it may seem most appropriate to study the prolific print media artifacts of women's and feminist presses. However, we did not examine women's publications because we were unable to find any that covered the sex passers in the databases we researched—although ironically *Ms.* did cover the Phipps case.

Generally, we ask: What frames did dominant and marginal media use to characterize these discoveries of passing? More specifically, we ask: What criteria did different constituencies advocate for the proper identification of "Black," "White," "Woman," and "Man"? Finally, what did these frames and criteria tell us about gender, sex, and media as practiced and theorized in the late 20th century in the United States? In order to answer these questions, we performed textual analysis on non-duplicated, newspaper and magazine articles that we discovered through multiple keyword searches on the *LEXIS/NEXIS, Ethnic Newswatch, Genderwatch,* and *Reader's Guide* databases. Notably, we have excluded from our data set discussion and debate generated by the successful Hollywood film, "Boys Don't Cry," which mixes fact and some fiction in its portrayal of the life, love, and death of Brandon Teena. We exclude these articles because of the film's occasional bouts of artistic license and because the mostly positive responses to its very sympathetic portrayal of Brandon Teena in the entertainment press would have greatly skewed our sample. Furthermore, we are interested in the initial response to the discovery of Brandon's female phenotype and the violence perpetrated, not the interweaving of the careers and lives of the stars of the movie and their reaction to the story. Additionally, we employ the concept of framing in order to excavate and characterize the discussions about race and biological sex identity that these discoveries of passing have occasioned. Following Entman (1993), we construe framing as the process of "selecting some aspects of a perceived reality and mak[ing] them more salient in a communicating text . . . to promote a particular problem definition, causal interpretation, moral evaluation, and/or treatment recommendation" for the described phenomenon (p. 52).

A comparison between marginal and dominant media coverage is justified on several accounts. First, the majority of media studies concerning race and gender focuses on dominant constructions of marginal identities (e.g., Lule, 1995; Parisi, 1998; Peer & Ettema, 1998; Sloop, 2000). Such scholarship is important in articulating the obstacles that marginal peoples face; however, it only tells part of the story. Identity construction is not a unidirectional process, and scholarship must reflect the importance and impact of marginal groups' narratives of identity or self-hood. Second, including marginal media production alongside dominant media texts reminds us that although the dominant media have great influence and reach in our society, the influence and reach of dominant media are not total (e.g., Flores & McPhail, 1997). Media resources produced by and for marginal peoples provide interpretations of events and identities that may run counter to dominant representations. Third, the comparison between marginal and dominant media discourses yields a richer account of the processes of interpretation, presentation, and representation of marginal and dominant identities. Exposed through this juxtaposition are competing histories, cultural memories, and understandings of power.

A second line of comparison is between race and sex passing. In this line of comparison, we follow Nakayama (1994, p. 163) who argues for "productive [scholarly] collusions between 'race,' gender, and sexuality." Both sex and race passing hold the potential to destabilize the regime of White male privilege. Furthermore, when both types of passers are "discovered," they expose the fast that despite the failure of the regime of visibility to tell us who is who, such failure is not sufficient to destroy the categories that have been confounded. Rather, the failure calls into action—and greater visibility—other methods of determining difference: legal, social and "scientific" norms and evidence are used to put the passer back into the right category and quell anxieties over blurred boundaries. Despite these similarities, our analysis reveals that oppressions are structured, experienced, and represented differently and that significant differences between these types of passing are borne from disparate histories and disparate in-group politics. As Robyn Wiegman (1995) argues, comparisons made by early feminists between the racism experienced by Blacks and sexism experienced by women were strategically useful but set up an over-simplified equation of oppression that elided White women's race privilege. In the next several sections of this essay, we examine the politics of passing and review relevant media studies on race, sex, and gender. We then examine both dominant and marginal media coverage of all three cases before explicating our conclusions.

The Politics of Passing

Scholars have defined passing variously. Those who view acts of passing as tragic or painful (e.g., Davis, 1991; Horton, 1994; Ramsey, 1976) typically accuse the passer of self-hatred and disloyalty. Those who view passing as playful and subversive (Ginsberg, 1996; Robinson, 1994; Tyler, 1994) note that passing performs a postmodern critique of identity and identity politics and engenders a "perverse pleasure" (Robinson, p. 736). Both the tragic/painful and postmodern/playful approaches are limited. Ambivalent, acts of passing generate both pain and pleasure, both subjugation and critique. Those who foreground the ambivalence of passing (Berlant, 1993; Helvie, 1997; Sheehy, 1999) recognize that passing can enact psychological or physical suffering *and* creative identity play for the passer, as well as elicit painful rage *and* surreptitious joy from the in-group.

As phenomena, passing and reactions to its discovery agitate contemporary concerns about constructions of identity and identity politics. Condemnations of essentialism, celebrations of performative, liminal identities, and concerns about cultural specifically and political action populate the landscape of current debates about identity politics. For better (as in the views of Diani, 1992, and Melucci, 1985) or for worse (as in the views of Cloud, 2001, and Gitlin, 1993, 1995), identity work is currently of great interest to practitioners and theorists of all political activism. Acts of passing expose both the performative dimensions of identity and the unreliability of visual regimes of identification built on scientific notions of race, sex and biology (Ginsberg, 1996, pp. 1–18). In addition, discoveries of passing reveal that more than self-esteem or community pride is at stake; that identity—who is who, and who gets to decide—is directly linked to material outcomes. Recent controversies over the 2000 U.S. Census's use of new racial categories reveal how the power to name groups and assign individuals to those groups affects many aspects of social policy and social justice. Affirmative action programs, civil rights regulation and enforcement, and the delivery of key health services depend, in part, on race, ethnic, sex identity labels. Furthermore, a lively scholarly conversation has emerged around the issue of passing and, more generally, hybrid or fluid identities. In literary studies, for example, scholars have shown much interest in 20th century fictional and autobiographical narratives of African Americans who pass as White (Favor, 1999; Wald, 2000; Berlant, 1993). These authors note that the dilemmas faced by characters in these texts reflect issues in the contemporary landscape of African American identity politics, observing that "we must push beyond skin color if we are to discuss who is black and how blackness is defined" (Favor, p. 2). Other recent works have coalesced around a few non-fictional, contemporary cases of passing, most notably the murder of Brandon Teena (Halberstam, 1998; Hale, 1998; Sloop, 2000).

Passing and catching someone in a pass make clearly visible the web of individual, state, society, and culture involved in maintaining identities. Passing is a transgression that inspires fear in the state and dominant social groups. Dominant groups and institutions desire the ability to survey and evaluate all subordinates with ease, thereby ensuring knowledge and readiness. As Ginsberg (1996) argues, "When 'race' is no longer visible, it is no longer intelligible: if 'white' can be 'black,' what is white? Race passing not only creates, to use Garber's term, a *category crisis* but also destabilizes the grounds of privilege founded on racial identity" (Ginsberg, p. 8). Likewise, sex passing "threaten[s] the security of male identity . . . [and] the certainties of identity categories and boundaries" (p. 13). When the passer is revealed, the result can be scandal, interrogation, legal procedures, violence, or even murder.

Communication scholars have examined passing along lines of class (Moon, 2000), sex (Sloop, 2000), sexual orientation (Spradlin, 1998), and race (Carlson, 1999; Hasian & Nakayama, 1998). Of particular relevance to this study, Hasian and Nakayama (1998) examine the legal and rhetorical dimensions of "Whiteness." In their analysis of courtroom argumentation and press coverage of the Susie Phipps case, the authors draw attention to the fictional and provisional nature of racial classifications, and they argue that efforts to refine and improve racial classifications for purposes of judgment actually perpetuate racial problems (p. 184). Sloop (2000) performs an analysis of mainstream media coverage in the aftermath of the murder of Brandon Teena and the trial of his murderers. While Sloop does not explicitly treat the case as an example of passing, his conclusions about the media's focus on deception and the incommensurability of theories that extol the fluidity of identity with people and institutions that demand a stable, intelligible identity (pp. 166–168, 170–172) point very much in that direction.

Below, we examine news coverage of three revelations of passing. Our analysis shows the similarities and differences between coverage of race and sex passing as well as the similarities and differences between dominant and marginal media coverage of these events.

Susie Guillory Phipps

Consider the case of Susie Guillory Phipps: according to Louisiana state records, her parents were born "colored" but died "white." She herself claimed, "I'm white. I'm going to be white. I've been white all my life and that's just it" (Schlangenstein, 1983), but discovered in 1977 that the State of Louisiana had recorded "colored" as her racial designation on her birth certificate. When for over a year the state of Louisiana refused to change her birth certificate to read "white," Phipps filed suit against the state, thus instigating public controversy over the standards and criteria for determining racial designations.

The fundamental obstacle to Phipps's effort to be designated as White was Louisiana's racial designation law. In 1970, Louisiana changed its racial designation laws and instituted the $1/32^{nd}$ rule, whereby anyone with $1/32^{nd}$ Black ancestry was considered legally Black. In 1981, Phipps's lawyer, Brian Begue, filed suit both to have the racial designation on her birth certificate changed and to rescind the states's "$1/32^{nd}$" formula of racial designation. Three days of testimony in 1982 included potentially damning narratives of somes of Phipps's elderly relatives who told the court that at least parts of the family had always considered themselves "colored." The state marshaled forth genealogical evidence that Phipps's great-great-great-great grandmother had been a freed slave named Margarita. Thus, with this and other evidence, the state's genealogist concluded that Susie Phipps had $3/32^{nd}$ "Negro ancestry." Although a geneticist testified that there was a chance Phipps had inherited no African genes from Margarita, the court denied her request to have the document changed.

Frames in Dominant Media

As the case made its way through the Louisiana court system, the dominant press did not consult or gather opinions or information from insiders in any meaningful way. As a result, the frames were constructed mainly from the views of the "dupe" class and the state. We identify three main frames in this coverage: (1) the case was a local, archaic anachronism; (2) the case was a bureaucratic and legal, not civil, issue; and (3) there exists a shadow world between races. These frames will be discussed below using evidence from the texts to illuminate the organization of the stories. Alternative frames from Black authors and publications will be used to show how dominant newspapers limited discussion of the complexities of the case.

LOCALIZING RACE AND MISCEGENATION LAWS Journalists repeatedly highlighted the fact that this case was "caused" by a 1970 Louisiana law. Some writers even declared that Louisiana was the last state in the United States to have an "equation for determining a person's race" (Jaynes, 1982, p. B16). Consistent iteration of the uniqueness of the Louisiana law served to contain the story of Susie Phipps firmly within the boundaries of her home state. One story included a map of the state of Louisiana with an inset of the area where Susie Guillory's family came from, pinpointing the problem safely within the state lines (p. B16). In the headline of a *People Magazine* article, Phipps was described as a "Louisiana Belle," invoking a chivalric heritage unique to the Southern region and implying that that quirky heritage inflects the character of the court case (Demaret, 1982). Other stories characterized Louisiana as "a state of many distinctions" (Herron, Wright, & Douglas, 1983, p. D4) and spoke of "a little local color" ("A Little Local

Color," 1982, p. E19). In *The New Yorker,* writer Calvin Trillin reminded readers that "from its earliest days as a French and Spanish colony, Louisiana has had a substantial number of residents who are not easily categorized racially by their appearance" (1986, p. 62). "The story," wrote Gregory Jaynes in the *New York Times,* "has elements of anthropology and sociology special to this region" (1982, p. B16). Only one story (Schlangenstein, 1983) hinted that a favorable court ruling might have national impact, but that sort of effect was not discussed. In summary, writers for dominant media did much to contain the significance of the Phipps case to the state of Louisiana or the region of the South, omitting its parallels in other states and minimizing its significance to a national conversation about race and law. On December 8, 1986, the U.S. Supreme Court refused to hear Phipps's case, further minimizing the potential for an extensive national conversation on racial identity.

Along with the verbal framing of Phipps's case as a Southern anomaly, the graphics themselves and the interplay between words and graphics served to reinforce the idea that this is a problem of the deep South and to encourage readers to judge for themselves how White or Black Phipps is. The photos in the newspapers were almost always full frontal shots of Phipps containing no obstacles to a view of her face and skin. She is totally available to scrutiny, with no shielding attorney, no protective husband to block the lens of the camera. The reader can easily peruse the photo without obstructions to visual "evidence" on her face or skin. In a piece that ran in the *New York Times,* Phipps was directly linked to the phrase "local color" by a headline that ran right above a large picture of her, suggesting that the locale of Louisiana is the only place that offers up faces such as hers ("A Little Local Color," 1982, p. E19).

People Magazine also chose to present multiple pictures of the woman they referred to as a "Southern Belle" in the headline (Demaret, 1982, pp. 155–156). A large close-up of Phipps opened the article, and subsequent pages featured her side-by-side with her White husband or White attorney, allowing the reader to compare their "authentic" skin to her questionable skin. Photos in a celebrity magazine like *People* are meant to invite the reader to imagine herself in intimate contact, up-close and personal, with the celebrity featured in the photo (Gabler, 1998). In this case, readers were not invited to measure her beauty or star power, but her Whiteness and/or Blackness. Would they be able to tell her ancestry from a close look like the one provided by the main photo? Could they imagine how her husband, working with her daily side-by-side in their business and having intimate relations after work, did not know the "truth" of her blood ancestry?

Before turning to the next frame, we would like to note that another "localization" occurred in the circumscription of questions of race to interrogations of blackness. That is, no journalists or editorialists asked the question, "What is white?" This failure can be seen as a reinforcement of the invisibility of Whiteness that, as Aida Hurtado suggests, allows the assumption that Whiteness is "natural" and "unproblematic" (1999, p. 228). Likewise, Diana Fuss notes that "in American culture, 'race' has been far more an acknowledged component of black identity than white; for good or bad, whites have always seen 'race' as a minority attribute" (in Bonnett, 1999, p. 212). The dominant press accounts of the Phipps case did not challenge the notion that race resides within "black blood" rather than in the regimes of White identity or privilege.

MAINTAINING INTEGRITY OF STATE RECORDS VS. MORAL INTEGRITY OF STATE LAWS In the dominant media, reporters emphasized the legal, bureaucratic processes that both gave rise to the case and promised to solve it. Headlines such as "Written Arguments Attack Racial Classification Law" (DeMers, 1983) and "Appeal Filed on Blood Law" (Schlangenstein, 1983) focused on various steps in the legal process. As discussed above, reporters paid much attention to the state's evidence that "proved" that it had accurately recorded and tracked the racial composition of the Guillory family. Thus, the burden was placed on Begue—in the papers and the courtroom—to prove why the state should change its time-honored record keeping practices. Only Phipps, her husband, and Begue spoke to the civil rights issues and expressed the ideal that states should allow citizens to name, and thus control, their personal identity. Quotations from Begue threatened the legal frame when he defended the right of the individual to self-designate and invoked the racist past of the designation laws. In depicting the drama of the courtroom, therefore, the legal question of whether or not the state's records are "accurate" was complicated from time to time with the question of whether it is right that the state can label an individual without her consent or knowledge. Despite these cracks in the frame provided by Phipp's defenders, the state's evidence was piled very high in the papers' reports: in 27 out of 45 stories her slave ancestor was mentioned, and 11 quoted testimony from her relatives that they considered themselves "colored." Only one story reported a geneticist's claim that the state could not prove that Phipps had inherited genetic material specifically from her slave ancestor (Jaynes, 1982, p. B16). None of the reporters ever posed the question: what evidence is necessary or legitimate in a case such as this? There was no description of what evidence could have proved her "White" to the state, but the judges (and implicitly the journalists) decided that Phipps does not have a sufficient amount of whatever it would be. Witness testimony quoted from the trial affirmed that those who are the products of interracial unions are colored, which was described in one witness's quote as "never white" (Trillin, p. 73).

Interestingly, the reporters who framed the story as one unique to the region failed to discover or note that the state of Louisiana had been dealing with the shortcomings of its 1/32nd law off and on since it was passed. Prior to Phipps, at least two other plaintiffs had demanded that the Bureau of Vital Statistics change their family members' birth certificates from "Negro" to "White" in the mid-1970's. (These cases are *Messina v. Ciaccio,* Court of Appeal of Louisiana, Fourth Circuit 290 So. 2d 339: 1974; and *Thomas v. Louisiana State Board of Health,* Court of Appeal of Louisiana, Fourth Circuit, 278 So. 2d: 1973.) In 1974 in the case *Messina v. Ciaccio,* Judge Samuel Lemmon of the Fourth Circuit decided that the Bureau of Vital Statistics had to change the birth certificate to read "white" because it had not met "the requirement for exactness established by the legislature in providing the 1/32nd Negro ancestry test" (*Messina v. Ciaccio,* 1974). The court stated that designations such as "mulatto" or "quadroon" as recorded by the Census and other agencies prior to the 1970 1/32nd law were not governed by strict blood percentage rules. Therefore, the judges ruled that the defendant's genealogical evidence—similar to that used against Phipps—was not sufficient to make a determination of how much Negro blood the plaintiffs had. This ruling was certainly a contrast to the rulings in the Phipps case, where the court did not challenge the genealogical evidence.

TRAPPED IN A "SHADOW WORLD" IN THE SOUTH   Dominant coverage of the Phipps case between 1982 and 1986 rarely acknowledged the existence of interracial people other than the plaintiff. When they did, the results were less than flattering. The quotations and descriptions reporters chose to include resonated with the long-standing stereotype that multiracial individuals will never fit into society. As G. Reginald Daniel notes in his recent book on multiracial identity in the United States, eugenicists, psychologists, and sociologists from the late 19th and well into the 20th century hypothesized that people of Black and White heritage would always experience a sense of being "betwixt and between" in a way that would translate into marginality and related pathologies of social dislocation and personal alienation (Daniel, 2001).

One of the two women with White and Black heritage featured in a *New York Times* article was presented with a statement from her personal writings that conveyed the idea that multiracial people will never fit in: "My mother says I am Creole. My teacher says I am Negro . . . Who am I?" (Jaynes, 1982, p. B16). Even quotations from Phipps's attorney fit this mold. One reporter chose to quote Begue describing Phipps as "emotionally white and legally black" (Hills, 1983), a description that reflects previous psychological theories that multiracial people would never be able to mentally reconcile their racial identities. In what registers as a concession to Phipps, Louisiana state attorney Westholz is quoted saying that "it is true that Susie is more white than black" (Demaret, 1982, p. 156). However, as Westholz said to a reporter in another article, Phipps was born as one of those "unfortunate people in between" Blacks and Whites (Debenport, 1984). Thus, the collection of quotations about Phipps and the few examples of interracial people's feelings reinforce the notion that these people don't fit acceptable categories and, by extension, are bound to experience problems fitting in to society at large.

The nebulousness of this in-between world is not entirely tragic, however, for individuals can exploit the ambiguities of interracial identity to improve their lot in life. Indeed, in addition to the narrative of Susie Phipps escaping and denying the colored identity shared by many of her family members, another story of escaping her roots emerged in the press: her rise from cousin-marrying rural poverty to small business affluence. *Time* magazine noted that Phipps is "married to a wealthy white crawfish merchant" ("Color Bind," 1983). Likewise, a *New York Times* reporter stated that Susie Phipps is "the wife of a well-to-do white businessman in Sulphur, La." (Marcus, 1983, p. A10). Phipps's marriage to her second husband was often mentioned with an accompanying phrase about his wealth, despite the fact that she was a partner in the business. Even those authors who did note her participation in the business signaled that she is a social climber in other ways. Trillin noted that for "colored Creoles" as light as the Guillory family, "it would not have been difficult to convince some of them of the advantage of simply marrying a white person and melting into the privileged caste. It's a process that is still going on" (1986, p. 68). In Trillin's accusation, Phipps exploits the indiscernibility of her body in order to improve her economic and social status. By stating that the process continues, he also intimated that other "colored Creoles" are circulating in White society unnoticed and, as a consequence, reaping the benefits of Whiteness.

Frames in Marginal Media

Having explicated and characterized what we discovered to be the three major frames in dominant media with regard to the Susie Phipps case, we now turn to texts created by the in-group, African Americans. The effects of the dominant or "dupe" frames can be better realized when juxtaposed with the alternative frames provided in the publications of the "insider" or "clairvoyant" group. Admittedly, we cannot gauge the clairvoyance of in-group members because none of them who speak in the texts claim the clairvoyance described by Robinson (1994). As a result, in this section we refer to "in-group members" rather than "in-group clairvoyants." We have identified three major frames in the Black press coverage of the Phipps case: 1) the case concerned civil rights, not merely bureaucratic technicalities; 2) Phipps is part of a long history of controversy involving mixed-race individuals; 3) Phipps's desire to be classified as White is an affront to Black communities.

CIVIL RIGHTS, NOT LEGAL TECHNICALITIES   Much like dominant media writers, Black writers and commentators amplified the legal dimensions of the Phipps case but with a twist. Rather than treat the case as a legal anomaly, they contextualized it within a larger rubric of civil rights cases. *Jet* magazine's coverage of the case, which consists of seven articles over a five-year period, began in 1982 and ended with the U.S. Supreme Court's decision in 1986 not to hear the case. *Jet* writers focused on how her case might bring greater justice to all Blacks. The magazine placed all of its articles in a section devoted to civil rights cases and other racial legal matters. In the first four pieces, *Jet* zeroed in on the absurdity of the 1/32nd statute, the need to abolish it, and the racist notion that "Black blood" impurifies "White blood" ("Ex-College Prexy," 1982, p. 23). The magazine used quotations from anthropologists and a prominent Black scholar that the state's blood quota had no scientific merit, highlighting the double standard of the law. Said Dr. Albert Dent: "it's discriminatory because it only classifies Blacks. If someone had a thirty-second of White blood in them, would they be classified as White?" (p. 23). The answer, of course, is no, not in a system where Black blood is considered simultaneously inferior and powerful. After repeating the statistic that many Whites have five-percent African genes, the article ended with a quotation from Dent that endorsed Phipps's claim to Whiteness because he believed that Whites in Louisiana ignorant of their Black genes would not want to be subject to the 1/32nd rule.

Jet's implicit endorsement of Phipps's fight against the state of Louisiana was not broad, however. *Jet*'s coverage focused on and lauded the dismantling of an unfair, racist statute, not Phipps's desire to be White. So, the magazine applauded when the state overturned the 1/32 law in 1983 ("La. Repeals," 1983; "La. Woman," 1983), but when Phipps's lawyer decided to pursue the task of eliminating racial labels on *all* birth certificates, the coverage changed. By 1984, opening paragraphs no longer presented the state's laws or legal decisions but instead focused on Phipps's desire to be designated White (e.g., "Woman Resumes Fight," 1984). Phipps's interest in eliminating the use of racial labels on any state documents conflicted with a key Black political interest—to ensure that the state records race in order to track and prosecute cases of racial discrimination. So began the implied critiques of Phipps's quest to change her state records. The sixth article in the series quoted the court's ruling at length, ending the article with the following statement: " '[Racial classification] provides statistics which are an essential tool for planning and monitoring the public health programs, affirmative action and other anti-discrimination measures,' the panel said" ("Louisiana Court," 1986, p. 5). The final article, as will be shown below, was particularly pointed in its critique of Phipps's goal to maintain and live a White identity.

RACIST HISTORY AS CONTEXT FOR PASSING   In contrast to the dominant media's "Southern Anomaly" frame, Black writers framed the Phipps case within a history of passing, racial double-standards, and a host of other laws that punished those who crossed the color line. In *Ebony* magazine, evidence of a nationwide obsession with passing, including laws against interracial marriage and other forms of social intercourse, was used to contextualize the Phipps case. The writer notes that, "Whatever the outcome of the Phipps case, the problem of racial classification will continue, for the national definition of race is still vague" ("What Makes You Black?," 1983, p. 118). *Ebony* also traced the problem of racial designation back to *Plessy v. Ferguson,* which created a national standard of hypodescent, or the "one-drop rule." Under hypodescent, the dominant society assigns a racially mixed person the identity that corresponds to the racial group that has the lowest social status (Root, 1996). In contrast to dominant accounts, *Ebony* announced that states other than Louisiana still have racial classification laws and guidelines (p. 116). For example, writers revealed that in Texas, the father's race determines that of the child; in West Virginia, the law is to follow the guidelines of the National Center for Health Statistics, whose code states that a child is recorded as "Black" if either parent is Black ("What Makes You Black?," 1983, p. 116). Dorothy Gilliam (1982) told readers that she "couldn't brush this [story] aside as a single eccentric's identity crisis," and that "this story is as old as the nation" (p. B1).

Furthermore, unlike the photos showcasing Phipps in the dominant press, the Black press contained a variety of visual representations. *Ebony* did not limit its photos to her case; rather, the magazine presents photos of other "passers" who have been caught up in the judicial system in previous decades. Thus the reader is invited to compare Phipps's appearance to other controversial figures from the past rather than alone and outside of the historical context as the White newspapers' photos did. In *Ebony,* she was presented as part of a lineage, so to speak, of liminal figures, but in the dominant press, she was put forth as a rarity to be examined alone.

It is notable that although the Black press did take pains to historicize the Phipps case, it did not mention the other challenges to the 1/32nd law. Perhaps this is because of discomfort with the plaintiffs' wish to be White rather than Black. The Black press has always been a champion of racial pride, and the act of passing or desiring to be another race is anathema to communication of pride. Transforming passing into a positive act is rare; Wald (2000) analyzed a series of articles in *Ebony, Jet* and *Negro Digest* in the 1950's that declared that passing was a dying practice in post-war America as middle class Blacks improved their economic and social positions. The declarations of Blacks light enough to pass that they were "through with passing" affirmed Black identity and disavowed the notion that being Black was inherently detrimental to one's economic and social well-being (Wald, pp. 116–151). Unlike the subjects in these "post-passing" narratives, the plaintiffs suing for White identity (albeit against a state using a racist double-standard for determining identity) do not communicate that Black identity is desirable.

PASSING AS CHALLENGE TO COMMUNITY INTEGRITY   With regard to the frame of interracial people trapped in a "shadow world," Black writers agreed in the sense that these are problematic people who have identity choices to make. Both implicitly and explicitly, Black authors indicated that all people with any African heritage should choose a Black identity—and be proud of it. The issue of pride, both personal and group-centered pride, became important for in-group writers. Susie Phipps was depicted as succumbing to self-hate caused by racism. "It's naïve to get caught up in this as an 'interesting' court case; it is having your head in the sand to be shocked. Susie Phipps is doing what many blacks are doing—running away from being black" (Gilliam, 1982, p. B1). For Black commentators, questions of individual choice and racial discrimination constituted the main focus; this case was seen as neither strictly nor primarily about procedures of law. Racial designation laws were described as took used against Blacks to secure White privilege. For Gilliam, the question was not if the state has an interest in recording Phipps's race, but that such mechanisms have been used as weapons to divide and psychologically damage Black people. Passing was portrayed as pathological and disrespectful to the Black community.

Like Gilliam, Smart-Grosvenor (1983) took Phipps to task for her—and her husband's—apparent racism. The article was peppered with implicit and explicit references to Phipps's internalized racism, beginning with the title, "Obsessed With 'Racial Purity,' " which could be applied both to the State of Louisiana and the plaintiff's state of mind. *Ebony,* like the *New York Times,* included testimony from her relatives that they considered the family colored, supporting the accusation that Phipps was trying to pass for White and run from her Blackness ("What Makes You Black?," 1983, p. 116). Smart-Grosvenor (1983) clearly believed that Phipps was knowingly passing and that her current personal quest for state-endorsed Whiteness was demeaning. "Blacks look on passing for economic reasons—so you can get a better job—with a bittersweet eye, but passing for white *just to be white* [italics added] is to most of us an anathema, no matter how little black blood you have" (p. 30). As this quotation reveals, passing is not all pleasure for in-group clairvoyants.

Jet's coverage, which was initially supportive of Phipps's quest to overturn the 1/32nd law, moved gradually toward a gentle implied critique of her personal motives. In the final *Jet* piece on Phipps, the opening sentence stated, "It looks as if Susie Guillory Phipps, 51, of Sulphur, La., might have to live with the official designation 'colored' rather than the label 'white' that she is seeking" ("Louisiana Woman Losing," 1987). And, whereas in previous articles all mentions of her slave ancestress were accompanied by the mention of the White slave owner who was also Phipps's ancestor, this article only mentioned Margarita. Describing the Supreme Court's refusal to hear the case, *Jet* wrote that the Court "would not get involved with Mrs. Phipps's argument," a statement that seemed to reduce her case to a personal vendetta rather than a wide-ranging legal problem of national significance. The article implied that Phipps should give it up and "live with" the knowledge—private and public—of her Blackness.

Despite their focus on the moral and social questions surrounding the case, Black writers did not offer any potential solutions to the problem of dual racial identity. Personal feelings of shame and group affinity were raised, and the influence of the state in these matters was spotlighted, but these reports left the reader with the same options as the dominant press. Furthermore, Black writers were invested in the notion that one has "Black blood" and that it makes you Black, no matter how small the fraction. Similar to the dominant press, the Black press barely confronted the court's role in constructing Whiteness and granting White identity. Black writers recognized the arbitrary 1/32nd quota as unjust and unfair, but not as part of the architecture of *White* identity; in these news narratives, the 1/32nd law was a generator of *Black* identity. As if in possession of some fantastically imagined gravitational density, one drop of Blackness dramatically pulled attention and emphasis away from the dominant end of the color hierarchy, leaving Whiteness to dissolve, unnoticed and unexamined. In sum, both dominant and Black texts contributed to the operation of Whiteness as a "strategic rhetoric" that renders invisible its nature as a rhetorical construction (Nakayama & Krizek, 1995). As we will see in our second and third cases, this pattern of reluctance to radically interrogate dominant categories discourages the creation and/or assignment of alternative identities for alleged passers.

Sean O'Neill and Brandon Teena

In 1993, Sean O'Neill, a 17 year-old boy in Colorado Springs, was known for being popular with the girls and having a volatile temper. After one of his girlfriends broke up with him, his temper got him into trouble. In September of 1994 during an argument on the phone, Sean told her he was going to kill her. The girl called the police to file a harassment charge, and the police came for Sean. When they asked him for an identification card, he handed them a Colorado ID made out to Sharon Clark. According to the police, Sean admitted there and then that he was a she. The police subsequently took Sean to a doctor who confirmed the presence of female genitalia. Soon after, Sharon Clark was charged with criminal impersonation and sexual assault. Four girls and their parents filed charges and went to court. During the trial, all of the girls who testified claimed they were completely fooled by Sean; one even insisted that they had sexual intercourse even though Sean denies ever using a dildo or other prosthesis to simulate a penis. Sean struck a deal with prosecutors for a reduced sentence, pleading guilty to second-degree sexual assault to face eight rather than fifty years in prison, and the judge reduced the sentence to probation.

Around the same time that Sean was becoming popular with girls in Colorado Springs, Brandon Teena was dating girls in Falls City, Nebraska, lavishing them with affection and expensive gifts. Unfortunately, Brandon's largesse was the product of forged checks. When the police arrested him for forgery in December of 1993, Brandon gave them an identification card with the name "Teena Brandon" on it, so they held him in the women's cell-block. After Brandon's new girlfriend, Lana Tisdel, and her ex-boyfriend, Marvin Nissen, posted bail, rumor began to spread that Brandon was a woman. To explain his occupancy in the women's cell-block, Brandon told Lana that he was a hermaphrodite, but this explanation did not satisfy everyone. At a Christmas party, Nissen and his friend, John Lotter, grabbed Brandon and stripped him of his pants and underwear, revealing labia and presumably a vagina, but not a penis. Later, they abducted Brandon, beating and raping him repeatedly. When he went to the police to press charges, the sheriff did not arrest the men even though they both had prior convictions for violent crimes. Furthermore, there was ample physical evidence of rape (Brandon had had an exam done at a hospital) and a savage beating (one of the assailants kicked Brandon so hard, the imprint of a boot was left in his back). A week later, on New Year's Eve, Nissen and Lotter went to the house where Brandon was staying with friends. They shot and stabbed Brandon and then shot his two friends. They were arrested within hours of the shooting and charged with murder, kidnapping, and rape.

Frames in Dominant Media

Although Brandon Teena's sex identity was never subjected to the scrutiny of a court, we have grouped these cases together because dominant news media treated the subjects similarly with respect to their sex identity. As one could guess, the dominant media had even less understanding for these cases than the Phipps "identity crisis." Three major frames emerged in dominant papers' coverage of Brandon and Sean's cases: 1) masquerade and deception; 2) the sex was not lesbian; 3) genitalia proves sex identity. Sloop (2000) discerns and describes all three of these frames in his analysis of mainstream media coverage of

Brandon Teena. They merit repetition here in order to confirm Sloop's findings about Brandon Teena but also to show that these frames were employed in dominant coverage of Sean O'Neill. In order not to replicate Sloop's work, we both provide different evidence from the Teena case and provide corroborating evidence from the Sean O'Neill case. Although the three frames that we discern were tightly constructed, the writers and editors had problems describing the case without exposing the complexities of dealing with persons who practice fluid gender identities.

MASQUERADING AS MEN Over and over again, the reporters covering these cases depicted Sharon and Teena as women *pretending to be* men, not women who *felt like,* and thus acted like, men. This finding confirms Sloop's (2000, pp. 170–172) observation about mainstream media coverage of Brandon Teena. The *Denver Post* described Sean O'Neill as "a 20-year-old *woman* who faced nearly 50 years in prison for allegedly sexually assaulting several young girls while *posing as a teenage boy* [italics added]" ("Plea Deal Made," 1995, p. B4), and never allowed Sean's self-description as male to enter the frame. The dominant press was very invested in depicting Brandon's "true" femaleness—using female pronouns and "Teena" as a first name when describing Brandon outside of quoted remarks—and focused intently on Brandon's own troubles with the law. The result was a portrait of an extremely troubled young woman who seemed destined for a tragic end. In feature-length articles in dominant publications, Brandon's multiple "deceptions," check forgery, use of stolen identity cards, and "passing" as a male with girlfriends were construed to have led him down a path of destructive behavior to his unmasking, rape, and death.

Photos of Brandon published in dominant periodicals were accompanied by captions that used female pronouns to describe the subject or stated that the pictured person was "Teena Brandon" rather than "Brandon Teena." *Playboy* (Konigsberg, 1995) and the *Chicago Tribune* (Worthington, 1994) used this strategy in their pictures. The *Playboy* article featured two head shots of Brandon with the caption "Dying to be a man: *Teena,* with fiancée Gina's name tattooed on *her* arm" (italics added, p. 197). The *Tribune* used a photo of Brandon lying on the floor, smiling at the camera, next to Lana Tisdel, who is also looking and smiling at the camera. The *Tribune's* caption stated *"Teena Brandon* (left) dated Lana Tisdel for a few weeks until Tisdel *found out Brandon was a woman"* (italics added, p. 1). In addition to declaring Brandon's gender as female through the use of the pronouns, the large photo of Brandon, the passer, next to his/her girlfriend, set up a comparison between the "real" female (Lana) and the "fake" male/passing female. Similar to the Phipps photos, where belittling, humorous headlines and captions (e.g. "A Little Local Color") signaled to the reader that there is a façade that needs to be dismantled, this picture of Brandon and Lana and its surrounding textual cues suggested that the picture's presentation of "reality" is faulty due to the passer's expertise in masking herself. The reader/spectator is guided to the position of potential dupe—and made an honorary in-group clairvoyant simultaneously. The reader/spectator "knows" the "true" identity because of the caption, headline and the subsequent story, but the picture and caption choices also allowed the reader to participate in the game of "would I have been fooled like Lana was?" For inexplicable reasons, readers were not invited to test their skills in reading Sean O'Neill's body, for no photos of him appeared in the dominant media.

NON-LESBIAN SEX BETWEEN WOMEN In the coverage of Sean O'Neill's case, the press strategically switched between "him" and "her" when depicting the defendant's identity and alleged transgressions. One reason for switching to the male pronouns and names when describing the girls' testimony about their sexual encounters was to classify their relationship with Sean as heterosexual. "'We had no clue at all,'" the 15-year-old's mother said. "'We were convinced the person was a boy. I saw this person probably every other day or so'" (Foster, 1994a, p. 8A). The girls were consistently depicted as ignorant of Sean's "true identity." A *Denver Post* reporter wrote "Several girls knew Clark as Sean O'Neill and testified that Sean 'kept "his" shirt on during their encounters'" ("Plea Deal Made," 1995, p. B4). Another headline highlighted one girl's testimony that Sean's "'sex act' fooled her for months" (Foster, 1994b, p. 12A).

Unlike Sean O'Neill's former girlfriend, Brandon's former girlfriends did not always use the male pronoun when describing their past sexual encounters, but the reporters took pains to emphasize that the girls were totally unaware of the "real sex" of their partner at the time. "'She was very convincing,' Brenda Tawzer says . . . 'and everybody believed she was a guy'" (Wheelwright, 1996, p. T7). Furthermore, Brandon was described as deliberately seeking out naïve partners who would not detect his female anatomy: "In Teena's estimation, Heather was a girl she could outsmart and win over" (Konigsberg, 1995, p. 194). The mixing of pronouns to describe the past and present muddied the frame a bit, but the continual return to the theme of masterful deception reinforced the frame that the girls believed they were engaged in heterosexual sex and are not lesbians—then or now (see also Sloop, 2000, pp. 175–179).

FEMALE GENITALIA IS PROOF OF FEMALE STATUS This last frame follows implicitly from the other two and is also reinforced explicitly. Reporters relayed that doctors confirmed that Sean and Brandon both had "normal" vaginas and breasts. There are no quotations from Sean, Brandon, queer activists, or others proposing that either person had any legitimate reasons to present himself as male. In the absence of such a challenge, biology—that is, genitalia-reigned as the unquestionable source of proof of Sean and Brandon's identity (see also Sloop, pp. 172–173).

Frames in Marginal Media

Examining queer coverage of the passers reveals significant contrasts with dominant coverage. Yet it also sheds light on the nuances of identity politics within queer communities. On the one hand, the queer press announced a political interest in labeling Brandon as a lesbian. On the other hand, Sean, who survived his unmasking, was given opportunity to speak and succeeded in complicating facile assignations of his sex and gender identities.[3] Three major frames emerged: 1) the passers' actions took place within a context of homophobia; 2) heteronormative identities are limiting and oppressive; 3) the passers present a challenge to the integrity of a queer community.

HOMOPHOBIC HISTORY AS CONTEXT One point of convergence in the queer press was that while queer writers did not necessarily endorse Sean and Brandon's failure to disclose their female bodies to their romantic partners, the writers defined public and state reactions to the two cases as ghastly exemplars of intense societal homophobia. Where the dominant press framed the cases as anomalous (never even mentioning the existence of the other "cross-dresser" despite the closeness of the two cases), the queer press cited them as examples of pervasive anti-queer sentiment and homophobic or gender violence. Most of the queer articles included extensive critiques of Sheriff Laux's response to Brandon's rape. The *Advocate* quoted Brandon's family and the New York Gay and Lesbian Anti-Violence Project's (AVP) damning evaluations of Falls City's law enforcement: "Says Terry Maroney, a spokeswoman for the AVP: 'I think it's clear as day that had they handled the rape case from the start, none of them would be dead'" (Ricks, 1994, p. 29). The *Lambda Book Report* mentioned Brandon's murder as an example of "one gender hate-crime after another," listing four other victims with him (Wilchins, 1997, p. 17). *off our backs* printed its piece on the case on a page reserved for reporting incidents of violence against women and revealed that Laux asked Brandon's family "What kind of sister did you have?" and "Why didn't she go back to Lincoln if she didn't like our law enforcement?" ("Violence News: Nebraska," 1994, p. 5). The sheriff's insensitivity was held up for scrutiny as evidence of institutionalized homophobia. Solidarity among queer writers about these two cases, however, breaks down along several lines.

OPPRESSIVE SOCIAL CATEGORIES EXPOSED Most articles in the queer press exposed oppressive social categories, but disagreement emerged over how far queers should extend this critique. Writers lamented the worst effects of heteronormativity-including compulsory heterosexuality, homophobia, and female femininity/male masculinity—and proclaimed or implied the need to defend gay and lesbian identities and to mobilize politically around them (e.g., "Deception on the Prairie," 1994; Minkowitz, 1994; Ricks, 1994). In this way, queer writers critiqued heteronormativity but did not extend critique to the categories of "gay" and "lesbian." Yet for a few writers (Minkowitz, 1995; Wilchins, 1997), even the valorized identities of "gay" and "lesbian" earned critical scrutiny and exposure for their oppressive qualities. This is most notable in Minkowitz's commentary on the Sean O'Neill case. Minkowitz stated the case "raises explosive questions" about sex, ethics, and identity (1995, p. 99). At one point she asked, "Does everyone have an obligation to reveal their [*sic*] gender—or to know it?" (p. 146). The simple fact of Sean's survival enabled the queer press to seek out and publicize his arguments and philosophy about his identity. In his own voice, Sean amplified his masculine identification, and Minkowitz, a self-identified lesbian, always referred to Sean as "Sean" and "he," not "Sharon" and "she." Minkowitz ended the piece with a discussion of transsexuality and queer theory, quoting queer activists and presenting the argument that "many lesbians and gay men have long argued that gender is socially constructed and changeable" (p. 146). In short, Minkowitz argued that the categories of "gay," "lesbian," and "bisexual" fail to account for the full range of sexual and gender identifications, and she suggested that "lesbian" cannot adequately describe Sean O'Neill.

PROBLEMATIC POSITION OF PASSER IN THE COMMUNITY The third major frame in queer coverage emerged from writers' efforts to make sense of Sean and Brandon and their status in the queer community. As in the previous frame, writers expressed disagreement. Queer voices in the media did not automatically side with the identity choices made by Brandon. Indeed, the *Advocate's* initial story about the Teena case was titled "Deception on the Prairie" ("Deception," 1994), echoing the emphasis on Brandon's and Sean's "crimes" of passing and fooling others in dominant press headlines like "Death of a Deceiver." We surmise, that, for the in-group, unwillingness to automatically side with Brandon and Sean derives in part from the pain of passing which in turn derives from the feeling that the passer does not want to be associated with the group and will do anything to escape it. Still, despite the pain, some within the in-group often "claimed" the passers as their own in order to illuminate the oppressions operating in the social, political, and legal responses to the passing discovery. Although friends and witnesses of Brandon's life in Nebraska switched between male and female names and pronouns to refer to their experiences with Brandon, the queer press was content to fix Brandon's identity as female. One implicit reason for doing this was to define Brandon as a lesbian—albeit a confused one—and to craft a narrative of homophobic murder. It seems that the queer press found it easier to make the claim that Lotter and Nissen perpetrated a hate crime against a "lesbian" than a person with gender dysphoria, a transgenderist, or some other descriptor.[4] The definition of Brandon as woman and (confused, closeted) lesbian opened up space to critique more easily the oppressive homophobic atmosphere of places like Falls City.

These two cases elicited very different responses from the queer press. While Brandon, a victim in a triple-homicide case, received significant coverage, Sean O'Neill garnered only one article. It is puzzling that only one reporter, Donna Minkowitz, covered both Brandon's murder and Sean O'Neill's criminal impersonation case. These two people's life stories were similar, their "crimes" occurred in the same region of the nation within ten months of each other, and court cases pertaining to them overlapped. They would seem to be a perfect pair for a journalist looking to comment on sex and gender in the 1990s or the emergence of "disturbing" sexual practices in the heartland. One could argue that the triple-homicide made Brandon's case more "newsworthy" than Sean's. However, there are important legal issues involved in the O'Neill case that did not arise in Brandon's, namely the issue of whether consensual sex can be viewed at a later date as assault. Minkowitz alone explored this issue, an issue that alarmed major civil rights organizations such as the National Organization for Women (NOW) and the Lambda Legal Defense Fund. That this debate was not noted by the dominant press and barely addressed in the queer press is notable; perhaps it signifies the discomfort both groups harbor toward people who extend their performance of the "opposite" sex (and "discordant" gender) to such a physically intimate level. The lack of coverage in the *Advocate, off our backs,* and other queer publications also may be due in part to O'Neill's refusal to identify as lesbian. Unlike Brandon, who was never subjected to sustained, public interrogation about his identity and loyalty to a queer community, Sean, alive and willing to speak publicly, disavowed a lesbian identity and disidentified with a queer community.

Photos used in the stories about Brandon reflect the strategy of rendering Brandon a female. Like the dominant press, the *Advocate* (Ricks, 1994) used female pronouns to describe Brandon in the photo captions. Utilizing the same photo as the *Tribune,* the *Advocate's* caption read, "Just prior to *her* murder, *Teena Brandon* (left) dated Lana Tisdel" (italics added, p. 28). Brandon's appearance and pose in the picture certainly could be interpreted as androgynous, if not masculine. The caption plus the opening sentence of the article, however, made it clear that the *Advocate* decided that Brandon's "true" or "real" identity is female. There was also a quotation in large type accompanying the photo that stated: "Everyone discovered he was *actually a woman* [italics added]" (p. 28). Because the quotation and caption warned the reader that Brandon was passing, seeing Brandon as female seemed to be the preferred reading of the photo.

In contrast, Donna Minkowitz's piece in the *Village Voice* did not label Brandon as female in all of the captions of its photos; rather, it employed a more fluid language to depict Brandon's short life and identity(ies). Captions accompanying the photos that document Brandon's successful "passing"—in shots with Lana and other girlfriends—used male pronouns to describe the pictured murder victim. Despite Minkowitz's willingness to mix and match the gender pronouns in the text of the story, the arrangement and order of the photos used in this story still emphasized the idea that Brandon did indeed pass as a man. The first page of the article featured four photos, arrange around blocks of text that form the column of a cross. The large caption proclaimed: "Brandon Teena *was a woman* [italics added] who lived and loved as a man. She was killed for carrying it off" (Minkowitz, 1994, p. 24). The photos that flank the cross (completed by the title of the story, "Love hurts," on the transverse of the cross) were of Brandon's former girlfriends and featured the women alone. The caption for this layout of photos read: "They say Brandon was the best boyfriend they ever dated. Clockwise from left: Reanna Allen, Daphne Gugat, Lindsay Claussen, and Gina Bartu, who was engaged to Brandon for three months."

It was not until the second page that the deceased was featured in a photo. In that photo, Brandon was with a new girlfriend, Lana Tisdel, looking at the camera playfully. The caption read, "*Brandon Teena* (right) teaching Lana Tisdel to play pool: '*He* knew how a girl liked to be treated'" (italics added, p. 25). The third page also sported a smaller picture of Brandon lifting another girlfriend with the caption "Brandon impressing *his* friends at his engagement party: *he* was worried about being thought of as a weakling" (italics added, p. 26). But below this photo was a quotation in large type from Brandon that stated " I can't be with a woman that way. That's gross,' Brandon told *her* best friend, Sara Lyon" [emphasis added] (p. 26). The captions' male pronouns, albeit liberating in that they affirm Brandon's chosen male identity during the moment the photo was taken, were contradicted by the large-type quotations and subheadlines that declared that Brandon had concealed a true, female identity. Similar to the photos and captions used to depict Susie Phipps, the pictures of Brandon included in these articles invited the reader to see if s/he could tell if the subject was passing. Furthermore, the captions suggested a preferred reading of each passer as "truly" belonging to a category that is the opposite of "her" passing identity.

Conclusions

Against the dominant media frames that portrayed Susie Phipps as trapped in a shadow world and her case as a local issues about legal technicalities, in-group writers and media outlets foregrounded the civil rights dimensions of her case and emphasized histories of racism and community integrity as larger contexts for understanding the case and its primary litigant. Visible through these frames are multiple, sometimes competing constituents of Black and White identity: blood percentages, genealogy, self-identification, and state documentation, for example. Ultimately, judges in the state of Louisiana upheld the integrity of state laws and state records and thus thwarted Phipps's effort to be(come) White. Dominant media frames about Sean O'Neill and Brandon Teena insisted that Sean and Brandon were women and thus lesbian deceivers; because of this deception, the sex between Sean and Brandon and their partners, although between two women, was not lesbian. Most of the queer press agreed that public reactions to the two exposed virulent homophobia and oppressive social categories. Yet queer writers struggled to make sense of Sean and Brandon, some claiming Sean and Brandon and some disidentifying with—and in Sean's case, ignoring—them. Criteria for determining their "true" identities boiled down to biology/genitalia and self-identification.

These frames and criteria of identity suggest several conclusions about gender, sex, race, and media practices in the late 20th century in the U.S. First, the comparison of dominant and marginal press reactions to cases of passing reveals that on the issue of passing there are major differences and a few notable similarities between dominant media and media that serve marginalized groups. The varying interests of these groups can serve to narrow the scope and length of debates over identity, and, by extension, affect the length and quality of discourses concerning these events and issues in the public sphere. In the Phipps case, the localizing of the story and the lack of editorial response in the dominant press cut off many avenues of discussion. Similarly, despite an acknowledgement of the larger historical and national implications of the case, the Black press did not explore the potential identity crises the case could elicit across the nation; rather, they depicted Susie Phipps and others like her as victims of self-hatred. The "one-drop rule" system of racial classification, although it is revealed to support a double standard in the Black press, is never challenged in the dominant press and is implicitly endorsed by the Black writers in the name of solidarity.

Likewise, in the dominant press Brandon Teena and Sean O'Neill were construed as criminals and anomalies, even though their cases occurred within ten months of each other. O'Neill's case was barely covered in the dominant papers, consisting of only short articles in regional newspapers. The Teena case had a longer life-span due in part to the triple-homicide that accompanied Brandon's "unmasking" (e.g., "Triple Murder," 1994). Unlike articles on the O'Neill and Phipps cases, articles on Brandon in both the dominant and queer presses went a bit further in their exploration of Brandon's sexual malleability, but many of these paths ended abruptly with implicit and explicit conclusions that assigned these individuals to relatively rigid sexual identities. Though the dominant and the alternative press did not agree on the range of available categories and on which labels to apply, they both reduced fluid individual identities to narrowed, socially approved categories.

The queer media's effort to classify the murder as a hate-crime is laudable: at the time these articles were written, sexual orientation only recently—in 1990—had been recognized as a protected class under legislation requiring the U.S. Department of justice to record hate crime statistics. Thus, we conclude that the queer press participated in progressive politics by framing the tragedy as a hate crime. Framing Brandon as a confused butch lesbian, however, is a restrictive act. As Hale (1998) writes, such a transformation "inadvertently turns a vagina into the actuality of gender categorization—as if biology was destiny after all, as if . . . we are all what our culture tells us our genitals mean, and as if genitals always, inevitably, outweigh agency" (p. 316). Framing Brandon as a lesbian produces the desired effect for the in-group—an icon to use in the fight against homophobia—but shuts down the possibilities of identity for the passer and others like him who are speechless in the in-group media narratives. In addition, Hale also cites that a similar violence is done to Brandon—who claimed several identifiers—when transgender communities rallied to protest dominant and queer coverage of the case and claimed Brandon as their own (p. 314). While their political mobilization is admirable and necessary to diversify discourses of sexual identity, pinning Brandon to any identity after his death is a dubious enterprise in limiting the meaning of that life and his relationships with others.

As Flores and McPhail (1997, p. 114) and critical rhetoricians Ono and Sloop (1995, p. 25) remind us, marginal peoples do not always (or necessarily frequently) produce oppositional or liberatory texts. The politics of identity seem to demand that individuals be labeled or choose labels that reflect their solidarity with a particular group or set of groups. People who exist on the margins of traditionally defined identity groups, however, do not have easy choices or "natural constituencies" to reference in their quest for recognition. The tensions between group and individual identity are highlighted in these cases, where larger, more established social groups aim to classify or re-classify individuals who clearly do not seek identification with those groups. Although we cannot propose an answer to this conundrum in this paper, we suggest that this is a major issue to which scholars and activists need to respond.

Comparisons of dominant and marginal media also expose the ambivalences of acts of passing. We noted earlier how scholars have described passing as playful and subversive, as painful and tragic, or both. Dominant media accounts of these three passing events uniformly emphasize the painful and tragic dimensions of passing. Most tragic are the consequences of Brandon's and Sean's actions. Because of their alleged violations at such an intimately physical level, mainstream writers consistently excoriate their actions. The social order generally, and their girlfriends specifically, suffer tragic consequences, but so do the passers—murder and incarceration. In-group media acknowledge a broader range of outcomes from passing. Black writers lament the damage to community pride and spirit resulting from passing for White, but they also recite histories of race passing in which the passers accrue material gains by fooling Whites. Similarly, queer writers ponder the possibility that gender and sex passing will destabilize social categories. These differences between dominant and marginal accounts of passing lead us to conclude that the effects of passing and discoveries of passing can only be assessed in a radically contextual manner.

A comparison of race and sex cases of passing parallels our comparison between dominant and marginal media and reveals that, despite academic notions to the contrary, many social groups are invested in fixing racial and sexual identities and depend on discrete categorization to maintain group interests and personal security (see Sloop, 2000, pp. 167–168, 184). Dominant social groups and the state want to fix identities to police boundaries of privilege and to enforce legal standards, standards that often disadvantage individuals and groups who are identified as having non-normative identities. For marginal groups, fixing identity can illuminate institutional racism and homophobia and make it easier to articulate civil rights agendas and establish a political presence. Blacks and queers, for example, are invested in a politics of identity to rally allies and fight injustices, injustices easier to locate and define when the potential victims ascribe to a discreet, often state-recognized identity. Supporting a politics of identity may be harder if group members want to perform more fluid, ambiguous, unnamable personae.

Thus, when a person is accused of performing the "wrong" identity, it prompts commentary and action not only from the state and dominant groups who feel "duped," but also from marginal in-groups who see a need to assert their identity and re-define the passer for their own agendas. In the aftermath of discovery, passers do not seem to fit in either community. They are coerced by the state and dominant society to admit to and perform a marginalized identity that may limit their lives: for example, Susie Phipps is forced to be documented as Black, Sean O'Neill must declare his anatomy as "female" on his driver's license, and Brandon Teena was subjected to horrible, violent acts and finally murdered. Although marginal in-groups attempt to appropriate the passers to fight for the redemption of marginal identities, Phipps ultimately is accused of being a race-traitor, and Sean is virtually ignored by the queer press after surviving discovery by the dominant group. Thus, the state, marginal groups, and dominant groups all pressure the alleged passer to conform to an accepted matrix of identities. Although the in-group uses this as a tool to critique oppressive double-standards of identity, the effect is still to foreclose the options of the passer.

A notable difference between the race and sex cases emerges in respect to what lines are being crossed by the alleged passers. Specifically, exposure of Phipps's alleged pass from Black to White conjures a distinctly different constellation of correlative demographics than does exposure of Sean and Brandon's alleged pass from female to male. This difference pivots on Robinson's (1994) claim that sex passing is easier than race passing, but we extend Robinson's recognition to show how in the aftermath of discovery of the pass, class is closely correlated to race while sexual orientation is closely correlated to sex. We noted above that most media coverage of the Phipps case eliminated the possibility for her to inhabit a discrete interracial identity; instead, she was construed as either Black or White. We also noted that one of the tropes of dominant coverage of the Phipps case was the parallel drawn between race passing and economic advancement. This correlation between race and class is neither surprising nor complicated as passing has often been recognized as a means to improve one's financial (and social) lot in life. Also not surprising but more complicated (in these cases, at least) is the correlation between sex and sexual orientation.

Earlier, we acknowledged our apparent conflation of sex and sexual orientation passing. (Indeed, our choice of queer media over women's/feminist media suggests such slippage.) An important question arises from our seeming slippage: Is passing for male equivalent to passing for heterosexual? The relation between sex and sexual orientation in the cases we examine is rather complicated and worth further commentary. For the passers themselves, we cannot respond to this question definitively. In Brandon's case, we side with Hale (1998) who claims that to impose a posthumous sexual identity onto Brandon is unjust. Furthermore, all of the evidence of Brandon's thoughts about sexuality and gender identity are mediated through third parties after his death, thus making it difficult to choose a definitive descriptor. Sean, however, survived the discovery of his passing and has given some first-hand information about his feelings about his identity. Tn the interview with Minkowitz (1995), Sean contests his ex-girlfriends' assertions that they were completely unaware of his female anatomy (including non-possession of a penis), suggesting that the "dupes" knowingly engaged in sexual acts with him. This assertion destabilizes the heterosexual framing of the girls' naïveté and implicitly queers them. Sean, however, never refers to himself as a lesbian, and Minkowitz describes him as using fluid, changing language when he refers to his sexuality. Although he tells the journalist that he now dates women who "know" about his anatomy, it is not necessarily correct to label his new romantic relationships as lesbian because he refuses that label. Nor does Sean label his new female romantic partners as heterosexual. Thus, Sean retains the male persona, but does not necessarily own the label heterosexual. The label queer might seem best for him, but the ambiguity surrounding his past and present sexuality points to an equally ambiguous answer to our question: one can pass for male, date women, but not pass for heterosexual, and one can begin that pass from a position that is not female or lesbian.

The answer to this question for the dupe class, as represented by the dominant press and those ex-girlfriends who claimed ignorance of the "true" identity of the passers, is that passing as male is passing as straight because this preserves the heterosexual identity of the allegedly duped young women. Indeed, many dominant media narratives implicitly or explicitly alleged that Brandon and Sean were homosexual women passing for heterosexual males. In the coverage of Brandon, the press raises the issue of gender dysmorphia and wonders whether Brandon was a self-hating lesbian. The heavy-handedness of the framing of Sean's case as one of criminal impersonation and the inclusion of the emphatic denials of parents and girlfriends reinforces the idea that this lesbian woman fooled heterosexual girls. So to the dupes, a queer female passes for straight and male to "dupe" "real" women or girls. The in-group press is split on the question of whether passing for male is always passing as a straight person. The lone article about Sean, as described above, leaves the question open for discussion. The in-group narrative for Brandon's case is not as fluid. Because many of the articles in the queer press present Brandon as "Teena Brandon" and "she" and intimate that "she" was a lesbian in a hostile environment, there is an implication that Brandon was a queer woman passing as a straight man in order to avoid homophobia.

We conclude with a final observation drawn from examination of these cases. There appears to be a need for a critical mass or threshold of visibility for those who perform identities that cannot be easily captured by our current norms and language. That is, these cases may have both been before their time and, in the case of Brandon Teena, since galvanized identity groups into publicity. When Susie Phipps's case was tried, there were not many people claiming to be "interracial" or "biracial" in the public eye. Today, a new generation of families has launched an impressive campaign to have mixed-race children identified as such on government records. The organized presence of advocacy groups and the celebrity of individuals who choose to embrace multiple racial heritages—Tiger Woods and Mariah Carey come to mind—in the 1990s was cause for one author to re-frame Susie Phipps as an example of multiracial identity (Tilove, 1992). The higher profile of interracial celebrities, children, and families provided a set of sources and texts for reporters in the '90s that earlier writers did not have. Additionally, Susie Phipps did not want the choice of "multiracial": she wanted to be White. White identity and the problematics of racial categorization are not completely resolved by the creation of new categories, even when they officially recognize mixed-race as a category.

Likewise, long after Brandon Teena was murdered, mainstream news media sought the opinions of a non-traditional identity group, Transsexual Menace (TM), to make sense of another murder case. Although a few reporters did mention transsexual as a possible marker for Brandon Teena, the voice of the transsexual community was not present in their reports. Indeed, disappointment with the gay and lesbian media's reports on the Teena case inspired the organization of TM a group dedicated to dismantling prejudices against transsexuals (Hale, 1998, p. 313). TM and other groups now provide lite dominant press with information, experiences, and opinions concerning transsexuality. In the case of the homophobic murder of Private Barry Winchell, the *New York Times* first reported that he was dating a "female impersonator" (Clines, 1999, p. A18). In a follow-up feature in the *New York Times Magazine,* however, Winchell's partner, Calpernia Addams, was described as a pre-op transsexual, and her uneasy position between "male" and "female" was explored (France, 2000).The inclusion of interviews with members of TM in this feature story served to problematize efforts by gay and lesbian activists to identify Winchell as a gay man who was killed for having a gay lover. The result was a much more complex picture of sex and gender identity than the articles concerning Brandon Teena, and, perhaps, a model for future stories about people whose identities are difficult to capture with our slow-to-transform language of racial and sexual identity. But the availability and understanding of the identity markers "transsexual" and "multiracial" to the media does not negate the dilemma of identity choice faced by those who do not ascribe to traditional racial or gender/ sex identities. For it is not the presence of "correct" labels for each individual's "true" category that is at issue here. It is the ability of individuals to move through different identity performances and to choose their identity performances that we believe ought to be the "lessons" of these case studies.

ENDNOTES

1. Recognizing that the term "queer" is problematic, nevertheless we employ the term to refer to a broad, diverse range of non-normative sexual identities. These identities include lesbian, gay, transgender and transsexual. Here it is important to explain the way in the two cases of alleged female-to-male passing ultimately become cases about queer identity and performance. Brandon and Sean convincingly perform masculine identities before their "true," female identities are exposed. Once exposed as female, Brandon and Sean become lesbians in the commentary of most mainstream media voices, and their effort to conceal their female identity is construed to be in the service of the larger goal of concealing their "lesbian" identity.

2. Although we use the terminology of "passing" and "passers" throughout the essay, we do not endorse the traditional deployment of these terms in order to judge the legitimacy of Phipps, Teena, and O'Neill's identity claims. That is, to say that Phipps "passed" for White is to imply that she *really is* Black. Rather, we use the terms because they are employed by both scholarly and lay commentators in controversies involving race, sex, and gender identities.

3. Throughout the essay, we employ Brandon and Sean as the first names of these two individuals and refer to them with masculine pronouns in deference to their own masculine self-nomination.

4. Here, we define transgenderist as "a person who is living full-time in a new gender role, but does not intend to have surgery" (Wilson, 2000). It is also important to note here that some transgender and transsexual activists prefer the term "gender euphoria," construed as enjoyment of one's gender affiliations and performances, to the American Psychological Association's clinical designation of "gender dysphoria," or gender identity disorder.

REFERENCES

Berlant, L. (1993). National brands/national body: *Imitation of Life.* In B. Robbins (Ed.), *The phantom public sphere* (pp. 173–208). Minneapolis: University of Minnesota Press.

Bonnett, A. (1999). Constructions of whiteness in European and American anti-racism. In R. D. Torres, L. F. Miron, & J. X. Inda (Eds.), *Race, identity, and citizenship: A reader* (pp. 200–218). Oxford: Blackwell Publishers.

Carlson, A. C. (1999). "You know it when you see it:" The rhetorical hierarchy of race and gender in *Rhinelander v. Rhinelander, Quarterly Journal of Speech, 85,* 111–128.

Clines, F. X. (1999, December 9). Killer's trial shows gay soldier's anguish. *New York Times*, p. A18.

Cloud, D. L. (2001). Doing away with Suharto—And the twin myths of globalization and New Social Movements. In R. Asen & D. C. Brouwer (Eds.), *Counterpublics and the state* (pp. 235–263). Albany: State University of New York Press.

Color bind: Louisiana reforms—sort of. (1983, July 18). *Time Magazine*, p. 17.

Daniel, G. R. (2001). *More than black: Multiracial identity and the new racial order.* Philadelphia: Temple University Press.

Davis, F. (1991). *Who is black? One nation's definition.* University Park: Pennsylvania State University Press.

Debenport, E. (1984, November 13). Round two in "block blood" appeal. United Press International, Tuesday AM cycle.

Deception on the prairie. (1994, February 8). *Advocate*, pp. 16–17.

Demaret, K. (1982, December 6). Raised white, a Louisiana belle challenges race records that call her "colored." *People Magazine*, pp. 155–156.

DeMers, J. (1983, February 4). Written arguments attack racial classification law. United Press International, Friday AM cycle.

Diani, M. (1992). The concept of social movement. *The Sociological Review, 40,* 1–25.

Entman, R. M. (1993). Framing: Toward clarification of a fractured paradigm. *Journal of Communication, 43,* 51–58.

Ex-college prexy calls Louisiana's race statute unscientific and biased. (1982, December 20). *Jet Magazine*, 23.

Favor, J. M. (1999). *Authentic blackness; The folk in the New Negro Renaissance.* Durham, NC: Duke University Press.

Flores, L. A., & McPhail, M. L. (1997). From black and white to *Living Color.* A dialogic exposition into the social (re)construction of race, gender, and crime. *Critical Studies in Mass Communication, 14,* 106–122.

Foster, D. (1994a, November 5). Girl, 15, finds "boyfriend" is a woman, *Rocky Mountain News*, p. 8A.

Foster, D. (1994b, December 24). Woman, accused of playing boyfriend to girls, to stand trial. *Rocky Mountain News*, p. 12A.

France, D. (2000, May 28). An inconvenient woman. *The New York Times Magazine*, 24–29.

Gabler, N. (1998). *Life the movie: How entertainment conquered reality.* New York: Knopf.

Gilliam, D. (1982, October 2). Black/white. *Washington Post*, p. B1.

Ginsberg, E. K. (1996). Introduction: The politics of passing. In E. K. Ginsberg (Ed.), *Passing and the fictions of identity* (pp. 1–18). Durham, NC: Duke University Press.

Gitlin, T. (1993). The rise of "identity politics"; An examination and a critique. *Dissent, 40,* 172–177.

Gitlin, T. (1995). *Twilight of common dreams.* New York: Henry Holt.

Halberstam, J. (1998). Transgender butch: Butch/FTM; Border wars and the masculine continuum. *GLQ 4,* 287–310.

Hale, C. J. (1998). Consuming the living, dis(re)membering the dead in the butch/FTM border lands. *GLQ 4,* 311–348.

Hasian, M. A., & Nakayama, T. K. (1998). The fictions or racialized identities. In J. M. & J. P. McDaniel (Eds.). *Judgment calls; Rhetoric, politics, and indeterminacy* (pp. 182–195). Boulder, CO: Westview Press.

Helvie, S. (1997). Willa Cather and Brandon Teena: The politics of passing. *Women and Language, 20,* 35–40.

Herron, C. R., Wright, M., &. Douglas, C. C. (1983, June 26). Louisiana drops racial fractions. *New York Times*, p. D4.

Hills, R. J. (1983, May 18). State's 1/32nd "Negro blood" law valid. United Press International, Wednesday AM Cycle.

Horton, M. (1994). Blackness, betrayal, and childhood: Race and identity in Nella Larsen's *Passing, CLA Journal, 39,* 31–45.

Hurtado, A. (1999). The trickster's play: Whiteness in the subordination and liberation process. In R. D. Torres, L. F. Miron, & J. X. Inda (Eds.), *Race, identity, and citizenship: A reader* (pp. 225–243). Oxford: Blackwell Publishers.

Jaynes, G. (1982, September 30). Suit on race recalls lines drawn under slavery. *New York Times*, p. B16.

Konigsberg, E. (1995, January). Death of a deceiver: Teena Renee Brandon. *Playboy*, 192–199.

LA repeals mathematical black blood classification. (1983, July 25). *Jet Magazine*, 42.

LA woman seeking repeal of "black blood" loses case. (1983, June 6). *Jet Magazine*, 5.

A little local color. (1982, September 19). *New York Times*, p. E19.

Louisiana court upholds race on birth certificates. (1986 January 13). *Jet Magazine*, 5

Louisiana woman losing her bid to be categorized as white. (1987, January 12). *Jet Magazine*, 66.

Lule, J. (1995). The rape of Mike Tyson: Race, the press and symbolic types. *Critical Studies in Mass Communications, 12,* 176–195.

Marcus, F. (1983, July 6). Louisiana repeals black blood law. *New York Times*, p. A10.

Melucci, A. (1985). The symbolic challenge of contemporary movements. *Social Research, 52*, 789–816.

Messina v. Clercio, 290 So. 2d 339 (4ᵗʰ Cir. La. Ct. App. 1974).

Minkowitz, D. (1994, April 19). Love hurts: Brandon Teena was a woman who lived and loved as a man; she was killed for carrying it off. *Village Voice*, pp. 24–30.

Minkowitz, D. (1995, October). On Trial: Gay? Straight? Boy? Girl? Sex? Rape? In the heart of Christian America, the case of a teen Don Juan(a) raises explosive questions. *Out Magazine*, 99–101; 140–146.

Moon, D. G. (2000). Interclass travel, cultural adaptation, and "passing" as a disjunctive inter/cultural practice. In M. J. Collier (Ed.), *International and Intercultural Communication Annual, 23*, 215–240.

Nakayama, T. K. (1994). Show/down time: "Race," gender, sexuality, and popular culture. *Critical Studies in Mass Communication, 11*, 162–179.

Nakayama, T. K., & Krizek, R. L. (1995). Whiteness: A strategic rhetoric. *Quarterly Journal of Speech, 81*, 291–309.

Ono, K. A., & Sloop, J. M. (1995). The critique of vernacular discourse. *Communication Monographs, 62*, 19–46.

Parisi, P. (1998). The *New York Times* looks at one block in Harlem: Narratives of race in journalism. *Critical Studies in Mass Communication, 15*, 236–254.

Peer, L., & Etterna, J. S. (1998). The mayor's race: Campaign coverage and the discourse of race in America's three largest cities. *Critical Studies in Mass Communication, 15*, 255–278.

Plea deal made in sex assaults. (1995, November 29). *Denver Post*, p. B4.

Ramsey, P. (1976). A study in "passing" novels of the nineteenth and early twentieth centuries. *Studies in Black Literature, 7*, 1–8.

Ricks, I. (1994, March 8). Heartland homicide. *Advocate*, 28–30.

Robinson, A. (1994). It takes one to know one: Passing and communities of common interest. *Critical Inquiry, 20*, 715–736.

Root, M. P. (Ed). (1996). *The multiracial experience: Racial borders as the new frontier.* Thousand Oaks, CA: Sage.

Schlangenstein, M. (1983, May 20). Appeal filed on blood law. United Press International, AM cycle.

Sheehy, J. (1999). The mirror and the veil: The passing novel and the quest for American racial identity. *African American Review, 33*, 401–415.

Sloop, J. M. (2000). Disciplining the transgendered: Brandon Teena, public representation, and normativity. *Western Journal of Communication, 64*, 165–189.

Smart-Grosvenor, V. (1983, June). Obsessed with "racial purity." *Ms.*, 28–30.

Spradlin, A. L. (1998). The price of "passing": A lesbian perspective on authenticity in organizations. *Management Communication Quarterly, 11*, 598–605.

Tilove, J. (1992, April 26). Racial identity in U.S. is mix of politics, fashion, and genetics, *Houston Chronicle*, p. A8.

Trillin, C. (1986, April 14). American chronicles: Black or white. *The New Yorker*, 62–78.

Triple murder has unusual twist. (1994, January 4). *Chicago Tribune*, p. 4.

Tyler, C.-A. (1994). Passing: Narcissism, identity, and difference. *Differences, 6*, 212–248.

Violence news: Nebraska. (1994, February), *off our backs*, 5.

Wald, G. (2000). *Crossing the line: Racial passing in twentieth-century U.S. literature and culture.* Durham, NC: Duke University Press.

What makes you black? (1983, January). *Ebony*, 115–118.

Wheelwright, J. (1996, February 20). The boyfriend. *The Guardian*, p. T6–7.

Wiegman, R. (1995). *American anatomies: Theorizing race and gender,* Durham, NC: Duke University Press.

Wilchins, R. (1997, April 30). On publishing: Out of the binary zoo. *Lambda Book Report*, p. 17.

Wilson, D. (2000). *Some transgender definitions.* Retrieved November 11, 2000. Available: http://www.firelily.com/gender/resources/defs.html.

Woman resumes fight over race on birth certificate. (1984, December 10). *Jet Magazine*, 39.

Worthington, R. (1994, January 17). Deadly deception: Teena Brandon's double life may have led to a triple murder. *Chicago Tribune*, pp. 1, 5 (Tempo section).

Voicing Your Opinion
In/Discernible Bodies: The Politics of Passing in Dominant and Marginal Media
Catherine R. Squires and Daniel C. Brouwer

1. How do the binary categories of sex/gender, man/masculine, and woman/feminine influence your understanding of the terms *passing* and *dupe?* Would or could these terms exist if we did not use labels to identify race, gender, and sexuality?

   _____

   _____

   _____

   _____

   _____

2. How might the general public obtain more information about issues pertaining to gender? Is there a risk in relying on popular press for information? Can you identify any problems in the ways that dominant and nondominant print media write about gender?

   _____

   _____

   _____

   _____

   _____

3. Respond to the following terms/phrases that are presented in the article: *homophobia, queer, marginal peoples, politics of identity.* In what other context have you encountered these terms/phrases? What is your personal definition of these terms/phrases? Would you expect to see these terms used in dominant media sources? Why or why not?

   _____

   _____

   _____

   _____

   _____

Conduct an Interview...

Instructions

Extend your understanding of gender in social systems by interviewing someone about a topic that pertains to gendered communication within educational settings, the workplace, or the media. Interview someone about a specific topic from one of these areas and then write a summary and analysis of that interview.

Choosing a Topic

Select a topic that pertains to broader topics covered in Part Five, *The Process of Understanding Gendered Social Systems.* You might want to review the articles in this section and/or your class notes to find a topic that interests you.

Guidelines for the Interview

Choose someone to interview. This should be a person who is an informed participant in the topic that you have chosen. Examples: a person who administers the sexual harassment policy at your university, a woman in a non-traditionally female job, a man in a non-traditionally male job, a teacher at a pre-school, a reporter or editor of your school newspaper. It is important that you choose someone who will be able to provide you with valuable information *about your topic.*

Set up the interview. You will need to spend between a half-hour and hour interviewing this person. Set up the time and location for the interview and be responsible about fulfilling this obligation. Make sure that you explain the purpose of the assignment to the interviewee and describe the *topic* that you are exploring.

Write your interview questions. Prepare ten questions to ask at the interview. These should be open-ended questions that allow your interviewee to respond with more than "yes" and "no" responses. You should anticipate that your interview might get off track from the structured questions; however, you should be *prepared* to ask all ten questions.

Conduct the interview. Be professional and prepared. Take close notes and be open to learning from this person. Listen carefully! You must ask for the interviewee's permission to audio or video tape the interview.

Writing about the Interview

1. An introduction that previews and explains your chosen topic.
2. A description of the interview that includes:
   - ✓ the date and time and place of the interview.
   - ✓ a short description of the interviewee. Include the reasons for choosing this person to interview.
   - ✓ a summary of the responses to the questions. This section of the paper may include verbatim statements or general descriptions of responses. You should provide a clear explanation of the content of the interview.
3. An analysis of the interview. Here you offer a thorough discussion of the *topic* of the paper. Think carefully and critically about what you have learned about your topic. Do not just *describe* what you have discovered; rather *evaluate* it for its impact on society. You should incorporate ideas from the interview with scholarly sources as well as your opinion.
4. A conclusion that summarizes your main points and offers concluding thoughts on the topic.

Suggestions

Be proactive about setting up your interview. Don't wait until the last minute!

Ask creative and engaging questions.

Be flexible and open to learning about your topic from the interviewee. Listen more than you talk.

6 The Process of Critiquing Gender

Important Things to Consider

We end our discussion of gender and communication by encouraging you to formulate and use a critical perspective when you study the topic of gender. In this section we introduce you to several social movements that pertain to the topic of gender fairness and equality. These movements are driven by men's and women's desires to redefine gendered expectations and maintain and/or establish gender equity.

The women's movement is a complex social movement that seeks to establish and maintain equitable laws, attitudes, policies, and human practices in regards to women. Members of this movement in the United States have argued for women's rights regarding voting, education, reproduction, workplace issues, sexual harassment, violence, and health (just to name a few!). It is sometimes called the women's rights movement or the feminist movement.

A few of the most significant events in the women's movement include the ratification of the Nineteenth Amendment to the U.S. Constitution that ensured that women would not be denied the right to vote; the right to receive minimum wage; the right to sit on a jury; the Civil Rights Act that included "sex" in its antidiscrimination language; and the passage of Title IX, which eliminates gender discrimination in educational settings.

The men's movement is relatively new in comparison to the women's movement. Members of this movement pursue equality for men in regard to parenting, divorce laws, wage and hiring practices, sexual harassment, and domestic violence. Another important goal of this movement is to develop and encourage productive and healthy definitions of *masculinity* and *manhood.* In keeping with this goal, members of a variety of men's organizations establish and support programs that encourage men to be strong family members and community leaders.

We have included three articles in this section. They will introduce you to both the women's movement and the men's movement, as well as expose you to the inherent conflicts embedded in gender activism.

Terms
Promise Keepers
Men's movements
Gender roles
Evangelical
Faith

GODLY MANHOOD GOING WILD?
Transformations in Conservative Protestant Masculinity

SALLY K. GALLAGHER AND SABRINA L. WOOD

This article is about a text, *Wild at Heart,* by John Eldredge, which sets up an idea of masculinity as essentially "heroic, slightly dangerous, alive and free." *Wild at Heart* is in direct contrast to the ideology of the Promise Keepers, a popular Christian men's organization. The authors asked men and women in conservative Protestant churches to read the book and provide them with feedback. Gender and age played a significant role in how people responded to the text.

This article assesses shifting ideals of masculinity among conservative Protestants focused on the current best seller, Wild at Heart, *by John Eldredge (2001). First, we compare Eldredge's notion of manhood as essentially "heroic, slightly dangerous, alive and free" with the ideals of responsible manhood central to much Promise Keepers literature. Second, we explore the salience of this shift for men's relationships with each other, their wives and female friends. Analysis of interview data with a sample of married men and women in two churches and one para-church campus ministry highlight the active and selective reading of religious texts across gender and age. Overall, Eldredge's "slightly dangerous" masculinity represents a re-articulation of the nineteenth century myth of the "self-made man" and is both a reaction against the rationalized nature of paid employment, as well as the responsible and "feminized" expectations of Promise Keepers' ideal of servant leadership and involved fatherhood.*

This article presents an analysis of shifting ideals of masculinity among conservative Protestants after the "demise" of the Promise Keepers. For over a decade, Promise Keepers ethos of responsible manhood dominated conservative Protestant rhetoric on manhood, fatherhood, and marriage. The "seven promises" of a Promise Keeper set the standard for evangelical men in terms of vibrant, expressive faith in Jesus Christ; commitment to the local church and its leadership; moral and sexual purity; unity across race and ethnicity; building strong marriages through "love, protection and biblical values"; and being held accountable for all of these through investing in relationships with a small group of like minded men (McCartney 1994). Yet from a high over a million attendees at twenty-two stadium conferences in 1996, the organization has struggled financially, reduced its focus on large conferences (450,000 attending in 1998 and less than half that number in 2003), and faded from the national visibility it held in the mid-1990s.

The question this article addresses, then, has to do with shifting interpretations of gender ideals within conservative Protestantism—most specifically, the vision of responsible manhood after the reorganization of the Promise Keepers. During the 1970s and 1980s evangelical gender debates focused on the implications of individualism and women's employment for notions of godly womanhood (Clark 1980; Cooper 1974; Elliot 1976; Getz 1977; Hurley 1981; Piper and Grudem 1991), and the case evangelical feminists had begun to make for mutual submission in marriage and women's ordination (Bilezikian 1985; Bristow

1988; Gallagher 2004a; Gundry 1980; Mickelsen 1986; Mollenkott 1977; Scanzoni and Hardesty 1974; Van Leeuwen 1990). By the late 1980s the focus had shifted away from increasingly refined theological debates to a wide range of practical advice intended to help evangelical couples balance and maintain a symbolic commitment to husbands' headship with the pragmatic egalitarianism that characterized the majority of evangelical households (Bartkowski 2001; Gallagher 2003, 2004b). Nearly all of this advice literature was addressed to women. That changed, however, in the early 1990s when men, masculinity and fatherhood appeared on the scene as the new focus of evangelical efforts to reinforce and strengthen "family values." Promise Keepers embodied this latter development (Bartkowski 2004; Mathisen 2001). As Promise Keepers developed into the dominant evangelical men's movement of the late twentieth century, evangelical publishers began to expand their marriage and parenting listings to include a growing number of books on how men also might more responsibly balance paid work and family, communicate better, be more involved at home, and more accountable to each other (McCartney 1997; Smalley & Trent 1992; Weber 1993, 1997).

In 2001, however, a book appeared that countered much of this emerging subcultural consensus about responsible manhood with the notion that masculinity is in essence "wild, dangerous, unfettered and free" (Eldredge 2001:12). The book was *Wild at Heart: Discovering the Secret of a Man's Soul,* by self-employed therapist, outdoorsman, former Focus on the Family employee, and father of three (boys), John Eldredge. It was an immediate success. The year after its publication, it sold over 200,000 copies and was the fourth best selling Christian book in the nation (Christian Booksellers Association 2004).

In the analysis that follows, we explore the symbolic and practical salience of the message of *Wild at heart* for evangelical notions of godly masculinity. We begin by systematically contrasting Eldredge's notion of godly manhood as essentially "heroic, slightly dangerous, alive and free" with the ideals of responsible manhood central to much of the Promise Keepers literature of the 1990s. Second, based on interviews with a cross section of conservative Protestant men and women, we explore the personal and practical salience of this shift in norms of masculinity for identity and men's relationships with each other, their wives and female friends. Data for this section of the analysis come from three sets of interviews with a sample of married men and women in two churches and with young adult men and women involved in a para-church evangelical campus ministry. Based on these interviews, we assess the degree to which Eldredge's "slightly dangerous" masculinity represents a re-articulation of the nineteenth century myth of the "self-made man" (Kimmel 1996; Rotundo 1994), and is both a reaction against the rationalized nature of paid employment (Schwalbe 1996), as well as the responsible and "feminized" expectations of Promise Keepers' ideal of servant leadership and involved fatherhood. As we will argue, ordinary evangelicals employ a flexible hermeneutic in interpreting popular texts, in the same way that they employ a range of hermeneutical approaches in interpreting biblical texts on family and gender (Bartkowski 1996, 2004; Gallagher 2003).

Contrasting Ideals for Godly Manhood

Although early research on Promise Keepers described the movement as an anti-feminist backlash intended to restore men to their rightful place as benign patriarchs within the family (Hackstaff 1999; Hardisty 1999; Messner 1997; Messner & Anderson 1998), a growing body of literature has begun to explore the poly-vocal and multi-dimensional ideals of masculinity articulated by movement leaders and participants (Bartkowski 2001, 2004; Lockhart 2000). Although less institutionally robust than in the 1990s, Promise Keepers rhetoric continues to frame men's expressiveness and nurturing as an extension of masculine leadership and authority within the household.

Bartkowski's (2001, 2004) analyses of this literature demonstrates the breadth of gender perspectives within the organisation. In addition to the Rational Patriarch model advocated in evangelical men's literature in the 1970s and 1980s (e.g. Christenson 1970; Cole 1982; Elliot 1981; Farrar 1990), Bartkowski identifies strands of PK literature in the 1990s—the expressive egalitarian; the tender warrior; and "multicultural man." Writing by Gary Oliver, *Real men have feelings, too* (1993), and Gary Smalley and John Trent's, *The hidden value of a man* (1992) typifies the first of these styles—the "expressive egalitarian." In these works, evangelical men are urged to communicate better with their wives, cultivate emotional vulnerability, and connect themselves to both their children and other men.

A second iteration of godly manhood Bartkowski identifies within PK literature is the "multicultural man" that draws on PK concerns with "racial reconciliation." PK authors recognize that historical and economic factors have played a role in creating and sustaining inequality, yet present the problem of racism as fundamentally one of personal sin. As a result, they argue that racial reconciliation is only possible through forgiveness and connection between individuals (Cooper 1995; Porter 1996; Washington and Kehrein 1997). (See Bartkowski (2004) and Allen (2000) for a more thorough analysis of this theme).

The third iteration of masculinity within PK literature is typified by the popular writings of Stu Weber (1993, 1997, 1998), in which he presents the case that authentic masculinity is characterized by four pillars: king, warrior, mentor and friend. At the center of godly masculinity is the responsibility to provide, protect, teach and love (1993:40–43). Like gender conservative evangelicals of an earlier generation Weber argues that these characteristics have been hard-wired into humanity by God, in dimorphic gender differences that mirror eternal spiritual realities and the very character of God. For Weber, "the core of masculinity is initiation—the provision of direction, security, stability and connection (1993:45)." It is also responsibility, particularly when marriage and fatherhood are involved.

> Husband. The noun form of husband means "manager." A husband is a "steward." A caretaker. The man responsible. In its verb form the term means "to direct, to manage." Those are strong terms that imply effective leadership. In a word, husbanding is responsibility. To be a husband is to be responsible (1993:88).

This image of responsible manhood expresses itself not only in protecting and directing family life, but also in loving "sacrificial" leadership, without domination.

> Manly love. Men must develop a thorough, biblical, manly love. Now what is that? In a word—*headship.* It is leadership with an emphasis upon responsibility, duty, and sacrifice. Not rank or domination (97).

While clearly nor advocating the egalitarian possibilities hinted at in the literature by "expressive egalitarians," Weber's pastoral concern for the struggles of dual career couples lends itself to a pragmatic masculinity that supports a modicum of flexibility in "roles" at home, as well as committed relationships with other men, while preserving notions of men's ultimate authority.

Alternatives to Responsible Manhood: Wildness and Following Your Heart

Every few years, a book appears that becomes "mandatory reading" within evangelical subculture. Unlike perennial favorites such as Dobson's works on parenting, these books create and are accompanied by a flash flood of marketing, videos, study guides, special editions, gift bindings, and seminars. Recent examples include *The prayer of Jabez* (Wilkenson 1999), *The purpose driven life* (Warren 2002), and the fictional *Left behind* series (LaHaye and Jenkins 1996). John Eldredge's *Wild at heart* is such a book. Since its publication in 2001 it has ranked in the top four best selling Christian books overall by the Evangelical Christian Publishers Association.[1] It was a finalist for the ECPA Book of the Year award in 2003, and winner of the ECPA Gold Medallion in Inspirational Books in 2003.

Given this enormous popularity, what is it about *Wild at heart* that has so captured the evangelical imagination? What model of godly manhood does Eldredge present, and how does it compare to the responsible and connected masculinity of much PK literature?

CONTRASTING *WAH* & PK IDEALS FOR MEN Compared to most PK literature, *Wild at heart* offers less connected masculinity, one directed by the passions of the heart rather than duty responsibility or accountability.[2] In fact, Eldredge offers his book as a counter point, if not antithesis, to Promise Keepers' ideas of connected and responsible masculinity.

> Do we really need another book for men? No. . . . We need permission. To be what we are—men made in God's image. Permission to live from the heart and not from the list of "should" and "ought to" that has left so many of us tired and bored. . . . So I offer this book, not as the seven steps to being a better Christian, but as a safari of the heart to recover a life of freedom, passion and adventure (xi–xii).

While never directly criticizing the Promise Keepers movement or its leaders, Eldredge's emphasis is clearly on the personal struggle of men to free themselves from feelings of inadequacy and move "westward into the wilderness" in their relationship with God, rather than their need to be responsible providers and leaders at church and at home. In one brief paragraph he supports the notion that men need each other, yet goes on to argue . . .

> Thanks to the men's movement the church understands now that a man needs other men, but what we've offered is another two-dimensional solution: "Accountability" groups or partners. Ugh. That sounds so old covenant: 'you're really a fool and you're just waiting to rush into sin, so we'd better post a guard by you to keep you in line.' We don't need accountability groups; we need fellow warriors, someone to fight alongside, someone to watch our back (175).

Like Weber, the book draws heavily on warrior metaphors. But whereas Weber argues that a godly man is a "tender warrior" who draws his strength from a community of men who are emotionally intimate and committed to "holding each other accountable," Eldredge downplays accountability in favor of men supporting each other in taking individual risks. He exaggerates Weber's "tender warrior" motif—bypassing initiation in favor of aggression as "part of the masculine *design* . . . (10)," arguing that "a man is a dangerous thing . . ." (82), whose "strength is wild and fierce (149)," who above all takes risks (202–03). For Eldredge, this iteration of masculinity is like God who also takes risks (in creation), and Jesus who was "fierce and wild and romantic to the core" (203).

Eldredge's vision of godly manhood is defined as much by what it is not as for what it is. The soul of a man is made for adventure (205). It is most emphatically not domestic. It thrives when it is embattled (141). For Eldredge, every man longs for " a great mission to his life that involves and yet transcends even home and family (141)." Finding that mission involves paying careful attention to one's own desires.

Following this adventure leads a man outside the household, into the wilderness. Men should "pay attention to our desire . . . to head into the wilderness" (207), because "the core of a man's heart is undomesticated *and that is good*" (4). Eldredge explains men's "wildness" by appealing to a detail in the Genesis creation account in which man is created *outside* the garden and brought in; while the woman is created *inside*. From this, he infers the basis of men's and women's essentially different natures—one uncultivated and "wild," the other domesticated. (One might as plausibly argue that the text demonstrates how Adam was incomplete until he was brought into the garden—that essential manhood is one that isn't finished until it is applied to the cultivation and nurture of growing things—but this is not the point Eldredge draws from the text.) Here, in the very beginning, lie the roots of male wildness, male aggression, and male desire for wilderness in which to roam free. Repeatedly posing Mr. Rogers and Braveheart as competing alternatives for manhood, Eldredge comes down firmly on the position that above all, godly men are not "nice."

> The whole crisis in masculinity today has come because we no longer have a warrior culture, a place for men to learn to fight like men. We don't need a meeting of Really Nice Guys; we need a gathering of Really Dangerous Men (175).

Eldredge pushes the metaphor further, writing specifically against anything associated with gentleness, meekness, humility or tenderness. The godly man "takes risks (202–03), "has a vision" (142), is "cunning" and "knows how to fight" both spiritual enemies (143), and for the heart of a woman (15). This latter theme, "the beauty to fight for" runs throughout the book. Every man "wants to be the hero to the beauty . . . he needs someone to fight *for* (15)." What prevents this heroism is the wounds men receive from fathers who undermine the very qualities that lie the center of authentic masculinity. Describing his own struggle to develop emotional intimacy with his wife, Eldredge writes, "Will you fight for her? That's the question Jesus asked me many years ago (192)."

Finally, Eldredge's message is tempered by occasional qualifications—godly manhood is "wild" but not irresponsible; it is "free" but not a solo enterprise; it is "slightly dangerous" but "the warrior is in this for good" (193). Echoing a theme that is central to PK accountability groups, Eldredge writes:

> Don't even think about going into battle alone. Don't even try to take the masculine journey without at least one man by your side. Yes, there are time a man must face the battle alone, in the wee hours of the morn, and fight with all he's got. But don't make that a lifestyle of isolation (174).

Yet against scattered statements encouraging community and cooperation stand illustration upon illustration of the solo hero battling unimaginable odds and stories of intensive counseling of individuals he has helped. These examples weigh clearly against the notion of men needing other groups of men—a theme that is central to much PK literature—or men being responsible, even submitting themselves, to the authority of a pastor or other spiritual leader. Rather than drawing their strength from an institution or community, Eldredge's godly man is more likely to struggle within and against the stultifying effects of established institutions.

Eldredge also hedges against the criticism that advocating male wildness promotes selfishness or irresponsibility.

> I'm not suggesting that the Christian life is chaotic or that a real man is flagrantly irresponsible. . . . What I am saying is that our false self demands a formula before he'll engage; he wants guarantee of success, and mister, you aren't going to get one. There comes a time in a man's life when he's got to break away from all that and head off into the unknown with God (213).

The "false self" that Eldredge alludes to here, is the self who is afraid to risk—the wounded self of the mythopoetic men's movement in which men are encouraged to find their true masculine hearts through retreat, workshops, and recognition of their inner warrior and wildman. (Kimmel 1996; Messner 1997; Schwalbe 1996). Sounding much like an evangelical version of Robert Bly, Eldredge argues that godly manhood takes risks and heads off "into the unknown with God." Authentic men are willing to take professional risks, as evidenced by Eldredge's account of leaving the security of Focus on the Family Ministries and became a freelance author and therapist. Nowhere does he provide any discussion of the risks of male wildness for women who live with truly dangerous men whose pursuit of their passions harms both wives and children (for a discussion of domestic violence in evangelical families see Nason-Clark and Kroeger 2004). Instead, wildness is understood as means to more authentic career choices and richer family life as men resist stagnation and are encouraged to engage in the dangerous business of living "free" in a rationalized world. Against the seven promises of a Promise Keeper, Eldredge writes:

> This is not a book about the seven things a man ought to do to be a nicer guy. It is a book about the recovery and release of a man's heart, his passions, his true nature, which he has been given by God. . . . If you are going to know who you truly are as a man, if you are going to find a life worth living, if you are going to love a woman deeply and not pass on your confusion to your children, you simply must get your heart back. You must head up into the high country of the soul, into wild and uncharted regions and track down that elusive prey (18).

Authority and Evidence in *Wild at Heart*

Although evangelicals and other conservative Protestants are often characterized as biblical literalists, much evangelical advice literature appeals as frequently to personal experience and popular culture as to the Bible. *Wild at heart* typifies this approach. Coding and counting these themes through the book shows nearly identical proportions of the text devoted to these three types of evidence—personal/autobiographical anecdotes, popular culture and the Bible. In emphasizing the "self evident" and "obvious" nature of his case and in drawing on personal experience as much as the Bible, *Wild at Heart* is a quintessentially evangelical text (Noll 1994). The heros in "Braveheart," "Saving Private Ryan" and "The Legends of the Fall" figure as dominantly as Moses, David and Jesus in his analysis. Perhaps most important is his use of material from Robert Bly's *Iron man,* whose work is highlighted nearly a dozen times in the book, and is clearly a key source for Eldredge's imaginative vision. Here in particular, *Wild at Heart* stands opposite that of PK author Stu Weber who mentions Bly, but writes scathingly about the mythopoetic men's movement, calling it self-indulgent and shallow, and contrasting its vision of self-involved masculinity to his challenge to evangelical men to prioritize wives and children above self and career (Weber 1993).

Interpreting *Wild at Heart*

Given the emphasis on responsible providing and involved fatherhood that is central to so much PK advice literature for men, and given the anti-promise keepers themes implicit within Eldredge's *Wild at heart*, what can we say about shifting ideals of masculinity among evangelical Protestants? How do ordinary readers interpret and apply the styles of masculinity advocated by this literature? To what extent are the readings of *Wild at heart* gendered—that is, do men and women read it in different ways? And how do age and marital status affect the personal meanings ordinary evangelicals draw from the book?

Research Methods

To answer these questions, we talked with a cross section of self-identified evangelical men and women, asking them what they thought about the book and how they saw themselves applying it in their own lives. More specifically, we interviewed a sample of married husbands and wives in two local congregations (a Presbyterian (PCUSA) and an Assemblies of God). We also talked with young adult men and women involved in an evangelical campus ministry.

The two sets of church-going men that we interviewed had studied the book together. At one church it was used as teaching material for a large Sunday school class of sixty to eighty men; in the other as the basis for discussion in an early morning men's Bible study of twelve to fifteen men. The men in the para-church fellowship did not read the book as part of a formal study group; rather the book was recommended and discussed informally among friends.

Because the early morning church bible study group had been meeting for years, and because the men and women in the para-church ministry frequently met for informal discussion we did group interviews with these three sets of respondents (interviewing men and women separately was a methodological decision that turned out to be strategically important in given the divergent responses that appeared across gender and age). Coordinating group meetings with the men who studied the book for Sunday school but were no longer meeting, and coordinating meetings with the wives of both groups of church-going men proved to be quite difficult. After multiple failed attempts, we interviewed the sample of men from the second church and the wives from both churches individually over the telephone.[3]

Among the married women in the local churches, only one had read the entire book. The remainder knew their husbands were reading it and a handful had discussed it with their husbands. None had been motivated to take time to read it themselves. Within the campus fellowship, the men who read the book were so passionate about its message that some of their female friends decided to read it themselves. As we describe below their reaction was passionate too, but of a different sort. The book spurred numerous heated debates about gender within the fellowship and led to a rethinking of both relationships and approaches to ministry on campus. In all, twenty men and nineteen women participated in these discussions (see Table 1 for sample description[4]). All interviews were recorded with permission and fully transcribed for analysis.

Multiple Meanings, Gender and Age

Two primary domains distinguished the meanings appropriated from reading *Wild at heart*—gender and age. Interpretations differed between younger and older men; and for women and men regardless of age.

Para-Church University Men

The men associated with the para-church ministry were unanimously positive in their overall reactions to the book. Ideas about men's "instinctive need" for adventure and women's need to be viewed as a "beauty to be rescued" echoed what most of them hoped or already thought were true about gender difference. As one young man explained

> [The book] made more sense than anything I ever read before, and it feels beneficial. I can be who I am . . . and chat should be beneficial to the women I'm around. . . . Men need to have a battle to fight, a beauty to rescue, adventure . . . What a women needs is for me to be alive and free and full of life. To be active and not passive. Any woman wants that, over me just checking out and not being there.

Table 1 Sample Characteristics

	Presbyterian	Pentecostal	Para-Church Organization	Total #
men n =	n = 9	n = 6	n = 5	20
x̄ age	58	52	23.2	
Women	n = 8	n = 6	n = 5	19
x̄ age	46	50	21.8	
% married	94	100	0	
% professional	80	80	—	
% Euro-American	100	100	80	
TOTAL #	17	12	10	39

Eldredge's imagery of men being made for risk and adventure was particularly salient. One young man said "I realized internally in my soul there were parts of me that were dying because everyone was communicating to me to be safe." Others argued that "men need to be 'slightly dangerous'" and to "stand up and not be afraid to show how much you care." For those in dating relationships and those hoping for relationships, images of masculine leadership and initiative rang true. They resonated with metaphors encouraging men to risk moving relationships forward to new levels of intimacy and commitment. As one of the men explained

> The point I came to was if I am dating her and I want to marry her, what is to honoring her? I am not just having fun, I am going to show that I am serious by going there and pursuing the "beauty." That's helped. Now she sees that I care and that I am serious.

This encouragement to "make a move" worked across levels of dating relationships—so that young men who were approaching decisions about marriage, as well as those just contemplating asking a woman out on a date heard a similar message—theirs was the responsibility to take the initiative and risk the danger of rejection and failure in their relationships with women. The rationale for this was the underlying belief that "women want to marry a man who has life and excitement—a purpose—not just someone who is a "yes" man." The notion that "what women want is a man who sees life as an adventure" was the kind of motivation some men needed to "take the risk" of a more personal relationship. When women protested this notion, arguing (as those in the fellowship had) that they would prefer to be partners in a joint adventure rather than join in one that is really "his" one of the men dismissed the objection as false consciousness and self-delusion.

> *All* the women I know, women who are strong women, who two years ago would never have expressed a desire to be beautiful or pursued, now they realize that's what they want. . . . there's a realization that it's actually true. All the women I know who are more mature will say. . . deep down, they want to be "the beauty" and be pursued. That's a fundamental difference between male desires and female desires. I think its what they really want, but they don't realize its what they want. They say they want someone who is safe originally, but down the road . . .

So compelling was the image of the beauty to be rescued that the same men who acknowledged "there's a range among women . . ." and argued that taking risk and adventure "aren't gender specific at all—he calls both men and women out," were nevertheless supportive of the notion that deep down, even if they don't realize it, what women really want is to beautiful and pursued.

Minimally critical of the book's gender messages, the men in the fellowship were much more concerned about the narrowness of Eldredge's vision across race and class. The theme of racial reconciliation (a major emphasis within Promise Keepers) had been a focus of the fellowship during the past year, and echoed in their comments on the "whiteness" of *Wild at heart.* They described how most of the book applied only to men who, like themselves and like Eldredge, were educated, white and relatively privileged. One who had grown up in a large urban area summarized this discussion by saying:

> I felt that he was writing to white men who live in the suburbs. Like where he tells the kid to punch the bully back. If you did that at my high school a kid might come at you with a baseball bat.

Most of Eldredge's metaphors for wild, adventurous, and even free masculinity seemed applicable only to the lives of privileged men. Adventuring in the West, counseling sessions with a family therapist, white water rafting and kayaking all seemed useful and exciting, but were hard to imagine as ordinary experiences for men across race and class. None of them, however, interpreted the inapplicability of much of the book to most men as a challenge to its basic premise—that men, by design, are slightly dangerous, alive and free.

Para-Church University Women

The women involved in the campus fellowship had quite a different reaction and set of perspectives on the book. If it made the young men cheer, it made the women cry. Literally. It made them cry; it made them angry. In short, they hated it.

Why this extraordinary difference? Like the men in the fellowship, the women also read *Wild at heart* as confirmation of gender stereotypes. Yet while this was good news for the men, it was acutely bad news for the women—especially the notion chat "everyone has to look like this."

> If everything in this book is "essential manhood" then I don't know what *I* am. . . . I don't have that much different an experience with my father [than he does with his]. I like to walk around outside, I like to get muddy, I like to get dirty, whatever. . . . in my world that doesn't make someone essentially a man or a woman.

The fellowship women found it initially problematic that Eldredge would presume to make such absolutist claims about a woman's essential nature and deepest needs. While not denying that being beautiful or desirable is important, they felt Eldredge exaggerated these characteristics. Women want to be beautiful as persons and partners, not passive beauties waiting to be rescued.

> When he talks about women's deepest desire as wanting to be considered beautiful after, I think that is two desires I have . . . but I think that my deepest desire is to have partnership and have someone to come along side and consider me an equal.

The women also voiced concern that Eldredge's model of femininity was simply an inversion of idealized masculinity, "as though for masculinity to increase, femininity must decrease, like a woman isn't whole." Although he does acknowledge variety among women and men (38), the overall message of the book was that masculinity is inherently strong, adventurous, risk taking and brave. Femininity, by association, seemed emptied of the possibility of those virtues.

> I get really mad when I hear femininity being described as the opposite of masculinity. It isn't. He builds this whole argument about what masculinity is, and femininity is the opposite. That's just not true.

The characteristics Eldredge argues are the essence of masculinity were some of the same characteristics women said they both saw and wanted to cultivate in themselves. They described "following Jesus" as a terrific adventure. It puzzled and disturbed them that in areas as diverse as evangelism and rock climbing, they would be passionate about things Eldredge argues are distinctly masculine. "What does this mean, I'm a man? I'm a bad woman? How am I supposed to respond to being told you're basically deluded about what you think it means to be a godly woman?" For them strength, courage, adventure seemed human, not gendered. And in both their lives and in the lives of their relatives and friends they saw enormous variation in character.

> He kept reiterating that there was this *masculine* journey and that . . . masculine aggression is a holy thing. I never considered just masculinity as aggressive. There might be something to that,

but I felt he was defining masculinity from his own experience. I could write the same from my own experience.

Not only did these women believe that love for adventure and risk taking are distributed to various degrees across women and men, they saw these as narrow caricatures of the real men with whom they were friends. In some cases, they thought "dangerous" and "free" might describe some of the men that they knew. But they also knew women who were like that and some men who were not.

> I am wondering and have been praying about a lot this: it feels like to talk about "godly gender" is almost a paradox or wrong, cause there is so much cultural influence that's hard to filter (out). God allows so much variation along gender lines than we would like to give him. I value the book because it wants to give these masculine men a place to dangerous that most churches don't allow, but I question whether it will allow for women to be this way, too . . . or for other men to say, "this doesn't fit me."

The young women were especially critical of the narrowness of Eldredge's vision of godly manhood. They were offended by his repetitive pitting of "Mr. Rogers" against "Braveheart" styles of masculinity. Not only did they think that manliness could be expressed in a wider range of activities than rafting, climbing and other outdoor adventures, they worried that these characteristics might not always be qualities God wanted to develop in a man's life. "What about compassion," "what about mercy" they wondered. "How is this supposed to help a man nurture children or care for the poor?" For them, "kindness" or "niceness" or even "meekness" were neither antithetical to their own ideals for godly manhood, nor were they synonymous with a man being a pathetic, weak or domesticated "nice guy."

Finally, the para-church women were highly critical of the degree to which Eldredge's image of godly manhood could be applied across race and class. Similar to the men, the women thought *Wild at heart* was written for a white middle-class audience. So thick is the book with examples of rafting, rock climbing, and bronco busting, that they could not imagine how it could be useful to men who were not white, privileged, outdoorsmen who could afford to cultivate such an adventurous lifestyle. As one woman explained

> I think that's really dangerous because not all men are like him at all. From my personal experience, my brother grew up in Hong Kong. He was never in the outdoors, he doesn't desire that at all. He came here when he was twelve, and he hated the idea of "be a man," be macho . . . have guns and play with frogs.

Even if economic resources were not a constraint on adventurous living, they could think of men they considered "Godly guys" who had no desire to go rafting or rock climbing. It seemed implausible that this image of aggressive manhood could apply to an entire world of men in multiple countries, cultures, and ethnicities.

Middle-Age Church-Going Men

Compared to those in the para-church fellowship, several interesting contrasts emerged in the interviews conducted with the mostly middle-age sample of church-going women and men. First, men from both churches were somewhat more temperate in their response to *Wild at heart.* For some, the moderation of the their enthusiasm reflected years of living with "real women." Other than the idea that all women want to be pursued—a notion interpreted as both leading to emotional as well as sexual intimacy—most of the married men were quick to identify Eldredge's gender ideals as unrealistically narrow. The romanticized notion of "a beauty to fight for" was appealing, but they laughed out loud at the thought that their wives, whom they'd seen living "outside the tower," were maidens locked away in distress.

> I think there are lots of models to be a man, so he generalizes what it would look like. Men in general, and women too, have a need to face challenge. It's not an exclusive thing. It might be played out more in men but I know lots of women who face challenges.

For some of the men, a little "wildness" seemed an attractive thing in women as well as men. The generalization seemed much too narrow, given the real and ideal of women they know.

> I think he really generalizes about what women want. Otherwise, why do we have stories from history of women who never marry, who contributed greatly in lives of adventure? Florence Nightingale: she spent her life waiting to be rescued [they laugh at the sarcasm]. . . . There's a painting in my office of a woman wrangler and *she* isn't waiting for anyone to rescue her. She's the un-stereotype of a woman. I really like it, it just points out what we men have thought about the stereotype role of woman. He generalizes way too much.

About a third of the men saw the book as sending different messages on both gender and accountability than they'd picked up in reading PK literature and attending PK events.

> I saw that crack on accountability groups. I've been to two or three PK events and think PK is a little more even handed and don't go after quite the same generalizations towards women. I see them as saying more "stick to the promises you have made to women, you promised to love them and provide for them, now get your tail to work and do it." I don't think PK is advocating at all for the Stone Age sort of stuff. I'm not sure Eldredge does either, but I think his views on women are a little outdated.

Although Eldredge is critical of the concept of PK style "accountability groups," reading the book together provided a context in which men could share areas of their lives they might never had otherwise. "It has been beneficial to get to know these guys. In how many churches do men see each other's faces Sunday after Sunday and don't know anything about each other. Maybe that is what fellowship is about." Reading the book as a group deepened their understanding of each other, provided opportunity to hear each other's life stories, and a context for sharing fears and struggles with family and career.

> It touched on a lot of subjects that men just don't want to talk about. It gets to the point and uses lots of illustrations so it was easy for all the guys to connect to what he was saying. It gave us a chance to talk about fear and relationships with wives and kids. Some guys just don't want to talk about this stuff cause their image is of being so cool or whatever. It's just hard for people to discuss some of this. But we had some really good discussions.

In sharing their personal struggles, a second area of contrast between older and younger men was their discussion of "the father wound." The younger men saw this as an area in which they should seek healing, while many of the older men had a difficult time identifying what the nature of this wound might be. For the few who felt they *had* been wounded, the damage appeared to be something they had already resolved. As one of the men in the AOG congregation explained:

> I was supposed to be teaching a Sunday school class on that section and both I and the other fellow couldn't figure out what to do with it because we just couldn't relate. Neither one of us felt like that described our relationships with our dads. And most of the guys we know who have had trouble have worked it out long ago.

Part of the difference between older and younger men's approach to the "father wound" is a difference in what older and younger men expect from their fathers. When older men talked about their fathers they expressed gratitude for their hard work and spoke fondly of the bonding trips they had taken together. As one man in his 80s expressed

> [Eldredge] put a big emphasis about wounding from the father and I tried and I just can't dig up anything. I think in terms of my father, he was very busy and we didn't spend a lot of time together, but I always felt supported and respected, and he gave me a lot of good advice in times when I needed it.

These varying generational expectations may have had some affect on how older and younger men approached the question of personal healing. One set of men who had read the book together talked about this portion of the book as a valuable opportunity to share about their fathers and childhoods with a group of other men. While appreciating the opportunity to share a part of their lives they might never had otherwise, the framework of a need to heal "the father wound" was not particularly salient.

On the other hand, the middle aged and older men *did* use this theme as an opportunity to rethink their relationship with their own children. Here it meant a chance to reconsider the degree to which they might be overly demanding or set unrealistic expectations for their children. It provided modest motivation for how they might approach asking their adult sons to forgive them for past mistakes, saying "One of the things this has prompted me to do is go back and talk to my kids . . . did I wound you? Was I too harsh? Did I neglect you?" Men with younger children were quick to point out how the book had provided them ammunition for countering their wives' concerns about doing risky and dangerous things with their children, to "go easy" on their sons, "connect more" and "mentor" their daughters.

Yet overall, the most important aspect of the book for the men in the church samples was the encouragement they received for taking risks in their jobs. Two thirds of the married men in our sample were white collar, highly paid professional men—most working in large bureaucratic corporations or in family businesses of their own. Their reading did nothing to discourage their sense of responsibility at home by taking off for the weekend into the wilderness. But did encourage them to rethink complacency at work and the dulling effects of years in a career.

> I think he's right that our society is trying keep people "safe." I think that's dangerous. The state tries to protect people from anything that could possibly conceivably hurt them. We are so afraid of risk that we risk losing the ability to act at all.

For one man in particular, the book was a real turning point in his career, providing the impetus to leave his high paying position in management and take several months to rethink what he really wanted to do with the second half of his life. More often, it reshaped how men described thinking about the balance of time and energy they were spending at work and at home.

> I'd read his other book, *Journey of desire,* and felt compelled to read this one when it came out. It spoke to where I've been the past two years, on a journey from being so independent and focused on me to being much more involved with my family and other men. My wife loves it: I've had a heart change. I'm definitely more available.

Along with being more involved at home and taking risks by scaling back careers, these older men made the case that perseverance, self-control and personal sacrifice—themes they thought were clear in the Promise Keepers literature they had read—were important aspects of godly manhood that *Wild at heart* neglected.

> I think he's right, but in my own estimate, these things in a man's heart are good but should be controlled. He doesn't say an awful lot about the matter of control, and there are all kinds of battles to be fought that aren't physical or even necessarily emotional. But they require real stamina in modern life, not just heroism.

Finally, one area of agreement between older and younger cohorts was the class and race biases of the book. It was hard for them to envision the book appealing to men in less privileged positions. One of them wondered aloud at how much money Eldredge had made from sales of the book and the degree to which "his brothers and sisters around the world were sharing in that."

Wives of Church-Going Men

The final sample of people with whom we talked were the wives of the middle aged and older men. The most remarkable thing about these interviews was their length—the women did not read the book, and so had very little to say about either it or how they saw it affecting their husband's lives. A couple of the wives had read parts of it. Only one had read the whole. When asked why, they said they "just never thought of it," "had other things to do," or "it seemed like a guys book, so I wasn't that interested." And so they didn't bother.

Still, even within these interviews, two points of contrast with the younger women's interviews emerged. First, several of the women did talk briefly (one at length) about how the book seemed good for their husbands' sense of being able to take risks at work. As we mentioned above, this translated into one wife encouraging her husband to leave his career. In most cases, however, women felt the book had helped their husbands in a general way to be willing to voice disagreement with supervisors or provide critical, but difficult, personnel reviews.

The most dramatic contrast that emerges out of the wives' interviews was their very different response to Eldredge's images of godly manhood and womanhood. For women in the Assemblies of God church, the emphasis on gender difference sounded both familiar and "right." "Men and women are different," they said. "Our society doesn't want to admit it, but they are. It was nice to hear someone say so." The married women with whom we talked were neither offended nor threatened by Eldredge's gender essentialism. Among those for whom the image of women as beauties desiring to be pursued did not ring true, they simply dismissed the entire line of argument as exaggerated and not particularly relevant.

> I think he may be right about some things, like how guys need to get out there and take risks. But I'm not like the women he describes. There's a lot more to both of us than that. What's important is that we both be willing to go out there and do whatever God wants us to do. Whether that's with our kids or jobs or whatever. Sometimes that gender stuff helps, sometimes it doesn't.

For married women who had already shared a number of years living with particular men, whether they agreed with Eldredge's gender essentialism or not, the overall impression of the book was that if it helped their husbands get in touch with other men, pay more attention to how they interacted with their kids, and gave them the push they needed to take hard stands at work, it was good. The rest of the story was not all that important.

Denominational Distinctives

While the most significant contrasts we identified were across age and gender, different ways of interpreting and appropriating the messages of *Wild at heart* were evident across religious tradition as well. Styles of discourse, metaphor and points of emphasis all subtly differed among men whose church culture, theology, style of worship and heroes of the faith were connected to broader Reformed or Pentecostal streams of Christianity. Men in the Assembly of God church were much more likely to use military and adventurer language in describing the role of men in family life, saying things like "the book really lays out who we are as men . . . what God designed us to be. . . . we're designed as men to be leaders and warriors." The warrior motif was applied to men being designed to fight both spiritual and relational battles, and appeared most prominently in AOG discussions of "putting on the armor of God," "going into battle," "being the spiritual leader," "the need for a man to lay down his life for his wife and kids" or more generally having "a beauty to rescue" because "God designed us to be that person." Clearly, the specific responsibilities of husbands and wives may have changed, but these men saw their primary responsibilities as extensions of the protector and provider husbands of the 1950s.

> Then men worked came home and worked and came home and did their jobs. Their role was to be the provider. It still is, but men are called to be bigger than that, to *be* Braveheart and Gladiator fighting for our families and the church. Somebody has to step up.

This model of strong masculine involved leadership appeared as a much-needed challenge to the "light weight" and "feminized" models of masculinity AOG men saw as coming to dominate American culture. In contrast, men affiliated with the Presbyterian church were less likely to spiritualize their struggles at home or work using metaphors of adventure, warfare or combat, but rather described these as areas in which God expected them to act responsibly vis à vis both family and employers.

The concerns these middle age church-going men also had with the book differed somewhat across denomination. For men connected with the Pentecostal church, two issues arose. First, the notion that *Wild at heart* might somehow encourage men to disregard their pastor's authority or the accountability of other men and opt to "fly solo." As one of the men, involved in leadership in the church expressed:

> Some things you have to take with a grain of salt, like his slamming the church-going man. What sells is controversy and some people picked it up because of that. Here's a guy who [sounds like he] attends church six or eight times a year and thinks he has all the answers. But he doesn't talk about who he's accountable to . . . I have guys throughout the United States where I never make a major move without consulting them and I didn't see any of that [in the book]. He doesn't talk about great times of fellowship with his men's leader, or major players in his life.

The men in the Presbyterian church also expressed concern that the book might encourage "solo Christianity," but the connection they thought was lacking was less a relationship of subordination to church leaders and more in a set of mutually supportive (and now somewhat more intimate) male friends.

> The guys by-and-large don't think its that great. Its not deep. But it does have some good ideas. I think they have appreciated the conversations and that we have beared our souls a little better. In a sense it validates his thesis that men need other men. So pastorally its been very worth while, cause I think the guys have talked more.

Clearly, these two approaches to authority within the church reflect the different denominational cultures of the Assembly of God and Presbyterianism in the United States. Moreover, in attitudes and policies regarding gender, specifically women in church leadership, men also differed. The men in the Presbyterian church were much more skeptical about the narrowness of the gender stereotypes and limited application across race and class than were men in the AOG church. In fact, none of the AOG men thought that Eldredge's gender stereotypes were particularly problematic. Although the image of women as needing to be pursued and rescued did not resonate as deeply as it did with the younger men, the men in the AOG study group were unanimous in their agreement that men and women are "just different"—an idea that confirmed their belief that husbands should be providers, protectors and spiritual leaders at home.

> As a husband and a father it showed me that my role is to provide opportunity to let my wife dance on the stage of life. Before it was all about me . . . my job, my influence, my money, how much I was earning. Now I see there has to be less of myself, dying to myself and my goals, my job. And now much more about my family.

Across denomination, reading the book increased men's awareness of the how much they were connected to family. Yet the degree to which gender differences were used to explain that connection was more prominent among the AOG men than the men at the Presbyterian church.

Finally, these middle aged church-going men differed in their thoughts about how the book was most useful or effective. Men in the Assembly, like the younger men in the para-church campus ministry, saw the book as a useful tool in evangelism as well as personal growth.

> I was very confident in my masculinity already . . . but you get a lot of guys who are into different things and there's no place for that in the church. Like you can separate your secular and sacred life. That's not right. If you can't use whatever you're into ministry wise, then maybe you ought to think again . . . maybe it shouldn't be in your life. So this weekend we're doing a "coast ride" for guys with bikes. Last time, we had 40 guys in leather with their Harleys, etc. Not your typical white shirt Baptist thing. We want all kinds of guys to know that the church is for them!

Or as another man put it:

> You know, the culture has evolved and if we don't evolve too, the gospel won't be heard. He puts the gospel in a way that men today can hear. It is very solid. The gospel has to be presented in the terms of the culture otherwise it won't have an impact. Just talking, like in traditional churches, from the scripture in a sermon—well, that's harder for men in our culture to hear. So Eldredge tells the gospel in a way that men today can hear. His word is something that God is using to raise up men and call them out.

In contrast, none of the men in the Presbyterian church described *Wild at heart* as a useful evangelism strategy. For them, its usefulness was found in help balancing commitments and enriching relationships with family and at work.

Although our sample is quite small, these differences across Pentecostal and non-Pentecostal men are consistent with findings from other research in which men and women in charismatic or Pentecostal churches tend to hold more essentialist notions of godly manhood and womanhood (Gallagher and Smith 1999, Gallagher 2003). Moreover they mirror specific denominational and theological distinctives: cultural relevance versus the "just talking from the scripture"; responsibility to church leadership versus responsibility to a group of men peers; spiritual warfare versus relational sensitivity; resisting domestication versus being involved fathers. In these ways, even this small sample points to the significance of embeddedness in a particular Christian theological story, in shaping how men interpret the particular stories they encounter in popular Christian advice literature.

Summary and Discussion

While this analysis is based on a small set of case studies across local church and para-church fellowships the findings speak to a number of broader theoretical and methodological issues within the sociology of religion.

First, it is clear that the social location of the reader has enormous influence over the messages heard and applied from family advice literature. By itself, this is hardly news. Each of us has a set of lenses with which we read that are colored by gender, age, ethnicity, class, cohort and history. These shape how particular themes are interpreted as meaningful, foci narrowed and ideas emphasized and adopted in the process of selecting, reading and remembering religious texts. When it comes to interpreting the bible, evangelicals are intensely concerned that they employ a hermeneutic that preserves ideas of biblical authority and inspiration, while also being sensitive to cultural-historic specifics that inform its application to everyday life. Questions of hermeneutics are given less attention when it comes to other religious texts, yet they are nonetheless active in shaping their interpretation. As our analysis demonstrates, readers are remarkably active and selective consumers of the messages presented in books such as *Wild at heart*. Just as they employ a range of hermeneutical approaches in interpreting the scriptures, so too do they employ a range of perspectives in interpreting popular evangelical texts.

Among the multiple sets of lenses that shape the appropriation of ideas, two emerged as particularly salient in affecting ordinary readers' interpretations of *Wild at heart*—gender and age. Both older and younger men understood the message of the book as a challenge to take risks in relationships. However, the younger men were more likely to emphasize and celebrate Eldredge's messages of gender difference as a relational strategy, while the older and middle-aged men focused on the need to take risks in their careers and in cultivating more nurturing relationship with their children. For men in the middle of their lives the book was less a confirmation of gender stereotypes than a challenge to resist complacency. Perhaps most importantly, it provided a coherently evangelical language with which to resist (or at least consider resisting) the stultifying effects of rationalization (Schwalbe 1996).

Gender was also, not surprisingly, enormously important in readings of *Wild at heart*. For younger women the ideal of femininity as passive antithesis and response to the agency of a man felt like an attack on their personhood. They dreamed of having their own adventures, not simply finding someone, whose adventure they could join. At a time in their lives when committed relationships are being formed, the narrowness of Eldredge's gender vision appeared more of a death trap, than a doorway to life. In contrast, the gender essentialism of *Wild at heart* hardly raised an eyebrow among middle-aged married women. They recognized the story, but ignored the plot line. Maybe he's right, maybe he's not—it made little difference. The real men with whom they shared their real lives appeared to be helped, and that was good enough.

From these interpretive strands, what more broadly can we learn about evangelical ideals for godly manhood? First, we are reminded that the range of masculinities and femininities among ordinary believers is much broader than those presented in most conservative Protestant family advice literature. More importantly, our analysis demonstrates that even narrow and gender essentialist messages can be read by ordinary believers as broader, more qualified, and more nuanced than the texts suggest. This selective appropriation of gender ideals highlights the need for researches to attend to multiple meanings as well as messengers, if we are to more adequacy describe and explain the workings of religion in everyday life.

Exploring the selective reading of these texts also helps explain the process through which evangelicals can be simultaneously symbolic traditionalists and pragmatic egalitarians (Gallagher 2003; Gallagher and Smith 1999) and "tack" between two seemingly contradictory sets of ideals (Bartkowski 2004). The most common expression of this process can be seen in cases where practice overrides literalist interpretation. The experience of married couples did not prevent them from hearing and even (in some cases) celebrating messages about essential gender difference. Their life can experience, however was a powerful filter that shaped how those messages were actually appropriated and applied. Among evangelicals for whom gender ideology does important subcultural religious boundary work, we are likely to see a shift toward ever greater spiritualization of the "rules" for men and women, and emphasis on partnership and effective communication in marriage rather than a "chain of command" and "God given roles." In these ways, the experience of ordinary evangelicals may be reshaping the production of evangelical culture as much as evangelical cultural producers shape the subculture itself.

Second, the selective reading and multi-vocal character of evangelical gender texts underscores the centrality of ideals of gender that are both essentialized *and* flexible to the subcultural strength of American evangelicalism (see Gallagher 2003; Smith 1998). The various interpretations and selective appropriation of ideas from books like *Wild at heart* reflect the very core of what makes evangelical subculture tick. Both methodologically and thematically it captures the essence of evangelical identity. Methodologically, it appeals to two domains of religious authority that are most salient to evangelicals—personal experience and the bible (Gallagher 2003). Eldredge, as do other evangelical authors, presents his argument as resting on evidence that is both self evident and obvious. In doing so, he stands well within a tradition of anti-intellectualism and "Scottish Common Sense Realism" that historian Mark Noll argues have long been characteristic of American Evangelicalism (Noll 1994). Thematically also borrows heavily (we might say shamelessly) from the ideas of popular culture. It re-articulates ideas of muscular Christianity (Kimmel 1996; Putney 2003; Rotundo 1994) that framed conservative Protestant gender debates nearly a century ago, and romanticizes the ideal of the independent "self-made" man from the same era. It repackages themes from the mythopoetic men's movement of the 1980s, translating these into the language and style that dominates evangelical self-help literature. The prominence of Robert Bly as an authority on masculine identity and the "father wound" highlights the degree to which *Wild at heart* borrows from this literature—problematizing the inner struggles of rationalized and emotionally isolated hegemonic manhood. Here, it stands somewhat in contradiction to much Promise Keepers literature, particularly the writing of Stu Weber, which emphasizes responsibility and stability and is critical of the perceived self-indulgence and self-centeredness of the men's movement (Weber 1993).

Overall, then, Eldredge's *Wild at heart* is a quintessentially evangelical text. It places non-negotiable, dimorphous gender identity at the center of the story. It appeals to the most salient sources of religious authority, the bible and personal experience, as the basis for believing these are true. And it links these truths to well known myths, movies and media, as though there were a kind of gender essentialist "common grace" through which the characteristics of masculinity and femininity can be clearly known. Thus, connecting religious gender identity to popular culture, Eldredge's *Wild at heart* speaks to the heart of evangelical identity and its mandate to be both orthodox and culturally relevant—to be both in but not of "the world."

For men, that struggle involves not so much the fight against irresponsibility or selfishness, but a fight against the fear of failure and the willingness to abandon one's deepest desires for personal security and safety. For Stu Weber's "tender warrior" the latter might be interpreted as the personal sacrifices of a responsible man; for Eldredge it is acquiescing to rationalization and the death of the soul. For evangelical men across generation and tradition, popular texts such as these offer an easily assessable narrative that provides a plot-line for framing significant decisions, encouragement for greater connectedness at home, and a vision for how manhood and faith should express themselves in the world.

ENDNOTES

1. In August 2004, *Wild at heart* was ranked #3 in overall best sellers by the Christian Booksellers Association (2004), just behind Rick Warren's *Purpose driven life* (2002) and newest book *You have what it takes: What every father needs to hear* (2004). It has been ranked #1 in the "Christian Living" category multiple times since publication.

2. The themes of desire, passion, and following one's heart appear in no fewer than eight books and workbooks by John Eldredge over the past seven years. Three of these—*The Sacred Romance* (Curtis and Eldredge 1997); *Journey of desire* (Eldredge 2000); and *Wild at heart* (Eldredge 2001)—were followed by the publication of an associated workbook, and were reissued as a set of "classics" in 2001. Since then, the *Wild at heart* phenomena has spawned numerous seminars, boot camps for men, and a video-book-tape-field guide boxed set for small group use (2003b). The theme of following one's heart continues in Eldredge's recent work (2002, 2003a).

3. In considering the effects of mixing interview techniques, it is possible that some of those interviewed in the group settings may have been be hesitant to speak as freely as they might in a personal interview. It is also possible for a few dominant individuals to limit the amount of input from less outspoken participants in a group. Two points give us some confidence that these potential problems did not

significantly undermine the quality of our data. First, the men and women we interviewed together had a history of meeting to talk about faith, relationships, American culture, etc., so that a significant degree of trust within the group was already established. Second, we encouraged all individuals to speak in an effort to prevent one or two leaders from dominating the group interviews. We began by offering each person opportunity to respond to opening questions about how they heard about the book and what they thought, liked and didn't like about it. We also made note to return to less outspoken members, asking their ideas about the particular aspect of the book under discussion. Moreover, it is possible that the men in the large Sunday school class and the wives of the church-going men (e.g. those respondents who were not part of any long term study or discussion group) were more open over the telephone than they might have been had we interviewed them in groups. However, we have no way to systematically assess the degree to which that was the case.

4. Nearly all of the men and women connected to the local churches were married. None of the young adults associated with the university para-church ministry were married (one woman was engaged and another couple were seriously dating). Most of the men and women in the church samples were in their late forties and early fifties; with two older couples in their late seventies. The overall age of the church sample was fifty-five years old. The young adults associated with the para-church college group ranged from nineteen to twenty-seven years old, with a mean age of about twenty-two. As in other samples of self-identified evangelical Protestants, our sample was middle and upper middle class, white, and fairly well educated (see Smith 1998).

REFERENCES

Allen, L. D. 2000. Promise keepers and racism. *Sociology of Religion* 16:55–72.

Bartkowski, J. P. 1996. Beyond biblical literalism and inerrancy. *Sociology of Religion* 57:259–72.

———. 2001. *Remaking the godly marriage.* New Brunswick, N.J.: Rutgers University Press.

———. 2004. *The Promise Keepers.* New Brunswick, N.J.: Rutgers University Press.

Bilezikian, G. 1985. *Beyond sex roles,* second edition. Grand Rapids, Mich.: Baker Book House.

Bristow, J. T. 1988. *What Paul really said about women.* San Francisco: Harper San Francisco.

Christenson, L. 1970. *The Christian family.* Minneapolis: Bethany.

Christian Booksellers Association. 2004. Online report: http://www.ecpa.org/ECPA/bestsell.html.

Clark, S. B. 1980. *Man and woman in Christ.* Ann Arbor, Mich.: Servant Publications.

Cole, E. L. 1982. *Maximized manhood.* New Kensington, Penn.: Whitaker House.

Cooper, D. 1974. *You can be the wife of a happy husband.* Wheaton, Ill.: Victor Books.

Cooper, R. 1995. *We stand together.* Chicago: Moody Press.

Curtis, B. and J. Eldredge. 1997. *The sacred romance.* Nashville: Thomas Nelson.

Eldredge, J. 2000. *Journey of desire.* Nashville: Thomas Nelson.

———. 2001. *Wild at heart.* Nashville: Thomas Nelson.

———. 2002. *Dare to desire.* Nashville: Thomas Nelson.

———. 2003a. *Waking the Dead.* Nashville: Thomas Nelson.

Eldredge, J. 2003b. *Wild at heart multi-media facilitator's kit.* Nashville: Thomas Media Group.

———. 2004. *What every man needs to hear.* Nashville, TN: Thomas Nelson.

Elliot, E. 1976. *Let me be a woman.* Wheaton, IL: Tyndale.

———. 1981. *Mark of a Man.* Wheaton, IL. Tyndale.

Farrar, S. 1990. *Point man.* Portland, OR: Multnomah.

Gallagher, S. K. 2003, *Evangelical identity and gendered family life.* New Brunswick, NJ.: Rutgers University Press.

———. 2004a. The marginalization of evangelical feminism. *Sociology of Religion* 65:215–37.

———. 2004b. Where are the anti-feminist evangelicals? *Gender & Society* 18:451–72.

Gallagher, S. K. & C. Smith. 1999. Symbolic traditionalism and pragmatic egalitarianism: *Gender & Society,* 13:211–233.

Getz, G. 1977. *The measure of a woman.* Ventura, CA.: Regal Books.

Gundry, P. 1980. *Heirs together.* Grand Rapids, MI: Zondervan.

Hackstaff, K. 1999. *Marriage in a culture of divorce.* Philadelphia, PA: Temple University Press.

Hardisty, J. 1999. *Mobilizing resentment.* Boston: Beacon Press.

Hurley, J. B. 1981. *Man and woman in biblical perspective.* Grand Rapids, MI: Zondervan.

Kimmel, M. 1996. *Manhood in America.* New York, NY: The Free Press.

LaHaye, T. and J. B. Jenkins. 1996. *Left behind.* Wheaton, IL: Tyndale House Publishers.

Lockhart, W. H. 2000. "We are one life," but not of one gender ideology. *Sociology of Religion,* 61:73–92.

Mathisen, J. A. 2001. The strange decade of the Promise Keepers. *Books & Culture* 7:36.

McCartney, B. 1997. *Sold out.* Waco, TX: Word.

———. 1994. *Seven promises of a Promise Keeper.* Colorado Springs, CO: Focus on the Family.

Messner, M. 1997. *The politics of masculinities.* Thousand Oaks, CA: Sage.

Messner, M. A. and C Anderson. 1998. Miles to go before they sleep. Paper presented at the Annual Meeting of the Pacific Sociological Association, August, San Francisco.

Mickelsen, A. 1986. *Women, authority and the bible.* Downers Grove, IL: InterVarsity Press.

Mollenkott, V. R. 1977. *Women, men and the bible.* Nashville, TN: Abingdon Press.

Nason-Clark, N. and C. C. Kroeger. 2004. *Refuge from abuse.* Downers Grove, IL: InterVarsity Press.

Noll, M. A. 1994. *The scandal of the evangelical mind.* Grand Rapids, MI: Eerdmans.

Oliver, G. 1993. *Real men have feelings too.* Chicago, IL: Moody Press.

Piper, J. and W. Grudem. 1991. *Recovering biblical manhood and womanhood.* Wheaton, IL: Crossway.

Porter, P. with W. T. Whalin. 1996. *Let the walls fall down.* Orlando, FL: Creation House.

Putney, C. 2003. *Muscular Christianity.* Cambridge, MA: Harvard University Press.

Rotundo, E. A. 1994. *American manhood.* New York, NY: Basic Books.

Scanzoni, L. D. and N. A. Hardesty. 1974. *All we're meant to be.* Waco, TX: Word.

Schwalbe, M. 1996. *Unlocking the iron cage.* New York, NY: Oxford University Press.

Smalley, G. and J. Trent. 1992. *The hidden value of a man.* Wheaton, IL: Tyndale House.

Smith, C. 1998. *American evangelicals.* Chicago, IL: University of Chicago Press.

Van Leeuwen, M. S. 1990. *Gender and grace.* Downers Grove, IL: InterVarsity Press.

Warren, R. 2002. *The purpose driven life.* Grand-Rapids, MI: Zondervan.

Washington, R. and G. Kehrein. 1997. *Break down the walls.* Chicago. IL: Moody Press.

Weber, S. 1993. *Tender warrior.* Sisters, OR: Multnomah Books.

———. 1997. *The four pillars of a man's heart.* Sisters, OR: Multnomah Books.

———. 1998. *All the king's men.* Sisters, OR: Multnomah.

Wilkenson, B. 1999. *The prayer of Jabez.* Sisters, OR: Multnomah Books.

Voicing Your Opinion
Godly Manhood Going Wild?: Transformations in Conservative Protestant Masculinity
Sally K. Gallagher and Sabrina L. Wood

1. The article discusses Stu Weber's description of "authentic masculinity" as characterized by four pillars: king, warrior, mentor, and friend. Respond to this description with your own ideas about masculinity. Do these words describe an "ideal" masculinity to you? Why or why not?

   _____

   _____

   _____

   _____

2. The results of the interview study in Gallager and Wood's article indicate that young, unmarried women had a negative response to the gender roles that are described in *Wild at Heart*. In contrast, the young unmarried men had a positive response to the described gender roles. Consider the reasons for the differences in the responses. Why did the men support the roles? Why did the women feel angry about them?

   _____

   _____

   _____

   _____

3. The article examines the ways that people learn and embody religious gender identity. What is your experience with this topic? Do you see evidence of religious gender roles in your family, your friends, or your community? How do the goals of religious gender identity fit within the broader goals of the women's and men's movements?

   _____

   _____

   _____

   _____

GENDER IS POWERFUL
The Long Reach
of Feminism

NANCY MACLEAN

This article is about the influence and impact of social movements from the turn of the twentieth century to the present. It focuses on the impact that feminism, labor movements, the Civil Rights movement, and the gay and lesbian movements have had on reconstructing gender issues in the United States. The article discusses the ways that feminism as a movement has changed the fabric of American work and family life.

O f all the movements of the Sixties, those involving gender, enlisted the largest number of participants and produced the deepest transformation in American society. Emboldened by the wider activism of the era, especially the black freedom movement, and spurred by seismic changes in the economy and family life, feminists attracted a growing following after 1966 as they set out to end the reign of gender inequality in American institutions and culture. Within a few years, lesbians and gay men too showed new daring in laying claim to the nation's core promises of freedom and equality. Public debate has since raged between supporters and opponents of these movements over a host of specific issues: the Equal Rights Amendment, abortion, affirmative action, gay school teachers, and more. Yet underlying the specific conflicts were profound alterations in political economy and culture that made gender issues matter as never before to activists on all sides—and to millions of ordinary citizens.

As is common with new social movements, early scholarship on second wave feminism took its cue from journalism and its inspiration from personal experience. Authors of the formative studies of the women's movement such as Jo Freeman and Sara Evans had themselves participated in the struggle, and so had intimate knowledge of their subjects. They showed, in the words of Evans' subtitle, "the roots of women's liberation in the civil rights movement and the New Left." Evans, in particular, focused on young women activists' recognition that "the personal is political" and showed how they used consciousness-raising discussion sessions to deepen understanding of the social roots of seemingly personal problems and develop innovative practices to address them, such as rape crisis centers.[1] Yet, rich as these works were, closeness to the events led to greater interest in immediate concerns than in the deep structure of change.

Most textbooks today follow early participants and journalists in taking a short view of the movement. The texts lead students to think that organizing for gender equality stopped after women won the vote in 1920 and suddenly "reawakened," the oft-used word, in the 1960s. Certainly there is some truth to this view, in the late Sixties, the ranks of women activists surged, their supporters multiplied many times over, and the pace of reform accelerated. Within just a few years, women won protection from employment discrimination, inclusion in affirmative action, abortion law reform, greater representation in media, equal access to school athletics, congressional passage of an Equal Rights Amendment, and much more.[2] Yet students are ill-served by the notion that such a powerful force came out of nowhere, or even that its main cause was the youth-led movements of "the Sixties."

Forty years have passed since some activists coined the phrase "women's liberation" and others formed the National Organization for Women (NOW). In that time a wealth of new scholarship has revealed the far deeper roots of these movements, both in social changes over generations and in political history reaching back to the early twentieth century. What made some kind of change in the gender order feel necessary to so many was, most immediately, the demise of the family wage system; the male breadwinner/ female homemaker model that shaped government policy and employer practices, even though it never described the reality of millions of American households. Just as important, however, were profound demographic changes sweeping every industrial society, infant mortality and birth rates declined, life expectancy surged, and women entered the paid labor force in massive numbers. In this context, popular understanding of marriage and the very meaning of life changed: no longer expecting to die soon after their last child left home, women came to want more from men, marriage, education, and themselves. That is why even countries that had no equivalent upheaval in the 1960s nevertheless generated their own variants of feminism as they sought to cope with these massive changes using the tools of the democratic process, above all, new public policies suited to changing family forms and individual life cycles.[3]

While one track of recent history reveals how a seemingly new movement accomplished so much so quickly, another provides a deep context for why so many welcomed feminism. The feminist movement, in other words, was not new at all. The ranks of self-described "feminism" dwindled after 1920, to be sure, as the elite, white National Women's Party made that label anathema to women working for wider social justice thanks to its leaders' single-minded quest for an Equal Rights Amendment, a gender-blind approach that threatened hard-won, gender-conscious reforms like protective legislation.[4] But tens of thousands of others continued to try to improve the lives of women between 1920 and 1965 through their work in the labor movement and in such organizations as the National Consumers League, the National Council of Negro Women, and the YMCA.[5]

This grassroots base made possible an ambitious organizing effort after World War II, a broad-based left-led coalition called the Congress of American Women. It joined women's equality to peace and wider social reforms, such as full employment, government sponsored child care facilities, and an end to racial segregation. CAW anticipated all of the agenda of second wave feminism save its sexual politics, and had more black women in leadership positions than any other feminist movement in U.S. history.[6] Such broad advocacy was enabled by changes in the infrastructure of American politics that began in the Progressive Era and expanded in the New Deal and war years. Feminism's goals and accomplishments depended on prior national commitment to a federal regulatory state to advance social citizenship, and on the mass membership organizations that ensured continued government commitment to a welfare state in the face of opposition from northern corporate Republicans and southern white supremacist Democrats.

One reason the Rip van Winkle account of feminism seemed plausible for so long was that the postwar Red Scare hurt organizing among women as it did labor and civil rights activism. CAW was a broad coalition, but communist women had played a key role in bringing it together. Under the harsh glare of investigation by the House Un-American Activities Committee and a demand by the attorney general that the organization must register as a "foreign agent," membership plummeted from a claimed high of 250,000 to just 3,000. Gerda Lerner, who later became a pioneer historian of women and president of the OAH, was then a rank-and-file CAW activist, a Jewish refugee from Nazism, and a Communist Party member herself. She burned all her records in terror of what the Right's new power portended. Most other groups doing innovative work for gender equality in 1940s and 1950s were affected in some way, and individual leaders became much more cautious. But many continued working, forming a human bridge between eras more propitious to activism as they labored quietly but steadily in arenas ranging from the American Civil Liberties Union to the United Auto Workers Women's Commission.[7]

This existing infrastructure helps explain how feminists were able to make such stunning headway after the formation of NOW and the take off to women's liberation. The wide array of leaders from earlier groups came together in the President's Commission on the Status of Women, which in turn spurred state-level women's commissions that became organizing centers. In 1963, the PCSW issued its major report calling for wide-ranging reform to end sex discrimination. Textbooks thus get it wrong when they credit Betty Friedan's best-selling 1963 book, *The Feminine Mystique,* for the rise of second wave feminism. What the book did, rather, was name what so many women were already feeling and invigorate those already acting. Friedan developed her expert aim, moreover, in the Popular Front of the 1940s as a labor-left journalist. Her book thus built on far more than her experience as a suburban wife and mother.[8]

Similarly, some of feminism's greatest policy victories in the 1960s and 1970s came as a result of using tools won by other movements. By far the most important was the employment section of the Civil Rights Act of 1964, Title VII, won by the black freedom movement to end occupational segregation. Women used it not only to enter good jobs of all kinds long closed to them but also to end pregnancy discrimination and fight sexual harassment. Indeed they raised foundational questions about gender and power

Figure 6.1
Protesting against the Federal Equal Rights Amendment outside the White House in the early 1970s. (Image courtesy of Library of Congress, *U.S. News and World Report* Collection, LC-U9-33389A-31/31A.)

with reverberations in every area of American life, Title VII also encouraged new coalitions between feminists and labor and civil rights groups of all kinds that expanded the constituency pushing for gender equity. Without a Title VII, NOW and small women's liberation never would have achieved so many successes so quickly, if they achieved them at all.[9]

Part of what made feminism so successful is the way that, almost from the outset, women in different situations developed their own variants and organized for the goals most important to them. As historian Nancy Cott wrote of the first wave, "feminism was an impulse that was impossible to translate into a program without centrifugal results."[10] The trite caricature of a white middle-class movement obscures this far more interesting history. From the beginning, black women inside and outside the movement put forth their own visions of gender justice, often with a particular focus on how the combined impact of racism and sexism hurt black families and harmed men as well as women. Latina feminists soon advanced a critique of *machismo* and of the constraining role of the Catholic Church in their communities. And so it went: Native American women, working-class women in trade unions. Jewish women, Catholic women, sex workers, older women, and women with disabilities all described what gender equality would mean from their vantage points and worked to achieve it.[11] Initial friction notwithstanding, over time these differences enriched the very definition of feminism while enlisting the commitment of a vast spectrum of Americans.[12]

Seen in the light of this older and broader story, the lesbian and gay quest for equality seems almost inevitable. It too responded to changes in family life and gender as it emphasized mutual love as the basis for domestic partnership, regardless of the sex of each partner. Like feminism, this movement built on foundations laid during the New Deal and World War II: newly accepted ideas about the rights of citizens and the role of government, newly powerful grassroots movements of labor and the left, massive same-sex armed forces, and a new capacity to enforce rights made possible by an expanded administrative state. It

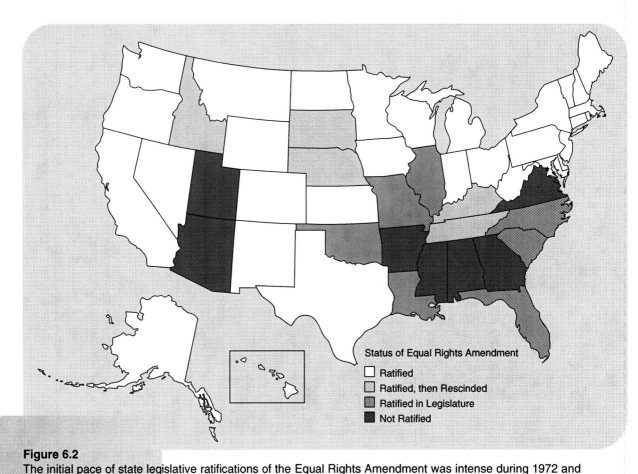

Figure 6.2
The initial pace of state legislative ratifications of the Equal Rights Amendment was intense during 1972 and 1973. This pace slowed in 1974 only three ratifications and only one in 1975.

was no accident that the first gay rights group, the Mattachine Society, was founded in the wake of World War II by left-wing activists such as Harry Hay, or that it identified gay rights with "our fellow minorities . . . the Negro, Mexican, and Jewish Peoples."[13]

The cold war had subdued this organizing, too, as it encouraged a "lavender scare" that cost more government workers their jobs than did the Red Scare itself. The State Department alone boasted in 1950 that it was firing one suspected homosexual a day.[14] But as in the case of women's equality, the social and cultural changes driving this movement were too powerful for repression to succeed over the long term. Thanks to being held back artificially in the 1950s, the gay liberation movement, like the women's movement, exploded with greater force in the 1960s—most dramatically in the four-night-long Stonewall riot in New York City in 1969. And the gay movement too generated a panoply of different organizations, the division of labor among which enabled the movement to work on various fronts—from creating its own media to changing municipal law, medical knowledge, and the practices of police and employers.[15]

For movement opponents, however, open homosexuality dramatized the separation of sexuality and reproduction that traditionalists already feared. It also showed how pliable gender was: its very existence implied there was no "natural" way for men or women to behave and so raised unprecedented question about gender hierarchy and the meaning of family. Further, what would it mean to grant equal rights for lesbians and gay men? That would require acknowledging the legitimacy of rights enforcement for others, too, beginning with blacks, something that conservatives in the North and South had long resisted. In short, on virtually every front that mattered to the right, this new movement seemed a particular challenge.[16]

With a focus on the deeper roots and larger stakes of these movements, it is easier to make sense of the phenomenon of mass antifeminism among women. Mobilized in 1972 by the veteran conservative activist Phyllis Schlafly in a group called STOP ERA, female antifeminism proved powerful enough to defeat the Equal Rights Amendment, which had sailed through both houses of Congress in 1972 after the surge of pro-equality activism. In my experience the paradox of women who fought gender equality is a great hook for teaching; it is hard to imagine, for example, African Americans organizing to fight passage the Civil Rights Act. On the face of it, it is so odd that students who yawn at feminism itself sit up to figure this out.

Solving the puzzle of why some women fought against equal treatment for their sex requires looking it how the family wage system and its breakdown drove gender-conscious politics of all kinds. Different groups of women came up with different answers to the decline of the family wage and the deep alterations in marriage and family because they stood in very different relation to these developments. Women who feel that they have benefited from the changes of recent years often become feminists, who try to further dismantle the old male dominated system in the name of equality and fairness. Yet many women who feel they have lost or will lose from the changes have rallied to the old system's defense.[17] Both reactions are understandable in a society that provides less of a social safety net than any other comparably developed nation. In western Europe, by contrast, which has more public policy supports for family well being and a stronger ethic of social solidarity, antifeminism is far weaker and there is no mass-based or influential analogue to America's religious right.[18]

Analysis of the deep structure of gender politics also helps to make sense of the prominent plate of issues of masculinity, femininity, family, and sexuality in other movements of the era not ostensibly concerned with gender. For example, historians have recently used gender analysis to reveal new dimensions of civil rights and black nationalism, the Chicano youth movement, and the conflict over the war in Vietnam. Their studies reveal how heated gender rhetoric signaled underlying concerns that influenced conduct once beyond the purview of women's history.[19]

This call for a new framework based on "the long women's movement" promises both challenges and opportunities for teachers of the U.S. survey.[20] It demands more of teachers, who will have to supply storyline, analysis, and documents that current textbooks do not. Most texts say little or nothing about women's organizing between 1920 and 1966, and almost none mentions the decisive role of the labor movement and broader progressive organizations, not explicitly feminist, in helping to advance women's equality. Taking the long view may also require sacrificing some of the attention-getting drama that dominates journalistic accounts. Time spent on media magnets like the demonstration at the 1969 Atlantic City Miss America Pageant may have to make room for how older women in the 1940s and 1950s worked for measures that would reduce the burden of the "double day" on working women, when few young people were paying attention. Given the widespread concern among today's students about how they will manage to combine employment and family commitments, that seems a fair trade.[21]

Indeed, the concept of a long women's movement offers pedagogical benefits that more than offset its start-up costs. Incorporating the best new scholarship, it introduces students to a cast of activists far more diverse than they meet in the worn-out stereotype of a "reawakened" white, middle-class movement based in the Northeast. The actors in these broader struggles look more like today's student bodies in class, race, religion, and region, if not in age, and therefore are more likely to hold their interest. Perhaps the most enticing advantage of "the long women's movement" framework for teachers, however, is that it reinforces earlier lessons by deepening student understanding of the present-day ramifications of the Progressive Era, the New Deal, the cold war, the civil rights movement, and the rise of political conservatism. It offers, that is, an opportunity for the ever-elusive synthesis. Not least, in a time of rapid worldwide economic restructuring and political disorientation, it provides students a better understanding of how momentous democratic change has really come about in the past.

ENDNOTES

1. Sara M. Evans, *Personal Politics: The Roots of Women's Liberation in the Civil Rights Movement and the New Left* (New York: Knopf, 1979); Jo Freeman, *The Politics of Women's Liberation: A Case Study of an Emerging Social Movement and Its Relation to the Policy Process* (New York: David McKay, 1975); also Alice Echols, *Daring to Be Bad: Radical Feminism in America, 1967–1975* (Minneapolis: University of Minnesota Press, 1989); Ruth Rosen, *The World Split Open: How the Modern Women's Movement Changed America* (New York: Viking, 2000).

2. For an overview, see Winifred D. Wandersee. *On the Move: American Women in the 1970s* (Boston: Twayne, 1988): Susan M. Hartmann. *From Margin to Mainstream: American Women and Politics since 1960* (New York: Alfred A. Knopf, 1989).

3. Barbara Ehrenreich, *The Hearts of Men: American Dreams and the Flight From Commitment* (New York: Anchor Books, 1983); Nancy MacLean, "Postwar Women's History: From the 'Second Wave' to the End of the Family Wage?" in *A Companion to Post-1945 America,* ed. Roy Rosenzweig and Jean-Christophe Agnew (London: Blackwell, 2002); Stephanie Coontz, *Marriage, a History: From Obedience to Intimacy, or How Love Conquered Marriage* (New York: Viking, 2005); Estelle Freedman, *No Turning Back: The History of Feminism and the Future of Women* (New York: Ballantine, 2003).

4. Nancy F. Cott, *The Grounding of Modern Feminism* (New Haven: Yale University Press, 1987); Leila Rupp and Verta Taylor, *Survival in the Doldrums: The American Women's Rights Movement, 1945 to the 1960s* (New York: Oxford University Press, 1987).

5. Vicki L. Ruiz, *Cannery Women, Cannery Lives: Mexican Women, Unionization, and the California Food Processing Industry, 1930–1950* (Albuquerque: University of New Mexico, 1987); Nancy F. Gabin. *Feminism in the Labor Movement: Women and the United Auto Workers, 1935–1975* (Ithaca: Cornell University Press, 1990); Deborah Gray White. *Too Heavy a Load: Black Women in Defense of Themselves, 1894–1994* (New York: W. W. Norton, 1998); Landon R. Y. Storrs, *Civilizing Capitalism: The National Consumers' League, Women's Activism, and Labor Standards in the New Deal Era* (Chapel Hill: University of North Carolina Press, 2000); Bruce Fehn, *Striking Women: Gender, Race and Class in the United Packinghouse Workers of America* (Iowa City: University of Iowa Press, 2003); Dorothy Sue Cobble, *The Other Women's Movement: Workplace Justice and Social Rights in Modern America* (Princeton: Princeton University Press, 2005). An excellent documentary that makes this case, is *Step by Step: Building a Feminist Movement* (Videocassette, Wisconsin Public Television, 1998; distributed by Women Make Movies).

6. Amy Swerdlow, "The Congress of American Women: Left-Feminist Peace Politics in the Cold War" in *U.S. History as Women's History: New Feminist Essays,* ed. Linda K. Kerber, Alice Kessler-Harris, and Kathryn Kish Sklar (Chapel Hill: University of North Carolina Press, 1995).

7. Gerda Lerner, *Fireweed: A Political Autobiography* (Philadelphia: Temple University Press, 2002); also Landon R. Y. Storrs, "Red Scare Politics and the Suppression of Popular Front Feminism: The Loyalty Investigation of Mary Dublin Keyserling," *Journal of American History* 90 (Sept. 2003): 491–524; Susan Lynn, *Progressive Women in Conservative Times: Racial Justice, Peace, and Feminism, 1945 to the 1960s* (New Brunswick: Rutgers University Press, 1992); Joanne Meyerowitz, *Not June Cleaver: Women and Gender in Postwar America* (Philadelphia: Temple University Press, 1994); Susan M. Hartmann, *The Other Feminists: Activists in the Liberal Establishment* (New Haven: Yale University Press, 1998).

8. Cynthia Harrison. *On Account of Sex: The Politics of Women's Issues, 1945–1968* (Berkeley: University of California Press, 1988); Daniel Horowitz, *Betty Friedan and the Making of "The Feminine Mystique": The American Left, the Cold War, and Modern Feminism* (Amherst: University of Massachusetts Press, 1998).

9. Hartmann, *The Other Feminists;* Nancy MacLean, *Freedom Is Not Enough: The Opening of the American Workplace* (Cambridge: Harvard University Press and the Russell Sage Foundation, 2006); also Cobble, *The Other Women's Movement.*

10. Cott, *Grounding of Modern Feminism,* 282.

11. For a sample, see Nancy Seifer, *"Nobody Speaks for Me!": Self-Portraits of American Working Class Women* (New York: Simon and Schuster, 1976); Asian Women United of California, *Making Waves: An Anthology of Writings By and About Asian American Women* (Boston: Beacon Press, 1989); Beverly Guy-Sheftall, ed. *Words on Fire: An Anthology of African-American Feminist Thought* (New York: The New Press, 1995); Alma M. Garcia, *Chicana Feminist Thought: The Basic Historical Writings* (New York; Routledge, 1997).

12. Freedman, *No Turning Back:* Sara M. Evans, *Tidal Wave: How Women Changed America at Century's End* (New York: Free Press, 2003): Benita Roth, *Separate Roads to Feminism: Black, Chicana, and White Feminist Movements in America's Second Wave* (New York: Cambridge University Press, 2004); Kimberly Springer, *Living for the Revolution: Black Feminist Organizations, 1968–1980* (Durham: Duke University Press, 2005).

13. Quote from "Statement of Purpose" in Van Gosse, *The Movements of the New Left, 1950–1975; A Brief History with Documents* (Boston: Bedford Books, 2005). 40; Allan Berube, *Coming out under Fire: The History of Gay Men and Women in World War Two* (New York: Free Press, 1990): Leisa D. Meyer, *Creating GI Jane: Sexuality and Power in the Women's Army Corps during World War II* (New York: Columbia University Press, 1996); John D' Emilio, *Sexual Politics, Sexual Communities: The Making of a Homosexual Minority in the United States, 1940–1970.* 2nd ed. (Chicago: University of Chicago Press, 1998); Martin Meeker, "Behind the Mask of Respectability: Reconsidering the Mattachine Society and Male Homophile Practice, 1950s and 1960s," *Journal of the History of Sexuality* 10 (Jan. 2001): 78–116.

14. David K. Johnson, *The Lavender Scare: The Cold War Persecution of Gays and Lesbian in the Federal Government* (Chicago: University of Chicago Press, 2004).

15. John D' Emilio, "After Stonewall." in his *Making Trouble: Essays on Gay History, Politics, and the University* (New York: Routledge, 1992), 234–74; *Creating Change; Sexuality, Public Policy, and Civil Rights,* ed. John D' Emilio, William B. Turner, Urvashi Vaid (New York: St. Martin's Press, 2000).

16. On the import of the separation of sexuality and reproduction, see John D' Emilio and Estelle B. Freedman, *Intimate Matters: A History of Sexuality in America* (New York: Harper & Row, 1988); on conservatives and civil rights, See MacLean, *Freedom In Not Enough,* esp. chaps. 2, 7, and 9.

17. Kristin Luker, *Abortion and the Politics of Motherhood* (Berkeley: University of California Press, 1984): Jane J. Mansbridge, *Why We Lost the ERA* (Chicago: University of Chicago Press, 1986): MacLean, "Postwar Women's History."

18. The best source of up-to-date information is the Institute for Women's Policy Research: <http://www.iwpr.org/>. For U.S. distinctiveness and its roots, see Barry D. Adam, "The Defense of the Marriage Act and American Exceptionalism: The 'Gay Marriage' Panic in the United States," *Journal of The History of Sexuality* 12 (April 2003): 259–76, esp. 265–66.

19. Vicki L. Crawford, et al., eds., *Women in the Civil Rights Movement: Trailblazers and Torchbearers, 1941–1965* (Bloomington: Indiana University Press, 1990); Scot Brown, *Fighting for US: Maulana Karenga, the US Organization, and Black Cultural Nationalism* (New York: New York University Press, 2003); Ramon A. Gutierrez, "Community, Patriarchy and Individualism: The Politics of Chicano History and the Dream of Equality." *American Quarterly* 45 (March 1993): 44–72; Joshua B. Freeman, "Hardhats: Construction Workers, Manliness, and the 1970 Pro-War Demonstrations," *Journal of Social History* (Summer 1993): 725–44; Robert D. Dean, *Imperial Brotherhood: Gender and the Making of Cold War Foreign Policy* (Amherst: University of Massachusetts Press, 2001); Justin David Suran, "Coming out against the War, Antimilitarism and the Politicization of Homosexuality in the Era of Vietnam." *American Quarterly* 53 (Sept., 2001): 452–488.

20. On "the long civil rights movement." see Jacquelyn Dowd Hall, "The Long Civil Rights Movement and the Political Uses of the Past." *Journal of American History* (March 2005): 1233–63; also *Time Longer than Rope: A Century of African American Activism. 1850–1950* ed. Charles M. Payne and Adam Green (New York: New York University Press, 2003).

21. For a model from the civil rights movement of how much is gained by changing the vantage point in this way, see Charles Payne, *I've Got the Light of Freedom: The Organizing Tradition and the Mississippi Freedom Struggle* (Berkeley: University of California Press, 1995).

Voicing Your Opinion
Gender Is Powerful: The Long Reach of Feminism
Nancy MacLean

1. Consider your own education on the women's movement and evaluate how much you know. Where did you learn about the women's movement? What events were highlighted in textbooks and classrooms? Did you learn about events that occurred between the first and second waves of the movement?

    _____

    _____

    _____

    _____

    _____

2. Feminist activists in the 1960s coined the phrase, "The personal is political." Respond to this statement with your own thoughts. How is the statement accurate or inaccurate? What are the benefits of thinking of personal issues as political? What are the risks?

    _____

    _____

    _____

    _____

    _____

3. Why do many people have a negative perception of the word *feminist?* Where do people learn about this word? Is there an opportunity to reconsider the word and develop more positive responses to it? Why or why not?

    _____

    _____

    _____

    _____

    _____

Terms

Sexism
Male privilege
Patriarchy
Domestic violence
Volunteer organizations
Feminism

MAULED BY MAVEN
Our Story of Involving
Men in the Movement

⚥

LAUREL MOHAN, ANGELA SCHULTZ, AND TRACI BOYLE

This article is about clashes that occur within a violence-prevention organization. Women volunteers report their experiences with institutional sexism and patriarchal frames when they attempt to include men in their work. The article looks at internalized sexism, male privilege, male voices, and organizations that seek to train individuals to deal with violence in society.

We didn't realize the risk we were taking when, in June of 2000 our three agencies collaborated to form the Men Against Violence Education Network (MAVEN) with the goal of involving men in our Community education and children's programs. We decided to recruit male volunteers for several reasons: We wanted children in our programs and people in the community to see positive relationships role modeled between men and women, and we know from experience that words spoken by men are often heard and taken more seriously than the same words spoken by women. Also, our agencies mission is to end violence against women and children, and we know that domestic violence will not end until all genders are involved.

We write this article to talk about what it's been like for us to involve men in the movement against domestic and sexual violence and to consider the way patriarchy shaped this experience. We write this to process and heal. We write this to share our story, to give voice to what creating space for men has been like for us. We write this in the hopes of opening up dialogues about involving men in the movement. Perhaps an examination of our experience with internalized sexism will open up a larger dialogue among feminists. Internalized sexism is something we've grappled with, in part because we haven't been involved in much feminist dialogue about it and have been caught off guard by the intensity and impact of our own ingrained sexism.

Trying to Train Men

We set out with the assumption that, among the four of us working on the project, our vast knowledge of community organizing, anti-oppression training, and volunteer coordinating, we could alter existing models to create an appropriate 40-hour training for male volunteers. The project quickly proved to be more than we expected. Our workloads doubled and the negative emotional impact of our work increased immeasurably due to the intensive of the sexism we experienced. As women we had spent our lives surviving sexism. As feminists we had spent years analyzing sexism. As activists, we had been struggling to dismantle sexism. We thought we knew sexism. MAVEN blindsided us. Much of the sexism that we write about in this article happens to all of us everyday, but has become so normalized that we are desensitized to it. Until we brought sexism under the magnifying glass of MAVEN and into the confined environment of the training, we really didn't know how much it could pervade our lives. We've made discoveries about how deeply it can impact us, how sinister and subtle it can be, how engrained it is in everyone, and how entrapped we can be by it, despite our awareness. Even though our world is male dominated, we've been able to create lives that have been built, for survival reasons, around self-created feminist communities. All of a sudden, to find ourselves as the leaders of this group of adult men was daunting and frightening.

Beginning the first night of training and continuing for the next year, we constantly dealt with different manifestations of the very trauma symptoms we had tried to leave behind in order to sustain ourselves in this work. Advocates in the movement against domestic violence know the symptoms of burnout: losing sleep, nightmares, fatigue, ambivalence and/or hypersensitivity to violence in our daily lives. These symptoms are manifestations of vicarious trauma, the cumulative impact of survivors stories and detailed reenactments. When the three of us writing this moved from our positions as direct service advocates in emergency shelters into the roles of outreach and prevention workers, we weren't expecting these indicators of trauma to come up and were surprised to be experiencing them on a whole new level where the traumatization is not vicarious, but direct.

Our First Clue

Our first indicator of how patriarchy would shape our entire experience with MAVEN presented itself before the training even began. After sending out a series of public service announcements about the training, we had a larger media response than we'd ever seen with any of our previous outreach efforts. Among much media attention was an interview by a reporter from *The Oregonian,* the largest newspaper in the state, which culminated in a front page article in the Metro section and a television appearance on "Good Day Oregon." On the one hand, it was exciting to have attention brought to the issue of community involvement in the movement and we had a large volume of calls from interested men. On the other hand, we resented the fact that we had never received this type of attention until men came into the picture. What about the women who started this movement as volunteers? What about the 25 years preceding this moment that had involved very few men? What about the lack of attention to domestic violence by the media, in general? While it frustrated us that all of this attention was more about men than the work that we have been doing for years, we focused on what we had set out to do and remained excited about gaining male allies.

This media experience as well as the following examples reflect a pervasive patriarchal pattern that women are not *heard* in our society, a standard we would continue to struggle with. There is a "text-book" illustration of this type of oppression where a person from a marginalized group has something to say, and a person with power doesn't hear them. Then another person with power restates the same idea and all of a sudden, it's heard by everyone in the room. This was something that we had all experienced in our lives as students, bartenders, partners to men, friends and daughters. But this scenario took on another dimension in MAVEN. In other aspects of our lives it has been easier to say something about it or to let it go because that's just the way it was and we could pick and choose our battles. In MAVEN, our aim is to have our male volunteers unlearn this behavior and we strive to interrupt it whenever we see it. At times the dynamics in the training room made that seem impossible. Many men were resistant, and some expressed feelings of vulnerability and others seemed to fear us as powerful women. It's common for people who are being confronted with their privilege to act defensively. This is something we are used to, but we were not prepared for how hard they would fight to maintain male supremacy, a battle made even scarier by the fact that we were outnumbered. There were 25 men in the room, many of whom constantly attacked what we were saying, raised their voices at us, and seemed to be in denial of the reality of sexism.

While we came into this training with the understanding that men's words are given more credence than women's, we imagined that the prospective volunteers had some awareness of this and were eager to learn from women. We'd assumed that 40-hours of training, some of which was done by men, would get our volunteers to an appropriate level of understanding. But after the first round of forty-hour training, one volunteer stated that he really didn't understand male privilege until he had heard a male author speak against it. In an attempt to interrupt his sexism, one of us asked. "Isn't it sexist that you went through a forty-hour training dealing with sexism and male privilege, led by women, and didn't hear any of it, and now you are saying you get it after hearing a man speak for two hours?" He gave no attention to her question, still not hearing her.

Not being heard was disconcerting but it led to a bigger stumbling block in the path of accomplishing what we wanted with MAVEN. It rendered us invisible as coordinators—as leaders our place was always challenged. For example, when talking about our interviewing and screening process with MAVEN volunteers, one man demanded that no one be turned away from getting involved. His demand seemed to come from the desire to keep MAVEN open to men who needed information and support. This felt like a direct attack to the purpose of MAVEN, which is to provide volunteers and to create a more effective process to maintain a safe space in the training and in our programs, for our programs. We have a serious responsibility to make sure that all volunteers are appropriate to work with children survivors. It felt like he didn't even have a concept of us as professionals who represent agencies and are accountable to the safety of all program participants. Rather, it seemed he saw as paramount the need for us, as women, to provide for the needs of men even before the needs of our clients.

The negation of us as leaders led to male volunteers taking ownership of MAVEN. Volunteers went as far as representing themselves as founders and leaders of MAVEN in the community. MAVEN was talked about by men without our three founding agencies ever being mentioned. Many volunteers voiced their vision for MAVEN as becoming an organization that offered services to men. Some men never mentioned to other people that MAVEN is a volunteer training but rather framed the project as a safe space for men to find their voices and heal. This misrepresentation of MAVEN and assumed ownership by some volunteers created misinformation in the community that we've had to work to untangle.

Comfort for Men?

While their desire for support services for men was pulling us away from our purpose, it came from a very valid need. Many men in the training seemed to be hurting either from having survived abuse as a child or young adult, or because they felt guilt from having abused adult partners. Perhaps these men came to MAVEN with the hope of finding solace. Some of the men came to training sessions needing to talk about abuse they had witnessed or experienced as children. As coordinators, we saw gaping wounds that had never been tended. We heard outpourings of child abuse that may have never been disclosed before. And while we ached for these men who were hurting, we were troubled that they saw themselves as being in a position to help others heal from similar pain, a leap that is too big to take.

Cultural conceptions of manhood don't allow much space for healing. These same conceptions label men as "fixers" who make any difficult situation tidy by becoming a knight-in-shining armor. Many of these men weren't ready to volunteer with MAVEN until some of those wounds had been tended, an issue that was difficult to address because there are no resources to offer men. The question was raised. "Why don't your agencies offer services for men?" Our response was, "Because our mission is to end violence against women and children and the overwhelming majority of family violence is perpetrated by men against women, and because much of our funding comes from the Violence Against Women Act," We constantly had to defend this with cited statistics and our agencies' philosophies. We encouraged the men to organize themselves and create the needed services. We even suggested that they look to the anti-domestic violence movement as a model from which to create such services, but their sexist expectation was that we would create these services for them. This was another attempt to pull us away from the mission that our agencies and the movement on the whole have had for the last 30 years; *To end violence against women and children.* They were tagging at the very core of what our agencies do and why we exist.

In addition to hearing about abuse these men had survived, we were overwhelmed and emotionally obliterated listening to their stories of their sexist behaviors and the abuse they had perpetrated. While we were asking men to work on unlearning their sexism, we were not expecting the extreme impact their stories would have on us. In one of the unlearning sexism sessions, the volunteers were asked by a male facilitator to "own" their sexist behavior by telling about a time that they exploited their male privilege. As the men went around the room stating what they had done, we sat in the back corner, shaking and holding back tears, fighting nausea and feeling like our heads were going to split open.

We also did not expect or encourage the volunteers to approach us to talk one-on-one about how their sexism hurt women. However, many men did this, seeking out the nurturing they seemed to expect from us as women. Some of these men were not appropriate to continue as volunteers, but we wanted to offer a place to continue the work they were starting on themselves. Batterers intervention classes do exist in our community but while these men would disclose abuse they had perpetrated, they would not hold themselves accountable enough to attend a class for batterers.

When a group discussion about services for men took place within the training, it was easier to steer them back on track. It was more of a challenge, however, on an individual level when a man would approach us to talk about his abuse issues, because we were not only dealing with his sexism in his expectation of us as caretakers, but also with our own internalized sexism. We sometimes found ourselves nurturing men who were hurting, rather than drawing boundaries and sticking to our jobs. This was one of many levels on which we were impacted by our own internalized sexism. Not only do men get the message that women fit into a specific gender role, in this case that of the nurturer, but we internalize that message as well. We found ourselves being intimidated, coerced, or otherwise falling into societal expectations of us as women. We didn't want to hurt their feelings, we didn't want to alienate anyone, and we didn't want to be called man-haters, so we nurtured these men, often taking time we did not have to listen to and support them.

Falling Prey to Sexism

The stereotype of women as nurturers was subtler than some of the other forms of sexism we experienced. There was a volunteer who manipulated, coerced, and pushed until a one-on-one meeting with a coordinator turned into an extremely uncomfortable date-like situation. After a string of other incidents, another coordinator called him with the purpose of making it clear that he was no longer welcome to participate in MAVEN in any way. He dominated the conversation, yelled at her, called her names, and accused MAVEN of oppressing men.

Another example where we fell prey to sexism was with a man who was able to take us in by the very same dynamics that we study about, teach about and work to prevent in our community. He would say horrific things about his own violence against women in training but would talk about how he's made concrete changes and showed a lot of excitement to be working on his issues. A lot of his disclosures felt very violating and scary for us. We eventually found out that he was actively perpetrating violence against a woman. The training was a way for him to get closer to the woman he was victimizing. This was manipulation. We were surprised to have found ourselves in this place, to have been manipulated by this man into thinking that he was a fantastic volunteer. We questioned our judgment as professionals because we missed the red flags and patterns. No matter how strong we were as a group of four women, we weren't as strong as his power to manipulate us.

This man was not the only volunteer who turned out to be a perpetrator and not the only one to hurt us with sexism. Initially we were bewildered that things like this could be happening to us. We sometimes found ourselves straying from focusing on holding MAVEN volunteers accountable for their actions and questioning ourselves. Why didn't we see the red flags? Why didn't we put a stop to things sooner? Why weren't we stronger? Although we are always working to counter the victim blaming of survivors, we struggle with blaming ourselves for their actions. These are two ways in which we are realizing that we still have ingrained in us the victim blaming and sexist ideals of our culture. So ingrained in fact, that it is a full twelve months after our first MAVEN training and we are just beginning to dissect this, to really see it for what it is. It has been a devastating realization to analyze what has happened in doing this work with men and to see that even as a group of strong women working together we could be overpowered by this web of sexist ideas, expectations of us as women, prescribed gender roles, and manipulate tactics. It has also been disheartening to realize that we are not as strong as we thought we were when we stepped out of self-created feminist communities.

On yet another level the realizations about our internalized sexism intensify when we start to consider how we feel writing this article. We struggle with feeling ashamed. We wonder what you think reading this. Do you think we are naïve for missing the warning signs that some of these men were abusive? Do you think we were clueless for taking this on with optimism? Do you think we are weak for nurturing these men? Are we foolish? Are we good feminists? Have we done the right thing trying to involve men? This fear of judgment does not come from our experiences with other women we have talked to about MAVEN: they have been nothing but supportive. These questions and feelings of shame come from within ourselves, but are a product of external messages about women. First, we are taught that if we are hurt or manipulated it is our fault as the victim. Second, we are taught that women are our own worst enemy. Third, we are taught that feminists are especially condemning people and should be feared. Not only do these three things not speak to our experience, but they do not even ring true intellectually. Yet they have been internalized so deeply that we find them boiling up inside of us as we write this, creating shame. Writing this article has been therapeutic in helping us to recognize more pieces of our own internalized sexism and in doing so, we feel ourselves growing into even stronger women. This article is an affirmation.

Realizing the role that internalized sexism played in our tribulations with MAVEN has quelled much of the anger with ourselves and has allowed us to focus on nurturing ourselves and each other rather than the men who have tried to demand it. Although being upset with ourselves has dissipated, the anger that we experienced during the training is still with us. We're angry at not having been heard, not been taken seriously as representatives of our agency and as experts in our field. We're angry that our agencies' mission and focus has been questioned, not respected. We resent having been hit on, yelled at, and being made to feel scared in our work. Many things continue to create rage within us: the domination of training space, lack of empathy for survivors of domestic and sexual violence, the inability to hear information about domestic violence, seeing participants verbally attack female presenters, and inappropriate sexual disclosures that clearly objectify women.

Overwhelmed with Emotions

As the MAVEN training went on, we found ourselves dealing with the most intense anger we had dealt with in years. One of us equated the intensity of anger to the way she felt nine years ago after two men tried to pull her into a van in broad day light while saying sexually violent things and no one made a move to help. At times we found ourselves saying how much we hated men even though as feminists we had worked so hard to not be "man-haters" in order to avoid accusations and knowing that hate is destructive and unproductive. We all dealt with this anger in different ways. It was interesting to see the way that we worked as team around it without ever having had made a deliberate decision around how to deal with it. As anger would boil up to a peak for one of us, the others would step forward calmly, taking on more responsibility, or dealing with a situation at hand. For example, the coordinator who had been coerced into a date-of-sorts with one volunteer never had to speak to him again. As the result of our teamwork, the others stepped in to deal with him. We flowed in and out being on the front line or retreating to cope with our overwhelming emotion. MAVEN impacted each of us professionally and personally in ways we did not expect, such as how it affected our sleep, our appetites, our health and our desire to do the work that we love. MAVEN has been a constant tug-of-war with burnout.

Among all of the difficulties and pain that has come with the process of MAVEN, there are reasons why this project is one that we all stick with. We have male allies now and we know that the information and tools MAVEN men learn in training is brought to the larger community. Social change is happening slowly as they incorporate what they've learned in their own lives and they spark discussions with their friends and neighbors and as they support survivors in their own lives. Without our own hearts and at the core of our agencies is the belief that social change is necessary to end violence against women and children. MAVEN has proven to further our social change mission.

There is a small but dedicated group of MAVEN volunteers who graduated from our first training. These men facilitate discussion groups for new MAVEN participants to process the information as well as an ongoing consciousness-raising group for training graduates. They have taken on a chunk of administrative and recruitment duties. They have stepped up to the plate when really tough issues have arisen, such as confronting men on inappropriate behavior and sexism, and have even been the ones to ask other men to leave the training. We have strong male allies where there were none before. We also now have some great men involved in our programs supporting children and speaking out in the community.

MAVEN has progressed. So much has changed as we've labored to make it work, responding to feedback from training participants and attempting to eliminate problems we've encountered. Our screening process has intensified, we've learned to listen to our collective gut more and have been much quicker to ask men to leave the training, and we've added more structured time to address unlearning sexism and male supremacy. Another change is the addition of more male trainers as co-facilitators and main presenters. While it has made our training so much more effective, it angers us that sexism makes male trainers more effective. While it's made us mad, it's made our lives a bit easier.

There are larger questions we've been considering, questions that we can't answer on our own. Is it appropriate to be involving men in the movement, especially knowing that we do so in part because it's sexism that makes men effective voices against violence? We're working within the patriarchal structure to further our message rather than focusing solely on dismantling the very structure of patriarchy. We're playing to that structure.

Is the movement at an appropriate place to be involving men in a volunteer capacity? It's happening in many cities, but there hasn't been a movement-wide discussion. Perhaps there should be more of a movement-wide examination of this issue. If men continue to become involved, how do we support each other and stay strong as women and how do we keep the movement focused? In our experience, it's so draining to deal with the sexism that comes with men's involvement. What if this drained some of our vital energy from providing services to survivors? Does sexism need to be dealt with before men are brought into the movement? Are we ready to deal with sexism coming from within the movement?

Conclusion

At one point we asked ourselves what the best part of MAVEN has been. The thing that stood out to all of us was each other, the women coordinators. On a professional level, MAVEN fortified the relationships among our Outreach and Volunteer programs and we are now partnering on other projects as well. On a personal level, we have developed strong relationships and have learned a lot from each other. We have been enormously supported by each other. MAVEN has been a challenge on so many levels, it had been incomprehensible at times in how it has made us feel and what we have witnessed. So much of this we could not have processed and understood on our own, let alone survived. But as a team that was possible and MAVEN was sustainable. And while the sexism we were experiencing sometimes made us feel like parts of us were dying, so much life comes from what we've made together. It's ironic that the best part of incorporating men into the movement has been the women.

Voicing Your Opinion
Mauled by MAVEN: Our Story of Involving Men in the Movement
Laurel Mohan, Angela Schultz, and Traci Boyle

1. The authors describe their personal struggles with *internal sexism* and explain how they felt responsible for nurturing and understanding the male volunteers. Is internal sexism something that you have experienced or witnessed in your life? How might women learn to resist this form of sexism? What needs to occur in our society in order for us to end internal sexism?

_____

_____

_____

_____

_____

2. How are women treated in groups and institutions? Do men listen to them? Do other women take their ideas as seriously as their men counterparts? Do the article's *many* examples of the dismissal of women sound accurate to you? Why or why not?

_____

_____

_____

_____

_____

3. Are men and women capable of working together in programs like MAVEN? Is it more effective if this type of activism is sex-segregated? Why or why not?

_____

_____

_____

_____

_____

Analyzing a Text . . .

Instructions

Write a research paper related to the study of gender and communication. This research will be in the form of a **critical textual analysis.** For this assignment, "text" is defined in a broad sense to include both print and non-print artifacts. You are asked to

1. Choose a **topic** that is of interest to you. Your topic must be developed using the list at the end of this assignment sheet. You should narrow down the broader topic to something more specific. (Example: "gendered violence" could be narrowed down to an analysis of violence toward women in music videos.)

2. Identify a **text** to analyze that pertains to that topic. Example of texts: If your chosen topic is "the representation of gender in print media," you may choose the swimsuit edition of *Sports Illustrated* as a text to analyze; if you choose "gender and the internet" as your topic, you might choose an internet website about eating disorders as your text. Other texts could include an art exhibit at a museum, a section of the Bible, a sexual harassment policy, a film, a TV program, lyrics of a song, etc.)

3. Choose a **framework or theory** to use to analyze your chosen text. Examples of theories: muted group theory, mothering theory, standpoint theory, social learning theory (or choose your own). Examples of frameworks: gender stereotypes, hegemonic masculinity, the hidden curriculum (or choose your own).

4. Find **scholarly sources** that help you to understand the text and/or your framework.

5. **Analyze** the text, and write a paper that documents the ideas that you have generated as you work through this analysis.

Paper Format

1. **Introduction:** Preview the topic in a way that captures the reader's attention. Also, state the purpose of your research and describe your text and framework of analysis.

2. **Summary of Sources:** Consult a **minimum** of three scholarly publications (published books or journal articles) that address questions relating to your topic, text, and framework of analysis. In addition to the three scholarly publications, you might choose to use sources such as popular magazines (e.g., *Time, Newsweek,* etc.) and internet websites; however, these should be used in addition to the three scholarly sources. Scholarly articles and books help you think through various issues you might want to discuss in your paper. There should be an obvious link between this information and the framework and analysis sections of your paper. You are likely to find this research in communication, literary studies, women's studies, history, media studies, or popular culture.

3. **Method:** Fully explain/describe your text and your framework of analysis.

4. **Analysis:** This is the most important section of your paper. Here you offer a critical view of the text that you have chosen to study. Think about what you have learned in relationship to the topic of gender and communication. Do not just *describe* what you have discovered; rather *evaluate* it for its impact on society. If you have chosen, for example, to analyze the use of gender language in an article from *Cosmopolitan* magazine, you should not just offer examples and samples, but also analyze the potential *impact* that this language has on men and women. In essence, you are offering a comprehensive understanding of the issues raised by your analysis of the text.

5. **Conclusion:** Summarize your main points and offer concluding thoughts on the topic.

Suggestions

Pick a topic that truly interests you and/or has an impact on your education or your life.

Take the time to find sources that help you investigate your topic in a thorough manner. Do not just "settle" for the first article that you find on the topic.

Allow yourself time to think carefully about the text that you are analyzing. Think before you write!

Remember to be analytical rather than descriptive.

Topics

Representations of gender in print media (newspapers, magazines)
Representations of gender in film
Representations of gender in television
Representations of gender in the music industry
Gender and the internet
Gendered violence
Sexual harassment
Gender in romantic relationships (heterosexual, gay, lesbian)
Gender in friendships (cross-sex and same-sex)
Gender in educational settings
Gender in the workplace